Contents at a Glance

Introduction 1

Book 1: Mindfulness 3
CHAPTER 1: Exploring Mindfulness in the Workplace 5
CHAPTER 2: Discovering the Benefits of Mindfulness 27
CHAPTER 3: Applying Mindfulness in the Workplace 47
CHAPTER 4: Practicing Mindfulness in the Digital Age 73

Book 2: Project Management 93
CHAPTER 1: Achieving Results 95
CHAPTER 2: Knowing Your Project's Audiences 113
CHAPTER 3: Clarifying Your Project 133
CHAPTER 4: Developing a Game Plan 157
CHAPTER 5: Keeping Everyone Informed 183

Book 3: Leadership 203
CHAPTER 1: Building Your Leadership Muscles 205
CHAPTER 2: Managing as a Leader 223
CHAPTER 3: Creating a Vision 243
CHAPTER 4: Leading across Cultures 267

Book 4: Time Management 277
CHAPTER 1: Organizing Yourself 279
CHAPTER 2: Setting Yourself Up for Success 285
CHAPTER 3: Valuing Your Time 297
CHAPTER 4: Focusing, Prioritizing, and Time-Blocking 307
CHAPTER 5: Controlling Email Overload 327

Book 5: Business Writing 335
CHAPTER 1: Planning Your Message 337
CHAPTER 2: Making Your Writing Work 359
CHAPTER 3: Improving Your Work 381
CHAPTER 4: Troubleshooting Your Writing 403
CHAPTER 5: Writing Emails That Get Results 425

Book 6: Presentations 447

CHAPTER 1: Creating Compelling Content................................... 449

CHAPTER 2: Honing Your Platform Skills 463

CHAPTER 3: Captivating Your Audience 487

CHAPTER 4: Keeping Your Audience Captivated........................... 503

CHAPTER 5: Ending on a High Note....................................... 517

Book 7: Negotiation 533

CHAPTER 1: Negotiating for Life... 535

CHAPTER 2: Knowing What You Want....................................... 547

CHAPTER 3: Setting Goals 567

CHAPTER 4: Asking the Right Questions................................... 577

CHAPTER 5: Closing the Deal 593

Index 617

Table of Contents

INTRODUCTION 1
    About This Book. 1
    Foolish Assumptions. 1
    Icons Used in This Book 2
    Beyond the Book 2

BOOK 1: MINDFULNESS 3

CHAPTER 1: **Exploring Mindfulness in the Workplace** 5
    Becoming More Mindful at Work 6
        Clarifying what mindfulness is. 6
        Taking a look at the background. 7
        Recognizing what mindfulness isn't 9
    Finding Out Why Your Brain Needs Mindfulness 12
        Evolving from lizard to spaceman. 13
        Discovering your brain's hidden rules 14
        Recognizing that you are what you think. 15
        Exploring your brain at work 18
    Starting Your Mindful Journey 21
        Being mindful at work yourself 22
        Overcoming common challenges 23
        Creating a mindful workplace 24
        Living the dream: Mindfulness at work 26

CHAPTER 2: **Discovering the Benefits of Mindfulness** 27
    Discovering the Benefits for Employees 27
        Increased mental resilience. 28
        Improved relationships. 31
        Honed mental clarity and focus 33
        Mindful leadership 35
    Looking at the Organizational Benefits of Mindfulness. 37
        Happier, more engaged employees 38
        Greater creativity. 39
        Increased productivity 41
        Improved decision making. 43
        Reducing staff turnover 45

CHAPTER 3: **Applying Mindfulness in the Workplace** 47
    Gaining Perspective in the Modern-Day Workplace. 47
        Engaging with a VUCA world 48
        Applying mindfulness in changing times .49

      Employing mindfulness for new ways of working 51

      Building resilience 53

  Adjusting Your Mental Mind-Set 55

      Focusing on the present moment. 55

      Treating thoughts as mental processes. 56

      Approaching rather than avoiding difficulties. 58

  Rewiring Your Brain 60

      Resculpting your brain to become more productive 61

      Increasing your present-moment circuitry 62

  Developing Mindfulness at Work 63

      Examining intentions and attitudes 63

      Remembering that practice makes perfect. 67

      Experimenting with mindfulness 68

      Acting ethically for the organization and its people. 69

      Living life mindfully 70

CHAPTER 4: **Practicing Mindfulness in the Digital Age** 73

  Choosing When to Use Technology 73

      Recognizing the pros and cons of technology. 74

      Rebalancing your use of technology. 76

  Communicating Mindfully 78

      Emailing mindfully. 81

      Phoning mindfully 82

      Using a smartphone mindfully 83

      Engaging with social media mindfully 85

      Writing mindfully. 85

  Using Technology Mindfully. 88

      Focusing on one task 89

      Discovering technology that enhances focus 90

BOOK 2: PROJECT MANAGEMENT 93

CHAPTER 1: **Achieving Results** 95

  Determining What Makes a Project a Project .95

      Understanding the three main components

      that define a project 96

      Recognizing the diversity of projects 97

      Describing the four stages of a project .98

  Defining Project Management. 100

      Starting with the initiating processes .101

      Outlining the planning processes 104

      Examining the executing processes 105

      Surveying the monitoring and controlling processes 106

      Ending with the closing processes 107

Knowing the Project Manager's Role 107
    Looking at the project manager's tasks 107
    Staving off excuses for not following a structured
    project-management approach 108
    Avoiding "shortcuts" 109
    Staying aware of other potential challenges 110
Do You Have What It Takes to Be an Effective Project Manager? 111
    Questions 111
    Answer key 112

CHAPTER 2: **Knowing Your Project's Audiences** 113
Understanding Your Project's Audiences. 114
Developing an Audience List 114
    Starting your audience list 114
    Ensuring a complete and up-to-date audience list. 118
    Using an audience list template 121
Considering the Drivers, Supporters, and Observers 122
    Deciding when to involve your audiences 124
    Using different methods to involve your audiences 127
    Making the most of your audiences' involvement 128
Displaying Your Audience List 128
Confirming Your Audience's Authority 129
Assessing Your Audience's Power and Interest 131

CHAPTER 3: **Clarifying Your Project** 133
Defining Your Project with a Scope Statement 133
Looking at the Big Picture: Explaining the Need for Your Project . . .136
    Figuring out why you're doing the project 136
    Drawing the line: Where your project starts and stops 146
    Stating your project's objectives 147
Marking Boundaries: Project Constraints 151
    Working within limitations 152
    Dealing with needs 154
Documenting Your Assumptions 155
Presenting Your Scope Statement 155

CHAPTER 4: **Developing a Game Plan** 157
Breaking Your Project into Manageable Chunks 157
    Thinking in detail 158
    Identifying necessary project work with
    a work breakdown structure 159
    Dealing with special situations 167
Creating and Displaying a WBS 170
    Considering different schemes 170
    Developing your WBS 171

Categorizing your project's work. 173
Labeling your WBS entries 174
Displaying your WBS in different formats .176
Improving the quality of your WBS. 178
Using templates. 179
Identifying Risks While Detailing Your Work 180
Documenting Your Planned Project Work. 182

CHAPTER 5: **Keeping Everyone Informed** 183
Successful Communication Basics 184
Breaking down the communication process. 184
Distinguishing one-way and two-way communication 185
Can you hear me? Listening actively. 186
Choosing the Appropriate Medium for Project Communication 188
Just the facts: Written reports 188
Move it along: Meetings that work 190
Preparing a Written Project-Progress Report 193
Making a list and checking it twice 193
Knowing what's hot (and what's not) in your report 194
Earning a Pulitzer, or at least writing an interesting report 194
Holding Key Project Meetings 198
Regularly scheduled team meetings. 199
Ad hoc team meetings 199
Upper-management progress reviews. 200
Preparing a Project Communications Management Plan 201

BOOK 3: LEADERSHIP 203

CHAPTER 1: **Building Your Leadership Muscles** 205
Putting Your Brain to Work 206
Using what you have. 206
Responding to situations flexibly 207
Taking advantage of fortuitous circumstances. 208
Making sense of ambiguous or contradictory messages 209
Ranking the importance of different elements. 209
Finding similarities in apparently different situations 210
Drawing distinctions between seemingly similar situations. 211
Putting concepts together in new ways 212
Coming up with novel ideas. 212
Communicating Effectively. 213
Speaking begins with listening 214
Eliciting the cooperation of others 215
Driving Yourself 215
Developing a Sense of Urgency. 216

Don't wait 216
Form a "kitchen cabinet". 217
Being Honest and Searching for the Truth 218
Displaying Good Judgment 218
Being Dependable and Consistent 218
Creating an Atmosphere of Trust 219
Encouraging a Learning Environment 220
Looking for Common Ground: The Type O Personality. 221

CHAPTER 2: **Managing as a Leader**. 223
Setting Reasonable Goals. 223
Delegating to Your Team 225
Knowing how to delegate. 225
Knowing what to delegate 229
Settling Disputes in Your Team 232
Allowing Your Team to Find Its Own Path .233
Leading When You Aren't Really the Leader 234
Leading as a follower 235
Leading when your position is honorary 238
Leading when you're not expected to succeed. 240

CHAPTER 3: **Creating a Vision**. 243
Where Do Visions Come From?. 243
Experience lets you visualize from the way you live 244
Knowledge lets you visualize from what you've learned. 244
Imagination helps turn randomness into a vision 245
Supplying the Human Element 246
A vision is a reminder of why you joined the group. 246
A vision attracts commitment and energizes people. 247
Establishing a Standard of Excellence 248
Helping You Stay Ahead of the Game 248
Becoming a visionary 249
Benchmarking everything 250
A Vision Links the Present to the Future 251
Building on the present 252
Envisioning the future. 252
A Vision Is a Doable Dream 253
Understanding what is doable. 253
Keeping the vision simple. 255
A Vision Is Not Just an Idea. 255
A vision depends on your ability to create a team 255
A vision depends on the ability to create a plan. 257
A Vision Is Based on Reality. 258
Thinking beyond available resources. 259
Responding to diminishing resources 260

A Vision Helps You Harness Opportunities 260
    Spotting an opportunity 261
    Searching out an opportunity 261
    Creating an atmosphere in which ideas flourish 262
    Moving from an idea to a plan. 263
A Vision Is Dynamic 265

CHAPTER 4: **Leading across Cultures** 267
Leading in a Diverse World 267
    Putting the diverse needs of your group first 269
    Listening to voices very different from your own. 269
    Eliciting cooperation from a diverse group 270
Emerging as a Leader from a Cultural Group 271
    Strive to want more. 272
    Toleration is a dirty word 272
Leading across International Divides 273
    Commit your brightest and best. 274
    Use the de minimus rule in making decisions 274
    Understand that capital doesn't make right 274
Leading in the Virtual Age 275

BOOK 4: TIME MANAGEMENT 277

CHAPTER 1: **Organizing Yourself** 279
Planning 279
    Achieving peace of mind 280
    Activating your subconscious mind 280
    The 1,000 percent return 281
    Assemble what you need 281
    Handle everything — once. 282
Grabbing the Three Keys to Personal Organization. 282
    Stepping back to evaluate 283
    Developing neatness habits. 283
    Refusing to excuse 284

CHAPTER 2: **Setting Yourself Up for Success** 285
Getting to Know Yourself 286
    Assessing your strengths and weaknesses 286
    Naming goals to give you direction 287
    Assigning a monetary worth to your time 287
    Identifying your rhythm to get in the zone 288
Following a System 289
    Scheduling your time and creating a routine 290
    Organizing your surroundings. 290

Overcoming Time-Management Obstacles 291
    Communicating effectively. 292
    Circumventing interruptions 292
    Getting procrastination under control 292
    Making decisions: Just do it 293
Garnering Support While Establishing Your Boundaries. 293
    Balancing work and time with family and friends 294
    Streamlining interactions with co-workers and customers. 294
Keeping Motivation High 295

CHAPTER 3: **Valuing Your Time** 297
Getting a Good Grip on the Time-Equals-Money Concept 298
Calculating Your Hourly Income 299
Boosting Your Hourly Value through Your Work Efforts 301
Making Value-Based Time Decisions in Your Personal Life. 302
    Deciding whether to buy time: Chores and responsibilities 303
    Making time-spending decisions: Leisure activities 303
    Looking at rewards 304
    Factoring in monetary and time costs 304
    Staying open to experiences and using time wisely. 306

CHAPTER 4: **Focusing, Prioritizing, and Time-Blocking** 307
Focusing Your Energy with the 80/20 Theory of Everything 308
    Matching time investment to return. 308
    The vital 20 percent: Figuring out where
    to focus your energy at work. 311
    Personal essentials: Channeling efforts in your personal life. . . .312
Getting Down to Specifics: Daily Prioritization 315
Blocking Off Your Time and Plugging in Your To-Do Items. 318
    Step 1: Dividing your day 319
    Step 2: Scheduling your personal activities. 320
    Step 3: Factoring in your work activities. 320
    Step 4: Accounting for weekly self-evaluation
    and planning time 321
    Step 5: Building in flextime 321
Assessing Your Progress and Adjusting Your Plan as Needed 322
    Surveying your results 322
    Tweaking your system 324

CHAPTER 5: **Controlling Email Overload** 327
Managing Email Effectively. 327
    Setting up filtering systems 328
Separating Your Work and Private Life 329
    Managing multiple email addresses. 329
    Organizing and storing email. 329

Responding to Email More Quickly. 330
    Employing an email response system 331
    Automating your responses. 333

BOOK 5: BUSINESS WRITING 335

CHAPTER 1: **Planning Your Message** 337
Adopting the Plan-Draft-Edit Principle 337
Fine-Tuning Your Plan: Your Goals and Audience 338
    Defining your goal: Know what you want .338
    Defining your audience: Know your reader. 340
    Brainstorming the best content for your purpose 344
    Writing to groups and strangers 345
    Imagining your readers 345
Making People Care 347
    Connecting instantly with your reader. 347
    Focusing on WIIFM 348
    Highlighting benefits, not features 349
    Finding the concrete and limiting the abstract 350
Choosing Your Written Voice: Tone 351
    Being appropriate to the occasion, relationship,
    and culture 352
    Writing as your authentic self 353
    Being relentlessly respectful 353
    Smiling when you say it 354
Using Relationship-Building Techniques 355
    Personalizing what you write. 356
    Framing messages with *you* not *I* 356

CHAPTER 2: **Making Your Writing Work** 359
Stepping into a Twenty-First-Century Writing Style 359
    Aiming for a clear, simple style 360
    Applying readability guidelines 361
    Finding the right rhythm. 364
    Achieving a conversational tone 366
Enlivening Your Language 368
    Relying on everyday words and phrasing 368
    Choosing reader-friendly words 369
    Focusing on the real and concrete 370
    Finding action verbs 372
    Crafting comparisons to help readers 373
Using Reader-Friendly Graphic Techniques 375
    Building in white space. 375
    Toying with type. 376

Keeping colors simple..377
Adding effective graphics....................................378
Breaking space up with sidebars, boxes, and lists...........378

CHAPTER 3: **Improving Your Work**.................................381
Changing Hats: Going from Writer to Editor...................381
Choosing a way to edit.....................................382
Distancing yourself from what you write....................384
Reviewing the Big and Small Pictures.........................385
Assessing content success.................................385
Assessing the effectiveness of your language..............386
Avoiding telltale up-down-up inflection...................388
Looking for repeat word endings...........................389
Pruning prepositions......................................392
Cutting all non-contributing words........................392
Moving from Passive to Active................................395
Thinking *action*...395
Trimming *there is* and *there are*.......................396
Cutting the *haves* and *have nots*.......................397
Using the passive deliberately............................397
Sidestepping Jargon, Clichés, and Extra Modifiers............398
Reining in jargon...398
Cooling the clichés.......................................400
Minimizing modifiers......................................401

CHAPTER 4: **Troubleshooting Your Writing**.......................403
Organizing Your Document.....................................403
Paragraphing for logic....................................404
Building with subheads....................................405
Working with transitions..................................406
Working in lists: Numbers and bulleting...................408
Catching Common Mistakes.....................................411
Using comma sense...412
Using *however* correctly.................................413
Matching nouns and pronouns...............................414
Weighing *which* versus *that*............................415
Pondering *who* versus *that*.............................416
Choosing *who* versus *whom*..............................416
Beginning with *and* or *but*.............................418
Ending with prepositions..................................418
Reviewing and Proofreading: The Final Check..................419
Checking the big picture..................................419
Proofreading your work....................................420
Creating your very own writing improvement guide.........422

CHAPTER 5: Writing Emails That Get Results 425

Fast-Forwarding Your Agenda In-House and Out-of-House 426
Getting Off to a Great Start 428
    Writing subject lines that get your message read 428
    Using salutations that suit 430
    Drafting a strong email lead 431
Building Messages That Achieve Your Goals 433
    Clarifying your own goals 433
    Assessing what matters about your audience 434
    Determining the best content for emails 437
Structuring Your Middle Ground 438
Closing Strong 440
Perfecting Your Writing for Email 441
    Monitoring length and breadth 441
    Styling it right 442
    Going short: Words, sentences, paragraphs 443
    Using graphic techniques to promote clarity 443
    Using the signature block 445

BOOK 6: PRESENTATIONS 447

CHAPTER 1: Creating Compelling Content 449

Getting Your Content Up to Par 450
    Determining your content's purpose 450
    Covering your points in priority order 451
    Navigating content 451
Adding Variety and Impact 452
    Using facts 453
    Giving examples 453
    Citing references 454
    Telling stories 454
    Going by the numbers 455
    Quoting experts 456
    Contrasting and comparing 456
    Giving demonstrations 457
    Defining terms 458
    Answering rhetorical questions 458
    Explaining yourself 459
    Making assumptions 460
    Showing testimonials 461
    Making analogies 461

CHAPTER 2: **Honing Your Platform Skills** 463

Using Your Voice to Command Attention .464

    Rule 1: Speak out loud 464

    Rule 2: Project your voice — without shouting 466

    Rule 3: Vary your volume 467

    Speaking softly. 468

    Adjusting your rate 468

    Adding a solid punch to a statement 470

    Pausing eloquently 470

Captivating Audiences with Your Eyes 472

    Understanding the importance of eye contact 473

    Speaking with your eyes. 474

    Keeping eye contact with a large audience 475

Finding the Right Posture. 475

    Giving a bad impression with the wrong posture. 475

    Standing tall 477

    Rocking and rolling 479

    Moving gracefully and purposefully 480

Making the Right Facial Expressions. 481

Gesturing Creatively 482

    Exploring gesture types 482

    Making a grand gesture 484

    Eliminating distracting gestures 485

CHAPTER 3: **Captivating Your Audience** 487

Touching on the Laws of Communication Impact 488

Starting with the Law of Primacy. 489

Starting Off on the Right Foot 491

    Making a dynamic first impression. 491

    Using mild-to-wild creativity. 492

Building Your Introduction. 496

    Sticking with tradition. 496

    Spicing it up 497

    Engaging the audience with questions. .498

    Adding a little humor 499

    Setting the stage 500

    Starting out bold and interesting 501

    Phrasing transitions 502

CHAPTER 4: **Keeping Your Audience Captivated** 503

Standing and Shouting Out: The Law of Emphasis and Intensity. . . .504

    Comparing and contrasting. 505

    Changing your voice 506

    Adding pizzazz 506

    Highlighting specific aspects 508

Using special effects 509
Telling a story. 509
Demonstrating your point 509
Propping up 510
Tech-ing out 510
Involving Your Audience: The Law of Exercise and Engagement. . . .511
Involving the audience 511
Encouraging interaction 512
Hitting Their Hot Buttons: The Law of Interest 513
Facing the Consequences: The Law of Effect 515

CHAPTER 5: **Ending on a High Note** 517
Concluding Effectively: The Law of Recency 518
Affecting Your Audience Right to the End 519
Conclude, don't include 519
Signal that the end is near 519
End it already 520
Be neither meek nor weak. 520
Leave with a strong message. 520
Giving a Tactical Conclusion. 521
Repeating a theme (with a twist). 521
Leaving them smiling 521
Offering impressive incentives 522
Engineering Your Conclusion with Building Blocks 524
Ending with motivation and inspiration. .525
Advocating a new strategic approach and direction 526
Giving the audience a happy ending 528
Offering an informational conclusion. 529

BOOK 7: NEGOTIATION 533

CHAPTER 1: **Negotiating for Life** 535
When Am I Negotiating?. 535
The Six Basic Skills of Negotiating. 536
Preparing 537
Setting goals and limits. 539
Listening 539
Being clear 540
Pushing the pause button 542
Closing the deal. 542
Handling All Sorts of Negotiations 543
When negotiations get complicated. 544
International negotiations 544
Negotiations between men and women .545
Negotiation on the phone and via the Internet 545

CHAPTER 2: Knowing What You Want 547

Creating Your Vision 548
   Envisioning your future 549
   Making a commitment 553
   Identifying your values 555
Deciding How You Are Going to Achieve Your Vision. 555
   The three-year plan. 556
   Putting your plan into action 558
Preparing Yourself for Negotiation. 559
   A is for alert 559
   Dressing for success 560
   Walking through the door 561
   Leaving enough time. 563
Defining Your Space 563
   Negotiating on your home turf 563
   Seating with purpose 564
   Planning the environment far in advance 565

CHAPTER 3: Setting Goals 567

Setting a Good Goal 568
   Getting active participation from every team member 570
   Keeping the goals on course 571
   Setting the right number of goals. 571
   Setting specific rather than general goals 572
   Setting challenging yet attainable goals. .572
   Prioritizing your goals 573
Separating Long-Range Goals from Short-Range Goals 574
Setting the Opening Offer 574
Breaking the Stone Tablet 575

CHAPTER 4: Asking the Right Questions 577

Tickle It Out: The Art of Coaxing Out Information 577
   Battling the jargon. 578
   Clarifying relativity. 579
Asking Good Questions: A Real Power Tool .580
   Avoid intimidation. 582
   Ask, don't tell 583
   Avoid leading questions 584
   Don't assume anything. 585
   Ask open-ended questions 587
   Ask again. 588
   Use your asks wisely 589
   Accept no substitutes 589

Dealing with Unacceptable Responses 590
Don't tolerate the dodge 590
Don't accept an assertion for the answer 590
Don't allow too many pronouns 591
Look for Evidence of Listening. 591

CHAPTER 5: **Closing the Deal**. 593
Good Deals, Bad Deals, and Win-Win Negotiating 594
Assessing the deal. 595
Creating win-win deals 597
Concessions versus Conditions. 599
What It Means to Close a Deal. 601
Understanding the Letter of the Law 602
Legal definition of a closed deal 602
Offers and counteroffers 603
Written versus oral contracts. 603
Legal protection before the contract 604
Recognizing When to Close 604
Knowing How to Close 605
The good closer 605
The only three closing strategies you'll ever need 606
Using linkage to close 607
Barriers to Closing. 609
Overcoming fears 609
Overcoming objections. 611
Closing When It's All in the Family. 613
When the Deal Is Done. 614
Review the process 614
Set up systems for checking the system .615
Remember to celebrate!. 616

INDEX. 617

Introduction

When was the last time you received an email and cringed at the muddled organization and horrible grammar? Or you felt so overwhelmed that your productivity plummeted? Or how about the last time you or a colleague were so nervous during a presentation that you came across as unprepared or worse — unprofessional?

Unfortunately, business professionals in all stages of their careers encounter these situations at one point or another. Although these instances may seem benign on the surface, they harm your professional reputation, which is hard to reverse. Would you want to do business with someone who is so unorganized that he constantly misses deadlines or turns in shoddy work because he's rushed? Of course not! Time management and having a solid organizational system are just a couple of the secrets to success that we discuss in this book.

About This Book

This book provides you with detailed information on topics that will help you gain the confidence needed to grow and advance in your professional life. You'll read about how practicing mindfulness can make you a more effective manager, how to craft the perfect written document that gets results, how to present like a pro, and more.

Foolish Assumptions

There's a time and a place for just about everything and assumptions are no different. First, we assume that you are a business professional and you're ready, willing, and able to devote some time and energy into your professional development.

We also assume that you have at least a general knowledge of the major software packages that businesses use and are interested in utilizing them to advance in your professional activities. If that's the case, this is the book for you!

Icons Used in This Book

Throughout this book, you'll find special icons to call attention to important information. Here's what to expect.

TIP

"If you see people falling asleep during your presentations, bang a book against the table to wake them up." Kidding!

This icon is used for helpful suggestions and things you may find useful at some point. No worries, though: No one will be falling asleep during your presentations if you take to heart the tip written here!

REMEMBER

This icon is used when something is essential and bears repeating. Again, this icon is used when something is essential and bears repeating. (See what we did there?)

TECHNICAL
STUFF

The little Dummies Man is information to share with the people who handle the technical aspect of things. You can skip technical-oriented information without derailing any of the hard work you're putting toward achieving your best professional self.

WARNING

Pay attention to these warnings to avoid potential pitfalls. Nothing suggested will get you fired or arrested (unless you do something like practice mindfulness *so well* that you start to nod off while driving or during meetings with the CEO — we can't help you there). If you see this icon, slow down and proceed with caution.

Beyond the Book

Although this book is a one-stop shop for your professional development, we can cover only so much in a set number of pages! If you find yourself at the end of this book thinking, "This was an amazing book! Where can I learn more about how to advance my career by working on my professional development?" head over to www.dummies.com for more resources.

For details about significant updates or changes that occur between editions of this book, go to www.dummies.com, search for *Career Development All-in-One For Dummies,* and open the Downloads tab on this book's dedicated page.

In addition, check out the cheat sheet for this book for tips on making presentations, making the most of your time, and more. To get to the cheat sheet, go to www.dummies.com, and then type *Career Development All-in-One For Dummies* in the Search box.

1
Mindfulness

Contents at a Glance

CHAPTER 1: Exploring Mindfulness in the Workplace.......... 5

Becoming More Mindful at Work 6

Finding Out Why Your Brain Needs Mindfulness 12

Starting Your Mindful Journey............................. 21

CHAPTER 2: Discovering the Benefits of Mindfulness......... 27

Discovering the Benefits for Employees 27

Looking at the Organizational Benefits of Mindfulness.......... 37

CHAPTER 3: Applying Mindfulness in the Workplace 47

Gaining Perspective in the Modern-Day Workplace............. 47

Adjusting Your Mental Mind-Set 55

Rewiring Your Brain 60

Developing Mindfulness at Work 63

CHAPTER 4: Practicing Mindfulness in the Digital Age 73

Choosing When to Use Technology 73

Communicating Mindfully 78

Using Technology Mindfully............................... 88

Chapter **1**

Exploring Mindfulness in the Workplace

n tough economic times, many organizations look for new ways to deliver better products and services to customers while reducing costs. Carrying on as normal isn't an option. Leaders must engage staff, and everyone needs to become more resilient in the face of ongoing change. For these reasons, more and more organizations offer staff training in mindfulness.

Major corporations, such as General Mills, have offered staff mindfulness training in recent years. Google and eBay are among the many companies that now provide rooms for staff to practice mindfulness during work time. Business schools such as Harvard Business School now include mindfulness principles in their leadership programs.

So what is mindfulness, and why are so many leading organizations investing in it?

Becoming More Mindful at Work

In this section, you discover what mindfulness is. More importantly, you also discover what mindfulness is not! You find out how mindfulness evolved and why it's become so important in the modern-day workplace.

Clarifying what mindfulness is

Have you ever driven somewhere and arrived at your destination remembering nothing about your journey? Or grabbed a snack and noticed a few moments later that all you have left is an empty wrapper? Most people have! These examples are common ones of *mindlessness*, or going on autopilot.

Like many humans, you're probably not present for much of your own life. You may fail to notice the good things in your life or hear what your body is telling you. You probably also make your life harder than it needs to be by poisoning yourself with toxic self-criticism.

Mindfulness can help you to become more aware of your thoughts, feelings, and sensations in a way that suspends judgment and self-criticism. Developing the ability to pay attention to and see clearly whatever is happening moment by moment doesn't eliminate life's pressures, but it can help you respond to them in a more productive, calmer manner.

Learning and practicing mindfulness can help you to recognize and step away from habitual, often unconscious emotional and physiological reactions to everyday events. Practicing mindfulness allows you to be fully present in your life and work and improves your quality of life.

Mindfulness can help you to

>> Recognize, slow down, or stop automatic and habitual reactions

>> Respond more effectively to complex or difficult situations

>> See situations with greater focus and clarity

>> Become more creative

>> Achieve balance and resilience at both work and home

REMEMBER

Mindfulness at work is all about developing awareness of thoughts, emotions, and physiology and how they interact with one another. Mindfulness is also about being aware of your surroundings, helping you better understand the needs of those around you.

Mindfulness training is like going to the gym. In the same way as training a muscle, you can train your brain to direct your attention to where you want it to be. In simple terms, mindfulness is all about managing your mind.

Taking a look at the background

Mindfulness has its origins in ancient Eastern meditation practices. In the late 1970s, Jon Kabat-Zinn developed Mindfulness-Based Stress Reduction (MBSR), which became the foundation for modern-day mindfulness. Figure 1-1 shows how it developed.

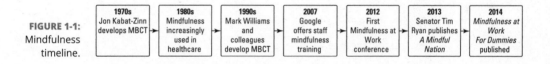

FIGURE 1-1: Mindfulness timeline.

1970s	1980s	1990s	2007	2012	2013	2014
Jon Kabat-Zinn develops MBCT	Mindfulness increasingly used in healthcare	Mark Williams and colleagues develop MBCT	Google offers staff mindfulness training	First Mindfulness at Work conference	Senator Tim Ryan publishes *A Mindful Nation*	*Mindfulness at Work For Dummies* published

In the 1990s Mark Williams, John Teasdale, and Zindel Segal further developed MBSR to help people suffering from depression. Mindfulness-Based Cognitive Therapy (MBCT) combined cognitive behavioral therapy (CBT) with mindfulness.

Since the late 1970s, research into the benefits of mindfulness has steadily increased. Recent studies have examined, for example, the effect of practicing mindfulness on the immune system and on those working in high-pressure environments.

Advances in brain-scanning technology have demonstrated that as little as eight weeks of mindfulness training can positively alter brain structures, including the amygdala (the fear center) and the left prefrontal cortex (an area associated with happiness and well-being). Other studies show benefits in even shorter periods of time.

Busy leaders who practice mindfulness have long extolled its virtues, but little research has existed to back up their claims. Fortunately, researchers are now increasingly focusing their attention on the benefits of mindfulness from a workplace perspective.

MBSR and MBCT are taught using a standard eight-week curriculum, and all teachers follow a formalized development route. The core techniques are the same for both courses. Most workplace mindfulness courses are based around MBCT or MBSR but tailored to meet the needs of the workplace.

Although MBSR and MBCT were first developed to help treat a range of physical and mental health conditions, new applications for the techniques have been established. Mindfulness is now being taught in schools and universities, and has even been introduced to prisoners. Many professional education programs, such as MBAs, now include mindfulness training.

Researchers have linked the practice of mindfulness to skills that are highly valuable in the workplace. Research suggests that practicing mindfulness can enhance

» Emotional intelligence

» Creativity and innovation

» Employee engagement

» Interpersonal relationships

» Ability to see the bigger picture

» Resilience

» Self-management

» Problem solving

» Decision making

» Focus and concentration

In addition, mindfulness is valuable in the workplace because it has a positive effect on immunity and general well-being. It has been demonstrated to relieve the symptoms of depression, anxiety, and stress.

ACT

In the late 1980s, research began by Steven Hayes and colleagues for another form of training called Acceptance and Commitment Theraphy (ACT). ACT combines mindfulness and acceptance with action-based strategies. In the last few years, ACT has begun to be adapted to meet the modern workplace, sometimes called Acceptance and Commitment Training.

Recognizing what mindfulness isn't

Misleading myths about mindfulness abound. Here are a few:

Myth 1: I will need to visit a Buddhist center, go on a retreat, or travel to the Far East to learn mindfulness.

Experienced mindfulness instructors are operating all over the world. Many teachers now teach mindfulness to groups of staff in the workplace. One-to-one mindfulness teaching can be delivered in the office, in hotel meeting rooms, or even on the web. Some people do attend retreats after learning mindfulness if they want to deepen their knowledge, experience peace and quiet, or gain further tuition, but doing so isn't essential.

Myth 2: Practicing mindfulness will conflict with my religious beliefs.

Mindfulness isn't a religion. For example, MBSR and MBCT are entirely secular — as are most workplace programs. No religious belief of any kind is necessary. Mindfulness can help you step back from your mental noise and tune into your own innate wisdom. Mindfulness is practiced by people of all faiths and by those with no spiritual beliefs. Practicing mindfulness won't turn you into a hemp-clad tofu eater, a tree-hugging hippie, or a monk sitting on top of a mountain — unless you want to be one of these people, of course!

Myth 3: I'm too busy to sit and be quiet for any length of time.

When you're busy, the thought of sitting and doing nothing may seem like the last thing you want to do. In 2010, researchers at Harvard University gathered evidence from a quarter of a million people suggesting that, on average, the mind wanders for 47 percent of the working day. Just 15 minutes a day spent practicing mindfulness can help you to become more productive and less distracted. Then you'll be able to make the most of your busy day and get more done in less time. When you first start practicing mindfulness, you'll almost certainly experience mental distractions, but if you persevere you'll find it easier to tune out distractions and to manage your mind. As time goes on, your ability to concentrate increases as does your sense of well-being and a feeling of control over your life.

Myth 4: Practicing mindfulness will reduce my ambition and drive.

Practicing mindfulness can help you become more focused on your goals and better able to achieve them. It can help you become more creative and gain new perspectives on life. If your approach to work is chaotic, mindfulness can make you more focused and centered, which in turn enables you to channel your energy more productively. Coupled with an improved sense of well-being, this ability to focus helps you achieve your career ambitions and goals.

Myth 5: If I practice mindfulness, people will take me less seriously and my career prospects will be damaged.

Some of the most successful and influential people in the world practice mindfulness. Senator Tim Ryan and Goldie Hawn, for example, are keen advocates of mindfulness. Practicing mindfulness doesn't involve sitting cross-legged on the floor — an office chair is fine. If you find it impossible to sit quietly and focus because you work in an open-plan office, or you're concerned about what others think, plenty of other everyday activities can become opportunities to practice mindfulness that nobody will notice. Walking, eating, waiting for your computer to boot up, or even exercising at the gym are all good opportunities to practice mindfulness. Mindfulness can be practicing with your eyes open, while you're moving around during the day.

Myth 6: Mindfulness and meditation are one and the same. Mindfulness is just a trendy new name.

Fact: Mindfulness often involves specific meditation practices. Fiction: All meditation is the same. Many popular forms of meditation are all about relaxation — leaving your troubles behind and imagining yourself in a calm and tranquil special place. Mindfulness helps you to find out how to live with your life in the present moment — warts and all — rather than run away from it. Mindfulness is about approaching life and things that you find difficult and exploring them with openness, rather than avoiding them. Most people find that practicing mindfulness does help them to relax, but that this relaxation is a welcome by-product, not the objective!

Training your attention: The power of focus

Are you one of the millions of workers who routinely put in long hours, often for little or no extra pay? In the current climate of cutbacks, job losses, and business efficiencies, many people feel the need to work longer hours just to keep on top of their workload. However, research shows that working longer hours does not mean that you get more done. Actually, if you continue to work when past your peak, your performance slackens and continues to do so as time goes on.

Imagine your job is to chop logs. After a while, your axe needs sharpening and your muscles need resting. If you keep going, you'll become inefficient and are more likely to have an accident. By taking a break and sharpening your axe, you can return to the job and get more done in less time. You'll probably enjoy the job more too. Mindfulness practice is like taking that break — you reenergize and sharpen your mind, ready for your next activity.

REMEMBER

Discovering how to focus and concentrate better is the key to maintaining peak performance. Recognizing when you've slipped past peak performance and then taking steps to bring yourself back to peak are also vital. Mindfulness comes in at this point. Over time, it helps you focus your attention to where you want it to be.

Focusing your attention may sound easy, but try thinking of just one thing for 90 seconds. It could be an object on your desk, a specific sound, or the sensation of your own breathing. Focus your full attention on your chosen object, sound, or sensation and nothing else. Then consider these questions:

>> Did you manage to focus your complete attention for the full 90 seconds, or did your mind wander and random thoughts arise?

>> Did you become distracted by a bodily pain or ache?

>> Did you find yourself getting annoyed with yourself, or annoyed with a sound such as a ticking clock or traffic?

You're not alone! Most people find this activity difficult at first. In truth, you're unlikely to ever be able to shut out all your mental chatter, but you can turn the volume down. Doing so enables you to see things more clearly, reduce time wasted on duplicated work, and stop your mind from wandering. Mindfulness offers you a way of getting more done in less time without burning yourself out.

Applying mindful attitudes

Practicing mindfulness involves more than just training your brain to focus. It also teaches you some alternative mindful attitudes to life's challenges. You discover the links between your thoughts, emotions, and physiology. You find out that what's important isn't what happens to you but how you choose to respond. This statement may sound simple, but most people respond to situations based on their mental programming (past experiences and predictions of what will happen next). Practicing mindfulness makes you more aware of how your thoughts, emotions, and physiology affect your responses to people and situations. This awareness then enables you to choose how to respond rather than react on autopilot. You may well find that you respond in a different manner.

By gaining a better understanding of your brain's response to life events, you can use mindfulness techniques to reduce your fight-or-flight response and regain your body's rest-and-relaxation state. You will see things more clearly and get more done.

Mindfulness also brings you face to face with your inner bully — the voice in your head that says you're not talented enough, not smart enough, or not good enough. By learning to treat thoughts like these as mental processes and not facts, the inner bully loses its grip on your life and you become free to reach your full potential.

These examples are just a few of the many ways that a mindful attitude can have a positive effect on your life and career prospects.

Finding Out Why Your Brain Needs Mindfulness

Recent advances in brain-scanning technology are helping us understand why our brain needs mindfulness. In this section, you discover powerful things about your brain: its evolution, its hidden rules, how thoughts shape your brain structure, and the basics of how your brain operates at work.

TECHNICAL STUFF

FACTS AND FIGURES

Size:

- Around 1,300 grams — that's over three times the size of a chimpanzee's, our closest animal relative.

- The human brain accounts for 2 percent of the body's weight but uses around 20 percent of its energy.

Energy consumption:

- A typical adult human brain runs on around 12 watts — a fifth of the power required by a standard 60 watt light bulb.

- Compared with most other organs, the brain is energy-hungry; but compared to manmade electronics, the brain is extremely efficient. IBM's Watson supercomputer depends on 90 IBM Power 750 servers, each of which requires around 1,000 watts.

Operating system:

- Energy travels to the brain via blood vessels in the form of glucose.

- The brain contains billions of nerve cells that send and receive information around the body.

- The brain never sleeps! It provides instant access to information on demand.

Performance:

- Neurons (brain cells that process and transmit information through electrical and chemical signals) fire around 5 to 50 times a second (or faster).

- Signals cross your brain in a tenth or hundredth of a second.

Evolving from lizard to spaceman

To understand how mindfulness works, you need to know some basics about the human brain. Over millions of years, the human brain has evolved to become the most sophisticated on the planet (see Figure 1-2).

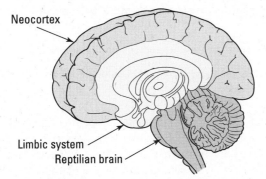

FIGURE 1-2:
Evolution of the human brain.

Neocortex

Limbic system
Reptilian brain

The oldest part of the brain is known as the *reptilian brain.* It controls your body's vital functions such as heart rate, breathing, body temperature, and balance. Your reptilian brain includes the main structures found in a reptile's brain: the brainstem and the cerebellum.

The middle part of your brain is known as the *limbic brain.* It emerged in the first mammals. It records memories of behaviors that produced agreeable and disagreeable experiences for you. The limbic system is responsible for your emotions and value judgments. The reptilian brain and limbic system are rigid and inflexible in how they operate. We call these two areas the *primitive brain.*

The newest part of our brain consists is the neocortex. It has deep grooves and wrinkles that allow the surface area to increase far beyond what could otherwise fit in the same size skull. It accounts for around 85 percent of the human brain's total mass. Some say that the neocortex is what makes us human. The neocortex is responsible for your abstract thoughts, imagination, and consciousness. For simplicity, we call it the *higher brain.* The higher brain is highly flexible and has an almost infinite ability to learn.

The primitive brain deals with routine tasks and needs little energy to operate quickly. The higher brain is incredibly powerful but requires a lot of energy to run and operates more slowly than the primitive brain. These differences explain why you often experience strong emotions or take action long before logic starts to kick in. It also explains the human tendency to work on autopilot (based on responses stored in the primitive brain) for much of the time.

Because you spend much of your time working on autopilot, you're often unaware of your thoughts, emotions, and physiology in the present moment. The following short activity is designed to help you recognize your routine responses and how changing them just slightly can make you more aware of them:

1. Sit in a different chair from usual in a meeting, park in a different spot in the car park, sleep on the other side of the bed, or use a different hand to write with.

2. Observe your thoughts, emotions, and bodily responses.

3. Identify how you felt. Did you find changing your behavior difficult? Did you feel awkward?

REMEMBER

Doing things differently can be hard because your mental programming is probably screaming, "You've got it wrong; that's not how you do it." Carrying out an activity in a new way involves conscious thought and thus engages your higher brain, which needs more energy to function. This explains why even small changes can feel difficult or uncomfortable.

Discovering your brain's hidden rules

Imagine yourself as one of your ancient ancestors — a cave dweller. In ancient times, you had to make life-or-death decisions every day. You had to decide whether it was best to approach a reward (such as killing a deer) or avoid a threat (such as a fierce predator charging at you). If you failed to gain your reward, in this example a deer to eat, you'd probably live to hunt another day. But if you failed to avoid the threat, you'd be dead, never to hunt again.

As a result of facing these daily dangers, your brain has evolved to minimize threat. Unfortunately, this has led to the brain spending much more time looking for potential risks and problems than seeking rewards and embracing new opportunities. This tendency is called the *human negativity bias.*

Try the following:

1. Think of six bad things that have happened recently.

2. Think of six good things that have happened recently.

3. Identify which task you found easiest.

Most people readily conjure up six bad things but struggle to think of six good things. The bad things dominate because the brain is primed to expend more energy looking for potential threats (bad things) than looking for opportunities (good things).

When your brain detects a potential threat, it floods your system with powerful hormones designed to help you evade mortal danger. The sudden flood of dozens of hormones into your body results in your heart rate speeding up, blood pressure increasing, pupils dilating, and veins in skin constricting to send more blood to major muscle groups to help you sprint away from danger. More oxygen is pumped into your lungs, and non-essential systems (such as digestion, the immune system, and routine body repair and maintenance) shut down to provide more energy for emergency functions. Your brain starts to have trouble focusing on small tasks because it's trying to maintain focus on the big picture to anticipate and avoid further threat.

Threat or risk avoidance is controlled by the primitive areas of your brain, which operate fast. This speed explains why, when you unexpectedly encounter a snake in the woods, your primitive brain decides on the best way to keep you safe from harm with no conscious thought, and you jump out of the way long before your higher brain engages to find a rational solution.

This process is great from an evolutionary perspective but can be bad news in modern-day life. Many people routinely overestimate the potential threat involved in everyday work such as a critical boss, a failed presentation, or social humiliation. The brain treats these modern-day "threats" in exactly the same way as your ancestor's response to mortal danger. This fight-or-flight response was designed to be used for short periods of time. Unfortunately, when under pressure at work, it can remain activated for long periods. This activation can lead to poor concentration, an inability to focus, low immunity, and even serious illness.

Mindfulness training helps you to recognize when you're in this heightened state of arousal and then reduce or even switch off the fight-or-flight response. It also helps you develop the skill to trigger at will your rest-and-relaxation response, bringing your body back to normal, allowing it to repair itself and increasing both your sense of well-being and your ability to focus on work.

Recognizing that you are what you think

For many years, it was thought that your brain became fixed once you reached a certain age. We now know that the adult brain retains impressive powers of *neuroplasticity*, the ability to change its structure and function in response to experience. It was also believed that, if you damaged certain areas of the brain (as a result of a stroke or other brain injury), you'd no longer be capable of performing certain brain functions. We now know that in some cases the brain can rewire itself and train a different area to undertake the functions that the damaged part previously carried out. The brain's hard wiring (neural pathways) change constantly in response to thoughts and experiences.

Neuroplasticity offers amazing opportunities to reinvent yourself and change the way you do and think about things. Your unique brain wiring is a result of your thoughts and experiences in life. Blaming your genes or upbringing; saying "It's not my fault; that's how I was born" is no longer a good excuse!

To take advantage of this knowledge, you need to develop awareness of your thoughts, and the effect that these thoughts have on your emotions and physiology. The problem is that, if you're like most people, you're probably rarely aware of the majority of your thoughts. Let's face it — you'd be exhausted if you were! Mindfulness helps you to develop the ability to passively observe your thoughts as mental processes. In turn, this allows you to observe patterns of thought and decide whether these patterns are appropriate and serve you well. If you decide that they're not, your awareness of them gives you the opportunity to replace them with better ways of thinking and behaving.

For example, if you arrive at work and think, "Oh no, I've got so many tasks on my to-do list. I'm never going to get them all done! I'm so inefficient." and so on, your brain is on a negative thought stream. Mindfulness helps you to catch yourself doing that and, instead, simply and more calmly move your attention to the first priority on your list of things to do.

Another common problem you may encounter is that you may *think* that your decisions and actions are always based on present-moment facts, but in reality they rarely are. Making decisions based on your brain's prediction of the future (which is usually based on your past experiences and unique brain wiring) is common. In addition, you see with your brain; in other words, your brain acts as a filter to incoming information from the eyes and chooses what it thinks is important. The problem is that you routinely make decisions and act without full possession of the facts. What happened in the past will not necessarily happen now; your predictions about the future could be inaccurate, leading to inappropriate responses and actions.

So, going back to the example of the long to-do list, if you're mindful, you can choose to do what's most important, rather than just automatically reacting to the last email you received.

REMEMBER

Practicing mindfulness helps you to see the bigger picture and make decisions based on present-moment facts rather than self-generated assumptions and fiction.

Here's another example. When you're under pressure, it's all too easy to fall into a thought spiral, with one thought driving the next. In the process, you develop your own story of what's going on around you, which can be wildly different from reality. For example, if you fail to get an invitation to a meeting at work you think you should attend, your thoughts might follow this pattern:

Why haven't they invited me?

They obviously think that my team and I have nothing to contribute.

Maybe they're discussing redundancies.

Maybe they haven't invited me because they're discussing making me redundant!

At my age, I'll never get another job!

How will I pay off the remainder of the mortgage?

This may mean my son has to drop out of college.

I'll ruin my son's life. I'm a dreadful father. I'm such a loser.

In reality, the failure to invite you was an administrative error, but your mind has created a detailed story, which your brain has treated as reality. As a result, your brain has triggered emotions (anger or fear), your body has become tense, and your heart rate has speeded up. Your emotions and physiology have a further effect on your thoughts and behavior, and so on.

Many people fall into this trap. Mindfulness helps you notice when your thoughts begin to spiral and take action to stop them spiraling down even further. You can observe what's going on in the present moment, and separate present-moment facts from self-created fiction. This ability gives you choices and a world of new possibilities.

Think of a person or situation that triggers your primitive brain's threat system. (Don't choose anything too scary or threatening!) Then:

1. **Observe what's going on in your head.** Identify patterns of thoughts, as if you were a spectator observing from the outside. What is it specifically that has triggered your primitive brain?

2. **Acknowledge your emotional response without judgment or self-blame.** Try to observe from a distance and see if you can reduce or prevent a strong emotional reaction by observing the interplay of your thoughts and emotions as if you were a bystander.

3. **Be kind to yourself.** You're human and just responding according to your mental wiring. Observe both your thoughts and emotions as simply mental processes, without the need to respond to them. Regarding them as thoughts not facts and being kind to yourself help to encourage your primitive brain to let go of the steering wheel and allow your higher brain to become the driver once more.

When developing new neural pathways, practice makes perfect. Changing your behavior or learning to do something new takes awareness, intention, action, and practice — no shortcuts exist! Understanding a few simple facts about how your brain works and making small adjustments to your responses can help you to create new and more productive neural pathways.

Exploring your brain at work

Before diving into more detail about mindfulness and how it could be of benefit to your work, you need to discover a little more about how your brain processes everyday work tasks.

Let's look at a real-life example. Jen is a senior manager working in a police training organization, where she is responsible for leading a team who develop doctrine (guidance and standards) for police forces across the country. Her job description includes the following desirable characteristics:

>> Organizational skills

>> Communication skills

>> Ability to manage conflicting priorities

>> Problem-solving skills

>> Decision-making skills

>> Relationship-building skills

>> Ability to manage change

One of the most challenging aspects of Jen's work is managing multiple and often conflicting demands. Because her role is national, she is responsible to multiple stakeholders working in different police forces and affiliate organizations. Problems sometimes arise when stakeholders think that their project is more important than other projects, and completion of that project by a certain date takes on an almost life-or-death importance in their minds. This elevated importance is often compounded by senior stakeholders taking sides and applying pressure. When this situation arises, Jen uses negotiation skills to try to resolve the issue. She gives the stakeholders a reality check, often along the lines of, "If I prioritize this, then I can't do that" or "If I do this first, that will be late."

At times like these, Jen notices her body tensing. She sometimes wakes at 2 a.m. trying to find a solution that resolves the conflict for all concerned. She sometimes experiences irritation and frustration at the inability of others to see the bigger picture. Her thoughts run along the following lines: "Either I'm not explaining it right or they're being obtuse"; "We're all supposed to be professionals, so why can't they behave as such?"; "No one will die if we're a few days late with this project"; and "Why are they acting so selfishly?"

What Jen is unaware of is the effect of one of the foundations of mindfulness training: non-judgmental observation of the interplay between her thoughts, emotions, and physiology. Her thoughts are triggering emotions, which are triggering a bodily response. Her bodily response (which she is largely unaware of) is having a tangible effect on her thoughts and decisions. Although she thinks that she's fully rational and in control when making decisions, in reality her emotions are also affecting her thoughts. If Jen were practicing mindfulness, she'd be much more aware of what's going on and able to choose alternative strategies that were better for her well-being and that might lead to wiser decisions.

Despite the fact that Jen is an experienced leader, calm, organized, and highly intelligent, her primitive brain has detected a possible threat to her social and professional status. Status — your place in the pecking order — is important to humans. Jen's amygdala (part of the limbic system in her primitive brain) triggers a fight-or-flight response. Her primitive brain is now in charge. Hijacked by emotions, her higher brain becomes helpless. In an attempt to keep her safe from harm, her primitive brain hijacks the driver's seat and she is reduced to being a passenger in the back seat, hanging on for dear life. Jen is in this position because her primitive brain switches off her higher brain, including the prefrontal cortex (PFC), shown in Figure 1-3. This vital part of your brain plays a huge role in decision making. The prefrontal cortex allows you to plan, create strategies, pay attention, learn, and focus on goals.

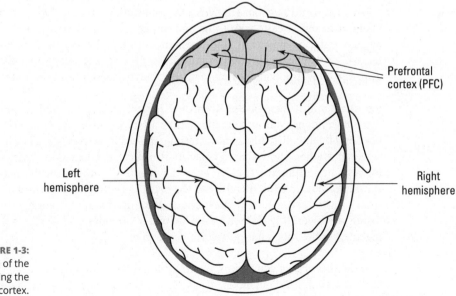

FIGURE 1-3:
Image of the brain showing the prefrontal cortex.

When finding out about mindfulness, you discover the interplay between your primitive brain's desire to keep you safe from harm and the effect of your sympathetic nervous system (which mobilizes your parasympathetic fight-or-flight response) on both your body and your ability to think clearly.

At times like this, Jen would benefit from a mindfulness exercise. She should focus her full attention on taking slow, deep breaths for a few minutes. Focusing her attention fully on the sensation of breathing will slow down or stop her mental chatter, which in turn will reduce the feeling of threat and trigger a lessening of her fight-or-flight response. In addition, her brain's PFC will get the oxygen it needs to regain control, and her primitive brain will hand back control to her PFC.

Of course, the rational PFC can't always prevent the primitive brain from engaging. This inability is because the primitive brain is more evolved and responds much more quickly than the highly powerful but slower and less-evolved higher brain. Mindfulness does not stop your rational higher brain from getting hijacked by your primitive brain, but it does make you much more aware of what's going on, much earlier. This awareness gives you choices in how to respond. You won't be forced to unconsciously default to primitive brain autopilot responses and actions. You have a choice!

Now we need to look at other elements of the brain that effect Jen's work and explore how mindfulness could be beneficial.

At times Jen feels as if she's hitting a brick wall when she's trying to find new solutions to old problems. When under pressure, defaulting to well-used, comfortable ways of doing things stored in the primitive brain is all too easy. Giving stock answers to questions may result. Mindfulness teaches you the benefits of taking time out to calm your mind and center yourself. Doing so can take as little as three minutes and can produce dramatic results. Allowing the brain to relax and let go of its frantic activity to solve the problem can deactivate the primitive brain's grip, and allow the higher brain to apply creativity and innovation to the problem.

Jen often multitasks, flitting from one project to another and juggling project work with phone calls and emails as they arise. She often finds herself becoming tired and having difficulty concentrating. The ability to multitask is a myth. Many research studies show that regular multitaskers get less done than those who focus on one thing at a time — even the people who think they're good at multitasking. Multitasking means that the brain is switching backward and forward from task to task, which wastes a huge amount of valuable energy. In addition, details are invariably lost with each switch. No wonder that Jen feels tired! She's making her life much harder than it needs to be.

Mindfulness shows you how to mentally stand back and observe what's going on around you and in your brain. It also helps you develop different approaches to life that are kinder to you and usually more productive. Mindfulness helps you observe and reduce the mental chatter that distracts you from your work, allowing you to focus on it more fully. By intentionally taking steps to recognize and avoid distractions and focusing your full attention on one task at a time, you can get things done more quickly, with fewer mistakes and less repetition. Using mindfulness techniques when you feel your attention waning can help you to restart work feeling refreshed and focused.

Mindfulness can also be useful in high-level meetings when emotions can sometimes be charged. Training in mindfulness would help Jen to observe the dynamics at play in such meetings more clearly. She'd probably recognize that in this situation, people are commonly motivated by the need to avoid potential threat (to status and social standing) and are unlikely to approach the task with an open mind and look for the best possible solution. Jen would also be aware of the two possible states of mind that people could be operating in.

In *avoidance mode,* people are motivated by the desire to avoid something happening. With their threat system activated, they may fail to see the bigger picture, be less able to think clearly, and be less creative in their ideas and solutions. Avoidance mode tends to be associated with increased activation of the right PFC. Excessive right-brain PFC activation is associated with depression and anxiety. Mindfulness cultivates an approach state of mind. Often the effort taken to avoid something happening is disproportionate to dealing with the thing you seek to avoid. An *approach mode* of mind is associated with increased left-brain PFC activation, which is connected with positivity and an upbeat approach to life. In approach mode, you're able to explore new possibilities and opportunities with an open mind.

When working in avoidance mode, cognitive thinking resources are diminished, making it harder to think and work things through. You're also likely to feel less positive and engaged. If Jen applied mindfulness to her work life, she'd be able to better manage her own emotions and subtly take steps to help reduce the sense of threat often permeating business meetings.

The brain can have a significant effect on how you work. Finding out about and practicing mindfulness gives you the tools you need to harness this knowledge to manage your mind better.

Starting Your Mindful Journey

Congratulations! The fact that you've picked up this book and started reading it means that you've already started your mindful journey. A good book is a great starting point, but nothing can replace experiencing mindfulness for yourself. As with learning anything new, you may find it difficult to know where to start. Learning mindfulness from an experienced teacher who can help you overcome obstacles and guide your development is advisable. The idea behind this book is to demonstrate *how* and *why* mindfulness can benefit you at work, and provide suggestions of how to apply simple mindfulness techniques to everyday work challenges.

Being mindful at work yourself

Getting caught up in the manic pace of everyday work life is common. You, like many workers, may feel under pressure to deliver more with fewer resources. You may also be keen to demonstrate what an asset you are to your company by working longer and longer hours, and being contactable round the clock.

Being mindful at work can involve as little or as much change as you're able to accommodate at this moment in time. At one end of the scale, you may simply apply knowledge of how the brain works and some mindful principles to your work. To gain maximum benefit, you need to practice mindfulness regularly and apply quick mindfulness techniques in the workplace when you need to regain focus or encounter difficulties. The choice is yours! The benefits you gain increase in line with the effort you put in. You should see a real difference after practicing mindfulness for as little as ten minutes a day for about six weeks.

At times, being mindful at work can involve an act of bravery — swimming against the tide by doing things differently. If the way you're currently working is leading to stress, anxiety, tiredness, or exhaustion, maybe you need to try something different. If you're tasked with being innovative and finding new ways of doing things, what makes you think that carrying on as you've always done will make this creativity possible? Humans dislike uncertainty and crave certainty. Defaulting to doing things as you've always done them is always easier, especially if they've become stored as habits in the primitive brain and can be repeated with little or no conscious thought.

Changing habits takes time and effort. For this reason, most mindfulness courses are taught weekly, over a five- to eight-week period. Each week you learn something new, practice it for a week, and then build new knowledge onto it the following week. When first learning to be mindful, most people find it easier to practice at home than at work. Practicing at home is simpler because controlling noise and disturbances at home is easier.

Following these initial practice sessions, most people then introduce a few short mindfulness techniques at work. Over time, as mindfulness becomes second nature to you, you'll develop the ability to practice wherever and whenever the opportunity arises. As your confidence builds and you apply mindfulness to your work further, others will probably notice changes in you. You may appear calmer, more poised, and better focused. Possibly your work relationships have improved. If you're lucky enough to be offered mindfulness sessions in work time, don't be surprised if people are curious, and ask you for tips and techniques to try out for themselves. Organizations that offer mindfulness classes often have a long waiting list of staff eager to attend.

Overcoming common challenges

Probably the most common challenges you face when learning mindfulness are concerns about what others think; finding the right time and place to practice; and breaking down habits and mind-sets to do things differently.

You now need to address each of these challenges in turn.

Dealing with concerns about what others think

In the past, mindfulness was often associated with Buddhism, spirituality, and new age ideas. This association was compounded by the fact that mindfulness was often taught only in Buddhist centers or local village halls. And, although MBSR had existed for over 40 years, and MBCT and ACT for about 20, they were used only in clinical settings and the general public was unaware of them. In addition, the media often confused mindfulness with other forms of meditation. Articles about mindfulness were often accompanied by pictures of people sitting cross-legged in the lotus position, their hands in prayer. This misleading image was almost certainly one of the reasons behind professionals' reluctance to come out of the mindfulness closet.

In recent years, mindfulness has been discussed in the White House, sampled at the World Economic Forum, and taught by major business schools. The press now feature mindfulness on a regular basis, and the pictures that accompany the articles are slowly becoming more representative of real-life mindfulness practice! As a result, more and more people are giving mindfulness a try, and integrating it into their workday.

Finding the right time and place to practice

If you're lucky enough to be offered mindfulness training by your organization, you quickly discover that mindfulness is unlike any other courses you've attended. Unlike most courses that employers routinely offer to staff, simply attending isn't enough. Classes help you understand the principles that underpin mindfulness and how mindfulness techniques work. They also provide you with a safe environment and guidance to try out different mindfulness techniques. However, the real learning usually happens outside work, as you practice it. You can't get fit without exercising, can you? The same applies to mindfulness. Think of mindfulness as a good workout for your brain; the more you practice, the easier it becomes.

On a typical workplace mindfulness course, you're taught a different technique each week, which you need to practice for at least six days before moving on to the next one. This process can prove to be one of the most challenging aspects of learning mindfulness. For many busy workers, their entire workday is scheduled, and this scheduling sometimes extends into their home life. With a mind-set of "so much to do and so little time," even finding 15 minutes a day can feel daunting. The question to ask yourself is, "Why am I doing this?" For many people, the answer is "because I cannot continue working in the way I do." If this is your reply, rearranging your life to make time for mindfulness is worthwhile.

TIP

Try not to think about mindfulness as just another thing that needs to be fitted into your busy life. Rather, view it as a new way to live your life. Think of the time you spend practicing mindfulness as "me time" — after all, this time is one of the rare moments in which you have nothing to do but focus on yourself.

Breaking down habits and mind-sets to do things differently

Habits are formed when you repeat the same thoughts or behaviors many times. Habits are highly efficient from a brain perspective because they're stored in the primitive brain, which can repeat them quickly without any conscious thought, using very little energy.

REMEMBER

Learning mindfulness may take effort, especially if you start to challenge your habits and patterns of thinking. Just as it takes time to form habits, so it takes time to replace old habits with different ways of thinking and being. With a little time and perseverance, you can find new ways of working that are more productive and better for your health and sense of well-being.

Creating a mindful workplace

Every great journey starts with just one step. A young single mother of three was once given the opportunity to climb Mount Everest. Three-quarters of the way up the mountain she became exhausted, felt overwhelmed by the whole journey, and declared that she could go no further. The trek leader calmly stood in front of her and asked whether she could see his footsteps in the snow ahead. She nodded in agreement. He told her that all she needed to do was put one foot in front of another, following his footsteps. By focusing on the present moment action of her feet, she was able to avoid worrying about the remainder of the journey. She made it to the summit — one of the greatest achievements of her life.

YOUR FIRST TASTE OF MINDFULNESS

If you're new to mindfulness, perhaps now is a good time to try the following little mindfulness exercise:

1. Sit on a chair in a comfortable posture. Try to sit upright rather than slouching, but you don't need to be tense or rigid.

2. Allow your eyes to close. If that's uncomfortable for you at the moment, simply cast your gaze downward.

3. Take three deep in and out breaths. As you breathe in, feel the sensation of your breath through your nose and into your body. As you breathe out, again feel the sensation of your breath leaving your body through your nose.

4. Now focus your attention on the sounds that surround you. They might be sounds in the room, elsewhere in the building, or outside the building. Try to treat them simply as sounds, using them as an anchor for your attention. There is no need to judge or categorize them; they are simply sounds.

5. Each time you notice that your mind has wandered off on a train of thought, which will certainly happen, turn your attention back to focusing your attention on sounds. It's important not to criticize or judge yourself for having a wandering mind — everyone has a wild mind! Just accept mind wandering as part and parcel of the process of mindfulness.

6. After a few minutes, focus your attention on any thoughts that may be going round your head. See if you can observe your thoughts simply as mental processes that come and go.

7. Finish with another three deep breaths — again, let those breaths be mindful by feeling each breath as it enters and leaves your body.

8. Slowly open your eyes if they've been closed and take a few moments to reflect on your experience. Notice how you feel having done this mindfulness exercise.

Mindfulness exercises like this can be difficult at first. Don't worry if you did not end the exercise relaxed and calm; everyone's experience is different. Like anything worth doing, mindfulness takes a little effort, but regular practice will pay dividends.

Getting caught up in planning the journey ahead is common, and at times you may feel overwhelmed by all the things you need to do and think about. When finding out about and practicing mindfulness for the first time, focus only on the next footstep, rather than the journey as a whole, is often the best approach. Try to let your mindful journey unfold, day by day, moment by moment. If you truly want your organization to become more mindful, you need to start by focusing on yourself. As you gain a deeper understanding of what mindfulness is, and start to experiment with integrating mindfulness into your life and work, you discover for yourself what works and what doesn't. Only then are you equipped to make a difference to your organization. The building blocks of a mindful organization are mindful employees who start to transform their organizations one step at a time.

Living the dream: Mindfulness at work

Sometimes the hardest part of a journey is taking the first step. In this book, you can find a wealth of information about mindfulness. You also discover mindful techniques for different situations that you may encounter at work and for different occupations.

The potential of mindfulness to transform the way you work and live your life is immense. The extent to which you benefit from it is entirely up to you and the effort that you're able to put into it.

REMEMBER

When discovering how to become more mindful, remember ABC:

>> **A** is for **awareness** — becoming more aware of what you're thinking and doing and what's going on in your mind and body.

>> **B** is for just **being** with your experiences — avoiding the tendency to respond on autopilot and feed problems by creating your own story.

>> **C** is for **choice** — by seeing things as they are you can **choose** to respond more wisely — by creating a gap between an experience and your reaction you can step out of autopilot and open up a world of new possibilities.

As with all new skills, the more you practice mindfulness, the easier it becomes. Canadian psychologist Donald Hebb coined the phrase "neurons that fire together, wire together." In other words, the more you practice mindfulness, the more you develop the neural pathways in the brain associated with being mindful.

Chapter **2**

Discovering the Benefits of Mindfulness

Mindfulness may appear to be the "in thing" at the moment, but does it have any substance? What are the actual benefits of mindfulness at work?

In this chapter, you uncover the positive effects of mindfulness for yourself. You discover the many positive changes that take place in your brain as a result of mindfulness practice. You find out why so many organizations are training their leaders and employees in mindfulness, and explore organizational ways of integrating mindfulness into the workplace to increase staff performance and well-being.

Discovering the Benefits for Employees

Being a mindful employee has many benefits. In this section, you find out how mindfulness changes your brain and how those changes make you more resilient, emotionally intelligent, and focused. If you're in a leadership position, you discover how mindfulness can make you more effective in your work, too.

Increased mental resilience

Resilience is the process of adapting well when you experience adversity, trauma, or a major source of stress. Resilience is sometimes described as the ability to bounce back from difficult experiences.

In the average workplace, mental resilience is essential. If you're resilient, you're able to deal with rapid changes and serious challenges rather than spiraling downward when faced with difficulties.

Resilience isn't a trait. You're not born with a certain amount of resilience and stuck with it. Instead, resilience involves a combination of thoughts, behaviors, and actions that you can learn. That's what makes resilience such an exciting concept.

Let's imagine you've been working on securing a bid for a huge project. You've been developing the presentation and report for months. You're under tremendous pressure to succeed and, when the day comes, your nerves get the better of you. You struggle to answer questions, as your mind goes blank. You lose the contract and your manager shouts at you in frustration and may even fire you. How would you feel? What would you think?

The following thoughts might arise from such a situation: "I failed. I'm so stupid. I messed up. What if I get fired? How will I pay my bills? I should have practiced more. What's wrong with me? I'm pathetic."

These thoughts emerge from the soup of emotions that's ignited by the stress you experienced. If you're unmindful, these thoughts persist and you're less able to bounce back from the experience. You feel increasingly worse and things can spiral downward.

From a mindful perspective, you notice that you're having these self-judgmental thoughts. You're then able to step back from them and see that, yes, the presentation didn't go well, but all the other things you're telling yourself are just thoughts arising from your negative feelings about the event — they aren't necessarily true. By acknowledging that feelings affect your thoughts, you can avoid reacting to the imagined threat and deal with the situation in a reasoned manner. You may choose to talk to your boss, explain what happened, and ask how to proceed — maybe you can give a presentation for a smaller project, or shift into a different role for the time being, or attend training in presentation skills. Over time, practicing mindfulness builds up your resilience to such workplace experiences and you'll be better able to deal with them.

Even the US army is using mindfulness to help build resilience in its recruits. Initial studies show that mindfulness helps to develop soldiers' mental fitness so that they're more able to make good decisions in stressful situations and less likely to suffer post-traumatic stress disorder.

Some people mistakenly think that resilient people don't experience distress — that's not true. When adversity strikes, experiencing mental and emotional pain is normal. Developing resilience, however, ensures that, over time, you're able to rebuild your life.

But, you may be wondering, how does mindfulness increase resilience in your brain? Research by Professor Richard Davidson and colleagues has discovered how mindfulness may help build resilience. They looked at people's brains when faced with a stressor and found that their amygdala (the part of the brain responsible for processing emotions and responding to fear) became activated, releasing stress hormones. The research participants also experienced negative, cyclical thoughts long after the stressor had passed. In those participants who practiced mindfulness, however, the activity of the amygdala reduced soon after the stressor was removed. Davidson states that better control of the amygdala may be the *key* to resilience.

Psychologist Barbara Fredrickson believes that mindfulness offers other ways to build resilience too:

>> **Acceptance:** You have the capacity to see what you can change and what you can't. In the preceding example, you can't change your presentation, but you can change your relationship to your thoughts that follow.

>> **Self-compassion:** You can be kind to yourself in the face of adversity. You find out how to be your own best friend rather than harshly criticize yourself. You see your difficulties as part and parcel of humanity's struggle with life's challenges, rather than a sense of you suffering alone. More than 200 studies show the positive benefits of self-compassion alone.

>> **Growth:** You are open to seeing difficulties as opportunities to learn and grow. Your mindset is open rather than fixed.

>> **Creativity:** In a more mindful state, the part of your brain geared toward creative thinking is active. You can come up with more novel solutions by visualizing different choices you could make, with consequent positive outcomes.

So, following an unsuccessful outcome to months of hard work, you may say to yourself, "Beating myself up is pointless. I worked hard, but I wasn't successful this time. I'm sure there are things I can discover from this experience. Perhaps

I could ask for feedback and tips from others. Then, after a few days of well-deserved rest, I can work on a different project."

Working in a resilient way isn't just for challenging circumstances. Mindfulness is a different way of being with your everyday experiences. You discover ways of living with awareness no matter what you're doing, seeking new challenges and looking forward to learning that may arise from them and drawing upon your insights for everything you do.

Here are five actions you can take to use mindfulness to help build your resilience:

>> **Help others.** Be mindful of the needs of others rather than just yourself. By seeking ways to help others when you're not so busy, you're more likely to be supported when going through difficulties yourself. For example, help John with his report, Michelle with her difficult team, or Jane with moving house over the weekend.

>> **Look after yourself.** In addition to helping others, help yourself too! Be mindful of how much sleep you're getting, how much exercise you're doing, and whether you're taking regular breaks. Muscles strengthen only if they have time to rest between activities. Your brain is the same.

>> **Nudge your mindset.** In any given moment, your brain receives far more information than it can actively be conscious of. So, rather than focusing the spotlight of your attention on what's not going well, focus it on the positives. What went well today? What are you grateful for? Think about it, make a note of it, or email someone close to you and share your appreciation. Your brain will thank you for it.

>> **Expect change.** If you practice mindfulness, you know that change is the only constant. When you try to focus on your breathing, your mind comes up with all sorts of thoughts. (See the nearby "Mindfulness of breath" sidebar.) If you can see that the nature of the world is change, and you seek to adapt to the change rather than avoid or run away from it, you're being more mindful and more resilient.

>> **Seek meaning.** When adversity strikes, after the initial period of sadness or anger, you do have a choice. You can sink into feeling sorry for yourself or look for an opportunity for growth. Post-traumatic growth obviously takes time but does usually happen. Look out for what you can discover from the challenges you're currently facing. For example, losing your job isn't nice but may allow you to decide on a new career path. Be mindful of the opportunities that arise for you.

MINDFULNESS OF BREATH

The mindfulness of breath exercise uses the breath as an anchor point on which to focus your attention. In this exercise, make sure that you do not try to *control* your breath — just *observe* it. The exercise isn't about relaxing (although many people do find it so). Rather, the exercise is about *falling awake,* becoming more aware of what's happening in your mind. Think of yourself as a kind scientist, inquisitively observing everything that's going on without judging or categorizing it.

Find somewhere quiet where you won't be disturbed. Read the following instructions, set a timer for 10 to 15 minutes, and guide yourself through the exercise. If possible, select a gentle alarm tone so that you don't jump out of your seat at the end of the exercise.

1. **Settle yourself in a chair where you can sit in a comfortable upright position.**

   Both feet should be firmly planted on the floor, with your shoulders relaxed and your head facing forward.

2. **Pay attention to the contact points between your body and the chair and floor.**

   Spend a few minutes exploring how your feet, legs, bottom, and any other areas in contact with the chair and floor feel.

3. **Notice how feelings arise and disappear.**

   If you notice nothing, that's fine. The important thing is checking in with yourself and just observing what's there.

4. **Now focus your attention on your breathing.**

   Notice how your chest and abdomen feel as the breath enters, pauses, and leaves your body. Observe how the air feels as it enters your nostrils, and leaves them.

   If your mind wanders, that's fine — minds do wander! Give yourself a pat on the back for having recognized that your mind has wandered and bring your attention back to where you want it to be. It doesn't matter if your mind wanders 100 times; the act of recognizing that your mind has wandered and bringing it back is what's important.

5. **Continue to use your breath as anchor within you for as long as you have time.**

   When your timer sounds, gently stretch your fingers and toes, and open your eyes, ready to start work again.

Improved relationships

You've probably had to work with people who are difficult to get along with. Maybe they are rude, critical, and rarely offer praise. They say the wrong thing at the wrong time. You wonder how they managed to get promoted in the company in the first place. You may even think that you're better off avoiding certain colleagues.

Relationships matter. A lot. In fact, the human brain is designed to be social. Learning, emotional processing, creativity, and insight are often enhanced when in conversation with others. If that's the case, why are workplace relationships so often fraught with difficulty? And how does mindfulness improve workplace relationships?

When you're mindful, you're better able to regulate your emotions. For example, Frank works for a large oil company and is responsible for the refining division. He talks to Samantha about her recent lateness at work. She starts giving excuses. This pattern repeats over several days. Eventually, in a fit of anger, Frank starts shouting at her. She shouts back. In the weeks that follow, Samantha does come into work early but refuses to do more than the minimum that's required of her. Behind Frank's back, she gossips about his ineffectiveness as a manager. Frank does the same to her. How could mindfulness have helped?

If Frank were more mindful, he'd have noticed the anger building up in him. As a result, he could have used mindfulness to acknowledge the feeling and make a choice. He could have chosen to speak to Samantha later in the day when he was more composed. At that time, he could go over the issue and explain why the company needs Samantha to be at work on time and the consequences of lateness. Listening to Samantha's reasons, he may discover a bigger underlying issue — maybe she's been working late on a particular project and feels she deserves a rest, or perhaps the pressure of deadlines makes it harder for her to both fall asleep at night and wake up in the morning. Seen in this bigger context, Frank is less likely to react with anger next time and more likely to develop positive working relationships with colleagues.

The second way that mindfulness improves relationships is by enhancing the ability to listen both to the words being said and the emotions behind them. Good communication is the very heart of relationships. With greater levels of mindful awareness, you become more adept at listening to both the words being spoken and how the person is feeling. You can also pick up someone's emotional signals by observing that person's body posture. If you're checking your text messages while someone's talking to you, you're multitasking — you're effectively saying to the other person that what he or she has to say isn't important and, as a result, the relationship slightly deteriorates. If you give that person your full attention, the relationship can develop instead.

Consider someone you know who is mindful. How does that person listen, talk, and move about? When you're in his or her company, do you feel comfortable? Most of us enjoy being with mindful people because they give us the time to speak. They listen non-judgmentally to our views and don't criticize. They understand the challenges we face. Being with someone like that makes us more mindful — mindfulness spreads.

You're better able to listen because mindfulness enhances focus. Research shows that the more you practice mindful exercises, the better your brain becomes at focusing on whatever it chooses to. Being better able to focus has obvious benefits when you're trying to listen to someone at work.

Mindfulness also helps you to step outside yourself. Rather than just thinking about yourself and what you need, you think about others more. For example, one corporate executive's brain was so frantically busy that his life was a blur. He had no chance of caring for others because he could hardly pay attention to what he had to do to look after himself. His relentless streams of thought made him see the world through cloudy glasses. Mindfulness helped him to step back from those thoughts, a bit like removing those glasses. The thoughts were still there, but they weren't as close and relentless. He was then better able to offer attention and care to his colleagues. He now finds colleagues often come to see him for personal advice. He's better able to see things from the perspective of other people — a vital skill in all relationships.

TIP

Use the following tips to be more mindful in your workplace relationships:

>> **Really connect.** Make a conscious effort to look people in the eye when they're speaking to you. Listen to their words and try to pick up on their emotions too. If you have the tendency to interrupt, resist it. Listen more and ask questions to clarify what the other people are saying.

>> **Take a mindful pause.** Stop and think before speaking to someone you find difficult. Notice whether you react emotionally to that person and, if you do, try to step back from your habitual emotions and thoughts. If you carry on doing what you've always done, you carry on getting what you've always got. Use the mindful pause and see what effect it has on the relationship.

>> **See things from their viewpoint.** Use mindful awareness to step back and see things from the other person's point of view. Maybe the person you're dealing with doesn't have the necessary social skills to cope with her staff. Possibly she makes rash decisions because she's anxious. Seen in this way, her behavior appears far less threatening and you may feel sorry for her rather than annoyed.

>> **Wish them well.** As you walk about in your workplace, rather than negatively judging people, or even being neutral toward them, you can wish them well. As you encounter people, think, "May you be well, may you be happy." After all, they're human beings just like you, and they want to be happy just like you. By wishing others well, you shift your attention away from your own worries and toward a more positive and mindful mindset. This may sound like a strange exercise to do, but it is certainly worth trying.

Honed mental clarity and focus

Imagine lying in a darkened room and shining a torch around. What you can see is whatever that spotlight is shining on.

Your mind works in the same way. Your attention is like a spotlight, and in a moment of mindfulness you can decide where to shine it. You can focus within yourself, on a particular part of your body, or even on your body as a whole. You can focus on your thoughts or emotions.

Focus is one of the most overlooked skills that humans possess. Most people think that focus is something they do or don't have. But that's not true. Your attention is like a muscle — the more you flex that brain muscle, the stronger it gets. With time and effort, the regions of your brain responsible for maintaining focus grow. And these changes happen within days, not years. Mindfulness offers a way to train that muscle in your brain so you can decide where you want to focus and stay focused for longer periods of time.

When you lack focus, you feel scattered. Your attention can get caught by another person's conversation, a thought about the event you attended yesterday, or just noise outside. The more your attention snags on other things, the less able you are to complete the tasks in front of you and you begin to feel inefficient. When you practice mindful exercises, your mind gradually shifts from being frazzled to being focused. You then become more efficient and, as a result, have more time to rest and relax.

One of the other benefits of greater focus is experiencing greater levels of happiness. Research suggests that people are at their happiest when they're fully focused on something — that is, not when they're relaxing watching TV at home or eating chocolate. That focus can be on anything: skiing downhill, painting a picture, or writing a sales report. When fully focused, people enter a flow state of mind, which results in a heightened feeling of well-being. As mindfulness develops your ability to focus, you're therefore more likely to be able to enter this flow state when working. And if you're happier, you're immediately more creative, productive, and confident.

TIP

How can you improve your focus in the workplace using mindfulness? Try these tips:

» **Start the working day with a short mindful exercise.** Try mindfulness of breath (see the "Mindfulness of breath" sidebar in this chapter) or a body scan (see the "Body scan" sidebar in Chapter 4). Even a mindful jog in the morning can help.

» **Avoid multitasking as much as possible.** If you can, do one task at a time and give it your full attention. Too much multitasking reduces your brain's ability to focus.

» **Feel your breathing whenever you remember.** Your breath is your anchor to bring you back to the present moment. If you're on the phone and find your mind keeps wandering, feel a few of your breaths to center yourself in the present.

» **Record your progress.** Keep notes on what you complete in each hour to make you more mindful of your use of time. You can then begin to focus more effectively in each hour that you use.

I PASSED MY TEST, THANKS TO MINDFULNESS!

A study published in 2013 in the *Mindfulness* journal (yes, a scientific journal dedicated to the subject does exist) measured the effect of a short mindfulness exercise on quiz scores following a lecture. One group of university students was taught a six-minute mindfulness exercise and another group wasn't. The mindfulness exercise predicted which students would pass the quiz!

Further analysis found that the mindfulness exercise was even more effective with a group of first-year students, perhaps because more of them were likely to have trouble focusing. The researchers were impressed with the changes that occurred in students following just a short mindfulness exercise and felt that more coaching could result in even bigger improvements in scores.

Mindful leadership

A mindful leader values both inner reflection and outer action. Rather than reacting automatically to everyday challenges, mindful leaders ensure that they're consciously making the right decision with awareness, compassion, and wisdom.

Mindful leadership does not mean that the leader is always practicing mindful exercises and walking around in a Zen-like bubble! A mindful leader is very much a person of action but understands the value of rest, reflection, and renewal.

A mindful leader can make a positive difference to an organization in these changing times. Because they're better able to see the bigger picture rather than just immediate threats or opportunities, an organization with mindful leaders can create solid corporate values and a clear mission statement.

Mindful leadership begins with self-awareness. These leaders are aware of their own thoughts, ideas, opinions, beliefs, and emotional state, from moment to moment. Through this self-awareness, they can challenge their interpretations to discover new solutions. And through this self-awareness, they're better able to relate and communicate with others — they have high levels of emotional intelligence.

For example, say that you're a manager in a medium-sized organization. Weeks ago, a meeting was scheduled in town, but a few hours before the meeting one of your employees says he wants to shift it to a different time. You're annoyed about the last-minute change and are about to send a scathing email to the employee. But then you stop. You take three mindful breaths and check on your inner state. You notice that you haven't had lunch, are in an irritable mood, and are emailing out of frustration, not to optimize the performance of your team. Instead, you pick up the phone, have a quick chat about meeting times in a calm voice, and all is resolved. You use discipline when necessary, not out of emotional anger.

Mindful leaders use the principles of mindfulness in their leadership approach. They are

>> Physically able to look after themselves and their workforce, understanding that mind and body are not separate.

>> Mentally focused, clear, and flexible. They use mindful exercises to train their brains to be in the moment and able to connect with others.

>> Emotionally intelligent. They're aware of their own emotional state as well as that of their team members. They can sensitively make choices based on these emotional states rather than make decisions without reflection.

>> Values driven. They're aware of their own values and align them with their work in an authentic way. In turn, they appreciate the importance of values in an organization.

>> Able to balance acceptance of what can't be changed and action to implement what can and needs to be changed.

>> Able to make time for stillness and reflection as well as time for activity and serving others.

>> Compassionate. They care for both themselves and their colleagues. They see other members of the team as equals and don't develop a false sense of superiority.

>> Passionate. They're driven by will to make their values real, helping others to fulfill their potential.

Research in mindful leadership is beginning to accelerate as mindfulness rapidly moves to the mainstream. A study by Ashridge Executive Education, ranked as one of the top 20 business schools in the world, looked at the effect of meditation on its members. It discovered that 90 percent of members found some form of benefit resulted from practices such as mindfulness.

Some of the benefits of mindful leadership are hard to measure but easy to see. Mindful leaders are more present, exude a sense of control, and make their employees feel more cared for.

If you're in a leadership position, whether you manage 2 people or 2,000, try the following exercise to help you be more mindful in just a few minutes:

1. **Practice a short mindful exercise.** Try mindfulness of breath for a few minutes. (See this chapter's "Mindfulness of breath" sidebar.)

2. **Spend a couple of minutes reflecting on your own state of mind.** Consider how you're feeling. What thoughts are popping into your mind?

3. **Think about your staff for a few minutes.** Consider what challenges they may be facing.

4. **Ask yourself: "How can I best look after myself now?"**

5. **Ask yourself: "How can I best look after my staff now?"**

Write down one idea for yourself and your staff, and if appropriate, carry them out. The exercise combines mindfulness and compassion. The mindfulness part helps you to tune into your current state. And the support part is an act of self-compassion. Finally, considering ways of supporting others shows compassion and leads to your staff feeling more valued. Looking after and appreciating your staff can help you get far more from them than a pay rise or promotion. Mindful leadership can develop this mindful, compassionate way of operating.

Looking at the Organizational Benefits of Mindfulness

A mindful organization is aware of and cares for its people, whether they are employees, volunteers, customers, or suppliers — whomever they work with. The organization understands the need to focus on revenue generation but in the long term rather than the short term. The company is based on sound ethical and sustainable values; it aims to make a positive difference to the world. When hard decisions about discipline or redundancy are necessary, the organization can make them but only after considering all other options. The organization encourages physical exercise and good nutrition, mental well-being through mindfulness classes, and emotional well-being through social interaction and training. To get the best out of people, working hours are flexible, as are many of the working practices. The organization celebrates success and fully engages the staff when making major changes and decisions about the organization's future. It helps the staff to do more of what they really enjoy and to find meaning in their work in a way that benefits both the individual and the organization.

An unmindful organization is highly focused on the short term. It may want to increase its profits for this quarter rather than care for its staff or customers. Its products or services may cause harm rather than provide value for its customers. Employees display a low level of interaction, communication, and emotional intelligence because they work in a climate of fear. The wrong people are in the wrong positions and are unclear about their roles and responsibilities. Working hours are long and unsustainable, and the organization frowns upon a healthy balance between work and home and social life. It does not respond effectively to changes taking place in its sector.

A mindful organization may sound idealistic. However, high levels of workplace stress, burnout, and inequality; a lack of creativity; unethical corporate behavior; and too much short-term focus on profit mean that creating a mindful organization isn't a luxury but an urgent necessity.

Happier, more engaged employees

Tony Hsieh founded a company called Zappos in 1999, which grew to $1 billion worth of sales in 2009. Hsieh says this success was the result of making customers happy — and he achieved that by making his employees happy. Tony also authored the popular — and worthwhile — business book, *Delivering Happiness: A Path to Profits, Passion, and Purpose* (Writers of the Round Table Press).

Zappos has a set of ten core values that the staff created together. They provide the foundation of the company's culture and are a guide to how to treat customers, suppliers, employees, and sales reps. These values are

>> Deliver WOW through service.

>> Embrace and drive change.

>> Create fun and a little weirdness.

>> Be adventurous, creative, and open-minded.

>> Pursue growth and learning.

>> Build open and honest relationships with communication.

>> Build a positive team and family spirit.

>> Do more with less.

>> Be passionate and determined.

>> Be humble.

Happiness isn't usually a term bandied about in a workplace environment. Traditionally, if you wanted to increase productivity, you made employees work harder or attend a time-management course, or looked for ways to automate tasks.

Mindfulness does make employees happy. So much so that the effects of happiness can be seen in brain scans! Happy people show greater activation in the left prefrontal cortex. Completing an eight-week mindfulness course has resulted in employees demonstrating greater activity in that part of the brain — the mindfulness literally made them feel happier.

But so what, you may ask. It transpires that happiness is linked to a host of benefits in the workplace. Happier staff are more productive and creative, take fewer sick days, and are more likely to be promoted. And greater happiness pays. For every employee, the New Economics Foundation predicts that an organization can save

>> $300, assuming a conservative 1 percent increase in productivity as a result of increased happiness

>> $125, assuming a reduction in sickness absence by just one day

>> $195, assuming a 10 percent reduction in staff turnover

That's $620 saved for every employee, each year. And that's a conservative esti-mate. If your organization has 1,000 employees, you can save well over half a million dollars a year!

So good work doesn't make you happy, but being happy creates good work.

TIP

Try the following tips to boost your happiness in the workplace using mindful-ness. Share them with your colleagues too!

>> Spend two minutes practicing mindfulness of breath (see the "Mindfulness of breath" sidebar in this chapter), then write down three things about your workplace for which you're grateful.

>> Go for a 15-minute mindful walk for every 1.5 hours of work you do. Master violinists were found to use this balance of work and rest to optimize their performance and well-being. Violinists who worked hard all day with fewer breaks were less successful.

>> Have a mindful conversation with the happiest colleagues at work. Happiness is contagious. If you're consciously present with happy colleagues at lunch, in your break, or over a quick drink after work, you feel happier.

>> Commit to doing at least one task mindfully when at work. Start small and build up from there.

>> Be mindful in the bathroom, if that's the only space available at work! Or ask the company to provide a room dedicated to quiet time and mindfulness.

Greater creativity

How important do you think creativity is in your organization? Is it important to innovate and find new ideas for products or services? Or do you simply keep doing the same thing and hope that your competitors won't catch up? Most people agree that, in the current economy, without innovation your competitors will soon overtake you. So, to be a successful organization, you need your employees' brains to be as creative as possible. Creative solutions not only help your organization, but also help to meet the needs of your customers.

Take a few moments to consider the stance of a creative brain — open, flexible, attentive, and not too stressed. In fact, when you're in a mindful state, the creative part of your brain is activated.

Mindfulness creates the ideal conditions in your brain for creative thought. When you're unmindful, you're on autopilot, thinking the same old thoughts. When you're mindful, you're more awake, energized, and aware of new ideas as they emerge.

A professor of architecture we know teaches mindfulness online. She finds that the more mindful she is, the more creative her work. She ran mindfulness sessions at a creativity and design conference, and the feedback was overwhelmingly positive — the designers loved the new way of using their minds to get the creative juices flowing. Even their designs are beginning to be more mindful — spacious, calming, and sustainable, with areas for individual quiet time.

Think back to the last time you had a creative idea. Were you feeling anxious or relaxed? Were you in the moment or mired in a fog of worries and concerns? Were you feeling happy or sad?

Psychologist Mihaly Csikszentmihalyi draws on 30 years' experience of researching mindfulness to identify the following five stages when engaged in the creative process:

>> **Preparation:** Immersion in an interesting problem that requires a creative solution

>> **Incubation:** A period of inner reflection

>> **Insight:** The "Aha!" moment when the solution begins to emerge

>> **Evaluation:** Deciding whether the solution can work

>> **Elaboration:** Turning the chosen solution into a final product

Mindfulness comes into play in all the different stages but is most important in the second, incubation. When an idea is being incubated, your mind needs to allow the problem to sink into your subconscious. The unconscious mind is far more creative than the slow logic of the conscious mind. Just think how creative and unusual dreams can be!

Mindfulness helps you to gradually step back from your conscious mind so that more creative ideas and solutions can emerge from your unconscious mind. The often creative, unconscious brain struggles to offer you new solutions because of a busy or negative mind-set. When your mind is more open and calm through mindfulness, creative solutions can rise up into your unconscious brain.

Try the following exercise to boost your own creativity at work. Then share them with your colleagues to help you develop a more mindfully creative team.

1. **Become mindful of the problem.** Be crystal clear about what you're trying to solve. As Einstein said, "If I had an hour to solve a problem, I'd spend 55 minutes thinking about the problem and 5 minutes thinking about solutions."

2. **Incubate.** Go for a mindful walk. Try practicing mindfulness of breath. At home, take a bath and just enjoy the experience. Be in the moment rather than trying hard to solve the problem with your conscious mind. Let go. Allow things to be. Reflect.

3. **Collect solutions.** Come up with as many solutions as possible, no matter how weird or wacky. They may not work, but write them all down nonetheless. Allow ideas to flow from your mind to the sheet of paper. Be utterly non-judgmental as you compile this list.

4. **Evaluate.** Consider each solution in turn and analyze whether it would work. Use mindfulness by being aware of each solution, one at a time. Avoid multitasking or other distractions. Take regular breaks as necessary. Keep your mind in optimal condition so you can make the right choice. Being mindful at this stage means that your brain can work in optimal conditions to achieve success.

Increased productivity

Productivity isn't just about accomplishing things. Productivity is also about choosing what you need to do and doing those activities at a time of day when your energy levels and focus are highest.

Productivity is about working smarter, not just harder. There's nothing wrong with working hard when at work — being lazy at work doesn't lead to a fulfilling life or an effective organization. Sorry, folks! But working smarter is about learning what you need to do and deciding how, when, and where to do it.

Mindfulness improves focus. One of the direct benefits of greater focus is increased productivity. You stop being distracted by other thoughts, a text message, or sounds in the office. Instead, you're able to keep your attention on whatever requires finishing.

Mindfulness of your own energy levels has a huge effect on productivity. As you become more mindful, you notice the subtle fluctuations in your energy levels. Noticing such things is an important skill. Everyone's energy rises and falls at different times of the day. When you recognize when your energy is at its peak, you can tackle your most challenging tasks. When your energy levels are naturally lower, you can use that time to chat with colleagues or take a break.

For example, if Gary knows that his energy levels peak in the morning and are lowest between 1 p.m. and 3 p.m., he can make sure that he spends his time writing that important report in the office before anyone else arrives. In the afternoon, satisfied with a productive morning's work, he can call up his managers in New York and catch up with progress over there. Without this knowledge, if Gary made calls and emailed all morning, by afternoon he'd struggle to write that report, end up working late in the office, get home late — and the cycle continues.

Your energy levels also increase because you experience less emotional reactivity. Mindfulness increases your emotional awareness. So when you feel low, frustrated, or angry, negative emotions don't creep up on you. You see the mood coming and accept the feeling. You know that moods coming and going is part of being human. When something happens at work to make you feel upset or angry, you discover how to deal with your emotion before speaking. You discover how to express your emotions without losing control of yourself. This way of behaving is much more energy efficient, which means that you have energy left over to productively complete your work. Mindfulness can also make you less emotional over petty things too — so other people's comments or behavior, which may have irritated you before, no longer do so.

Practicing mindfulness also gives you more energy because you worry less. Your brain uses up 20 percent of your energy even though it comprises only 2 percent of your body weight. Think back to the last time you spent a few minutes worrying — did you feel energized or drained afterwards? Most people feel drained. When you're mindful, you're more focused on the moment and what needs to be done and you don't waste energy worrying. Remember: Worry is like a rocking chair — it gives you something to do but never gets you anywhere. Mindfulness exercises help you to reduce your worrying.

Finally, one of the skills you develop with mindfulness is the ability to step back from whatever you're doing and see the context within which your task fits. How often have you completed a task, only to later discover that you were doing it the long way? Or that you'd already performed the task before? By being mindful, your mind has the flexibility to step back from time to time to see the bird's-eye view. Taking a quick overview means that you don't waste your time doing unnecessary tasks. Productivity isn't just about doing what needs doing; it's also about not doing what doesn't need doing!

The following short exercise helps you to mindfully consider the circumstances that prompted you to be particularly productive. Follow these steps:

1. **Think back to an occasion on which you were really productive.** What time of day was it? Where were you? Try to visualize yourself in that moment in time.

2. **Describe your state of mind.** Were you mindful or unfocused; in the present moment or thinking about the past or the future; judgmental or non-judgmental; curious or bored; calm or excited?

3. **Remember how much effort you put into achieving that level of productivity.**

Your responses to these prompts may help you to be more productive in the future. Try to re-create those conditions and see what happens.

TIP

Here are a few tips for making your organization more productive:

>> Dedicate a room to quiet time, mindfulness, prayer, or meditation. Taking a break in this room gives the staff time to reflect and recharge their batteries.

>> Discourage working late. Working long hours reduces efficiency and productivity and has a negative effect on employees' home life, which inevitably affects their work life too.

>> Encourage all staff to attend a mindfulness workshop and ensure that they have access to online courses, books or e-learning. Even a 1 percent increase in productivity more than pays back the cost of the training and resources.

Improved decision making

All CEOs know that high-quality decisions can make or break their organization. When managers make effective decisions, their staff work more efficiently, they feel more in control, and the results can be seen in sustainable income for long-term growth.

Good decisions lead to

>> Increased opportunities for growth

>> Higher revenue

>> Healthier, happier employees

>> Ability to hire the best employees for each role

>> Improved quality of products and services for customers

You can make good decisions when your brain is functioning optimally. You can read all you like about decision theory, but if your brain isn't working optimally, you fail to take all factors into account and make bad decisions.

Think back to the last time you came home after a tough day at work. What sort of decisions did you make? Did you decide to eat a healthy fruit salad, go for a swim, meditate, and phone a friend who needed cheering up? Or did you eat too much chocolate, slump in front of the TV, and snap at your partner? The latter scenario is more likely — because your brain wasn't able to make good decisions. A brain starved of rest overtook your long-term goals of losing weight or being healthy or socializing more. This situation is called decision fatigue. The more decisions you make, without adequate breaks, the less effective your decisions will be. One way of countering decision fatigue is practicing mindfulness exercises.

Another way in which mindfulness can help with decisions is by switching off the autopilot response in your brain. When operating without mindfulness, all your decisions are automatic and based on previous decisions. They lack freshness and don't have access to any new information. If the employees of an organization are more mindful, they can spot new ideas, see the activities of competitors, notice a need for, say, younger consumers, and make a different decision — and thus move the company forward successfully.

JUDGES ARE SIX TIMES NICER AFTER LUNCH

A study conducted in 2010 by Columbia and Ben-Gurion universities looked at 1,112 judicial rulings over 10 months. The rulings related to granting prisoners parole. An amazing pattern was found. Judges were up to six times more likely to grant parole just after lunch. About 60 percent were granted parole at the start of the day, but this figure gradually declined. Just before lunch, prisoners had by far the lowest chance of being granted parole; and immediately after lunch, the figure went back up to about 60 percent. The break and some food appear to refresh the judges' brains and they were more likely to make the difficult decision to set the post-lunch prisoner free.

This study demonstrates the effect of taking regular breaks and eating properly on decision-making ability. It also shows how sensitive the decision-making brain is. Through mindfulness, you can energize your brain with a minibreak during the day and improve your decision making too. Mindfulness directly affects the way your brain works, activating the prefrontal cortex. So, when faced with an important decision, take a few moments to be mindful so that your decisions are based on reason rather than emotional reaction.

Kodak provides an example of a company's inability to see beyond habitual ideas. The company went bankrupt, mainly because CEO after CEO decided not to take the plunge into the digital photography market, despite all the signs showing that this was the way to go. Ironically, an engineer at Kodak invented the digital camera, but the company decided not to pursue the concept. Kodak's competitors jumped on the digital bandwagon, and the rest is history.

A more mindful management could have helped Kodak. With a better ability to see the big picture and a willingness to let go of what didn't work, maybe Kodak could have gone on to be a leader in the digital photography market. But because it stuck to its habitual pattern of using chemicals to develop photographs, it lost almost everything.

For day-to-day decisions, try the five-step approach shown in Figure 2-1.

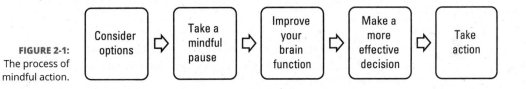

FIGURE 2-1: The process of mindful action.

By taking a mindful minute, you can optimize your brain function, reduce decision fatigue, and make better decisions.

TIP

Bear these tips in mind to improve your decision making:

>> Ensure that you schedule meetings at a time of day when people's energy levels are high, making mindful awareness more likely.

>> If you're chairing a meeting, take a mindful pause before you start, to ensure that you're in the right state of mind. End the meeting if you notice people's attention beginning to wane.

>> Remember that you're a human being, not a machine. You can't keep making decisions all day and expect them to be of a high standard. Take a mindful break every 90 minutes, even if just for a minute.

Reducing staff turnover

High employee turnover hits the bottom line. The cost of replacing an employee can cost up to twice that employee's salary. Consider the time involved in recruitment as you screen candidates and the loss of productivity as the new employee learns the ropes. Maybe the new employee won't work out and you have to repeat the process. On top of that, constant staff changes can negatively affect staff morale.

Mindfulness can help lower staff turnover by helping employees to cope better with stress. Stress can lead to illness and ultimately result in people being on long-term sick leave. But even for the staff who aren't overwhelmed by stress, mindfulness can build their resilience and improve their performance, which will make them feel more valued.

Too much stress leads to burnout. According to Professor Marie Asberg, burnout is the end of an exhaustion funnel when you gradually stop doing things that you deem unimportant, such as practicing mindfulness, exercising, and socializing, and instead obsess about your workplace outcomes. Research carried out in 2009 with doctors found that practicing mindfulness decreased burnout rates in this cohort.

Prevention is better than cure. Yet most organizations focus on fixing their staff after they become ill rather than preventing stress-related illness in the first place. Most employers spend 200 to 300 percent more on managing ill heath than on prevention.

Research by the iOpener Institute found that increasing employee well-being in one company reduced staff turnover by 46 percent and reduced sickness absence by 19 percent. Mindfulness is one way of increasing well-being and reducing staff turnover.

TIP

Use the following mindful tips to help lower staff turnover:

>> **Measure your staff's well-being and then implement means to improve it.** The University of Pennsylvania's Authentic Happiness website, at www.authentichappiness.sas.upenn.edu/, has lots of well-being question-naires that you could try.

>> **Set up a regular mindfulness group for all staff to attend for free in the workplace.**

>> **Identify those in your staff who may be susceptible to burnout.** Ensure that they have access to more regular mindfulness courses and other forms of help.

>> **Train managers in mindfulness so they're better able to listen to their staff.** Being better listened to makes employees feel more cared for and they're less likely to leave the organization as a result. Not being appreciated and listened to are two causes of high staff turnover.

>> **Help employees to maintain a work/life balance.** A nationwide survey found that 20 percent of employees left their job as a result of poor work/life balance and 20 percent because of workplace stress. Mindfulness can help improve productivity so employees can get home earlier, thus improving their work/life balance and reducing their stress levels.

Chapter **3**

Applying Mindfulness in the Workplace

M indfulness is all well and good, but how do you apply it effectively in the workplace? That's exactly what you find out in this chapter. You also discover why mindfulness is more important than ever in the modern workplace and discover lots of practical ways to start "mindfulnessing" within minutes!

Gaining Perspective in the Modern-Day Workplace

Fifty years ago, a sizeable proportion of the population got a job and worked for that organization until they retired. The key benefit resulting from this scenario was a sense of security and stability — they knew what to expect.

For students looking for a job today, things are very different. A recent survey of workers found that one in three remains in a job for less than two years. This massive change in people's working lives is bound to have an effect — sometimes positive but often negative. In this section, you discover how mindfulness can help you deal with uncertainty in the workplace.

Engaging with a VUCA world

To understand the modern workplace and how mindfulness can help you deal with it, consider the VUCA acronym. Originally used by the military, VUCA is now used in business. VUCA stands for

- » **Volatility:** The high speed and complicated dynamics of change in modern organizations and the markets that they work in. The digital revolution, global competition, and connectivity are all contributing to higher levels of volatility.

- » **Uncertainty:** The lack of predictability and the prospect of surprise facing many employees. In uncertain situations, forecasting becomes difficult and decision making becomes more challenging.

- » **Complexity:** The wide range of ideas, information, and systems that cause confusion and chaos in an organization lead to complexity.

- » **Ambiguity:** The lack of clarity about what is actually happening in the organization as well as the environment in which the organization operates.

To give you an idea of the VUCA world, consider the average working day of Kate, a senior executive. Her alarm goes off at 5 a.m. She turns on her phone as she wakes up, and it immediately starts buzzing. She skims through and half-answers emails as she gets dressed, and has a quick cup of coffee and a piece of toast. She jumps into her car and mentally compiles a to-do list on the journey. Half of the emails she read earlier appear urgent, so she wants to deal with them immediately. However, the complexity of the issues makes it almost impossible for her to decide which one to do first. Juggling between phone calls, emails, and routine tasks and meetings, she has no time for lunch. She works till late into the evening, keeping herself going with lots of coffee. To ensure that she remains awake for the journey home, she blasts out music on her iPod. As she travels, her phone keeps buzzing with more emails. Kate grabs a takeout dinner, eats it in front of the television, and then goes to bed. She answers a few more emails before turning off the light and then tries to sleep. Unsurprisingly, sleep eludes her as she tosses and turns, going over everything that's happened during the day and worrying about how she's going to function the next day if she doesn't get to sleep soon.

Kate's working day is certainly volatile, uncertain, complex, and ambiguous. How can mindfulness help her? Following are a few changes she can make to her day that require almost no time and increase her effectiveness and efficiency:

- » During breakfast, Kate can keep her phone switched off and eat her toast being mindfully aware of its taste, perhaps looking out into her garden as she does so. The meal would be finished a bit quicker (because she isn't simultaneously dealing with emails) and the time saved can be used to check emails later in the office.

>> She can take three mindful breaths before setting off in her car. Driving with mindful awareness, focusing solely on the road ahead rather than mentally planning her day, means that her mind is rested and ready for work.

>> Arriving at the office, she can again take a few deep mindful breaths, instantly calming her fight-or-flight mechanism if she's had a difficult journey.

>> As she waits for her computer to start, she can enjoy a mindful stretch in her chair. She can then organize her priorities for the day rather than allow her attention to be captured immediately by emails.

>> She can allot time for dealing with emails — after she gets her most challenging task out of the way. She can then feel more in control of her day and attend to the most difficult job while her mind is still fresh.

>> She can mindfully walk to meetings. Rather than rushing, she can walk a little slower, feeling her feet as she does so. Walking in this way will settle her mind, and her subsequent air of calmness will make attendees more willing to listen to her.

>> She can prioritize lunch. Going to a quiet place and eating her lunch with full attention ensures that she digests the food properly. She can leave her phone on her desk to avoid the temptation of checking emails and texts while she eats.

>> She can do her best to give her full attention to colleagues when she's talking to them. Taking subtle, deeper breaths occasionally will make her more patient because the breaths switch on her relaxation response.

>> She can ensure that she goes home on time rather than working late. What she achieves in three hours late at night can be done in an hour when she's fresh the next morning.

Leaving work on time after a 9-to-5 day can take courage if it flies in the face of your office culture. Sheryl Sandberg, ex-Google executive and current chief operating officer of Facebook, leaves the office at 5.30 p.m. You may think that following her example is impossible, but at least consider it. Leaving work earlier, despite making you feel guilty, makes you much more efficient the next day. Finishing work on time is partly a mind-set.

Resilience, the ability to effectively manage adversity, is the key to managing VUCA at work.

Applying mindfulness in changing times

The current rate of change in the workplace is faster than at any other time in history. The last 15 years have seen an explosion in communications technology and social networking and a rapid rise in economic growth in the emerging economies of India, China, Russia, and Brazil. These changes have a big effect on the workplace and affect employees at all levels. How can mindfulness help in managing these changes?

Change isn't always easy. Sometimes change in the workplace can be met with resistance. The human brain works through habit, which creates a sense of famil-iarity and security. Poorly managed change can make people feel threatened, so they resist it.

Mindfulness is about being aware of the emotional effect of change. You need to prepare employees in advance, providing relevant training if necessary. Following the change, you must be a good listener and respond quickly if employees express frustration or distress.

A unique way of thinking about change is provided by a deeper understanding of the principles of mindfulness. Most mindfulness teaching stresses that the world is in a constant state of flux. Mindfulness exercises demonstrate this perpetual change. Try focusing on one of your senses for more than a few minutes and notice the variety of thoughts, feelings, bodily sensations, and distractions that you experience.

A MINDFUL MINUTE

Although this exercise is called the mindful minute, you can extend it if time permits. Follow these steps:

1. **Center yourself (about 20 seconds).**

   Feel your feet in contact with the ground. Imagine that your feet are rooted to the ground and that your legs are like tree trunks, firmly supporting you in place. Use your feet as an anchor for your attention.

2. **Acknowledge what's going on (about 20 seconds).**

   Now focus your attention on everything that's going on — the thoughts entering your mind, sounds, smells, and bodily sensations. Acknowledge your experiences and let them go without judging or getting involved, just noticing the present moment.

3. **Take a mindful pause (about 20 seconds).**

   Now focus your attention on nothing but your breath. Feel the breath coming in and the breath going out. If thoughts arise, kindly acknowledge them and let them go.

Many people find that this exercise helps to create a short space between the busy-ness of their working mind and the present moment state that's ideal for mindful communications.

The universe is constantly changing. Atoms are continually moving; in fact, scientists are unable to achieve absolute zero, the temperature at which atoms stop moving. If constant change is the way of the world, you need to expect some in your own life. Resisting that change leads to pain.

Expect and embrace the change that is bound to come. If you find yourself reacting with sadness or anger to that change, give yourself the time and space to work through those emotions using mindfulness exercises.

TIP

To better manage change in the workplace, try these tips:

» **Expect change:** If you're clinging to the hope that change won't happen, you're living with greater fear and anxiety. Instead, simply expect change to happen at work. When change doesn't happen, be pleasantly surprised.

» **Embrace change:** Jack Welch, ex-CEO of General Electric, advises, "Change before you have to." Try to see change as an opportunity. Write down the benefits of the change and view them as a chance to manage that change.

» **Anchor yourself in the present:** When you're faced with a torrent of change, you can easily feel flustered. One way of coping with that change is through mindfulness exercises. Even one deep breath taken mindfully can switch on your parasympathetic nervous system, which makes you more relaxed and grounded.

Change can be challenging. But in our experience, regular mindfulness practice makes managing external changes easier because you realize that, beyond your changing thoughts and emotions, a deeper sense of peace, calm, and spaciousness exists that is simply your own awareness. That awareness is always the same, ever present and unchanging. When faced with too much change, you can take refuge in mindfulness to rest your body, mind, and emotions in your own, unchanging awareness. Figure 3-1 shows how mindfulness can help you tune in to that unchanging awareness.

Employing mindfulness for new ways of working

The essence of working with mindfulness is simple: Pay attention to the task at hand. By giving work your full attention, the quality and quantity of what you do improves. But there's more to mindful working than just outcomes. Your level of focus improves, and you give less attention to your normal worries and concerns.

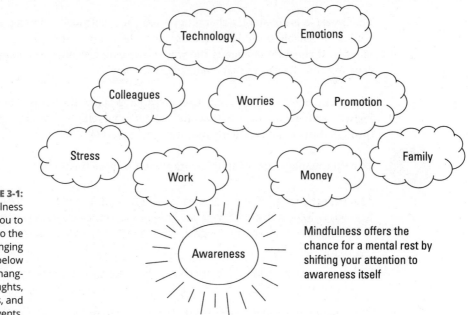

FIGURE 3-1:
Mindfulness helps you to tune into the unchanging awareness below constantly changing thoughts, emotions, and events.

Mindfulness offers the chance for a mental rest by shifting your attention to awareness itself

TIP

In addition to working with attention, you need to find moments in the day to recharge your mind. The ideal time is between the end of one task and the start of another. After spending an hour writing emails, you can spend a couple of minutes feeling the weight of your body on the chair and your feet on the floor. This mindful awareness of your bodily sensations focuses you on the present moment and is restful for your mind. You feel more energized and prepared for the next task. After a two-hour meeting, you can do a mini-mindfulness exercise, such as a mindful minute or a three-step body check (see the nearby sidebars) after everyone has left the room.

Communication is a fundamental aspect of the workplace. On top of giving attention to your own work, and allowing yourself short periods of rest in between, you need to be able to communicate effectively with others. Businesses are called *companies* — they involve the *companionship* of others. As you become more mindful, you're better able to simultaneously identify the emotions of others and be aware and in control of your own emotions. As a result of this heightened emotional intelligence, people will feel drawn to you and will be more willing to work with you. A recent survey of 2,600 managers found that 75 percent of them were more likely to promote an employee demonstrating emotional intelligence than one with a high IQ.

Unmindful use of technology is also affecting success in the workplace. Laptops and phones mean that you can take your work home with you. If you're not in control of your behavior, you can end up working through all your waking hours. That's not good for you or your work. Having time away from work gives your brain a rest and an opportunity to recharge. Chapter 4 covers how to use technology in a more mindful way.

THREE-STEP BODY CHECK

You can do this version of the body scan anywhere, as long as you have a chair, three minutes to spare, and are unlikely to be disturbed. It's quick and easy to do at your desk.

You can do this exercise with your eyes open in soft focus (just slightly opened and looking downward) or closed. Sit in a comfortable, upright position with your feet firmly on the floor, and follow these steps:

1. **Feet, legs, and lower body.**

   Center yourself by focusing on the sensation of taking three slow breaths. Notice the sensations you experience, such as heat, cold, or tingling, when you focus your full attention on your feet. Pause to observe and then repeat with your legs, followed by your bottom.

2. **Chest and arms.**

   Repeat as in Step 1, but focus on your chest and internal organs, followed by your arms.

3. **Shoulders and head.**

   Repeat as in Step 1, but focus on your neck and shoulders. Follow this with your jaw, nose, facial skin, and scalp.

Finish centering yourself by focusing on the sensation of taking three slow breaths.

Building resilience

Too many challenges at work makes you feel overwhelmed and frustrated. In response, you trigger your fight-or-flight mechanism. This threat response, if switched on for too long, leads to inefficient use of your brain and disease in your body. Building resilience is a way of managing challenges more effectively.

Take the example of Thomas Edison, legendary inventor of the light bulb. He famously said that each time he failed, he didn't view the experiment as a failure; rather he saw it as another way that didn't work. Seeing failed attempts as stepping stones to success is an example of a resilient attitude. Edison bounced back from attempts that didn't work to discover what did work. He certainly thrived on success, inventing the phonograph, motion picture, and telegraph.

The achievements of Edison may appear hard to emulate. He seemed to be almost born with a positive attitude and destined for success. And, as far as we know, he didn't formally practice mindfulness! How can mindfulness help you?

As you become more mindful, your tendency to ruminate declines. *Rumination* is how much you think about and dwell on your problems. Rumination is like a broken record that keeps replaying itself — that argument you had with your colleague, that error you made in your presentation. If you ruminate, you overthink about situations or life events.

Mindfulness may be one of the most effective ways to reduce ruminative thinking because you become more aware of your thought patterns and more skillful at stepping back from unhelpful thoughts.

CARROTS, EGGS, AND COFFEE BEANS

Once upon a time, a daughter complained about her enormous troubles to her mother. The mother took her to the kitchen and began boiling three pots of water. In the first pot she put some carrots, in the second she put some eggs, and in the third she put some coffee beans. The pots boiled away. After 10 minutes, she took the carrots, eggs, and some coffee out and asked the daughter what she noticed about them.

The daughter felt the carrots — they were soft and soggy. She broke the egg and discovered it was hard inside. And she sipped the coffee — it tasted delicious. "What does this all mean?" asked the daughter.

Her mother explained that each experienced the same adversity — boiling water. The carrots started off strong but became soft. The egg was initially fragile, but now had become hardened on the inside. But the coffee was unique — the coffee beans had flavored the water beautifully.

The mother asked the daughter, "When adversity knocks on your door, are you a carrot, an egg, or a coffee bean?"

Consider this question yourself. When faced with adversity, are you like the carrot — hard and strong but wilting when faced with adversity? Or are you like the egg — fluid on the inside at first but becoming hard of heart on the inside, even though you look the same on the outside?

Or are you like the coffee bean? The coffee bean is changed by the adversity itself, releasing a rich aroma. When faced with hardship, can you rise to the challenge and change the circumstance or your attitude to meet the difficulty? Can you use adversity to enhance what you can offer the world?

An online experiment conducted in 2013 with the BBC and the University of Liverpool and involving over 32,000 participants found that people who didn't ruminate or self-blame demonstrated much lower levels of depression and anxiety, even though they'd experienced many negative events.

Mindfulness helps you to spot those little troubling negative thoughts before they grow too large. And mindfulness helps you to naturally see tough situations at work as challenges to be faced and overcome rather than avoided. If you're feeling overwhelmed by adversity, mindfulness won't offer a quick fix. But dealing with each challenge step by step and combining mindfulness with help from colleagues or a coach means that you can begin to thrive at work.

Think of those in your workplace who seem to thrive on change and whom you respect. Identify

>> Their attitudes and beliefs

>> The kind of language they use to describe a change in the workplace

>> The sort of hours they work and what they do to rest and recharge

>> How mindful (present) they are when at work

Spending time talking with those who thrive on change in the workplace can help you to see things from their perspective.

Adjusting Your Mental Mind-Set

When some people discover mindfulness, their mindset shifts 180 degrees. Before that first lesson in mindfulness, they were completely goal-orientated. But after that lesson, they discover that life is to be enjoyed not only in the future, after attaining all their goals, but also right now, here in the present moment.

Nothing is wrong with achieving success and attaining goals, but not at the expense of the here and now. Ironically, by living in a more present-focused way, you are better able to achieve success. The best way to prepare for the future is to live in the present.

Focusing on the present moment

We know that our most successful coaching, training, and writing sessions occur when we're fully in the present. Think of an Olympic athlete, someone operating at the highest level of performance. She's very much in the present moment. Have you ever seen a top Olympic athlete look as if her mind is wandering when she's performing? She's fully present because being that way optimizes her success. Take the 100-meter sprint. Once the athlete starts running, she's wholly in the here and now, which leads her to success.

Everyone experiences being fully in the moment at some point. Consider the last time you were fully present at work — what were you doing? How did you feel? How productive were you?

TIP

Here are a few tips to help you be more mindfully present at work:

>> **Do something different.** Work can be filled with habits and routines. You sit at the same desk, open the same program, speak to the same people about the same issues. Shake things up a bit. Take a different route to work. Eat something different for lunch or speak to someone on the phone whom you normally email. Doing something new makes you switch from autopilot to a more present-moment awareness.

>> **Savor.** Living in the present moment can be highly enjoyable. Present-moment living means that you can stop waiting for success in the future. Instead, enjoy the simple pleasures in each moment — the taste of your sandwich, the color of the autumn leaves on your route to work, the simple smooth feeling of your breath. Don't dismiss these everyday pleasures — they boost your mood and mental well-being.

>> **Know that you can always find out more.** No matter what you do, room for improvement always exists. Ellen Langer, professor of psychology at Harvard University, says we stop paying attention to something when we think that we know it all. When musicians in an orchestra are told to make their performance subtly different, they enjoy the performance more — and so does the audience. By noticing something new, you have space to explore, discover, and grow — and you shift straight back into the moment. Make work an adventure by seeking to discover subtly new ways to perform your tasks.

Treating thoughts as mental processes

Some people estimate that they have up to 60,000 thoughts a day. If you've tried practicing mindfulness exercises already, you probably think that's an underestimate. In the East, the brain's tendency to constantly go from one thought to another is called the *monkey mind* because it resembles a monkey swinging from branch to branch.

Thoughts can be great. Through the power of thinking, humans have managed to achieve feats way beyond what any other animal on Earth has accomplished.

We've created cities, designed planes, and landed on the moon. Unfortunately, we've also designed nuclear weapons and heavily polluted the planet.

Thoughts have another disadvantage on a personal level. If all your thoughts are taken to be true and those thoughts are self-critical, your mental well-being suffers. As a result, your performance at work declines too.

Try this thought bubble exercise:

1. **Picture bubbles floating away in the sky.** Maintain this image for one minute.

2. **Imagine that every thought you have can float away in one of those bubbles.**

3. **Let your mind wander.** Each time a thought pops into your head, imagine it drifting away in a bubble. Continue to do this for a few minutes. You may have lots of thoughts or very few. It doesn't matter.

How did you find this exercise? Did your thoughts float away? More importantly, were you able to observe your thoughts? If you were, you've demonstrated that you are not your thoughts — you can observe them from a distance.

The thought bubble and similar exercises help to show you an important mindfulness skill: the ability to step back from your thoughts. You may have all sorts of thoughts popping into your head in the workplace, such as

>> I'm useless in meetings.

>> I can't handle this project. It's too big for me.

>> What if Mike tells Michelle about my report? I'll miss my chance at promotion.

>> I hate working with David. He's too slow for me.

These types of thoughts have an effect on your emotions, bodily sensations, and ability to accomplish your work.

Mindfulness offers a solution. As you become more mindful, you notice these thoughts more often. You are then able to step back from them, seeing them as mental processes in your mind rather than absolute truths.

TIP

Being able to step back from your thoughts takes practice, especially in the hustle and bustle of the workplace. For this reason, try out some of these exercises when you're not under too much pressure. When your brain gets the hang of how to watch and step back from unhelpful thoughts, you've gained a powerful and life-changing skill.

In the old days of personal development, self-help gurus promoted positive thinking. For most people, slapping positive thoughts on top of negative beliefs means they just slip off! Instead, you need to become aware of those negative beliefs and see them for what they are — just thoughts.

Use the following exercise to deal with your thoughts and mind state when you're judging things negatively. It's a simple process but has long-lasting effects once it becomes a habit for you.

You can deal with your negative thoughts by following these three simple steps:

1. **Notice your thoughts.** Focus particularly on unhelpful thoughts about yourself, others, or your workplace.

2. **Step back from your thoughts.** See them as simply mental processes arising in your mind that aren't necessarily true. You can imagine them on clouds, in bubbles, or floating away like leaves in a stream. The idea is to create a sense of distance between you and your thoughts — not just to get rid of them.

3. **Refocus your attention on the task or person in front of you.** The more mindfulness exercises you practice, the better your brain gets at dealing with negative thoughts.

Approaching rather than avoiding difficulties

Do you love the taste of chocolate but don't like the taste of cauliflower? If so, you tend to approach chocolate more positively than you do cauliflower. If you could scan your brain when you see these two different foods, you'd probably see different patterns emerging.

Suppose that work causes you anxiety. You worry about all the meetings you have to attend, the deadlines you have to meet, and the colleagues you have to deal with. How do you cope with that feeling of anxiety? Should you continue to face up to the challenges at work and just get on with the uncomfortable feeling of anxiety, or should you avoid anything that makes you feel that way?

You can avoid the feeling by working even harder so that your attention is completely focused on the task in hand and not on your anxiety. Or you can go for a drink every evening after work, causing the emotional sensation to reduce. Or you can start eating every time that feeling arises, so your attention is focused on the food instead of your anxiety.

All these strategies help you avoid the feeling of anxiety in the workplace. Unfortunately, none of them work over the long term. The feeling of anxiety is still there and requires an increasing number of avoidant strategies to help you suppress it.

Mindfulness is about approach rather than avoidance. It helps you to approach unpleasant feelings at a pace that's right for you.

Approaching difficult emotions when you've always found a way to avoid them isn't easy at first. To help you get better at doing so, you need to approach your feeling as you'd approach a kitten. You don't rush toward a kitten because it would get frightened and run away. You approach a kitten slowly. First you walk toward it and then you crouch down so that you don't look too big. Next, you reach out and gently stroke it. The kitten begins to trust you and eventually you can pick it up.

Treat whatever emotion you're dealing with in the same way. Notice where you're holding the feeling in your body. Approach the feeling slowly and tentatively, with a sense of curiosity. Gradually you come to fully feel the sensation, just as it is. This experience is like having a kitten in your hand. Unlike a kitten, however, the feeling is likely to change as you approach it.

Sometimes it grows; sometimes it dissolves. But that's not the point. The point is that you're *willing* to feel that emotion and approach rather than avoid it. This empowering move leads to greater emotional regulation — you have control over your emotion rather than the emotion controlling you.

Approaching emotions involves a process of non-judgmental acceptance — a key aspect of mindfulness. When you're practicing mindfulness, you're endeavoring to experience thoughts, emotions, sensations, and events as they are in the moment, without trying to judge them as good or bad, desirable or undesirable.

REMEMBER

Approach a challenge rather than avoid it, if you can, and discover how to accept the sensations that it produces. Being able to approach your difficulties makes you feel more confident and less likely to let emotions control your life.

Have a go at this five- to ten-minute mindful exercise on managing difficulties:

1. **Sit comfortably and spend a couple of minutes focusing your attention on your breathing or the sounds around you.**

2. **Think of something in the workplace that scares you a little.**

   Bring to mind a difficult presentation, an aggressive colleague, or the thought of losing your job, for example.

3. **Notice any tension in your body resulting from your sense of anxiety.**

4. **Approach that sensation in your body slowly and gently.**

5. **Try feeling the sensation together with your breathing.**

6. **Be aware that you're approaching rather than avoiding the feeling — a mindful step. Notice whether the feeling changes or stays the same from one breath to the next.**

7. **Refocus on your breathing alone for a couple of minutes before ending the exercise.**

TIP

Try this exercise whenever you find yourself using avoidant strategies to deal with difficult emotions.

Rewiring Your Brain

Your brain is made up of neurons, which are like wires that carry electrical current from one place to another. Each neuron is connected to many others. The brain is the most complex organism in the known universe and scientists still have very little idea about how it works.

In the 1970s, many students were taught that the brain gradually deteriorates as a person gets older. The prevailing view was that the brain can't improve itself and that neurons die off as you age. That view was incorrect! We now know that you can create new connections in your brain at any age.

Your brain is unique and shaped by your daily experiences and what you pay attention to. If you're a violinist, the part of your brain that maps touch in your fingers is actually larger. If you're a taxi driver, the part of your brain responsible for spatial awareness is more pronounced. And if you're a mindfulness practitioner, the areas of your brain that control focus and manage emotions are more powerful, and the area responsible for higher levels of well-being (the left prefrontal cortex) is more.

An explosion of interest in the study of mindfulness has recently occurred. Centers for mindfulness have been established at numerous universities all over the world. Examples include the UMASS Medical School for Mindfulness, UCLA's Mindful Awareness Research Center, and the UCSD Center for Mindfulness. Figure 3-2 shows the growth in publications on mindfulness between 1980 and 2013.

Throughout this minibook you read about insights into the effects of mindfulness on the brain. This section describes findings from the world of neuroscience.

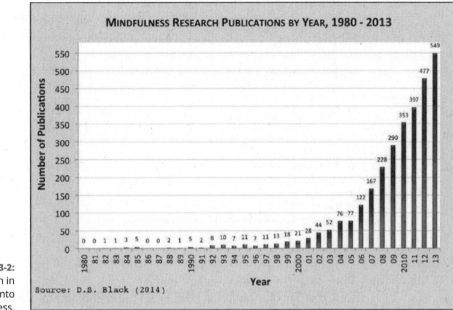

FIGURE 3-2:
Growth in research into mindfulness.

Source: DS Black, Mindfulness Research Guide

Resculpting your brain to become more productive

Most people feel that their mind is all over the place. In fact, some people who practice mindfulness even think that the exercises make them less focused! Studies show that the opposite is true. When you sit down to be mindful, you're much more likely to notice each time your mind becomes distracted. Usually, your mind is so focused that you don't even realize it.

Brain scans reveal that even after just a week or so of daily mindfulness practice, the parts of the brain dedicated to the paying attention (which include the parietal and prefrontal structures) become more activated. In other words, you are actively improving your brain's ability to pay attention. Longer-term practitioners appear to have more permanent changes in the brain, showing a greater propensity to be in the present moment even when in a resting state.

In his most recent book, *Focus: The Hidden Driver of Excellence* (Harper Paperbacks), psychologist Daniel Goleman argues that incessant use of technology, such as emails and text messages, has rendered young people increasingly distracted. He goes on to say that current research suggests that mindfulness exercises enable the brain to rewire itself and become more focused.

Goleman identifies three types of focus that are required for different types of tasks:

>> **Concentration:** Focusing on one thing only and blocking out distractions — ideal for completing tasks requiring your full attention

>> **Open presence:** Being receptive to all incoming information — ideal if you're in a leadership position that requires you to see the big picture and identify how all the different activities help the organization achieve its goals

>> **Free association:** Letting go of your old ideas and allowing your mind to drift — ideal when tapping into your creativity

Mindfulness directly helps to strengthen the networks in your brain associated with concentration and open presence, and allows you to choose to engage in free association when you need to.

Increasing your present-moment circuitry

Children love stories. Adults love stories. Have you ever wondered why? The brain is designed to be hooked by stories. Stories switch on the visual part of your brain. Because stories are formed of connecting ideas, they tune into the connections in your own brain.

Some people refer to the brain as a story-telling machine. Think about when you first wake up in the morning. Your mind is blank and then, suddenly, whoosh! Who you are and where you live and that long to-do list come to mind.

Your storytelling mind is the default network in your brain. In other words, your brain's normal mode is to tell you stories about yourself and others. For example, "I need to finish this project by noon, then I need to have a chat with Paul before I get dressed to meet my editor. I must make sure that I'm on time. That hotel we're meeting in looks very big. I hope we can find a table. I wonder if my co-author can join us . . . ?"

That's the storytelling brain at work — not always terribly exciting and often repetitive. But mindfulness is different and much more interesting. If your brain is in a more mindful state, you're focused on the present moment, which engages a different circuitry in your brain. You can access the present moment right now by noticing the sensations that your body is experiencing as it sits. Do you start to become aware of your poor posture or notice tension in your neck? You can now start to notice information from the world around you: the coolness of the book you're holding, the size of the tree outside, the wispy clouds and hints of a blue sky beyond. That's present-focused attention.

When you're more present-moment focused, rather than running on your default network all the time, you're more in control of your life. Instead of finding yourself aimlessly surfing the web, you can catch yourself and choose to get on and finish your work. If you're lost in thought after thought, you can't make a choice about what you're doing until you snap out of the dream. Mindfulness offers you that choice.

Try this exercise to help you become more present-moment focused:

1. **Make a concerted effort to engage your present-moment focus for the next 8 hours or workday.**

   If you think 8 hours will be too challenging, try 1 hour.

2. **Use any free moments in the day to focus your attention on your bodily sensations and breathing or smells, tastes, and sights.** In any given moment when you'd usually let your mind wander, choose one of the preceding and observe. Focus your attention on just that one thing.

3. **Record your observations.** What did you discover or notice? Is your mind more clear and focused? How did you cope with the distractions that your mind created?

Developing Mindfulness at Work

This section describes some of the key principles of true mindfulness, which are important both in the workplace and beyond. Some of these principles have emerged from ancient practices, developed by millions of people over thousands of years. Take a few moments to consider the key aspects of mindfulness at work and whether these ideas resonate with you.

Examining intentions and attitudes

Mindfulness is much more than just paying attention in the present moment. Mindfulness has three aspects: intention, attention, and attitude.

Intention is clarifying what you hope to get from mindfulness. Your intention when introducing mindfulness in the workplace may be to

» Increase focus

» Encourage creativity

» Reduce anxiety or stress

» Improve well-being

» Increase productivity

» Generate bigger profits

» Find greater meaning in your work

» Improve relationships at work

» Develop resilience

Your intentions play a huge role in your mindfulness practice. You may practice mindfulness for personal reasons or to benefit your team, your organization, or even the world!

Your intentions in everyday life may be so subtle that you don't recognize just how important they are. For example, take the example of breaking a window. A thief may break your window to enter and steal something from your home. A firefighter, however, may break your window to enter your home and rescue you from a fire. The action is the same but the intention is different. In the same way, being clear about your intention has a big effect on your practice.

At first, you may practice mindfulness for yourself, and that's fine. But as you develop your practice, you may like to consider being mindful for the benefit of others too. For example, you might practice mindfulness to

» Improve relations in your work team

» Be more productive so you can serve your customers better

» Be more emotionally intelligent so you can relate more effectively with your colleagues

» Help calm the anxious atmosphere in the office

These intentions aren't right or wrong, but they may help you to find greater meaning in your mindfulness practice and working life. And people whose sense of meaning is connected to their work tend to be happier, healthier, and more successful in their role — a triple whammy! See the nearby "Job, career, or call-ing" sidebar for more on what motivates people at work.

In addition to intention, your attitudes are also important. Jon Kabat-Zinn, co-developer of mindfulness-based approaches in the West, recommends developing the following attitudes to life.

JOB, CAREER, OR CALLING?

Amy Wrzesniewski, Associate Professor of Organizational Behavior at Yale University's School of Management, conducted fascinating research on how you approach your work. She may have found the key to happiness and meaning in the workplace. She explored the following three orientations toward work:

- **Job:** If you fall into this category, you view work as a means to an end. You receive pay to support your family, hobbies, or other pleasures outside of work. You seek work that doesn't interfere with your personal life. It's just a job.

- **Career:** In this category, you seek work where you have an opportunity to rise up the ladder. If no chance for promotion or development exists, you move to a different workplace. You're interested in success and prestige. You want new titles and the social standing that comes with the career.

- **Calling:** If you see your work as a calling, you see work as integral to your life. Your work is a form of self-expression and personal passion. You're more likely to find work meaningful and be more satisfied in both your work and life in general. If work is your calling, you'd probably say that you'd do the work even if you didn't get paid for it.

These categories aren't exclusive — you may have a calling for your work but also seek good pay and career prospects. And no right or wrong job orientation exists — you may prefer to find more meaning outside your work.

The incredible finding is that it doesn't matter what type of work people do — the orientations seem to be evenly spread, one third each. So a personal assistant may see his work as a job (I want to get paid and get out of here), a career (I hope this job leads to extra training and a chance to work with the vice president), or a calling (I enjoy making my boss's life run smoothly and seeing her achieve her goals). It's the mind-set that counts.

Being non-judgmental

Your mind is constantly judging experiences as good or bad. Mindfulness practice offers time for you to let go of those internal judgments and just observe whatever you're experiencing, accepting the moment as it is.

Being patient

Mindfulness requires patience. You need to bring your attention back to the present again and again. If you're naturally impatient, mindfulness is probably the best training you can undertake! But it won't be easy. You need to experience sitting with the discomfort of impatience. With time, the feeling dissolves. Being non-judgmental with your feelings helps you to accept and be with them, no matter how impatient you feel.

Adopting a beginner's mind

If you adopt a *beginner's mind*, you undertake each mindfulness practice as if the experience was a completely new one. And not only mindfulness — to work with a beginner's mind means that you approach your work with freshness — as if you've never done this kind of work before. Adopting this attitude helps you to switch off your habitual, automatic ways of doing things. As you become more experienced in mindfulness, the beginner's mind is particularly important. Always practice mindfulness as if you're a beginner!

Developing trust

Mindfulness takes time to show its benefits. In that time, you need to be able to trust the process. If you're going through a difficult time at work, you also need to be able to trust your own inner capacity to work through the challenge with the support of mindfulness, together with any other support that you can access. Trust is about believing that things can be better. And with that mind-set, you're willing to try something new. Developing trust involves noticing and respecting your doubts but not letting them run away with you. Great scientists need to trust that their experiments may lead to new discoveries; otherwise they wouldn't bother trying them in the first place. Try to adopt the trusting and open attitude of a scientist as you learn to be more mindful.

Learning to be non-striving

To strive means trying to reach a future goal, whether it's an internal goal of feeling happier or more focused or an external goal of achieving financial success. Striving engages the "doing mode" in your brain. In this state, you experience a sense of inherent dissatisfaction with the way things are in the present moment. This dissatisfaction drives the action to achieve the goal.

Mindfulness is about non-striving. To be mindful, you need to let go of your constant desire to achieve. Just be with whatever experiences show up; simply observe them with curiosity and make no judgments. You don't have to feel calm or relaxed; you simply need to be present in your moment-to-moment experiences as best you can.

Being accepting

Acceptance is a fundamental aspect of mindfulness. To accept means to stop fighting with your present-moment experience and just be aware of whatever is happening. For example, if you feel discomfort in your body when you're practicing mindfulness, and shifting your posture doesn't ease it, just acknowledge the sensation and let it be. Giving presentations may make you feel anxious. Mindfulness lets you acknowledge the anxiety as an interesting feeling and then ignore it.

Letting go

Consider what you're holding on to. A job that isn't right for you? Ways of working that are no longer effective? Even more importantly, are you holding on to ideas that are limiting your potential, such as "I can't handle this project" or "I'll never be able to give a speech"? Perhaps you need to let go of your old ideas.

Letting go is an act of freedom. When you let go of old ideas, beliefs, people, jobs, or ways of working, you create space for the new. When practicing mindfulness, you need to let go of each stream of thought that you notice. The process is a continuous movement of observation and letting go.

Sometimes mindful awareness results in a complete sense of letting go and being in your moment-to-moment experience, with full acceptance, total peace, and joyful effortlessness. If this experience ever happens to you, remember to let it go too!

Remembering that practice makes perfect

Early scientific research into mindfulness investigated the effect it had on monks, who practice mindfulness for years. Brain scans revealed that monks' brains operate far more effectively than those of people who don't practice mindfulness. The researchers also found that the more practice a monk had undertaken, the greater the number of positive changes. Monks have an incredible ability to focus, can manage their emotions very well, experience lots of positive emotions (that's why they're always smiling!), and rarely, if ever, lose their temper.

The good news is that you don't need to become a monk to benefit from mindfulness. Positive changes have been observed in the brains of people who've been practicing mindfulness for just 10 to 20 minutes a day for a few days.

Daily practice is the key. Consider the process of discovering how to ride a bike. If you spend just 1 minute a day practicing, you eventually get better but doing so takes years! If you practice for 20 minutes a day with a teacher, you may be able to ride within a week or two. Once you get the hang of riding a bike, you need regular practice to be able to cycle faster. You may need to train with a coach, read books about cycling, meet other cyclists to share ideas, and so on.

Mindfulness is similar. You need to practice regularly, and the more time you can dedicate to being mindful, the better you get at it. You can start slowly with short mindful exercises and gradually build up to longer sessions. If you want to get really good at mindfulness, you need to read about it, get a coach or trainer, and practice diligently.

Experimenting with mindfulness

What makes a good scientist? Someone who has a theory, tests it, and perseveres until it's proven. Think of your workplace as a laboratory — time to pop on your lab coat! Think of your job as a place where you can test the effect of mindfulness on the quality of your work, your relationships with colleagues, your productivity, or whatever outcome you're hoping for. You're much more likely to adopt mindfulness if you find out that the exercises work.

Use these steps to monitor the effects of your mindfulness practice:

1. **Record how things are for you now, without mindfulness.** You can record how much work you achieve every hour, how well you're getting on with your colleagues, how focused you are, or even how much you're enjoying your work at the end of each day. Measure whatever you're interested in ultimately changing. As with any good budding scientist, keep clear records. Enter data on a spreadsheet, note data in a journal, or record findings on your phone.

2. **Integrate mindfulness into your work for a few weeks.** You can do a 10-minute mindfulness exercise at the start of the day, enjoy three mindful pauses spread out over the day, or set reminder alarms on your phone to be mindful and focused while you're working. Continue to record your productivity or whatever else you're measuring.

3. **Analyze your results.** What effect did mindfulness have on whatever you're measuring? Note what worked for you and stick with it. The longer you practice, the more effective your mindfulness will be.

REMEMBER

Don't take these results too seriously. It takes a lot longer than a few weeks to reap benefits. Many people, when they first start practicing mindfulness, notice more of their own negative thoughts and patterns than positive ones. But after that initial dip, they're better able to focus and to ignore negative thoughts and modify unhelpful behaviors. So you may want to experiment for a few months before drawing any conclusions.

Acting ethically for the organization and its people

To behave in an ethical manner means doing what you consider to be right. Being ethical is vital for all parts of the organization, but especially so for its leaders. If the leaders of your company are unethical, other employees are tempted to follow suit. The example set by leaders holds far more weight than all the words in the ethics handbook.

Not only is acting ethically important in itself, it has numerous benefits:

>> **Safeguarding assets:** If your organization has an ethical culture, the staff respects the company's assets. So office supplies won't go missing and employees won't use the phone for personal conversations. When employees feel proud of their organization and work with integrity, they respect the company's supplies and equipment.

>> **Quality of decision making:** Decisions are often based on ethical choices. The more tempting decision may not be the most ethical one. Ethical decisions based on transparency and accountability lead to the long-term health of the organization.

>> **Public image:** An ethical organization is far more attractive to the general public. When unethical actions come to light, a company's image can be destroyed overnight. The public would like to see you value your staff, the environment, and those less fortunate rather than value profits alone.

>> **Teamwork:** If your organization communicates its values and ethics to employees, they can better align their own values with those of the company. When these positive values are authentic and acted upon, employees feel proud of their organization and what it stands for. The quality and quantity of work increase alongside increased intrinsic motivation.

Examples abound of multinationals incurring huge financial losses as a result of acting unethically. Lack of corporate integrity can bring down an entire organization.

Mindfulness can affect the ethical stance of everyone in the organization. Ethics are ultimately based on decisions. When mindful, you're more aware of the decision you're making and the effect that it has. As all decisions contain an element of emotion, you can use mindfulness to focus on emotions that result in more ethically sound decisions.

Marc Lampe, a professor at the University of San Diego, argues that mindfulness improves cognitive awareness and emotional regulation, positively contributing to ethical decisions.

Common sense agrees. Mindfulness is based on attitudes such as compassion, curiosity, and self-awareness. The non-reactive and caregiving stance that mindfulness promotes is bound to lead to morally sensitive choices in the workplace.

Living life mindfully

To get the best results, mindfulness needs to be practiced at home as well as at work. If you live mindfully when you're traveling, at home, with friends, or engaging in hobbies, you're more likely to be mindful when you're at work.

If you're training to run a marathon, you don't just eat healthily during the day and then pig out in the evening — you need to live a healthy life. To develop mindfulness, you need to *live* mindfully.

TIP

Here are a few tips for practicing mindfulness at home:

>> **When conversing with your partner, give him or her your full attention.** Notice your tendencies to interrupt, argue, or ignore. Instead, make a concerted effort to step back and see your partner afresh, with a sense of gratitude for what the person offers to the relationship. See relationship interactions as a chance for you to grow and develop rather than a means to fix or change the other person. Seeing the faults in others is often much easier than recognizing your own shortcomings.

>> **When you're with your children, know that love and attention go hand in hand.** When you play with them, listen to their stories about school or help them with their problems. Doing so makes your children feel more loved. You can't always give them your undivided attention, of course, but if you usually do some work in the evening and always see your kids as a distraction, redress your priorities.

>> **Housework is a great way to practice mindfulness.** The work doesn't involve too much thinking, the processes are repetitive, and there's a clear focus for attention. Take ironing, for example. Rather than trying to finish it as quickly as possible, take your time. Enjoy the heat coming off the shirt, the sensation of the iron gliding over the material, the smell of a freshly washed garment, and the beauty of a pressed shirt. Focusing your attention in this way is not only satisfying but also another way to deepen your mindfulness.

>> **Cook and eat with awareness.** Taking time to cook a meal is a wonderful discipline. Every time you chop a tomato, feel the knife slicing through it. Listen to the onion sizzling in the frying pan and smell the freshly cooked herbs. Cooking is a great way to develop your mindful awareness and improve your health because you, not some restaurant chef, decide how much sugar and fat goes into your cooking. Use fresh, organic, local ingredients when you can and enjoy the taste of your meal. Eating slowly, tasting each morsel, and being grateful to have food available is all part of mindful cooking and eating.

>> **Be aware of your phone, TV, and Internet usage.** If your work involves looking at screens all day, take a screen break when you get home. Spend more time talking to your family and friends; set aside time for walking, reading, or going to the theater. Ensure that you have things to do on your calendar that involve getting out and about.

To live mindfully is to live with greater wisdom and compassion. Wisdom is about the choices you make and your attitudes to life. Compassion is responding kindly to your own suffering and that of others. Mindful awareness helps you to wake up to your own life and make living and working with greater wisdom and compassion a reality. You're able to act with greater integrity and respond with increased empathy. You're in tune with your inner values and are sensitive to the needs and values of others.

Reflect on the following questions and jot down your thoughts in a journal:

>> **Think about the wisest people you know.** What sort of work do they do? How do they behave when they're at work? What is their attitude to life? How mindful are they when they're at work, at home, or with friends? How balanced is their lifestyle? Spend time with them and share what you think of them. Find out how they came to be so wise.

>> **Think about the kindest, friendliest, or happiest people you know.** How do they behave when they're with others? What sort of words do they use? How do they measure success? Try spending more time with them and find out what they do to develop these positive qualities.

Chapter **4**

Practicing Mindfulness in the Digital Age

This chapter helps you manage one of the most beneficial but also most challenging aspects of living in the information age — digital technology. Mindfulness offers you the presence of mind to be able to choose when to use technology, to identify what sort of technology you need, and to recognize when a more offline, human approach is called for. When you do use technology, you discover how mindfulness offers a way of working with it that involves a greater degree of presence, wisdom and compassion.

Choosing When to Use Technology

Technology includes any application of scientific knowledge for practical purposes. In the industrial age, technology was dominated by mechanical machinery driven by the steam engine. But in the twenty-first century, your daily life is probably dominated by digital technology. The recent explosion in the use of digital technology is affecting every organization in some way.

The evolution of the human brain didn't take modern technology into account. So these changes are creating a big challenge, even for the powerhouse that resides in your skull. The pervasive use of technology often means that you may not even question your use of email or texting to communicate, but mindfulness offers you a chance to momentarily reflect before you immerse yourself in sending another deluge of messages out into the web.

Recognizing the pros and cons of technology

Digital technology certainly has many benefits in the workplace. Communication via texts and instant messaging is immediate. Video conferencing means that time isn't wasted on traveling to meetings. Work can be completed on the move. With laptops and smartphones, you can stay connected and keep working in planes, trains, and automobiles. And with the processing power of computers, technology is used to manage huge amounts of data from customers to help you decide how best to serve their needs.

Does the use of technology have any drawbacks? We think so, especially if you use it unskillfully. Here are a few disadvantages that are often overlooked:

>> **Compulsive use of digital communication:** Email can change from a tool to an addiction, as detailed in the "Checking messages can be addictive" sidebar. Constant checking of email, even when other tasks are more pressing, wastes both time and energy and ultimately reduces the company's productivity.

>> **Reduced ability to focus:** Too much use of technology can make you distracted, as you jump from one task to the next. A lack of extended time working on just one task reduces your brain's ability to focus.

>> **Less face-to-face time:** The more time you spend using technology, the less time is available for face-to-face meetings. This reduction in human contact can make working relationships a little shallower and result in lower levels of trust and understanding between people.

>> **Inefficiency resulting from multitasking:** With technology comes the temptation to multitask. Multitasking leads to reduced productivity and a lack of satisfaction.

Mindfulness can help you to notice your new relationship with technology so that you're more in control rather than being a slave to your digital devices.

CHECKING MESSAGES CAN BE ADDICTIVE

Do you find yourself constantly checking your emails throughout the day and evening? Can you resist reading that text message on your phone so you can get on with your work? If not, the culprit is probably dopamine, which is a chemical released in your brain.

The latest research shows that dopamine causes seeking behavior — that is, it makes you seek out things to address your basic needs, such as food, sex, and warmth. But dopamine also makes you seek out facts, making you curious about new ideas. Dopamine activates your goal-directed behavior.

This seeking behavior is rewarded by a separate but complimentary system called the opioid system. So, as an example, say that dopamine makes you seek chocolate. When you get the chocolate, your brain rewards you with opioids.

Texts, emails, Twitter, and Google all offer you instant gratification for whatever you're seeking. If you feel a bit lonely, you start seeking companionship. The ping of a new email makes you feel wanted, and a bit of your pleasure chemical is instantly released. You feel momentarily satisfied, but your desire to check email again returns immediately. Suddenly you can't stop texting, emailing, or surfing online.

What makes technology particularly addictive? Three elements:

- **A cue triggers dopamine.** The sound of the text or ping of the email activates a cue — an important requirement for dopamine release. Your seeking behavior begins!

- **Unpredictability is a key element in dopamine activation.** The sound of a text being delivered means you have a message from someone, but you don't know who and you don't know what it contains. The desire to check that message right now, no matter what you're doing, is fueled by dopamine.

- **Short messages boost dopamine.** Because the information doesn't reveal all the information you desire, just an alluring snapshot, texts, WhatsApp messages, and tweets make the experience short and super addictive. You text back or click the link to find out more — and the seeking continues.

All this stimulation and seeking behavior is draining and depletes your attention. Constantly checking your digital devices affects your productivity because you can't focus. So, what can you do about it?

Turning off the cues is the easiest way to remove the temptation. Without hearing the arrival of emails, texts, and tweets, you're less likely to keep checking. Also, consider leaving your phone behind from time to time or blocking your Internet access occasionally.

Rebalancing your use of technology

Using technology too much is a problem. If you're used to checking your phone every minute of the day for messages, you may struggle to concentrate when in a meeting or listening to your boss. Inefficient habits when online may mean that you end up surfing from one website to another instead of completing your tasks. And deciding to always communicate via technology rather than meeting face to face can lead to a loss of opportunities to discuss new ideas and create a deeper and more trusting relationship with colleagues or customers.

Having described the downside to overuse of digital devices in the preceding section, you need to recognize that an aversion to technology can be an issue too. If you're the CEO of the organization and decide not to make best use of technology, your competitors may surpass you. Using outdated technology may frustrate your staff and mean that you struggle to attract the talent you need to succeed.

A balanced approach is the answer. Most companies have embraced the use of technology, and that's probably a good thing. But you may not know how to use technology in a more mindful way so that you're not in a constant state of distraction or miscommunicating with others as you respond on a purely emotional level. A set of strategies is urgently required in the workplace to help individuals make more conscious choices in their use of technology.

One of the most effective ways of managing your technology is having downtime — time when you switch off from technology. Computers are different from humans. Computers work best if they're never switched off. They can go on and on working without rest. If you stay connected and switched on without time to recharge, however, you will burn out. Your attentional resources will deplete rapidly, as will your energy levels, enthusiasm, and intelligence. So having a few minutes, a few hours, a few days, and sometimes a few weeks away from technology is key to your success. For more on this topic, see the "Dealing with information overload" sidebar.

DEALING WITH INFORMATION OVERLOAD

Alvin Toffler coined the term *information overload* in 1970. He predicted that access to large amounts of information would cause people problems — and he was right! Information overload is an ever-worsening problem in the workplace. It occurs when you take in more information than you're able to process, which then results in you delaying decisions or just making incorrect decisions.

Referring to this time period as the information age isn't accurate. Information has been available since the invention of the printing press hundreds of years ago. The difference now is the massive amount of information available to pretty much everyone. Computers continue to store and are able to share more and more information, but the human mind can manage only so much. The human brain has evolved over millions of years to manage our everyday environment, but the technology that allows us to view the written word and visual images on screen has been around for only a few decades — the brain hasn't had time to properly evolve in relation to these environmental changes.

The problem of information overload can easily spread in the workplace. For example, if one person has too much information in his email inbox, he may share it or pass it to others without processing that information effectively. Then more and more people are overloaded with too many emails to deal with and too little time.

Consuming up to 100,000 words a day, via email, websites, social media, and other digital sources isn't unusual. Accessing this amount of information can take up to 12 hours. The need to manage this relentless onslaught on the brain is one reason why mindfulness is gaining popularity in the West.

Managing information overload isn't easy. Here are a few solutions for mindfully dealing with information overload in the workplace:

- **Spend time disconnected.** That way, no new information can come in and you can start and complete one task at a time. Use mindful breaths between and during tasks to keep you in the present moment.

- **Ask people specific, clear questions so that you receive clear-cut answers.** Listen with mindful awareness so you know exactly what they said.

- **Keep communication short.** Rather than writing long emails and having extended phone conversations, limit your time and get to the point! If you don't, you'll finish your work late and limit your free time. Quality, not quantity, counts.

- **Schedule face-to-face time every day.** Meeting with someone and having a more relaxed chat gives you a break from text and allows you to recharge your brain.

- **Read information that you need to know rather than what you want to know.** Save fun reading for your spare time and focus on completing your essential tasks first. Doing so prevents you taking in too much information, feeling unfocused, and being unmindful as a result.

Mindfulness gives you choices. Without mindfulness, you can spend hours flitting from website to website and email to email while your high-priority work gets left behind. Mindfulness exercises help you to wake up. Mindfulness gives you the presence of mind to switch off and be more creative, constructive, and conscious in your working life.

Here are a few ways to create digital downtime, based on how much time you have available:

>> **A few minutes:** Take a break for a few minutes every half-hour or so if you work on a computer all day. Taking a step back, concentrating on a few deep, conscious breaths, and walking around are good for your body and mind.

>> **A few hours:** When the workday is over, take a break from the screen. It's common for people to work at a screen all day, and relax at home by watching another screen. Refresh yourself by socializing, doing a mindfulness practice, taking up a hobby, or participating in sport.

>> **A few days:** Take time off from technology every week. Aim for at least one day off per week if possible; Saturday is a good day for many people. See whether you can leave your phone behind, avoid checking email or social media, and do something more natural and energizing for you.

>> **A few weeks:** If you can, take a few weeks vacation at least once a year. While on vacation, see if you can have an extended period of time away from phones, computers, and so on. This is probably when you'll have your creative juices flowing as your mind comes up with unique solutions for challenges you've been facing in the workplace or home life. If you're connected digitally every day, you'll be amazed at how clear your mind becomes following a break from all that for a week or so.

Communicating Mindfully

Communication lies at the heart of being human. In the workplace, you're bound to be communicating often with others. And when you're not communicating with others, you're communicating with yourself, being aware of your thoughts, emotions, and even sensations in your body.

Mindful communication is about bringing a greater level of conscious awareness and reflection to how you communicate. With greater awareness, you're better able to understand what others want to express to you, as well as able to choose when and how to communicate your own thoughts.

Communication has been transformed by technology. Whereas in the past face-to-face conversations were the only way to communicate, you can now share your thoughts in lots of different ways. With the advent of the telephone, a person on the other side of the world could be reached in a few moments. And with the creation of the Internet came not only email but also live video chat via platforms such as Skype and Google Hangout — and free to boot! More recently, communication has taken another step with the creation of social media, dominated by Facebook, Twitter, and LinkedIn.

Face-to-face conversations are now just one option and are often the option less chosen because of the required time investment. Are face-to-face meetings worth the effort? Regular face-to-face interactions build up social networks in the brain through subtle visual cues and signals. If you spend thousands of hours online, you miss out on this training. Young people growing up in the modern age may have a reduced ability to socialize resulting from lack of face time.

Face-to-face communication has many inherent benefits that aren't so easy to access online or over the phone. These benefits include the following:

- » **The personal touch:** When you've met a colleague, customer, or supplier in person, the relationship changes. You're more likely to keep in touch and you have a clear image associated with that name. The in-person meeting can lead to conversations, ideas, and insights that would never be discussed in other ways.

- » **Non-verbal communication:** Spending time face-to-face means that you pick up all sorts of clues from a person's body language that you won't get via other forms of communication. This point is key. A pause when you mention the new deal may tell you that the other person is reluctant to commit to it. If you manage a salesperson via email alone, you never pick up that she speaks too loudly and quickly. You don't understand the pressure your designer is under until you see his face. With this extra information, you can make better decisions.

- » **Teams work better when together:** Research described in the *Journal of Computer-Mediated Communication* found that teams working face-to-face made fewer errors and reported improved teamwork and performance.

- » **Dealing with tricky situations:** When a situation is slightly emotionally charged, a face-to-face conversation can work best. Positive non-verbal communication can help to diffuse unnecessary tension. Online communication may cause the difficulties to spiral into bigger problems if not nipped in the bud.

According to management guru Peter Drucker: "The most important thing in communication is to hear what isn't being said."

Mindful communicators choose what is the most effective form of communication and then give that communication their full attention. Mindful communication also keeps in mind the limits of the medium of communication.

HEY YOU, FOCUS HERE!

In an interview, Daniel Goleman, a world expert on emotional intelligence in the workplace and author of *Focus: The Hidden Driver of Excellence,* explained that two main types of attention exist: top down and bottom up. Top-down attention is intentional, conscious focus. Bottom-up attention is living on autopilot, being distracted by every ping of an email and ding of a text.

Technological devices are designed to capture your attention; as a result, becoming more mindful is increasingly important as a means of keeping your brain on task, enabling you to do the work that you find interesting and meaningful. Daniel recommends that each time you notice that you're scrolling through Facebook, checking emails, or texting unnecessarily, you simply guide your attention back to your work. Each time you guide your attention in this way, you strengthen the networks in your brain that allow you to focus in the moment. Directing your attention back to work is like practicing mindfulness of breath, in which you notice when your mind has wandered into thoughts and then gently guide your attention back to the present moment.

Following are seven forms of communication, rated hierarchically according to the level of feedback they provide, from least to most:

1. **Instant messaging:** Expect instant replies. Little or no emotion. Fast.

2. **Text:** Very short; great for catching attention but too short for any meaningful communication. No emotional communication to couch the words spoken. The same message can potentially be read as positive or negative.

3. **Email:** Lacks any emotional feedback. Neutral emails can be read as negative or rude.

4. **Social media:** Some forms include emotional feedback, but the stream of messages often scatter the attention thinly.

5. **Telephone:** Tone of voice can provide much more feedback than preceding methods. Needs to be used more, not less.

6. **Video chat:** Probably the best form of technology-based communication. Facial expression enhances the information exchanged. Some of the social network parts of your brain receive feedback and engage.

7. **Face-to-face meeting:** The ultimate form of communication. Tone of voice, body posture, speed of speech, and a wide range of facial expressions are clearly observable. No risk of technology breakdown. A handshake or friendly hug, together with eye contact, increase trust and improve well-being. Slow.

Emailing mindfully

Email is both incredibly convenient and incredibly stressful. As the existence of over 5 billion email accounts demonstrates, however, it is certainly popular.

Here are some facts about email:

>> Over 100 trillion emails are sent every year.

>> The average office worker spends over a quarter of his or her day dealing with emails.

>> The average employee sends and receives 116 emails a day.

Email is a tool for your own use. When you check email when you need to and respond efficiently, all may be well. But you may be in the habit of checking email too often, hoping for that next interesting message to come flying through.

Mindful emailing is using email with greater awareness and wisdom. The purpose of using email is to communicate for the benefit of both you and your recipient.

TIP

Try these tips to help you use email more mindfully and productively:

>> **Make a brief emailing plan.** Use a notebook to jot down who you plan to send emails to and a few brief points that you want to make each day. Then write those emails first. You can check new emails later. Making a plan may take only a couple of minutes but can save you hours of time reading and replying to unimportant emails.

>> **Watch out for email addiction.** Decide in advance how many times a day you're going to check your emails. For some people, once is enough; for others, once an hour is necessary. Unless your primary role is dealing with emails, you need to ensure that you're not in the habit of constantly checking your inbox. If you find that even sticking to a nominal number of checks a day isn't working, write down the actual times of day that you're going to open your inbox. Imposing discipline on yourself in this way helps you retrain your mind so that you focus on what's in front of you rather than being constantly distracted by often unnecessary messages.

>> **Breathe before sending.** Before you send an email, take three mindful breaths. Doing so helps you to become more mindful, gives you an opportunity to reflect on what you've written, and helps you to stay focused. Give it a try!

>> **See your email from the other person's perspective.** After you've taken your mindful breaths (see preceding point), imagine how the other person will feel when she reads your email. You may decide that it needs editing before you send it. You may even give her a call instead!

Chade-Meng Tan, the man behind mindfulness programs at Google, recalls one staff member who tried this technique. Apparently, when this person described having tried something different and made a phone call, everyone in the room gasped! At Google, technology obviously rules.

>> **Send at least one positive email every day.** Focusing on the good helps to rebalance your brain's natural negativity bias and makes both you and your recipient feel better. Praise an employee for settling into the team so quickly, thank your boss for her help with the report yesterday, or congratulate Michelle on her sales presentation. A positive email is a great way to start the day.

Control your emails; don't let them control you. Choose whom you want to respond to instead of reacting to every new email that lands in your inbox. Cultivate good email habits, such as limiting the time you spend on them and focusing only on those that are essential. Above all, be mindful and present as you deal with emails. Use your favorite mindful exercises before and after emailing to help you achieve greater focus.

TIP

Turn off your message notifications, so that you aren't alerted each time a new one arrives. Doing so is your first step toward reducing the amount of time you waste in this way.

Phoning mindfully

One day, Mark wanted to do something different. When he received a routine email from Sarah in accounts, he decided to phone the sender rather than simply email his response. The phone seemed to ring for quite some time before a tentative voice said, "Hello?" Mark told the woman that he was the Mark she'd been emailing for years but had never spoken to. They went on to have a pleasant conversation. Sarah said the call made her feel less like a machine and more like someone who actually works with other people. That encounter was certainly a wake-up call for Mark!

Mindful phoning means bringing a greater degree of awareness to the process of being on the phone. With mindful phoning, you need to be aware of several things:

>> What the other person is saying

>> That person's tone of voice

>> What you want to say

>> Your state of mind

>> What you want to achieve from the conversation

>> How you can be of help to the other person

Try this exercise the next time you make a phone call:

1. **Take a few moments to be mindful.**

   Practice a short mindful pause by feeling your breathing or your bodily sensations or connecting with one of your senses.

2. **Write down the aims of the conversation you're about to have.**

   This task takes only a few seconds.

3. **Stand up.**

   If you usually sit down all day facing a computer, making a phone call provides a great opportunity to get to your feet and move your body around a bit.

4. **Listen more than you speak.**

   Make sure that you listen to the other person's tone of voice as well as the words.

5. **Be aware of your emotions.**

   If the conversation makes you feel anxious or angry, notice the feeling in your body. Feel the emotion with your breathing and then speak from your wise mind rather than reacting automatically to your feelings, saying things you may later regret. Try to tap into greater levels of mindfulness as the conversation progresses. Breathing mindfully can help!

6. **End the conversation when you need to, rather than dragging it out unnecessarily.**

TIP

The key to mindful phoning is to do a short mindful exercise before phoning. Then you'll be more focused and present during the call itself.

Using a smartphone mindfully

Smartphones are pretty smart. They can check emails, update social media, surf the web, take photos and make videos, edit videos, upload to YouTube, write a blog post, access loads of apps, work with documents, enable video chat, manage your calendar, help you find a restaurant, use global maps with GPS, tell you the time anywhere on the planet, let you read and listen to books, buy products, and even learn mindfulness! Oh, you can make phone calls too.

Smartphones are particularly addictive and can drain your mental focus and creativity when used excessively. A study of 1,600 managers conducted at Harvard University revealed that

>> 70 percent check their phone within an hour of waking up.

>> 56 percent check their phone in the hour before they go to sleep.

>> 51 percent check their phone continually when they're on holiday.

Compulsively checking your smartphone becomes a problem when it starts interfering with your everyday life. Reading your emails instead of listening to someone speaking in a meeting is one example. But what about scanning through your Facebook updates when you're listening to a customer on the phone — such behavior may cost you and your company lost revenue.

If you think that you need an injection of mindfulness to bring your smartphone habits under control, try these tips:

TIP

>> **Be conscious.** When you feel the desire to check your emails or suddenly find yourself gazing at your beloved iPhone, ask yourself what emotion you're feeling. What emotion are you trying to avoid? Anxiety, boredom, or loneliness, perhaps?

>> **Be disciplined.** Turn off your device in certain situations, such as when you're driving, attending meetings, playing with your children, and eating supper with your partner — all the key moments in your day when focus is called for.

>> **Ride the wave.** When you feel an urge to check your phone, take mindful breaths and be with the feeling rather than acting on it. Your compulsion should gradually weaken.

>> **Don't give up.** If you relapse into your 24/7 phone-checking habit, don't feel defeated. Try again. You don't need to beat yourself up about it. Your smartphone is addictive, so be friendly to yourself and try again.

If you can afford to do so, use one phone for work and another for your personal life. That way you can literally switch off from work at the end of the day.

TIP

Here are a few strategies to help you manage your smartphone with mindfulness:

>> Don't check your messages in the morning or evening.

>> Switch off notifications on your phone except those for text messages.

>> Set your phone on airplane mode whenever you're focusing on a piece of work.

>> Turn off your phone when attending meetings, going for a walk, or enjoying time with friends.

Engaging with social media mindfully

Social media, such as Facebook, Twitter, and LinkedIn, has changed the way many businesses operate. Entire companies have emerged to help organizations manage their social media — the way they connect with their customers and suppliers. And traditional advertising is finding itself working less effectively because social media is far more interactive, engaging, and fun for consumers.

Here are some key principles to consider when using social media in a way that means personal and business use overlap, as often happens in small to medium-sized organizations:

>> **See business social media as part of your working day.** Just as it would be rude to start checking your emails when your partner is talking to you, so too is using social media for business purposes.

>> **Update at set times.** Update social media using apps such as Buffer or HootSuite so that you reduce the time you spend turning on and off all the separate social media channels.

>> **Be friendly.** You can easily end up seeing people as just another number. They're not — behind each connection is a human being. If they have a comment or question, do respond. If you've too many messages to respond to individually, acknowledge their comments in a group response.

>> **Seek to make genuine connections rather than superficial contacts.** Customers will feel better for it, and so will you. And those connections may lead to more business.

>> **Give more than you receive.** Seek to help others. If someone has a question that isn't directly related to your business, you can still help. Just as you wouldn't ignore someone in person who asked you a question, don't ignore the person when online either.

Writing mindfully

Pretty much every modern business in the world has a presence on the Internet. And websites need content. Although such content is increasingly in the form of video and audio, the Internet is still awash with the written word. To be successful online, you need to be able to write well or hire someone with that skill.

Writing effectively is also important for communication. Emails, text messages, reports, and even presentations involve writing. How can you write in a way that engages your readers? And what does mindfulness have to contribute to the art of writing?

The following points relate to writing in a mindful way:

» **Look after yourself.** Writing well requires that your brain to be working at its optimal level. You can't achieve this state for long if you're feeling tired, hungry, cold, or stressed out. Go to bed on time and get enough sleep. Eat something every few hours, and make sure that meals contain plenty of fruit and vegetables. Keep a bottle of water to hand — the brain works much better when properly hydrated. Make sure that the room is at a comfortable temperature; you'll feel more relaxed as a result. Finally, if you're under a lot of pressure, take regular breaks and find time to socialize and exercise. Even if you're facing a big deadline, try to prioritize breaks and make time for mindfulness practice. Doing so will make you more efficient.

» **Remember that timing is everything.** Keep a time journal to identify at what time of day you're most efficient. Then do your writing at that time. You need to make that time sacrosanct — avoid phone calls, meetings, emails, and any other distractions.

» **Focus with mindfulness exercises.** Practice mindfulness exercises as often as you can. Use the mindful body scan (see the nearby "Body scan" sidebar) or do some informal mindfulness when you're walking or eating. Try to connect with your senses whenever mindfulness comes to mind.

» **Remove outside distractions.** To be able to write well, you need to focus. Block out as many distractions as you can. Silence your phone; don't tell other people where you're working; close all other programs on your computer.

» **Manage your inner critic.** You need to take in hand that inner voice that judges everything you do. The process of writing really wakes it up! Fortunately, you can use mindfulness to manage your inner critic. First, you notice those negative thoughts, and then you say to yourself "inner critic" and smile. Smiling sends a signal to your brain (neurons connect the brain to the muscles you use to smile) that you're not scared of that voice. Fighting or frantically running away from your inner critic can exacerbate its judgmental voice. Each time you address your inner critic in this way, you weaken its power until eventually, if you're lucky, it dies.

» **Write non-judgmentally.** Mindfulness means moment-to-moment non-judgmental awareness. So, try a period of time just writing down whatever comes into your head, without judging it. Don't correct sentences, delete words, or fix spellings. Just go with the flow and write. Doing so is a true mindfulness process — being in the moment and allowing whatever arises to be as it is. Later, you can go back and correct your mistakes.

BODY SCAN

The body scan is all about getting back in touch with your body. Your body has more of an effect on your mind than you may expect. Mindfulness of your body sensations encourages you to shift into approach mode rather than work in avoidance mode.

Read the following exercise, and select a quiet place where you won't be disturbed. Then set a timer so you won't worry about drifting off, and follow these steps:

1. **Sit on a comfortable chair, with your feet firmly on the floor.**

   Ensure that your back is upright and comfortable and your head is looking forward. Your arms can rest on the arms of the chair or your lap. Remain aware of your posture throughout the exercise if you can, and correct yourself if you notice that you're slouching.

2. **Focus your attention on your breath.**

   Feel the sensations of your breath coming in and your breath going out. Do so for approximately ten in and ten out breaths.

3. **Focus your attention on the toes of your right foot.**

   Identify whether you can feel any sensations, such as hot, cold, or tingling. See whether you can feel your toes in contact with your socks or shoes. Spend a few moments exploring your toes, and then repeat the process with your left foot. If you can't feel any sensation, just notice the lack of sensation.

4. **Compare your right and left toes.**

   Do they feel any different?

5. **Focus your attention on the soles of your feet.**

   Start with your right sole, and identify what you feel. Repeat the process with your left sole, and then compare the sensations you experienced with your right and left soles.

   If at any point during the exercise you feel any discomfort, treat it as an opportunity to explore what's going on. Approach the discomfort with kindness and curiosity. What does it feel like; what sensations arise? What thoughts enter your mind? What emotions are you experiencing? Then try letting go of the discomfort as you breathe out.

6. **Focus on your lower leg.**

   Spend time exploring the right lower leg, then the left, and then compare the two.

(continued)

(continued)

7. Focus on your knees.

Examine the sensations in your right knee, then your left knee, and then compare the two.

8. Focus on your thighs and bottom.

Explore how they feel when in contact with the chair.

9. Try to explore the sensations in your internal organs.

Focus on your liver, kidneys, stomach, lungs, and heart. You may not notice any sensation at all — and that's okay.

10. Focus on your spine.

Move up your spine slowly, focusing briefly on one vertebra at a time.

11. Focus on your right arm.

Identify the sensations in your right arm, then your left arm, and then compare the two.

12. Focus on your neck and shoulders.

If you experience any tension or discomfort, try letting it go as you breathe out.

13. Focus on your jaw and facial muscles.

Identify all the feelings and sensations.

14. Focus on your scalp.

Finish with your head. You've now worked your way from the bottom to the top of your body.

TIP

If you write on a computer, lots of software is available to help you stay focused. For example, Microsoft Word has Focus mode, in which you see only the document you're writing; all other windows disappear — ideal for you budding mindful writers out there! Another option is Ommwriter — available for Mac, PC, and iPad.

Using Technology Mindfully

Can technology be used mindfully? We think that anything done with awareness, wisdom, and compassion is a form of mindfulness. Although mindfulness has traditionally been associated with more natural surroundings, there's no reason why mindfulness can't be applied between uses of and while using technology.

Technology can help to make you *more* mindful. Various phone apps, computer programs, and online courses encourage greater mindfulness. Even a few computer games show you how to be more mindful or remind you to tune into your breathing.

Focusing on one task

Multitasking is impossible. When you think you are multitasking, you are actually switching from one task to another, creating the illusion of doing several tasks at once. Multitasking is often an inefficient way of working.

Are you a so-called multitasker? If so, you're not alone — nowadays most people try and use multitasking to finish more work in less time. Multitasking can become particularly prevalent when using technology. But the strategy often backfires. The process can also lead to you feeling unfocused, making mistakes, and getting wound up.

Here are some common examples of multitasking when using technology that lead to less efficiency rather than more:

>> **Having lots of windows open on your computer:** Having too many windows open not only slows down your computer, making your work take longer to do, but also makes you more likely to move between one task and another, rather than finishing one task and then starting the next.

>> **Emailing while working:** Most people leave their email program open all day and reply to messages as they arrive. Doing so distracts you from your work and can leave you feeling frazzled by the end of the day. Try turning off your email notifications for a day to see what happens.

>> **Sending texts while crossing the road:** Typing a text message needs your full attention. You're breaking the law if you use your mobile phone while driving, for good reason — you can't concentrate fully on two things at once. The same applies to crossing the road.

>> **Using your phone or computer while eating lunch:** Make time for a break at lunch. Applying a mere 15 minutes of mindfulness helps you make better choices about what you eat and aids your digestion. If 15 minutes is too hard for you, try just a few minutes of eating without distractions. Your entire afternoon may go more smoothly if your lunchtime is a bit more mindful.

>> **Using digital technology while driving:** It can be tempting to check emails, send texts, and see who's up to what on Facebook while behind the wheel. If you lack mindful awareness, you may easily develop this dangerous habit.

GATHERING OF MINDS AT WISDOM 2.0

The Wisdom 2.0 Conference in San Francisco started as a small gathering in 2009. The event focuses on living with greater presence, compassion, and wisdom in the digital age. It addresses the great challenge of our age: to live connected to one another through technology in ways that are beneficial to our own well-being, effective in our work, and useful to the world. The conference brings together leaders from the field of technology with teachers from the wisdom communities, such as mindfulness or yoga practitioners.

Wisdom 2.0 has flourished and thousands of people from over 30 countries have attended. Speakers have included the CEOs of the Ford Motor Company and LinkedIn, the founders of Twitter, PayPal, eBay, and Facebook, and mindful teachers Eckhart Tolle, Jon Kabat-Zinn, and Jack Kornfield. If you can't attend, you can find videos of many of the excellent talks online at www.wisdom2summit.com or on www.youtube.com.

If you're a multitasker and are convinced that doing several tasks works for you, so be it. But if you feel that life is too frantic and would like to explore a different way of working, give single-tasking a try, even for short blocks of time. Do one thing at a time with your full attention, and see what happens. Start with 10 minutes or 30 minutes — whatever you can manage.

TIP

Try keeping just one browser window open at a time on your computer. Doing so makes you feel more focused and efficient. Complete the task you need to do with that window and then close it.

Discovering technology that enhances focus

As well as all the methods of discovering mindfulness that are available online, programs to enhance your focus also exist. They block Internet access or analyze how you've used your time while on the computer. A few of these programs are described next.

SelfControl

SelfControl for Mac (http://selfcontrolapp.com) is a free program that you can use to block whatever websites you find yourself wasting time on. So, for example, you can block access to your Facebook and Twitter accounts as well as your email, for a time period of your choice. You might use this program for several hours during the day when you need to focus on writing or just need a break.

Freedom

The Internet itself can seem like a distraction sometimes. The Freedom program (www.macfreedom.com) works on the iPhone, the iPad, and Mac and Windows, and blocks complete access to the Internet for whatever period of time you choose.

RescueTime

If you use your computer a lot, RescueTime (www.rescuetime.com/) may be a good program for you. It runs in the background and keeps a record of how long you spend using different programs during the day. It then uses the data to calculate your productivity. The program presents graphs to show you at which parts of the day you were most productive, and which periods of time you spent surfing the Internet, reading blogs, and so on. The amount of detailed feedback this program provides is fascinating. The basic version of the program is free.

2

Project Management

Contents at a Glance

CHAPTER 1: Achieving Results 95

Determining What Makes a Project a Project 95

Defining Project Management 100

Knowing the Project Manager's Role 107

Do You Have What It Takes to Be an Effective
Project Manager? 111

CHAPTER 2: Knowing Your Project's Audiences 113

Understanding Your Project's Audiences 114

Developing an Audience List 114

Considering the Drivers, Supporters, and Observers 122

Displaying Your Audience List 128

Confirming Your Audience's Authority 129

Assessing Your Audience's Power and Interest 131

CHAPTER 3: Clarifying Your Project 133

Defining Your Project with a Scope Statement 133

Looking at the Big Picture: Explaining the Need
for Your Project 136

Marking Boundaries: Project Constraints 151

Documenting Your Assumptions 155

Presenting Your Scope Statement 155

CHAPTER 4: Developing a Game Plan 157

Breaking Your Project into Manageable Chunks 157

Creating and Displaying a WBS 170

Identifying Risks While Detailing Your Work 180

Documenting Your Planned Project Work 182

CHAPTER 5: Keeping Everyone Informed 183

Successful Communication Basics 184

Choosing the Appropriate Medium for
Project Communication 188

Preparing a Written Project-Progress Report 193

Holding Key Project Meetings 198

Preparing a Project Communications Management Plan 201

Chapter **1**

Achieving Results

S uccessful organizations create projects that produce desired results in established time frames with assigned resources. As a result, businesses are increasingly driven to find individuals who can excel in this project-oriented environment.

Because you're reading this book, chances are good that you've been asked to manage a project. So, hang on tight — you're going to need a new set of skills and techniques to steer that project to successful completion. But not to worry! This chapter gets you off to a smooth start by showing you what projects and project management really are and by helping you separate projects from nonproject assignments. This chapter also offers the rationale for why projects succeed or fail and gets you into the project-management mind-set.

Determining What Makes a Project a Project

No matter what your job is, you handle a myriad of assignments every day. For example, you may prepare a memo, hold a meeting, design a sales campaign, or move to new offices. Or you may make the information systems more user-friendly, develop a research compound in the laboratory, or improve the organization's public image. Not all these assignments are projects. How can you tell which ones are and which ones aren't? This section is here to help.

Understanding the three main components that define a project

A *project* is a temporary undertaking performed to produce a unique product, service, or result. Large or small, a project always has the following three components:

>> **Specific scope:** Desired results or products

>> **Schedule:** Established dates when project work starts and ends

>> **Required resources:** Necessary number of people and funds and other resources

REMEMBER

As illustrated in Figure 1-1, each component affects the other two. For example: Expanding the type and characteristics of desired outcomes may require more time (a later end date) or more resources. Moving up the end date may necessitate paring down the results or increasing project expenditures (for instance, by paying overtime to project staff). Within this three-part project definition, you perform work to achieve your desired results.

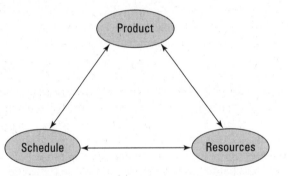

FIGURE 1-1:
The relationship between the three main components of a project.

Although many other considerations may affect a project's performance (see the later section "Defining Project Management" for details), these three components are the basis of a project's definition for the following three reasons:

>> The only reason a project exists is to produce the results specified in its scope.

>> The project's end date is an essential part of defining what constitutes successful performance; the desired result must be provided by a certain time to meet its intended need.

>> The availability of resources shapes the nature of the products the project can produce.

A Guide to the Project Management Body of Knowledge, 6th Edition (*PMBOK 6*), published by Project Management Institute, elaborates on these components by

>> Emphasizing that *product* includes both the basic nature of what is to be produced (for example, a new training program or a new prescription drug) and its required characteristics (for example, the topics that the training program must address), which are defined as the product's *quality*

>> Noting that *resources* refers to funds, as well as to other nonmonetary resources, such as people, equipment, raw materials, and facilities

PMBOK 6 also emphasizes that *risk* (the likelihood that not everything will go exactly according to plan) plays an important role in defining a project and that guiding a project to success involves continually managing tradeoffs among the three main project components — the products to be produced and their characteristics, the schedule, and the resources required to do the project work.

Recognizing the diversity of projects

Projects come in a wide assortment of shapes and sizes. For example, projects can

>> **Be large or small**

- Installing a new subway system, which may cost more than $1 billion and take 10 to 15 years to complete, is a project.

- Preparing an ad hoc report of monthly sales figures, which may take you one day to complete, is also a project.

>> **Involve many people or just you**

- Training all 10,000 of your organization's staff in a new affirmative-action policy is a project.

- Rearranging the furniture and equipment in your office is also a project.

>> **Be defined by a legal contract or by an informal agreement**

- A signed contract between you and a customer that requires you to build a house defines a project.

- An informal promise you make to install a new software package on your colleague's computer also defines a project.

>> **Be business-related or personal**

- Conducting your organization's annual blood drive is a project.

- Having a dinner party for 15 people is also a project.

REMEMBER

Regardless of the individual characteristics of your project, you define it by the same three components described in the previous section: results (or scope), start and end dates, and resources. The information you need to plan and manage your project is the same for any project you manage, although the ease and the time to develop it may differ. The more thoroughly you plan and manage your projects, the more likely you are to succeed.

Describing the four stages of a project

Every project, whether large or small, passes through the following four stages:

- **Starting the project:** This stage involves generating, evaluating, and framing the business need for the project and the general approach to performing it and agreeing to prepare a detailed project plan. Outputs from this stage may include approval to proceed to the next stage, documentation of the need for the project and rough estimates of time and resources to perform it (often included in a project charter), and an initial list of people who may be interested in, involved with, or affected by the project.

- **Organizing and preparing:** This stage involves developing a plan that specifies the desired results; the work to do; the time, cost, and other resources required; and a plan for how to address key project risks. Outputs from this stage may include a project plan that documents the intended project results and the time, resources, and supporting processes needed to create them.

- » **Carrying out the work:** This stage involves establishing the project team and the project support systems, performing the planned work, and monitoring and controlling performance to ensure adherence to the current plan. Outputs from this stage may include project results, project progress reports, and other communications.

- » **Closing out the project:** This stage involves assessing the project results, obtaining customer approvals, transitioning project team members to new assignments, closing financial accounts, and conducting a post-project evaluation. Outputs from this stage may include final, accepted, and approved project results and recommendations and suggestions for applying lessons learned from this project to similar efforts in the future.

For small projects, this entire life cycle can take just a few days. For larger projects, it can take many years! In fact, to allow for greater focus on key aspects and to make it easier to monitor and control the work, project managers often subdivide larger projects into separate phases, each of which is treated as a miniproject and passes through these four life cycle stages. No matter how simple or complex the project is, however, these four stages are the same.

REMEMBER

In a perfect world, you complete one stage of your project before you move on to the next one; and after you complete a stage, you never return to it again. But the world isn't perfect, and project success often requires a flexible approach that responds to real situations that you may face, such as the following:

- » **You may have to work on two (or more) project stages at the same time to meet tight deadlines.** Working on the next stage before you complete the current one increases the risk that you may have to redo tasks, which may cause you to miss deadlines and spend more resources than you originally planned. If you choose this strategy, be sure people understand the potential risks and costs associated with it.

- » **Sometimes you learn by doing.** Despite doing your best to assess feasibility and develop detailed plans, you may realize you can't achieve what you thought you could. When this situation happens, you need to return to the earlier project stages and rethink them in light of the new information you've acquired.

- » **Sometimes things change unexpectedly.** Your initial feasibility and benefits assessments are sound and your plan is detailed and realistic. However, certain key project team members leave the organization without warning during the project. Or a new technology emerges, and it's more appropriate to use than the one in your original plans. Because ignoring these occurrences may seriously jeopardize your project's success, you need to return to the earlier project stages and rethink them in light of these new realities.

Defining Project Management

Project management is the process of guiding a project from its beginning through its performance to its closure. Project management includes five sets of processes, which are described in more detail in the following sections:

» **Initiating processes:** Clarifying the business need, defining high-level expectations and resource budgets, and beginning to identify audiences that may play a role in your project

» **Planning processes:** Detailing the project scope, time frames, resources, and risks, as well as intended approaches to project communications, quality, and management of external purchases of goods and services

» **Executing processes:** Establishing and managing the project team, communicating with and managing project audiences, and implementing the project plans

» **Monitoring and controlling processes:** Tracking performance and taking actions necessary to help ensure project plans are successfully implemented and the desired results are achieved

» **Closing processes:** Ending all project activity

As illustrated in Figure 1-2, these five process groups help support the project through the four stages of its life cycle. Initiating processes support the work to be done when starting the project, and planning processes support the organizing and preparing stage. Executing processes guide the project tasks performed when carrying out the work, and closing processes are used to perform the tasks that bring the project to an end.

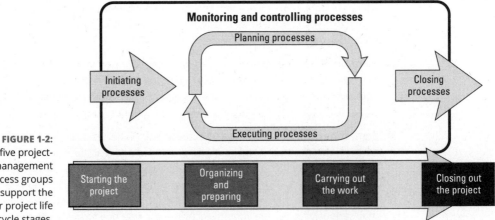

FIGURE 1-2: The five project-management process groups that support the four project life cycle stages.

Figure 1-2 highlights how you may cycle back from executing processes to planning processes when you have to return to the organizing and preparing stage to modify existing plans to address problems you encounter or new information you acquire while carrying out the project work. Finally, you use monitoring and controlling processes in each of the four stages to help ensure that work is being performed according to plans.

REMEMBER

Successfully performing these processes requires the following:

>> **Information:** Accurate, timely, and complete data for the planning, performance monitoring, and final assessment of the project

>> **Communication:** Clear, open, and timely sharing of information with appropriate individuals and groups throughout the project's duration

>> **Commitment:** Team members' personal promises to produce the agreed-upon results on time and within budget

Starting with the initiating processes

All projects begin with an idea. Perhaps your organization's client identifies a need; or maybe your boss thinks of a new market to explore; or maybe you think of a way to refine your organization's procurement process.

Sometimes the initiating process is informal. For a small project, it may consist of just a discussion and a verbal agreement. In other instances, especially for larger projects, a project requires a formal review and decision by your boss and other members of your organization's senior management team.

REMEMBER

Decision makers consider the following two questions when deciding whether to move ahead with a project:

>> *Should* **we do it?** Are the benefits we expect to achieve worth the costs we'll have to pay? Are there better ways to approach the issue?

>> *Can* **we do it?** Is the project technically feasible? Are the required resources available?

If the answer to both questions is "Yes," the project can proceed to the organizing and preparing stage (see the following section), during which a project plan is developed. If the answer to either question is a definite, ironclad "No," under no circumstances should the project go any further. If nothing can be done to make it desirable and feasible, the decision makers should cancel the project immediately. Doing anything else guarantees wasted resources, lost opportunities, and a frustrated staff. (Check out the later sidebar "Performing a benefit-cost analysis" if you need extra help determining the answer to the first question.)

Suppose you're in charge of the publications department in your organization. You've just received a request to have a 20,000-page document printed in 10 minutes, which requires equipment that can reproduce at the rate of 2,000 pages per minute.

You check with your staff and confirm that your document-reproducing equipment has a top speed of 500 pages per minute. You check with your suppliers and find out that the fastest document-reproducing equipment available today has a top speed of 1,000 pages per minute. Do you agree to plan and perform this project when you know you can't possibly meet the request? Of course not.

PERFORMING A BENEFIT-COST ANALYSIS

A *benefit-cost analysis* is a comparative assessment of all the benefits you anticipate from your project and all the costs required to introduce the project, perform it, and support the changes resulting from it. Benefit-cost analyses help you to

- Decide whether to undertake a project or decide which of several projects to undertake

- Frame appropriate project objectives

- Develop appropriate *before* and *after* measures of project success

- Prepare estimates of the resources required to perform the project work

You can express some anticipated benefits in monetary equivalents (such as reduced operating costs or increased revenue). For other benefits, numerical measures can approximate some, but not all, aspects. If your project is to improve staff morale, for example, you may consider associated benefits to include reduced turnover, increased productivity, fewer absences, and fewer formal grievances. Whenever possible, express benefits and costs in monetary terms to facilitate the assessment of a project's net value.

Consider costs for all phases of the project. Such costs may be nonrecurring (such as labor, capital investment, and certain operations and services) or recurring (such as changes in personnel, supplies, and materials or maintenance and repair). In addition, consider the following:

- Potential costs of not doing the project

- Potential costs if the project fails

- Opportunity costs (in other words, the potential benefits if you had spent your funds successfully performing a different project)

The farther into the future you look when performing your analysis, the more important it is to convert your estimates of benefits over costs into today's dollars. Unfortunately, the farther you look, the less confident you can be of your estimates. For example, you may expect to reap benefits for years from a new computer system, but changing technology may make your new system obsolete after only one year.

Thus, the following two key factors influence the results of a benefit-cost analysis:

- How far into the future you look to identify benefits
- On which assumptions you base your analysis

Although you may not want to go out and design a benefit-cost analysis by yourself, you definitely want to see whether your project already has one and, if it does, what the specific results of that analysis were.

The excess of a project's expected benefits over its estimated costs in today's dollars is its *net present value (NPV)*. The net present value is based on the following two premises:

- **Inflation:** The purchasing power of a dollar will be less one year from now than it is today. If the rate of inflation is 3 percent for the next 12 months, $1 today will be worth $0.97 one year from today. In other words, 12 months from now, you'll pay $1 to buy what you paid $0.97 for today.

- **Lost return on investment:** If you spend money to perform the project being considered, you'll forego the future income you could earn by investing it conservatively today. For example, if you put $1 in a bank and receive simple interest at the rate of 3 percent compounded annually, 12 months from today you'll have $1.03 (assuming 0 percent inflation).

To address these considerations when determining the NPV, you specify the following numbers:

- **Discount rate:** The factor that reflects the future value of $1 in today's dollars, considering the effects of both inflation and lost return on investment
- **Allowable payback period:** The length of time for anticipated benefits and estimated costs

In addition to determining the NPV for different discount rates and payback periods, figure the project's *internal rate of return* (the value of the discount rate that would yield an NPV of 0) for each payback period.

Rather than promising something you know you can't achieve, consider asking your customer whether she can change the request. For example, can she accept the document in 20 minutes? Can you reproduce certain parts of the document in the first 10 minutes and the rest later?

During some projects, you may be convinced that you can't meet a particular request or that the benefits of the project aren't worth the costs involved. Be sure to check with the people who developed or approved the project. They may have information you don't, or you may have additional information that they weren't aware of when they approved the request.

WARNING

Beware of assumptions that you or other people make when assessing your project's potential value, cost, and feasibility. For example, just because your requests for overtime have been turned down in the past doesn't guarantee they'll be turned down again this time.

Outlining the planning processes

When you know what you hope to accomplish and you believe it's possible, you need a detailed plan that describes how you and your team will make it happen. Include the following in your project-management plan:

>> An overview of the reasons for your project. (See Chapter 3 of this minibook.)

>> A detailed description of intended results. (Chapter 3 of this minibook explains how to describe desired results.)

>> A list of all constraints the project must address. (Chapter 3 of this minibook explores the different types of constraints a project may face.)

>> A list of all assumptions related to the project. (Chapter 3 of this minibook discusses how to frame assumptions.)

>> A list of all required work. (Chapter 4 of this minibook discusses how to identify all required project work.)

>> A breakdown of the roles you and your team members will play.

>> A detailed project schedule.

>> Needs for personnel, funds, and nonpersonnel resources (such as equipment, facilities, and information).

>> A description of how you plan to manage any significant risks and uncertainties.

>> Plans for project communications. (Chapter 5 of this minibook discusses how to keep everyone who's involved in your project up-to-date.)

>> Plans for ensuring project quality.

TIP

Always put your project plans in writing; doing so helps you clarify details and reduces the chances that you'll forget something. Plans for large projects can take hundreds of pages, but a plan for a small project can take only a few lines on a piece of paper (or a tablecloth!).

The success of your project depends on the clarity and accuracy of your plan and on whether people believe they can achieve it. Considering past experience in your project plan makes your plan more realistic; involving people in the plan's development encourages their commitment to achieving it.

WARNING

Don't let the pressure to get fast results convince you to skip the planning and get right to the tasks. Although this strategy can create a lot of immediate activity, it also creates significant chances for waste and mistakes.

TIP

Be sure your project's drivers and supporters review and approve the plan in writing before you begin your project (see Chapter 2 of this minibook). For a small project, you may need only a brief email or someone's initials on the plans. For a larger project, though, you may need a formal review and signoff by one or more levels of your organization's management.

Examining the executing processes

After you've developed your project-management plan and set your appropriate project baselines, it's time to get to work and start executing your plan. This is often the phase when management gets more engaged and excited to see things being produced.

Preparing

Preparing to begin the project work involves the following tasks:

>> **Assigning people to all project roles:** Confirm the individuals who'll perform the project work and negotiate agreements with them and their managers to make sure they'll be available to work on the project team.

>> **Introducing team members to each other and to the project:** Help people begin developing interpersonal relationships with each other. Help them appreciate the overall purpose of the project and explain how the different parts will interact and support each other.

>> **Giving and explaining tasks to all team members:** Describe to all team members what work they're responsible for producing and how the team members will coordinate their efforts.

>> **Defining how the team will perform its essential functions:** Decide how the team will handle routine communications, make different project

decisions, and resolve conflicts. Develop any procedures that may be required to guide performance of these functions.

>> **Setting up necessary tracking systems:** Decide which system(s) and accounts you'll use to track schedules, work effort, and expenditures and then set them up.

>> **Announcing the project to the organization:** Let the project audiences know that your project exists, what it will produce, and when it will begin and end.

REMEMBER

Suppose you don't join your project team until the actual work is getting underway. Your first task is to understand how people decided initially that the project was possible and desirable. If the people who participated in the start of the project and the organizing and preparing stages overlooked important issues, you need to raise them now. When searching for the project's history, check minutes from meetings, memos, letters, emails, and technical reports. Then consult with all the people involved in the initial project decisions.

Performing

Finally, you get to perform the project work! The performing subgroup of the executing processes includes the following:

>> **Doing the tasks:** Perform the work that's in your plan.

>> **Assuring quality:** Continually confirm that work and results conform to requirements and applicable standards and guidelines.

>> **Managing the team:** Assign tasks, review results, and resolve problems.

>> **Developing the team:** Provide needed training and mentoring to improve team members' skills.

>> **Sharing information:** Distribute information to appropriate project audiences.

Surveying the monitoring and controlling processes

As the project progresses, you need to ensure that plans are being followed and desired results are being achieved. The monitoring and controlling processes include the following tasks:

>> **Comparing performance with plans:** Collect information on outcomes, schedule achievements, and resource expenditures; identify deviations from your plan; and develop corrective actions.

>> **Fixing problems that arise:** Change tasks, schedules, or resources to bring project performance back on track with the existing plan, or negotiate agreed-upon changes to the plan itself.

>> **Keeping everyone informed:** Tell project audiences about the team's achievements, project problems, and necessary revisions to the established plan.

Ending with the closing processes

Finishing your assigned tasks is only part of bringing your project to a close. In addition, you must do the following:

>> Get your clients' approvals of the final results.

>> Close all project accounts (if you've been charging time and money to special project accounts).

>> Help team members move on to their next assignments.

>> Hold a post-project evaluation with the project team to recognize project achievements and to discuss lessons you can apply to the next project. (At the very least, make informal notes about these lessons and your plans for using them in the future.)

Knowing the Project Manager's Role

The project manager's job is challenging. For instance, she often coordinates technically specialized professionals — who may have limited experience working together — to achieve a common goal. Although the project manager's own work experience is often technical in nature, her success requires a keen ability to identify and resolve sensitive organizational and interpersonal issues. This section describes the main tasks that a project manager handles and note potential challenges she may encounter.

Looking at the project manager's tasks

Historically, the performance rules in traditional organizations were simple: Your boss made assignments; you carried them out. Questioning your assignments was a sign of insubordination or incompetence.

But these rules have changed. Today your boss may generate ideas, but you assess how to implement them. You confirm that a project meets your boss's (and your organization's) real need and then determine the work, schedules, and resources you require to implement it.

Handling a project any other way simply doesn't make sense. The project manager must be involved in developing the plans because she needs the opportunity to clarify expectations and proposed approaches and then to raise any questions she may have *before* the project work begins.

The key to project success is being proactive. Instead of waiting for others to tell you what to do, you should

>> Seek out information because you know you need it.

>> Follow the plan because you believe it's the best way.

>> Involve people whom you know are important for the project.

>> Identify issues and risks, analyze them, and elicit support to address them.

>> Share information with the people you know need to have it.

>> Put all-important information in writing.

>> Ask questions and encourage other people to do the same.

>> Commit to your project's success.

Staving off excuses for not following a structured project-management approach

Be prepared for other people to fight your attempts to use proven project-management approaches. You need to be prepared for everything! The following list provides a few examples of excuses you may encounter as a project manager and the appropriate responses you can give:

>> **Excuse:** Our projects are all crises; we have no time to plan.

Response: Unfortunately for the excuse giver, this logic is illogical! In a crisis, you have limited time and resources to address critical issues, and you definitely can't afford to make mistakes. Because acting under pressure and emotion (the two characteristics of crises) practically guarantees that mistakes will occur, you can't afford not to plan.

>> **Excuse:** Structured project management is only for large projects.

Response: No matter what size the project is, the information you need to perform it is the same. What do you need to produce? What work has to be accomplished? Who's going to do that work? When will the work end? Have you met expectations?

Large projects may require many weeks or months to develop satisfactory answers to these questions. Small projects that last a few days or less may take only 15 minutes. Either way, you still have to answer the questions.

>> **Excuse:** These projects require creativity and new development. They can't be predicted with any certainty.

Response: Some projects are more predictable than others. However, people awaiting the outcomes of any project still have expectations for what they'll get and when. Therefore, a project with many uncertainties needs a manager to develop and share initial plans and then to assess and communicate the effects of unexpected occurrences.

Even if you don't encounter these specific excuses, you can adapt the response examples provided here to address your own situations.

Avoiding shortcuts

The short-term pressures of your job as a project manager may encourage you to act today in ways that cause you, your team, or your organization to pay a price tomorrow. Especially with smaller, less formal projects, you may feel no need for organized planning and control.

WARNING

Don't be seduced into the following, seemingly easier shortcuts:

>> **Jumping directly from starting the project to carrying out the work:** You have an idea and your project is on a short schedule. Why not just start doing the work? Sounds good, but you haven't defined the work to be done!

Other variations on this shortcut include the following:

● **"This project's been done many times before, so why do I have to plan it out again?"** Even though projects can be similar to past ones, some elements are always different. Perhaps you're working with some new people or using a new piece of equipment. Take a moment now to be sure your plan addresses the current situation.

● **"Our project's different than it was before, so what good is trying to plan?"** Taking this attitude is like saying you're traveling in an unknown area, so why try to lay out your route on a road map? Planning for a new project is important because no one's taken this particular path before. Although your initial plan may have to be revised during the project, you and your team need to have a clear statement of your intended plan from the outset.

>> **Failing to prepare in the carrying out the work stage:** Time pressure is often the apparent justification for this shortcut. However, the real reason is that people don't appreciate the need to define procedures and relationships before jumping into the actual project work.

>> **Jumping right into the work when you join the project in the carrying out the work stage:** The plan has already been developed, so why go back and revisit the starting the project and the organizing and preparing stages? Actually, you need to do so for two reasons:

- To identify any issues that the developers may have overlooked

- To understand the reasoning behind the plan and decide whether you feel the plan is achievable

>> **Only partially completing the closing stage:** At the end of one project, you often move right on to the next. Scarce resources and short deadlines encourage this rapid movement, and starting a new project is always more challenging than wrapping up an old one.

However, you never really know how successful your project is if you don't take the time to ensure that all tasks are complete and that you've satisfied your clients. If you don't take positive steps to apply the lessons this project has taught you, you're likely to make the same mistakes you made in this project again or fail to repeat this project's successful approaches.

Staying aware of other potential challenges

WARNING

Projects are temporary; they're created to achieve particular results. Ideally, when the results are achieved, the project ends. Unfortunately, the transitory nature of projects may create some project-management challenges, including the following:

>> **Additional assignments:** People may be asked to accept an assignment to a new project in addition to — not in lieu of — existing assignments. They may not be asked how the new work might affect their existing projects. (Higher management may just assume the project manager can handle everything.) When conflicts arise over a person's time, the organization may not have adequate guidelines or procedures to resolve those conflicts.

>> **New people on new teams:** People who haven't worked together before and who may not even know each other may be assigned to the same project team. This lack of familiarity may slow down the project because team members may

- Have different operating and communicating styles

- Use different procedures for performing the same type of activity

- Not have time to develop mutual respect and trust

» **No direct authority:** For most projects, the project manager and team members have no direct authority over each other. Therefore, the rewards that usually encourage top performance (such as salary increases, superior performance appraisals, and job promotions) aren't available. In addition, conflicts over time commitments or technical direction may require input from a number of sources. As a result, they can't be settled with one, unilateral decision.

Do You Have What It Takes to Be an Effective Project Manager?

You're reading this book because you want to be a better project manager, right? Well, before you jump in, we suggest you do a quick self-evaluation to determine your strengths and weaknesses. By answering the following ten questions, you can get an idea of what subjects you need to spend more time on so you can be as effective as possible. Good luck!

Questions

1. Are you more concerned about being everyone's friend or getting a job done right?

2. Do you prefer to do technical work or manage other people doing technical work?

3. Do you think the best way to get a tough task done is to do it yourself?

4. Do you prefer your work to be predictable or constantly changing?

5. Do you prefer to spend your time developing ideas rather than explaining those ideas to other people?

6. Do you handle crises well?

7. Do you prefer to work by yourself or with others?

8. Do you think you shouldn't have to monitor people after they've promised to do a task for you?

9. Do you believe people should be self-motivated to perform their jobs?

10. Are you comfortable dealing with people at all organizational levels?

Answer key

1. Although maintaining good working relations is important, the project manager often must make decisions that some people don't agree with for the good of the project.

2. Most project managers achieve their positions because of their strong performance on technical tasks. But after you become a project manager, your job is to encourage other people to produce high-quality technical work rather than to do it all yourself.

3. Believing in yourself is important. However, the project manager's task is to help other people develop to the point where they can perform tasks with the highest quality.

4. The project manager tries to minimize unexpected problems and situations through responsive planning and timely control. When problems do occur, the project manager must deal with them promptly to minimize their impact on the project.

5. Though coming up with ideas can help your project, the project manager's main responsibility is to ensure that every team member correctly understands all ideas that are developed.

6. The project manager's job is to provide a cool head to size up the situation, choose the best action, and encourage all members to do their parts in implementing the solution.

7. Self-reliance and self-motivation are important characteristics for a project manager. However, the key to any project manager's success is to facilitate interaction among a diverse group of technical specialists.

8. Although you may feel that honoring one's commitments is a fundamental element of professional behavior, the project manager needs both to ensure that people maintain their focus and to model how to work cooperatively with others.

9. People should be self-motivated, but the project manager has to encourage them to remain motivated by their job assignments and related opportunities.

10. The project manager deals with people at all levels — from upper management to support staff — who perform project-related activities.

» **Identifying drivers, supporters, and observers**

» **Using an effective format**

» **Determining who has authority in your project**

» **Prioritizing your audiences**

Chapter **2**

Knowing Your Project's Audiences

O ften a project is like an iceberg: Nine-tenths of it lurks below the surface. You receive an assignment and think you know what it entails and who needs to be involved. Then, as the project unfolds, new people emerge who may affect your goals, approach, and chances for project success.

You risk compromising your project in the following two ways when you don't involve key people or groups in your project in a timely manner:

» You may miss important information that can affect the project's performance and ultimate success.

» You may insult people. And you can be sure that when people feel that you have slighted or insulted them, they will take steps to make sure you don't do it again!

As soon as you begin to think about a new project, start to identify people who may play a role. This chapter shows you how to identify these candidates; how to decide whether, when, and how to involve them; and how to determine who has the authority, power, and interest to make critical decisions.

Understanding Your Project's Audiences

A *project audience* is any person or group that supports, is affected by, or is interested in your project. Your project's audiences can be inside or outside your organization, and knowing who they are helps you

>> Plan whether, when, and how to involve them.

>> Determine whether the scope of the project is bigger or smaller than you originally anticipated.

You may hear other terms used in the business world to describe project audiences, but these terms address only some of the people from your complete project audience list. Here are some examples:

>> **A *stakeholder list* identifies people and groups who support or are affected by your project.** The stakeholder list doesn't usually include people who are merely interested in your project.

>> **A *distribution list* identifies people who receive project communications.** These lists are often out-of-date for a couple of reasons. Some people remain on the list simply because no one removes them; other people are on the list because no one wants to run the risk of insulting them by removing them. In either case, having their names on this list doesn't ensure that these people actually support, are affected by, or are interested in your project.

>> ***Team members* are people whom the project manager directs.** All team members are stakeholders and, as such, are part of the project audience, but the audience list includes more than just team members.

Developing an Audience List

As you identify the different audiences for your project, record them in an audience list. Check out the following sections for information on how to develop this list.

Starting your audience list

A project audience list is a living document. You need to start developing your list as soon as you begin thinking about your project. Write down any names that occur to you; when you discuss your project with other people, ask them who they think may be affected by or interested in your project. Then select a small group of the audiences you identify and conduct a formal brainstorming session. Continue to add and subtract names to your audience list until you can't think of anyone else.

In the following sections, you discover how to refine your audience list by dividing it into specific categories and recognizing important potential audiences. This section ends with a sample to show you how to put together your own list.

Using specific categories

To increase your chances of identifying all appropriate people, develop your audience list in categories. You're less likely to overlook people when you consider them department by department or group by group instead of trying to identify everyone from the organization individually at the same time.

REMEMBER

Start your audience list by developing a hierarchical grouping of categories that covers the universe of people who may be affected by, be needed to support, or be interested in your project. You might want to start with the following groups:

>> **Internal:** People and groups inside your organization

- **Upper management:** Executive-level management responsible for the general oversight of all organization operations

- **Requesters:** The person who came up with the idea for your project and all the people through whom the request passed before you received it

- **Project manager:** The person with overall responsibility for successfully completing the project

- **End users:** People who will use the goods or services the project will produce

- **Team members:** People assigned to the project whose work the project manager directs

- **Groups normally involved:** Groups typically involved in most projects in the organization, such as the human resources, finance, contracts, and legal departments

- **Groups needed just for this project:** Groups or people with special knowledge related to this project

>> **External:** People and groups outside your organization

- **Clients or customers:** People or groups that buy or use your organization's products or services

- **Collaborators:** Groups or organizations with whom you may pursue joint ventures related to your project

- **Vendors, suppliers, and contractors:** Organizations that provide personnel, raw materials, equipment, or other resources required to perform your project's work

- **Regulators:** Government agencies that establish regulations and guidelines that govern some aspect of your project work

- **Professional societies:** Groups of professionals that may influence or be interested in your project

- **The public:** The local, national, and international community of people who may be affected by or interested in your project

TIP

Continue to subdivide these categories further until you arrive at job titles or position descriptions and the names of the people who occupy them. (The process of systematically separating a whole into its component parts is called *decomposition*, which you can read about in Chapter 4 in this minibook.)

THE TRUE PURPOSE OF THE AUDIENCE LIST

Suppose your boss had assigned you a project that you have to finish in two months. You immediately develop an audience list, following the steps in this chapter, but, much to her horror, the list included more than 150 names! How are you supposed to involve more than 150 people in a two-month project? You might conclude that the audience list is clearly of no help.

In fact, your audience list has served its purpose perfectly. Identifying the people at the outset who would affect the success of your project gives you three options:

- Plan how and when to involve each person during the project.

- Assess the potential consequences of not involving one or more of your audiences.

- Discuss extending the project deadline or reducing its scope with your boss if you realize that you can't ignore any of the audiences.

The audience list itself doesn't decide whom you should involve in your project. Instead, it specifies those people who may affect the success of your project so you can weigh the benefits and the costs of including or omitting them.

Considering often overlooked audiences

As you develop your audience list, be sure not to overlook the following potential audiences:

>> **Support groups:** These people don't tell you what you should do (or help you deal with the trauma of project management); instead, they help you accomplish the project's goals. If support groups know about your project early, they can fit you into their work schedules more readily. They can also tell you information about their capabilities and processes that may influence what your project can accomplish and by when you can do so. Such groups include

- Facilities

- Finance

- Human resources

- Information technology (IT)

- Legal services

- Procurement or contracting

- Project management office

- Quality

- Security

>> **End users of your project's products:** *End users* are people or groups who will use the goods and services your project produces. Involving end users at the beginning of and throughout your project helps ensure that the goods and services produced are as easy as possible to implement and use and are most responsive to their true needs. It also confirms that you appreciate the fact that the people who will use a product may have important insights into what it should look like and do, which increases the chances that they'll work to implement the products successfully.

In some cases, you may omit end users on your audience list because you don't know who they are. In other situations, you may think you have taken them into account through *liaisons* — people who represent the interests of the end users. (Check out the nearby sidebar "Discovering the real end users" for a costly example of what can happen when you depend solely on liaisons.)

>> **People who will maintain or support the final product:** People who will service your project's final products affect the continuing success of these products. Involving these people throughout your project gives them a chance to make your project's products easier to maintain and support. It also allows them to become familiar with the products and effectively build their maintenance into existing procedures.

DISCOVERING THE REAL END USERS

A major international bank based in the United States had spent millions of dollars revising and upgrading its information system. Project personnel had worked closely with special liaisons in Europe who represented the interests of the local bank personnel who would be entering and retrieving data from the new system. When the bank introduced the upgraded system, they discovered a fatal problem: More than 90 percent of the local bank personnel in Europe were non-English speaking, but the system documentation was written in English. The enhanced systems were unusable!

The system designers had spent substantial time and money working with the liaisons to identify and address the interests and needs of the end users. However, the liaisons had raised only issues from their own experience instead of identifying and sharing the needs and concerns of the local bank personnel. Because English was the primary language of all the liaisons, they failed to consider the possible need to prepare system instructions in multiple languages. Putting the local bank personnel on the audience list along with the liaisons would have reminded the project personnel not to overlook their special needs.

Examining the beginning of a sample audience list

Suppose you're asked to coordinate your organization's annual blood drive. Figure 2-1 illustrates some of the groups and people you might include in your project's audience list as you prepare for your new project.

Ensuring a complete and up-to-date audience list

Many different groups of people may influence the success of or have an interest in your project. Knowing who these people are allows you to plan to involve them at the appropriate times during your project. Therefore, identifying all project audiences as soon as possible and reflecting any changes in those audiences as soon as you find out about them are important steps to take as you manage your project.

REMEMBER

To ensure your audience list is complete and up-to-date, consider the following guidelines:

Category			
Level 1	Level 2	Level 3	Level 4
Internal	Upper Management	Executive Oversight Committee	
		VP, Sales and Marketing	
		VP, Operations	
		VP, Administration	
	Requester	VP, Sales and Marketing	
		Manager, Community Relations	
	Project Team	Project Manager	
		Team Members	Customer Service Rep
			Community Relations Rep
			Human Resources Rep
	Groups Normally Involved	Finance	
		Facilities	
		Legal	
		Human Resources	
	Groups Just for this Project	Project Manager and Team Members from last year's blood drive	
External	Clients/Customers	Donors	Prior
			New
		Hospital and medical centers receiving blood from the drive	
	Vendors, Contractors	Attending nurses, food-service provider, facility's landlord, local blood center	
	Regulatory Agencies	Local board of health	
	Professional Societies	American Medical Association	
		American Association of Blood Banks	
	Public	Local Community	
		Local media	Local newspapers
			Local TV stations
			Local radio stations

FIGURE 2-1: The beginning of a sample audience list for an annual blood drive.

>> **Eventually identify each audience by position description and name.** You may, for example, initially identify people from sales and marketing as an audience. Eventually, however, you want to specify the particular people from that group — such as *brand manager for XYZ product, Sharon Wilson* — and their contact information.

>> **Speak with a wide range of people.** Check with people in different organizational units, from different disciplines, and with different tenures in the organization. Ask every person whether he or she can think of anyone else you should speak with. The more people you speak with, the less likely you are to overlook someone important.

>> **Allow sufficient time to develop your audience list.** Start to develop your list as soon as you become project manager. The longer you think about your project, the more potential audiences you can identify. Throughout the project, continue to check with people to identify additional audiences.

>> **Include audiences who may play a role at any time during your project.** Your only job at this stage is to identify names so you don't forget them. At a later point, you can decide whether, when, and how to involve these people (see the later section "Considering the Drivers, Supporters, and Observers").

>> **Include team members' functional managers.** Include the people to whom the project manager and team members directly report. Even though functional managers usually don't perform project tasks themselves, they can help ensure that the project manager and team members devote the time they originally promised to the project and that they have the resources necessary to perform their project assignments.

>> **Include a person's name on the audience list for every role she plays.** Suppose your boss plans to provide expert technical advice to your project team. Include your boss's name twice — once as your direct supervisor and once as the technical expert. If your boss is promoted but continues to serve as a technical advisor to your project, the separate listings remind you that a new person now occupies your direct supervisor's slot.

>> **Continue to add and remove names from your audience list throughout your project.** Your audience list evolves as you understand more about your project and as your project changes. Plan to review your list at regular intervals throughout the project to identify names that should be added or deleted. Encourage people involved in your project to continually identify new audiences as they think of them.

>> **When in doubt, write down a person's name.** Your goal is to avoid overlooking someone who may play an important part in your project. Identifying a potential audience member doesn't mean you have to involve that person; it simply means you have to consider him or her. Eliminating the name of someone who won't be involved is a lot easier than trying to add the name of someone who should be.

Using an audience list template

An *audience list template* is a predesigned audience list that contains typical categories and audiences for a particular type of project. You may develop and maintain your own audience list templates for tasks you perform, functional groups may develop and maintain audience list templates for tasks they typically conduct, or your organization's project management office may develop and maintain templates for the entire organization.

Regardless of who maintains the template, it reflects people's cumulative experiences. As the organization continues to perform projects of this type, audiences who were overlooked in earlier efforts may be added and audiences who proved unnecessary removed. Using these templates can save you time and improve your accuracy.

Suppose you prepare the budget for your department each quarter. After doing a number of these budgets, you know most of the people who give you the necessary information, who draft and print the document, and who have to approve the final budget. Each time you finish another budget, you revise your audience list template to include new information from that project. The next time you prepare your quarterly budget, you begin your audience list with your template. You then add and subtract names as appropriate for that particular budget preparation.

REMEMBER

When using audience list templates, keep the following guidelines in mind:

>> **Develop templates for frequently performed tasks and for entire projects.** Audience list templates for kicking off the annual blood drive or submitting a newly developed drug to the Food and Drug Administration are valuable. But so are templates for individual tasks that are part of these projects, such as awarding a competitive contract or printing a document. Many times, projects that appear new contain some tasks that you've performed before. You can still reap the benefits of your experience by including the audience list templates for these tasks in your overall project audience list.

>> **Focus on position descriptions rather than the names of prior audiences.** Identify an audience as *accounts payable manager* rather than *Bill Miller*. People come and go, but functions endure. For each specific project, you can fill in the appropriate names.

>> **Develop and modify your audience list template from previous projects that worked, not from initial plans that looked good but lacked key information.** Often you develop a detailed audience list at the start of your

project but don't revise the list during the project or add audiences that you overlooked in your initial planning. If you update your template with information from an initial list only, your template can't reflect the discoveries you made throughout the earlier project.

>> **Encourage your team members to brainstorm possible audiences before you show them an existing audience list template.** Encouraging people to identify audiences without guidance or restrictions increases the chances that they'll think of audiences that were overlooked on previous projects.

>> **Use templates as starting points, not ending points.** Make clear to your team that the template isn't the final list. Every project differs in some ways from similar ones. If you don't critically examine the template, you may miss people who weren't involved in previous projects but whom you need to consider for this one.

>> **Reflect your different project experiences in your audience list templates.** The post-project evaluation is an excellent time to review, critique, and modify your audience list for a particular project.

WARNING

Templates can save time and improve accuracy. However, starting with a template that's too polished can suggest you've already made up your mind about the contents of your final list, which may discourage people from freely sharing their thoughts about other potential audiences. In addition, their lack of involvement in the development of the project's audience list may lead to their lack of commitment to the project's success.

Considering the Drivers, Supporters, and Observers

After you identify everyone in your project audience, you need to determine which of the following groups those people fall into. Then you can decide whether to involve them and, if so, how and when.

>> **Drivers:** People who have some say in defining the results of your project. You're performing your project for these people.

>> **Supporters:** The people who help you perform your project. Supporters include individuals who authorize or provide the resources for your project as well as those who work on it.

>> **Observers:** People who are neither drivers nor supporters but who are interested in the activities and results of your project. Observers have no say in your project, and they're not actively involved in it. However, your project may affect them at some point.

Separating audiences into these three categories helps you decide what information to seek from and share with each audience, as well as to clarify the project decisions in which to involve them.

Suppose an IT group has the job of modifying the layout and content of a monthly sales report for all sales representatives. The vice president of sales requested the project, and the *chief information officer* (CIO — the boss of the head of the IT group) approved it. As the project manager for this project, consider categorizing your project's audiences as follows:

>> **Drivers:** The vice president of sales is a driver because he has specific reasons for revising the report. The CIO is a potential driver because she may hope to develop certain new capabilities for her group through this project. Individual sales representatives are all drivers for this project because they'll use the redesigned report to support their work.

>> **Supporters:** The systems analyst who designs the revised report, the training specialist who trains the users, and the vice president of finance who authorizes the funds for changing the manual are all supporters.

>> **Observers:** The head of the customer service department is a potential observer because he hopes your project will lead to an improved problem-tracking system this year.

WARNING

Beware of supporters who try to act like drivers. In the preceding example, the analyst who finalizes the content and format of the report may try to include certain items that she thinks are helpful. However, only the real drivers should determine the specific data that goes into the report. The analyst just determines whether including the desired data is possible and what doing so will cost.

REMEMBER

Keep in mind that the same person can be both a driver and a supporter. For example, the vice president of sales is a driver for the project to develop a revised monthly sales report but also a supporter if he has to transfer funds from the sales department budget to pay for developing the report.

The following sections help you identify when you need to involve drivers, supporters, and observers, and how to keep them involved.

INCLUDING A PROJECT CHAMPION

A *project champion* is a person in a high position in the organization who strongly supports your project; advocates for your project in disputes, planning meetings, and review sessions; and takes whatever actions are necessary to help ensure the successful completion of your project.

As soon as you start planning, find out whether your project has a champion. If it doesn't, try to recruit one. An effective project champion has the following characteristics:

- Sufficient power and authority to resolve conflicts over resources, schedules, and technical issues

- A keen interest in the results of your project

- A willingness to have his or her name cited as a strong supporter of your project

Deciding when to involve your audiences

Projects pass through the following four stages as they progress from an idea to completion (see Chapter 1 of this minibook for detailed explanations of these stages):

>> Starting the project

>> Organizing and preparing

>> Carrying out the work

>> Closing the project

Plan to involve drivers, supporters, and observers in each stage of your project's life cycle. The following sections tell you how you can do so.

Drivers

Keeping drivers involved in your project from start to finish is critical because they define what your project should produce, and they evaluate your project's success when it's finished. Their desires and your assessment of feasibility can influence whether you should pursue the project. Check out Table 2-1 to see how to involve drivers during the four stages of your project.

TABLE 2-1   **Involving Drivers in the Different Project Stages**

Stage	Involvement Level	How to Involve
Starting the project	Heavy	Identify and speak with as many drivers as possible. If you uncover additional drivers later, explore with them the issues that led to the project; ask them to identify and assess any special expectations they may have.
Organizing and preparing	Moderate to heavy	Consult with drivers to ensure your project plan addresses their needs and expectations. Have them formally approve the plan before you start the project work.
Carrying out the work	Moderate	As the project gets under way, introduce the drivers to the project team. Have the drivers talk about their needs and interests to reinforce the importance of the project and help team members form a more accurate picture of project goals. In addition, have the team members talk to the drivers to increase the drivers' confidence that the team members can successfully complete the project. While performing the project work, keep drivers apprised of project accomplishments and progress to sustain their ongoing interest and enthusiasm. Continually confirm that the results are meeting their needs.
Closing the project	Heavy	Have drivers assess the project's results and determine whether their needs and expectations were met. Identify their recommendations for improving performance on similar projects in the future.

Supporters

Involving supporters from start to finish is important because they perform and support the project work; supporters need to know about changing requirements so they can promptly identify and address problems. Keeping them actively involved also sustains their ongoing motivation and commitment to the project. Check out Table 2-2 to see how to involve supporters during your project's four stages.

Observers

After you choose the observers with whom you want to actively share project information, involve them minimally throughout the project because they neither tell you what should be done nor help you do it. Table 2-3 shows how you may keep observers involved.

TABLE 2-2   **Involving Supporters in the Different Project Stages**

Stage	Involvement Level	How to Involve
Starting the project	Moderate	Wherever possible, have key supporters assess the feasibility of meeting driver expectations. If you identify key supporters later in the project, have them confirm the feasibility of previously set expectations.
Organizing and preparing	Heavy	Supporters are the major contributors to the project plan. Because they facilitate or do all the work, have them determine necessary technical approaches, schedules, and resources. Also have them formally commit to all aspects of the plan.
Carrying out the work	Heavy	Familiarize all supporters with the planned work. Clarify how the supporters will work together to achieve the results. Have supporters decide how they'll communicate, resolve conflicts, and make decisions throughout the project. Throughout the project, keep supporters informed of project progress, encourage them to identify performance problems they encounter or anticipate, and work with them to develop and implement solutions to these problems.
Closing the project	Heavy	Have supporters conclude their different tasks. Inform them of project accomplishments and recognize their roles in project achievements. Elicit their suggestions for handling similar projects more effectively in the future.

TABLE 2-3   **Involving Observers in the Different Project Stages**

Stage	Involvement Level	How to Involve
Starting the project	Minimal	Inform observers of your project's existence and its main goals.
Organizing and preparing	Minimal	Inform observers about the project's planned outcomes and time frames.
Carrying out the work	Minimal	Tell observers that the project has started and confirm the dates for planned milestones. Inform observers of key project achievements.
Closing the project	Minimal	When the project is done, inform observers about the project's products and results.

TIP

Because observers don't directly influence or affect your project, be sure to carefully manage the time and effort you spend sharing information with them. When deciding whom to involve and how to share information with them, consider the following:

>> Their level of interest in your project

>> The likelihood that your project will affect them at some point in the future

>> The need to maintain a good working relationship with them

See the "Assessing Your Audience's Power and Interest" section, later in this chapter, for information on what to consider when deciding how to involve different audiences.

Using different methods to involve your audiences

Keeping drivers, supporters, and observers informed as you progress in your project is critical to the project's success. Choosing the right method for involving each audience group can stimulate that group's continued interest and encourage its members to actively support your work. Consider the following approaches for keeping your project audiences involved throughout your project:

>> **One-on-one meetings:** One-on-one meetings (formal or informal discussions with one or two other people about project issues) are particularly useful for interactively exploring and clarifying special issues of interest with a small number of people.

>> **Group meetings:** These meetings are planned sessions for some or all team members or audiences. Smaller meetings are useful to brainstorm project issues, reinforce team member roles, and develop mutual trust and respect among team members. Larger meetings are useful to present information of general interest.

>> **Informal written correspondence:** Informal written correspondence (notes, memos, letters, and emails) helps you document informal discussions and share important project information.

>> **More formal information-sharing vehicles:** Information resources such as project newsletters or sites on the organization's intranet may be useful for sharing nonconfidential and noncontroversial information with larger audiences.

>> **Written approvals:** Written approvals (such as a technical approach to project work or formal agreements about a product, schedule, or resource commitment) serve as records of project decisions and achievements.

Flip to Chapter 5 in this minibook for additional suggestions for sharing information about your project's ongoing performance.

Making the most of your audiences' involvement

To maximize your audiences' involvement and contributions, follow these guide-lines throughout your project:

>> **Involve audiences early in the project planning if they have a role later.** Give your audiences the option to participate in planning even if they don't perform until later in the project. Sometimes they can share information that'll make their tasks easier. At the least, they can reserve time to provide their services when you need them.

>> **If you're concerned with the legality of involving a specific audience, check with your legal department or contracts office.** Suppose you're planning to award a competitive contract to buy certain equipment. You want to know whether prospective bidders typically have this equipment on hand and how long it will take to receive it after you award the contract. However, you're concerned that speaking to potential contractors in the planning stage may tip them off about the procurement and lead to charges of favoritism by unsuccessful bidders who didn't know about the procurement in advance.

Instead of ignoring this important audience, check with your contracts office or legal department to determine how you can get the information you want and still maintain the integrity of the bidding process.

>> **Develop a plan with all key audiences to meet their information needs and interests as well as yours.** Determine the information they want and the information you believe they need. Also decide when to provide that information and in what format. Finally, clarify what you want from them and how and when they can provide it.

>> **Always be sure you understand each audience's *what's in it for me* (WIIFM).** Clarify why seeing your project succeed is in each audience's interest. Throughout your project, keep reminding your audiences of the benefits they'll realize when your project is complete and the progress your project has made toward achieving those benefits.

Displaying Your Audience List

You're concerned with two issues when developing the format and content of your audience list:

>> Increasing your confidence that you identified all appropriate audiences

>> Helping others suggest people not on the list who should be included and people on the list who possibly should not

Figure 2-2 shows a sample audience list format you might want to use for your audience list. The format includes three major categories of information:

>> The hierarchical structure of the categories in which audiences are located

>> The specific identifiers of each audience (job title and name)

>> The audience's role with regard to the project (driver, supporter, or observer; see the earlier section "Considering the Drivers, Supporters, and Observers")

Note: You can add additional columns on the right for optional information, such as email and phone.

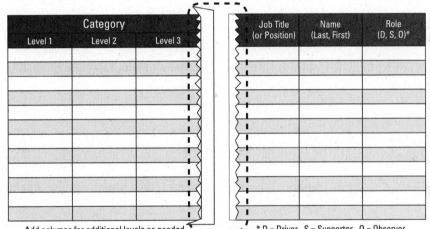

FIGURE 2-2:
Sample audience
list format.

Add columns for additional levels as needed   * D = Driver   S = Supporter   O = Observer

Confirming Your Audience's Authority

In project terms, *authority* refers to the overall right to make project decisions that others must follow, including the right to apply project resources, expend funds, or give approvals. Having opinions about how an aspect should be addressed is different from having the authority to decide how it will be addressed. Mistaking a person's level of authority can lead to frustration as well as wasted time and money.

Confirm that the people you've identified as audiences have the authority to make the decisions they need to make to perform their tasks. If they don't have that authority, find out who does and how to bring those people into the process.

At the beginning of the carrying out the work stage in your projects, take the following steps to define each audience member's authority:

1. **Clarify each audience member's tasks and decisions.**

   Define with each person his tasks and his role in those tasks. For example, will he just work on the task, or will he also approve the schedules, resource expenditures, and work approaches?

2. **Ask each audience member what his authority is regarding each decision and task.**

   Ask about individual tasks rather than all issues in a particular area. For example, a person can be more confident about his authority to approve supply purchases up to $5,000 than about his authority to approve all equipment purchases, no matter the type or amount.

   Clarify decisions that the audience member can make himself. For decisions needing someone else's approval, find out whose approval he needs. (Ask, never assume!)

3. **Ask each audience member how he knows what authority he has.**

   Does a written policy, procedure, or guideline confirm the authority? Did the person's boss tell him in conversation? Is the person just assuming? If the person has no specific confirming information, encourage him to get it.

4. **Check out each audience member's history of exercising authority.**

   Have you or other people worked with this person in the past? Has he been overruled on decisions that he said he was authorized to make? If so, ask him why he believes he won't be similarly overruled this time.

5. **Verify whether anything has recently changed regarding each audience member's authority.**

   Do you have any reason to believe that this person's authority has changed? Is he new to his current group or position? Has he recently started working for a new boss? If any of these situations exists, encourage the person to find specific documentation to confirm his authority for his benefit as well as yours.

Reconfirm the information in these steps when a particular audience's decision-making assignments change. Suppose, for example, that you initially expect all individual purchases on your project to be at or under $2,500. Bill, the team representative from the finance group, assures you that he has the authority to approve such purchases for your project without checking with his boss. Midway through the project, you find that you have to purchase a piece of equipment for $5,000. Be sure to verify with Bill that he can personally authorize this larger expenditure. If he can't, find out whose approval you need and plan how to get it.

Assessing Your Audience's Power and Interest

An audience's potential effect on a project depends on the power he or she can exercise and the interest the person has in exercising that power. Assessing the relative levels of each helps you decide with whom you should spend your time and effort to realize the greatest benefits.

Power is a person's ability to influence the actions of others. This ability can derive either from the direct authority the person has to require people to respond to her requests *(ascribed power)* or the ability she has to induce others to do what she asks because of the respect they have for her professionally or personally *(achieved power)*. In either case, the more power a person has, the better able she is to marshal people and resources to support your project. Typically, drivers and supporters have higher levels of power over your project than observers do.

On the other hand, a person's *interest* in something is how much she cares about it, is curious about it, or pays attention to it. The more interested a person is in your project, the more likely she is to want to use her power to help the project succeed.

You can define an audience's relative levels of power and interest related to your project as being either *high* or *low*. You then have four possible combinations for each audience's relative levels of power and interest. The particular values of an audience's power and interest ratings suggest the chances that the audience may have a significant effect on your project and, therefore, the relative importance of keeping that audience interested and involved in your project.

TIP

Most often, you base the assessments of an audience's power over and interest in your project on the aggregated individual, subjective opinions of several parties: you, your team members, your project's other audiences, people who have worked with the audience on other projects, subject matter experts, the audience himself or herself, or a combination. If you assign a value of *1* to each individual rating of *high* and *0* to each individual rating of *low*, you'd rate an audience's power or interest as *high* if the average of the individual assessments were 0.5 or greater and *low* if the average were below 0.5.

Figure 2-3 depicts a *power-interest grid*, which represents these four possible power-interest combinations as distinct quadrants on a two-dimensional graph.

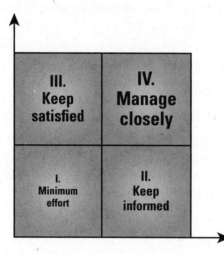

FIGURE 2-3:
Involving audiences with different levels of power and interest in your project.

As the project manager, you should spend a minimal amount of time and effort with audiences who have low levels of both power and interest (quadrant I). Spend increasingly greater amounts of time and effort with audiences that have a low level of power and a high level of interest (quadrant II) and a low level of interest and a high level of power (quadrant III), respectively. You should spend the most time and effort keeping audiences with high degrees of both power and interest (quadrant IV) informed and involved. (Check out Chapter 5 of this minibook for different ways to communicate with your project's audiences.)

Chapter **3**

Clarifying Your Project

All projects are created for a reason; someone identifies a need and devises a project to address that need. How well the project ultimately addresses that need defines the project's success or failure.

This chapter helps you develop a mutual agreement between your project's requesters and your project team about the project's goals and expectations. It also helps you establish the conditions necessary to perform the project work.

Defining Your Project with a Scope Statement

A *scope statement* is a written confirmation of the results your project will produce and the constraints and assumptions under which you will work. Both the people who requested the project and the project team should agree to all terms in the scope statement before project work begins.

A good scope statement includes the following information:

» **Justification:** A brief statement regarding the business need your project addresses

>> **Product scope description:** The characteristics of the products, services, and/or results that your project will produce

>> **Acceptance criteria:** The conditions that must be met before project deliverables are accepted

>> **Deliverables:** The products, services, and/or results that your project will produce (also referred to as *objectives*)

>> **Project exclusions:** Statements about what the project will not accomplish or produce

>> **Constraints:** Restrictions that limit what you can achieve, how and when you can achieve it, and how much achieving it can cost

>> **Assumptions:** Statements about how you will address uncertain information as you conceive, plan, and perform your project

REMEMBER

Think of your scope statement, when viewed with the other components of your project plan, as a binding agreement in which

>> You and your team commit to producing certain results. Your project's requesters commit that they'll consider your project 100 percent successful if you produce these results.

>> You and your team identify all restrictions regarding your approach to the work and the resources you need to support your work. Your project's requesters agree that there are no restrictions other than the ones you've identified and that they'll provide you the support you declare you need.

>> You and your team identify all assumptions you made when setting the terms of your scope statement. Your project's requesters agree that, if any of these assumptions prove to be invalid, you may have to modify some or all of your project plans.

A well-written scope statement is an important resource for helping to manage stakeholder expectations.

REMEMBER

Of course, predicting the future is impossible. In fact, the further into the future you try to look, the less certain your predictions can be. However, your scope statement represents your project commitments based on what you know today and expect to be true in the future. If and when situations change, you have to assess the effect of the changes on all aspects of your project and propose the necessary changes to your scope statement. Your project's requesters always have the option of either accepting your proposed changes (and allowing the project to continue) or canceling your project.

DOCUMENTS RELATED TO THE SCOPE STATEMENT

Your organization may use a number of other documents, such as the ones listed here, to address issues similar to those included in the scope statement. When you use these other documents as sources of information to prepare or describe your project plan, be careful to note how they differ from the scope statement:

- **Market requirements document:** A formal request to develop or modify a product. This document (typically prepared by a member of your organization's sales and marketing group) may lead to the creation of a project. However, in its original form, this document reflects only the *desires* of the person who wrote it. It doesn't reflect an assessment of whether meeting the request is possible or in the organization's best interest, nor is it a commitment to meet the request.

- **Business requirements document:** A description of the business needs that a requested product, service, or system must address.

- **Technical requirements, specifications document, or product requirements document:** A description of the characteristics that the products and services produced must have.

- **Project request:** A written request for a project by a group in the organization. The project request indicates a desire for a project rather than a mutual agreement and commitment to perform it.

- **Statement of work:** A narrative description of products, services, or results to be supplied by a project.

- **Project profile:** A document that highlights the key information about a project, sometimes also called a *project summary* or a *project abstract.*

- **Project charter:** A document issued by upper management that formally establishes a project and authorizes the project manager to use organizational resources to perform project activities.

- **Work order:** A written description of work that people or groups in your organization will perform in support of your project. The signed work order focuses on work performance rather than overall project outcomes.

- **Contract:** A legal agreement for providing specified goods or services.

Looking at the Big Picture: Explaining the Need for Your Project

Understanding the situation and thought processes that led to your project's creation helps ensure that you and your project successfully meet people's expectations. This section helps you clarify your project's justification and the desired deliverables.

Figuring out why you're doing the project

When you take on a project, *why* you're doing it may seem obvious — because your boss told you to. The real question, however, isn't why you chose to accept the assignment but why the project must be done (by you or anyone else) in the first place.

The following sections help you identify people who may benefit from your project so you can then determine how their expectations and needs help justify the project.

Identifying the initiator

Your first task in discovering your project's underlying justification is to determine who had the original idea that led to your project (this person is called the *project's initiator*). Project success requires that, at a minimum, you meet this person's needs and expectations.

REMEMBER

Identifying your project's initiator is easy when he's the person who directly assigns it to you. More likely, however, the person who gives you the project is passing along an assignment she received from someone else. If your project has passed through several people before it reaches you, you may have difficulty determining who really had the initial idea. Not to mention, the original intent may have become blurred if people in the chain purposely or inadvertently changed the assignment a little as they passed it on.

MAKING A POSITIVE FIRST IMPRESSION: THE PROJECT TITLE

To accomplish a successful project, a group of focused and motivated people must effectively and efficiently work together to produce an agreed-upon set of desired results. From the beginning of the project, these people must have all the information they need to perform their assigned tasks, as well as the motivation and commitment to overcome any challenges they may encounter as they proceed with their project work. One of the first items you can use to develop these essential information-sharing and commitment-building processes is your project's title.

Although one important use of the project title is to serve as an identifier for project information and materials, the title, if written well, can also serve to

- Announce your project's existence
- Reveal what the project is about
- Stimulate curiosity and interest in the project
- Evoke positive feelings about the project

For the title to accomplish these goals, the following must happen:

- People must read the title.
- The title must include information about the project's intended results.
- People must be able to relate to the title.
- People must remember the title.

You can help ensure that your title meets all these requirements by adhering to the following guidelines when writing it:

- Know your audience — their interests, knowledge, and communication preferences.
- Keep the title to one sentence.
- Make it reader-friendly by printing it in a sufficiently large font in a color that contrasts effectively with its background.
- Make it a mini-abstract of your project by stating the main intended results.
- Include the most important words first.
- Triple-check that all information is accurate.
- Remove unnecessary words (like *a* and *the*) and any redundant information.
- Minimize your use of technical jargon and acronyms.

(continued)

Clarifying Your Project

(continued)

If you aren't feeling especially creative, consider asking the marketing or graphics department for some ideas or soliciting the assistance of team members and others you might know.

Whether or not you acknowledge it, your project title will affect people's knowledge and feelings about your project. You can choose to write a title that will influence people in ways that you want, or you can write it with no consideration for how it will affect your project's potential audience. Just know that not considering how it will affect others doesn't mean it won't affect them.

To determine who came up with the original idea for your project, take the following steps:

1. **Ask the person who assigns you the project whether he originated the idea.**

2. **If that person didn't initiate the idea, ask the following questions:**
   - Who gave her the assignment?
   - Who else, if anyone, was involved in passing the assignment to her?
   - Who had the original idea for the project?

3. **Check with all the people you identified in Step 2 and ask them the same questions.**

4. **Check the following written records that may confirm who originally had the idea:**
   - Minutes from division-, department-, and organization-wide planning and budget sessions
   - Correspondence and email referring to the project
   - Reports of planning or feasibility studies

   A *feasibility study* is a formal investigation to determine the likely success of performing certain work or achieving certain results.

   In addition to helping you identify the people who initiated your project, these written sources may shed light on what these people hope to get from it.

5. **Consult with people who may be affected by or are needed to support your project; they may know who originated the idea.**

Be as specific as possible when specifying your project initiator. In other words, don't write "The sales department requested promotional literature for product Alpha." Instead, write "Mary Smith, the sales representative for the northeast region, requested promotional literature for product Alpha."

TIP

Be sure to distinguish between drivers and supporters as you seek to find your project's initiator (see Chapter 2 in this minibook for more information about drivers and supporters):

>> *Drivers* have some say when defining the results of the project. They tell you what you *should* do.

>> *Supporters* help you perform your project. They tell you what you *can* do.

For example, the vice president of finance who requests a project to upgrade the organization's financial information systems is a project driver. The manager of the computer center who must provide staff and resources to upgrade the organization's information systems is a project supporter.

Sometimes supporters claim to be drivers. For example, when you ask the manager of the computer center, he may say he initiated the project. In reality, however, the manager authorized the people and funds to perform the project, but the vice president of finance initiated the project.

Recognizing other people who may benefit

Although they may not have initiated the idea, other people may benefit from your completed project. They may be people who work with, support, or are clients of your project's drivers, or they may have performed similar projects in the past. They may have expressed interests or needs in areas addressed by your project in meetings, correspondence, or informal conversations.

Identify these other people as soon as possible to determine what their particular needs and interests are and how you can appropriately address them. These additional audiences may include people who

>> Know the project exists and have expressed an interest in it

>> Know it exists but don't realize it can benefit them

>> Are unaware of your project

Identify these additional audiences by doing the following:

>> Review all written materials related to your project.

>> Consult with your project's drivers and supporters.

>> Encourage everyone you speak to about the project to identify others who may benefit from it.

As you identify people who can benefit from your project, also identify people who strongly oppose it. Figure out why they oppose your project and whether you can address their concerns. Take the time to determine whether they may be able to derive any benefits from your project, and, if they can, explain these benefits to them. If they continue to oppose your project, make a note in your risk-management plan about their opposition and how you plan to deal with it.

Distinguishing the project champion

A *project champion* is a person in a high position in the organization who strongly supports your project; advocates for your project in disputes, planning meetings, and review sessions; and takes necessary actions to help ensure that your project is successful.

Sometimes the best champion is one whose support you never have to use. Just knowing that this person supports your project helps other people appreciate its importance and encourages them to work diligently to ensure its success.

Check with your project's drivers and supporters to find out whether your project already has a champion. If it doesn't, work hard to recruit one by looking for people who can reap benefits from your project and who have sufficient power and influence to encourage serious, ongoing organizational commitment to your project. Explain to these people why the success of your project is in their best interest and how you may need their specific help as your project progresses. Assess how interested they are in your project and how much help they're willing to provide.

Considering those who will implement the project's results

Most projects create a product or service to achieve a desired result. Often, however, the person who asks you to create the product or service isn't the one who'll use it.

Suppose your organization's director of sales and marketing wants to increase annual sales by 10 percent in the next fiscal year. She decides that developing and introducing a new product, XYZ, will allow her to achieve this goal. However, she won't go to all your organization's customers and sell them XYZ; her sales staff will. Even though they didn't come up with the idea to develop XYZ, the sales staff may have strong opinions about the characteristics XYZ should have — and so will the customers who ultimately buy (or don't buy!) the product.

To identify the real users of project products and services, try to do the following early in your project planning:

>> Clarify the products and services that you anticipate producing.

>> Identify exactly who will use these products and services and how they'll use them.

After you identify these people, consult with them to determine any additional interests or needs they may have that your project should also address.

Determining your project drivers' expectations and needs

The needs that your project addresses may not always be obvious. Suppose, for example, that your organization decides to sponsor a blood drive. Is the real reason for your project to address the shortage of blood in the local hospital or to improve your organization's image in the local community?

The needs your project must satisfy to successfully achieve its purpose are termed your project's *requirements*.

When you clearly understand your project's requirements, you can

>> Choose project activities that enable you to accomplish the true desired results (see Chapter 4 in this minibook for information on identifying project activities).

>> Monitor performance during and at the end of the project to ensure that you're meeting the real needs.

>> Realize when the project isn't meeting the real needs so that you can suggest modifying or canceling it.

When you're initially assigned a project, you hope you're told the products you're supposed to produce and the needs you're supposed to address. However, often you're told what to produce (the outcomes), but you have to figure out the needs yourself.

REMEMBER

Consider the following questions as you work to define your project's requirements:

>> **What needs do people want your project to address?** Don't worry at this point whether your project can address these needs or whether it's the best way to address the needs. You're just trying to identify the hopes and expectations that led to this project in the first place.

>> **How do you know the needs you identify are the real hopes and expectations that people have for your project?** Determining people's real thoughts and feelings can be difficult. Sometimes they don't want to share them; sometimes they don't know how to clearly express them.

When speaking with people to determine the needs your project should address, try the following techniques:

>> Encourage them to speak at length about their needs and expectations.

>> Listen carefully for any contradictions.

>> Encourage them to clarify vague ideas.

>> Try to confirm your information from two or more independent sources.

>> Ask them to indicate the relative importance of addressing each of their needs.

The following scheme is useful for prioritizing a person's needs:

>> **Must have:** The project must address these needs, at the very least.

>> **Should have:** The project should address these needs, if at all possible.

>> **Nice to have:** It would be nice for the project to address these needs, if doing so doesn't negatively affect anything else.

See whether your organization performed a formal benefit-cost analysis for your project. A *benefit-cost analysis* is a formal identification and assessment of the following (see Chapter 1 in this minibook for details):

>> The benefits anticipated from your project

>> The costs of performing your project and using and supporting the products or services produced by your project

The benefit-cost analysis documents the results that people were counting on when they decided to proceed with your project. Therefore, the analysis is an important source for the real needs that your project should address.

Confirming that your project can address people's needs

Although needs may be thoroughly documented (see the preceding section), you may have difficulty determining whether your project can successfully address those needs. On occasion, companies fund formal feasibility studies to determine whether a project can successfully address a particular need.

Other times, however, your project may be the result of a brainstorming session or someone's creative vision. In this case, you may have less confidence that your project can accomplish its expected results. Don't automatically reject a project at this point, but do aggressively determine the chances for success and the actions you can take to increase these chances. If you can't find sufficient information to support your analysis, consider asking for a formal feasibility study.

REMEMBER

If you feel the risk of project failure is too great, share your concerns with the key decision makers and explain why you recommend not proceeding with your project.

Uncovering other activities that relate to your project

Your project doesn't exist in a vacuum. It may require results from other projects, it may generate products that other projects will use, and it may address needs that other projects also address. For these reasons, you need to identify projects related to yours as soon as possible so you can coordinate the use of shared personnel and resources and minimize unintended overlap in project activities and results.

Check the following sources to identify projects that may be related to yours:

>> Your project's audiences

>> Centrally maintained lists of projects planned or being performed by your organization

>> Organization-wide information-sharing vehicles, such as newsletters or your organization's intranet

>> The project management office (PMO)

>> Upper-management committees responsible for approving and overseeing your organization's projects

>> The finance department, which may have established labor or cost accounts for such projects

>> The procurement department, which may have purchased goods or services for such projects

>> The information technology department, which may be storing, analyzing, or preparing progress reports for such projects

>> Functional managers whose people may be working on such projects

Emphasizing your project's importance to your organization

How much importance your organization places on your project directly influences the chances for your project's success. When conflicting demands for scarce resources arise, resources usually go to those projects that can produce the greatest benefits for the organization.

Your project's perceived value depends on its intended benefits and people's awareness of those benefits. Take the following steps to help people understand how your project will support the organization's priorities:

>> **Look for existing statements or documents that confirm your project's support of your organization's priorities.** Consult the following sources to find out more about your organization's priorities:

- **Long-range plan:** A formal report that identifies your organization's overall direction, specific performance targets, and individual initiatives for the next one to five years

- **Annual budget:** The detailed list of categories and individual initiatives that your organization will financially support during the year

- **Capital appropriations plan:** The itemized list of all planned expenditures (over an established minimum amount) for facilities and equipment purchases, renovations, and repairs during the year

- **Your organization's key performance indicators (KPIs):** Performance measures that describe your organization's progress toward its goals

When you review these documents, note whether your project or its intended outcome is specifically mentioned.

In addition, determine whether your organization has made specific commitments to external customers or upper management related to your project's completion.

>> **Describe in your brief statement of justification how your project relates to the organization's priorities.** Mention existing discussions of your project from the information sources mentioned in the preceding point. If your project isn't specifically referenced in these sources, prepare a written explanation of how your project and its results will affect the organization's priorities.

Occasionally, you may have a hard time identifying specific results that people expect your project to generate. Perhaps the person who initiated the project has assumed different responsibilities and no longer has any interest in it, or maybe the original need the project was designed to address has changed. If people have trouble telling you how your project will help your organization, ask them what would happen if you didn't perform your project. If they conclude that it wouldn't make a difference, ask them how you can modify your project to benefit the organization. If they don't think your project can be changed to produce useful results, consider suggesting that the project be canceled.

Organizations are consistently overworked and understaffed. Spending precious time and resources on a project that everyone agrees will make no difference is the last thing your organization needs or wants. More likely, people do realize that your project can have a positive effect on the organization. Your job, then, is to help these people consistently focus on the valuable results your project has to offer.

Being exhaustive in your search for information

In your quest to find out what your project is supposed to accomplish and how it fits into your organization's overall plans, you have to seek information that is sensitive, sometimes contradictory, and often unwritten. Getting this information isn't always easy, but following these tips can help make your search more productive:

>> **Try to find several sources for the same piece of information.** The more independent sources that contain the same information, the more likely the information is to be correct.

>> **Whenever possible, get information from primary sources.** A *primary source* contains the original information. A *secondary source* is someone else's report of the information from the primary source.

Suppose you need information from a recently completed study. You can get the information from the primary source (the actual report of the study written by the scientists who performed it), or you can get it from secondary sources (such as articles in magazines or scientific journals by authors who paraphrased and summarized the original report).

The further your source is from the primary source, the more likely the secondary information differs from the real information.

>> **Look for written sources because they're the best.** Check relevant minutes from meetings, correspondence, email, reports from other projects, long-range plans, budgets, capital improvement plans, market requirement documents, and benefit-cost analyses.

>> **Speak with two or more people from the same area to confirm information.** Different people have different styles of communication as well as different perceptions of the same situation. Speak with more than one person, and compare their messages to determine any contradictions.

If you get different stories, speak with the people again to verify their initial information. Determine whether the people you consulted are primary or secondary sources (primary sources tend to be more accurate than secondary ones). Ask the people you consulted to explain or reconcile any remaining differences.

» **When speaking with people about important information, arrange to have at least one other person present.** Doing so allows two different people to interpret what they hear from the same individual.

» **Write down all information you obtain from personal meetings.** Share your written notes and summaries with other people who were present at the meeting to ensure that your interpretation is correct and to serve as a reminder of agreements made during the meeting.

» **Plan to meet at least two times with your project's key audiences.** Your first meeting starts them thinking about issues. Allow some time for them to think over your initial discussions and to think of new ideas related to those issues. A second meeting gives you a chance to clarify any ambiguities or inconsistencies from the first session. (See Chapter 2 in this minibook for more information on project audiences.)

» **Practice active listening skills in all your meetings and conversations.** See Chapter 5 in this minibook for information on how to practice active listening.

» **Wherever possible, confirm what you heard in personal meetings with written sources.** When you talk with people, they share their perceptions and opinions. Compare those perceptions and opinions with written, factual data (from primary sources, if possible). Discuss any discrepancies with those same people.

Drawing the line: Where your project starts and stops

Sometimes your project stands alone, but more often it's only one of several related efforts to achieve a common result. You want to avoid duplicating the work of these other related projects, and, where appropriate, you want to coordinate your efforts with theirs.

Your description of your project's scope of work should specify clearly where your project starts and where it ends. Suppose your project is to develop a new product for your organization. You may frame your project's scope description as follows:

> This project entails designing, developing, and testing a new product.

If you feel your statement is in any way ambiguous, you may clarify your scope further by stating what you will not do:

> This project won't include finalizing the market requirements or launching the new product.

To make sure your project's scope of work description is clear, do the following:

>> **Check for hidden inferences.** Suppose your boss has asked you to design and develop a new product. Check to be sure she doesn't assume you'll also perform the market research to determine the new product's characteristics.

>> **Use words that clearly describe intended activities.** Suppose your project entails *the implementation of a new information system.* Are you sure that everyone defines *implementation* in the same way? For instance, do people expect it to include installing the new software, training people to use it, evaluating its performance, fixing problems with it, or something else?

>> **Confirm your understanding of your project's scope with your project's drivers and supporters.**

Suppose that you have an assignment to prepare for the competitive acquisition of certain equipment. You develop a plan to include the selection of the vendor, awarding of the contract, and production and delivery of the equipment. Your boss, however, is stunned with your project estimate of six months and $500,000. He thought it would take less than two months and cost less than $25,000.

After a brief discussion with your boss, you realize that your job was to select the potential vendor, not place the order and have the equipment manufactured and delivered. Although you clarified your misunderstanding, you still wondered aloud, "But why would we select a vendor if we didn't want to buy the equipment?"

You missed the point. The question wasn't whether the company planned to buy the equipment. (Certainly the intention to buy the equipment was the reason for the project.) The real question was whether the project or a different project in the future would purchase the equipment.

Stating your project's objectives

As mentioned previously in this chapter, *objectives* are outcomes your project will produce (they're also referred to as *deliverables*). Your project's outcomes may be products or services you develop or the results of using these products and services. The more clearly you define your project's objectives, the more likely you are to achieve them. Include the following elements in your objectives:

>> **Statement:** A brief narrative description of what you want to achieve

>> **Measures:** Indicators you'll use to assess your achievement

>> **Performance targets:** The value(s) of each measure that define success

Suppose you take on a project to reformat a report that summarizes monthly sales activity. You may frame your project's objective as follows:

Statement	Measures	Performance Targets
A revised report that summarizes monthly sales activity	Content	Report must include total number of items sold, total sales revenue, and total number of returns for each product line.
	Schedule	Report must be operational by August 31.
	Budget	Development expenditures are not to exceed $40,000.
	Approvals	New report format must be approved by the vice president of sales, regional sales manager, district sales manager, and sales representatives.

WARNING

Sometimes people try to avoid setting a specific target by establishing a range of values that defines successful performance. But setting a range is the same as avoiding the issue. Suppose you're a sales representative and your boss says you'll be successful if you achieve $20 million to $25 million in sales for the year. As far as you're concerned, you'll be 100 percent successful as soon as you reach $20 million. Most likely, however, your boss will consider you 100 percent successful only when you reach $25 million. Although you and your boss appeared to reach an agreement, you didn't.

The following sections explain how to create clear and specific objectives, identify all types of objectives, and respond to resistance to objectives.

Making your objectives clear and specific

REMEMBER

You need to be crystal clear when stating your project's objectives. The more specific your project objectives, the greater your chances of achieving them. Here are some tips for developing clear objectives:

>> **Be brief when describing each objective.** If you take an entire page to describe a single objective, most people won't read it. Even if they do read it, your objective probably won't be clear and may have multiple interpretations.

>> **Don't use technical jargon or acronyms.** Each industry (such as pharmaceuticals, telecommunications, finance, and insurance) has its own vocabulary, and so does each company within that industry. Within companies, different departments (such as accounting, legal, and information services) also have their own jargon. Because of this proliferation of specialized languages, the same three-letter acronym (TLA) can have two or more meanings in the same organization! To reduce the chances for misunderstandings, express your objectives in language that people of all backgrounds and experiences are familiar with.

>> **Make your objectives SMART, as follows:**

- **Specific:** Define your objectives clearly, in detail, with no room for misinterpretation.

- **Measurable:** State the measures and performance specifications you'll use to determine whether you've met your objectives.

- **Aggressive:** Set challenging objectives that encourage people to stretch beyond their comfort zones.

- **Realistic:** Set objectives the project team believes it can achieve.

- **Time sensitive:** Include the date by which you'll achieve the objectives.

>> **Make your objectives controllable.** Make sure that you and your team believe you can influence the success of each objective. If you don't believe you can, you may not commit 100 percent to achieving it (and most likely you won't even try). In that case, it becomes a wish, not an objective.

>> **Identify all objectives.** Time and resources are always scarce, so if you don't specify an objective, you won't (and shouldn't) work to achieve it.

>> **Be sure drivers and supporters agree on your project's objectives.** When drivers buy into your objectives, you feel confident that achieving the objectives constitutes true project success. When supporters buy into your objectives, you have the greatest chance that people will work their hardest to achieve them.

  If drivers don't agree with your objectives, revise them until they do agree. After all, your drivers' needs are the whole reason for your project! If supporters don't buy into your objectives, work with them to identify their concerns and develop approaches they think can work.

Probing for all types of objectives

When you start a project, the person who makes the initial project request often tells you the major results she wants to achieve. However, she may want the project to address other items that she forgot to mention to you. And other (as yet unidentified) people may also want your project to accomplish certain results.

REMEMBER

You need to identify *all* project objectives as early as possible so you can plan for and devote the necessary time and resources to accomplishing each one. When you probe to identify all possible objectives, consider that projects may have objectives in the following three categories:

>> Physical products or services

>> The effects of these products or services

>> General organizational benefits that weren't the original reason for the project

Suppose that your information technology department is about to purchase and install a new software package for searching for and analyzing information in the company's parts-inventory database. The following are examples of objectives this project may have in each category:

>> **Physical product or service:** The completed installation and integration of the new software package with the parts-inventory database

>> **The effect of the product or service:** Reduced costs of inventory and storage due to timelier ordering facilitated by the new software

>> **A general organizational benefit:** Use of the new software with other company databases

REMEMBER

An objective is different from *serendipity* (a chance occurrence or coincidence). In the previous example of the new software package, consider that one project driver won't be completely satisfied unless the software for the parts-inventory database is also installed and integrated with the company's product-inventory database. In this case, installing the system on the company's product-inventory database must be an objective of your project so you must devote specific time and resources to accomplish it. On the other hand, if your audience will be happy whether you do or don't install the software on the second database, being able to use the software on that database is serendipity — meaning you shouldn't devote any time or resources specifically to accomplishing it.

Determining all project objectives requires you to identify all drivers who may have specific expectations for your project. See Chapter 2 in this minibook for a discussion of the different types of audiences and tips on how to identify each one.

Anticipating resistance to clearly defined objectives

Some people are uncomfortable committing to specific objectives because they're concerned they may not achieve them. Unfortunately, no matter what the reason, not having specific objectives makes knowing whether you're addressing (and meeting) your drivers' true expectations a lot more difficult. In other words, when your objectives aren't specific, you increase the chances that your project won't succeed.

REMEMBER

Here are some excuses people give for not defining their objectives too specifically, along with suggestions for addressing those excuses:

>> **Excuse 1: Too much specificity stifles creativity.**

Response: Creativity should be encouraged — the question is where and when. Your project's drivers should be clear and precise when stating their objectives; your project's supporters should be creative when figuring out ways to meet those objectives. You need to understand what people *do* expect from your project, not what they *may* expect. The more clearly you can describe your objectives, the more easily you can determine whether (and how) you can meet them.

» **Excuse 2: Your project entails research and new development, and you can't tell today what you'll be able to accomplish.**

Response: Objectives are targets, not guarantees. Certain projects have more risks than others. When you haven't performed a task before, you don't know whether it's possible. And if it is possible, you don't know how long it will take and how much it will cost. But you must state at the outset exactly what you want to achieve and what you think is possible, even though you may have to change your objectives as the project progresses.

» **Excuse 3: What if interests or needs change?**

Response: Objectives are targets based on what you know and expect today. If conditions change in the future, you may have to revisit one or more of your objectives to see whether they're still relevant and feasible or whether they, too, must change.

» **Excuse 4: The project's requestor doesn't know what she specifically wants her project to achieve.**

Response: Ask her to come back when she does. If you begin working on this project now, you have a greater chance of wasting time and resources to produce results that the requestor later decides she doesn't want.

» **Excuse 5: Even though specific objectives help determine when you've succeeded, they also make it easier to determine when you haven't.**

Response: Yep. That's true. However, because your project was framed to accomplish certain results, you need to know if your project achieved those results. If it didn't, you may have to perform additional work to accomplish them. In addition, you want to determine the benefits the organization is realizing from the money it's spending.

Marking Boundaries: Project Constraints

You'd like to operate in a world where everything is possible — that is, where you can do anything necessary to achieve your desired results. Your clients and your organization, on the other hand, would like to believe that you can achieve everything they want with minimal or no cost to them. Of course, neither situation is true.

Defining the constraints you must work within introduces reality into your plans and helps clarify expectations. As you plan and implement your project, think in terms of the following two types of constraints:

>> **Limitations:** Restrictions other people place on the results you have to achieve, the time frames you have to meet, the resources you can use, and the way you can approach your tasks.

>> **Needs:** Requirements you stipulate must be met so you can achieve project success.

This section helps you determine your project's limitations and needs.

Working within limitations

Project limitations may influence how you perform your project and may even determine whether or not you (and your project's drivers and supporters) decide to proceed with your project. Consult with your project's drivers and supporters to identify limitations as early as possible so you can design your plan to accommodate them.

Understanding the types of limitations

Project limitations typically fall into several categories. By recognizing these categories, you increase the chances that you'll discover all the limitations affecting your project. Your project's drivers and supporters may have preset expectations or requirements in one or more of the following categories:

>> **Results:** The products and effect of your project. For example, the new product must cost no more than $300 per item to manufacture, or the new book must be fewer than 384 pages in length.

>> **Time frames:** When you must produce certain results. For example, your project must be done by June 30. You don't know whether you can finish by June 30; you just know that someone expects the product to be produced by then.

>> **Resources:** The type, amount, and availability of resources to perform your project work. Resources can include people, funds, equipment, raw materials, facilities, information, and so on. For example, you have a budget of $100,000; you can have two people full time for three months; or you can't use the test laboratory during the first week in June.

>> **Activity performance:** The strategies for performing different tasks. For example, you're told that you must use your organization's printing department to reproduce the new users' manuals for the system you're developing. You don't know what the manual will look like, how many pages it'll be, how

many copies you'll need, or when you'll need them. Therefore, you can't know whether your organization's printing department is up to the task. But at this point, you do know that someone expects you to have the printing department do the work.

Be careful of vague limitations; they provide poor guidance for what you can or can't do, and they can demoralize people who have to deal with them. Here are some examples of vague limitations and how you can improve them:

>> **Time frame limitation:**

- **Vague:** "Finish this project as soon as possible." This statement tells you nothing. With this limitation, your audience may suddenly demand your project's final results — with no warning.

- **Specific:** "Finish this project by close of business June 30."

>> **Resource limitation:**

- **Vague:** "You can have Laura Webster on your project part time in May." How heavily can you count on her? From Laura's point of view, how can she juggle all her assignments in that period if she has no idea how long each one will take?

- **Specific:** "You can have Laura Webster on your project four hours per day for the first two weeks in May."

When people aren't specific about their constraints, you can't be sure whether you can honor their requests. The longer people wait to be specific, the less likely you are to adhere to the limitation and successfully complete your project.

Looking for project limitations

Determining limitations is a fact-finding mission, so your job is to identify and examine all possible sources of information. You don't want to miss anything, and you want to clarify any conflicting information. After you know what people expect, you can determine how (or whether) you can meet those expectations. Try the following approaches:

>> **Consult your audiences.** Check with drivers about limitations regarding desired results; check with supporters about limitations concerning activity performance and resources.

>> **Review relevant written materials.** These materials may include long-range plans, annual budgets and capital appropriations plans, benefit-cost analyses, feasibility studies, reports of related projects, minutes of meetings, and individuals' performance objectives.

>> **When you identify a limitation, note its source.** Confirming a limitation from different sources increases your confidence in its accuracy. Resolve conflicting opinions about a limitation as soon as possible.

Addressing limitations in the scope statement

List all project limitations in your scope statement. If you have to explore ways to modify your project plan in the future, this list of limitations can help define alternatives that you can and can't consider.

You can reflect limitations in your project in two ways:

>> **Incorporate limitations directly into your plan.** For example, if a key driver says you have to finish your project by September 30, you may choose to set September 30 as your project's completion date. Of course, because September 30 is the outside limit, you may choose to set a completion date of August 31. In this case, the limitation influences your target completion date but isn't equivalent to it.

>> **Identify any project risks that result from a limitation.** For example, if you feel the target completion date is unusually aggressive, the risk of missing that date may be significant. Your goal is to develop plans to minimize and manage that risk throughout your project.

Dealing with needs

As soon as possible, decide on the situations or conditions necessary for your project's success. Most of these needs relate to project resources. Here are a few examples of resource-related needs:

>> **Personnel:** "I need a technical editor for a total of 40 hours in August."

>> **Budget:** "I need a budget of $10,000 for computer peripherals."

>> **Other resources:** "I need access to the test laboratory during June."

TIP

Be as clear as possible when describing your project's needs. The more specific you are, the more likely other people are to understand and meet those needs.

Sometimes you can identify needs early in your project planning. More often, however, particular needs surface as you create a plan that addresses the drivers' expectations. As your list of needs grows, check with your project's supporters to decide how the new needs can be met and at what cost. Check with your project's drivers to confirm that the estimated additional cost is justified, and modify your project documentation to reflect any changes in planned results, activities, schedules, or resources.

Documenting Your Assumptions

As you proceed through your planning process, you can identify issues or questions that may affect your project's performance. Unfortunately, just identifying these issues or questions doesn't help you address them.

TIP

For every potential issue you identify, make assumptions regarding unknowns associated with it. Then use these assumptions as you plan your project. Consider the following examples:

>> **Issue:** You don't have a final, approved budget for your project.

Approach: *Assume* you'll get $50,000 for your project. *Plan* for your project to spend up to, but no more than, $50,000. Develop detailed information to demonstrate why your project budget must be $50,000, and share that information with key decision makers.

>> **Issue:** You don't know when you'll get authorization to start work on your project.

Approach: *Assume* you'll receive authorization to start work on August 1. *Plan* your project work so that no activities start before August 1. Explain to key decision makers why your project must start on August 1, and work with them to facilitate your project's approval by that date.

Note: Don't forget to consider all project assumptions when you develop your project's risk-management plan.

Presenting Your Scope Statement

Figure 3-1 presents an example of how you can display your scope statement in a table format. In this example, the information in the statement is grouped by major categories, starting with a brief statement of the justification for the project and its importance to the organization, moving through the specific results the project is intended to produce, and finishing with important constraints and assumptions that will define the environment in which the project is performed.

This table format is effective for the following reasons:

>> The category headings serve as reminders of the information you should include in the document.

Project Title		Project Manager	Date: (mm/dd/yy)
			/ /

SCOPE STATEMENT

Justification	(To be written by the document's author)
	Brief statement of the reason for the project (to be summarized from the project charter)

Objectives/Deliverables (continue on additional pages as necessary)

Statement (continue on additional pages as necessary)

1.	(To be written by the document's author)

Product Scope Description/Product Acceptance Criteria	
Measures	Performance Targets
1.1. (To be written by the document's author)	1.1.1. (To be written by the document's author)
1.2.	1.1.2.
Etc. (Continue on additional pages as necessary)	Etc. (Continue on additional pages as necessary)

Constraints	
Limitations	
1.	
2.	(To be written by the document's author)
3.	
Etc.	(Continue on additional pages as necessary)
Needs	
1.	(To be written by the document's author)
2.	
3.	
Etc.	(Continue on additional pages as necessary)

Assumptions	
1.	(To be written by the document's author)
2.	
3.	
Etc.	(Continue on additional pages as necessary)

Approvals

Project Manager	Client	Other
Date	Date	Date

FIGURE 3-1:
Sample scope
statement.

>> The prepared format presents the information in the document in a logical
order for the reader to digest.

>> The category headings make it easy for readers to find the particular informa-
tion they are seeking.

>> The premeasured space for each category of information encourages you to
choose your words carefully and keep the length of your entries to a
minimum.

Chapter **4**

Developing a Game Plan

The keys to successful project planning and performance are completeness and continuity. You want to identify all important information in your project plan and address every aspect of your project while it's in progress.

Describing in detail all the tasks required to complete your project helps you accomplish them. Your description of project work provides the basis for scheduling, planning resources, defining roles and responsibilities, assigning work to team members, capturing key project performance data, and reporting on completed project work. This chapter helps you break down your project work into manageable pieces.

Breaking Your Project into Manageable Chunks

Two major concerns when starting a new project are remembering to plan for all important pieces of work and accurately estimating the time and resources required to perform that work. To address both issues, you should develop a logical framework to define all work that's necessary to complete the project.

Suppose you're asked to design and present a training program. You and a colleague work intensely for a couple of months developing the content and materials, arranging for the facilities, and inviting the participants. A week before the session, you ask your colleague whether he's made arrangements to print the training manuals. He says that he thought you were dealing with it, and you say that you thought he was dealing with it. Unfortunately, neither of you arranged to have the manuals printed because you each thought the other person was handling it. Now you have a training session in a week, and you don't have the time or money to print the needed training notebooks.

How can you avoid a situation like this one? By using a structured approach in the organizing and preparing stage of your project to identify all required project work. The following sections explain how to accomplish this task by subdividing your project's intermediate and final products into finer levels of detail and specifying the work required to produce them.

Thinking in detail

The most important guideline to remember when identifying and describing project work is this: Think in detail! People consistently underestimate the time and resources they need for their project work because they just don't recognize everything they have to do to complete it.

Suppose you have to prepare a report of your team's most recent meeting. Based on your past experience with preparing many similar reports, you quickly figure you'll need a few days to do this one. But how confident are you that this estimate is correct? Are you sure you've considered all the work that writing this particular report will entail? Will the differences between this report and others you've worked on mean more time and work for you? How can you tell?

The best way to determine how long and how much work a project will take to complete is to break down the required project work into its component deliverables, a process called *decomposition*. (A *deliverable* is an intermediate or final product, service, and/or result your project will produce. See Chapter 3 in this minibook for more information on project deliverables, or *objectives*, as they're often called.)

The greater the detail in which you decompose a project, the less likely you are to overlook anything significant. For example, creating the report in the preceding example actually entails producing three separate deliverables: a draft, reviews of the draft, and the final version. Completing the final version of the report, in turn, entails producing two deliverables: the initial version and the edited version. By decomposing the project into the deliverables necessary to generate the final report, you're more likely to identify all the work you need to do to complete the project.

TIP

Follow these two guidelines when decomposing your project:

>> **Allow no gaps.** Identify all components of the deliverable you're decomposing. In the example of creating a meeting report, if you have *allowed no gaps,* you'll have the desired final product in hand after you've produced the draft, the reviews of the draft, and the final version. However, if you feel that you'll have to do additional work to transform these three subproducts into a final product, you need to define the subproduct(s) that this additional work will produce.

>> **Allow no overlaps.** Don't include the same subproduct in your decomposition of two or more different deliverables. For example, don't include completed reviews of the draft by your boss and the vice president of your department as parts of the draft (the first deliverable) if you've already included them with all other reviews under reviews of the draft (the second deliverable).

Using these guidelines as you specify the parts and subparts of your project decreases the chance that you'll overlook something significant, which, in turn, helps you develop more accurate estimates of the time and resources needed to do the project.

Identifying necessary project work with a work breakdown structure

Thinking in detail is critical when you're planning your project, but you also need to consider the big picture. If you fail to identify a major part of your project's work, you won't have the chance to detail it! Thus, you must be both comprehensive and specific.

Figure 4-1 shows how you can depict necessary project work in a *work breakdown structure* (WBS), a deliverable-oriented decomposition of the work required to produce the necessary project products and achieve the project's objectives. The different levels in a WBS have had many different names. The top element is typically called a *project* and the lowest level of detail is typically called a *work package.* However, the levels in between have been called *phases, subprojects, work assignments, tasks, subtasks,* and *deliverables.* In this minibook, the top-level box (the Level 1 component) is a *project,* the lowest level of detail is a *work package,* and the elements in between are *Level 2 components, Level 3 components,* and so forth. A work package is comprised of activities that must be performed to produce the deliverable it represents.

Specifically, Figure 4-1 shows that you can subdivide the entire project, represented as a Level 1 component, into Level 2 components and then subdivide some or all Level 2 components into Level 3 components. You can continue to subdivide all the components you create in the same manner until you reach a point at which you think the components you defined are sufficiently detailed for planning and management purposes. These Level *n* components, where *n* is the number of the lowest-level component in a particular WBS branch, are called *work packages.*

Developing a Game Plan

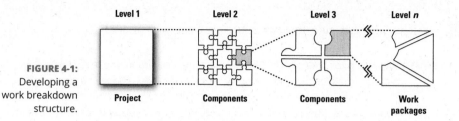

FIGURE 4-1:
Developing a
work breakdown
structure.

Level 1   Level 2   Level 3   Level *n*

Project   Components   Components   Work packages

Suppose you're responsible for a project titled *Training Program Creation and Presentation* that entails creating and presenting a new training program for your organization. To get started, you develop a WBS for this project as follows:

1. **Determine the major deliverables or products to be produced.**

   Ask yourself, "What major intermediate or final products or deliverables must be produced to achieve the project's objectives?"

   You may identify the following items:

   - Training program needs statement

   - Training program design

   - Participant notebooks

   - Trained instructor

   - Program testing

   - Training program presentation

   Creating the WBS with deliverables rather than activities is important because

REMEMBER

   - It reinforces that in almost all instances, you achieve project success by producing desired outcomes, not by performing certain activities.

   - It creates a link between the scope statement and the WBS, which helps ensure that you identify and perform all required work (and only work that is, in fact, required).

2. **Divide each major deliverable from Step 1 into its component deliverables.**

   If you start with *Training program needs statement,* ask, "What intermediate deliverables must I have so I can create the needs statement?"

   You may determine that you require the following:

   - Interviews of potential participants

   - A review of materials discussing the needs for the program

   - A report summarizing the needs this program will address

3. **Divide each intermediate deliverable from Step 2 into its component parts.**

If you start with *Interviews of potential participants,* ask, "What deliverables must I have to complete these interviews?"

You may decide that you have to produce the following deliverables:

- Selected interviewees
- Interview questionnaire
- Interview schedule
- Completed interviews
- Report of interview findings

But why stop here? You can break each of these five items into its component parts and then break those pieces into even more parts. How far should you go? The following sections can help you answer that question.

Asking four key questions

Determining how much detail you need isn't a trivial task. You want to describe your work in sufficient detail to support accurate planning and meaningful tracking. But the benefits of this detail must justify the additional time you spend developing and maintaining your plans and reporting your progress.

REMEMBER

Asking the following four questions about each WBS component can help you decide whether you've defined it in enough detail:

>> Do you require two or more intermediate deliverables to produce this deliverable?

>> Can you estimate the resources you need to perform the work to produce this deliverable? (Resources include personnel, equipment, raw materials, money, facilities, and information.)

>> Can you accurately estimate how long producing this deliverable will take?

>> If you have to assign the work to produce this deliverable to someone else, are you confident that person will understand exactly what to do?

If you answer yes to the first question or no to any one of the other three, break down the deliverable into the components necessary to produce it.

Your answers to these questions depend on how familiar you are with the work, how critical the activity is to the success of your project, what happens if something goes wrong, whom you may assign to perform the activity, how well you know that person, and so on. In other words, the correct level of detail for your WBS depends on your judgment.

TIP

If you're a little uneasy about answering these four questions, try this even simpler test: Subdivide your WBS component into additional deliverables if you think either of the following situations applies:

>> The component will take much longer than two calendar weeks to complete.

>> The component will require much more than 80 person-hours to complete.

Remember that these estimates are just guidelines. For example, if you estimate that it will take two weeks and two days to prepare a report, you've probably provided sufficient detail. But if you think it will take two to three months to finalize requirements for your new product, you need to break the deliverable *finalized requirements* into more detail because

>> Experience has shown that there can be so many different interpretations of what is supposed to occur during these two to three months that you can't be sure your time and resource estimates are correct, and you can't confidently assign the task to someone to perform.

>> You don't want to wait two or three months to confirm that work is on schedule by verifying that a desired product has been produced on time.

Making assumptions to clarify planned work

Sometimes you want to break down a particular WBS component further, but certain unknowns stop you from doing so. How do you resolve this dilemma? You make assumptions regarding the unknowns. If, during the course of your project, you find that any of your assumptions are wrong, you can change your plan to reflect the correct information.

Regarding the *Training Program Creation and Presentation* project example presented previously in this section — suppose you decide that the *Completed interviews* deliverable from Step 3 needs more detail so you can estimate its required time and resources. However, you don't know how to break it down further because you don't know how many people you'll interview or how many separate sets of interviews you'll conduct. If you assume you'll interview five groups of seven people each, you can then develop specific plans for arranging and conducting each of these sessions. In most situations, it's best to consider a guess in the middle of the possible range. To determine how sensitive your results are to the different values, you may want to analyze for several different assumptions.

TIP

Be sure to write down your assumption so you remember to change your plan if you conduct more or less than five interview sessions. See the discussion in Chapter 3 of this minibook for more information about detailing assumptions.

Focusing on results when naming deliverables

Whenever possible, name a deliverable based on the result you need to achieve rather than the activity you need to perform to achieve that result. For example, you might title a deliverable that signifies completion of a needs assessment survey you have to conduct in one of two ways:

>> Survey completed

>> Needs assessment finished

Both options state that something has been finished. However, although the deliverable *Survey completed* indicates that a survey was performed, it doesn't explain what type of information the survey was supposed to obtain or whether it successfully obtained that information. On the other hand, *Needs assessment finished* confirms that the information from the completed survey successfully fulfilled the purpose for which it was intended.

Using action verbs to title activities

Use action verbs in the titles of activities that make up a work package to clarify the nature of the work the activities entail. Action verbs can improve your time and resource estimates, your work assignments to team members, and your tracking and reporting because they provide a clear picture of the work included in the activities and, thereby, the work packages of which they are a part.

Consider the assignment to prepare a report after a team meeting. Suppose you choose *Draft report* to be one of its work packages. If you don't break down *Draft report* further, you haven't indicated clearly whether it includes any or all of the following actions:

>> Collecting information for the draft

>> Determining length and format expectations and restrictions

>> Writing the draft

>> Reviewing the draft yourself before officially circulating it to others

But if you simply break down the work package into two activities that are titled "Design the draft report" and "Write the draft report," your scope of work is instantly clearer. A few well-chosen words at this level go a long way.

Developing a Game Plan

Developing a WBS for large and small projects

You need to develop a WBS for very large projects, very small projects, and everything in between. Building a skyscraper, designing a new airplane, researching and developing a new drug, and revamping your organization's information systems all need a WBS. So, too, do writing a report, scheduling and conducting a meeting, coordinating your organization's annual blood drive, and moving into your new office. The size of the WBS may vary immensely depending on the project, but the hierarchical scheme used to develop each one is the same.

REMEMBER

Occasionally, your detailed WBS may seem to make your project more complex than it really is. Seeing 100 tasks (not to mention 10,000) on paper can be a little unnerving! However, the WBS doesn't create a project's complexity; it just displays that complexity. In fact, by clearly portraying all aspects of your project work, the WBS simplifies your project.

Check out the sidebar "Conducting a survey using a WBS" for an illustration of how a work breakdown structure helps you develop a more accurate estimate of the time you need to complete your work.

CONDUCTING A SURVEY USING A WBS

Suppose your boss asks you to estimate how long it will take to survey people regarding the characteristics they would like to see in a new product your company may develop. Based on your experience doing similar types of assessments, you figure you'll need to contact people at the company headquarters, at two regional activity centers, and from a sampling of current clients. You tell your boss that the project will take you between one and six months to complete.

Have you ever noticed that bosses aren't happy when you respond to their question of "How long will it take?" with an answer of "Between one and six months"? You figure that finishing any time before six months meets your promise, but your boss expects you to be done in one month, given some (okay, a lot of) hard work. The truth is, though, you don't have a clue how long the survey will take because you have no idea how much work you have to do to complete it.

Developing a WBS encourages you to define exactly what you have to do and thereby improves your estimate of how long each step will take. In this example, you decide to conduct three different surveys: personal interviews with people at your headquarters, phone conference calls with people at the two regional activity centers, and a mail survey of a sample of your company's clients. Realizing you need to describe each survey in more detail, you begin by considering the mail survey and decide it includes five deliverables:

- **A sample of clients to survey:** You figure you need one week to select your sample of clients if the sales department has a current record of all company clients. You check with that department, and, thankfully, it does.

- **A survey questionnaire:** As far as this deliverable is concerned, you get lucky. A colleague tells you that she thinks the company conducted a similar survey of a different target population a year ago and that extra questionnaires from that effort may still be around. You find that a local warehouse has 1,000 of these questionnaires and — yes! — they're perfect for your survey. How much time do you need to allow for designing and printing the questionnaires? Zero!

- **Survey responses:** You determine that you need a response rate of at least 70 percent for the results to be valid. You consult with people who've conducted these types of surveys before and find out that you have to use the following three-phased approach to have an acceptable chance of achieving a minimum response rate of 70 percent:

  1. Initial mailing and receiving of questionnaires (estimated time is four weeks)

  2. Second mailing and receiving of questionnaires to non-respondents (estimated time is four weeks)

  3. Phone follow-ups with people who still haven't responded, encouraging them to complete and return their surveys (estimated time is two weeks)

- **Data analyses:** You figure you'll need about two weeks to enter and analyze the data you expect to receive.

- **A final report:** You estimate you'll need two weeks to prepare the final report.

Now, instead of one to six months, you can estimate the time you need to complete your mail survey to be 15 weeks. Because you've clarified the work you have to do and how you'll do it, you're more confident that you can reach your goal, and you've increased the chances that you will!

Note: To develop the most accurate estimates of your project's duration, in addition to the nature of the work you do, you need to consider the types and amounts of resources you require, together with their capacities and availabilities. However, this example illustrates that using just a WBS to refine the definition of your project's work components significantly improves your estimates.

Understanding a project's deliverable/activity hierarchy

Figure 4-2 shows a portion of the *deliverable/activity hierarchy* for the project of surveying people to determine the characteristics a new product your organization may develop should have (refer to the nearby sidebar "Conducting a survey using a WBS" for details on this example). As illustrated in the figure, a project's deliverable/activity hierarchy is comprised of three types of components:

>> **Deliverables:** Intermediate or final products created during the performance of the project (see Chapter 3 of this minibook)

>> **Work packages:** Deliverables at the lowest point in each branch of the hierarchy that can be further subdivided into activities

>> **Activities:** Work that's performed to produce a deliverable

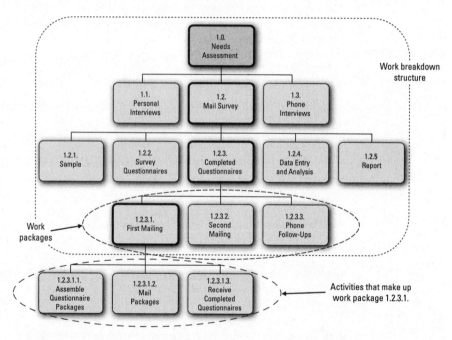

FIGURE 4-2:
The hierarchy of deliverables and activities for surveying people.

The WBS is the portion of the hierarchy that contains the deliverables (from the topmost level down to and including all work packages) that will be produced during the project. The activities that make up the work packages are recorded in a comprehensive activity list. While not considered to be part of the WBS, each activity is a component of a work package, so you need to identify it as such. (For convenience, you should include activities in the WBS dictionary under the work package to which they relate; see the later section "Documenting Your Planned Project Work" for details on the WBS dictionary.)

Dealing with special situations

With a little thought, you can break down most WBS elements into components. However, in some situations, like the ones described in the following sections, you have to get creative.

Representing conditionally repeating work

Suppose your project contains a deliverable (such as an approved report) that requires an unknown number of repetitive cycles (such as reviewing and revising the latest version of the draft report) to produce, each of which generates at least one intermediate deliverable. In reality, you write the report and submit it for review and approval. If the reviewers approve the report, you obtain your deliverable of an approved report and proceed to the next phase of your project (such as a distributed report). But if the reviewers don't approve the report, you have to revise it to incorporate their comments and then resubmit it for a second review and approval. If they approve the second draft, you obtain your deliverable of an approved report and proceed to the next phase of your project. But if they still don't approve your report, you have to repeat the process (or try to catch them in a better mood).

Revising the draft is *conditional work*; it will be completed only if a certain condition (in this case, not receiving the reviewers' approval) comes to pass. Unfortunately, a WBS doesn't include conditional work; you plan to perform every piece of work you detail in your WBS. However, you can indirectly represent conditional work in the following two ways:

>> **You can define a single deliverable as an *Approved report* and assign it a duration.** In effect, you're saying that you can create as many *Reviewed but not approved versions of the report* as necessary (each of which is an intermediate deliverable) to obtain the final reviewed and approved version within the established time period.

>> **You can assume that you'll need a certain number of revisions and include the intermediate deliverable created after each one (a different *Reviewed but not approved version of the report*) in your WBS.** This approach allows more meaningful tracking.

REMEMBER

Whichever approach you choose, be sure to document it in your project plan.

Assuming that your project needs three reviews and two revisions doesn't guarantee that your draft will be good to go after only the third review. If your draft is approved after the first review, congratulations! You can move on to the next piece of work immediately — that is, you don't perform two revisions just because the plan assumed you would have to!

However, if you still haven't received approval after the third review, you continue to revise it and submit it for further review until you do get the seal of approval you need. Of course, then you have to reexamine your plan to determine the effect of the additional reviews and revisions on the schedule and budget of future project activities.

REMEMBER

A plan isn't a guarantee of the future; it's your statement of what you will work to achieve. If you're unable to accomplish any part of your plan, you must revise it accordingly (and promptly).

Handling work with no obvious break points

Sometimes you can't see how to break a piece of work into two-week intervals. Other times that amount of detail just doesn't seem necessary. Even in these situations, however, you want to divide the work into smaller chunks to remind yourself to periodically verify that your current schedule and resource estimates are still valid.

KEEPING A CLOSE EYE ON YOUR PROJECT

A number of years ago, a young engineer was asked to design and build a piece of equipment for a client. He submitted a purchase request to his procurement department for the raw materials he needed and was told that, if they didn't arrive by the promised delivery date in six months, he should notify the procurement specialist he was working with so she could investigate the situation. He was uneasy about waiting six months without checking periodically to see whether everything was still on schedule, but being young, inexperienced, and new to the organization, he wasn't comfortable trying to fight this established procedure. So he waited six months.

When he didn't receive his raw materials by the promised delivery date, he notified the procurement specialist, who, in turn, checked with the vendor. Apparently, there had been a major fire in the vendor's facilities five months earlier, and production had just resumed the previous week. The vendor estimated his materials would be shipped in about five months!

He could have divided the waiting time into one-month intervals and called the vendor at the end of each month to see whether anything had occurred that changed the projected delivery date. Although checking periodically wouldn't have prevented the fire, the engineer would have known about it five months sooner and could have made other plans immediately.

In these instances, arbitrarily define intermediate milestones to occur every two weeks that are defined as "progress confirmed as being on schedule" or "expenditures confirmed as being on budget." Check out the sidebar "Keeping a close eye on your project" for an illustration of why it's important to have frequent milestones to support project tracking and how to deal with WBS components that have no obvious break points.

Planning a long-term project

A long-term project presents a different challenge. Often the work you perform a year or more in the future depends on the results of the work you do between now and then. Even if you can accurately predict the work you'll perform later, the further into the future you plan, the more likely it is that something will change and require you to modify your plans.

When developing a WBS for a long-term project, use a *rolling-wave approach,* in which you continually refine your plans throughout the life of your project as you discover more about the project and its environment. This approach acknowledges that uncertainties may limit your plan's initial detail and accuracy, and it encourages you to reflect more accurate information in your plans as soon as you discover it. Apply the rolling-wave approach to your long-term project by taking the following steps:

1. **Break down the first three months' work into components that take two weeks or less to complete.**

2. **Plan the remainder of the project in less detail, perhaps describing the work in packages you estimate to take between one and two months to complete.**

3. **Revise your initial plan at the end of the first three months to detail your work for the next three months in components that take two weeks or less to complete.**

4. **Modify any future work as necessary, based on the results of your first three months' work.**

5. **Continue revising your plan in this way throughout the project.**

REMEMBER

No matter how carefully you plan, something unanticipated can always occur. The sooner you find out about such an occurrence, the more time you have to minimize any negative effect on your project.

Issuing a contract for services you will receive

Generally speaking, you use a WBS that you include in a contract for services to be provided to you by another person or organization differently from the way

Developing a Game Plan

you use one to guide project work that you or your organization performs itself. When you perform the project yourself, the WBS provides the basis for developing detailed project schedules, estimating personnel and other resource requirements, detailing the project roles and responsibilities of project team members, and assessing all aspects of the ongoing work. However, when you manage a contract with an external organization that's performing the project for you, you use the WBS to

>> Support responsive progress assessment to help ensure that the overall project is on track to finish on time and within budget.

>> Provide the contractor with a framework for tracking and reporting periodic assessments of project schedule achievement and resource expenditures.

>> Confirm that product, schedule, and resource performance is sufficient to justify the making of scheduled progress payments.

In addition, you don't want the WBS to unduly restrict the contractor's ability to use his experience, skills, and professional judgment to achieve the results detailed in the contract. Typically, developing the WBS to two or three levels of detail is sufficient to meet the preceding needs without creating unnecessary restrictions.

Creating and Displaying a WBS

You can use several schemes to develop and display your project's WBS; each one can be effective under different circumstances. This section looks at a few of the most common schemes and provides some examples and advice on how and when to apply them.

Considering different schemes

The following five schemes (and their examples) can help you subdivide project work into WBS components:

>> **Product components:** Floor plan, training manuals, or screen design

>> **Functions:** Design, launch, review, or test

>> **Project phases:** Initiation, design, or construction

>> **Geographical areas:** Region 1 or the northwest

>> **Organizational units:** Marketing, operations, or facilities

Project phases, product components, and functions are the most often used.

When you choose a scheme to organize the subelements of a WBS component, continue to use that same scheme for all the subelements under that component to prevent possible overlap in categories. For example, consider that you want to develop finer detail for the WBS component titled *Report.* You may choose to break out the detail according to function, such as *Draft report, Reviews of draft report,* and *Final report.* Or you may choose to break it out by product component, such as *Section 1, Section 2,* and *Section 3.*

WARNING

Don't define a WBS component's subelements by using some items from two different schemes. For instance, for the component *Report,* don't use the subelements *Section 1, Section 2, Reviews of draft report,* and *Final report.* Combining schemes in this way increases the chances of either including work twice or overlooking it completely. For example, the work to prepare the final version of Section 2 could be included in either of two subelements: *Section 2* or *Final report.*

TIP

Consider the following questions when choosing a scheme:

>> **What higher-level milestones will be most meaningful when reporting progress?** For example, is it more helpful to report that *Section 1* is completed or that the entire *Draft report* is done?

>> **How will you assign responsibility?** For example, is one person responsible for the draft, reviews, and final report of Section 1, or is one person responsible for the drafts of Sections 1, 2, and 3?

>> **How will you and your team members actually do the work?** For example, is the drafting, reviewing, and finalizing of Section 1 separate from the same activities for Section 2, or are all chapters drafted together, reviewed together, and finalized together?

Developing your WBS

How you develop your WBS depends on how familiar you and your team are with your project, whether similar projects have been successfully performed in the past, and how many new methods and approaches you'll use. Choose one of the following two approaches for developing your WBS based on your project's characteristics:

>> **Top-down:** Start at the top level in the hierarchy and systematically break WBS elements into their component parts.

This approach is useful when you have a good idea of the project work involved before the actual work begins. The top-down approach ensures that you thoroughly consider each category at each level, and it reduces the chances that you overlook work in any of your categories.

>> **Brainstorming:** Generate all possible work and deliverables for this project and then group them into categories.

Brainstorming is helpful when you don't have a clear sense of a project's required work at the outset. This approach encourages you to generate any and all possible pieces of work that may have to be performed, without worrying about how to organize them in the final WBS. After you decide that a proposed piece of work is a necessary part of the project, you can identify any related work that is also required.

TIP

Whichever approach you decide to use, consider using stick-on notes to support your WBS development. As you identify pieces of work, write them on the notes and put them on the wall. Add, remove, and regroup the notes as you continue to think through your work. This approach encourages open sharing of ideas and helps all people appreciate — in detail — the nature of the work that needs to be done.

The top-down approach

Use the following top-down approach for projects that you or others are familiar with:

1. **Specify all Level 2 components for the entire project.**

2. **Determine all necessary Level 3 components for each Level 2 component.**

3. **Specify the Level 4 components for each Level 3 component as necessary.**

4. **Continue in this way until you've completely detailed all project intermediate and final deliverables.**

    The lowest-level components in each WBS chain are your project's work packages.

The brainstorming approach

Use the following brainstorming approach for projects involving untested methods or for projects you and your team members aren't familiar with:

1. **Identify all the intermediate and final deliverables that you think your project will produce.**

    Don't worry about overlap or level of detail.

    Don't discuss wording or other details of the work items.

    Don't make any judgments about the appropriateness of the work.

2. **Group these items into a few major categories with common characteristics and eliminate any deliverables that aren't required.**

   These groups are your *Level 2* categories.

3. **Divide the deliverables under each Level 2 category into groups with common characteristics.**

   These groups are your *Level 3* categories.

4. **Use the top-down method to identify any additional deliverables that you overlooked in the categories you created.**

5. **Continue in this manner until you've completely described all project deliverables and work components.**

   The lowest-level components in each WBS chain are your project's work packages.

Categorizing your project's work

Although you eventually want to use only one WBS for your project, early in the development of your WBS, you can look at two or more different hierarchical schemes. Considering your project from two or more perspectives helps you identify work you may have overlooked.

Suppose a local community wants to open a halfway house for substance abusers. Figures 4-3 and 4-4 depict two different schemes to categorize the work for this community-based treatment facility. The first scheme classifies the work by product component, and the second classifies the work by function:

>> Figure 4-3 defines the following components as Level 2 categories: staff, facility, residents (people who'll be living at the facility and receiving services), and community training.

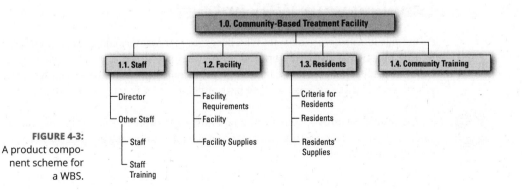

FIGURE 4-3:
A product component scheme for a WBS.

>> Figure 4-4 defines the following functions as Level 2 categories: planning, recruiting, buying, and training.

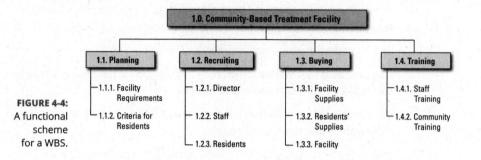

Both WBSs contain the same lowest-level components or work packages.

When you think about your project in terms of major functions (rather than final product components), you realize that you forgot the following work:

>> Planning for staff recruiting

>> Buying staff supplies

>> Planning for your community training

After you identify the work components you overlooked, you can include them in either of the two WBSs.

WARNING

Be sure you choose only one WBS before you leave your project's planning phase. Nothing confuses people faster than trying to use two or more different WBSs to describe the same project.

Labeling your WBS entries

As the size of a project grows, its WBS becomes increasingly complex. Losing sight of how a particular piece of work relates to other parts of the project is easy to do. Unfortunately, this problem can lead to poor coordination between related work efforts and a lack of urgency on the part of people who must perform the work.

TIP

Figure 4-5 illustrates a scheme for labeling your WBS components so you can easily see their relationships with each other and their relative positions in the overall project WBS:

>> The first digit (1), the Level 1 identifier, indicates the project in which the item is located.

>> The second digit (5) indicates the Level 2 component of the project in which the item is located.

>> The third digit (7) refers to the Level 3 component under the Level 2 component *1.5.* in which the item is located.

>> The fourth and last digit (3) is a unique identifier assigned to distinguish this item from the other Level 4 components under the Level 3 component *1.5.7.* If *1.5.7.3. Materials Ordered* isn't subdivided further, it's a work package.

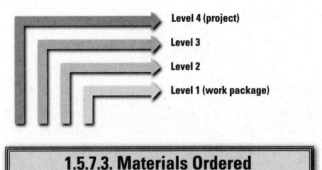

Level 4 (project)

Level 3

Level 2

Level 1 (work package)

FIGURE 4-5:
Identifying your WBS components.

1.5.7.3. Materials Ordered

TIP

When you're ready to label the activities that fall under a given work package, use a combination of the WBS code of the work package and a unique code that specifically refers to each activity. For example, suppose an activity under the work package 1.5.7.3. is *Prepare list of items to order.* You may give this activity the identifier code depicted in Figure 4-6. In this instance, the first four digits of the activity code are the WBS code for the work package of which this activity is a part. The fifth digit distinguishes this activity from the others in work package 1.5.7.3.

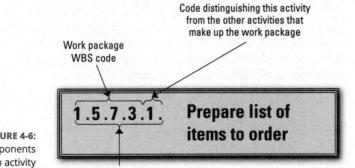

Code distinguishing this activity from the other activities that make up the work package

Work package WBS code

1.5.7.3.1. **Prepare list of items to order**

Activity code

FIGURE 4-6:
The components of an activity code.

Displaying your WBS in different formats

You can display your WBS in several different formats. This section looks at three of the most common ones.

The organization-chart format

Figure 4-7 shows a WBS in the *organization-chart format* (also referred to as a *hierarchy diagram* or a *graphical view*). This format effectively portrays an overview of your project and the hierarchical relationships of different WBS components at the highest levels. However, because this format generally requires a lot of space, it's less effective for displaying large WBSs.

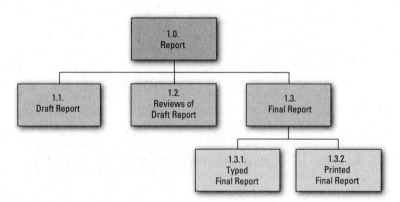

FIGURE 4-7:
Your WBS in the
organization-
chart format.

The indented-outline format

The *indented-outline format* in Figure 4-8 is another way to display your WBS. This format allows you to read and understand a complex WBS with many components. However, you can easily get lost in the details of a large project with this format and forget how the pieces all fit together.

TIP

Both the organization-chart format and the indented-outline format can be helpful for displaying the WBS for a small project. For a large project, however, consider using a combination of the organization-chart and the indented-outline formats to explain your WBS. You can display the Level 1 and Level 2 components in the organization-chart format and portray the detailed breakout for each Level 2 component in the indented-outline format.

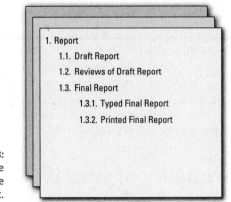

FIGURE 4-8:
Your WBS in the indented-outline format.

```
1. Report
    1.1. Draft Report
    1.2. Reviews of Draft Report
    1.3. Final Report
          1.3.1. Typed Final Report
          1.3.2. Printed Final Report
```

The bubble-chart format

The *bubble-chart format* in Figure 4-9 is particularly effective for displaying the results of the brainstorming approach to develop your WBS for both small and large projects (see the earlier section "The brainstorming approach"). You interpret the bubble-chart format as follows:

>> The bubble in the center represents your entire project (in this case, *Report*).

>> Lines from the center bubble lead to Level 2 breakouts (in this case, *Draft report, Reviews of draft,* and *Final report*).

>> Lines from each Level 2 component lead to Level 3 components related to the Level 2 component. (In this case, the Level 2 component *Final report* consists of the two Level 3 components *Typed final report* and *Printed final report.*)

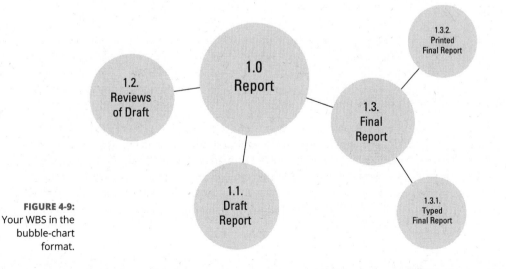

FIGURE 4-9:
Your WBS in the bubble-chart format.

Developing a Game Plan

The freeform nature of the bubble-chart format allows you to easily record thoughts generated during a brainstorming session. You can also easily rearrange components as you proceed with your analysis.

WARNING

The bubble-chart format isn't effective for displaying your WBS to audiences who aren't familiar with your project. Use this format to develop your WBS with your team, but transpose it into an organization-chart or indented-outline format when you present it to people outside your team.

Improving the quality of your WBS

You increase the chances for project success when your WBS is accurate and complete *and* when people who will be performing the work understand and agree with it. The following guidelines suggest some ways to improve your WBS's accuracy and acceptance:

>> **Involve the people who'll be doing the work.** When possible, involve them during the initial development of the WBS. If they join the project after the initial planning, have them review and critique the WBS before they begin work.

>> **Review and include information from WBSs from similar projects.** Review plans and consult people who've worked on projects similar to yours that were successful. Incorporate your findings into your WBS.

>> **Keep your WBS current.** When you add, delete, or change WBS elements during your project, be sure to reflect these changes in your WBS. (See the "Documenting Your Planned Project Work" section, later in this chapter, for more about sharing the updated WBS with the team.)

>> **Make assumptions regarding uncertain activities.** If you're not sure whether you'll do a particular activity, make an assumption and prepare your WBS based on that assumption. Be sure to document that assumption. If your assumption proves to be wrong during the project, change your plan to reflect the true situation. (See the sections "Making assumptions to clarify planned work" and "Representing conditionally repeating work" for more about assumptions.)

REMEMBER

>> **Remember that your WBS identifies only your project's deliverables; it doesn't depict their chronological order.** Nothing is wrong with listing deliverables from left to right or top to bottom in the approximate order that you'll create them. In complex projects, however, you may have difficulty showing detailed interrelationships among intermediate and final deliverables in the WBS format. The purpose of the WBS is to ensure that you identify all project deliverables.

Using templates

A *WBS template* is an existing WBS that contains deliverables typical for a particular type of project. This template reflects people's cumulative experience from performing many similar projects. As people perform more projects, they add deliverables to the template that were overlooked and remove deliverables that weren't needed. Using templates can save you time and improve your accuracy.

Don't inhibit people's active involvement in the development of the WBS by using a template that's too polished. Lack of people's involvement can lead to missed activities and lack of commitment to project success.

This section looks at how you can develop a WBS template and improve its accuracy and completeness.

Drawing on previous experience

By drawing on previous experience, you can prepare your WBS in less time than it takes to develop a new WBS and be more confident that you've included all essential pieces of work.

Suppose you prepare your department's quarterly budget. After doing a number of these budgets, you know most of the work you have to perform. Each time you finish another budget, you revise your WBS template to include new information you gleaned from the recently completed project.

The next time you start to plan a quarterly budget, begin with the WBS template you've developed from your past projects. Then add and subtract elements as appropriate for this particular budget preparation.

Improving your WBS templates

The more accurate and complete your WBS templates are, the more time they can save on future projects. This section offers several suggestions for continually improving the quality of your WBS templates.

When using templates, keep in mind the following guidelines:

>> **Develop templates for frequently performed tasks as well as for entire projects.** Templates for the annual organization blood drive or the submission of a newly developed drug to the Food and Drug Administration are valuable. So are templates for individual tasks that are part of these projects, such as awarding a competitive contract or having a document printed. You can always incorporate templates for individual pieces of work into a larger WBS for an entire project.

>> **Develop and modify your WBS template from previous projects that worked, not from initial plans that looked good.** Often you develop a detailed WBS at the start of your project, but you may forget to add intermediate or final deliverables that you overlooked in your initial planning. If you update your template from a WBS that you prepared at the *start* of your project, it won't reflect what you discovered *during* the performance of the project.

>> **Use templates as starting points, not ending points.** Clarify to your team members and others involved in the project that the template is only the start for your WBS, not the final version. Every project differs in some ways from similar ones performed in the past. If you don't critically examine the template, you may miss work that wasn't done in previous projects but that needs to be done in this one.

>> **Continually update your templates to reflect your experiences from different projects.** The post-project evaluation is a great opportunity to review and critique your original WBS. At the end of your project, take a moment to revise your WBS template to reflect what you found.

Identifying Risks While Detailing Your Work

In addition to helping you identify work you need to complete, a WBS helps you identify unknowns that may cause problems when you attempt to perform that work. As you think through the work you have to do to complete your project, you often identify considerations that may affect how or whether you can perform particular project activities. Sometimes you have the information you need to assess and address a consideration and sometimes you don't. Identifying and dealing effectively with information you need but don't have can dramatically increase your chances for project success.

Unknown information falls into one of two categories:

>> **Known unknown:** Information you know you need that someone else has

>> **Unknown unknown:** Information you know you need that neither you nor anyone else has because it doesn't exist yet

REMEMBER

You deal with known unknowns by finding out who has the information you need and then getting it. You deal with unknown unknowns by using one or more of the following strategies:

>> Buying insurance to minimize damage that occurs if something doesn't turn out the way you expected

>> Developing contingency plans to follow if something doesn't turn out the way you expected

>> Trying to influence what the information eventually turns out to be

In the project *Conducting a survey* discussed in the "Conducting a survey using a WBS" sidebar, presented previously in this chapter, you figure you'll need a week to select a sample of clients to survey if the sales department has a current customer relationship manager (CRM) program listing all the company's clients. At this point, whether the listing exists is a *known unknown* — it's unknown to you, but if it exists, someone else knows about it. You deal with this unknown by calling people to find someone who knows whether such a listing does or doesn't exist.

You experience a different situation when you become aware that the person who managed the CRM program has left the job. As part of your *Conducting a survey* project, you need to have the new person work with the list and you're concerned that he doesn't know that it's part of his job.

Whether or not the operator knows it's his job is an unknown unknown when you prepare the WBS for your project plan. You can't determine beforehand that the first person would leave the company and the new one wouldn't be properly trained because it's an unintended, unplanned act (at least you hope so).

Because you can't find out for certain whether or not this occurrence will happen, you consider taking one or more of the following approaches to address this risk:

>> **Develop a contingency plan.** For example, in addition to developing a scheme for the computerized selection of names directly from the original database, have the statistician who guides the selection of the sample develop a scheme for selecting names randomly by hand from the database.

>> **Take steps to reduce the likelihood that only one person knows what is going on with the CRM.** For example, check with the department head to see whether another employees can be trained to run the CRM program.

Of course, if you feel the chance that only one operator will know how to run the program is sufficiently small, you can always choose to do nothing beforehand and just deal with the situation if and when it actually occurs.

Developing the WBS helps you identify a situation that may compromise your project's success. You then must decide how to deal with that situation.

Documenting Your Planned Project Work

After preparing your project WBS, take some time to gather essential information about all your work packages (lowest-level WBS components), and keep it in the *WBS dictionary* that's available to all project team members. You and your team will use this information to develop the remaining parts of your plan, as well as to support the tracking, controlling, and replanning of activities during the project. The project manager (or her designee) should approve all changes to information in this dictionary.

The WBS dictionary can contain but isn't limited to the following information for all WBS components:

>> **WBS component title and WBS identification code:** Descriptors that uniquely identify the WBS component

>> **Activities included:** List of all the activities that must be performed to create the deliverable identified in the work package

>> **Work detail:** Narrative description of work processes and procedures

>> **Schedule milestones:** Significant events in the component's schedule

>> **Quality requirements:** Desired characteristics of the deliverables produced in the WBS component

>> **Acceptance criteria:** Criteria that must be met before project deliverables are accepted

>> **Required resources:** People, funds, equipment, facilities, raw materials, information, and so on that these activities need

TIP

For larger projects, you maintain the entire WBS — including all its components from Level 1 down to and including the work packages —in the same hierarchical representation, and you keep all the activities that make up the work packages in an activity list or in the WBS dictionary or in both. Separating the WBS components in this way helps you more easily see and understand the important interrelationships and aspects of the project deliverables and work.

On smaller projects, however, you may combine the deliverable-oriented WBS components and the activities in each work package in the same hierarchical display.

» Deciding how to share news

» Writing your project-progress report

» Getting familiar with different meeting styles

» Creating a project communications plan

Chapter **5**

Keeping Everyone Informed

I magine standing at one end of a large room filled with assorted sofas, chairs, and tables. You've accepted a challenge to walk to the other end without bumping into any of the furniture. But as you set off on your excursion, the lights go off and you have to complete your trip in darkness, with only your memory of the room's layout to guide you.

Sounds like a pretty tough assignment, doesn't it? How much easier it would be if the lights went on every few seconds — you could see exactly where you were, where you had to go, and where the furniture got in the way. The walk would still be challenging, but it would be much more successful than in total darkness.

Surprisingly, many projects are just like that walk across the room. People plan how they'll perform the project — who will do what, by when, and for how much — and they share this information with the team members and other people who will support the project. But as soon as the project work begins, people receive no information about their progress, the work remaining, or any obstacles that may lie ahead.

Effective communication — sharing the right messages with the right people in a timely manner — is a key to successful projects. Informative communications support the following:

>> Continued buy-in and support from key audiences and team members

>> Prompt problem identification and decision making

>> A clear project focus

>> Ongoing recognition of project achievements

>> Productive working relationships among team members

Planning your project communications enables you to choose the appropriate media for sharing different messages. This chapter can help you keep everyone in the loop so no one's left wondering about the status of your project.

Successful Communication Basics

Have you ever played the game of telephone with a group of people sitting around a table? The first person at the table has a written message, and the object of the game is for the group to transmit that message accurately to the last person at the table by having each person in turn whisper the contents of the message to the next person in line. The rules are simple: No one other than the first person can see the original written message, and each person must ensure that only the next in line hears the message she whispers. Invariably, the message received by the last person bears little, if any, resemblance to the original message because, even in this controlled setting, a myriad of factors influence how well people send and receive messages.

Sadly, sometimes this type of miscommunication can occur in a project-management environment. But don't worry! This section is here to help. It explores important parts of the communication process, distinguishes different types of communication, and offers suggestions to improve the chances that the message a receiver gets is the one the sender intended to give.

Breaking down the communication process

Communication is the transmitting of information from a sender to a receiver. Whenever you communicate, during the life of a project or at any other time, your goal is to ensure that the right person correctly receives your intended message in a timely manner.

REMEMBER

The process of transmitting information includes the following components:

>> **Message:** The thoughts or ideas being transmitted.

>> **Sender:** The person transmitting the message.

>> **Encoded message:** The message translated into a language understandable to others. (This language may consist of words, pictures, or actions.)

>> **Medium:** The method used to convey the message. (The different mediums are described in detail in the later section "Choosing the Appropriate Medium for Project Communication.")

>> **Noise:** Anything that hinders successfully transmitting the message. (Noise may include preconceived notions, biases, difficulty with the language used, personal feelings, nonverbal cues, and emotions.)

>> **Receiver:** The person getting the message.

>> **Decoded message:** The message translated back into thoughts or ideas.

Depending on the nature of a particular communication, any or all of these elements can affect the chances that the sender receives the message as intended.

Distinguishing one-way and two-way communication

Certain types of communication are more effective for transmitting particular types of information. The two main types are

>> **One-way communication:** Going from the sender to the receiver with no opportunity for clarification or confirmation that the receiver received and correctly understood the intended message. This type of communication can be effective for presenting facts, confirming actions, and sharing messages that have little chance of being misinterpreted.

One-way communications are either push or pull:

• **Push:** Proactively distributed to particular people; examples include memos, reports, letters, faxes, and emails.

• **Pull:** Available to people who must access the communications themselves; examples include Internet and intranet sites, knowledge repositories, and bulletin boards.

>> **Two-way communication:** Going from the sender to the receiver and from the receiver back to the sender to help ensure that the intended audience

received and correctly interpreted the message. Examples include face-to-face discussions, phone calls, in-person group meetings, interactive teleconferences, and online instant messaging. Two-way communication is effective for ensuring that more complex content is correctly received and for conveying the sender's beliefs and feelings about the message.

Can you hear me? Listening actively

The one skill that most strongly influences the quality of your communications is your ability to listen actively. Although you can assume that the information contained in a message and the format in which it's presented affect how well that message is received, you can find out whether the recipient received the message as you intended by listening carefully to the recipient's reactions.

Active listening is exploring and discussing a message that's being sent to help ensure that the message is understood as intended. If you're sending a message, you should encourage your intended recipient to use active listening techniques to help ensure that she correctly understands your message. If you're receiving a message, you should use these techniques to verify to yourself that you have correctly received the intended message.

Because listening to and observing your recipient's response to a message you sent her involves information flowing first from you to the recipient and then from the recipient back to you, active listening is, by definition, a form of two-way communication.

Active listening techniques include the following:

>> **Visualizing:** Forming a mental picture of the content of a message. Forming this picture gives the receiver the opportunity to identify pieces of the message that may be missing or misunderstood, as well as to seek additional information that may improve the overall understanding of the original message.

Consider that you've been asked to redesign the layout of your group's offices to create a more open environment that will encourage people to feel more relaxed and to engage in more informal working group discussions. To help clarify what's expected, you may try to visualize how the office environment will look and how people will behave after the changes in the layout are made. In particular, you may think about the following:

• Whether you'll have to use the existing furnishings or you'll be able to buy new ones

- Where people might hold informal meetings

- How much soundproofing partitions of differing heights will provide

As you try to visualize these different parts of the new office layout, you realize that the following aspects aren't quite clear to you:

- Will window offices have couches or just chairs?

- How many people should be able to sit comfortably in an office?

- Should you install white noise machines?

As you talk with people to find answers to your questions, you get a better idea of what your boss does and doesn't want.

» **Paraphrasing:** Explaining the message and its implications, as the receiver understands them, back to the sender in different words than the original message. To be most effective, the receiver should repeat the message in her own words to give the sender the best chance of identifying any misinterpretations.

Consider that your boss asks you to prepare a report of your company's recent sales activity by the end of the week. Many aspects of this request are unclear, such as the time period the report should cover, the specific time by when the report must be finished, the format in which you should prepare the report, and so forth. To clarify these items, you can paraphrase the request back to your boss as follows:

"I'd like to confirm that you're asking me to prepare for you a PowerPoint presentation on the company's total gross and net sales of products a, b, and c for the period from January 1 to March 31 of this year and that you'd like me to have it for you by this coming Friday at 5:00 p.m."

» **Checking inferences:** Clarifying assumptions and interpretations that the receiver makes about the message received.

Consider the previous example in which your boss asks you to redesign the layout of your group's offices. As you start to calculate the numbers of desks and chairs you'll need in the new arrangement, you realize you're assuming that the group will have the same number of people now and after the move. Instead of making this assumption, you can check with your boss to find out how many people he would like you to plan for as you design the new layout.

REMEMBER

Active listening is particularly useful in situations that are emotionally charged, situations in which understanding is critical, situations in which consensus and clarity are desired in resolving conflict, and situations in which trust is sought.

Choosing the Appropriate Medium for Project Communication

When deciding how to communicate with your team and your project's audiences, choosing the right medium is as important as deciding what information to share (check out Chapter 2 of this minibook for a detailed discussion of project audiences). Your choice of medium helps ensure that people get the information they need when they need it.

Project communications come in two forms:

>> **Formal:** Formal communications are planned and conducted in a standard format in accordance with an established schedule. Examples include weekly team meetings and monthly progress reports.

>> **Informal:** Informal communications occur as people think of information they want to share. These communications occur continuously in the normal course of business. Examples include brief conversations by the water cooler and spur-of-the-moment emails you dash off during the day.

WARNING

Take care not to rely on informal communications to share important information about your project because these interchanges often involve only a small number of the people who should hear what you have to say. To minimize the chances for misunderstandings and hurt feelings among your project's team members and other audiences, follow these guidelines:

- Confirm in writing any important information you share in informal discussions.

- Avoid having an informal discussion with only some of the people who are involved in the topic.

Formal and informal communications can be either written or oral. The following sections suggest when to use each format and how to make it most effective.

Just the facts: Written reports

Unlike informal oral communication, written reports enable you to present factual data efficiently, choose your words carefully to minimize misunderstandings, provide a historical record of the information you share, and share the same message with a wide audience.

Although written reports have quite a few benefits, they also have some draw-backs that you need to consider:

>> They don't allow your audience to ask questions to clarify the content, meaning, or implication of your message.

>> With written reports, you can't verify that your audience received and interpreted your message as you intended.

>> They don't enable you to pick up nonverbal signals that suggest your audience's reactions to the message.

>> They don't support interactive discussion and brainstorming about your message.

>> You may never know whether your audience reads the report!

TIP

Keep the following pointers in mind to improve the chances that people read and understand your written reports (see the later section "Preparing a Written Project–Progress Report" for specifics on writing this special type of communication):

>> **Prepare regularly scheduled reports in a standard format.** This consistency helps your audience find specific types of information quickly.

>> **Stay focused.** Preparing several short reports to address different topics is better than combining several topics into one long report. People are more likely to pick up the important information about each topic.

>> **Minimize the use of technical jargon and acronyms.** If people are unfamiliar with the language in your report, they'll miss at least some of your messages.

>> **Use written reports to share facts, and be sure to identify a person or people to contact for clarification or further discussion of any information in the reports.** Written reports present hard data with a minimum of subjective interpretation, and they provide a useful, permanent reference. A contact person can address any questions a recipient has about the information or the reasons for sharing it.

>> **Clearly describe any actions you want people to take based on information in the report.** The more specifically you explain what you want people to do, the more likely they are to do it.

>> **Use different approaches to emphasize key information.** For example, print key sections in a different color or on colored paper, or mention particularly relevant or important sections in a cover memo. This additional effort increases the chances that your audience will see the report *and* read it.

>> **After you send your report, discuss one or two key points that you addressed in it with people who received it.** These follow-up conversations can quickly tell you whether your recipients have read your report.

When you come across people who clearly haven't read your report, in addition to following the other suggestions in this section, explain to them the specific parts of the document that are most important for them to review and why. Then tell them that you'd like to set up a follow-up meeting with them to discuss any questions or issues they may have regarding the information contained in those parts of the document.

>> **Keep your reports to one page, if possible.** If you can't fit your report on one page, include a short summary (one page or less) at the beginning of the report (check out the nearby sidebar "Keep it short — and that means you!").

Move it along: Meetings that work

Few words elicit the same reactions of anger and frustration that the word *meeting* can provoke. People consider meetings to be everything from the last vestige of interpersonal contact in an increasingly technical society to the biggest time waster in business today.

KEEP IT SHORT — AND THAT MEANS YOU!

Be careful of the "yes, but" syndrome, in which you think an idea sounds great for others, but your *special* situation requires a different approach. In a training program a number of years ago, the speaker suggested that project reports should be one page or less. Most people agreed that doing so made sense, but one participant rejected the notion. He proceeded to explain that his project was so important and so complex that he sent his boss monthly project reports that were a minimum of ten pages. "And," he added, "My boss reads every word."

A few weeks after the training session, the speaker had the opportunity to talk to this participant's boss about an unrelated matter. In the course of the conversation, he happened to mention his frustration with a person on his staff who felt his project was so important that he had to submit monthly progress reports no fewer than ten pages. He said that he usually read the first paragraph, but he rarely had time to review the reports thoroughly. He added that he hoped this person had listened carefully to the suggestion that reports fit on one page!

You've probably been in meetings where you wanted to bang your head against the wall. Ever been to a meeting that didn't start on time? How about a meeting that didn't have an agenda or didn't stick to the agenda it did have? Or how about a meeting at which people discussed issues you thought were resolved at a previous meeting?

REMEMBER

Meetings don't have to be painful experiences. If you plan and manage them well, meetings can be effective forms of communication. They can help you find out about other team members' backgrounds, experiences, and styles; stimulate brainstorming, problem analysis, and decision making; and provide a forum to explore the reasons for and interpretations of a message.

You can improve your meetings by using the suggestions in the following sections. (In addition, check out the later section "Holding Key Project Meetings" for tips on planning different types of meetings.)

Planning for a successful meeting

TIP

To have a good meeting, you need to do some pre-meeting planning. Keep these pointers in mind as you plan:

>> **Clarify the purpose of the meeting.** This step helps you ensure that you invite the right people and allows attendees to prepare for the meeting.

>> **Decide who needs to attend and why.** If you need information, decide who has it, and make sure they attend the meeting. If you want to make decisions at the meeting, decide who has the necessary authority and who needs to be part of the decision making, and make sure they attend.

>> **Give plenty of notice of the meeting.** This step increases the chances that the people you want to attend will be able to do so.

>> **Let the people who should attend the meeting know its purpose.** People are more likely to attend a meeting when they understand why their attendance is important.

>> **Prepare a written agenda that includes topics and their allotted discussion times.** This document helps people see why attending the meeting is worth their time. The agenda is also your guideline for running the meeting.

>> **Circulate the written agenda and any background material in advance.** Doing so gives everyone time to suggest changes to the agenda and to prepare for the meeting.

>> **Keep meetings to one hour or less.** You can force people to sit in a room for hours, but you can't force them to keep their minds on the activities and information at hand for that long. If necessary, schedule several meetings of one hour or less to discuss complex issues or multiple topics.

Conducting an efficient meeting

How you conduct the meeting can make or break it. The following tasks are essential for conducting a productive meeting:

>> **Start on time, even if people are absent.** After people see that you wait for latecomers, everyone will come late!

>> **Assign a timekeeper.** This person reminds the group when a topic has exceeded its allotted time for discussion.

>> **Assign a person to take written minutes of who attended, which items you discussed, and what decisions and assignments the group made.** This procedure allows people to review and clarify the information and serves as a reminder of actions to be taken after the meeting.

>> **Keep a list of action items that need further exploration, and assign one person to be responsible for each entry.** This step helps ensure that when you meet to discuss these issues again, you have the right information and people present to resolve them.

>> **If you don't have the right information or the right people to resolve an issue, stop your discussion and put it on the list of action items.** Discussing an issue without having the necessary information or the right people present is just wasting everyone's time.

>> **End on time.** Your meeting attendees may have other commitments that begin when your meeting is supposed to end. Not ending on time causes these people to be late for their next commitments or to leave your meeting before it's over.

Following up with the last details

Your meeting may be over, but your work isn't finished. Make sure you complete the following post-meeting tasks to get the greatest benefit from the session:

>> **Promptly distribute meeting minutes to all attendees.** These minutes allow people to reaffirm the information discussed at the meeting when it's still fresh in their minds, and minutes quickly remind people of their follow-up tasks.

Try to distribute the minutes within 24 hours of the meeting, and ask recipients to let you know if they have any corrections or additions.

>> **Monitor the status of all action items performed after the meeting.** Because each action item is itself a miniproject, monitoring its progress increases the chances that people successfully complete it.

REMEMBER

Don't just talk about the suggestions outlined in the preceding sections for making your meetings more effective. Discussing them can't improve your meetings. Act on them!

Preparing a Written Project-Progress Report

The *project-progress report* is a project's most common written communication. The report reviews activities performed during a performance period, describes problems encountered and the corrective actions planned and taken, and previews plans for the next period.

This section helps you identify the audience for your project-progress report, provides pointers on what to include in your report, and suggests how to keep that content interesting so it doesn't put your team to sleep.

Making a list and checking it twice

A project-progress report is a convenient way to keep key audiences involved in your project and informed of their responsibilities. Decide who should get regularly scheduled project-progress reports by answering the following questions:

>> Who needs to know about your project?

>> Who wants to know about your project?

>> Whom do you want to know about your project?

REMEMBER

At a minimum, consider providing project-progress reports to your supervisor, upper management, the client or customer, project team members, and other people who are helping you on the project, as well as to people who are interested in or who will be affected by the project's results.

Knowing what's hot (and what's not) in your report

Preparing the project-progress report gives you an opportunity to step back and review all aspects of your project so you can recognize accomplishments and identify situations that may require your early intervention. Be sure to include some or all of the following information in your project-progress report for each performance period:

>> **Performance highlights:** Always begin your report with a summary of project highlights, such as "The planned upper-management review was successfully conducted on schedule" or "Our client Mary Fisher approved our training outline according to schedule." (Just remember to keep it to one page!)

>> **Performance details:** Describe the activities, outcomes, milestones, labor hours, and resource expenditures in detail. For consistency, identify each activity by its work breakdown structure (WBS) code (see Chapter 4 in this minibook for details).

>> **Problems and issues:** Highlight special issues or problems that you encountered during the period and propose any necessary corrective actions.

>> **Approved changes to the plan:** Report all approved changes to the existing project plan.

>> **Risk-management status:** Update your project risk assessment by reporting on changes in project assumptions, the likelihood of these updated assumptions occurring, and the effect of those updated assumptions on existing project plans.

>> **Plans for the next period:** Summarize major work and accomplishments that you have planned for the next performance period.

Figure 5-1 contains an example of a project-progress report format. Although you can expand each section of information, depending on the nature of your project, remember that the longer the report is, the less likely your intended audience is to read and understand it.

Earning a Pulitzer, or at least writing an interesting report

When you write your project-progress report, make sure it's interesting and tells the appropriate people what they need to know. After all, you don't want your report to end up as a birdcage liner. Use the following tips to improve the quality of each of your project-progress reports:

Monthly Progress Report			
Project Name	Project Number	Project Manager (First)　　　(Last)	
Period Covered / / – / / (From)　　　(To)	Date Report Submitted / /	Report Prepared by (First)　　　(Last)	

Performance Highlights

Major Accomplishments	Major Issues Encountered

Detailed Performance

Milestone/Activity		Start Date		End Date		Comments
WBS Code	Name	Planned	Actual	Planned	Actual	

Approved Changes to Plan Made during Period

Risk-Management Status

Plans for Next Period

FIGURE 5-1:
Example of a
project-progress
report.

» **Tailor your reports to the interests and needs of your audiences.** Provide
only the information that your audience wants and needs. If necessary,
prepare separate reports for different audiences. (See Chapter 2 of this
minibook for more on defining your project's audiences.)

>> **If you're preparing different progress reports for different audiences, prepare the most detailed one first and extract information from that report to produce the others.** This approach ensures consistency among the reports and reduces the likelihood that you'll perform the same work more than once.

>> **Produce a project-progress report at least once a month, no matter what your audience requests.** Monitoring and sharing information about project progress less often than once per month significantly increases the chances of major damage resulting from an unidentified problem.

>> **Make sure that all product, schedule, and resource information in your report is for the same time period.** Accomplishing this may not be easy if you depend on different organization systems for your raw performance data.

If you track project schedule performance on a system that you maintain yourself, you may be able to produce a status report by the end of the first week after the performance period. However, your organization's financial system, which you use to track project expenditures, may not generate performance reports for the same period until a month later.

Address this issue in your project's start-up phase. Determine your sources for status data, the dates your updated data is available from each source, and the time periods that the data applies to. Then schedule your combined analysis and reporting so that all data describes the same time period.

>> **Always compare actual performance with respect to the performance plan.** Presenting the information in this format highlights issues that you need to address.

>> **Include no surprises.** If an element requires prompt action during the performance period (if, say, a key person unexpectedly leaves the project team), immediately tell all the people involved and work to address the problem. However, be sure to mention the occurrence and any corrective actions in the progress report to provide a written record.

>> **Use your regularly scheduled team meetings to discuss issues and problems that you raise in the project-progress report.** Discuss any questions people have about the information in the project-progress report. (However, don't read verbatim to people from the written report they've already received — and, you hope, read!)

USING A PROJECT DASHBOARD

To make your written project-progress reports most effective, you want to include the greatest amount of information in the least amount of space. A *project dashboard* is an information display that depicts key indicators of project performance in a format that resembles an instrument panel on a dashboard. This format can convey the project's overall progress and highlight particular problems that require further attention.

When designing a dashboard for your project, take the following steps:

1. **Select the major categories of information.**

   Typical information categories that reflect important aspects of project performance include

   - **Results:** Desired products your team has produced to date

   - **Performance to schedule:** Dates that your team achieved milestones and started and completed activities compared to the schedule plan for milestones and activities

   - **Performance to resource budgets:** Labor hours, funds, and other resources your team has used to date compared to their budgeted amounts

   - **Risk management:** Current status of factors that may unexpectedly impede project performance

2. **Choose specific indicators for each information category.**

   Choose these indicators with the project's drivers and supporters. For example, a project that develops an operations manual for a piece of equipment may have the following indicators:

   - **Results:** The number of manual chapters written or the number of people who have approved the final manual

   - **Performance to schedule:** The number of milestone dates you've met and the number you've missed

   - **Performance to resource budgets:** The ratio of funds expended to those budgeted for all completed activities

   - **Risk management:** The number of original risks that may still occur or the number of new risks you've identified during the project

(continued)

(continued)

3. **Select the format for each indicator.**

You can display indicators in a table, bar graph, pie chart, or speedometer format. In addition, indicators often have a traffic light format:

- **Green light:** The element is proceeding according to plan.

- **Yellow light:** One or more minor problems exist.

- **Red light:** One or more serious situations require immediate attention.

Determine the specific criteria for green-, yellow-, and red-light status for each indicator in consultation with the project's drivers and supporters.

The following illustrations depict the types of displays in a project dashboard.

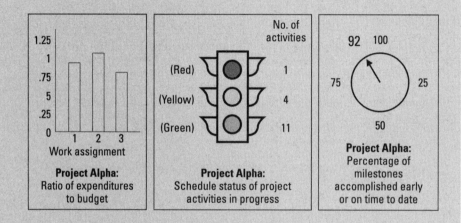

Project Alpha:
Ratio of expenditures to budget

Project Alpha:
Schedule status of project activities in progress

Project Alpha:
Percentage of milestones accomplished early or on time to date

When creating a dashboard for your project, be sure to

- Work with the intended audiences of a report to select the categories, indicators, and their display formats.

- Always present *actual* indicator values alongside *planned* values.

- Keep the project dashboard report to one page or less.

Holding Key Project Meetings

Active, ongoing support from all major project audiences gives you the greatest chance for achieving project success. To gain that support, continually reinforce your project's vision and your progress toward it, and help your project's audiences understand when and how they can most effectively support your efforts. This section looks more closely at the three types of meetings you may hold during your project.

Regularly scheduled team meetings

Regularly scheduled team meetings give members an opportunity to share progress and issues and to sustain productive and trusting interpersonal relationships. These meetings also provide an opportunity to reaffirm the project's focus and to keep team members abreast of activities within and outside the project that affect their work and the project's ultimate success. Recognizing that most people work on several projects at the same time, these meetings can reinforce the team's identity and working relationships.

TIP

Consult with team members to develop a meeting schedule that's convenient for as many people as possible. If some people can't attend in person, try to have them participate in a conference call.

In addition to following the suggestions for productive meetings in the section "Move it along: Meetings that work," observe the following guidelines when planning and conducting regular team meetings:

>> Even though your team meetings are held regularly, before each meeting, prepare a specific agenda, distribute it beforehand, and solicit comments and suggestions.

>> Before the meeting, distribute the project-progress report for the most recent performance period (take a look at the previous section, "Preparing a Written Project-Progress Report," for details on this report).

>> Distribute any other background information related to topics on the agenda before the meeting.

>> Limit discussions that require more in-depth consideration; deal with them in other forums.

>> Start on time and end on time.

>> Prepare and distribute brief minutes of the meeting within 24 hours after its end.

Ad hoc team meetings

Hold ad hoc team meetings to address specific issues that arise during your project. An ad hoc meeting may involve some or all of your team's members, depending on the topic. Because issues often arise unexpectedly, do the following as you plan an ad hoc meeting:

>> Clarify the issue and what you hope to achieve at your meeting.

>> Identify and invite all people who may be interested in, affected by, or working on the issue.

>> Clearly explain the meeting's purpose to all meeting invitees.

>> Carefully document all action items that the attendees develop at the meeting, and assign responsibility for their completion.

>> Share the results of an ad hoc meeting with all team members who may be affected by the results, who have an interest in them, and/or whose support you need to implement them.

Upper-management progress reviews

An *upper-management progress review* is a meeting that a senior manager usually presides over, a project manager runs, and team members and representatives of all functional areas attend. This review gives you the chance to tell upper management about your project's status, its major accomplishments, and any issues that require their help. The review is also an opportunity for you to note ways to keep the project in line with major organization initiatives.

REMEMBER

Take every opportunity to help upper management remember why your project is important to them. They may have approved your project only months ago, but chances are your project is now just one of many activities in your busy organization.

TIP

Get the most out of your upper-management progress review by observing the following tips:

>> Identify the interests of your audience and explain how your project is meeting those interests.

>> Keep your presentation short; choose a few key messages and emphasize them.

>> Highlight key information but be prepared to go into more detail on issues if anyone asks you to do so.

>> Use both text and graphics to convey important information.

>> Allow time for questions.

>> Present updated information on project risks, and explain how you're addressing them.

>> Distribute a brief handout at the meeting that summarizes the key points of your presentation.

>> After the meeting, distribute notes that highlight issues raised and actions that you agreed on during the review.

Preparing a Project Communications Management Plan

With the diversity of audiences that will be looking for information about your project and the array of data you'll be collecting, it's essential that you prepare a project communications management plan to avoid duplication of effort and to ensure that nothing falls through the cracks.

A project *communications management plan* is a document that specifies all project communications generated throughout the project, their target audiences, their information content, and their frequency. Prepare an initial version of your project communications management plan in the starting the project stage of your project, and update it as needed in the carrying out the work stage. (Flip to Chapter 1 in this minibook for details on the distinct stages of a project.)

At a minimum, your plan should specify the following for all project communications:

>> **Target audience:** The people whose information needs are addressed through the project communication. (Check out Chapter 2 in this minibook for a discussion of how to identify and classify project audiences.)

>> **Information needs:** The information that the target audience wants and/or needs.

>> **Information-sharing activity:** The specific type of information-sharing activity to be used to transmit information to the target audience — written reports, presentations, and meetings, for example. (Check out the section "Choosing the Appropriate Medium for Project Communication" for more on when different types of information-sharing activities should be used.)

>> **Content:** The specific data to be shared in the project communication.

>> **Frequency:** When the information-sharing activity occurs (can be either regularly scheduled or ad hoc).

>> **Data collection:** How and when the data for the report is collected.

3

Leadership

Contents at a Glance

CHAPTER 1: Building Your Leadership Muscles 205

Putting Your Brain to Work 206

Communicating Effectively. 213

Driving Yourself 215

Developing a Sense of Urgency. 216

Being Honest and Searching for the Truth 218

Displaying Good Judgment 218

Being Dependable and Consistent 218

Creating an Atmosphere of Trust 219

Encouraging a Learning Environment 220

Looking for Common Ground — The Type O Personality. 221

CHAPTER 2: Managing as a Leader 223

Setting Reasonable Goals. 223

Delegating to Your Team 225

Settling Disputes in Your Team 232

Allowing Your Team to Find Its Own Path 233

Leading When You Aren't Really the Leader 234

CHAPTER 3: Creating a Vision 243

Where Do Visions Come From?. 243

Supplying the Human Element 246

Establishing a Standard of Excellence 248

Helping You Stay Ahead of the Game 248

A Vision Links the Present to the Future 251

A Vision Is a Doable Dream 253

A Vision Is Not Just an Idea. 255

A Vision Is Based on Reality 258

A Vision Helps You Harness Opportunities 260

A Vision Is Dynamic. 265

CHAPTER 4: Leading across Cultures 267

Leading in a Diverse World 267

Emerging as a Leader from a Cultural Group 271

Leading across International Divides 273

Leading in the Virtual Age 275

» **Keeping people in the loop**

» **Making sound decisions**

» **Finding the middle ground**

Chapter **1**

Building Your Leadership Muscles

You may wonder why some people seem to become leaders naturally and effortlessly, whereas others don't. You've probably heard reverent whispers that so-and-so is a *natural leader*, but leadership is situational, not hereditary. Believing that certain people are destined for leadership is easy, however, if those people have personality traits that lend themselves to leadership.

Although some come naturally by personality traits common to leaders, personality traits can be developed, too. Think of it this way: Some people have to work hard to develop a good golf swing, while others seem to naturally have a knack for it. Similarly, with perseverance and work, anyone can develop his or her own leadership traits. (And people who work diligently to develop an ability often end up better than those who just get by on their natural abilities.)

In this chapter, we focus on ten of the most important traits common to great leaders. Developing these traits in your everyday life tells everyone you meet that you have the ability to lead.

Putting Your Brain to Work

To make use of the cliché, you don't have to be a rocket scientist or a brain surgeon to be a leader. Many leaders are not highly schooled, but they are intelligent, and one of the most interesting things about their intelligence is that they can take a limited amount of information and translate it into a workable set of skills. Think of leaders as something like MacGyver, the television character that Richard Dean Anderson played for several years. No matter what situation he got himself into, he was able to find a way to use little more than his handy Swiss Army knife and a roll of duct tape to improvise a solution. His skill was that he could imagine the things at hand to be other things.

Using what you have

Intelligence is critical to leadership because synthesizing information is often necessary to create a vision. When a group comes to you for leadership, their goals are often unformed or poorly formed. But intelligence enables you to start from a set of unknowns or with very limited information and proceed to a known outcome.

TEST YOUR LEADERSHIP IQ

Here's a little quiz. Look at the following list and ask yourself whether you do these things often, sometimes, or never. Give yourself a point if you do them all the time, add no points if you do them sometimes, and take away a point if you never do them. Ready?

1. I respond to situations flexibly.

2. I take advantage of fortuitous circumstances.

3. I can make sense out of ambiguous or contradictory messages.

4. I can recognize the importance of different elements of a situation.

5. I can find similarities between situations despite differences that may separate them.

6. I can draw distinctions between situations despite similarities that may link them.

7. I can synthesize new concepts by taking old concepts and putting them together in new ways.

8. I can come up with new ideas.

If you've scored four or more points, you are probably already known as a leader. If you've scored two or three points, you have good leadership potential. If you score one or fewer, you have some work to do on your leadership intelligence skills.

The quarterback of a football team is usually the leader of the team. Some quarterbacks, such as John Elway or Doug Flutie, distinguish themselves with their improvisational skill. They can direct traffic on the field while linebackers are rushing at them, and set up a receiver for a critical play with nothing more than hand signals and eye movements even after the set play has fallen apart. They use the information at hand to create something new and move their teams forward toward the goal line.

TIP

A leader is required to have a vision, which is a fancy word for a purpose and a goal or goals for followers. Creating that vision means recognizing what is possible for the group you are leading, which itself requires intelligence in the form of the ability to assess the skills of the group.

Responding to situations flexibly

Taking in new information and adjusting your response to a particular situation requires intelligence. Instead of responding in a knee-jerk way, an intelligent person responds flexibly, based on circumstances and needs.

Here's a situation: You own a vacation house and you've been away from it for a while. Your brother-in-law, who is looking after the house, has turned down the heat in the wintertime to save you money, even though the area where your house is located is prone to short-term power outages. The power has gone off in your house, the pipes have frozen, and then the power has come back on. By the time you arrive, the frozen pipes have burst, and the furnace is merrily pumping hot water through all the leaks and flooding your house. What do you do?

If your first response is "I scream and curse the Fates," you are not responding to the situation flexibly. If you threaten to divorce your spouse, who brought into your life the idiot who did this to you, you're not doing yourself any good, either. But if you open the door and a river pours out, along with a cloud of steam, and you run downstairs to the basement to shut off the furnace and then go out and find a couple of pails and mops and begin cleaning up, you are responding to the situation flexibly.

The goal is to prevent further damage. The effort requires that you elicit cooperation from your spouse, so you can't yell or make sarcastic remarks. And you need to listen to your spouse, who may have some additional ideas to contribute to drying out the house.

The flooded house example is leadership at a very local, personal level, to be sure, but it is no different from the situation that faced Bob Saldich. In 1983, Saldich became president of Raychem, then a $2 billion California manufacturer of electronics products, after spending more than 20 years rising through the ranks of the company. One of the products that Saldich had been a champion of before he became the president was Raytel, a connection system for linking fiber-optic cables to the home. On the surface, Raytel was just the kind of product that could propel Raychem forward at a critical time when its sales were flagging.

As president, Saldich knew he couldn't push Raytel through the company just because it was his right to do so. He began to look at Raytel through leader's eyes, and his analysis was that the project would cost more than the company could afford before it might be successful, it might take too long to bring to the marketplace, and it could be superseded by other approaches from competitors. So he killed the Raytel project, took a $200 million writedown, and moved on to rebuild the company by cutting costs and adding other new products. Said Saldich about his move, "When you are a product champion, you look at projects one way. But when you become responsible for the fortunes of the whole company, you have to reassess everything. You have to be flexible in the face of new circumstances."

Taking advantage of fortuitous circumstances

The Roman poet and playwright Virgil once said that fortune favors the brave. He didn't mean bravery in the heroic sense, but rather in the opportunistic sense. You not only have to be smart enough to adapt to new information with flexibility, but you also have to have the courage to seize opportunities when they present themselves. Often, the opportunity appears when you do nothing more than reshuffle existing information.

Take, for example, Sam Walton, the founder of Walmart. When he was working for the Ben Franklin stores, that chain served areas that were economically marginal, or what demographers call "C" counties. Walton noticed that a lot of the customers of the stores were from out of the area, from towns and villages that were even more disadvantaged than the towns Ben Franklin stores served. So he asked permission to open a store in a "D" county — a place that is the bottom of the barrel economically. When the company denied Walton's request, he quit and opened his first Walmart. He reasoned, rightly, that no matter where people live, they have the same needs. They have to buy toothpaste and shaving cream and shoelaces and all the other little things that go into making life normal. If they could buy them without traveling a great distance or paying more money, they would become loyal customers.

Walton took advantage of a lack of flexibility on the part of his employer to create the largest retailing empire in history. He also listened to his customers and created a circumstance for them to cooperate with him — his store opened in their town in return for their patronage. And finally, he put his customers above himself by not charging a premium price even though it cost him more to get his goods to more remote locations. By opening several stores in an area at once, Walton was able to get manufacturers to absorb the extra costs through bulk-order discounts.

Making sense of ambiguous or contradictory messages

In Greek mythology, one of the great tests of leadership was a visit to the Oracle of Delphi. The oracle was a prophetess of the Temple of Apollo. This temple, at the foot of the steep slope of Mount Parnassus, was considered the center of the universe. When a leader or a warrior went to the oracle, she would descend into the basement of the temple and chew on the leaves of the laurel plant until she went into a trance. Her priests then translated her trance words into what was often highly ambiguous verse.

How the hero or leader interpreted the riddle determined whether he succeeded or failed. So it is with modern leaders. They get information from many sources. Much of it is contradictory, hazy, or ambiguous at best. Modern leaders may hear many messages from a group waiting to be led, including the hostile "Who are you to think you can lead us?" message.

REMEMBER

A good leader listens to all the information and then sorts through it. You test contradictory messages by asking for more information in order to find the truth. Martin Puris, former chairman of the advertising agency Ammirati Puris Lintas, called this concept "piercing the fog," and Lintas believes that a leader's most important job is "the relentless search for the truth."

Often, to get at the truth, a leader has to elicit the cooperation of people who don't necessarily want to provide the answers. Working with uncooperative people may require leaders to restrain a natural tendency toward anger and place the need to solve the group's problems ahead of their own egos. Leaders use their intelligence to interpret riddles and to come up with the correct answers.

Ranking the importance of different elements

What happens when you are given all the information you need and all the information is truthful, but the problem itself is breathtakingly complex? Again, a trip back to mythology is in order. In 333 BCE, while Alexander the Great was marching through Anatolia — what is today the Asian part of Turkey — he reached the gates of Gordium, the ancient capital of Phrygia. There, he was shown the chariot of the city's founder, Gordius, with the chariot's yoke lashed to a pole of the city's gate by means of an intricate knot with its end hidden. According to local legend, this knot could be untied only by the future conqueror of Asia. Alexander drew his sword and sliced the knot in half. The phrase "cutting the Gordian knot" has come to mean a bold-stroke solution to a complicated problem.

WARNING

The story of a quick cut to the Gordian knot is entertaining, and although quick thinking is often called for in real crises, bold strokes often end in disaster. A true leader knows how to rapidly sort through the disparate elements of a problem and focus on the most important component of a complex and interlocking set of facts.

Rather than slice through the Gordian knot, a strong leader often asks for yet more information. When Louis V. Gerstner, Jr., left McKinsey & Company to join American Express as executive vice president of its Travel Related Services (TRS) Division, he already knew a lot about the core of its business — credit cards. At McKinsey, he had spent almost five years consulting with TRS. Yet when he landed at American Express, according to Harvard Business School professor John P. Kotter, he "shocked the people running the card organization by bringing them together within a week of his appointment . . . and then proceeding to question all of the principles by which they conducted their business."

Gerstner used that same procedure when he became president of the TRS Division and later vice chairman of American Express, and again at RJR Nabisco, when he became chairman in 1989, and yet again at IBM, when he became CEO in 1993. Gerstner is insistent that senior management provide him with as much information as possible, and he frequently asks questions much farther down in the ranks of management round out his knowledge of a problem. When Gerstner acts, he is much more likely to be decisive, because he has listened to everything rather than just what was told to him.

Finding similarities in apparently different situations

One of the normal characteristics of intelligence is a talent for analogies. You may remember these exercises from when you were taking the Scholastic Aptitude Test (SAT) in high school. Analogies compare pairs of words, such as black::white as evil::?. Analogous intelligence in leaders is the ability to draw on prior experience, no matter how tenuous the connection is, to find a similarity that you can use to solve a problem.

TIP

You are often a leader in your everyday life, even though you don't realize it. You can draw upon your everyday experiences and use analogies to lend insight into more complicated problems. People call this skill *common sense.* Here is an example of what we mean: If you've planned a wedding and your boss asks you to plan a meeting, draw on the wedding experience to make the meeting successful. If you're asked to head a task force and you've been a Little League coach, remember that the members of your task force are looking to you for the same kind of coaching as your players did.

Drawing distinctions between seemingly similar situations

You can find differences among situations just as often as you can find similarities, and a good leader learns to recognize when A is not like B and emphasize the differences over what the two have in common. For example, humans and chimpanzees have more than 98 percent of their DNA in common, yet you wouldn't put a chimp in charge of getting a rocket to the moon. Conversely, human beings share more than 99.999 percent of their DNA with each other, yet the most minute differences give us our individuality and act as a yawning chasm between people. The same thing is true of situations: Every situation you encounter is the same, yet different.

As the great engineer and thinker Buckminster Fuller once said, "Unity is plural and, at minimum, is two." Situations are similar to people. You can do the same thing a hundred times, but the moment you begin to treat it as routine, something can change and gum up the works. For example, a physician who has done a thousand heart bypass operations may begin to work on automatic pilot. Maybe on the next chest, the doctor could face a heart that's in reversed position. Failing to recognize the difference could lead to disaster.

TIP

An effective leader recognizes that situations rarely repeat themselves exactly, and so will make minor adjustments and not always do whatever was done before, "because it worked so well at the time."

In 1992, Rally's, a small hamburger chain located in the Midwest and the South, began to expand nationally. The company needed a way to emphasize the differences between its generic burger and the generic burgers sold by the two giants. Ed McCabe, the brilliant advertising executive who has created many memorable campaigns, analyzed the fast-food market and concluded that the menus at McDonald's and Burger King had become too complicated and too expensive. In a brilliant series of commercials that drew on the differences between Rally's simple, inexpensive menu and the large chains' complicated, expensive menus, McCabe helped propel Rally's sales from a negligible amount to more than 5 percent of the total burger market. The commercials also forced the chains into a price war that was ultimately detrimental to Rally's, which could not absorb the losses.

What is important in this area of leadership is not the ultimate consequence, but the ability to find the minute differences that can give you an advantage, even a temporary one.

Putting concepts together in new ways

Along with analogies, one of the components of intelligence is the ability to synthesize new knowledge by putting together time-tested concepts in new ways. Take, for example, the *80-20 rule*, which says that 20 percent of your customers account for 80 percent of your business. In the 1990s, Mercer Management Consulting used that old idea to help its clients examine their retailing relationships, which helped manufacturers realign their marketing channels to make them more efficient and more profitable.

The 80-20 idea is an old one, but when combined with a new idea — channel relationships — it takes on a new life. Out of Mercer's take on the 80-20 rule has come the idea of selling into the channels where you sell the most. Many Mercer clients have withdrawn from small mom-and-pop retailers and cut more profitable deals with large category-killer retailers, trading per item profit for much larger unit volumes.

Leaders are often expected to synthesize goals. In fact, much of what people who write about leadership call *vision* is really about the synthesis of ideas and information into a new direction.

Coming up with novel ideas

According to Ecclesiastes, "There is no new thing under the sun," yet sometimes leadership calls for *inspiration,* the novel thinking that enables you to strike off in a new direction, even more than it calls for vision. When you are faced with a situation in which no existing solution will provide you with a clear advantage, you have to invent something entirely new. In 1988, with the Cold War more than 40 years old, "everything that could have been thought of had been thought of and tried," said one German diplomat with regard to the question of German reunification. But remember: Leadership is situational, and situations change.

In 1988, West German Chancellor Helmut Kohl recognized that the Soviet Union was in serious danger of riots from food shortages because of a series of harsh winters and the economic hardship caused by Russia's prolonged war with Afghanistan. Kohl proposed a simple solution: He would deliver several hundred million dollars' worth of food, especially meat, to the Russians if they would allow reunification talks with East Germany to proceed without further hindrance. Mikhail Gorbachev, who needed peace in Russia more than he needed

East Germany, took the opportunity, and the result was an almost overnight end to nearly 45 years of Soviet control of the eastern half of Germany. Kohl came up with a novel idea, and the world changed.

Communicating Effectively

First and foremost, a leader has to keep the vision in the minds of his or her followers in every conversation, whether in a spoken or unspoken manner. When a leader is speaking as a leader, and not as a friend or confidante, he or she needs to remind people in a simple and straightforward manner and without a lot of additional explanation why they are being asked to turn the vision into reality.

In his book, *Leadership IQ: A Personal Development Process Based on a Scientific Study of a New Generation of Leaders* (John Wiley and Sons, Inc.), Emmett C. Murphy says that the leaders he has researched have mastered the art of conversation.

> *As we eavesdropped on their conversations with the stakeholders in their organizations — a high-tech marketing manager talking with a recently hired sales associate, a cardiac care nurse conversing with her supervisor, a team of municipal council members discussing economic development with local businesspeople — we saw that they had followed well-crafted scripts in all their communications.*

Murphy doesn't mean literal scripts. Instead, he means that the structure to communication between leaders and followers tends to remain the same even when the circumstances or situation changes.

In other words, a leader has to find a kind of shorthand to remind the group of the goal. Often, such shorthand appears in our everyday lives as slogans. The problem with slogans is that they have been overused by advertising, so people tend to distrust them. Consumers may want to be sold on something, but they want to know the difference between a lofty goal and an impetus to purchase.

REMEMBER

The responsibility of leadership is to communicate the vision so clearly that no room is left for doubt among those who must execute it.

Leaders must not only explain, but they must also motivate their followers. In ancient Greece, when Aeschines finished speaking, people said, "He spoke well." But after Demosthenes spoke to them, they cried, "Let us march (into battle against Philip of Macedon's army)!" To inspire people enthusiastically to do what is necessary to ensure success, a business leader must articulate the very reasons the people have gathered to form an enterprise. A community leader must do the same thing, and you — no matter what kind of role you play — certainly need to motivate people in your everyday life.

How do you learn to speak to motivate? It all starts with our primary building blocks: eliciting the cooperation of others, listening well, and placing others above yourself. You look at these issues in the following sections.

Speaking begins with listening

A good speaker almost invariably is someone who can listen to or read the mood or tenor of an audience, even when the audience is not communicating verbally. Good speakers can sense nervousness, restlessness, or hostility among a group, and they learn to use the mood of the crowd to their own advantage.

Listening also involves asking questions and paying attention to the answers. If the first characteristic of leadership is high intelligence, that intelligence must be applied. You read about the relentless search for the truth that a leader goes through when crafting a vision or goals for the group earlier in this chapter. That search is a combination of asking questions, listening to the answers, and then processing the information.

WARNING

FIXING THE PROBLEM RATHER THAN FIXING THE BLAME

You can think of the difference between focusing on goals and focusing on faults in this way: In the world of Internet commerce, transactions can be online or offline. In an online transaction, you complete the transaction at the moment you sign off. Buying an airline ticket on the web, for example, is an online transaction. Your seat has to be locked up by the reservations computer at the time the transaction is completed. But buying a book on the web is an offline transaction. The sale looks the same, but no book is instantly pulled from a shelf. Instead, at the end of the day, perhaps hours after you've signed off, your order goes to a warehouse, where it is then pulled and processed.

Solving problems and assigning blame operate the same way. When you find a problem and solve it, you are completing an online transaction because you have not interrupted the flow of events. You are working to keep movement toward the vision going along a smooth trajectory with a minor course adjustment. The determination of who exactly was responsible for the mistake that led to your vision going off course can be handled offline after the goal has been achieved. Stopping what you're doing to assign blame is one of the most dangerous things a leader can do, because it breaks the flow of events, and controlling the flow is one of the things that a leader needs to do to maintain leadership of a group.

Eliciting the cooperation of others

Eliciting the cooperation of others is the process of offering something for something. As a song from the 1960s says, "Nothing from nothing leaves nothing. You gotta have something if you want to be with me." Implicit in what a leader does is trading a goal or vision focused on the future for struggle and hard work in the present. The goal has to be real and attainable, and it must fit the needs of the people being led.

For example, when a company is losing money and the rest of its industry is growing by 15 percent a year, it does no good for a CEO to set 20 percent growth as next year's goal. First, the executive has to find out why the company is losing money while its competitors are profiting — that's listening. Then the chief has to set an attainable goal, which may be stopping the hemorrhaging of cash. Then and only then can the company think about moving forward, which becomes a next goal. Even then, the goal cannot be outlandish; it needs to be attainable.

TIP

How does a speaker put the needs of others above his or her own? By speaking to the concerns and needs of the person you are talking to rather than your own. Early on, you have to acknowledge how hard a person is working toward a shared goal or vision, not talk about your own difficulty in leading. You must focus on the group's sacrifices and the importance of the mission, and you have to discover how to refrain from finding fault even while you are looking for the source of the roadblocks to completing the mission. This method sounds contradictory, but it isn't. Blaming people is distracting; finding the fault, correcting it, and moving on is not.

Driving Yourself

The drive to succeed is composed of aggressiveness, self-confidence, and the ability to communicate. All these traits have to be present, balanced, and focused on the problem at hand, or the result can be a disaster. A leader who is only aggressive often substitutes short-term tactical advantage for a longer-term gain, to the company's disadvantage, whereas someone who lacks confidence is likely to reverse a decision or look for another course of action at the first sign of trouble. Another real-world example illustrates this concept.

MILK OR BUTTERMILK

To see what can happen when a leader learns confidence, consider Malcolm Forbes. Before Forbes became the editor and publisher of *Forbes Magazine,* he was known, and ridiculed, for his indecisiveness. During Forbes's unsuccessful run for governor of New Jersey, his opponent said that Forbes was so wishy-washy that he couldn't decide whether to have milk or buttermilk for breakfast. When Forbes took over the magazine his father had founded, it was deeply in the red and needed self-confident leadership. Forbes created a persona, a public image of self-confidence — with his motorcycles and ballooning — that helped remake the magazine as "The Capitalist Tool " and made it highly successful. In private, he remained a shy and hesitant speaker all his life, but whenever Malcolm Forbes was in the public eye, he moved with ease and confidence.

Originally, MCI was conceived as a microwave radio system that would allow truckers to communicate with each other while they were on the road. But making the system work required a connection to AT&T's lines, permission that the telephone company refused to give. Almost any other person would have given up in the face of AT&T's clear monopoly power, but William McGowan, founder and chairman of MCI, insisted that the fledgling company's headquarters be moved to Washington so that he could lobby MCI's case with the Federal Communications Commission (FCC) and Congress. As a result, McGowan thought of MCI less as a phone company and more as "a law firm with an antenna on top." McGowan's drive to succeed not only made MCI successful but also changed the nature of telephone service in the United States.

Developing a Sense of Urgency

Generally, business visions are born of a change in the marketplace that suddenly creates an opportunity. What separates a more successful company from a less successful one? The better leader has a sense of urgency about translating the vision into a business. A good leader doesn't wait for information but instead seeks it out. A great leader begins assembling a team and determining what resources are necessary to make the idea a success even while information is still coming in.

Don't wait

At Chrysler, prior to its merger with Daimler–Benz, the top leadership would meet together for lunch nearly every day. The purpose of the lunch was not to talk about company problems but rather to shoot the breeze. However, within these informal conversations were often heated discussions about how people were using their cars and what types of vehicles people may want next.

Bob Lutz, then president and vice chairman of Chrysler, says that the give-and-take in these meetings was far more important than any formal market research study because it focused the best and brightest minds in the company on the future without putting anything at stake. "There's a lot you can do informally to move your company forward," says Lutz. "By the time an idea gets to the formal proposal stage, we ought to be able to say yes, because everybody already knows everything they need to know. Once a proposal is formally approved, then we move as rapidly as possible to getting the car into production."

Just because a leader has a sense of urgency does not mean that a good leader such as Lutz or Chrysler chairman Bob Eaton relies on hunches or intuition. Some leaders do, but the better leaders depend on systematic planning to guide them. Once a Chrysler car has moved beyond informal discussions and into the formal planning process, the planning process takes over, and every car is planned out in exactly the same way. Systematic planning is also required to start a business. Though businesses may be different, starting all businesses requires most of the same steps — planning, determining needs, and raising or allocating money.

Form a "kitchen cabinet"

TIP

The best way to stay on top of information so that you can maintain your focus on goals and maintain your sense of urgency about reaching them is to form what President Andrew Jackson called a "kitchen cabinet" of advisors. These advisors are people who can not only act as a sounding board for ideas but can also form the nucleus of a team after all the information for making a go-ahead decision is available. This committee is not a clique or an elite palace guard, but a wide-ranging group of people who have ideas and knowledge in diverse areas. You can call upon them for advice and, when necessary, for help in making the connections that will help you reach your goal.

TIP

TAKE YOUR TIME: THINK IT OVER

Intellectual honesty is perhaps the toughest trait for a leader to acquire. If you are at the top and you truly believe Harry Truman's old maxim, "The buck stops here," you may well believe that you have to have all the answers because you have the final say. Not so. A leader is allowed to say "I don't know" and ask for as many options as are needed to arrive at the best answer. After a decision is made and action is set in motion, it is too late for new information, so take the time to be rigorous in your search for the truth and discover how to recognize it when you see or hear it.

Being Honest and Searching for the Truth

Leading well requires that people be honest when they look at information and resist their own biases, even when they think they already know the answer.

Since its founding at the end of the 1960s, Leon Hirsch had been the near-dictatorial owner of U.S. Surgical. He had relied almost solely on his own ideas of where the market for surgical staplers was going, but in 1994, faced with a sharp downturn in sales and mounting losses, Hirsch did an uncharacteristic thing. He went to his employees and asked them for ideas on how to fix the company. He asked each section head had to come up with ways to save money, and formed a team of senior executives to explore new avenues for the company. The result was a remarkable turnaround in sales and profitability. Hirsch could not have accomplished his turnaround without being intellectually honest to an extreme (in this case, admitting that he didn't have all the answers) and without surrendering his own long-held beliefs about the future of U.S. Surgical.

Displaying Good Judgment

Leaders are generally responsible people. One of the things that people look for in a leader is his or her willingness to accept responsibility from early on, and people tend to judge potential leaders by how well they meet their responsibilities. Continuing to rise as a leader means that you continually exercise prudent judgment and don't allow yourself to fall into extreme situations. It means that you always keep the needs of the group in mind and that you don't commit the group to a potentially disastrous course of action. That's what was meant before, during the discussion about sizing your vision to the capabilities of the group. If you gamble everything, you risk losing everything. But if you gamble a little and lose a little, you can figure out what you did wrong and try again.

TIP

Good judgment goes out the window only in the most dire life-and-death circumstances, when failing to take a chance may result in the demise of the group. As a leader, even then you must communicate the options available to the group and persuade them that gambling everything is in their best interests.

Being Dependable and Consistent

Woody Allen once opined, "Ninety percent of success is simply showing up." He meant that reach a goal, you have to attack it consistently. A leader cannot be mercurial, whimsical, or wishy-washy. After a vision or goal has been selected and clearly articulated, you do not serve the needs of the group by altering course. Such indecision leads only to confusion and consternation among your followers.

Dependability is itself a form of good judgment. Of course, because a leader is dependable doesn't mean that a leader needs to be stubborn. Circumstances change constantly, and today's decision, made with the best information available, can mean tomorrow's disaster if external events change significantly. But consistency means that you follow the rules of leadership in a regular way. You are always searching for the truth, always listening, always working on the things necessary to keep your group cooperating toward its goal. You do not withdraw support from people on whom you depend.

Creating an Atmosphere of Trust

Consistency and dependability, especially when they accompany the basic requirements of leadership, breed trust among followers. If you know that the leader of your group is always going to listen to what you have to say — he or she may not follow your advice but you know you'll get a full and fair hearing — and that your leader is always going to find a way to elicit your cooperation, you are far more likely to trust that person than someone who doesn't communicate this way.

TRUST IS SACRED

TIP

How does a leader create an atmosphere of trust? Perhaps the most important way is to learn how to keep confidences. If you are told something that is meant to be kept secret, you have to learn to keep conversations as privileged information unless you are told otherwise. In intelligence agencies, the rigid classification system is based upon a "need to know."

Conversely, you also have to learn how to disseminate information in a way that keeps all your followers completely in the loop. At Colgate-Palmolive, CEO Reuben Mark knows that it is impossible to personally tell all his thousands of employees what the company is planning to do next, so he prepares meticulously detailed briefings for key executives. He gives them briefing materials so that they can brief the next level of executives down, and so on, until everybody in the company who may be affected by a decision has been told. Employees are told exactly what they need to know by the leader above them, and no communication is missed. Colgate uses that system successfully to launch its products on a worldwide basis.

TIP

As parents are fond of telling their children, trust is earned. However, as parents often find out — to their chagrin — trust is a two-way street. The parents' actions must be consistent if a developing child is going to learn to trust his or her parents. A parent who constantly changes the rules regarding what is expected and what rewards and punishments are meted out is a parent who is discouraging a child's trust. Conversely, children have to turn the lessons their parents teach them into instinctive behavior before a parent can learn to fully trust the child and extend privileges and responsibilities.

Encouraging a Learning Environment

Perhaps the most important thing that a leader can do to ensure that a goal or vision is achieved over a long term is to promote group learning. *Group learning* is one of those terms that management consultants like to throw around, but it really means that as whole group gets smarter, the leader makes better decisions. When a leader makes the effort to keep everyone informed, to communicate new information rather than hoard it — in other words, when the leader places the needs of the group above his or her own — the entire group benefits in ways that cannot be calculated. In turn, the leader benefits, because with better information, members of the group are far more likely to come up with new ideas for solving problems that were previously thought to be intractable.

TIP

SHARE INFORMATION

Group learning means that the leader has to learn from the group as well as being a teacher. Because leaders often respond to the needs of multiple groups, the information the leader learns from one group can often be conveyed to another, which improves the knowledge of all. The leader becomes a conduit for information so that all groups understand a problem from the same perspective. For this kind of give-and-take to happen, the leader must be a fast learner who is able to absorb new lessons and then apply them in the service of reaching a goal.

Looking for Common Ground: The Type O Personality

A curious thing about good leaders is that they are generally likable. They know how to get along with people — not just the people who follow them or admire them, but people who have every reason to despise them. They do not rise to the bait and fight with their enemies; rather, they seek to find common ground with their foes, knowing that a well-considered compromise can benefit both sides.

A poor leader will push opponents until they are forced to respond, often with disastrous consequences to both the person doing the pushing and the group they are leading.

At times, of course, a leader cannot get along with everyone. When you make the judgment that someone in the group is seriously impairing the group's ability to move forward, you need to take corrective action, which may mean putting the needs of the group above the process of cooperation.

LEARN TO LIKE PEOPLE

How do you find common ground with anyone? You can start by taking Will Rogers's maxim "I never met a man I didn't like" to heart. Liking people makes listening to what they have to say possible. When you begin to really listen, you'll see that with the exception of dealing with madmen, a grain of reason and legitimacy is evident in nearly any position.

Your job as a leader is to offer a point of retreat or an out for your opponent at the place where his or her position is least reasonable. If an opponent attacks your leadership, you are pulled away from reaching the goal of the group. You descend into a fight to maintain your leadership, and you wind up sacrificing the group's needs to your own.

» Setting goals and measuring your progress

» Settling disputes among team members

» Helping your team find its own path

» Finding a way to lead when you're not an official leader

Chapter **2**

Managing as a Leader

L eading is about decision making. And, as you discover in this chapter, one of the most important decisions you can make is to let your team make the decisions.

Setting Reasonable Goals

A leader's primary responsibility is setting goals. The first rule is, "Learn to be realistic about the goals you set." When Peter Derow was president of *Newsweek* back in the early 1970s, a piece of advice he used to hand out was, "Take care in how you set your goals. If you set them too high and don't reach them, you will be seen as a failure. If you set them lower and then exceed your goals, people will look at you as a hero." Derow could have added, "Don't set them too low, or management will think you're too timid."

REMEMBER

Matching goals to your group's abilities requires planning and perspective, as well as a critical and honest evaluation of your team, the resources you've been given, and where in the pack of competitors you currently sit. If your Little League team finished in last place last summer, telling the kids that they can win the championship this year is probably unreasonable and is likely to put too much pressure on them. On the other hand, if your team was in last place and lost the great majority of games by two runs or less, the addition of one more good pitcher and slightly better fielding, along with the maturity, experience, and better coordination that comes with age, may indeed send you to Williamsport, Pennsylvania, the site of the Little League World Series. But that should be a privately held hope, not a goal that you're going to sell to the team. Realistically, you have to believe that with improvement, you can win half of the games that you previously lost.

How do you set reasonable goals? Keep in mind the maxim, "Things take time." Even the most charismatic leader can't improve a bad situation overnight. You should want to, and you should bring the drive and commitment that says you will seize any opportunity to reach your ultimate goal; but you don't want to burn out your team on false hopes and wasted labor before they have reached the ultimate goal. Instead, tell your team what your ultimate goal is and set up a series of milestones, which, if you accomplish them, teammates can look upon as mini-goals that they've achieved.

TIP

How you measure your goals is as important as the goals themselves. If you choose the wrong targets, or if you allow others to select your goals for you, you greatly increase your chances that you will not measure up. Conversely, if you take a strong, leadership role in setting your goals, you will show yourself to be accountable for your success or failure up front, but you will also have a better understanding of what is expected of you, because you will have participated in the decision-making process.

THE THEORY OF RELATIVITY

If the senior leaders of your company have given you a Mission Impossible, work with them to readjust their expectations. A marketing executive at a financial services software firm was given the job of increasing his company's sales by 30 percent annually. His bonus and stock options depended upon his ability to hit that number. When the stock markets took a tumble during the summer of 1998, it became impossible for him to hit that target. For 1999, the CEO reiterated the target, and said, "Forget about 1998. It was a bad year. I won't pay you a bonus, but I won't fire you, either." The marketing executive said, "You're calculating wrong. We increased sales by 12 percent when the market demand for our product was declining by 20 percent. 'Relative to the market' we grew our sales by 32 percent." His boss thought it over and paid him the bonus.

Remember the following:

>> As a leader, you want people to judge you not on an absolute basis but on a relative basis — relative to how your competitors are doing.

>> As a leader, you want to be able to find multiple measurements of performance rather than a single measurement. Your superiors may have given you a sales target that proves impossible to reach. However, if you can show that you lowered your cost of selling or your cost of new customer acquisition, or increased customer loyalty as measured by a retention rate, you will live to fight another day, because those are all indicators of progress, both to your team and to your superiors.

Delegating to Your Team

Although many new managers are reluctant to delegate authority, fearing that it may cause them to lose control or that others may perceive them as weak, nothing could be further from the truth. Properly delegated authority is one of the most useful tools a leader possesses to build team spirit, motivation, and cohesion.

A good leader spends a lot of time at the beginning of the planning process, ensuring that every team member has a delegated task. Your job is to make team members feel wedded to your team's goals (see the preceding section, "Setting Reasonable Goals"). Delegating authority is one of the best ways to do that.

Knowing how to delegate

So much of delegating is wrapped up with choosing whom to delegate authority to that the primary rule of delegating is "Don't get bogged down by people." You are leading people, of course, but as a leader, you have to learn how to avoid the inevitable squabbles that arise out of personality conflicts, charges of favoritism, jealousy, and dishonesty. When we say "don't get bogged down by people," we mean "don't allow yourself to be distracted by all the petty aspects of human behavior."

TIP

When you assume a new leadership role, ask for an organizational chart so that you know the reporting lines of authority. However, that's just a start. Also ask around to find out who has the real power, and revise your chart accordingly to reflect the way decisions and resources flow in your area.

SWOT your staff

Your first step in assuming a new leadership role is to conduct a *SWOT analyses*, which means identifying the strengths, weaknesses, opportunities, and threats of the most important members of your team. In the beginning, as you review personnel files, forget about job titles. Look instead at strengths and weaknesses.

>> **What do previous leaders say about your team members?** Do they identify particular people as obstacles, or say that your team is easy to work with? Do they identify people with important knowledge, or people who are especially effective? Ask about these things to get a fix on the capabilities of the group.

>> **Do you see any discernible patterns?** Have several previous leaders told you the same things about the group? If so, there could be an institutionalized pattern of behavior, which might make the group more effective and cohesive — or be the group's undoing.

>> **Do any glaring weaknesses stand out?** Does the group consistently meet its goals, or are there constant struggles? If so, where are those struggles focused? Is it particular individuals or is it an entire department?

>> **Do the team members have particular strengths?** Skills such as written and oral presentation skills, analytical capabilities, decisiveness in action, and good judgment may indicate leadership potential, regardless of functional specialty.

>> **Are some team members brilliant but don't fit in?** These may be team members to whom you want to delegate a special project to give them the encouragement to become a vital member of your team.

TIP

You should also complete a sober assessment of your own strengths and weaknesses, and you ought to be looking at people who can fill in for you where you're weak. If you have come this far as a leader, you probably know your skills as well as the areas that need improvement. Look around your group to find people who complement your strengths and who can help you overcome your weaknesses, and give them responsibility for doing those things you don't do particularly well.

After conducting a SWOT analysis, go through your goal-setting and planning process (Chapter 3 in this minibook covers goal setting and planning in detail). At the same time, do a SWOT analysis of your competitive situation. Try to do the analysis in terms of the skills needed to reach the goal. For example, if you're a market laggard with a superior product, your analysis tells you that you have to communicate your message better. Do you have a superior communicator on your team? No matter what that person's functional title is, you want that person sitting in when the marketing department and the advertising agency are planning strategy.

Try to find out from the next level of management above you who is earmarked for promotion. Every organization has people who, fairly or not, are protected and seem to have a clear track for advancement. Compare the actual work performance of such people with what has been said about them. If it is equal, give them more responsibility. If their work performance is sub par, find something for them to do that has significant ceremonial meaning but won't bog down your mission or the team's ability to accomplish its goals. If there is such a person in your organization, the best use of that person will often be as a bridge to higher management, to help buy your team more resources.

CHOOSING UP SIDES

The problem for leaders comes when people who want to be chosen for a task besiege the leader. Do you remember when you were a kid and you were choosing up sides for a game? The two people who did the choosing, usually the two best athletes who functioned as team captains, had to make quick decisions about whom they wanted for their sides. Not only did they choose on the basis of athletic skills in descending order (the best players were picked first, the worst players were left for last), but they also took into account factors such as trust (whether they had previous playing experience with one person over another), and convoluted factors such as whether in order to get player A (who was great) you had to pick player B, player A's best friend (who was awful). Finally, after sides were chosen up, the captain had to find something for each person to do. In softball, that meant that the good hitters were at the top of the lineup and the poor hitters were at the bottom. And the people with good hands played infield, while the clumsiest players got stuck out in right field where they would do the least damage and could spend time praying that no ball would be hit in their direction.

Choosing up sides and assigning positions in a game is a simple leadership experience compared to delegating authority in a large organizational situation, or even in a volunteer setting. You may often manage to others' expectations; therefore, the roles and tasks that you assign and delegate may often seem to be less likely under your control. Delegating authority is something like choosing up sides with someone standing to one side who has both veto and insistence power. "You can have player A, but you can't have player B under any circumstances, even if he or she wants to be on your team and is a perfect fit."

Moreover, many of the people you may deal with already have well-defined jobs. If you're being charged with running a division, the sales people don't want to suddenly have to do finance, and the finance people don't want to get their hands dirty with production, despite the fact that it may help the entire organization.

Recruit stars when you can; train employees when you can't

You will inevitably find holes in your team. Like the football coach who needs an extra linebacker or the baseball coach who needs a good shortstop to plug up the gap in the infield, you may find that you need specific role players to meet your goals.

Where do you find them? They may exist in another division of your company, but more than likely, they work for your competitors or are people in subordinate positions who want to step up and embrace the challenge of more responsibility. To convince such people that they want to work for you, you need to demonstrate to them that your team and your workplace can provide certain advantages. These include the following:

TIP

>> **Provide a feeling of participation.** To ignore the talents and knowledge of the people you hire, because of rigid job designs or a tight hierarchical structure, is to throw away a significant resource. The best companies actively seek out the knowledge of their workers to lower costs, to improve the design of their products, to make them more competitive, and to aid in decision making.

Any company can get more out of its employees by designing processes that bring worker knowledge to the attention of top management without the filtering that often goes on through middle management. One of the best ways to do this is to reward managers who bring the suggestions and ideas of their workers to the attention of management, and to make it a basis by which their performance is measured.

>> **Provide opportunities for advancement.** Under the right circumstances, everyone is capable of advancement. Great leaders create the mechanisms for all their team members not only to excel but also to find the level at which they can do their best work. Great leaders also add responsibility to their team members when they are ready for it, to keep them involved and committed.

>> **Meet the personal needs of your employees.** Not so long ago, the workplace was homogeneous in almost every way. Not only were all the employees white males, but they lived in similar neighborhoods and had nuclear families with parents who were able to take care of themselves and with children who could be allowed a fair degree of independence because the streets were quiet and safe. The world is different now, and it is unlikely to become so homogeneous ever again. With workplace diversity comes a wide range of work habits and outside-of-work needs.

TIP

A company that wants to get the greatest commitment from its workers must be fully prepared to meet those needs and to minimize the inevitable distractions that life now brings to the workplace. How? By providing day care, a range of health care options, flextime, and job sharing. When you take on the responsibility for a team, you take on the responsibility for people's lives.

You have a right to expect discipline and concentration on the job, but you have to do the things necessary to encourage the behavior you expect.

» **Encourage diversity.** Diversity is no longer a matter of enlightened social policy. It is a necessity. Not enough talented people are available for any enterprise to cut itself off from any potential pool of applicants. Becoming an equal opportunity employer is a mechanism by which an enterprise gives itself the best chance of remaining competitive. In practice, diversity is harder to achieve than most people believe, because managers tend to hire people whom they are comfortable with. Diversity requires your personal commitment, and the commitment of every leader in your company.

To make diversity a success, you also have to commit yourself to

- Training and development from the time new hires enter your company.

- Creating models of appropriate behavior in the company.

- Nudging people into opportunities that they may think are beyond their present skills.

- Providing ongoing training and ongoing support.

» **Equip your workplace properly.** In an age of sophisticated machines and computer and communication networks, a company that does not equip its people with the proper tools can't remain competitive. The proper tools include the proper training. Employees should be trained not just to be minimally competent at their jobs but also to excel at them. The pressures of competition are too relentless to lose time to poor training.

» **Make your workplace safe.** Workplace safety should never be an afterthought. Safety must be designed into the tools, content, and structure of every job. Whether it is machinery that does not physically threaten the lives of your employees or breaks built into the day to prevent fatigue and stress that may lead to injuries, maintaining a safe workplace has a direct and positive effect on the profitability of your enterprise, as well as an indirect effect in lower insurance premiums charged to your overhead costs. Today, many companies believe that safety is an issue that affects only heavy industrial companies and those that handle hazardous materials. This is simply not so. Any workplace where work is repetitive and where the measurement of productivity is pure throughput is a workplace waiting for an accident or repetitive motion stress injuries to happen.

Knowing what to delegate

If you have managed the *who* of delegating and you think your team is in reasonably good shape, it's time to tackle the *what* of delegating. You need to determine how to break your plan down into goals and a mission. (Some call these *strategy* and *tactics,* but strategy is only a component of a goal and does not include the ultimate destination.) Then, delegate everything that has to do with the mission. (See Chapter 3 of this minibook for more on missions.) Create committees to handle each aspect of the mission, and have the relevant people in these committees report all new information on a timely basis.

Give your subordinates the chance to embrace the responsibilities you have given them. In other words, you want them to lead. Your role, during the development of the mission, involves supervising, mediating, mentoring, and controlling resources. You want your team to demonstrate its ability to execute the mission.

Track how well the team executes the mission. You may have to intervene. To know when you should take this step, sit in on any committee meeting where a problem is beginning to crop up: Listen, help, and, if necessary, take temporary control.

Rethink your problems

You want your team to be capable of solving its own problems wherever possible. But what do you do when someone comes to you and says, "I've tried everything, but it still doesn't work"?

Often, a problem that stymies everyone is a problem that is stated incorrectly. To quote the Danish mathematician Piet Hein, "The solution to a problem lies in its definition." Hein was once hired by a large Danish department store to work on the problem of moving people quickly in and out of the store's excellent cafeteria. The store could lower the quality of the food, but that could have had an effect on overall store sales. Or the store could hire ushers to shoo away loiterers. Instead, Hein helped a chair designer develop a dining room chair whose shape would be comfortable for no more than about 20 minutes. If people sat on them any longer, they would begin to suffer excruciating pain in their bottom. The chairs were made, and turnover increased as desired.

You need to think the same way. If you have an intractable problem, go back to the beginning and attempt to recast the problems in terms you may be able to solve, before you begin to think about calling in high-priced consultants. Often, rethinking a problem means accepting responsibility for a new situation. For example, car manufacturers wrestled for years to design better bumpers to protect cars and their drivers in low-speed crashes. It was only when designers began to realize that it was more important to protect the occupant than the car that rethinking led to padded dashboards, recessed instruments, a redesign of the steering wheel to protect the chest, and the addition of seat belts and then air bags to protect drivers and front seat passengers.

How do you go back to the beginning? You can approach an intractable problem in a number of ways. For example:

>> **Reverse engineer.** If you're making a product that isn't selling well, go out and buy a couple of examples of a competitor's product that's outselling yours. Take it apart. Figure out not only why it's better, but also attempt to figure out how it was made. Almost always, you will gain clues to how your competitor solved a problem that you cannot.

>> **Reverse market.** Perhaps your product isn't selling well because it's being sold in the wrong places, by the wrong people, or in the wrong way. Again, look at what your competitor is doing. Ask around about how your competitor's product is being sold and where. Look at your competitor's brochures and advertising. They'll provide clues about where your competitor thinks the market is heading.

>> **Hold an open competition.** If your own group cannot solve a problem, open it up to other people in your company. Post it on the company bulletin board and offer a prize for a solution. This will spur people to put in time off the clock to find a solution to your problem, and may flush out someone who should become a member of your team.

>> **Recast the problem.** Often, the way a problem is stated inhibits a solution. For example, if you say that you want to raise your profits by 10 percent, you'll look for areas where you can cut costs or increase sales. But if all those avenues have been tried, and no more profit can be wrung out, you may want to ask the questions, "Which are my most profitable sales channels? Can I create a promotion that's limited to those so that a small incremental gain in sales in those channels yields a large increase in sales and profitability?" This is an example of recasting the problem in a small way, looking at the source of profits rather than the profits themselves.

Run a play clock in your head

TIP

As a leader, you ultimately want to be able to delegate anything that doesn't impair or hinder your ability to lead or that will interfere with your ability to make decisions at a critical time. Just as a quarterback keeps a kind of clock in his head that tells him how much time he has to get rid of the ball by throwing it or handing it off, as a leader, you have to keep multiple clocks going in your head to let you know when to intervene in the various components needed for your team to reach its goals.

You can keep the clock in a few ways. The obvious way is to put up a chart with all of a project's deadlines on your wall, or record them in your diary. But deadlines are artificial, so an effective leader will advance deadlines a bit. If you need a completed marketing plan within a month, give the person who has to complete it three weeks. That way, if problems arise, your team member will have a week for revisions without imperiling other parts of your project.

Moreover, learn to schedule small reviews before projects are to be completed. If a project is especially complex, there should be a schematic that contains all the steps needed for completion and the order in which tasks need to be finished. If you break down the schematic finely enough and then monitor the completion of each piece, you'll quickly notice where problems arise.

This leads inevitably to the question, when do you take over? As the leader, your sense of timing will have almost everything to do with the confidence you have in your team, based on your experience with it, and almost nothing to do with actual schedules. You have to learn to develop a feel for when to intervene that's based on observation, conversations with team members, and the needs of the mission. An effective leader tends to intervene early, but not so early that he or she demoralizes the members of the team. Remember: You want them to do the work. You're there to set the team on its path and to encourage the team members to follow it.

Settling Disputes in Your Team

As a leader, one of your responsibilities is to maintain an orderly environment. This means listening to and mediating disputes that may arise (some of which concern themselves with the mission, but many more of which are personality-centered) and eliciting the cooperation of your team members to get them to cooperate when they are feeling torn apart from the group by their own concerns. You also need to get team members to act like leaders by asking them to place the needs of the mission above their own.

Your first question in settling any dispute should always be, "Is this about the mission or about people?" Many disputes come to you in the form of "Joe is impairing the mission because he's taking too much personal time while the rest of us are sitting here working our butts off trying to find an answer to this vexing problem." Before you come down on Joe, here's what you need to do:

1. **Review the work of the team members to try to find out why they are having difficulty.**

   This may sound counterintuitive, but it isn't. Make Joe's presence at the team meeting that you're attending mandatory, as an indication to the team members that they can talk about the problems only in terms of structures — no personalities allowed. If someone insists that Joe's absence is the problem, do not ask Joe to defend himself. Ask that person to demonstrate specifically that Joe's absence has caused a missed deadline or inferior work, or has in some way damaged the mission.

   The kinds of questions you need answered are, "What exactly is the problem that cannot be solved?" "Is Joe's presence critical to the solutions?" "Is this a team comfort issue or is it a mission issue?" You can determine quickly whether it is a "Joe" problem — that he is not really pulling his weight — or whether some larger issue exists.

2. **Find out whether you can supply the team with more resources.**

   Because your role as a leader is to keep the team moving toward its goal, helping the team members by getting more resources or by rethinking processes accomplishes that. If resources aren't the issue, work with them to help them rethink the problem (see the section, "Rethink your problems," earlier in this chapter).

3. **Then and only then talk privately to Joe.**

   Find out why he has been taking excess time away from the problem. If he has a legitimate reason, you can change his responsibilities — assign him to a different team or give him the time he needs to take care of his personal issues. If his reasons are not legitimate, you can still take whatever action you deem appropriate without harming the mission or the goals.

Concentrate on solving problems. Avoid assessing blame.

Your next question should be, "Is this an essential problem?" Many times, problems are brought to leadership solely because team members want to be assured that their problems — and they — have the leader's attention. The problem isn't significant enough to warrant the leader's intervention, but if a team member or a group is feeling neglected, the problem becomes magnified. This is where "leadership by walking around" comes in handy. If you make it a point to visit regularly with each group and ask about progress and problems, instead of waiting for trouble to come to you, you reassure people that you have their best interests and welfare at heart.

Your final question should be, "What will it take to get this problem fixed?" You should put that question back to the group and encourage the team members to come up with a solution, and then work with them to make the solution a reality. Often, groups will take the easy way out and answer, "Give us more resources." Your first response should be, "What have you done to solve the problem with the resources at hand?" and "Is there any guarantee that if I give you more resources, the problem will be resolved?" Make the team members prove their case, and if they cannot, sit down with them and go through a rethinking process.

Allowing Your Team to Find Its Own Path

One of the most satisfying aspects of being a leader is giving your team the confidence necessary for it to solve its own problems. When that happens, you have achieved what every leader wants to achieve — leading a group of self-motivated people capable of selecting its own goals and implementing them. That group relies on the leader for vision, and sometimes for counsel, but it is capable of moving on its own. For a group to get to that point, a leader has to constantly ask the team

>> Where do you want to go?

>> What do you think of as legitimate goals?

>> How do you assess your own strengths and weaknesses?

After you can answer these questions about your team, allow them increasing latitude in setting their goals and defining their mission. A leader with a team is much like a parent with teenagers. You know that you're not always going to be around to run their lives, so your responsibility is to equip them as well as possible with your values, test them by giving them responsibility, and allow them to test themselves by accepting it.

Leading When You Aren't Really the Leader

Lech Walesa — one of the founders of Poland's Solidarity movement and its long-time leader — once said that "you become free by acting free." The same is true of leading. You become a leader by acting like a leader. You don't need the title or the authority. You need only to be willing to embrace responsibility — to be able to elicit cooperation from people, listen to their needs, and then place those needs above your own.

Making yourself a leader when you aren't one doesn't mean running around, as General Alexander Haig reputedly did after the assassination attempt on President Reagan, yelling, "I'm in charge. I'm in charge." It does mean acting on the moment and helping to pull your team together.

Situational leaders are people who rise to leadership status because the time and circumstances are right for them. They meet the opportunity when it arises. But every time is potentially right for leadership, and every circumstance holds within it the potential for leadership opportunity. Don't sit around waiting for someone to discover your leadership potential. Instead, begin making your reputation as a leader.

The way to become a leader is to view every situation as a leadership situation. Change takes place because people who are not leaders in any accepted sense take on the role of leadership to lead other like-minded people toward a desirable goal. This section looks at the notion that you can lead as a follower, that you can exert real leadership even when your title is honorary, and that you can succeed when others expect you to fail. In all three cases, you can demonstrate your leadership abilities in a way that draws positive attention to you.

Leading as a follower

Leading as a follower begins with a simple idea: No matter how little of your work responsibility is under your control, you always retain control of your dignity as an individual. Most Americans no longer work in extremely dangerous or hostile work environments, but many people still work on jobs where they have little control over their job content or their workplace. Most current workplace struggles, as a consequence, are no longer about the right to unionize or bargain collectively — although union organization is important when workers feel completely disenfranchised — but about the right to human dignity on the job.

We are surrounded by a steady barrage of news about lawsuits — from sexual harassment and discrimination to repetitive motion injuries and work rules that prohibit placing personal objects around your workspace. All of these are human dignity issues. Many of these problems wind up as lawsuits because the company or organization did not recognize that its workplace was changing or that entrenched interests resented the changes.

Improve even the simplest things

TIP

Often, the simplest thing you can do to add to the dignity of the workplace is to clean it up and make it more cheerful. Many people take the attitude that physical conditions in the workplace are solely the responsibility of management, and that they should not be spending their own time and money for the benefit of the company. But putting together a work detail one weekend to paint the walls of your office a brighter color, instead of waiting for maintenance to do it three years from now, can brighten everyone's attitude, both through the doing and through the end result. It will also make an impression on your group's leader and make him or her more receptive to your next suggestion about ways to improve work flow or profits.

Use information to build team spirit

As we note throughout this book, an effective leader is someone who pursues information so that he or she can make the best possible decisions. But often, information is valuable not for what it can do for you but for what it can do for others.

THE JAYCEE WAY OF ASKING

Learning how to ask for change is probably the most important component of leading when you're not in a leadership position. The best way to approach a request is to act as if you are making a presentation as a leader. How do you do this? Look to the Jaycees for a model.

The United States Junior Chamber, the Jaycees, encourage volunteerism among their members, but they use volunteering as a leadership training ground. The Jaycees expect every member to develop a project that he or she can complete on behalf of the community. Their model for how to go about that is excellent for learning to lead while you're still a follower.

The Jaycee model starts with a project statement, which defines the project and the benefits that it brings the community. This is equivalent to writing a statement of vision. "I want to build a new playground on the vacant lot on Main Street because it will provide a safer place for the kids in the nearby housing project to gather, and it will rid the neighborhood of a weed-infested, bottle strewn vacant lot" may be such a statement. Or, "I want to organize a group to redecorate the office on our own time, with the resulting benefit of improved workplace morale and productivity."

The next thing the Jaycees ask of their members is an action plan. What materials do you need? What is the cost? Who is doing the work? What required approvals, permits, and such do you need? Who is responsible for the project on an ongoing basis? What are its long-term benefits?

These are the same elements that go into any business plan. The Jaycees choose from many projects they receive on the basis of originality and resourcefulness: Who manages to do the most for the community at large with the lowest expenditure and the highest local and team involvement? The entire Jaycee experience is meant to replicate as closely as possible what a leader does in terms of eliciting cooperation from a diverse group and placing the needs of others above himself.

You don't have to join the Jaycees to be effective, though. You simply need to want to lead, no matter what your actual position. You have to want to improve the lives of the people around you, and you have to want to give something of yourself to others.

For example, every person in your office or plant has a birthday. Take the responsibility of acknowledging those milestones, with a card and a brief ceremony. Everybody has important family moments. You should acknowledge these events also. If your company has a newsletter, take the responsibility for your group to supply it with information. If there isn't a newsletter, start one, even if it is just a photocopied single sheet of paper. You can contribute to the cohesiveness of the group by showing co-workers how much they have in common, and you can also help to build team spirit.

Always ask on behalf of the group

TIP

Doing any of these things may ultimately improve your leverage with management when you want to ask for a bigger, more significant change. But when you do ask for a significant change, such as upgraded training, ask on behalf of the group, not yourself. If you couch your request in terms of how the group benefits, it may be taken more seriously. To demonstrate leadership in these situations, it has to be clear to whomever you're speaking that you represent the goal or needs of a group, not yourself alone. Group aspirations are why the need for leadership exists, after all.

Get your group involved in the community

TIP

Companies and organizations exist within their larger communities, so take it upon yourself to improve your group's ties to the community as a whole. The public relations department or the head of the company may be making charitable grants, but that doesn't stop you from organizing a group to help in an area where you think you can do some good. A playground near your workplace may need some cleanup or improvement. You can organize it. If there is an accident or a local disaster, you can help with organizing a fund-raising effort. Is there a mentoring program or a literacy program to which you can contribute? All of these are opportunities to demonstrate leadership and involvement.

Most companies and organizations attempt to portray themselves as at least outwardly benevolent. So take advantage of that fact to gain volunteer time and access to company resources. It may get you noticed by higher levels of management.

BANNING LAND MINES

Jody Williams did volunteer work for the Vietnam Veterans of America, an organization that raises money for veterans programs. After talking to a large number of veterans who were victims of land mines, and after reading about the large number of children whose hands and feet were being blown off by land mines planted years before, Williams decided to find out more about the subject. She found dispirited support for a treaty banning mines, and took it upon herself to create something called the International Campaign to Ban Landmines. She became the coordinator of an effort that spans hundreds of organizations in more than 100 countries. Her leadership resulted in an international treaty banning such mines, which has been signed by more than 120 nations. For her efforts, she received the Nobel Peace Prize in 1997.

Get a logo

TIP

If you are indeed a team, get yourself a team logo. At NASA, every space mission has its own logo, and mission members wear their logo patches proudly, to let other people know what projects they are working on.

A researcher at *Newsweek International* had 12-dozen shirts made up with the *Newsweek* logo, and the words "The International Newsmagazine" emblazoned across the front. He sent them out to reporters and correspondents around the world and to other selected friends, including a photographer who wound up doing a highly publicized model shoot with the magazine. The shirts promoted the separate identity of *Newsweek International* and helped turn a stepchild publication into a powerhouse of its own. The idea won him the attention of management so that when he proposed a new publication, they listened to his ideas.

Don't pick fights with your bosses

Workplace dignity provides fertile ground for leadership opportunities. This *doesn't* mean actively seeking out confrontations with management. It means looking for ways to add to the value of the worker in the workplace.

Leading when your position is honorary

Under any number of circumstances, someone may name you as a leader but you may have no real authority. Probably the most common form of honorary leadership, the one that nearly everyone experiences at one time or another during adult life, is serving on a jury. This responsibility is an awesome one, because you're being asked to decide the fate of another human being, one who has been accused of committing a wrongful act. Most people attempt to avoid serving on juries — it takes too much time away from their regular lives, the cases are often arcane and complex, and most jurors have little sympathy for the situations that put them in the jury box. But a leader embraces responsibility, and leadership in the jury room is critical if justice is going to be done.

Basic leadership skills are critical to juries. Listening well means you have to pay attention to the proceedings. You can't doze off, and you must try to keep your personal feelings in check because they may color what you hear and what you see. Eliciting the cooperation of others is critical because after you're inside the jury room, you're going to have to build a consensus for conviction or acquittal in a criminal trial, or find for the plaintiff or the defendant in a civil trial. Placing the needs of others above yourself means that you have to give careful consideration to all the evidence, because the future of a fellow human being is at stake.

As another example, suppose you helped raise money for the local volunteer fire department and were so effective that the group names you "Honorary Chief."

Aside from the plaque, what does that mean? If you really care about the fire department, it means that you now have an opportunity to add to its leadership. The real chief is responsible for running the department on a day-to-day basis, ensuring that the firefighters properly maintain equipment and that the department is ready to meet all its responsibilities. But every chief has a wish list — a group of things he or she wishes to do if more time, money, or both are available. You can help the chief prioritize the list and then make the top item the focus of your next fund-raising effort, for example. Or, if the funds are available and the chief's time isn't, you can take charge of a project, such as organizing training seminars.

With any honorary title goes a *grant of opportunity*. Think of a grant of opportunity as a gift of money. How will you spend your new position? What will you do with it? Will you simply enjoy it until it's gone, or will you attempt to use it to improve your life and the lives of people around you?

To appreciate what a grant of opportunity means, think about Prince Charles and the late Princess Diana. Look past their stormy relationship and her tragic death to their roles as honorary leaders.

While Prince Charles waits to assume Britain's throne, he is severely constrained in what positions he can take by British law; Prince Charles has nevertheless managed to become an increasingly important force in England. He has become an impassioned supporter of the arts and of good architecture, and favors all sorts of charitable organizations with his patronage. He proves that you can lead well even without a title.

Princess Diana proved to be an even more inspirational leader, with even less of a title. Following her acrimonious divorce from Charles, she was essentially cut off from the flow of opportunities that go with being royal in England. She took up the cause of eradicating land mines internationally and helped to mobilize world opinion to a treaty banning such weapons of destruction. Her death played a large role in gaining recognition for the work of the International Campaign to Ban Landmines and probably accelerated the Nobel Prize given to the group and Jody Williams. (See the "Banning land mines" sidebar, earlier in this chapter.)

Perhaps you think that it's easy to be a leader when you have public image advisors and all the mechanisms of the media at your disposal. But Princess Diana could as easily have chosen a more commercial path, like her sister-in-law Sarah Ferguson. She didn't, and you don't have to be a princess in the glare of the spotlight to do good when the opportunity presents itself.

Any time you're given an honorary title, take it as a grant of opportunity to do something besides stand on the dais beaming. Whatever you choose to do may be unexpected, and it may be more than anyone did before. It may also reinforce the good feeling that led the group to make you its honorary leader in the first place.

WARNING

Keep in mind, however, that you're not really the leader, and you have to suggest and offer rather than plan and command. You have to prepare yourself for the real leader to say no, and you have to make certain that you in no way threaten the real leader of your group.

Leading when you're not expected to succeed

Welcome to the Department of Lost Causes. Because of the nature of organizations, even failing and dying organizations need leadership, lest they sell the furniture, close the offices, and let their workers go. An organization in its death throes is a sorry sight, especially if the organization has a proud history.

If it should come to pass that you're chosen to lead such an organization or group, what do you do? You could refuse, and allow the group to fail without you, or you can accept, even if you know that your chances of resurrecting the group are slim to none. If you choose to accept, you have to make sure that you won't get the blame for the group's failure, even if your turnaround efforts are unsuccessful.

Rally the troops

It is important for you to meet with your group as soon as you have taken on the leadership role. Let the group members know that you are aware that things are grim, but that if they give you their support, even temporarily, you can at least attempt to find a workable course of action, which may include an orderly shutdown. People who work for a company often freeze up at the possibility that they may lose their jobs, for example, so it's your job to explain to them that even if that happens, you will do all you can on their behalf.

HOMEMAKERS FOR PEACE

In the early 1970s, two homemakers, one Protestant and one Catholic, were appalled by the sectarian violence in Northern Ireland. The pair, Betty Williams and Mairead Corrigan, formed an organization, Peace People, to begin a dialogue between women and children of the warring factions, reasoning that if hatred could be overcome in the home, it may be overcome in the streets. The pair's success led them to be recognized in 1976 with the Nobel Peace Prize.

In this, you're much like a doctor who is attending a dying patient. On the one hand, you want to do everything possible to save the patient; on the other hand, you want to know when it is time to cease heroic intervention in favor of making the patient's last moments as comfortable as possible.

Follow the money

Every organization depends on a flow of funds, so the very first thing you should do is have someone audit the books. This way you know how much money is really in the till and how it has been spent. Announce and publish your results to the entire membership. If you find that there has been no wrongdoing, your publication of the results may spur some members to increase their contributions. If there has been poor administration, you have given yourself and others valuable information about why things are going badly, and can begin to correct them.

Choose a short-term goal

After you know the money and the people situations, develop a short-term goal. That goal will almost inevitably involve the funds of the organization. If there are problems that you can fix by spending money, spend it. If there are problems that you can fix by not spending, stop spending.

The second short-term goal is rebuilding trust. If you have a failing business, you have to rebuild trust with your customers. If you have a church with dwindling membership, you have to rebuild trust with the community. If you have a sports league whose membership is dwindling, you have to rebuild trust with the remaining members. They are your greatest allies in helping you to grow again.

Know when events are beyond your control

Say your church is dwindling because of a demographic shift in your neighborhood. It used to be Baptist, and suddenly there is a huge influx of new Indian immigrants, all Hindus, into the community. They may not want to pray at your church, but if you can, invite them to take part in the activities you sponsor. If you set up a group that helps them learn about the community or obtain assistance from the local social service agencies, you may help give your own church some new life.

But what happens when events are beyond your control? The demographic and lifestyle shifts that change so many communities, and the "creative destruction" of market forces almost inevitably mean that no group lasts forever. Under the circumstances, you have to be like the pilot of a plane that is crashing. Keep the wings level even as you crash, so that when somebody does the postmortem, he or she will say that you acted diligently and prudently and that nobody could have done more.

Failure can be a stepping-stone to success at a later time — if you handle the failure well and learn from your mistakes.

» Staying ahead of your competitors through your vision

» Planning for the future by establishing a vision

» Harnessing potential opportunities with a vision

» Keeping your vision dynamic

Chapter **3**

Creating a Vision

With just a little training, people can learn to operate in a cooperative manner, without the imposition of leaders. A group can be trained to set its own goals, implement its own mission, and move to action just as if it had a leader, but with responsibilities shared among all members of the group. So why bother with leaders at all? Why not just train people in their tasks, integrate those tasks with other jobs and roles, and set a whole group in motion?

Invariably, situations arise that require something more than group thinking and collective action. A challenging problem may require a new direction, or a group may have been successful in its mission but reached a dead end. In both cases, the group needs something that it can't supply: *vision.*

Where Do Visions Come From?

Successful leaders provide vision to a group. Leaders communicate to their followers the overarching, doable dream that's somehow different from the present reality. That vision is what keeps everyone on track and is the touchstone against which the mission and goals of the group are judged.

As long as the circumstances facing a group remain constant, a group can operate pretty well without a leader. Even if circumstances change somewhat, the entire group can adjust to the change if the change is gradual. But when people are confronted by the potential of radical changes in their future, or when they feel that they need a dramatic change, they need the quality of vision offered by a strong leader. Vision is what defines a future and allows groups to seek continued growth and challenge.

A vision comes from three places:

» Experience

» Knowledge

» Imagination

All three are related, but each is different. The following sections explain how these factors combine to create a vision.

Experience lets you visualize from the way you live

If you're working on an assembly line in an uncomfortable position, a lot of formal education isn't necessary to figure out that standing rather than bending over all the time would reduce the pain in your back at the end of every work shift. That's exactly what workers at Volvo figured out on their own about two decades ago. When they asked the company to improve the ergonomics of their jobs, the company complied by building a new factory at Uddevalla. In the new factory, the assembly line raised and lowered cars so that the part that was being worked on was always at mid-arm height, eliminating work fatigue. When women began working on the line a few years after the plant was opened, the company redesigned all its assembly tools, so that they would fit into a woman's hands and multiplied a woman's mechanical advantage to equal a man's.

Knowledge lets you visualize from what you've learned

Knowledge is the reason you go to school. A large body of knowledge cannot be taught by experience alone. Sometimes, acquiring knowledge from books is the best way. Reinventing the wheel isn't necessary when you can learn the process by which the wheel was first invented. After you have acquired knowledge, you see the world in a different light.

When Wilbur and Orville Wright were young, they were great kite flyers, and they were fascinated with the flight of birds and the rush of air currents. But it wasn't until they had some physics in school that they discovered Bernoulli's Principle, which taught them that the differential between air flowing over a curved surface and air flowing over a flat surface would cause lift. Bernoulli's Principle, not experience, allowed them to design a wing that would support heavier-than-air flight.

Imagination helps turn randomness into a vision

Imagination springs from the randomness of life, because it synthesizes knowledge and experience, but it's also connected to desire. By taking your life experience and factoring in all the possibilities and all the ways that you can see yourself and the world, your imagination allows you to grasp the possibility that waits just over the horizon. Think of the Jay and the Americans song "Only in America." They sing, "Only in America can a kid without a cent/Get a break and maybe grow up to be president."

Luck and possibility are intertwined because a change in luck can determine your possibilities. And possibility is the stuff of visions. Think of the Horatio Alger stories that were popular in nineteenth-century America. Young Horatio is a plucky lad who does everything right — he sells newspapers to support his poor mother, he studies hard, and always looks for opportunity — but it isn't until he saves a rich man's daughter that his fortune turns.

Is Horatio Alger just the stuff of myth? Consider David Sarnoff, a young boy who worked his way up from the ghettos of New York's Lower East Side, and studied what was then the newly discovered invention called radio, until he landed a job as a radio operator at the station atop New York's John Wanamaker department store. In 1912, while he was manning his post, the distress signal from the sinking *Titanic* came over his receiver in Morse code. Sarnoff stayed awake for more than two days, coordinating rescue efforts and relaying news to the nation's newspapers. The head of General Electric, who was aboard the ship and survived, told young Sarnoff that if he ever had an idea for a business, GE would finance it. That idea came a decade later, when companies began to broadcast sound over radio waves. Sarnoff went to GE and, with its financial resources, founded the Radio Corporation of America (RCA), the pioneer in the coast-to-coast presentation of radio programming and the Microsoft of the pre-Depression Roaring Twenties.

Supplying the Human Element

The philosopher Pierre Teilhard de Chardin once wrote that the greatest force for the advancement of the human species is "a great hope held in common." That's what a vision is. It's what moves people to action, and, because of their action, it's what allows an organization to make progress.

Almost by definition, people are believers. They may not be religious — they may, in fact, be atheists — but almost everyone believes in something. To lack belief is to lack the will to live, and when people lack the will to live, they often turn to a charismatic leader who gives them something — anything — to believe in. When people feel sufficiently hopeless and threatened, they turn to an individual who promises that they can have a better life, even if it means at the expense of someone else's life. That is at once the great weakness and the great strength of belief. After you believe, you're willing to go to great lengths to protect your belief.

Vision supplies people with something in which to believe. Martin Luther King Jr.'s "I Have a Dream" speech crystallized in the minds of millions of Americans the vision of racial peace and diversity and gave momentum to the civil rights movement. King had both the vision and the courage to express his vision. King paid the ultimate price for his vision, but his words and dreams continue to provide a positive goal to race relations in the United States.

Leadership often focuses on seemingly mundane tasks — raising profitability, fixing a problem, expanding the membership of a group, or winning a championship. Any of these things can be accomplished without belief. They are, after all, just tasks that can be mastered by hard work and discipline. And people will often decide that it's in their own best interest to provide the hard work needed to accomplish a task, without the pushing and prodding of a leader, if only to see something through to completion. But to truly move forward — to achieve a higher purpose — a group must be committed to the leader's vision.

A vision is a reminder of why you joined the group

You can't gain the commitment of followers for long without a vision. Inevitably, things go wrong.

>> A star player is injured and the team's season looks like it's going down the drain.

>> A competitor comes out with an improved product, and your carefully thought-out sales plan goes up in smoke.

A vision reminds everyone why they are members of your group, and why they are struggling. A vision tells people that no matter what happens, their struggle is worthwhile. By supplying a vision, a leader can hold a group together, even when things go wrong. The group accepts that whatever setbacks it may be suffering, the object of the vision means that they can achieve ultimate success.

When George Washington spent the winter of 1777–1778 in Valley Forge, Pennsylvania, his troops were starving and the desertion rate was high. The Continental Congress had not appropriated money to pay the army, provisioning of the army had been mismanaged, and the soldiers could see across to English-held areas, where people were well fed. One day, near Christmas in 1777, Washington told his army that every man had the right to decide for himself whether to return home, but that, if they did, the dream of liberty and freedom from England would be lost forever. Almost no one left Valley Forge, even though staying meant enduring one of the worst winters on record, and nearly starving to death. The common belief in liberty, coupled with improved training, turned Washington's army of 11,000 men from a ragtag bunch of rebels into an efficient fighting force when they left their encampment the following June. Their belief in Washington's vision had seen them through.

Whether your group is an entrepreneurial company, a volunteer group, a team, or a large, established company, if it does not have a clearly articulated vision, maintaining the group's cohesiveness for very long will be difficult. Before joining a group, learn as much as you can about its vision for the future. If you don't subscribe to this vision, remaining true to the group's mission as a follower or member will be close to impossible.

TIP

Remember, whether you're a leader or a follower, you should gain as complete a knowledge of the group's vision as possible.

A vision attracts commitment and energizes people

People need a significant challenge, something they can commit to that is worthy of their best efforts. Getting people to make an emotional investment in the pursuit of an incremental gain in quarterly profits is never easy, but people are willing, even eager, to commit voluntarily and completely to something they perceive as truly worthwhile. Every enterprise faces obstacles in its development and growth, but without a shared vision, people will not willingly endure what is necessary to turn an idea into a successful enterprise. A shared vision makes them more than willing to sacrifice time, effort, and energy on behalf of the enterprise.

In that context, a vision is a rallying point for people. Often, a vision that can be crafted into a well-articulated story attracts followers to a movement all by itself, even without a leader having to actively recruit members. For example, when Charles and Maurice Saatchi started their advertising agency, Saatchi & Saatchi, in the late 1980s, they were considered to be so much in the forefront of their business that resumes flooded through the door. Not only that, but companies in related fields, such as market research and public relations, begged to be acquired by the brothers, so that they could be part of the Saatchi's vision, as it changed the face of advertising in the United Kingdom, and then around the world.

Establishing a Standard of Excellence

Most people want to be thought of as doing a good job, to have the feeling that they are effectively advancing the organization's purposes, and to be recognized for their contributions. To do so, they have to be clear on what those purposes are and when an action is likely to advance them. A vision spells out the purposes of the organization. It tells employees, suppliers, customers, and competitors what you stand for, and where you see yourself going now and in the future. A vision establishes a standard for everyone to live up to, and lets people benchmark their own progress within an organization.

TIP

At salary review time in your company, write a memo that may loosely be titled, "What I Have Done for You Lately." In that memo, outline your achievements in helping the organization reach its current goals. This kind of memo will help your superiors see why you deserve a raise. But if you really want to be promoted, you should include a section in your memo addressing the ways in which you have helped the organization advance its vision even further.

Helping You Stay Ahead of the Game

A good leader, while managing in the present, is always looking ahead to see what threats are just over the horizon, and what opportunities are there, as well. Vision is a kind of distant, early-warning radar that is set two steps into the future, like a chess player anticipating her response to all the possible moves an opponent may make, and knowing the outcome of the move after that as well. Good leaders train themselves to keep looking toward the horizon and beyond it, while maintaining a firm linkage to the present and to reality.

Becoming a visionary

A vision requires a visionary, someone who can see what may become possible if only one or two things fall into place. The visionary, who is usually — but not always — the leader, has to look at existing events for his or her group and be able to say, "We can do a lot better and a lot different if X and Y can be made to happen."

Here's a look at two visionaries:

>> Gordon Moore, Robert Noyce, and Andrew Grove had the vision to create a computer on a chip — the microprocessor. But they were able to have that vision only because an entire sequence of events had already taken place that suggested to them that their vision was doable.

First, the transistor had to be invented. Then, the integrated circuit, which placed a number of transistors together onto a single piece of silicon, came along. Then, a number of integrated circuits, each with their own logic, or software, had to be put together. During this time, from 1948, when the transistor was invented, until 1971, when Intel, the company they created, introduced the 4004 microprocessor, thousands of engineers at many companies had to work out the processes of continually shrinking the size of each transistor, so that more and more of them could be placed into an ever smaller space. Fulfilling the vision of creating a microprocessor was impossible until all the previous steps had taken place.

But Moore, who was the visionary in the group, saw that it could be done. He had plotted the density of transistors onto silicon chips and had developed something that is now known as "Moore's Law," which states that the number of transistors on a chip doubles every 18 months. Moore figured, rightly, that at a certain point in the doubling, the number of circuits that could be made would be large enough to duplicate the functions of a hard-wired computer memory.

>> Mel Farr, a running back for the Detroit Lions during the 1980s, had a vision of becoming a successful black businessman after he retired from football. Because the Lions are owned by William Clay Ford, a descendant of Henry Ford and an executive of the Ford Motor Company, and because Detroit is the Motor City, Farr thought that the best way to success was through a car dealership. But he discovered that there were few African-American–owned dealerships at the time. A combination of lack of capital and a general

reluctance to sell cars in black neighborhoods had made it difficult for African-American entrepreneurs to move into auto retailing.

Farr examined the problem and determined that the poor credit histories of his customers, perhaps more than anything, were the greatest deterrent to their owning new cars. So he began with used cars, and instituted a tough repossession policy on people who missed their car payments. At the same time, he designed programs to help customers budget their money better, so that there would be less likelihood that they would miss a payment. Farr's business grew steadily, and he acquired a Ford dealership in 1975, eventually increasing his company to a chain of 11 dealerships.

Farr's vision from the beginning was not simply to become successful but to become involved in auto sales. His connections and star status with the Detroit Lions ensured that he would get the chance, and then he made the most of the opportunity after he had it.

Benchmarking everything

Keeping ahead of the competition also entails keeping up with them. Don't be afraid to admit that someone else is doing something better than you are and to take advantage of that person's example.

TIP

As a leader, you're responsible for having a complete knowledge not only of your own group's resources but of the widest possible resources available. Gordon Moore, from Intel, was building on the work of thousands of others, and so should you. If you're running a community group, you should make it your business to find out which other groups — anywhere — are running programs similar to yours, and you should learn from the best. If your Sunday school attendance is down, for example, and you have taken on the role of principal of the school, contact your synod or diocese or synagogue council and find out where Sunday school attendance is up, and then go off and learn what they're doing that you're not.

This process is called *benchmarking*, because it comes from the idea that the best practices are a benchmark for everyone to emulate. But when you benchmark, don't confine your imagination just to Sunday schools. Think about other kinds of programs where attendance is vital, and where people have worked hard to improve it, for example. You may come up with something like a computer user group, or you may even want to take a look at a company whose sales have suddenly begun to improve by double-digit amounts. What are they doing right? Can you use their methods? These questions are the ones you should be asking yourself.

WHEN VISION FAILS

A good example of what happens when vision fails were the sky-high stock market valuations of Internet companies. In 1989, right after the U.S. government decided that it would allow its ARPANET computer communications system to be opened to general use by the public, large companies could have taken over the Net and its communications protocols (which make up the World Wide Web), for next to nothing. But nobody wanted to make even the small investment required, because companies realized that the Net was slow and fragmentary, and that there were still only a couple of million personal computers in homes. The argument was, "How many people want to spend their lives scurrying around the web looking for things?"

But a group of small start-ups, led chiefly by America Online, reasoned that they had little to lose (except some investor money) and much to gain, if web use caught on. Scores of other small entrepreneurs had the same idea, and before long, the Internet was flooded with services, tens of millions of people had hooked up, and companies began using email in place of the telephone for intercompany communications. Internet use skyrocketed, and large companies began to realize that if they wanted to survive into the future, they would have to buy into the burgeoning Net economy. In the meantime, however, the price of entry had risen dramatically. Companies such as America Online and Amazon had developed huge customer bases, which larger, better established companies were willing to pay billions of dollars to have access to. That access price is reflected in the stock prices of e-business companies. If established companies had had some vision of the Internet's potentials, they would have bought in early, made the necessary investments, and reaped the benefits of growth themselves.

That's what vision is all about. It's the ability to see what isn't there in terms of what is. Any established company could have seen that the Internet would grow to become very large at some point. But because leaders of large enterprises become averse to taking risks, they couldn't see far enough over the horizon to know at what point they should make their investment, and so they missed out on a once-in-a-century opportunity.

A Vision Links the Present to the Future

There is an old saying, "The future is now," and whoever first said it probably had vision in mind. A vision is a bridge between the present and the future. Because enterprises are increasingly complex, you can easily lose focus while you're caught up in the pressures of simply getting the job done. A vision moves an organization and its people beyond the status quo and keeps all its people sharply focused on why they are doing what they're doing in the first place. The vision sustains and constantly renews their commitment, keeping the organization moving toward the future, focused on new ideas and services, and keeps them contributing not only to the operation of the organization but to its progress as well.

Building on the present

We're reminded of some old advice about telling jokes: You can't go over the head of the audience. That's a simple way of saying that people have to understand a joke's frame of reference before they can find a joke funny. The same thing is true for visions. If you're in the clothing business, and you assemble your workers and tell them you've decided to turn your company into an Internet service provider, they're going to look at you as though you've just gone bonkers. Nobody in the room knows how to do that, and so your vision for a new enterprise probably means that they are all going to get fired so that you can hire an entirely new team.

Because visions are doable dreams, they have to be able to take advantage of the resources you have on hand, or those you may logically be able to get. You can have the best idea and easy access to venture capital, but if you don't have the experience, persuading others to let you do what you think you want to do will be difficult. The best business plan in the world and the ablest people are not enough if no linkage exists between what those people are doing in the present and what they propose to do in the future.

Envisioning the future

Most people have difficulty seeing tomorrow, let alone next week or ten years from now. But successful leadership requires you to envision the future and persuade other people that your dream is both realizable and worth pursuing. This is a two-step process. First, your vision must be realistic and doable. We're not talking about get-rich-quick schemes here. Many people have interesting visions that are immediately dismissed by their friends, family, or co-workers as pie-in-the-sky, or unrealistic, or beyond the scope of their resources. Listen carefully to what people are telling you and see whether you can connect the dots in your mind to create the vision that you see.

The second part of the process is your ability to convince others that your vision is worth pursuing. Often, a person who has a vision isn't a leader at the time the vision appears. He or she has to articulate the vision, and by doing so attract followers who believe in the vision strongly enough to help make it a reality. In articulating a vision, the person emerges as a leader. In other cases, a group has a goal that it can't reach and needs someone to help get them there, and so a leader comes on board. Then the vision does not belong to the leader alone but to the group as a whole, and cooperation is generally easier to come by.

A Vision Is a Doable Dream

In the first part of this chapter, you read about the need for a vision, which is often the dream of a single individual who sees an opportunity to create change, or sees a need for a product or service, an application of a technology, an opportunity to create a more effective organization, or an opportunity to right a wrong.

But the transformation of a vision into reality can often be a complex process. Many visions, though doable in theory, require tremendous technological or social changes to become reality. This section shows you how to do that.

Of all the elements that a leader must successfully execute, a clear vision is perhaps the most important. Remember *Man of La Mancha* and Don Quixote's "Impossible Dream," in which he was trying to right the unrightable wrong, beat the unbeatable foe? A vision is just the opposite. A vision is a doable dream based on the realities of a group's strengths and resources. Far from being wide-eyed and dreamy, a leader's vision is sober and reflective.

Understanding what is doable

What is doable? The physicist Isidor I. Rabi, who worked on the Manhattan Project and later won a Nobel Prize, once said, "With enough money, you can even suspend the laws of Nature. Temporarily!" What he meant was that if a thing could be imagined, it could be done. You have to figure out the cause, whether the price is too great to pay for the result, and, finally, whether the result is sufficiently permanent to justify the effort. Those are often hard to know in the short term, but what makes certain leaders great is the persistence of their vision. For example:

» Carbon paper was invented in the late 1800s, shortly after the invention of the typewriter. Carbon paper had been in use for about 50 years, and was the accepted form of duplicating, when Chester Carlson decided in the 1930s that a better way to produce copies quickly had to exist. Carlson's idea, a process that he initially called electrophotography, slowly evolved over a decade into a process called xerography (Greek for "dry writing"). By the time electrophotography became xerography, in the late 1940s, Carlson's original work had been supplemented by the work of hundreds of engineers and scientists from the Battelle Memorial Institute in Columbus, Ohio. It then took the Haloid Company, which bought the process from Battelle and Carlson, another two years to create a machine that could actually make copies, but the resulting company, renamed Xerox, began with Chester Carlson's vision.

» In the case of McDonald's restaurants, the initial vision of a good hamburger restaurant belonged to Dick and Mac McDonald, two brothers who opened the first "Golden Arches" hamburger stand in San Bernardino, California, in

1948. But it was Ray Kroc, a man who sold malted milk machines, who was so impressed by the constant traffic around the McDonald brothers' hamburger stand that he kept coming back, trying to figure out why it attracted so much more business than other hamburger stands in town. Kroc finally figured out that it was not quality alone, but consistency — the ability to become efficient and profitable by doing the same things the same way over and over — that was making the McDonalds wealthy. With this in mind, he went to the McDonald brothers in 1954 and persuaded them to let him sell franchises that would exactly duplicate their methods. A year later, Kroc opened his first McDonald's in Des Plaines, Illinois, and built the concept of repeatable consistency into a multibillion-dollar company. The McDonald brothers were doing what came naturally, but it was Kroc who had the inspirational vision to figure out exactly what made McDonald's, and not some other hamburger chain, worth replicating.

» In 1905, Sarah Breedlove, a black washerwoman, had an idea for a product that would straighten the curly hair of African-American people, and began to sell it locally in St. Louis, where she lived. It was a modest success until she hit upon the idea of hiring other people to sell her product as agents. By 1910, she had nearly 3,000 agents selling her hair straightener and other beauty products developed for African Americans. Having married Charles J. Walker in 1906, she named her company the Madame C.J. Walker Company and moved its headquarters to Indianapolis, where she became America's first African-American millionaire.

What all of these visions share in common is that they began with ideas, usually for products. But it was not the idea that attracted followers; it was the *outcome* of the idea. People weren't attracted to the way McDonald's made and sold hamburgers, but to the hamburgers themselves. People were attracted to the idea that black women could gain more freedom in their hairstyles rather than to a sales device.

HEIGH-HO, HEIGH-HO!

Consider Walt Disney's vision for Disneyland. Here is how he wrote it: "The idea of Disneyland is a simple one. It will be a place for people to find happiness and knowledge. It will be a place for parents and children to spend pleasant times in one another's company: a place for teachers and pupils to discover greater ways of understanding and education. Here the older generation can recapture the nostalgia of days gone by, and the younger generation can savor the challenges of the future. Here will be the wonders of Nature and Man for all to see and understand." That is a clearly articulated vision, and it has carried Disneyland and Walt Disney World along for decades.

Keeping the vision simple

A vision should be both simple and straightforward. People who are asked to help turn a vision into reality should be able to understand what the vision is, without a lot of additional explanation, and should have an innate sense that the vision is doable even before they begin to explore what's necessary to make it so.

In a sense, a vision represents an interesting paradox: Visions are not obvious before they are articulated, or they would already exist. But after they are spoken, or put down on paper, they should inspire an "Aha!" or "But, of course!" from whomever is asked to help make the vision a reality. One obvious indicator of whether you want someone on your team to help make your vision a reality is how quickly he or she can grasp both the uniqueness and the obviousness of your vision.

A Vision Is Not Just an Idea

Although many visions begin as ideas, a vision is different from an idea. Ideas are abundant. Almost everybody has them at one time or another. An idea that becomes a vision begins with the desire to bring the idea to reality. Many people's ideas never get beyond the "What if . . ." or "I wish I could . . ." stage, because they don't have the energy, the will, or the ability to carry their idea forward. To turn a vision into reality requires leadership, the willingness to embrace the responsibility for getting the job done.

Many more ideas are abandoned after a bit of research, when people discover that a reasonable approximation of what they want to do, or what they wish, already exists. But a few ideas become fully fledged visions when, with a little help from other people, a leader manages to translate an idea into reality. A vision depends on the ability to create a plan and a team, and the ability to meld the two into an organization that can bring success to the marketplace. By marketplace, we don't mean only the world of business. We mean a marketplace of ideas and a marketplace of social responsibility.

The following sections examine the components of vision.

A vision depends on your ability to create a team

Most ideas come from the knowledge, experience, or imagination of a single individual. Edwin Land of Polaroid, Chester Carlson of Xerox, Fred Smith of FedEx,

Creating a Vision

and many others are singular individuals who had a defining idea of a product or service. But shaping a vision from an idea is seldom the work of a single individual. Every single personal vision that was translated into a successful and sustainable enterprise was done by bringing together a group of forward-looking, knowledgeable people who understood the nature of the idea, its implications for the future, and the knowledge, resources, and leadership needed to make it work.

Perhaps the single best example of the kind of team it takes to turn a vision into a successful enterprise is the saga of Apple Computer. The idea for a cheap, affordable personal "computer for the rest of us" was not new. Companies such as Altair had been selling kit computers almost from the moment the microprocessor was invented in 1978, even though the computers didn't do very much and were lacking in the features we think of as typical of personal computers. But Steve Jobs and Steve Wozniak, two kit-computer builders, thought that they could mass-produce a low-cost computer that did more. Their early effort, the Apple I, was a hand-built machine, but their second device, the Apple II, incorporated major changes gleaned from a visit to Xerox's famed Palo Alto Research Center (PARC). Xerox had developed an advanced computer called the Star nearly a decade earlier that incorporated all the features we expect to see in a personal computer — a graphical user interface, a mouse, a large screen, WYSIWYG (what you see is what you get) word processing, and more.

When they went out looking for money to finance their vision, their venture capitalists put together a team and really went to work. With Jobs in command of the vision, they teamed the new company with Regis McKenna, a public relations specialist, who designed the company's logo, and Mike Markkula, a savvy finance man who helped keep expenses under control. With additional team members handling software, and Frog Design providing hardware design integration, the first product, the Apple II, was a hit almost from the beginning. As the product was introduced, other members, such as Jay Chiat, who created the company's innovative advertising, were brought on to the team. Without the total team effort, the personal computer would have remained an artifact in a garage, and Silicon Valley would not be the driving force it is today.

One of the best ways to learn about team building is to play Fantasy Baseball, in which you join a baseball league that exists only on paper. Each person in the league is a manager, and each person is given a certain amount of money to "spend" on personnel. Managers "buy" players until their roster is filled and their money exhausted. The players are actual major leaguers. As each day's major league scores and batting averages are recorded, you get the production of the roster members of your team. So if you were smart enough to put both Mark McGwire and Sammy Sosa on your team at the start of the 1998 season, you would have received all their home runs and all their strikeouts as well. The object of Fantasy Baseball is to force you to think about real players in real situations, and to force you to put those players together in optimal conditions.

When you're attempting to translate an idea into a vision, you have to do the same thing. You begin with a clean sheet of paper and a question: "If there were no restrictions on resources, where could I go and what could I do?" Such questions eliminate, for the moment, all the arguments from potential naysayers about why your idea can't possibly work, and why your vision should be discarded, or reduced in scope. By asking a no-limits question, you confront physicist Isidor I. Rabi's statement that there are no limits, except the laws of nature, and that even those can be overcome for a while if you want to spend the money.

Over the following weeks and months, if you investigate your idea, research it, and learn as much as possible about what it may take to bring it to fruition, a vision may emerge that has a chance of succeeding. As you're doing your research, you're beginning to know what types of knowledge you don't have, and what knowledge and experience will be essential to making your vision into a reality. As the leader, it's your job to begin building a team.

You have to pencil in a name and responsibilities to fill in each gap in your knowledge. If you're intent on providing shelter for the homeless, for example, you have to get someone who knows about permits for homeless shelters, an architect, a banker or some type of money person, someone who has worked with the homeless and knows their needs, and someone who can be an advocate of your project to people who can help you. Each one of those people will be able to help you make your vision a reality, and each will help you shape your original vision and give it the limitations and scope that will make the project doable.

Because the process of building a vision generally involves the people who have to carry it out, team building helps you achieve a consensus and a common commitment at the early stages of a project that are needed to take a vision from a dream to a reality.

A vision depends on the ability to create a plan

As you go from an idea or a dream to a vision, you will slowly begin the process known as *planning*. The purpose of planning is to answer this question: "What should we be doing and how should we do it?" William Ouchi, a consultant who wrote *Theory Z: How American Business Can Meet the Japanese Challenge* (published by Perseus Books), has observed that Japanese firms spend about 80 percent of the time required to launch a new business in planning, and only 20 percent in execution, whereas most American firms spend 20 percent of their time in planning and the rest of the time floundering around, struggling to execute properly. To give any organization its best possible chance of success, you must develop an idea, within the knowledge and experience of the team, and within the context of its marketplace — where it is now and where it's likely to be five years from now. That plan will determine whether your vision is doable, and whether it can become a reality.

Information — we want information!

Good planning begins with collecting information. Information is not a set of half-baked hunches, nor is it the personal opinions of the members of the team. It's composed of what Harold Geneen, the former chief executive of ITT, called unshakable facts. Said Geneen, "No matter what you think, try shaking it to be sure."

In addition to the facts, planning rests on an agreed-upon set of assumptions about the marketplace, your resources, and your knowledge and skills. If you don't have agreement on these areas, your planning will never have a firm foundation, and you will constantly be shifting emphasis.

Planning is everybody's business

Planning requires the participation of every member of your team. If people don't participate, you'll never know whether they have wholly bought into the assumptions inherent in the vision or not. Spend time with all the team members so that you know their point of view going into the creation of an enterprise. When you're turning a vision into a business, you're likely to find many things that you haven't anticipated. One of them should not be sudden and late opposition from members of your own team.

Proper planning involves finding out what your resources are, and aligning those resources with your vision. Proper planning is also the opposite. If you're bent on your vision, you must make a list of the resources you're going to need to make your vision a reality, and couple that with a list of where to find the resources you need. If you need money, you need to develop a comprehensive list of venture capitalists and bankers. If you need experts, you should be talking to the best and the brightest in your field, asking them for recommendations.

A Vision Is Based on Reality

Having a vision when you have little or no hope of bringing it to reality doesn't do you much good. All successful visions begin with a sober assessment of the strengths and resources of the group. Those strengths are people, capital, location, intellectual property, desire, market share, and previous success, no matter what kind of enterprise you're leading. (This may require a little analogizing on your part.) If you're coaching a team, you may ask yourself what that has to do with market share. Your winning record is your market share. Your playbook is your intellectual property, your recruiting ability is your capital, and your players are your people. Your desire to win, of course, is desire.

>> The belief that Robert Noyce, one of the founders of Intel, had in his ability to create a microprocessor was based on the fact that he had already co-invented the integrated circuit in 1958. He was one of those thousands of engineers who had worked out the problems of cramming transistors into a small space. Noyce and his partners, Gordon Moore and Andy Grove, had all worked together for another semiconductor company, and they had gained not only experience in running a business enterprise but also an understanding of each other's skills, strengths, and weaknesses, and they had learned to trust each other. Each had specific experience to contribute to the new enterprise — Noyce's technical skill, Moore's long-range planning abilities, and Grove's knowledge of manufacturing. Without those strengths and resources, the company they created, Intel, may not have turned their vision of creating a microprocessor into a reality.

>> By the time Mel Farr, the former Detroit Lion professional-football-player-turned-car-dealer, had opened his first new car dealership in a lower-income neighborhood, he had already proved to skeptical automobile companies that he could sell used cars in Detroit successfully, and that he had developed practices to ensure that his customers had credit records similar to those in suburban neighborhoods. Each new step that Farr took in widening his vision was based on his prior experience and on the growing resources of his company.

A vision is not short-term. A vision is something that will carry you through the achievement of several short-term goals, to achieve some sort of enduring greatness or distinction, something for which your group or enterprise will be known and remembered. It can be as simple as the desire to open and operate the best French restaurant in the neighborhood, the restaurant that everybody talks about and that will cause people to line up for reservations. Or it could be the goal of establishing an employment agency that helps large companies effectively recruit minorities. Every vision is different because it's based on the experiences, strengths, and resources of the person having the vision. But all visions should be the same in that they are a challenge — a call to action — to the people who will formulate a plan to execute the vision.

Thinking beyond available resources

In addition to recognizing the abilities of existing resources, a good leader thinks beyond the available resources. If you're running a company that makes toothpaste, you have to consider resources from all over the world. You have to consider your intellectual property to be your formula, but also the work that researchers may be doing elsewhere that may cause you to consider changing your formula. The point is, you can't look only at what you have. You must also look at what you may have if you were a little bigger or a little richer. A good leader is always a little covetous of what is just over the hill and wants to take his group there.

Responding to diminishing resources

The best vision in the world, coupled with the savviest knowledge and the deepest experience, can't help you if your resource base is cut or diminished. What happens, for example, when a rival company comes in and hires away your most knowledgeable workers? What happens when you're running a soccer league and a group of parents set up a rival league that is better-funded than yours? What happens when you own the best restaurant in town and decide to open another branch, but the community won't okay your zoning request?

Any good leader has to respond to diminishing resources — or any new situation. Leaders have to be resourceful, which means that they have to find new ways to do the things they were doing before, or new ways to do new things, if they want to put a vision into practice.

You should never be hindered by the word "no" if there is something that you really want to do — assuming, of course, that what you want to do is legal, moral, and ethical (if not, then you should always be deterred by the word "no"). A way to turn a vision into a reality always exists.

A Vision Helps You Harness Opportunities

Don't think that opportunities are rare — they are abundant and have always been in every age. The magazine *Business Week*, for example, started in 1929, at the beginning of the Great Depression. The great failure of companies and individuals is not that they lack for ideas, but that so few ideas are well thought out and planned. We live in a society of abundance, but that abundance still rests on a product failure rate of greater than 90 percent.

Forget the phrase "Opportunity knocks only once." The reality is that opportunity is a steady hammer on your windows and doors, a constant noise that you spend most of your time attempting to block out by stuffing cotton in your ears. Opportunities are everywhere, if you can learn to recognize them for what they are.

Most opportunities arise in one of three ways, covered in the following sections.

Spotting an opportunity

In 1980, IBM was looking for a way to respond to the growing strength of Apple Computer, Inc., but did not want to invest the resources to invent a personal computer of its own. Bill Gates told IBM that he could do it to a very tight deadline at a very low cost. Gates bought the rights to QDOS (short for "quick and dirty operating system") for $50,000 from Seattle programmer Tim Paterson, renamed it the Microsoft Disk Operating System (MS-DOS), and resold the rights to use it to IBM. Gates spotted an opportunity and created a giant company out of it.

Opportunities are out in the world all the time. All you need to do is open your eyes. Debbi Fields was walking through a mall with her husband and suddenly had a hankering for a chocolate chip cookie. She couldn't get one anywhere at the mall, so she said, "If I have a hankering, maybe other people will, too. And if I can fresh bake them, the smell will attract customers." Out of that idea came a vision for Mrs. Field's Cookies, one of the great franchise hits of the 1980s. It wasn't a giant leap for mankind, but it satisfied a genuine need.

If you want to get an idea of what kind of opportunity exists, take a trip to a big city and walk the streets for a few days. Look at the great number and variety of the shops, and every time you see a store that looks like nothing you've ever seen before in your own hometown or your local mall, go in and look at the merchandise. Take along a notebook and make notes. We guarantee that you'll come back home with at least a hundred ideas.

Searching out an opportunity

If a business is making money for one firm, it means that at least enough of a market exists for one, but it probably means that untapped market potential is available for a competitor. Never be deterred by someone else's success. In fact, that ought to spur you to try to emulate it, and then beat it. Some of the most successful businesses began as me-too operations that one-upped existing companies.

The same thing goes for social organizations. Just because a successful charity exists in town doesn't mean that it's immune from competition. If you don't like the way the organization goes about its work, join it, and learn as much as you can about how the organization works (and doesn't work) and where and how the money is spent. You'll find the organization's weaknesses, and doing so will help you develop a plan for your own charity that will allow you to offer the same or better service at a lower cost, which ultimately will help you attract sponsorship. Your overhead and effectiveness will be your selling point.

Creating an atmosphere in which ideas flourish

In 1944, Minnesota Mining and Manufacturing Company chief executive William McKnight decided that the company could not rely solely on Scotch tape for its future. So he created a policy that encourages innovation, saying, "Management that is destructively critical when mistakes are made kills initiative, and it is essential that we have many people with initiative if we're to continue to grow." Today 3M expects its engineers and technical people to spend up to 15 percent of their time tinkering with new products. This time, called *bootleg time,* has been responsible for the creation of thousands of successful new products, such as Post-it notes and reflective, glow-in-the-dark tape.

Employees deep within every organization often have ideas about new products or services — and about possible new directions for your enterprise — but they simply haven't been asked to contribute. As a leader, your job is to ask them. You have to find a way — beyond the typical suggestion box — to get your people to come up with new ideas that move your enterprise's vision forward.

Many firms pay employees for suggestions that save or make money. But firms should also get into the habit of developing vision quest competitions. If leadership can articulate its vision — and it should if it's effective leadership —it should hold a competition every few years in which employees are encouraged to write about how they would extend the vision over a succeeding five- or ten-year period. Ask people what challenges they think the firm is going to face and how the firm may deal with those challenges. You'll get a lot of expected answers, but you may find a future leader deep in the pack. If you find such a visionary, put him or her in charge of developing the vision into a plan.

During the 1970s, Corning Glass Works hired Robert Christopher, formerly an editor at *Time* and *Newsweek,* to become its house visionary. Christopher spent some time learning about the glass business, and then he spent time exploring the American political, economic, and social structure. One of his ideas — that Corning develop solar heat exchangers — was considered good enough for the company to turn it into a business. Although the idea ultimately did not prove workable — the price of oil plummeted by the time the heat exchanger was developed, so that solar power diminished as a viable, marketable product — the company proved that it could generate new visions and turn them into reality.

CHECKLIST FOR LAUNCHING AN ENTERPRISE

Perhaps your vision involves launching a new business. Before doing so, double-check that you have the knowledge, expertise, and experience to successfully launch a new enterprise.

- Do you know your market? Nothing happens without sales. And sales come only with good marketing. Who are your customers going to be? Where are they located? Do you know what quantities they will buy? At what prices? Through what channels? Remember, these questions apply to nonprofit organizations as well as to products and services that are going to be sold for a profit.

- Do you have an essential expertise? If you open a restaurant, for example, do you know how to cook or manage a dining room? If you want to launch a high-tech business, can you be the technical whiz? Remember that "if wishes were horses, beggars would ride." It's not enough to have the desire to do something. You have to have some practical expertise, or the chance of acquiring it, before you can hope to turn a vision into reality.

- Do you know how to run an enterprise? If you've never been a leader at any level, it's hard to start at the top. You need to acquire some experience leading and turning visions into reality at some level, and then continue acquiring experience. This is what is known as the *scale problem.* If your only experience is in running a ten-person enterprise, leading a thousand people will be substantially more difficult for you. You should beg off, and take on a hundred-person task first.

If you have a great idea for an enterprise but not enough skills, consider finding a partner who shares your values and your enthusiasm for the idea, and who complements your skills and knowledge. Many successful businesses, including Apple, Intel, Hewlett-Packard, and Microsoft, started that way. Remember: It takes a team to turn a vision into reality. Very few people can do it by themselves.

Moving from an idea to a plan

Good planning begins with collecting information and testing assumptions. Unfortunately, many enterprises fail because leaders, in their enthusiasm for an idea, fail to plan or test. To succeed, the idea that underlies a vision should be able to answer the following questions:

> **» Why should customers buy your product or service?** What is the significant difference between your product and its competition? Why should a person buy from you rather than from someone else? A product or service does not

have to be limited to a company. If you're starting a new church or synagogue, or contemplating starting a charter school, you will be offering a vision of the delivery of a service. Why is yours different from — and better than — what people can already get? Until you can answer that question convincingly to the satisfaction of a potential member or customer, you don't have an enterprise.

» **Will it last? Is it enduring or a fad?** You'd be surprised at how many things fit the phrase "It seemed like a good idea at the time." Before you invest a lot of time and effort, take the trouble to investigate whether conditions are likely to change in the near future that will make your product or service obsolete.

» **Will competition let you survive?** What is the experience of others in your chosen competitive field? Who are the big players? Will they ignore you, try to force you out of business, or offer to buy you out? These questions are not ones to be answered lightly. Many excellent ideas never make it to the marketplace simply because their developers did not have the resources to see their idea through to victory and were squeezed out by better-financed competition. When you're contemplating starting a new enterprise — whether it's a business or a charitable organization — you have to ask yourself what the barriers to entry are. If they are low enough for you to enter, will they be low enough to attract additional competitors? And what about resources? If your major resource is people, your competitor may simply be able to outspend you and lure your best people away.

» **Can it be profitable?** Good enterprises require good profits. If you're starting a business, will it provide you with enough profit margin to allow you to maintain a steady pace of growth in the face of rising competition? If you're running a nonprofit, are you running it efficiently enough so that you can increase your levels of service without taxing the membership? Can you generate enough social profit to attract additional donations for your good work? That should be your goal, and if your enterprise is going to operate on a shoestring, you should rethink how you're doing your work.

» **Can it be implemented?** Are you using the right technology? Can you find the right people? Can you repeat what you're doing consistently? Can your enterprise be financed adequately? Turning a vision into reality requires resources. You should be able to design into your planning document a large margin for error, on the assumption that things are going to go wrong along the way. If you rely on a key person, what happens if a car hits him or her? Can you replace the person quickly? Make a depth chart so that you'll know whom to turn to in the event of the unforeseen.

Likewise, what happens when you're working furiously on a technology and a new technology turns out to work better than yours? Can you shift gears fast enough, or will you be dead in the water even before you start? You should make it your business not to be taken by surprise by events.

>> **Can the enterprise grow?** Most enterprises, except specialty retail businesses and local social service agencies, ultimately fail if they don't grow. Does your enterprise have the potential to continue growing? Will your success lead to other products and to leadership in its field? Do you have a plan to move your enterprise from a local to a regional to a national level? You should be thinking of the next stage even while you're busy planning the current stage of your enterprise.

>> **Will being in this enterprise satisfy your needs?** Start by asking yourself the question, "What would I do if I had no limits?" Then, after you've finished the planning process — but before you begin to implement your vision — ask yourself, "Do I really want to do this?" Implementing a vision takes time, energy, and commitment. It may require you to spend countless hours away from your family and friends. It may put you in contact with a lot of stubborn, tiresome people. If you're not prepared to "live the vision," think seriously about whether you should be leading the charge, or whether you need to find someone else to be the leader while you take on the role of *consigliere* — the behind-the-scenes advisor.

In turn, ask yourself whether your idea-turned-vision really inspires you to do your best. Does it fit your lifestyle? Will it meet your long-term goals? Is it worth the effort? Whatever you decide to undertake, remember that executing a vision takes maximum, unswerving commitment. Other people will be counting on you and pinning their hopes on your leadership. If you can't embrace that responsibility, rethink your position.

A Vision Is Dynamic

In many organizations, leaders know that their tenure is limited so a common tendency is to not want to make plans too far into the future. "After all," the leader reasons, "I'm not going to be here to see my plans carried out, and I don't want my vision to become a burden and an imposition on the person who succeeds me." This idea is wrong-headed. Because you don't know much about the quality of the people who may succeed you, giving your group or organization a very strong vision is always important so that they have a constant sense of mission and an expanding sense of possibility.

In fact, one of the jobs of a good leader is to spread a sense of vision throughout the organization. It's not enough for the leader alone to have a vision. That vision must be integral to everything that every member of the group does, so that when new challenges or opportunities arise, somebody — not necessarily the leader of the moment — will recognize that the time has arrived for an expansion or a change of vision.

Many leaders are reactive or hierarchical, which is to say that they are in the wrong place or are there at the wrong time. Such leaders often lack vision, but they can be effective nonetheless — if the situational leader before them provided them with a solid vision.

Because visions change, you should review the driving forces of your group on a regular basis. Say, for example, that you're trying to open the best day-care center in the area, and after a lot of hard work, you did exactly that. Now what do you do? Do you improve the existing facilities to the point where they are "gold-plated" — that is, filled with expensive and unnecessary luxuries — or do you attempt to expand your day-care vision to new sites so that other parents can have access to the same high-quality facilities?

Chapter **4**

Leading across Cultures

I nclusion is a big part of what leadership has become and is about. A smart leader wants to put together the best possible team, but the definition of *best* has changed over the years. Winning is still the ultimate goal. However, smarter people have begun to question what the idea of winning really means. In this chapter, you look at ways to become a leader of a wider, more inclusive group of people.

Leading in a Diverse World

Not by right, but by statistical preponderance, a leader is still more than likely a white male — and in many enterprises, a middle-aged white male who has spent a good portion of his career leading other white males. When women talk about "glass ceilings" and minorities talk about invisible barriers, at least part of what they're talking about is the fact that the biggest determinant in being given a leadership position is often time in grade. People are promoted from below in most organizations, and women and minorities may not yet have large enough numbers in the white-collar work force to have become visible as leaders, although their numbers are rising as time goes on.

The need for organizations and groups to compete for resources in a free market-place puts the heat on any leader to find ways to bring the best resources in the direction of his or her group. Women and minorities are important customers who spend real money and are quick to pick up on the hypocrisy of a leadership group wanting something and giving little in return.

The power of consumers — of goods, services, and volunteer activity — is probably one of the two or three factors most responsible for the profound shift in the way we perceive leaders and the demands we make on them. The power of consumers gives followers almost unlimited bargaining power, and thanks to the likes of people such as Martin Luther King, Jr., and Jesse Jackson, Sr., what they have bargained for the most is a seat at the table of power.

The civil rights and women's rights struggles of the 1960s through the 1980s have given way to the struggle to become truly inclusive. No longer is it enough to take a token person from a minority group — like the schoolyard captain forced to take one or two unpopular players onto his team — and put that person in a place where she will be visible but have no real input. One of the great benefits of diversity when it is truly practiced is the way it enlarges the context in which you work. Other cultures, other points of view, and other ways of doing things can add immeasurably to a team's problem-solving skills and to its creativity.

For a typical white male organizational leader, the trick is to translate this knowledge into an active reality. How do you manage people who are different from you, without appearing patronizing or condescending? How do you communicate to people whose cultures and work habits may be substantially different from your own or what the team needs?

Likewise, if you are not a white male — if you are female, a member of a minority group, or both, you can't allow yourself to fall into the same sad ruts that older-style leaders have wandered. You cannot decide to favor your group just because you want to help people "make up for lost time" or because you have some notion of getting even. You still have to figure out how to build the best team, so that may mean including the best-experienced white males.

Start with the basics: Leadership is about eliciting cooperation from others, and listening to and putting the needs of others above your own needs. To lead in a diverse organization, you need to reverse the order of those three fundamentals.

Why reverse the order of the fundamentals? The more homogeneous and like-minded a group is, the easier it is to elicit cooperation. The more diverse a group is, the greater the number of variables, so this task is the most difficult and requires the most time and effort. The same thing goes for listening. If your group is a lot like you, you'll have a pretty good idea of what they are going to tell you. But if it's a diverse group, you're going to have to learn how to listen to different voices and actually hear them from their own viewpoint, not only your own. But putting others above yourself is the easiest thing to do when a group is diverse. Elevating the group is the most direct way for a leader to show that he or she is human and is willing to give encouragement and commitment at a human level to the group.

Putting the diverse needs of your group first

The first and simplest question you have to ask yourself as a leader in a diverse world is, "If I am leading people who are different from me, what do they need to be able to work up to the level that I require?"

You may need to supply different tools, as the Volvo people found when they began hiring women to work in their car plants and discovered that conventional hand tools didn't fit a woman's hands. Or you may need to supply special equipment, ramps, and transportation, as a number of companies have found in bringing wheelchair-bound workers into their factories. You may need to expand medical benefits policies if you have workers who are HIV-positive. The point is, if you have workers who have special needs, they'll be more preoccupied with those needs than your needs or the team's needs until you can do something to improve their situations.

So begin from the perspective that it's your responsibility as a leader to help your team solve its problems. If you're about to hire a significant number of Hispanic workers, what do you need to know about their needs? Do they need bilingual training, or can your operating instructions be translated into Spanish? What are their social needs (such as dealing with a suspicious Immigration and Naturalization Service)? Do they need help finding affordable housing? The group may change, but the reality is the same: You must start by understanding what the group needs and then getting those needs fulfilled.

Listening to voices very different from your own

Because you hired a group with an aim toward diversity, you want to profit from that diversity, which begins with listening. You know how you do things. But how do different members of the group solve similar problems? It may be that for each new method you have to teach, you'll learn one new thing, if you are open to that possibility. You should make it a practice to regularly review your business practices, with an eye on learning from your group.

Some people argue that the best way to deal with diversity is to create a neutral business world, a kind of artificial climate where all team members obey an objective set of rules whatever their background while they are members of the team, and that at the end of the day, everyone goes his or her separate way. The logic of this view sounds appealing, but it's based in fiction.

The fiction says that rules are objective. But rules by their nature are *subjective,* made for the convenience of smoothing transactions between and among individuals. In the ideal world, rules are based on conventions that have evolved through give and take, custom, and negotiation, and everyone agrees on the rules. But an ideal world doesn't exist and never did. There is no such thing as neutral business ground, only rules that one group can force another to accept. So accept the subjectivity of rules and conventions, and modify them to fit the needs of the group.

A good example of how subjectivity works in current practice is the ongoing struggle by large, Western-dominated organizations such as the International Monetary Fund and the World Bank to impose economic and business conduct rules on nations that come to both organizations in need of money. Governments are forced to accept a broad range of "reforms" which often serve to do little more than set in play extreme economic and cultural displacement across whole societies, all in the name of neutral business and lending rules.

TIP

A better way of dealing with the differences can be found in the Grameen Bank, a micro-lending organization founded in Bangladesh in 1983. The Grameen Bank started by making tiny loans — usually around $100 — to Bengalis, often women, who wanted to start their own businesses. The borrowers had to be scrupulous about their repayments, and in fact, were. The loan loss rates for the bank are almost nil. The idea of the Grameen Bank has been successfully translated to the United States, where such neighborhood banks as the South Shore Bank in Chicago now have their own community lending operations that are sensitive to the needs of individuals.

Eliciting cooperation from a diverse group

Ever heard the Latin phrase *quid pro quo?* It means "this for that," and in a diverse world, the best way to elicit cooperation is to be able to trade. Because there's no such thing as a neutral business ground, you have to be willing to trade things that are non-critical to your team's ability to get a task accomplished for a diverse team's cooperation in and adherence to methods that will help it reach its goals.

Trading is more important in diverse groups than among homogeneous groups because, among people who are culturally similar, norms and behavior are usually accepted and agreed upon as a condition of existence. So, for example, until well into the 1960s, every white male who went to work in an office in the United States understood that he had to wear a white shirt, a suit, and a tie. But as the workplace became more diverse, new entries didn't have that knowledge. A conventional leader may impose the white shirt and suit culture on all new hires, "because that's the way it's always been done around here," but a better, more effective leader may learn to trade part of the dress code for a willingness of diverse members to take an additional training seminar on their own time.

As the leader, you have the final say on how your team is going to do its job, but that doesn't mean that you need to rigidly impose your ways upon the group when you can persuade it by trading favor for favor, and by using your abilities as a coach and mentor to bring the team around to your way of doing things.

Use your leadership position in a positive way. After all, you are the leader because you know what you are doing and have the vision. Solicit the views of team members, but persuade them that you have a lot to teach them and that if they are willing to learn from you, they are far more likely to achieve their goals.

Emerging as a Leader from a Cultural Group

In a 1984 interview, the French feminist writer Simone de Beauvoir said, "The moment a woman gets power, she loses the solidarity she had with other women. She will want to be equal in a man's world and will become ambitious for her own sake." de Beauvoir perfectly encapsulates the problems of cultural diversity in that quote. If you are different, do you have to surrender that which is different to participate in a group larger than your own, and do you have to surrender your differences completely if you want to become a leader of a larger group than your own?

These questions are powerful and important because they go to the heart of what we expect of leaders. The basis upon which people give trust to a leader often begins and ends with familiarity. "He's one of us," and "she represents our values" are the kinds of sentiments you often hear when you question people about why they will choose one person over another as a leader in an open election. Those feelings put a burden on a would-be leader who is different to minimize their differences or erase them to be accepted and find a place in mainstream society.

With ethnic white males in the US, the subjugation of differences was relatively easy. Dropping the extra vowels from your last name, changing the way you dressed, getting some elocution lessons to eradicate a less-than-desirable accent, and going to night school for more education were all surefire pathways to success for a generation of post-war Jews, Italians, Poles, and Greeks.

Women and non-white minorities, however much they may want to follow along the same path as ethnic whites, cannot. There exists, for want of better words, a visibility problem. A woman in a room full of men, even in a leadership position, is strikingly different in dress, appearance, and mannerisms than her male colleagues. A dark-skinned person amidst a sea of white faces stands out conspicuously, no matter how much everyone believes that race doesn't matter. Often, for a non-white, non-male person in a white-male dominated business world, moving up the organizational ladder evokes loneliness and separation from that individual's own group.

How does an organization deal with leadership issues when there are internal diversity problems? Perhaps the simplest way is for the topmost leaders of organizations to mentor someone who is different from them all the way to the top. CEOs at both Time Warner and American Express have mentored blacks into senior executive roles, while other companies, such as Mattel and Columbia Pictures, have simply jumped women into senior executive positions and demanded that their male colleagues make the adjustment. This is using the power of leadership to impose diversity upon an organization.

TIP

A second, more practical way is to practice diversity from the ground up. Make it a policy to hire from a wide pool of people. Many companies hire from the same couple of dozen schools all the time, because that's where their recruits have come from in the past. Make the effort to open up recruiting to other schools, even if it means that you have to forego a trip to your alma mater or you have to turn down someone in the company who wants you to hire a relative.

Strive to want more

Hiring from a wide pool immediately raises the question of quotas. Should you set aside a certain number of places for minorities? Should your hiring practices force you to hire in such a way that your workforce mirrors the population as a whole? The answer to both questions is emphatically "no." Hire whom you want, but learn to *want* more. Learn to *want* diversity. Learn to *want* other talents, other skills, and other points of view. Learn to appreciate the benefits of seeing your own group through the eyes of others. If women and minorities want to work for your organization or enterprise because they view it as a means to meet their own rising expectations, you should learn to allow your own expectations to rise along with theirs.

Toleration is a dirty word

One of the greatest stumbling blocks to creating a diverse workplace is *toleration.* The definition of the word is "the act of permitting that which is not established or accepted." Toleration at the very least is condescension. It implies that your way of doing things is better, but that for the sake of peace, you will allow another way to co-exist with your own. But your message of implied superiority is always going to grate upon those being tolerated, and it will degrade the cooperation they are likely to give.

TIP

Instead, as a leader, if you really want to promote diversity in your organization, you have to go systematically through all your organization's methods and procedures and either change them if they make no sense or explain them if they do. For example, say you operate a chemical plant, and a Hispanic male with a droopy mustache and a degree in chemical engineering comes to you for a position. If you tell him that it is a condition of his job that he has to shave off his mustache, without explaining that he cannot have any facial hair that may interfere with the safety respirator he may have to wear, you have done him a disservice that he won't soon forget. You may even face a charge of discrimination and a lawsuit. But you have to enforce that rule with everyone. No long hair among your women employees, or anyone, for that matter. These are rules that make sense within the safety context of the job.

But if a rule exists because of tradition or someone's exaggerated sense of what a business place should look like, think seriously about scrapping those rules. Dress codes, for example, are one of the largest areas of contention among minority employees, as is hair length and hair style. People simply do not all have to look alike to be able to get their work done. Such rules are a vestige of the old-fashioned command economy and should be allowed to die the death they deserve.

Leading across International Divides

Almost everything said so far about how you lead when your group is internally diverse is even more critical when you're involved in international situations. To the normal cultural differences amongst your own group, you now have to add differences in language, customs, legal structures, standards, and other oddities, such as work rules and holidays. On the other hand, there are some simple rules about working cross-culturally on an international basis. Because of all the biases we choose to ignore or refuse to acknowledge when we are dealing within our group, we freely admit to them when we are dealing with people who are obviously different.

Commit your brightest and best

When you are putting together an international team, you want your smartest, most flexible people at hand. You want people who have the capacity to learn what the differences are that separate you from your foreign colleagues and who are able to accommodate themselves to those differences. The Romans once said that the definition of being civilized was the ability to live comfortably in another person's culture. So look for civilized people when you are forming your team.

Being civilized begins with *civility*, which is the granting of consideration to others. You will know by experience with your team who are the people who can quietly adjust to new situations, and who are the people who whine, complain, scream, or stamp their feet. Keep the first group and leave the rest home.

Sell participation in an international team as an adventure. Even the most civilized people are often reluctant to commit to something that takes them away from hearth and home, so an international team assignment has to be worth their while in some way that appeals to them. Find out what each person needs, and help him or her achieve it.

Use the de minimus rule in making decisions

When you are working within a multinational or international context, you are going to find yourself up against different rules and regulations. In Germany, for example, boilerplate can be no less than a certain thickness. In England, it has to be at least a certain thickness, but one that is less than the German standard. Whose standard should prevail? If you use the de minimus rule — the minimum standard — you can't go wrong. Your German colleagues will continue to make their boilerplate thicker, because that's the way they do it, but they will not be violating the terms of your agreement by doing so. The added expense is entirely on their shoulders.

When you are sitting down with an international group to plan a mission, getting such issues in the open early is important. Language alone causes its share of misunderstandings.

Understand that capital doesn't make right

A cynical version of the Golden Rule states, "Whoever has the gold makes the rules." That version has undermined more international cooperation than probably any other idea, because people who have capital seem to believe that they have the right to set the rules for an enterprise. "I'm contributing most of the money, so we should do things my way" is the logic.

But there are assets beyond money. Markets are gold, and access to markets is worth at least as much as the investment required to open them up. People are assets, because they represent an opportunity for you to elicit their cooperation in the service of your cause. Knowledge of local customs is an asset, because these customs are integral to the fabric of the lives of the people you want to reach, so respecting local customs and assisting at the local level is imperative for international team success.

When you're deciding how to make your enterprise work internationally, discard the idea that only money counts. Money, although important, is only a small part of a larger equation.

Leading in the Virtual Age

Increasingly, people do not come together in the physical sense to act as teams or to meet as groups. They network. They use the Internet, phones, and computers to cooperate with each other on projects they want to achieve in common. Leading in the Age of the Internet requires at the same time more skills and fewer skills, because certain things that conventional leaders struggle with are already givens.

Start with the need to communicate. Although smart leaders should communicate frequently and in writing, virtual leaders do that of necessity, because their communication is bound by a keyboard and by the structures of databases and spreadsheets. What you share is there for all your team to see, so you have to learn how to write well, how to make your thoughts clear and concise, and how to set internal deadlines, so that people don't just stack your email messages up in their in-boxes and then later throw them away. The Internet has the benefits of a formal logic structure, and virtual leaders take advantage of that structure.

The Internet also favors planners. Writing a business plan for a Net-based enterprise is easier than for many other types of business enterprise because there are software limitations on presentation. Short of writing your own planning program, you are going to use an off-the-shelf program, so you are going to accept the conventions and limitations implicit in the program you choose.

Timeliness is also not a problem on the Net. Because virtual organizations operate in a 24/7 world, the time that you communicate and share is less important than the fact that you do it. As a virtual leader, your major responsibility is sharing and managing the flow of information and then building validity checks into the information you receive, so that your plan does not go GIGO — garbage in, garbage out.

Diversity is also easier in a virtual enterprise. The person who is somehow unacceptable within the confines of an organization suddenly becomes wholly acceptable when he is working remotely. All you have to face is his structured written communication, and you judge him solely upon timeliness and results. There is no longer an arbitrary standard of whether he is "like the boss" in the sense of appearance or class or education. There is simply the question of whether he can meet a work standard.

On the down side, virtual corporations lack a certain human intimacy and camaraderie. Yes, people share jokes over the Internet all the time, and you can always phone. But a joke is not the same when it appears with a routing list of over a hundred names as when someone puts his arm on your shoulder and pulls you close to him, to deliver the punch line.

Virtual leaders thus have to focus even harder on listening (which in this case means learning to read between the lines) and communicating (which means picking up the phone and talking with people, or getting on a plane and visiting them) to maintain team rapport. Eliciting the cooperation of people who are working remotely is also more difficult, because measuring the effect of the incentives you are offering is more difficult.

Time
Management

4

Contents at a Glance

CHAPTER 1: Organizing Yourself 279

Planning 279

Grabbing the Three Keys to Personal Organization. 282

CHAPTER 2: Setting Yourself Up for Success. 285

Getting to Know Yourself 286

Following a System 289

Overcoming Time-Management Obstacles. 291

Garnering Support While Establishing
Your Boundaries 293

Keeping Motivation High 295

CHAPTER 3: Valuing Your Time. 297

Getting a Good Grip on the
Time-Equals-Money Concept. 298

Calculating Your Hourly Income 299

Boosting Your Hourly Value through
Your Work Efforts 301

Making Value-Based Time Decisions
in Your Personal Life. 302

CHAPTER 4: Focusing, Prioritizing, and Time-Blocking 307

Focusing Your Energy with the
80/20 Theory of Everything 308

Getting Down to Specifics: Daily Prioritization 315

Blocking Off Your Time and Plugging
in Your To-Do Items 318

Assessing Your Progress and Adjusting Your
Plan as Needed 322

CHAPTER 5: Controlling Email Overload 327

Managing Email Effectively. 327

Separating Your Work and Private Life 329

Responding to Email More Quickly. 330

Chapter **1**

Organizing Yourself

Time management boils down to a mindset of focusing on your priorities, goals, and objectives for a specific time period — a week, a day, or even an hour. It's the awareness that you are the one who lays claim to your success with the allotment of time you have for today.

Time management is a set of skills that are learned over time. Skills such as time blocking, single handling, and controlling interruptions don't provide you with overnight success, nor can you implement or perfect them quickly. They require patience to fail, adjust, proceed, and then repeat the process many times. But by sticking with it, you can accomplish what you need to without too much stress and panic, and maybe have a little extra time left over.

This minibook is about taking control of the time you have in each day. Effective time management requires a little introspection, some good habits and organizational skills, and a handful of logistical and tactical tools. So take some time and get ready to learn how to manage it successfully.

Planning

The planning process for a project, your workday, or even a vacation is more vexing than the execution. Many people invest countless hours planning that perfect vacation to Hawaii. They research the different island options, review recreation activities, lodging, air travel, dining options . . . the list is endless. But few people plan their day or week with such zeal.

You have to fall in love with planning. You are likely faced each day with tasks you would rather not do, but frequently they seem to be high priorities. For example, most salespeople don't wake up each morning saying, "How exciting! Today I get to call people I don't know and ask for their business!" Most parents don't get up and say in an excited tone, "I get to remind my seventh-grade son ten times to make sure he packs his homework before he goes to school!"

This is where planning brings big dividends to your life. Before your day begins — maybe the night before — plan to do the toughest but most important things first. Tough tasks usually become more challenging to complete as the day progresses and more projects, deadlines, and emergencies crop up. So a good rule is to clear out the tough tasks first.

The sheer act of planning is the key to unlocking creativity, problem solving, mental strength, and clarity. It also increases your mental and physical energy because you see the pathway to a productive day.

REMEMBER

The better you use planning strategies and techniques, the more you can avoid procrastinating away what you don't want to do. At its base level, planning is simply creating a list. You increase your productivity by more than 25 percent by simply writing down what you need to accomplish. The advantages of creating a list are described next.

Achieving peace of mind

Create your list as you wind down for the day so that you're ready to take on tomorrow. You'll be more likely to rest and relax, knowing that tomorrow is planned. You will sleep better knowing that your time and tasks are under control.

Activating your subconscious mind

You trigger your subconscious mind while you sleep. Because you have created your list, your subconscious works on that list while you rest. Your subconscious mind turns the challenges and problems over and over like a rotisserie, and eventually it comes up with strategies and solutions.

Have you ever gone to bed with a problem or challenge only to wake up with a couple of new ideas on how to solve them? Your subconscious mind created those ideas while you slept. Always give your subconscious something to do at night by handing it a list.

The 1,000 percent return

Planning always provides a large payoff. Many studies have indicated that for every minute of planning you save ten minutes in execution, for a 1,000 percent return on your time!

If you have $10,000 and get a 1,000 percent return in one year, at the end of the year you would have $100,000. If you receive a 1,000 percent return the next year, you would have $1,000,000. The initial investment went from $10,000 to $1,000,000 in less than two years. That's the type of return you can receive each day from planning properly.

We've all thought, "I'm too busy to plan." But even if you forced yourself to plan everything in excruciating detail, you most likely would not invest more than a few minutes a day in the entire process. Strange as it may sound, sometimes you may need to slow down to speed up. Planning is the only pathway to greater productivity and quality of life.

The wasted time and mistakes you make are most likely related to a lack of planning. The most epic failures have commonality in lack of planning.

Assemble what you need

After you have planned out your day, a project, or even dinner, you then need to gather your materials to start and complete the project. For example, Colin frequently cooks with his kids, Annabelle and Wesley. They get so excited that when they decide which recipe to make together that they are instantly ready to crack the eggs and start mixing. Colin has to slow them down to read the recipe, gather all the ingredients, the measuring cups, pans to bake in, bowls, hand mixer, and so on. He wants all the tools on the counter in an organized fashion for a couple of reasons.

Perhaps a trip to the store is necessary for a missing ingredient. That certainly will add time to the project. Or they could decide to cook something else for which they have all the ingredients, saving a trip. By assembling all that is needed, they save considerable time not wandering around the kitchen from pantry to refrigerator to food preparation area. And they save cleanup time because the mess is concentrated in one area rather than all over the kitchen.

REMEMBER

Before you start on anything, ask yourself these key questions:

>> What data or information would complete this task quicker?

>> Is there some information I don't have that would save me time for this project?

>> Do I have everything I need?

The cycle of planning to gathering to implementation is the cycle of success and efficiency. If you have to gather resources after you've begun implementation, or go back to planning because your execution is stalled, the waste of time in backtracking is a significant loss.

Handle everything — once

In today's world, we deal with less paper because of electronic documents, but even electronic documents are often handled and reviewed multiple times before being acting on. The shuffling and reshuffling happens inside your computer, so it seems far more efficient. The truth is you can just store more stuff easily so your productivity can really plummet.

Because we can store so much in electronic files, many of us keep rather than purge. You can be more efficient with your time if you throw away documents, files, and papers that are not relevant to your life, family, business, or goals. Ask yourself, "Is there a negative consequence to throwing this out now?" If the answer is "No," throw it out now.

If you need this information in the future, is there another place you could easily access it? Information is readily available, so keeping it because you might need it in the future only overloads you with files, documents, and stuff.

Grabbing the Three Keys to Personal Organization

Your personal organization is one of the largest influences of success and happiness in your life. Your personal organization skills and systems help you feel more fulfilled, become more productive, and achieve a mental state of well-being.

To improve your personal organization, you should learn three skills: Step back to evaluate, develop neatness habits, and refuse to excuse.

Stepping back to evaluate

Evaluating key work areas can reveal a lot about the person working there. By stepping back from your desk or work area, you can ask the questions, "What type of person works at this desk? Is she organized or unorganized? Does it appear that she has an effective system in getting work done? What changes should she make in her organization? Would I trust this person with an important task based on this work environment? What are the reasons I would or wouldn't?"

You need to have an honest evaluation with yourself, as if you hired a third party or neutral authority to review your workspace. What do you see, and what would he or she see? Then repeat that process for your home office. Would an outsider view it as a productive environment? What does your briefcase, computer files, car, closet, house, yard, and garage look like? Who is the person who would live in this manner? Would you entrust this person with an important task to be completed?

Developing neatness habits

For some of us, developing the habit of neatness is tough. There is no question that we can save time and increase productivity by organizing or even cleaning up our workspace. We all need a sense of order and organization to feel calm, relaxed, and in control of our surroundings. Your actual work environment can create a feeling of pleasure and satisfaction or stress and frustration. By instituting order and neatness, you can increase your productivity.

When you create this ordered environment, your self-esteem increases. You're more self-confident in a successful outcome. That self-confidence emotion creates a willingness to be creative, innovate, try new things, and take risks. You feel more in control with more power.

All this neatness removes the roadblocks of frustration and generates more energy. The higher energy level taps into your resources and determination to accomplish the task at hand faster and more efficiently. Establishing neatness habits has far-reaching benefits, reducing your time while increasing your well-being and the results you achieve.

Refusing to excuse

"Refuse to excuse" should be a life mantra and not applied only to time management. Too many people let themselves off the hook with excuses of why tasks and chores didn't get finished or why these folks didn't accomplish their mission. People who are messy frequently make excuses to justify or cover up a mess. "That's just the way I am," or "I know where everything is," or "I work better this way."

When you review the time spent, messy people are deluding themselves into thinking they know where everything is located. Frequently a large part of their day is spent trying to find or remember where they put things, instead of being productive at the office or home.

Refuse to excuse a messy desk or work environment for this week. If you have to clear your desk to be able to start on a project, just do it. Take the one task or tool you need to work on, and clear the rest off your desk. If you have to put everything else in drawers, cabinets, closets, waste baskets, or even on the floor, do it. Test this on yourself. Unclutter your space. Utter no excuses for a few days, and see how productive you become.

» Building a solid system of time management

» Facing up to time management's biggest challenges

» Applying time-management skills to all facets of your life

Chapter **2**

Setting Yourself Up for Success

Time is the great equalizer — everyone has the same amount in a day. No matter who you are, where you live, and what you do, you clock the same 24-hour cycle as the next person. One person may be wealthier than another, but that doesn't earn him or her a minute more than the poorest people on the planet.

If that simple fact seems a bit discouraging, think of it this way: You may not have the power to get yourself more time, but you *do* have the power to make the most of it. You can take your 365 days a year, 7 days a week, and 1,440 minutes in a day and invest them in such a way that you reap a return that fulfills your life and attracts the success you dream of.

That's what this minibook is about: taking control of how you spend your time to make sure you're using it how you really want to. You really are in control of your time, even though you don't always feel like it — even if you have a job that demands overtime; even if you have kids who keep you in the carpool loop; even if you have dreams and goals that involve developing new skills or furthering your education.

All in all, discovering how to manage your time well is part mental restructuring and part creating a system. Effective time management requires a little introspection, some good habits and organizational skills, and more than a few logistical and tactical tools. But all are achievable, so if you have the time — and we assure you that you do — get ready for a journey that's certain to, if not buy you more time, show you how to make the absolute most of the 24 hours in your day.

Getting to Know Yourself

Although everyone gets the same number of hours to work with each day, what people don't have in equal amounts are other valuable assets: skill, intelligence, money, ambition, energy, passion, attitude, even looks. All these unique reserves play into your best use of time. So the better you understand yourself — your strengths, weaknesses, goals, values, and motivations — the easier it is to manage your time effectively. In this section, you look at your strengths and goals, think about how much your time is worth, and observe personal energy and behavior patterns that affect your focus throughout the day.

Assessing your strengths and weaknesses

Chances are that by this point in your life, you've discovered some skills that you come to naturally or perhaps have worked hard to acquire. Maybe you're a master negotiator. Or a whiz with numbers. You may be a good writer. Or you may have a silver tongue. Whatever your strengths, developing the handful that brings you the most return on your efforts, propelling you forward to attain your goals, is a more productive course of action than trying to be the best at everything. For most people, these strengths typically number no more than a half-dozen.

In addition to pinpointing your strengths, you need to identify the areas where your skills are lackluster. Then figure out which tasks are essential for meeting the goals you want to accomplish, and build those skills.

REMEMBER

Invest time in honing and maintaining your strengths, and improve the weaknesses that you need to overcome to reach your goals. To be successful, you need to be selective.

Naming goals to give you direction

You know how it is: When you're working toward something, keeping your focus is much easier. A man may want to lose weight, for example, but perhaps he struggles to stick to a diet or exercise plan. But if his son's wedding is looming three months away, he may be more inspired to stay on track, cutting back on second helpings and getting in time for workouts.

REMEMBER

Your goals can serve as inspiration in adopting good time-management skills. After all, managing your time isn't really a benefit in and of itself, but managing your time so you can spend more of it doing what's important to you *is* — whether you're saving for a retirement of travel and adventure or buying the house in the perfect neighborhood.

Using your aspirations to fire up your time-management success means you have to identify your goals and keep them in the front of your mind. Pinning down what's most important to you may require some soul searching. Write down your goals — all of them — and follow these guidelines:

TIP

» **Cast a wide net.** Go for the big goals, such as joining the Peace Corps, as well as the not-so-big ones, such as getting an energy-efficient car next year.

» **Think big.** Don't rein in your dreams because they seem unrealistic.

» **Be as descriptive as possible.** Instead of "build my dream house," flesh it out: Where is this house? How big? What features does it have? What does it look like? When do you want to move in?

» **Don't limit goals to a single category.** Think about goals for your career, your personal life, your social situation, your financial status, and any other facet of life that's important to you.

The process of goal seeking can be a fun and energizing experience.

Assigning a monetary worth to your time

Most people think about the value of their time as it relates to on-the-job activity. The fast-food worker knows he earns a minimum wage per hour. The freelance artist advertises a per-hour rate. The massage therapist charges for her services in half-hour and hour increments. But to be truly aware of the value of your time, you need to carry this concept into your personal life as well. The value of time in your personal life is at least as valuable as the time in your work life. In some cases, personal time is priceless.

THROWING AWAY MONEY

A man in a parking lot was throwing pennies on the ground. When asked what he was doing, he replied that he had just read about a multimillionaire who had calculated his worth, and based on the value of an hour of his time, he determined that it wasn't worth the few seconds it'd take for him to pick up a dollar bill from the sidewalk. This person, however, had decided that although it was worth his time to pick up a dollar, he could afford to part with a few pennies.

I think he missed the point, but there's a lesson in this experience: You're always on the clock. Time is money, and yours has a value. Giving away your precious time without a sense of its value is like throwing money on the sidewalk. By knowing what your time is worth, you can prioritize the tasks that yield the greatest return, delegating or eliminating the tasks that provide little to no return on your time investment.

REMEMBER

One of the most important points to remember as you work through this minibook is that it's okay not to accomplish everything. What's critical is making sure that you do the important things. By assigning value to your time and using the skills you acquire from this minibook, you can clearly identify what's important and make conscious wise choices. For example, if you need to save another $200 per month because you want to start an account for your children's college education, you may determine that putting in an extra shift at work may not be worth the loss of time with your family, even at time-and-a-half pay. Or if you detest yard work, paying someone else $50 to cut your grass may be a fair trade for the extra two hours of time watching the game.

Identifying your rhythm to get in the zone

Athletes talk about being *in the zone,* a place where positive results seem to stick like a magnet. Well, the zone isn't some magical place where wishes come true. Anyone can get there, without a lucky token or fairy dust. What it takes is focus, singular focus.

If you know your rhythms — when you're most on, what times of day you're best equipped to undertake certain tasks — you can perform your most important activities when you're in the zone. Everyone works to a unique pace, and recognizing that rhythm is one of the most valuable personal discoveries you can make. Some of the aspects you need to explore include the following:

BREAKOUT! SHARPENING YOUR FOCUS WITH TIME OFF

About ten years ago, as Amanda was evaluating her sales results, she puzzled over a drop in numbers at the tenth week when she'd been working without a break. It didn't take her long to realize that her lower results reflected a drop in focus. And it was a pattern she could see in previous months. She realized the best course of action, rather than gutting it out, was to get out. She needed a vacation.

She also found that she didn't need a full week's vacation to return to work revitalized and refreshed. She simply needed a mini-break, about five days over the course of a long weekend to step away from the work routine and see the world through another lens, whether holing up with her family or making an escape to the beach.

In the last few years, that span of time spent at work has been reduced from ten weeks to nine. The drop might be attributed to age, increased responsibility, pre-teen and teen children, or a few of ongoing health issues. However, she has learned that getting out is still the best course of action.

To this day, she outlines her entire year in advance, now based on the nine-week rhythm. This ensures that she uses her time for maximum benefit. She is either working at a high level or is out recharging herself for five days to come back strong.

» How many hours can you work at a high level each day?

» What's your most productive time of the day?

» How many weeks can you work at high intensity without a break?

» How long of a break do you need so you can come back focused and intense?

Following a System

Effective time management requires more than good intent and self-knowledge. To keep your time under careful control, you need a framework. In your arsenal of time-management ammunition, you want to stock organizational skills, technology that helps keep you on track, and planning tools that help you keep the reins on your time, hour by hour, day by day, week by week, and so forth.

Establishing a solid system you can replicate is a key to succeeding in managing your time. Systems, standards, strategies, and rules protect your time and allow you to use it to your best advantage. These skills are applicable whether you're the company CEO, a salesperson, a midlevel manager, an executive, or an administrative assistant. No matter your work or your work environment, time management is of universal value.

Scheduling your time and creating a routine

Sticking to a time-scheduling system can't guarantee the return of your long-lost vacation days, but by regularly tracking your meetings, appointments, and obligations, you reduce your odds of double-booking and scheduling appointments too close. And by planning, you make sure to make time for all the important things first.

You might want to try the time-blocking system, in which you put your priorities first (starting with routines and then moving to individual tasks/activities) before scheduling commitments and activities of lesser importance.

Such time-management techniques are just as applicable to the other spheres of your life. There's a reason why you are advised to plug in your personal commitments first when filling in your time-blocking schedule: Your personal time is worthy of protection, and you can further enhance that time by applying time-management principles.

Organizing your surroundings

A good system of time management requires order and organization. Creating order in your world saves time wasted searching for stuff, from important phone numbers to your shoes. But even more, physical order creates mental order and helps you perform more efficiently.

Yes, your workspace should be clean and orderly, with papers and folders arranged in some sort of sequence that makes items easy and quick to find. Your desk should be cleared off, providing space to work. Your important tools — phone, computer — ought to be within reach. And your day planner, of course, should be at your fingertips. Your briefcase, your meeting planner, even your closet has an effect on your time-management success.

THE SCHEDULE WILL SET YOU FREE

Too many people feel that all this structure is too restrictive. They think the freedom they seek with their schedules and their lives is contained in a more flexible environment. They're afraid establishing a routine will keep them wrapped in the chains of time.

However, most people waste too much time figuring out each individual day on the fly. They react to the day rather than respond. Reacting is a reflex action that turns over your agenda to others, and can't possibly lead to freedom. Responding is a disciplined act of planning that determines where and how you'll invest your time.

For example, suppose you have a set place in your schedule to respond to phone calls and problems. You've established the routine of dealing with these issues in predetermined time slots. You can hold off on your response until later — when you're calmer, more focused, and in a problem-solving frame of mind — instead of reacting because you're dealing with the issue now.

Planning how to spend your time, which at first glance seems opposed to freedom, is the only pathway to the true mastery of time. With the right routine come simplicity, productivity, and freedom. The "what am I going to work on today?" or "what's my schedule today?" never happens. And when you get the important work out of the way, you free yourself to do what you really enjoy.

If you're a free spirit and what we're suggesting just fried your circuits, start with a small amount of routine. Ask yourself, "Can I establish a daily routine to try it out? What can I do without having it send me into withdrawal?" Then implement a new routine every week. You'll add more than 50 new pieces of structure to your schedule in a normal work year and see a significant improvement in your freedom.

Overcoming Time-Management Obstacles

Anyone can conquer time management, but it's not always easy. Sometimes your days feel like a video game, where you're in constant threat of being gobbled up on your course to the finish line. But instead of cartoon threats, your obstacles are your own shortcomings (poor communication skills, procrastination, and the inability to make wise and quick decisions), time-wasting co-workers and bosses, phone and people interruptions, and unproductive meetings. You discover how to overcome these obstacles in this section.

Communicating effectively

Communicating effectively is one of the best ways to maximize your time. One of the biggest time-wasters on company time is, no surprise, talking with co-workers. But what may be a surprise is that the abuse *isn't* a function of weekend catch-up discussions that take place at the water cooler or the gossip circle at the copy machine. Rather, it's the banter at the weekly staff status reports, the drawn-out updates of projects that never seem to conclude, the sales presentations that get off track. It's all the meetings that could be as brief as ten minutes but somehow take an hour or more.

At your disposal, however, is an amazing weapon for taming these misbehaving encounters: your words. With a few deft remarks, you have the power to bring these meetings to a productive close.

Circumventing interruptions

Interruptions creep into your workday in all sorts of insidious manners. Besides the pesky co-worker stepping into your office with "Got a sec?" interruptions come in the form of unproductive meetings, phone calls, hall conversations that drift into your office and distract you, and the email icon on your screen. You now have more of these interruptions than ever before. You get sidetracked by instant messaging and social media such as Facebook and Twitter. The list of five-minute-here-and-there interruptions is endless.

Additionally, most poor time managers interrupt themselves by trying to do too much at once. Study after study supports that multitasking isn't the most effective work style. The constant stops and starts disrupt a project, requiring startup time each time you turn back to the task. Being a good time manager at work depends on how you create, craft, and implement your interruption system and strategy. Each day, interruptions cost hours of lost productivity for businesses.

Getting procrastination under control

Sometimes, it's tempting to use interruptions as an excuse to postpone a project or a task. How nice to have someone else to blame for not getting started! And before you know it, you've found so many good reasons not to do something that you've backed yourself into a tight 11th-hour corner, and the pressure is on.

Say you're writing a 400-page book and you have ten months to complete the project. You have almost a year to put this thing together. Looking forward, your task requires you to complete 40 pages per month — little more than a page a day. That's too easy! You can afford to put it off for a while. Wait for a couple of months, and then you'll need to produce 50 pages a month. Still doable. But at some point, *doable* starts to morph into *impossible.* But when? When you're down to four months and pressured to crank out 100 pages per month? Or do you wait until the last minute and find yourself struggling to complete nearly 15 pages per day?

Procrastination has a lot of causes, but most of the reasons to procrastinate leave you headed for trouble.

Making decisions: Just do it

One of the easiest things to put off is making a decision. Even sidestepping the smallest decisions can lead to giant time-consumption. Think about it: You scroll through your email and save one to ponder and respond to later. You revisit a few times and still can't bring yourself to a commitment. So you get more email from the sender. To stave off making a decision, you ask a couple of questions, which requires more time and attention. By the time the issue is resolved and put to bed, you may have invested five times more attention than if you'd handled it at once.

Many factors create the confusion and uncertainty that prevent you from making sound but quick decisions. Often, part of the struggle is having too many options. Most people have a tough enough time choosing between pumpkin and apple pie at the Thanksgiving table. But every day, you're forced to make decisions from choices as abundant as a home-style cafeteria line. Having options is usually a good thing, but too much choice is overwhelming, even paralyzing.

Being able to handle email, paperwork, and tasks leverages your time. Being able to decide on a course of action, whether you handle an issue or delegate it to someone else, creates a surplus of time.

Garnering Support While Establishing Your Boundaries

Sometimes your family, friends, and co-workers are your biggest challenge to managing your time successfully. Whose phone calls interrupt your train of thought when you're on a roll? Who expects you home for dinner, despite a pressing proposal deadline? For whose meetings do you have to take a break from your critical research?

Yet despite all the challenges they throw your way, these same folks can also serve as your allies as you pursue the quest of better time use. Getting them on board and perceiving them as comrades in shared goals is a great way to offset the interruptions that they also inevitably bring to the table.

Balancing work and time with family and friends

All work and no play, as they say, means something is askew with your life balance. Recognize that although your job and career are critical components of who you are, they're also a means to support aspects of your life that, we suspect, are more important to you: your personal life, which includes your family, your friends, your community, and your leisure and social activities.

REMEMBER

If you find yourself constantly putting in long hours at work for months on end, something's off-kilter: Either you're not managing your time effectively, or something's wrong with your job. No one — not even Wall Street lawyers — should be putting in 70-hour weeks on a regular basis. A 70-hour workweek leaves little time for sleep, recreation, family, or relationships.

The first step to creating time-management success in out-of-balance times is to recognize the potential in advance; stress is reduced if you plan for out-of-balance times. The next step is to approach your family. Getting their support is critical for success.

It's important to determine and discuss the time frame. In time management, short out-of-balance time periods likely won't hurt your health or relationships. And at the end of the out-of-balance time period, offer a reward that's shared by all: a reward that your family or friends can experience together. Discuss the reward and come to a consensus so everyone benefits, not just you or your business.

Streamlining interactions with co-workers and customers

Most people find themselves in a work environment in which they regularly interact with others, whether co-workers, business associations, or customers. The workday is rife with opportunities for interruption, distraction, and time wasting. In addition to the phone calls and cubicle pop-ins, you have business appointments, associates who keep you waiting, or meetings that are unfocused and poorly run.

Maintaining control of your time at work requires you to develop some ways to manage meetings, appointments, and other work interactions so they're as efficient and productive as possible. Whether you initiate the interaction or are merely a participant, you can have some control over the meeting.

If you're in sales or a customer service capacity, in such positions, taking control of your time is a little more challenging. To make the sale, you want to take as much time as your prospect wants. And when addressing a service issue, your most important objective is to make the customer happy. But you can be successful in sales and serve your clients well and still keep control of your time.

Keeping Motivation High

According to Earl Nightingale, the dean of the personal development industry, "Success is the progressive realization of a worthy goal or worthy ideal." His definition doesn't confine achievement to a fixed point but instead presents success as a journey. Like most goals, mastering your time-management skills isn't something that happens overnight.

TIP

Throughout the process of working to improve the way you manage your time, you'll occasionally encounter points where you start feeling disappointed, wondering whether your efforts are paying off. Whenever you hit those lows — and you will — remember to give yourself credit for every step you make in the right direction. One great way to stay motivated is to link incentive to inducement: In other words, reward yourself. For example, if you complete certain actions that tie to your goals, give yourself Friday afternoon off. Or savor an evening on the couch with a good movie or dinner at a favorite restaurant. Do whatever serves as an enticing reward.

Take motivation to the next level by involving others in the reward. Let your spouse know that an evening out awaits if you fulfill your week's goals before deadline. Tell the kids that if you spend the next few evenings at the office, you can all head for the amusement park on Saturday. This strategy is a surefire way to supercharge your motivation.

As you work through this difficult but worthy bout of self-improvement, keep your mind on the positive side and remember two simple truths:

>> You're human.

>> Work always expands to fill the time you allow for it.

No matter how productive you are, whether you have just a few things to accomplish or a sky-high pile on your desk, and whether you leave work on time or stay late, there's always something that doesn't get done. So don't get hung up on those things you don't accomplish — just keep your eyes on the goal, prioritize accordingly, delegate what you can, and protect your boundaries carefully so you take on only as much as you know you can handle while still remaining satisfied with all parts of your life. When you start to get frustrated about the never-ending flow of work that comes your way, remind yourself that you're blessed with more opportunities than time — and that's not a bad place to be.

» **Calculating the value of your time**

» **Getting more out of the time you have**

Chapter **3**

Valuing Your Time

D epending on your values, different kinds of numbers may be important to you: To some, it's cholesterol count and blood pressure figures; to others, it's the number of years they've been married. To many, the total in the retirement account is the number-one number, and some people zero in on the amount left on their mortgage.

But we contend that your per-hour worth should be among the top-of-mind numbers that are important to you — no matter what your values or priorities are — even if you don't earn your living on a per-hour rate. Knowing the value of your time enables you to make wise decisions about where and how you spend it so you can make the most of this limited resource according to your circumstances, goals, and interests.

Obviously, the higher you raise your per-hour worth while upholding your priorities, the more you can propel your efforts toward meeting your goals, because you have more resources at your disposal — you have either more money or more time, whichever you need most.

This chapter guides you toward optimizing your value so you can reap the rewards and attain what's most important to you. The chapter starts by showing you why your hourly value is crucial to effective time management. From there, you calculate the overall value of your time based on your employment income. (If you have an hourly job, you can skip that section.) Then you decide how to leverage your time and money, both in your career efforts and in your personal choices, so you can boost your hourly value and get the most out of your time investment.

Getting a Good Grip on the Time-Equals-Money Concept

Your per-hour value translates to your quality of life, both now and in the future. Your income not only influences how you spend your nonworking hours but also determines how much leisure time you have to spend.

As you can imagine, your hourly value reaches beyond the basics: It effects your health, too. For instance, studies show that lower-income earners have more health problems, including heart disease and diabetes, which are often attributed to poor diets and a lack of medical care. Also, low-income earners have less free time to invest in exercise because they have to invest more time to provide for the basic needs of their family. Additionally, the challenge of trying to make ends meet can cause great stress, leading to not just physical illness but also to depression and other mental health problems.

And though it's important to live in the present, it's also important to keep an eye toward the future. How well you prepare does have an effect on your quality of life right now. Making enough money to be able to save for retirement and other major life expenses — including a child's education — results in a sense of comfort and safety about your future.

Your personal time has value, too. And by having a grip on the value of your work hours, you gain a better grasp on what your downtime is worth. After all, most people work so they can make the most of their personal time, whether they're devoting it to family, hobbies, volunteer work, travel, or education.

For example, Sharon sells real estate in Virginia. She has more than doubled her income in the last few years. Her challenge is balancing her thriving business with her true priorities in life — her boys and husband. Because she has raised her hourly rate in business, some of the *home tasks*, such as laundry, meal shopping and preparation, and house cleaning, need to be reevaluated as to their value.

Because of these tasks, she was staying up late or getting up early to complete them. These *normal* activities caused her to work longer hours, miss opportunities in business, and feel detached from the family fun because she needed to get the laundry done or the house cleaned. After discussing the situation with a time coach, she realized that she could hire someone to clean the house, do the laundry, and prep a few meals a week for the cost of one to two sales per year. She just needed to trade her time from a lower-value activity to a higher-value activity.

REMEMBER

When you recognize that your free time has a monetary value, just as your work time does, you gain the perspective you need to make choices:

>> Is the extra money you gain by working overtime worth giving up your holiday with your family?

>> Could you go part-time and stay at home with your small children?

>> Can you afford to take a leave of absence to do a volunteer stint in Haiti?

>> Should you take on a freelance project that means giving up all your free time for three months to fund your dream trip to Bali?

But what is an hour of your personal time worth? Well, that's not a question you can easily answer. How do you put a price on time with your young children? Or apply a dollar value to travel experiences that bring you in touch with new worlds? Or equate the quiet therapy of a walk in the woods with the stress of a work presentation?

The harsh truth is that you don't get paid for not working. But that doesn't mean your personal time has no monetary value. Just thinking about your time as a commodity with a value helps you sort through and recognize the activities that are most important to you. (For information on valuing your personal time, see the later section "Making Value-Based Time Decisions in Your Personal Life.")

Calculating Your Hourly Income

No matter your occupation, everyone sells time for a price; it's just a lot more transparent in some situations than others. Most obvious are individuals who receive a wage or a fee based on the hours they work, including minimum-wage workers and self-employed individuals such as tutors, house cleaners, and consultants.

What you are paid per hour is based on the activities you do and the skill you bring to the marketplace. A pilot, by that nature of the skill and what pilots do, has more value than a flight attendant. Fewer people could pilot the plane than serve as a flight attendant.

If you are a lower-wage earner, it's because the job you currently have does not have the value to pay you more. If you stay in the present position, you might gain raises over time, but there will be a limit. A fast-food counter worker will not be paid $50 an hour . . . ever.

Your objective should be to raise your value so you can advance to a higher-value job that pays more. Too many people focus on the wrong area. A low-wage job is there to help you acquire skills and show aptitude, passion, drive, and commitment. No one is supposed to stay at that pay for his or her whole life. What we are paid for our time starts at minimum wage. Wage ladders enable you to climb up to higher compensation levels, but you have to do the climbing!

Other people advertise their prices based on a per-project basis, but in reality base that fee on an estimate of project hours the job takes. Freelance writers, for instance, may charge $1,500 to write a promotional brochure, but that amount is likely a reflection of the writer's value of his or her time at a certain figure — say, $75 per hour multiplied by 20 hours of production time.

Some businesses and professions charge customers based on an hourly rate, although workers don't directly receive that per-hour fee. Instead, their salary or compensation is based on the revenue the company can bring in based on those hours. Law firms and plumbers, for example, may charge for their services on an hourly basis and pay their employees a salary or a per-hour rate.

TIP

If you earn a salary, you may not perceive yourself as having an hourly rate. But everyone does. Here's how to calculate your hourly income. This number doesn't affect how you're paid, but it puts you in touch with what an hour of your work time brings you.

1. **Calculate the number of hours you work per week:**

   (Work hours/day × days/week) + overtime = hours/week

   To be completely accurate, calculate your hourly rate based on the hours you actually work. If you consistently put in more than 40 hours a week (most salaried folks aren't paid overtime for additional hours worked), add those hours to your total. Here's an example:

   8 hours/day × 5 days/week + 2 hours overtime = 42 hours/week

2. **Figure out how many hours you work per year.**

   Work hours/week × weeks/year = hours/year

   Make sure you subtract time off. For instance, if you take three weeks of vacation each year, subtract that from your total number of weeks worked. If your salary is based on a three-week vacation and an average 42-hour workweek, here's how many hours you work per year:

   42 hours/week × 49 weeks/year = 2,058 hours/year

3. **Divide your gross salary by the number of hours you work per year:**

   Salary ÷ hours/year = hourly income

   For instance, $80,000 divided by 2,058 hours is $38.87.

Boosting Your Hourly Value through Your Work Efforts

REMEMBER

Money isn't the scarcest and most valuable resource; time is. You can make more money in plenty of ways, but you can't add more minutes to an hour. You have a limited amount of this precious commodity, so you want to protect it and spend it as if it's your own personal trust fund.

Most people think that if they work more hours, they'll automatically make more money. That's faulty thinking: You can devote more hours to work, but if you invest the hours in the wrong actions, you gain nothing — and you lose time.

The solution may be to ask for more money for your time. Some workers have a good deal of control over their hourly income and can therefore charge more per hour for their services. The freelance writer can raise her hourly rate from $65 to $70 and bring in an additional $50 on a ten-hour project. A tax accountant can increase the fee for income tax preparation from $450 to $510. If he needs six hours to prepare the average income tax return, the accountant just gave himself an increase from $75 to $85 an hour.

However, the simple fact is that most people don't have the luxury of raising their income at will. So what's the next best step? Change how you use your time so you get the best return on investment — after all, what you do with your time leads to greater prosperity.

To increase your hourly value, you have to decide whether you'll work toward earning more money or earning more time. Then focus on performing high-value activities to achieve that goal; the process of discovering the important actions or items you can invest your time in can help you change your hourly rate. The decision of how to increase your hourly value — whether to work toward generating more money in the same amount of time or generating the same amount of money in less time — depends on your circumstances:

>> If you're in a commission or bonus compensation structure, you can increase productivity to earn additional income.

>> If you're in a salary-based position, you can find ways to be more productive within the 40-hour workweek and reduce the additional hours you put in.

However, if your job doesn't enable you to increase your hourly value, whether in terms of money or time, you have bigger decisions to make. Other changes you can make to directly effect your income are to simply do the following:

>> Find a similar job at a company that pays a bigger salary or offers more freedom with your work hours.

>> Improve your performance and earn a raise or a promotion. Know, however, that the success of your efforts toward a raise or promotion is ultimately up to the higher-ups.

TIP

When evaluating time-for-money trades, be sure not to limit your definition of *return* to money: Ask yourself whether the exchange improves the quality of your life. Look at how your life would change outside of work if you were to double or triple your hourly rate. If what you're trading for dollars does any of the following, it's a good trade.

>> Increases your ability and opportunity to earn more money

>> Increases your amount of family time

>> Decreases your work hours

>> Enhances your physical and mental fitness

>> Provides an opportunity for someone who needs it

>> Removes something you don't enjoy or don't do well from your life

So that's a simple look at the overall strategy behind improving your return on investment. Chapter 4 in this minibook takes you through the specifics, helping you schedule your to-do list each day so you make sure all your efforts align with your goals.

Making Value-Based Time Decisions in Your Personal Life

When you consider the way you live your personal life, divide your focus into two categories: chores/responsibilities, and leisure time. Although personal time may seem straightforward, there really is a difference between chores and leisure activities, and the way you approach your time-management decisions hinges on that difference. But however you spend your personal time, you can assign that time a value equal to your work worth — even though no one's paying you — to help you decide how to spend it.

Deciding whether to buy time: Chores and responsibilities

When you have a handle on the value of your time in hourly increments (see the earlier section "Calculating Your Hourly Income"), you have the information you need to make better time choices. The chores have to be done, whether you do them, or delegate, or even pay someone else to do them. The question with chores is whether you want to do them yourself or exchange dollars for someone else to do them. You have to ask, "Is the cost of the time this task would take me greater than or less than the cost to hire someone to do the work?" Here, you're simply comparing numbers. Think of the laundry list of household chores and personal errands that can eat up every bit of personal time you have. If you could pay someone to do some of those tasks at a rate equal to or well below your hourly rate, wouldn't that be a good return on investment?

All time in life is a trade. You are trading your time for something you desire, want, or need. The evaluation is based on your value of time and enjoyment of a particular action or activity. For example, if you have all kinds of free time on the weekend — and you enjoy being out in the yard — paying someone else to cut your grass may be a money-time trade that has no value for you. But if you would rather not touch a mower, an edger, or a weed whacker ever again, paying a professional to do yard work might be worthwhile.

If you love to garden but hate cleaning the house, and cleaning the house takes you four hours ($200 if your time is worth $50 per hour), why *not* pay a house-cleaning service $100 to buy back the four hours it would take you to do it all? And you buy yourself four blissful hours puttering over your zinnias and scarlet runner beans.

Making time-spending decisions: Leisure activities

With leisure activities, your decision simply hinges on whether you want to do them at all. Unlike chores, which you have to deal with in some way, you can get away with forgoing certain pastimes. When you're faced with decisions on whether to accept an invitation or volunteer for a committee or do any other activity, that can affect your leisure time.

Looking at rewards

REMEMBER

A leisure activity has to bring you as much joy or value as your hourly income rate. Some things you do will be priceless, whereas others are worthless or even less than worthless because they drain you rather than fill you up. So with leisure activities, you aren't comparing numbers — you simply decide whether a given activity is worth your hourly value. Consider the value of the activity in terms of

>> Your personal enjoyment

>> The service you want to do for someone

>> The support to those who are less fortunate than you

>> The desire to pay it forward

>> The legacy you want to leave to others

Factoring in monetary and time costs

Another factor to consider when choosing leisure activities is the cost of your free time. Often, that time isn't so free — you undertake activities that require some recreational funds. When you have to pay to enjoy certain recreational or leisure activities, take the cost of the activity and add it to the monetary time-cost you'd have to pay for the activity. In short, would you pay the cost in your hourly value (plus any costs of the activity itself) to participate in that activity?

Say your income equates to $35 an hour. If an acquaintance you're not all that crazy about invites you to her jewelry party on a weeknight, you'd be looking at, say, a two-hour cost of $70, plus any money you'd spend while there. Should you go? Probably not, if this acquaintance really isn't someone you prefer to spend your time with.

Or how about this scenario? A local nonprofit asks you to be on a committee that requires an average of ten hours per month. Total value: $350 worth of your time each month. Is the value earned from your time donation worth the cost to you? How does it factor into your overall goals? Do you enjoy being on the committee and do you feel passionate about the nonprofit's mission? Do you have other more important things you have to tend to first?

HELPING KIDS UNDERSTAND THE TIME-VERSUS-MONEY BALANCE

Business travel can eat up a lot of the personal time you count on for recreation and renewal. You may still tie up your workday at 5:30 p.m., but instead of going home to the family, you retreat to your hotel room for the night. And your weekend may be consumed with long travel days to get home.

The following anecdote shows how one father explained to his child the balance between time and work. Allan was getting ready to leave for a week of speaking engagements. His 5-year-old son, Carl, was crying and begging him not to go. Allan knew that he couldn't *not* go, so after all his reassurances weren't working to stop Carl's tears, he went out on a limb and tried to reason with his son.

He explained to that he had already promised the people that he would be there and it wouldn't be right for him not to show up. Allan then assured Carl that if he wanted him to, he'd be willing to stop speaking and spend more time at home. But the entire family would have to make some changes: They would have to sell their home and buy a smaller one because Daddy would be making less money. They would need to cut some things out of the budget, such as some vacations, eating out, toys — the new bike Carl had been asking for. Allan wound up his explanation and asked his son gently, "Do you understand?" Carl looked at him thoughtfully for a second and then said, "Bye, Dad. See you later." And off he ran.

The money-to-time-value consideration extends to even the seemingly most mundane of activities — for example, dining out. Going out to a two-hour dinner with a family of four may rack up $80 or more. If you earn $80 in one hour, this may seem like a fair trade — you're paying $80 for something that would cost you $160 in time. But if your income is $20 per hour, you're essentially paying $80 for something that's worth only $40 in time. That may seem steep for a midweek convenience grab; however, if you're celebrating your child's first straight-A report card, it may feel like a fairer trade.

How about a week of vacation? Travel, hotel, and food on the road can add up fast. If you and your partner total up $3,000 in expenses for a beach resort getaway, at $80 an hour, that's 37.5 hours — not quite a week's worth of work hours . . . and not a bad deal, you may think. The fact of the matter is this: The decision of whether an activity is worth its cost is subjective. That idea is certainly empowering and freeing, as long as you make conscious choices about where you dole out your hours.

Staying open to experiences and using time wisely

The process of evaluating your leisure time is meant to help you use your time well, not to limit your experiences. If you're unsure about a certain activity but you had fun and found it worthwhile in the past, you should probably go. Also consider going if it's part of your current or future goals. If you enjoy the people but not an activity, you can suggest a change of venue and make the outing more worthwhile.

If you give up activities and find yourself mindlessly wasting the time you gained in front of the TV or online, you likely need more clarity in your goals. Or your goals may not be compelling enough.

» **Prioritizing activities**

» **Developing the habit of time-blocking**

» **Staying on the road to successful time-blocking**

Chapter **4**

Focusing, Prioritizing, and Time-Blocking

What you do with your time is more important than how much time you have. Just as recognizing and understanding your life goals helps you achieve successful time-management skills, the effective use of your time goes a long, long way to shortening the journey to those goals. By investing your time with care and consideration, your journey toward your dreams is certain to be a smoother road. In fact, an old time-management adage says that for every minute you invest in planning, you save ten minutes in execution. Spend an hour planning your trip, and you'll free up ten hours — to achieve better business results, reduce stress, and add quality time at home.

The best way to achieve your goals is to prioritize them and develop an ordered plan to reach them. A universally recognized method for maximizing productivity, called the *80/20 rule,* has proven successful time and again, for more than 100 years. This chapter explains the general concept and show you how to apply it — at work, at home, in your relationships, and beyond.

People who are most productive have another common trait: They treat everything in life as an appointment. These people value their time and the activities to which they commit, whether business or personal. They lend importance to their duties, commitments, and activities by writing them down and giving them a time slot, whether they're one-time occurrences or regular activities. They even make appointments with themselves.

To ensure you act on your priorities in the order that's most important to you, you need to follow a method to your scheduling — and that's what this chapter is all about. Here, you match your overall time investment to your goals, prioritize your tasks, and create a schedule to take you safely to your destination.

Focusing Your Energy with the 80/20 Theory of Everything

In 1906, Vilfredo Pareto noted that in his home country of Italy, a small contingency of citizens — about 20 percent — held most of the power, influence, and money — about 80 percent, he figured. That, of course, meant that the other 80 percent of the population held only 20 percent of the financial and political power in the country. Pareto found a similar distribution in other nations. In the 1940s, Joseph M. Juran applied the same 80:20 ratio to quality control issues, and since then the business world has run with idea of the "vital few and trivial many."

The basic principle that in all things, only a few are vital and many are trivial is known as the *80/20 rule* (also referred to as the *Pareto principle*), and you can apply it to almost any situation. We've heard it used in the workplace ("20 percent of my staff makes 80 percent of the revenue") and even by investors ("20 percent of my stocks generate 80 percent of my income"). You can also apply the 80/20 rule to time management, as explained in this section.

Matching time investment to return

Generally speaking, only 20 percent of those things that you spend your time doing produces 80 percent of the results that you want to achieve. This principle applies to virtually every situation in which you have to budget your time to get things done — whether at work, at home, in your relationships, and so on.

REMEMBER

The goal in using the 80/20 rule to maximize your productivity is to identify the key 20 percent activities that are most effective (producing 80 percent of the results) and make sure you prioritize those activities. Complete those vital tasks above all else and perhaps look for ways to increase the time you spend on them.

In this section, you discover how to implement the 80/20 rule.

Step 1: Sizing up your current situation

Before you can do any sort of strategizing, you need to take a good, honest look at how you use your time. For people who struggle with time management, the problem, by and large, lies in the crucial steps of assessing and planning. Start your assessment with these steps:

1. **Observe how you currently use your time.**

   Through the observation process, you can discover behaviors, habits, and skill sets that both negatively and positively affect your productivity. What do you spend most of your day doing? How far down the daily to-do list do you get each day?

2. **Assess your personal productivity trends.**

   During which segments of the day are your energy levels the highest? Which personal habits cause you to adjust your plans for the day?

3. **Take a close look at the interruptions you face on a regular basis.**

   During what segments of the day do you experience the most interruptions? What sort of interruptions do you receive most frequently, and from whom?

Later in the chapter, in "Blocking Off Your Time and Plugging in Your To-Do Items," you find out how to control and plan for your time through time-blocking your day.

Step 2: Identifying the top tasks that support your goals

Some folks tend to follow the squeeze-it-in philosophy: They cram in everything they possibly can — and then some. These people almost always end up miserable because they try to do so much that they don't take care of their basic needs and end up strung out in every possible way. The quality of what they do, as well as the amount of what they do, suffers as a result of their ever-increasing exhaustion.

To work efficiently, you need to identify your 80 percent — the results you want to achieve. Break out your list of goals. Take a good look at your top 12 goals and identify the tasks you need to do that align with those goals. If your number-one goal is to provide your kids with an Ivy League education, for example, your priorities are less likely to center around taking twice-yearly vacations to the Caribbean and more likely to revolve around investing wisely and encouraging your offspring to do well in school (can you say "full-ride scholarship"?).

After you identify what you need to do — your vital few — spend a bit more time in self-reflection to double-check that you've correctly identified your goals and essential tasks. One of the biggest wastes of time for people is changing direction, priorities, objectives, and goals. Successful people and successful time managers take the direct route from point A to point B.

Here's what to ask yourself about these key tasks:

>> How much time do you devote to those activities? Do you devote 20 percent? Less? More?

>> What are you doing with the remainder of your time?

>> How much return are you getting for the investment on the remainder?

Step 3: Prioritizing your daily objectives

After you identify the tasks and activities that you need to accomplish to achieve your goals, assign a value to those goals so you can decide how to order your daily task list.

Take the scenario of sending your kids to an Ivy League school, mentioned in the preceding section: Even though another of your priorities is to be home for your kids, you — as a nonworking parent who values the type of education you want to provide for your young child more than the short-term joy of being a stay-at-home parent — may decide to return to the workforce as you see tuitions skyrocketing. You can make this decision because you have a clear idea about how you rank your priorities. This clarity may help direct you to a job with hours compatible with your kid's schedule.

To personalize how you prioritize your goals at work, follow these steps:

1. **Look at your long-term career goals.**

   Do you want to advance to a particular career level? Do you want to achieve a particular income? Or is your goal to fine-tune your skill set before figuring out where you want to go next?

2. **Review your company's priorities.**

   Having a solid understanding of the company's priorities, goals, objectives, and strategic thrusts guides your own prioritization so you can get the edge on the company's competition. To get a global perspective, review your company's mission statement and its published corporate values and goals, and see how they pertain to your position. Ask your direct supervisor for further elaboration on these statements and on his or her priorities so you can make sure you align yours accordingly.

The vital 20 percent: Figuring out where to focus your energy at work

Used effectively, the 80/20 rule can increase your on-the-job performance. From boardroom to lunchroom, executive suite to mailroom, this time-management principle can help you accomplish the most important tasks in less time and help you advance in your career.

REMEMBER

The 20 percent investment in the 80 percent of results remains relatively constant. What's truly important for success changes very little within a given profession. The two global objectives of any successful business are profit and customer retention. What differs among professions is how those global objectives translate to match individual objectives.

For example, here's how the 80/20 rule factors into some major job categories:

>> **Ownership/executive leadership:** As an executive or owner, your most important role is to establish the vision, goals, and benchmarks for the business. What are the core values and core purpose for the business? What are the goals for the year and then next quarter? What are the most pressing problems that need to be solved? What are the strengths, weaknesses, opportunities, and threats the company or marketplace is experiencing? You then have to convey those answers consistently in clear terms for your lieutenants to follow and hold the lieutenants accountable to the standards.

>> **Sales:** For sales professionals, lead generation leads to 80 percent of your return. Without new leads and new prospects to sell to, your customer and prospect base remains fixed to your current clients. So in sales, your most important tasks are prospecting and following up on leads; you should put a priority on securing and conducting sales appointments and building personal relationships.

Don't forget your existing client base as well. They usually follow the same 80/20 rule, where 20 percent of them contribute 80 percent of the revenue. Spend your time with this group to increase sales and referrals.

>> **Management:** For those in leadership positions, your vital 20 percent is the coaching and development of people. You use coaching strategies to encourage and empower your employees, and you monitor your staff's adherence to the company's strategic plans. In addition, you help your employees acquire the knowledge, skills, attitude, and actions to advance their careers.

>> **Task- or service-based roles:** This group of people varies the most because it's the broadest. To identify your vital tasks, take a look at your company's objectives, your department's objectives, and your own objectives to get a well-rounded picture of how your role fits into the bigger picture. Then decide

which of your job responsibilities increase sales or improve customer retentions.

After that, consider the value of the product or service you offer, and weigh the importance of quality versus speed or quantity — your ultimate goal is to serve your customers better so you retain and grow your relationships with them. (If you're not sure how much weight each element deserves, talk to your supervisor about where you should focus your efforts.)

- If quality takes higher priority, ask yourself how you can deliver a better product or service in the amount of time you're given.

- If delivery speed or quantity is more important, ask yourself how you can deliver that product more efficiently while maintaining quality.

>> **Administration:** If you're in an administrative role, your goal is to enhance the company's performance, whether you're supporting frontline sales staff or assisting the corporate leadership in steering the business toward profit. If you're in sales support, how can you help free up the salespeople to do more selling? Can you fill out reports for the salespeople? Research new market opportunities and get contact information? Can you repeat that help for the sales manager in reports and better tracking of the salespeople's numbers so the manager can do more coaching and shadowing of the salespeople?

If you're working in customer service, is there a recurring customer service problem that needs to be solved? Can you identify it? Can you find at least two solutions to the problem and bring them to your boss for review? You can make yourself an indispensible asset to the company with these actions and save time for yourself and your superiors as well.

Personal essentials: Channeling efforts in your personal life

The 80/20 rule isn't strictly business related, so don't lose sight of its influence on your personal life. In fact, the 80/20 rule can have the greatest effect at home. For most, personal and family life is the realm that matters most. But with all the demands of work and the outside world, it often takes the back seat. By categorizing and ordering your personal priorities, you can customize your approach to the people and priorities in your home life and make the most of your time spent with family, hobbies, leisure, and friends.

When factoring in your personal priorities, think of a variety of areas, such as time with loved ones, a worthy cause, your faith, education, and future plans. This section covers the two areas of prioritization that affect most people (for other situations, follow the general process outlined previously in "Matching time investment to return").

SETTING UP FAMILY TRADITIONS

Joan and Dirk adhere to two traditions that don't take much time but reap huge dividends in the closeness they feel with one another and the partnership in responsibilities that they share. The first is that Saturday each week is date night. They have a standing babysitter, and even with Dirk's travel schedule, they rarely miss a Saturday-night date. They also walk together each evening after dinner. This enables them to share, interact, and exercise all with one activity.

The children and their father also have a few longstanding traditions to foster nurturing relationships with each other. Dirk and his son have Boy's Breakfast Out at least two Friday mornings per month. They spend about 90 minutes talking and laughing, and then Dirk takes his son to school. His daughter loves to have tea parties, so he sets aside time to sit among her stuffed animals and toys while she serves tea in doll-sized cups. They don't spend as long at this activity, because sitting in a low stool for longer than 45 minutes is murder on his back! But she, too, eagerly anticipates teatime with Daddy.

The family has two other traditions. Friday night is Family Friday. They do something as a family, whether it's watching the local high school football game, catching a movie, or having dinner out. Sunday night is game night. They turn off all electronics and play cards or board games together.

Your 20 percent time traditions may differ from these, depending on the age, interests, and unique traits of your loved ones at home. The important thing is to find out what brings the biggest return, greatest connection, and best memories.

Although you may understand how the 80/20 rule applies to your home relationships, putting it into practice remains a challenge. Work on this with each passing day.

Investing wisely in your personal relationships

One of the great things about the 80/20 rule is that it doesn't apply only to task-oriented items — it's also about the quality of your time and the energy you put into what you choose to do with it. If you have a significant other, for example, consider how 20 percent of all the time you spend with him or her shapes 80 percent of your relationship with that person.

TIP

Outside of work, personal relationships are number one, so always consider them first, before you even start thinking about chores. Evaluate your connection with each of the important people in your life, both family and friends. In this way, you can customize your approach to the people and priorities in your home life instead of lumping everything into the generalized category of "home" and perhaps not giving any individual or activity its due attention. When dealing with people, ask yourself these questions to help you identify the 80/20 balance:

» How can you invest your time with this person to create a better relationship?

» What's most important to this loved one, and how can you serve and support these needs?

Many other questions can help get you to the root — or the 20 percent — of actions that produce a bumper crop of love, security, appreciation, and experience that build meaningful relationships at home. For example, if you're raising children, you may ask yourself these questions as well:

» How can you invest your time to nurture this child's developing interests?

» How can you show that you value this child in a way that is meaningful to him or her?

» What do you need to do each week to teach this child an important life skill?

» What shared activities allow you to serve as a positive example?

» What can you do to create a positive family memory?

Balancing crucial household tasks with at-home hobbies

Face it: Your days are filled with tasks that don't bring much return on investment. Whether it's doing the laundry or filling out paperwork, there are loads of those necessary-but-not-monumental duties that you'll never be able to eliminate. And in your personal life, these activities may include housework, home maintenance, or walking the dog.

However, you can apply the 80/20 rule to help balance how you invest your time in chores so it aligns with your hobbies. Which activities bring you the biggest return? For example, do you spend every summer evening and weekend on your back patio, entertaining or simply admiring your backyard and flower garden? Then for you, trimming, mowing, planting, and weeding may be a wise way to invest that vital 20 percent of your time. If, however, you get more enjoyment from traveling to new places, you may allocate that time to budgeting for and planning exciting vacations.

TIP

Cooking, cleaning, shopping, laundry, yard work, bill paying, and other tasks are essential, but that doesn't mean that *you* have to do them — sometimes, the added cost of hiring help is worth the time it frees in your schedule. If you gain no joy or fulfillment whatsoever in cleaning or household maintenance, or feel you simply don't have the time or energy to do all of this without sacrificing your most important priorities, hire out those responsibilities. Sure, a cost is involved, but you buy back time to spend on the activities that mean the most to you. So send out the laundry if it frees you up to explore new menus in the kitchen, or bring in a personal chef if you'd rather be out in the garden planting tomatoes.

If you can hire someone who makes far less money than you do to do something you don't enjoy, hire out the task immediately. If you can work a few more hours and increase your pay or set yourself up for promotion sooner, work the extra hours and hire the help. In the end, you'll be doing something you enjoy rather than something you despise.

The 80/20 rule doesn't stop there — you can also apply it to the quality of those tasks or hobbies and the results they have on your well-being. If you're a gardener, for example, think about the 20 percent of your efforts that bring forth the 80 percent of your pleasure and satisfaction from gardening. For example, maybe you don't need to sculpt a perfectly arranged flower garden to reap the personal benefits — the very act of digging your hands into the earth may give you the greatest sense of joy. So focus on the act of planting more than on the planning and shopping.

REMEMBER

Don't forget to include those activities that support and improve your physical, mental, and emotional health. Those activities that keep you sane, happy, and fit may seem insignificant when taken one at a time. But if they start getting squeezed out of the schedule, you just may start to see that sanity, happiness, and health start slipping. Be sure to account for all those little pleasures that add texture to your life, such as reading, study, yoga, or a weekly facial.

Getting Down to Specifics: Daily Prioritization

After you identify the vital few tasks you need to accomplish to meet your top 12 goals, break them down a bit further into daily to-do items. Then prioritize them to make sure you accomplish the most important tasks first, identifying which ones you must do on a given day. In that way, you progressively work through all the minor tasks that lead to the greater steps that, in time, lead you to achieving your goals. Here's how:

1. **Start with a master list.**

   Write down everything you need to accomplish today. Don't try ranking the items at this point. You merely want to brain dump all the to-do actions you can think of. You may end up with 20, 30, even 50 items on your list: tasks as mundane as checking email and as critical as presenting a new product marketing plan to the executive board. Or if you want to fill work on your personal to-do list, the items may range from buying cat food to filing taxes before midnight.

WARNING

Remember to account for routine duties that don't have a direct effect on your company's mission or bottom line: turning in business expense reports, typing and distributing meeting minutes, taking sales calls from prospective printing vendors. Neglecting to schedule the humdrum to-do items creates a destructive domino dynamic that can topple your well-intentioned time-block schedule.

2. **Determine the A-list.**

   Focusing on consequences creates an urgency factor so you can better use your time. Ask yourself, "What, if not done today, will lead to a significant consequence?" Designate these as *A activities.* If you have a scheduled presentation today, that task definitely hits the A-list. The same is true for filing your tax return if the date is April 15. Buying cat food probably doesn't make this list — unless you're out or have a vindictive cat.

3. **Categorize the rest of the tasks.**

   Now move on to B-level tasks, activities that may have a mildly negative consequence if not completed today. C tasks have no penalty if not completed today, followed by D tasks: D is for *delegate.* These are actions that someone else can take on. Finally, E items are tasks that could be eliminated, so don't even bother writing an E next to them — just cross them out.

4. **Rank the tasks in each category.**

   Say you've categorized your list into six A items, four B items, three C items, and two D items. Your six A tasks obviously move to the top of the list, but now you have to rank these six items in order: A-1, A-2, A-3, and so forth.

TIP

If you have trouble ordering several top priorities, start with just two: Weigh them against each other — if you could complete only one task today, which of the two is most critical? Which of the two best serves your 80/20 rule? Then take the winner of that contest and compare it to the next A item, and so on. Then do the same for the B and C items.

As for the D actions? Delegate them! Everyone likes to think he or she is indispensable, but for most people, the majority of their duties could be handled by someone else. That's where the *85/10/5 rule* — first cousin to the 80/20 rule — comes into play: You tend to invest 85 percent of your time doing tasks that anyone else could do, and 10 percent of your time is devoted to actions that some people could handle. Just 5 percent of your energy goes to work that only you can accomplish. But whether at home or at work, this doesn't mean you can kick back and leave 95 percent of your responsibilities to someone else. It simply helps you home in on the critical 5 percent, allocate your remaining time to other activities that bring you the greatest satisfaction, and recognize those tasks that are easiest to delegate.

REMEMBER

Now you're ready to tackle your to-do list, knowing that the most important tasks will be addressed first (see the nearby sidebar, "Rocking out: Putting the A-list tasks in place," for the importance of prioritizing). Don't expect to complete as large a number of cross-offs as you may be used to. Because you're now focused on more important items — which likely take more time — you may not get as many tasks completed. However, a measure of a great day is whether you wrap up all the A-list items. If you follow this system and consistently complete the As, we can assure you success. Why? Because the B and C items quickly work their way to As — and you always get the most important things done.

ROCKING OUT: PUTTING THE A-LIST TASKS IN PLACE

Steven Covey, A. Roger Merrill, and Rebecca R. Merrill illustrated the importance of prioritizing tasks in their book *First Things First* (Simon & Schuster) with a simple metaphor. In short, a guest lecturer was speaking to a group of students when he pulled out a 1-gallon, wide-mouthed Mason jar, set it on a table in front of him, and began filling it with about a dozen fist-sized rocks. When the jar was filled to the top and no more rocks would fit inside, he asked the class whether the jar was full, to which they unanimously replied, "Yes."

He then reached under the table and pulled out a bucket of gravel, dumping some of it into the jar and shaking the jar, causing pieces of gravel to work themselves down into the spaces between the big rocks. He asked the group once more whether the jar was full, to which one suspicious student responded, "Probably not."

Under the table he reached again, this time withdrawing a bucket of sand. He started dumping in the sand, which sank into all the spaces left between the rocks and the gravel. Once more, he asked the question "Is the jar full?" "No!" the class shouted. "Good!" he said, grabbing a pitcher of water and pouring it in until the jar was filled to the brim.

He looked up at the class and asked, "What is the point of this illustration?" One eager beaver raised his hand and said, "The point is no matter how full your schedule is, if you try really hard, you can always fit some more things into it!"

"No," the speaker replied. "The truth this illustration teaches us is if you don't put the big rocks in first, you'll never get them in at all."

Don't assume that you just move the Bs and Cs up the next day. You need to complete the entire process each day. Some of the Bs will move up, but others will stay in the B category. Some of the Cs — due to outside pressure, your boss, or changed deadlines — may leapfrog the Bs and become As.

Blocking Off Your Time and Plugging in Your To-Do Items

After you identify and order your priorities (see the preceding sections), you place them into time slots on your weekly calendar, broken into 15-minute segments — this process is commonly called *time-blocking.* You might not discover a better system for managing time on a daily, weekly, monthly, yearly, and lifelong basis.

Like exercise, time-blocking can be tricky because it requires a lot of thought and adjustment, both in the initial stage where you're doing it for the first time and for a while thereafter, when you're developing the skill. Everybody knows what day two after the beginning of a new fitness program feels like: Stiff joints and sore muscles have you moving like the Tin Man after a rainstorm. At first you may feel like you'll never achieve the goals you've set, but sticking to the daily program eventually brings the results you want. Figuring out how to best manage your time depends on two factors:

>> **Consistent, diligent practice:** If you want to build those time-blocking muscles, you have to not only work them regularly but also increase the weight, stress, and pressure as you progress. Understanding the key to managing your minutes, hours, days, weeks, and so on takes repetition.

REMEMBER

Don't panic when you find yourself a little stressed or sore from all your time-blocking exercises. It's simply a sign that your efforts to build those skills are working.

>> **A span of time to improve:** Achieving a level of time-blocking mastery does take time — a minimum of 18 months and as much as 24 months. Why so long? Because you're developing a complex skill. A typical day has you switching from refereeing an argument between your kids to making an important presentation to the corporate executives, and from putting together your department's annual budget to paying for your groceries in the checkout line. That's a lot to orchestrate, and even Handel didn't write his *Messiah* overnight. If you accept that time-blocking skills require time to develop, you're more likely to remain motivated. Your objective is to make measureable progress in reasonable time.

REMEMBER

Everyone needs some ongoing reinforcement, repetition, and refresher course of the time-blocking principles shared here.

Implementing time-blocking to help organize your schedule takes a bit of time, but you reap huge dividends on that initial investment. This section walks you through a general outline of the process.

Step 1: Dividing your day

To start, you need a daily calendar or Google Calendar divided into 15-minute increments. Why such small bites of time? Because even 15 minutes can represent a good chunk of productive activity. Losing just two or three of these small blocks each day can diminish your ability to meet your goals, from finishing that project at work to writing your bestselling (you hope) memoir.

On that blank schedule, begin by dividing your day; draw a clear line between personal time and work time. When you take this step, you're creating work-life balance from the start. Don't take it for granted that Saturday and Sunday are time off just because you work a Monday-through-Friday workweek. Block it into your schedule, or work activities may creep into your precious downtime. The more you take action on paper, the more concrete the time-block schedule becomes.

TIME-BLOCKING: MAKING SMALL INVESTMENTS IN A BIG SUCCESS

Time-blocking doesn't require a huge commitment to produce results. For example, a few years ago, Sarah, a top sales performer, exploded her sales by more than 125 percent in one year! Time-blocking played an important role in her success. When asked what percentage of the time she had managed to adhere to her time-blocking schedule, she confessed that she'd stuck to the schedule only 35 percent of the time. The undeniable truth is that a little goes a long way. As you continue to use your time-blocking skills, that percentage increases, and your productivity grows accordingly.

Another salesperson, Mike, increased his contacts by ten per day after adopting time-blocking. These ten additional contacts led to an increase of five leads per week. He averages one appointment for every 2.5 leads and has a 50-percent close ratio on appointments. So from ten contacts per day, he gains one extra sale a week. At an average $5,000 commission per sale, he has the potential to increase his income by $250,000 a year (with two weeks off per year). How's that for results?

TIP

Apprehensive about drawing a line between work and personal time because you're wary of having to tell a business associate you can't attend a business function that extends into personal time? Not to worry. You don't have to tell a client that your Tuesday-morning workout is more important than a breakfast meeting with her — simply say you're already booked at that time. That's all the explanation you owe, and our experience shows that professional colleagues who want to do business with you respect your boundaries.

Step 2: Scheduling your personal activities

Blocking out personal activities first gives weight to these activities and ensures that they won't be overtaken by obligations that have lesser importance in the long run. Personal obligations are almost always the first thing most people trade for work; because of that, you should hold fast and tight to the personal area so it doesn't get away from you. Another advantage? You help establish a reasonable end to your workday. If you're scheduled to meet at a friend's for Texas Hold 'Em on Thursday nights, you're more motivated to wrap up your project in enough time to cut the deck.

Scheduling personal activities is twofold:

1. **Schedule routine activities you participate in.**

   Do you have dinner together as a family every night? A weekly date night with your significant other? Do you want to establish family traditions? Don't just assume these activities will happen — give them the weight they deserve and block out the time for each one. Don't forget to include your extracurricular activities here: All those PTA groups, fundraising committees, nonprofit boards, and other volunteer commitments get plugged in as well.

2. **Schedule personal priorities that aren't routine.**

   Put those personal agenda items first before filling in your day with tasks and activities that don't support those priorities.

Step 3: Factoring in your work activities

Begin with the activities that are a regular part of your job and then factor in the priorities that aren't routine. Whether you're a company CEO, a department manager, a sales associate, an administrative assistant, or an entry-level trainee, you're responsible for performing key tasks and activities each day and week. They may include daily or weekly meetings. Or maybe your responsibility is scheduling meetings for others. You likely have to prepare for these appointments. Perhaps you have to write and turn in reports or sales figures on an ongoing basis.

You may have to call someone for information routinely. If you report to work daily and always spend the first hour of your day returning phone calls, time-block it into your schedule.

Step 4: Accounting for weekly self-evaluation and planning time

Your goals — whether a one-year business plan or long-range retirement vision — warrant routine checkups. Consider them as rest stops on your journey: Are you still on the right road? Is a detour ahead? Have you discovered a more direct route?

Use weekly strategic planning sessions — ideally for Friday afternoon or the end of the workweek — to review your progress toward those near-future business projects as well as your larger career aspirations or personal goals. This time is an opportunity to review the previous week and jump-start the upcoming week. Spend 15 to 30 minutes daily and then take a 90-to-120-minute session on self-evaluation and planning at the end of the week.

REMEMBER

This strategic planning time is probably your most valuable time investment each week. It gives you a tremendous wrap-up for the week and a good start to next week, and it reinforces your vision for your long-term success. It also enables you to go home and spend time with your family in the right frame of mind.

Step 5: Building in flextime

Plug segments of time into your schedule every few hours to help you minimize the fallout from unplanned interruptions or problems. About 15 or 30 minutes is enough time to work in at strategic intervals throughout your day. Knowing that you have this free block of time can help you adhere to your schedule rather than get off track.

TIP

As you begin to build your time-blocking skills, insert 30-minute flex periods into your schedule for every two hours of time-blocked activity. This may seem like a lot of flextime, but if it allows you to maintain the rest of your time-block schedule and maintain or increase your productivity, it's worth the investment. Our experience is that the best time for flextime is after you've put in a couple of hours of your most important work — whether sales calls, report preparation, or meeting a deadline.

WARNING

Don't schedule flextime right before you go into an important activity time: You're more likely to get distracted and fail to get started with your critical business. Schedule it after the work — then you can use it, if necessary, to resolve any unforeseen problems.

Assessing Your Progress and Adjusting Your Plan as Needed

Becoming comfortable with time-blocking takes time, and achieving a glitch-free schedule that you can work with for a stretch may take a half-dozen revisions. Even then, routinely evaluate your time-blocking efforts and adjust them periodically to make sure you're getting the desired results. You don't need to make a huge time investment — you can check yourself with a few minutes a day or use 15 to 30 minutes of your weekly time to review your results. Ask yourself the following:

>> What took you off track this week?

>> What interruptions really affected your success with your time?

>> Is someone sabotaging your time-block?

>> What shifts would help your efficiency?

This section describes this review in detail.

Surveying your results

One way to determine your effectiveness at time-blocking is to check results. In as little as two weeks from when you launch your time-blocking schedule, you can probably see where you need minor adjustments. The best way to keep tabs on results is to track them on an ongoing basis. Conduct both a weekly review that focuses on the past week and a periodic review of where you stand in relation to your overall goals.

The weekly review is a time for you to replay the video of the week, looking at the highs and lows. You'll have days where you want to pull your hair out because you face so many problems and distractions. You'll also have days that are smooth as silk. What were the differences in those days besides the outcome?

As for the periodic review, review your job description, key responsibilities, and the ways in which your performance and success are measured. Then ask yourself these questions:

>> Are you moving closer toward achieving your goals?

>> Can you see measurable progress in reasonable time?

>> Are you monitoring your performance well enough to see improvement?

>> What changes do you need to adopt now to increase your speed toward reaching the goal and reduce the overall amount of time you invest?

Your success in meeting your objectives tells you whether the time-blocking is working for you.

Looking at measurable goals

If you can measure your goals in terms of numbers (dollars or sales, for example), checking your results is a cinch. As a salesperson, for example, you may follow your sales numbers or commissions results over several months to get a good understanding of the effectiveness of your time-blocking efforts. Or suppose you're a magazine editor who's evaluated on consistently meeting weekly publication deadlines; if your goal is to publish three articles per month in national magazines, you can assume that your time-blocking efforts require some tweaking if your review reveals that you're getting only one story in print.

Evaluating qualitative goals

If your goals aren't easily measured in terms of dollars or sales, you may need to get creative in developing your own tally for results. Family and personal goals are difficult to measure, but you can likely gain a good sense of how your efforts are tracking by just paying attention to your daily life and how you feel about it, rating your day on a 1-to-10 scale. Are your kids comfortable talking and spending time with you? Do they look forward to being with you? Are you on friendly terms with the people in your community activities? Do you and your spouse laugh together more often than you argue?

You can also turn to other measuring sticks, which are especially useful in the workplace:

>> What went well this week? What could you have done better?

>> Did you accomplish what you really needed to do? How many high-priority items did you carry over to the next day or week? (See the earlier section titled "Getting Down to Specifics: Daily Prioritization" for more on prioritizing.)

>> How would you rate your week on a 1-to-10 scale, with 1 being utterly overwhelmed and dissatisfied, and 10 being completely in control of and happy with how you spend your time?

>> How do you feel you performed at work? How does your supervisor feel you're performing?

>> Did you meet your goals at home?

>> Has what you've accomplished this week positioned you better to achieve your long-range goals?

>> What are the key improvement areas for you next week?

>> What adjustments to your long-range plans do you need to make?

>> What's diverting you from your schedule?

>> Were you unrealistic in your time estimates for tasks?

>> What segment of the day or activity is tipping your schedule off track?

REMEMBER

As you're reviewing your results, be careful to do so with an open, observant mind, not a judgmental one. Give yourself a couple of weeks before you resolve to change your schedule. Doing so helps you get through a long enough period of time to account for anomalies.

Tweaking your system

Looking back at your personal behaviors and skills and the interruptions you routinely face, identify two or three steps you need to take to increase your success. Here are a couple of tips to point you in the right direction:

>> **If you're not completing the most important tasks or working toward the most important efforts each day:** Weed out some of the trivial tasks to make room for the most important ones. (For help doing that, see "Getting Down to Specifics: Daily Prioritization," earlier in this chapter.)

>> **If your most productive times of day are filled with trivial tasks:** Shift the tasks and the time slots you fit them in. (Your trouble is time-blocking, so refer to the "Blocking Off Your Time and Scheduling and Plugging in Your To-Do Items" section.)

After you figure out what you need to change, you can adjust your schedule accordingly. Unfortunately, there are no one-size-fits-all set of answers to help you figure out what to change — those decisions depend on your job requirements, your personal strengths and weaknesses, your personal goals and desires, and the amount of control you have over the aspects you'd like to improve. Some questions, however, can help steer you in the right direction.

REMEMBER

Remember the adage "Grant me the serenity to accept the things I cannot change, courage to change the things I can, and the wisdom to know the difference"? You can apply it to the way you manage your time. If you can balance the results you expect to achieve (more productivity, greater efficiency, reduction in time worked, and greater sales) with the results you need to achieve, you'll be successful.

Following are some examples of quick evaluation questions that can help you make the most effective, results-oriented changes to your schedule:

>> **What's the standard?** Do you have a sales quota that needs to be met? Are you completing the priorities of your boss? Going home, how are you feeling about your progress?

>> **How accurate does the time-block schedule need to be?** In time-blocking, a little goes a long way. The real question is how well you did this week with the most important activities — the vital 20 percent of the 80/20 rule.

>> **How much have you improved?** How have you improved since you started working your time-block? How large is the improvement? Would you be happy if you improved each week for a year at this level?

>> **With additional revision, how much additional productivity would you gain?** Before revising a time-block schedule, look at the anticipated return on investment. Is this change going to bring significant benefit in productivity, efficiency, or personal satisfaction?

>> **How good is good enough?** Where is the point where you'll achieve diminishing returns on your effort? At some point, further refining your schedule can lead to reduced results. Where do you think that will happen?

WARNING

Perfectionism is a scourge of people who are trying to achieve more with their time. The obsession with revising, redoing, and readjusting one's time-block schedule every few days — or even hours — leads to frustration. In your time-blocking, clearly define the line of success so you can achieve your goals without going overboard.

Chapter **5**

Controlling Email Overload

You might receive less email because you communicate more on social media platforms such as Facebook, Twitter, or Instagram. Or you may have become frustrated with so much email and spam that you vowed to dramatically cut the volume of messages. Whichever category describes you, this chapter helps you reduce, remove, and reclaim your email box.

Managing Email Effectively

If all the email correspondence you've ever received, sent, saved, responded to, forwarded, and deleted were turned into paper mail, your output alone could probably fill a U.S. Postal Office. Of course, you don't keep it all, but you might let your email accumulate at times, perhaps until your system notifies you that your mailbox has exceeded its limit.

A good tool is only as good as the person wielding it. If you know how to use email properly, it can make your productivity output hum. If not, you can end up sabotaging your efforts to accomplish things. This section helps you rein in the all-too-often unwieldy paperless communication system.

Setting up filtering systems

Even militant time masters can lose hours of productive time to email — and much of that email isn't even work-related. Sometimes it's not even something you *want* to receive, yet you still have to dig your way through the sludge to see what the email is regarding.

TIP

Spam is only one factor that adds to the deluge of email you find in your inbox on a daily basis. If you're like most people, you probably authorized or even requested most of the promotional email you receive. Here are some tips to slow the flow of spam and other incoming email that clutters your inbox:

>> **Unsubscribe from newsletters or mailing lists that you no longer read.** When you were starting your organic garden last spring, a weekly email about composting tips seemed like a great idea. Now you find that you almost always delete it without opening. Time to put that idea to bed.

>> **Think twice before signing on for new mailing lists.** You may appreciate a monthly newsletter about one of your hobbies. But instead of bulking up your inbox, why not add the website to your favorites list and visit when it's convenient for you?

>> **When ordering online, seek out the check box that confirms your agreement to receiving email — and deselect it.** Called the *negative option* response, many merchants include a box on the order form that indicates, "Yes, I want to receive regular notices about your company's special offers." That box is already selected, for your "convenience." In order to get nothing, you must take action and get rid of that mark.

>> **When visiting or leaving personal or contact information on a website, always check the privacy policy to confirm that your information won't be sold.** You can usually find a link to the privacy notice at the bottom of the web page or next to where you enter your information.

>> **Install spam-filtering software on your computer.** Remember, though, that these programs typically don't remove the spam; they simply filter it to your junk folder so you can review or delete it.

WARNING

Don't ever respond to spam. You may hope that your polite request to remove you from the mailing list will stop the mailings, but most often the opposite happens. Your reply confirms that your email address is a valid one. You may start getting even more email, and your address may be sold to other annoying spam-senders. Clicking an opt-out link can also put you at risk if the email is spam, so let your spam software do its job and leave it at that.

Separating Your Work and Private Life

It's important (and healthy) to keep your home and work lives separate. And one way to do that is to create different emails for your job and your personal correspondence. Setting up email accounts through services such as Gmail is easy and enables you to have all personal emails, newsletters, and store offers sent to a specific personal account.

Just about every email service or software (such as Outlook or Thunderbird) has ways to filter all the mail you receive. Check each one for the steps necessary to make sure you see the mail you want, and reroute the spam and other unwanted mail. This is a timesaver for both your personal life and your and work life.

Managing multiple email addresses

You might think that using multiple emails can exponentially create frustration and confusion. If done correctly, however, it can be a huge timesaver. The process takes a little upfront design time and organization of what email to use with different people and offers.

We don't recommend forwarding all emails from different email addresses to one central warehouse location for email. We see many people do this, but it defeats the purpose and efficiency of using multiple addresses in the first place. It does allow you to easily leave one of your email addresses behind if you or a sender gets hacked or the address gets sold to a spammer.

If you are an executive, a key decision maker, or an entrepreneur, marketers and salespeople are targeting you. You are the big fish they want to land as an account. If your email address is posted on your website or can easily be figured out by looking at all the others posted on your or your company's website —such as bigfish@ dontbotherme.com — you are bound to get a volume of solicitation emails on a regular basis. Route those emails to key staff members, who can review them, respond as necessary, and forward the ones that require your direct attention. Use a "secret" email that only your best clients and key strategic partners have access to. This enables you to save large amounts of time when reading and responding to emails.

Organizing and storing email

Managing, organizing, categorizing, and filing your email is a practice that can serve you much like maintaining a well-organized paper filing system. Many of your email messages, especially business correspondence, are probably important to you as references.

Your email program includes many valuable tools that help you keep information as close as the click of a mouse. Most email programs include various folder and filing systems that serve as a virtual lateral file cabinet — but searching and finding what you want is a lot easier with just a little experience. You can sort and store your email by a number of categories, grouping them by sender, date, project, importance, or subject. Here are just some ways you can use the features your email service or software provides:

TIP

>> Set up your email program so that certain messages — periodic newsletters, for example — automatically route to a specific folder. (This tool works on the same concept as spam blockers, except these items go in a folder you want to see.) With the help of filtering software, you can flag specific email addresses and automatically send them to a folder — or even delete them — before they reach your inbox. Most people use only a small portion of what their filtering features can do. Take a few minutes to explore your options — setting up filtering takes only a few minutes.

>> Create a new-arrivals folder, defining *new* as a day, a week, or whatever you determine.

>> Establish a dump folder that you clean out once a month or as often as you choose.

>> Don't look at all the email in the dump folder before you dump them. That takes too much time. You've filtered them enough to be able to let them go.

>> Make specific project folders where you can save relevant email, providing a record of all conversations for the future. When you no longer need the file because the project is long completed, you can delete it. This setup also functions as a great backup system.

>> Employ the search function to track down any correspondence about a certain topic. For example, if you're looking for an email outlining details for a trip to the Bahamas, you can type "Bahamas" in the search field and all inbox email with *Bahamas* somewhere in the body or subject line will come up.

Responding to Email More Quickly

Do you have days when you receive hundreds of emails, even after using the filtering techniques described previously? Receiving only what you need to deal with is only half the battle. You must create a system that shrinks the response time and investment if you still get a large volume of emails.

If you are set to craft a long email response, ask yourself if it could be quicker to pick up the phone and place a call. You can talk faster than you can type. If you don't need documentation of the correspondence, you might be able to shave half the time by calling and speaking rather than writing out an email.

The other option is sending a voice text or video email. If you have a webcam you can create video email quickly using a service such as BombBomb. In less time than it takes to craft a medium-length email, you can record the video in Bomb-Bomb. While it's finishing the processing of the video, you can write the short text subject line, cut and paste the email address to send it to, and then press the Send button. You just saved time and improved the quality of the communication.

When responding to a long email with many questions and points of clarification, create an opening greeting at the top of the email and then instruct the person that your responses follow in red, or blue, or whatever color you choose. This enables you to avoid scrolling up and down when you craft your response and allows you to refer to the question because it's on the screen right in front of you.

Employing an email response system

Performing triage is an excellent way to approach your email responses. Some mail you get is dead on arrival; other messages are of interest to you but not critical to address immediately; and others need your attention right now. When you receive 100 or more new messages a day, you need a good email management system.

When you open up your mailbox, resort to the three Ds: *delete, do it,* or *defer.* Every email fits into one of these categories.

Delete

Although your computer doesn't take up any more space if you have 10 or 10,000 emails, the clutter of useless, obsolete, irrelevant correspondence in your inbox can *seem* like a mile-high stack of stuff you have to carry with you.

Keep your inbox clean by discarding any email that's unimportant or long-obsolete. As for the advertisements, forwarded jokes, urban myths, and the string of thanks, you're-welcome, have-a-good-day, see-you-after-work correspondence, read them (or don't) and delete immediately.

Also delete without opening any email with a subject line that seems too good to be true or seems like a marketing pitch from an unknown sender. How realistic is it to think that some company has sought *you* out to offer you an opportunity to make millions? And if a deal is really so incredible, would the advertiser really need to tell you that? Probably not. Beware of any email with subject lines containing misspelled words or words with symbols in place of letters (such as *Fr** Mon!y*). Spammers do this to try and bypass spam filters.

REMEMBER

Knowing how to delete helps everyone in your company. When employees share a network, the server fills up when everyone retains all email, which can stop the flow of inbound email for the entire company. Most networks establish a limit to the size of individual inboxes and send notices when you get close to the limit. Then it's time for some major housecleaning. Better to keep up with the cleaning rather than let it build up.

Do it

Nike coined the phrase "Just do it." That's not bad advice for email management, either. Of course, this *do it* response is critical if the matter is urgent or must be done today, but it's also a sound strategy for most other email, too. If a message warrants a response, do it. Now. Answer the question. Forward the message. Transfer the to-do to your task list or schedule. Send a response. If you need little more than a click or a minute or two to respond, file, or forward, then don't waste time by keeping it for later.

Just as with mail or papers in your inbox, the best strategy is to handle it once (see Chapter 4 in this minibook) and then get it off your plate.

Defer

For those email messages that aren't critical-care matters, it may make sense to set them aside to address after you pass through all your correspondence. So you *don't* forget and leave them buried in your inbox to be remembered too late, immediately place these email messages in an appropriate folder so they'll pop up later for your attention. Messages that fall into this category may include personal email that you want to read carefully and to which you want to take time to craft a response. They can also include flexible-timeline projects that don't have to be done today or even this week.

Actually, there's a fourth D: *delegate.* It falls in the defer category. Although you can simply click the Forward button and send the message along with instructions for carrying out the requested action, the reliability of email is suspect enough that you want to remind yourself to follow up if you hear nothing back from the delegate.

Automating your responses

The ability to plan with email communication saves you loads of time. If you regularly field the same FAQs numerous times during the week or day, it may make sense to craft template emails of standard responses. Place these templates in a folder where you can easily access them, and you're ready to cut and paste your reply, using the form language and making personal tweaks as necessary. For example, if you get queries from clients about the status of their projects, you may put together a standard response informing them that you're attending to their project and will get in touch with them by such-and-such a date.

TIP

Don't forget about the automated message function when you're out of the office. Set up a message with the pertinent details: when you'll return, whether you'll be checking email, when people can expect to hear from you, and who they can contact if they need immediate assistance.

5
Business Writing

Contents at a Glance

CHAPTER 1: Planning Your Message 337

Adopting the Plan-Draft-Edit Principle 337

Fine-Tuning Your Plan: Your Goals and Audience 338

Making People Care 347

Choosing Your Written Voice: Tone 351

Using Relationship-Building Techniques 355

CHAPTER 2: Making Your Writing Work 359

Stepping into a Twenty-First-Century Writing Style 359

Enlivening Your Language 368

Using Reader-Friendly Graphic Techniques 375

CHAPTER 3: Improving Your Work 381

Changing Hats: Going from Writer to Editor 381

Reviewing the Big and Small Pictures. 385

Moving from Passive to Active. 395

Sidestepping Jargon, Clichés, and Extra Modifiers 398

CHAPTER 4: Troubleshooting Your Writing 403

Organizing Your Document 403

Catching Common Mistakes 411

Reviewing and Proofreading: The Final Check 419

CHAPTER 5: Writing Emails That Get Results 425

Fast-Forwarding Your Agenda In-House and Out-of-House 426

Getting Off to a Great Start 428

Building Messages That Achieve Your Goals. 433

Structuring Your Middle Ground. 438

Closing Strong 440

Perfecting Your Writing for Email 441

Chapter **1**

Planning Your Message

Think for a minute about how you approached a recent writing task. If it was an email, how much time did you spend considering what to write? A few minutes? Seconds? Or did you just start typing?

Now bring a more complex document to mind: a challenging letter, proposal, report, or marketing piece. Did you put some time into shaping your message before you began writing — or did you just plunge in?

This chapter demonstrates the power of taking time before you write to consider *whom* you're writing to, *what* you truly hope to achieve, and *how* you can deploy your words to maximize success.

Adopting the Plan-Draft-Edit Principle

Prepare yourself for one of the most important pieces of advice in this book: Invest time in planning your messages. That means *every* message, because even an everyday communication such as an email can have a profound effect on your success. Everything you write shows people who you are.

How many times have you received an email asking for something, but the message was badly written and full of errors? Or a long, expensively produced document with an abrupt and sloppy email cover note? A poorly written email doesn't help the cause — whatever the cause is.

No, you shouldn't lean back in your chair and let your mind wander into blue-sky mode before writing every email. The planning we recommend is a step-by-step process that leads to good decisions about what to say and how to say it. It's a process that will never fail you, no matter how big (or seemingly small) the writing challenge. And it's simple to adopt — in fact, you may experience surprising immediate results. You may also find that you enjoy writing much more.

This strategic approach has no relation to how you learned to write in school, unless you had an atypical teacher who was attuned to writing for results, so start by tossing any preconceived ideas about your inability to write over the side.

When you have a message or document to write, expect to spend your time this way:

» Planning — one third

» Drafting — one third

» Editing — one third

In other words, give equal time, roughly speaking, to the jobs of deciding what to say (the content), preparing your first draft and finally, and fixing what you wrote.

See Chapter 2 in this minibook for no-fail writing strategies and Chapter 3 for editing tips and tricks.

Fine-Tuning Your Plan: Your Goals and Audience

A well-crafted message is based on two key aspects: your goal and your audience. The following section shows you how to get to know both intimately.

Defining your goal: Know what you want

Your first priority is to know exactly what you want to happen when the person you're writing to reads what you've written. Determining this is far less obvious than it sounds.

Consider a cover letter for your resume. Seen as a formal but unimportant necessity toward your ultimate goal — to get a job — a cover letter can just say:

Dear Mr. Blank, here is my resume — Jack Slade

Intuitively you know that isn't sufficient. But analyze what you want to accomplish and you can see clearly why it falls short. Your cover letter must yield the following results:

>> Connect you with the recipient so that you're a person instead of one more set of documents

>> Make you stand out — in a good way

>> Persuade the recipient that your resume is worth reading

>> Show that you understand the job and the company

>> Set up the person to review your qualifications with a favorable mind-set

You also need the cover letter to demonstrate your personal qualifications, especially the ability to communicate well.

If you see that your big goal depends on this set of more specific goals, it's obvious why a one-line perfunctory message can't succeed.

A cover letter for a formal business proposal has its own big goal — to help convince an individual or an institution to finance your new product. To do this, the letter's role is to connect with the prospective buyer, entice him to actually read at least part of the document, predispose him to like what he sees, present your company as better than the competition, and show off good communication skills.

How about the proposal itself? If you break down this goal into a more specific subset, you realize the proposal must demonstrate the following:

>> The financial viability of what you plan to produce

>> A minimal investment risk and high profit potential

>> Your own excellent qualifications and track record

>> Outstanding backup by an experienced team

>> Special expertise in the field

>> In-depth knowledge of the marketplace, competition, business environment, and so on

REMEMBER

Spelling out your goals is extremely useful because the process keeps you aligned with the big picture while giving you instant guidelines for content that succeeds. Because of good planning on the front end, you're already moving toward *how* to accomplish what you want.

WARNING

To reap the benefit of goal definition, you must take time to look past the surface. Write every message — no exceptions — with a clear set of goals. If you don't know your goals, don't write at all.

Invariably one of your goals is to present yourself in writing as professional, competent, knowledgeable, empathetic, and so on. Create a list of the personal and professional qualities you want other people to perceive in you. Then every time you write, remember to be that person. Ask yourself how that individual handles the tough stuff. Your answers may amaze you. This technique isn't mystical; it's just a way of accessing your own knowledge base and intuition. You may be able to channel this winning persona into your in-person experiences, too.

Defining your audience: Know your reader

You've no doubt noticed that people are genuinely different in countless ways — what they value, their motivations, how they like to spend their time, their attitude toward work and success, how they communicate, and much more. One ramification of these variables is that they read and react to your messages in different and sometimes unexpected ways.

TIP

As part of your planning, you need to anticipate people's responses to both your content and writing style. The key to successfully predicting your reader's response is to address everything you write to someone specific, rather than an anonymous, faceless anyone.

When you meet someone in person and want to persuade her to your viewpoint, you automatically adapt to her reactions as you go along. You respond to a host of clues. Beyond interruptions, comments, and questions, you also perceive facial expression, body language, tone of voice, nervous mannerisms, and many other indicators. (Check out *Body Language For Dummies,* 3rd Edition by Elizabeth Kuhnke to sharpen your ability to read people.)

REMEMBER

Obviously a written message lacks all in-person clues. So for yours to succeed, you must play both roles — the reader's and your own. Doing this isn't as hard as it may sound.

GENERATION GAPS: UNDERSTANDING AND LEVERAGING THEM

In business today, understanding young people is important to older ones, and vice versa. If you're a member of Generation X or Generation Y, understanding Baby Boomers is especially useful because they still constitute more than 70 percent of business owners and probably a similar percentage of all top jobs.

You may quibble about the following descriptions — especially of your own cohort — but the generalizations are still illuminating. Supplement these ideas with your own observations and you discover ways to make higher-ups happy without necessarily compromising your own values:

- **Baby Boomers** (born 1946 to 1964) are highly competitive and define themselves by achievement. Many are workaholics. They respect authority, loyalty, position, and patience with the hierarchy and slow upward progress. They would like today's young people to advance the same way they did: earning rewards gradually over time. They are good with confrontation and prefer a lot of face-to-face time, so hold meetings often. They resent younger people's perceived lack of respect, low commitment level, expectations of fast progress, and arrogance about their own superior technology skills. And careless writing! Well-planned and proofed messages score high points with Boomers, and they are more likely to prefer long, detailed accounts. They like phone calls but resent telephone run-arounds and response delays.

- **Generation X'ers** (born 1965 to 1980) are literally caught in the middle. They are often middle managers and may constantly translate between those they report to and those who report to them. They are hard working, individualistic, committed to change, and technologically capable, but lack the full enthusiasm toward technological solutions of Gen Y. They value independence and resourcefulness (having been the first latchkey children) and like opportunities to develop new skills and receive feedback. Their preferred communication mode is generally email, the short efficient kind. They'd rather skip the meetings.

- **Generation Y members** (born after 1980) expect their technical skills and input to be recognized and rewarded quickly. They are highly social and collaborative, preferring to work in teams, and like staying in touch with what everyone is doing. They want to be given responsibility but also like structure and mentoring. They don't see the point of long-term commitment and expect to spend their careers job-hopping. Generation Y'ers prefer to interact through texting, instant messaging, and social media, and will use email as necessary, rather than in-person or telephone contact. A subgroup, the Millennials (born 1991 or later), are even more technocentric in their communication preferences.

Unless you're sending a trivial message, begin by creating a profile of the person you're writing to. If you know the person, begin with the usual suspects, the demographics. Start by determining the following:

>> How old? (Generational differences can be huge! See the sidebar "Generation gaps: Understanding and leveraging them.")

>> Male or female?

>> Engaged in what occupation?

>> Married, family, or some other arrangement?

>> Member of an ethnic or religious group?

>> Educated to what degree?

>> Social and economic position?

After demographics, you have *psychographic* considerations, the kind of factors marketing specialists spend a lot of time studying. Marketers are interested in creating customer profiles to understand and manipulate consumer buying. For your purposes, some psychographic factors that can matter follow:

>> Lifestyle

>> Values and beliefs

>> Opinions and attitudes

>> Interests

>> Leisure and volunteer activities

You also need to consider factors that reflect someone's positioning, personality, and in truth, entire life history and outlook on the world. Some factors that may directly affect how a person perceives your message include the following:

>> Professional background and experience

>> Position in the organization: What level? Moving up or down? Respected? How ambitious?

>> Degree of authority

>> Leadership style: Team-based? Dictatorial? Collaborative? Indiscernible?

>> Preferred communication style: In-person? Short or long written messages? Telephone? Texting? PowerPoint?

- >> Approach to decision-making: Collaborative or top-down? Spontaneous or deliberative? Risk-taker or play-it-safer?

- >> Information preferences: Broad vision? Detailed? Statistics and numbers? Charts and graphs?

- >> Work priorities and pressures

- >> Sensitivities and hot buttons

- >> Interaction style and preferences: A people person or a systems and technology person?

- >> Type of thinking: Logical or intuitive? Statistics-based or ideas-based? Big picture or micro oriented? Looking for long-range or immediate results?

- >> Weaknesses, perceived by the person or not: Lack of technological savvy? People skills? Education?

- >> Type of people the person likes — and dislikes

TIP

Do you know, or can you figure out, what your reader worries about? What keeps him up at night? What is his biggest problem? When you know a person's deepest concerns, you can effectively leverage this information to create messages that he finds highly compelling.

And of course, your precise relationship to the person matters — your relative positioning; the degree of mutual liking, respect and trust; the *simpatico* factor.

No doubt you're wondering how you can possibly take so much into consideration, or why you want to. The good news is, when your message is truly simple, you usually don't. More good news: Even when your goal is complex or important, only some factors matter. We're giving you a lengthy list to draw on because every situation brings different characteristics into play. Thinking through which ones count in your specific situation is crucial.

For example, say you want authorization to buy a new computer. Perhaps your boss is a technology freak who reacts best to equipment requests when they have detailed productivity data — in writing. Or you may report to someone who values relationships, good office vibes, and in-person negotiation. Whatever the specifics, you need to frame the same story differently. Don't manipulate the facts — both stories must be true and fair.

REMEMBER

You succeed when you take the time to look at things through the other person's eyes rather than solely your own. Doing so doesn't compromise your principles. It shows that you're sensible and sensitive to the differences between people and helps your relationships. It shows you how to frame what you're asking for. See the section "Framing messages with *you* not *I*" later in this chapter for more on these techniques.

Brainstorming the best content for your purpose

Perhaps defining your goal and audience so thoroughly sounds like unnecessary busywork. But doing so helps immeasurably when you're approaching someone with an idea, a product, or a service that you need her to buy into.

Suppose your department is planning to launch a major project that you want to lead. You could write a memo explaining how important the opportunity is to you, how much you can use the extra money, or how much you'll appreciate being chosen for the new role. But unless your boss, Jane, is a totally selfless person without ambition or priorities of her own, why would she care about any of that?

You're much better off highlighting your relevant skills and accomplishments. Your competitors for the leadership position may equal or even better such a rundown, so you must make your best case. Think beyond yourself to what Jane herself most values.

A quick profile (see the preceding section) of Jane reveals a few characteristics to work with:

>> She likes to see good teamwork in people reporting to her.

>> She's a workaholic who is usually overcommitted.

>> She likes to launch projects and then basically forget about them until results are due.

>> She's ambitious and always angling for her next step up.

Considering what you know about Jane, the content of your message can correspond to these traits by including the following:

>> Your good record as both a team player and team leader

>> Your dedication to the new project and willingness to work over and beyond normal hours to do it right

>> Your ability to work independently and use good judgment with minimal supervision

>> Your enthusiasm for this particular project, which, if successful, will be highly valued by the department and company

Again, all your claims must be true, and you need to provide evidence that they are: a reminder of another project you successfully directed, for example, and handled independently.

Your reader profile can tell you still more. If you wonder how long your memo needs to be, for example, consider Jane's communication preferences. If she prefers brief memos followed by face-to-face decision-making, keep your memo brief but still cover all the points to ensure that you secure that all-important meeting. However, if she reacts best to written detail, give her more info up front.

REMEMBER Reader profiling offers you the chance to create a blueprint for the content of all your messages and documents. After you've defined what you want and analyzed your audience in relation to the request, brainstorm the points that may help you win your case with that person. Your brainstorming gives you a list of possibilities to review. Winnowing out the most convincing points is easy — and organizing can involve simple prioritizing, as you see in Chapter 2 of this minibook.

TIP Thinking through how to profile your reader works the same way if you're writing a major proposal, business plan, report, funding request, client letter, marketing piece, PowerPoint presentation, or networking message. Know your goal. Figure out what your audience cares about. Then think widely within that perspective.

Writing to groups and strangers

Profiling one person is easy enough, but you often write to groups rather than individuals as well as to people you haven't met and know nothing about. The same ideas discussed in the preceding section apply with groups and strangers, but they demand a little more imagination on your part.

TIP Here's a good tactic for messages addressed to groups: Visualize a single individual — or a few key individuals — who epitomize that group. The financier Warren Buffet explained that when writing to stockholders he imagines he's writing to his two sisters: intelligent but not knowledgeable about finance. He consciously aims to be understood by them. The results are admirably clear financial messages that are well received and influential.

Like Buffet, you may be able to think of a particular person to represent a larger group. If you've invented a new item of ski equipment, for example, think about a skier you know who'd be interested in your product and profile that person. Or create a composite profile of several such people, drawing on what they have in common plus variations. If you're a business strategy consultant, think of your best clients and use what you know about them to profile your prospects.

Imagining your readers

Even when an audience is new to you, you can still make good generalizations about what these people are like — or, even better, their concerns. Suppose you're

Planning Your Message

a dentist who's taking over a practice and you're writing to introduce yourself to your predecessor's patients. Your basic goal is to maintain that clientele. You needn't know the people to anticipate many of their probable concerns. You can assume, for example, that your news will be unwelcome because long-standing patients probably liked the old dentist and dislike change and inconvenience, just like you probably would yourself.

You can go further. Anticipate your readers' questions. Just put yourself in their shoes. You may wonder

>> Why should I trust you, an unknown entity?

>> Will I feel an interruption in my care? Will there be a learning curve?

>> Will I like you and find in you what I value in a medical practitioner — aspects such as kindness, respect for my time, attentiveness, and experience?

TIP

Plan your content to answer these intrinsic questions and you can't go wrong. Note that nearly all the questions are emotional rather than factual. Few patients are likely to ask about a new doctor's training and specific knowledge. They're more concerned with the kind of person he is and how they'll be treated. This somewhat counterintuitive truth applies to many situations. The questions are essentially the same for an accountant or any other service provider.

When writing, you may need to build a somewhat indirect response to some of the questions you anticipate from readers. Writing something like "I'm a really nice person" to prospective dental patients is unlikely to convince them, but you can comfortably include any or all of the following statements in your letter:

I will carefully review all your records so I am personally knowledgeable about your history.

My staff and I pledge to keep your waiting time to a minimum. We use all the latest techniques to make your visits comfortable and pain-free.

I look forward to meeting you in person and getting to know you.

I'm part of your community and participate in its good causes such as . . .

REMEMBER

Apply this strategy to job applications, business proposals, online media, and other important materials. Ask yourself, whom do I want to reach? Is the person a human resources executive? A CEO? A prospective customer for my product or service? Then jot down a profile covering what that person is probably like as well as her concerns and questions. Everyone has a problem to solve. What's your reader's problem? The HR person must fill open jobs in ways that satisfy other people. The CEO can be counted on to have one eye on the bottom line and the other on the big picture — that's her role. If you're pitching a product, you can base a prospective customer profile on the person for whom you're producing that product.

TIP

If you're an entrepreneur, building a detailed portrait of your ultimate buyers is especially important to your success. The more you know about your prospects, the better you can deliver what they need.

Making People Care

Sending your words out into today's message-dense world is not unlike tossing your message into the sea in a bottle. However, your message is now among a trillion bottles, all of which are trying to reach the same moving and dodging targets. So your competitive edge is in shaping a better bottle — or, rather, message.

Any message you send must be well crafted and well aimed, regardless of the medium or format. The challenge is to make people care enough to read your message and act on it in some way. The following sections explore the tools you need to ensure your bottle reaches its target and has the effect you desire.

Connecting instantly with your reader

Only in rare cases these days do you have the luxury of building up to a grand conclusion, one step at a time. Your audience simply won't stick around.

REMEMBER

The opening paragraph of anything you write must instantly hook your readers. The best way to do this is to link directly to their central interests and concerns, within the framework of your purpose.

Say you're informing the staff that the office will be closed on Tuesday to install new air-conditioning. You can write:

> *Subject: About next Tuesday*
>
> *Dear Staff:*
>
> *As you know, the company is always interested in your comfort and well being. As part of our company improvement plan this past year, we've installed improved lighting in the hallways, and in response to your request that we . . .*

Stop! No one is reading this! Instead, try this:

Subject: Office closed Tuesday

We're installing new air-conditioning! Tuesday is the day, so we're giving you a holiday.

I'm happy the company is able to respond to your number 1 request on the staff survey and hope you are too.

TIP

One of the best ways to hook readers is also the simplest: Get to the point. The technique applies even to long documents. Start with the bottom line, such as the result you achieved, the strategy you recommend, or the action you want. In a report or proposal, the executive summary is often the way to do that, but note that even this micro version of your full message still needs to lead off with your most important point.

Note in the preceding example that the subject line of the email is part of the lead and is planned to hook readers as much as the first paragraph of the message. Chapter 5 in this minibook has more ideas of ways to optimize your emails.

Focusing on WIIFM

The marketing acronym *WIIFM* stands for *what's in it for me*. The air-conditioning email in the preceding section first captures readers by telling them that they have a day off and then follows up by saying that they're getting something they wanted. Figuring out what's going to engage *your* readers often takes a bit of thought.

REMEMBER

To make people care, you must first be able to answer the question yourself. Why *should* they care? Then put your answer right in the lead or even the headline.

If you're selling a product or service, for example, zero in on the problem it solves. So rather than your press release headline saying

New Widget Model to Debut at Expo Magnus on Thursday

Try

Widget 175F Day-to-Night Video Recorder Ends Pilfering Instantly

If you're raising money for a non-profit, you may be tempted to write a letter to previous donors that begins like many you probably receive:

For 75 years, Little White Lights has been helping children with learning disabilities improve their capacities, live up to their potential, and feel more confident about their educational future.

But don't you respond better to letters that open more like this?

> *For his first five years of school, Lenny hated every second. He couldn't follow the lessons, so he stopped trying and even stopped listening. But this September Lenny starts college — because the caring people and non-traditional teaching at Little White Lights showed him how to learn. He's one of 374 children whose lives we transformed since our not-for-profit organization was established, with your help, nine years ago.*

The second version works better not just because it's more concrete but also because it takes account of two factors that all recipients probably share: a concern for children, and a need to be reassured that their donations are well used.

Highlighting benefits, not features

REMEMBER

People care about what a product or service can do for them, not what it is.

>> *Features* describe characteristics — a car having a 200 mph engine; an energy drink containing 500 units of caffeine; a hotel room furnished with priceless antiques.

>> *Benefits* are what features give us — the feeling that you can be the fastest animal on earth (given an open highway without radar traps); the ability to stay up for 56 hours to make up all the work you neglected; the experience of high luxury for the price of a hotel room, at least briefly.

Benefits have more to do with feelings and experiences than data. Marketers have known the power of benefits for a long time, but neuroscientists have recently confirmed the principle, noting that most buying decisions are made emotionally rather than logically. You choose a car that speaks to your personality instead of the one with the best technical specs, and then you try to justify your decision on rational grounds.

REMEMBER

The lesson for business writing is clear: People care about messages that are based on what matters to them. Don't get lost in technical detail. Focus on the effect of an event, an idea, or a product. You can cover the specs but keep them contained in a separate section or as backup material. Approach information the way most newspapers have always done (and now do online as well). Put what's most interesting or compelling up front and then include the details in the back (or link to them) for readers who want more.

Finding the concrete and limiting the abstract

The Little White Lights example in a previous section demonstrates how to effectively focus on a single individual and simultaneously deliver a powerful, far-reaching message. One concrete example is almost always more effective than reams of high-flown prose and empty adjectives.

Make things real for your readers with these techniques:

>> **Tell stories and anecdotes.** They must embody the idea you want to communicate, the nature of your organization, or your own value. An early television show about New York City used a slogan along the lines, "Eight million people, eight million stories." A good story is always there, lurking, even in what may seem everyday or ordinary. But finding it can take some thinking and active looking.

>> **Use examples — and make them specific.** Tell customers how your product was used or how your service helped solve a problem. Give them strong case studies of implementations that worked. Inside a company, tell change-resistant staff members how another department saved three hours by using the new ordering process, or how a shift in benefits can cut their out-of-pocket healthcare costs by 14 percent. And if you want people to use a new system, give them clear guidelines, perhaps a step-by-step process to follow.

>> **Use visuals to explain and break up the words.** Readers who need to be captured and engaged generally shy away from uninterrupted type. Plenty of studies show that people remember visual lessons better, too. Look for ways to graphically present a trend, a change, a plan, a concept, or an example. In a way that suits your purpose and medium, incorporate photographs, illustrations, charts, graphs, and video. When you must deliver your message primarily in words, use graphic techniques such as headlines, subheads, bullets, typeface variations, and icons — like those in this book!

>> **Give readers a vision.** Good leaders know that a vision is essential, whether they're running companies or running for public office. You're usually best off framing your message in big-picture terms that make people believe the future will be better in some way. Don't make empty promises; instead, look for the broadest implications of an important communication and use details to back up that central concept and make it more real. Focusing a complicated document this way also makes it more organized and more memorable — both big advantages.

>> **Eliminate meaningless hyperbole.** What's the point of saying something like, "This is the most far-reaching, innovative, ground-breaking piece of industrial design ever conceived"? Yet business writing is jampacked with empty, boring claims.

WARNING

Today's audiences come to everything you write already jaded, skeptical, and impatient. If you're a service provider and describe what you do in words that can belong to anyone, in any profession, you fail. If you depend on a website and it takes viewers 20 seconds to figure out what you're selling or how to make a purchase, you lose. If you're sending out a press release that buries what's interesting or important, you're invisible. The solution: Know your point and make it fast!

TIP

Go for the evidence! Tell your audience in real terms what your idea, plan, or product accomplishes in ways they care about. Show them how

>> The product improves people's lives

>> The non-profit knows its money is helping people

>> The service solves problems

>> You personally helped your employer make more money or become more efficient

Proof comes in many forms: statistics, data, images, testimonials, surveys, case histories, biographies, and video and audio clips. Figure out how to track your success and prove it. You end up with first-rate material to use in all your communication.

Choosing Your Written Voice: Tone

Presentation trainers often state that the meaning of a spoken message is communicated 55 percent by body language, 38 percent by tone of voice, and only 7 percent by the words. Actually, this formula has been thoroughly debunked and denied by its creator — the psychologist Albert Mehrabian — but it does imply some important points for writing.

WARNING

Written messages come without body language or tone of voice. One result is that humor — particularly sarcasm or irony — is risky. When readers can't see the wink in your eye or hear the playfulness in your voice, they take you literally. So refrain from subtle humor unless you're really secure with your reader's ability to get it. Better yet: Be cautious at all times because such assumptions are dangerous.

But even lacking facial expression and gesture, writing does carry its own tone, and this directly affects how readers receive and respond to messages. Written tone results from a combination of word choice, sentence structure, and other technical factors.

Also important are less tangible elements that are hard to pin down. You've probably received messages that led you to sense the writer was upset, angry, resistant, or amused — even if only a few words were involved. Sometimes even a close reading of the text doesn't explain what's carrying these emotions, but you just sense the writer's strong feelings.

REMEMBER

When you're the writer, be conscious of your message's tone. Consistently control tone so it supports your goals and avoids undermining your message. You've probably found that showing emotion in the workplace rarely gives you an advantage. Writing is similar. Tone conveys feelings, and if you're not in control of your emotions when you write, tone betrays you.

The following sections explore some ways to find and adopt the right tone.

Being appropriate to the occasion, relationship, and culture

Pause before writing and think about the moment you're writing in. Obviously if you're communicating bad news, you don't want to sound chipper and cheery.

Always think of your larger audience, too. If the company made more money last month because it eliminated a department, best not to treat the new profits as a triumph. Current staff members probably aren't happy about losing colleagues and are worried about their own jobs. On the other hand, if you're communicating about a staff holiday party, sounding gloomy and bored doesn't generate high hopes for a good time. The same is true if you're offering an opportunity or assigning a nuisance job: Make it as enticing as possible.

REMEMBER

Just as in face-to-face situations, the moods embedded in your writing are contagious. If you want an enthusiastic response, write with enthusiasm. If you want people to welcome a change you're announcing, sound positive and confident, not fearful or peevish and resentful — even if you don't personally agree with the change.

TIP

Make conscious decisions about how formal to sound. After you work in an organization for a while, you typically absorb its culture without noticing. (In fact, most organizations don't realize that they have a culture until they run into problems when introducing change or a high-level hire.) If you're new to the place, observe how things work so you can avoid booby-trapping yourself. Read through files of correspondence, emails, reports, as well as websites and online material. Analyze what your colleagues feel is appropriate in content and in writing style. How formal is the communication for the various media used? Adopt the guidelines you see enacted.

WARNING

Every passing year seems to decrease the formality of business communication. Just as in choosing what to wear to work, people are dressing down their writing. This less formal style can come across as friendlier, simpler, and more direct than in earlier years — and should. But business informal doesn't mean you should address an executive or board member casually, use texting or abbreviations your reader may not understand, or fail to edit and proofread every message. Those are gaffes much like wearing torn jeans to work or to a client meeting.

And you want to be especially careful if you're writing to someone in another country — even an English-speaking one. Most countries still prefer a formal form of communication.

Writing as your authentic self

Never try to impress anyone with how educated and literate you are. Studies show that people believe that those who write clearly and use simple words are smarter than those whose writing abounds in fancy phrases and complicated sentences.

TIP

Authentic means being a straightforward, unpretentious, honest, trustworthy person — and writer. It doesn't mean trying for a specific writing style. Clarity is always the goalpost. This aim holds true even for materials written to impress. A proposal, marketing brochure, or request for funding gains nothing by looking or sounding pompous and weighty.

Being relentlessly respectful

REMEMBER

Never underestimate or patronize your audience, regardless of educational level, position, or apparent accomplishment. People are sensitive to such attitudes and react adversely, often without knowing why or telling you. In *all* work and business situations, take the trouble to actively demonstrate respect for your reader. Specifically, do the following:

>> Address people courteously and use their names.

>> Close with courtesy and friendliness.

>> Write carefully and proofread thoroughly; many people find poorly written messages insulting.

>> Avoid acronyms, jargon, and abbreviations that may be unfamiliar to some readers.

>> Never be abrupt or rude or demanding.

>> Try to understand and respect cultural differences.

Planning Your Message

Apply these guidelines whether you're writing to a superior, a subordinate, or a peer. You don't need to be groveling to an executive higher up the chain than you are (in most cases), though often you should be more formal. Nor should you condescend to those lower down. Consider, for example, how best to assign a last-minute task to someone who reports to you. You could say the following:

> *Madge, I need you to read this book tonight and give me a complete rundown of the content first thing tomorrow. Thanks.*

Or:

> *Madge, I need your help — please read this book tonight. The author is coming in tomorrow to talk about engaging us. I'm reading another of his books myself and if we can compare notes first thing tomorrow, I'll feel much more prepped. Thanks!*

Either way, Madge may not be thrilled at how her evening looks, but treating her respectfully and explaining *why* you're giving her this intrusive assignment accomplishes a lot: She'll be more motivated, more enthusiastic, more interested in doing a good job, and happier to be part of your team. At the cost of writing a few more sentences, you improve her attitude and perhaps even her long-range performance.

Smiling when you say it

People whose job is answering the phone are told by customer service trainers to smile before picking up the call. Smiling physically affects your throat and vocal chords, and your tone of voice. You sound friendly and cheerful and may help the person on the other end of the phone feel that way.

The idea applies to writing as well. You need not smile before you write (though it's an interesting technique to try), but be aware of your own mood and how easily it transfers to your messages and documents.

REMEMBER

Your feelings of anger, impatience, or resentment might be well grounded, but displaying them rarely helps your cause. People dislike negative, whiny, nasty messages that put them on the defensive or make them feel under attack.

Suppose you've asked the purchasing department to buy a table for your office and were denied without explanation. You could write to both your boss and the head of purchasing a note such as the following:

> *Hal, Jeanne: I just can't believe how indifferent purchasing is to my work and what I need to do it. This ignorance is really offensive. I'm now an associate manager responsible for a three-person team and regular meetings are essential to my . . .*

Put yourself in the recipients' places to see how bad the effect of such a message can be — for you. At the least, you're creating unnecessary problems; at worst, perhaps permanent bad feelings. Why not write the following instead, and just to the purchasing officer:

Hi, Hal. Do you have a minute to talk about my request for a small conference table? I was surprised to find that it was denied and want to share why it's important to my work.

REMEMBER

The best way to control your tone is to let emotion-laden matters rest for whatever time you can manage. Even a ten-minute wait can make a difference. Overnight is better, if possible, in important situations. You're far more likely to accomplish what you want when you come across as logical, reasonable, and objective. Positive and cheerful is even better.

Sometimes the challenge isn't to control bad feelings, but to overcome a blah mood that leads your writing to sound dull and uninspired when you need it to sound persuasive and engaging. Knowing your own daily patterns is helpful, so you can focus on the task that requires the most energy when you're most naturally up.

TIP

If you don't have the luxury of waiting for a good mood to hit before writing, try the following method. Churn out the basic document regardless of your spirits. Later, when you're feeling bouncier, inject the energy and enthusiasm that you know the original message is missing. Typical changes involve switching out dull passive verbs and substituting livelier ones, picking up the tempo, editing out the dead wood, and adding plusses you overlooked when you felt gray. Chapter 2 in this minibook is chock-full of ideas to enliven your language.

People naturally prefer being around positive, dynamic, enthusiastic people, and they prefer receiving messages with the same qualities. Resolve not to complain, quibble, or criticize in writing. People are much more inclined to give you what you want when you're positive — and they see you as a problem-solver rather than a problem-generator.

Using Relationship-Building Techniques

REMEMBER

Just about everything you write is a chance to build relationships with people you report to and even other people above them in the chain, as well as peers, colleagues, customers, prospects, suppliers, and members of your industry. More and more, people succeed through good networking. In a world characterized by less face-to-face contact and more global possibilities, writing is a major tool for making connections and maintaining them.

As with tone, awareness that building relationships is always one of your goals puts you a giant step ahead. Ask yourself every time you write how you can improve the relationships with that individual. A range of techniques is available to help.

Personalizing what you write

In many countries, business emails and letters that get right down to business seem cold, abrupt, and unfeeling. Japanese writers and readers, for example, prefer to begin with the kind of polite comments you tend to make when meeting someone in person: "How have you been?" "Is your family well?" "Isn't it cold for October?" Such comments or questions may carry no real substance, but they serve an important purpose: They personalize the interaction to better set the stage for a business conversation.

TIP

Creating a sense of caring or at least interest in the other person gives you a much better context within which to transact business. If you've thought about your audience when planning what to write (see the previous section, "Defining your audience: Know your reader"), you can easily come up with simple but effective personalizing phrases to frame your message. You can always fall back on the old reliables — weather and general health inquiries. If communication continues, you can move the good feelings along by asking whether the vacation mentioned earlier worked out well, or if the weekend was good — whatever clues you can follow up on without becoming inappropriate or intrusive. The idea works withgroups, too: You can, for example, begin, "I hope you all weathered the tornado okay."

Some techniques you can use to make your writing feel warm are useful but may not translate between different cultures. For example, salutations like *Hi, John* set a less formal tone than *Dear John*. Starting with just the name — *John,* — is informal to the point of assuming a relationship already exists. But both ways may not be appropriate if you're writing to someone in a more formal country than your own. A formal address — *Mr. Charles, Ms. Brown, Dr. Jones, General Frank* — may be called for. In many cultures, if you overlook this formality and other signs of respect, you can lose points before you even begin.

Similarly, it feels friendlier and less formal to use contractions: *isn't* instead of *is not, won't* instead of *will not*. But if your message is addressed to a non-native English speaker or will be translated, contractions may be confusing.

Framing messages with *you* not *I*

Just accept it: People care more about themselves and what they want than they do about you. This simple-sounding concept has important implications for business writing.

Suppose you're a software developer and your company has come up with a dramatically better way for people to manage their online reputations. You may be tempted to announce the following on your website:

We've created a great new product for online reputation management that no one ever imagined possible.

Or you could say this:

Our great new Product X helps people manage their online reputation better than ever before.

The second example is better because it's less abstract and it makes the product's purpose clear. But see if you find this version more powerful:

You want a better way to solve your online reputation management challenges? We have what you need.

TIP

When you look for ways to use the word *you* more, and correspondingly decrease the use of *I* and *we*, you put yourself on the reader's wavelength. In the case of the new software, your readers care about how the product can help them, not that you're proud of achieving it.

The principle works for everyday email, letters, and online communication too. For example, when you receive a customer complaint, instead of writing the following:

We have received your complaint about . . .

You're better off writing this:

Your letter explaining your complaint has been received . . .

Or:

Thank you for writing to us about your recent problem with . . .

Coming up with a *you* frame is often challenging. Doing so may draw you into convoluted or passive-sounding language — for example, "Your unusual experience with our tree-pruning service has come to our attention." Ordinarily we recommend a direct statement (such as, "We hear you've had an unusual experience with . . . "), but in customer service situations and others where you want to relate to your reader instantly, figuring out a way to start with *you* can be worth the effort and a brief dip into the passive. (See Chapters 2, 3, and 4 in this minibook for ways to expand your resource of techniques for fine-tuning your tone through word choice, sentence structure, and customized content.)

REMEMBER

In every situation, genuinely consider your reader's viewpoint, sensitivities, and needs. Think about how the message you're communicating affects that person or group. Anticipate questions and build in the answers. Write within this framework and you will guide yourself to create successful messages and documents. When you care, it shows. And you succeed.

Chapter **2**

Making Your Writing Work

Your writing style probably took shape in school, where literary traditions and formal essays dominate. This experience may have led you to believe that subtle thoughts require complex sentences, sophisticated vocabulary, and dense presentation. Perhaps you learned to write that way — or maybe you didn't. Either way: The rules of academic writing don't apply to the business world.

Real-world business writing is more natural, reader-friendly, and easier to do than academic writing — especially after you know the basics covered in this chapter.

Stepping into a Twenty-First-Century Writing Style

REMEMBER

In business you succeed when you achieve your goals. You need to judge business writing the same way — by whether it accomplishes what you want. The following characteristics of business writing work:

>> **Clear and simple:** Except for technical material directed at specialists, no subject matter or idea is so complex that you cannot express it in clear, simple

language. You automatically move forward a step by accepting this basic premise and practicing it.

>> **Conversational:** Business writing is reader-friendly and accessible, far closer to spoken language than the more formal and traditional style. It may even come across as casual or spontaneous. This quality, however, doesn't give you a free pass on grammar, punctuation, and the other technicalities.

>> **Correct:** Noticeable mistakes interfere with your reader's ability to understand you. Further, in today's competitive world, careless writing deducts points you can't afford to lose. People judge you by every piece of writing you create, and you need to live up to your best self. However, good contemporary writing allows substantial leeway in observing grammatical niceties.

>> **Persuasive:** When you dig beneath the surface, most messages and documents ask something of the reader. This request may be minor ("Meet me at Restaurant X at 4") to major ("Please fund this proposal; a million will do."). Even when you're just asking for or providing information, frame your message to suit your reader's viewpoint. Writing for your audience is covered in depth in Chapter 1 of this minibook.

All these indicators of successful business communication come into play in everything you write. The following sections break down the various components of style into separate bits you can examine and adjust in your own writing.

Aiming for a clear, simple style

Clarity and simplicity go hand in hand: Your messages communicate what you intend with no room for misunderstanding or misinterpretation. This requires the following:

>> Words your reader already knows and whose meanings are agreed upon — no forcing readers to look up words, no trying to impress

>> Sentence structure that readers can easily follow the first time through

>> Well-organized, logical, on-point content without anything unnecessary or distracting

>> Clear connections between sentences, paragraphs, and ultimately ideas, to make a cohesive statement

>> Correct spelling and correct grammar

REMEMBER

Writing with the preceding characteristics is transparent: Nothing stands in the way of the reader absorbing your information, ideas, and recommendations. Good business writing for most purposes doesn't call attention to itself. It's like a good makeup job. A woman doesn't want to hear, "Great cosmetology!" She hopes for "You look beautiful." Similarly, you want your audience to admire your thinking, not the way you phrased it.

TIP

One result of following these criteria is that people can move through your material quickly. This is good! A fast read is your best shot at pulling people into your message and keeping them from straying off due to boredom. These days, people are so overwhelmed and impatient that they don't bother to invest time in deciphering a message's meaning. They just stop reading.

Creating an easy reading experience is hard on the writer. When you write well, you do all the readers' work for them. They don't need to figure out anything because you've already done it for them. Make the effort because that's how you win what you want.

Applying readability guidelines

Guidelines for business writing are not theoretical. They're practical and supported by research studies on how people respond to the written word. Fortunately, you don't have to read the research. Most word-processing software, including Microsoft Word, and several websites have digested all the data and offer easy-to-use tools to help you quickly gauge the readability of your writing.

Several readability indexes exist (see the sidebar "Readability research: What it tells us"). In this section, we focus on the Flesch Readability Index because it's the index that Microsoft Word uses. The Flesch Readability Index predicts the percentage of people likely to understand a piece of writing and assigns it a grade level of reading comprehension. The grade level scores are based on average reading ability of students in the US public school system. The algorithm for the Flesch Readability Index is primarily based on the length of words, sentences, and paragraphs.

TIP

Word's version of the Index also shows you the percentage of passive sentences in a selection, which is a good indicator of flabby verbs, indirect sentence structure, and cut-worthy phrases. See the section "Finding action verbs," later in this chapter, for more on activating sentences that contain passive verbs.

Matching reading level to audience

TIP

Whatever readability index you use, your target numbers depend on the audience you're writing to (one more reason to know your readers).

Making Your Writing Work

Highly educated readers can obviously comprehend difficult material, which may lead you to strive for text written at a high educational level for scientists or MBAs. But generally this isn't necessarily a good idea. For most business communication — email, letters, proposals, websites — most readers (yourself included) are lazy and prefer easy material.

At the same time, usually you don't want to gear your use of language to the least literate members of your audience. So take any calculations with many grains of salt and adapt them to your audience and purpose. (The average reader in the US is pegged at a 7th- to 9th-grade reading level, depending on which study you look at.)

TIP

When you want to reach a diverse group with a message, you can segment your audience, just like marketers, and craft different versions for each. If a company needs to inform employees of a benefits change, for example, it may need different communications for top managers, middle managers, clerical staff, factory workers, and so on. Beyond assuming varying reading comprehension levels, you may need to rethink the content for each as well.

Assessing readability level

If you're writing in Microsoft Word 2010, to find the Readability Index choose File⇨Options⇨Proofing. (In Office 365, go to Word⇨Preferences⇨Spelling & Grammar.) In the When Correcting Spelling and Grammar in Word section, select the Check Grammar with Spelling and Show Readability Statistics options. Thereafter, whenever you complete a spelling and grammar check, you see a box with readability scores.

Several readability tests are available free online, including www.readability-score.com. On most sites, you simply paste a chunk of your text into a box and have the site gauge readability.

Example *print media* targets for general audiences follow:

>> Flesch reading ease: 50 to 70 percent

>> Grade level: 10th to 12th grade

>> Percentage of passive sentences: 0 to 10 percent

>> Words per sentence: 14 to 18, average (some can consist of one word, while others a great many more)

>> Sentences per paragraph: Average three to five

READABILITY RESEARCH: WHAT IT TELLS US

Serious studies to figure out what produces easy reading began in the early twentieth century and continue to be done in many languages in addition to English. The most influential researchers have been Rudolph Flesch — for which the Flesch Readability Index is named — and Robert Gunning, who more picturesquely called his measurement system the Fog Index. Both worked with American journalists and newspaper publishers in the late 1940s to lower the reading grade level of newspapers. And sure enough, newspaper readership went up 45 percent.

Recent grade-level ratings of what we read are illuminating. Overall, the simpler and clearer the language, the higher the readership. A few examples of necessary grade levels follow:

- Most romance novels: 7
- Popular authors, including Stephen King, Tom Clancy, and John Grisham: 7
- The UK's *Sun* and *Daily Mirror:* 9
- *The Wall Street Journal:* 11
- *Sydney Sun-Herald:* 12
- *London Times:* 12
- *The Guardian:* 14
- *Times of India:* 15
- Academic papers: 15 to 20
- Typical government documents: Over 20

A recent British university study applied readability criteria to online newspapers and the results mirror print studies: *The Sun* was easiest to read and *The Guardian* the most difficult.

For online media, the targets are tighter. Reading from a screen — even a big one — is physically harder for people, so they are even less patient than with printed material. Sentences work best when they average 8 to 12 words. Paragraphs should contain one to three sentences.

Select a section or an entire document of something you wrote recently in Word or for a website. Review the Readability Statistics to find out if you need to simplify your writing. If the statistics say that at least a 12th-grade reading level is required (on many Word programs, the index doesn't show levels above 12) and less than 50 percent of readers will understand your document, consider rewriting. Or do the same if you used more than 10 percent passive sentences.

The next section provides lots of suggestions for rewriting, but for now consider any or all of the following:

>> Substitute short, one or two syllable words for any long ones.

>> Shorten long sentences by breaking them up or tightening your wording.

>> Break paragraphs into smaller chunks so that you have fewer sentences in each.

>> Look for words that are a form of the verbs *have* or *to be* (*is, are, will be,* and so on). These verbs are weak and often result in passive verb construction.

>> Review the rewrite to make sure that your message still means what you intended and hasn't become even harder to understand.

Then recheck the statistics. If the figures are still high, repeat the process. See if you can get the grade level down to 10, then 8. Try for less than 10 percent passive. Compare the different versions.

Finding the right rhythm

You may wonder whether basing your writing on short simple sentences produces choppy and boring material reminiscent of a grade school textbook. Aiming for clear and simple definitely should not mean dull reading.

Becoming aware of rhythm in what you read, and what you write, can improve your writing dramatically. Like all language, English was used to communicate orally long before writing was invented, so the sound and rhythm patterns are critical to how written forms as well as spoken ones are received.

Think of the worst public speakers you know. They probably speak in a series of long, complex sentences in an even tone that quickly numbs the ear. Good speakers, by contrast, vary the length of sentences and their intonation. As a writer, you want to do the same.

REMEMBER

In everything you write, aim to build in a natural cadence. Rhythm is one of the main tools for cajoling people to stay with you and find what you write more interesting. Just begin each sentence differently from the previous one and try alternating short, plain sentences with longer ones that have two or three clauses.

Good public speakers vary the lengths of their sentences to keep listeners' ears engaged. They avoid long, complex sentences, and they know that short punchy words and phrases need to be doled out carefully for maximum effect. As a writer, you want readers to have a similar experience.

Fixing the short and choppy

Even a short message benefits from attention to sentence rhythm. Consider this paragraph:

> *John: Our screw supply is low. It takes three weeks for orders to be filled. We should place the order now. Then we won't have an emergency situation later. Please sign this form to authorize this purchase. Thank you. — Ted*

And an alternate version:

> *John: Our screw supply is low. It takes three weeks for orders to be filled, so we should place the order now to avoid an emergency later. Please sign the attached form to authorize the purchase. Thanks. — Ted*

REMEMBER

For long documents, varying your sentence length and structure is critical. Few people will stay with multiple pages of stilted, mind-numbing prose.

Notice too that when you combine some short sentences to alternate the rhythm, easy ways emerge to improve the wording and edit out unneeded repetition. You may choose to go a step further and write a third version of the same message:

> *John: I notice that our screw supply is getting low. Since an order will take three weeks to reach us, let's take care of it now to avoid an emergency down the line. Just sign the attached authorization and we're all set. — Ted*

Leaving aside how this was edited, which is discussed in the next chapter, notice how much more connected the thoughts seem, and how much more authoritative the overall message feels. With little rewriting, the writer comes across as a more take-charge, efficient professional — someone who is reliable and cares about the entire operation, rather than just a cog going through the motions.

Fixing the long and complicated

Many people have a problem opposite to creating short, disconnected sentences. Maybe you tend to write lengthy complicated ones that end up with the same result: dead writing.

Making Your Writing Work

TIP

The solution to never-ending strings of words is the same — alternate sentence structures. But in this case, break up the long ones. Doing this produces punchier, more enticing copy.

A number of basically good writers don't succeed as well as they might because they fall into a pattern that repeats the same rhythm, over and over again. An example taken from an opinion piece written for a workshop:

> *I strongly support efforts to improve the global economy, and naturally may be biased toward the author's position. While this bias may be the reason I responded well to the piece in the first place, it is not the reason why I consider it an exceptional piece of writing. Not only is this article extremely well researched, its use of cost-benefit analysis is an effective way to think about the challenges.*

The monotonous pattern and unending sentences serve the ideas poorly. One way to rewrite the material:

> *I strongly support efforts to improve the global economy and this probably inclined me to a positive response. But it's not why I see it as an exceptional piece of writing. The article is extremely well researched. Further, its cost-benefit analysis is an effective way to think about the challenge.*

Again, simply varying the sentence length and structure quickly improves the overall wording and flow. Notice that you can take liberties with the recommended short-long-short sentence pattern and use two short sentences, then two more complex ones, for example.

Spend ten minutes with a recent piece of your writing that's at least half a page long. Scan it for rhythmic patterns. You may find a balanced flow with varying types of sentences. Or you may see sets of short, choppy sentences. Experiment with recombining some of them into longer ones. If you find too many long, convoluted sentences, break some of them up so short, terse ones are interspersed. Read the reworked text in its entirety and see whether it reads better.

REMEMBER

Everyone has particular ways of writing that leave room for improvement. Strive to recognize your own weaknesses and you'll be a giant step closer to better writing because you can apply fix-it techniques as part of your regular self-editing process. You can draw on a bunch of methods in Chapter 3 of this minibook.

Achieving a conversational tone

New business writers are often told to adopt a conversational tone, but what does that mean? Business correspondence written during the nineteenth century and even most of the twentieth seems slow, formal, and ponderous when you read it now. Today's faster pace of life results in a desire for faster communication, both in terms of how you deliver messages and how quickly you're able to read and deal with them.

REMEMBER

Conversational tone is something of an illusion. You don't really write the way you talk, and you shouldn't. But you can echo natural speech in various ways to more effectively engage your audience.

Rhythm, described in the preceding section, is a basic technique that gives your copy forward momentum and promotes a conversational feeling. Sentence variety engages readers while unrelieved choppy sentences or complicated ones kill interest.

Additional techniques for achieving conversational tone include the following:

>> **Infuse messages with warmth.** If you think of the person as an individual before you write, content that's appropriate to the relationship and subject will come to you, and the tone will be right.

>> **Choose short, simple words.** Rely on the versions you use to *talk* to someone, rather than the sophisticated ones you use to try and impress. See the later section "Choosing reader-friendly words" for examples.

>> **Use contractions as you do in speech.** For example, go with *can't* rather than *cannot,* and *I'm* rather than *I am.*

>> **Minimize the use of inactive and passive forms.** Carefully evaluate every use of the *to be* verbs — *is, was, will be, are,* and so on — to determine if you can use active, interesting verbs instead.

>> **Take selective liberties with grammatical correctness.** Starting a sentence with *and* or *but* is okay, for example, but avoid mismatching your nouns and pronouns.

>> **Adopt an interactive spirit.** As online media teaches, one-way, top-down communication is so yesterday. Find ways in all your writing to invite active interest and input from your reader.

If you ignore the preceding guidelines — and want to look hopelessly outdated — you can write a long-winded and lifeless message like the following:

Dear Elaine:

I regret to communicate that the meeting for which we are scheduled on Tuesday at 2 p.m. must be canceled. Unfortunately the accounting information anticipated for receipt on Friday will not be able to meet the delivery deadline.

I am contemplating an appropriate rescheduling. Please inform my office of your potential availability at 3 p.m. on the 2nd. — Carrie

Yawn — and also a bit confusing. Or you can write a clear, quick, crisp version like this:

> *Elaine, I'm sorry to say we're postponing the Tuesday meeting. The accounting info we need won't be ready till Wednesday. Bummer, I know.*
>
> *Is Thursday at 3:00 okay for you? — Carrie*

TIP

Although the second example feels casual and conversational, these aren't the actual words Carrie would say to Elaine in a real phone conversation. This exchange is more likely:

> *Hi. How are you? Listen, we got a problem. The project numbers are running way late. I won't have them till Wednesday. Yeah. So no point meeting Tuesday. How's Thursday look?*

Online copy often works best when it carries the conversational illusion to an extreme. Pay attention to the jazzy, spontaneous-style copy on websites you love. The words may read like they sprang ready-made out of some genie's lamp, but more than likely a team of copywriters agonized over every line for weeks. Spontaneous-reading copy doesn't come easy: It's hard work. Some people — frequent bloggers, for example — are better at writing conversationally because they practice this skill consciously.

The next time you encounter bloggers or online writers whose voices you like, copy some text and paste it into a blank word-processing document (to separate the words from all the online bells and whistles). Read through the words carefully and analyze what you like in terms of words, phrases, and sentences. See if you can identify how the writers pull off their appealing breezy style.

Enlivening Your Language

The most important guideline for selecting the best words for business writing may seem counterintuitive: Avoid long or subtle words that express nuance. These may serve as the staple for many fiction writers and academics, but you're not striving to sound evocative, ambiguous, impressive, or super-educated. In fact, you want just the opposite.

Relying on everyday words and phrasing

The short everyday words you use in ordinary speech are almost always best for business writing. They're clear, practical, and direct. They're also powerful enough to express your deepest and widest thoughts. They're the words that reach people emotionally, too, because they stand for the most basic and concrete things people care about and need to communicate about. For example, *home* is a whole different story than *residence,* and *quit* carries a lot more overtones than *resign.*

Make a list of basic one- and two-syllable words. Almost certainly, they come from the oldest part of the English language, Anglo-Saxon. Most words with three or more syllables were grafted onto this basic stock by historical invaders: the French-speaking Normans and the Latin-speaking Romans for the most part, both of whom aspired to higher levels of cultural refinement than the Britons.

If you were raised in an English-speaking home, you learned Anglo-Saxon words during earliest childhood and acquired the ones with Latin, French, and other influences later in your education. Scan these previous two paragraphs and you know immediately which words came from which culture set.

REMEMBER

For this reason and others, readers are programmed to respond best to simple, short, low-profile English words. They trigger feelings of trust (an Anglo-Saxon word) and credibility (from the French). Obviously, I don't choose to write entirely with one-syllable words. Variety is the key — just as with sentences. English's history gives you a remarkable array of words when you want to be precise or produce certain feelings. Even in business English, a sprinkling of longer words contributes to a good pace and can make what you say more specific and interesting. But don't forget your base word stock.

TIP

If you're writing to a non-native English speaking audience, you have even more reason to write with one- and two-syllable words. People master the same basic words first when learning a new language, no matter what their original tongue, so all new English-speakers understand them. This applies to less educated readers too. Given the diverse and multicultural audiences many of your messages must reach, simplicity of language should rule.

This principle holds for long documents such as reports and proposals as much as for emails. And it's very important for online writing such as websites and blogs. When you read on-screen, you have even less patience with multi-syllable sophisticated words. Reading (and writing) on smartphones and other small devices makes short words the *only* choice.

Choosing reader-friendly words

The typical business English you see all the time may lure you toward long, educated words. Resist!

Consciously develop your awareness of short-word options. Clearer writing gives you better results. Opt for the first and friendlier word in the following pairs:

Use	Rather than
help	assistance
often	frequently
try	endeavor
need	requirement
basic	fundamental
built	constructed
confirm	validate
rule	regulation
create	originate
use	utilize
prove	substantiate
show	demonstrate
study	analyze
fake	artificial
limits	parameters
skill	proficiency
need	necessitate

The longer words aren't bad — in fact, they may often be the better choice. But generally, make sure that you have a reason for going long.

Focusing on the real and concrete

Concrete nouns are words that denote something tangible: a person or any number of things, such as cat, apple, dirt, child, boat, balloon, computer, egg, tree, table, and Joseph.

Abstract nouns, on the other hand, typically represent ideas and concepts. They may denote a situation, a condition, a quality or an experience. For example: catastrophe, freedom, efficiency, knowledge, mystery, observation, analysis, research, love, and democracy.

REMEMBER

Concrete nouns are objects that exist in real space. You can touch, see, hear, smell, or taste them. When you use concrete nouns in your writing, readers bring these physical associations to your words, and this lends reality to your thoughts. Moreover, you can expect most people to take the same meaning from them. This isn't true of abstract words. Two people are unlikely to argue about what an apricot is, but they may well disagree on what exactly *independence* means.

TIP

When your writing is built on a lot of abstract nouns, you are generalizing. Even when you're writing an opinion or philosophical piece, too much abstraction doesn't fire the imagination. A lot of business writing strikes readers as dull and uninspiring for this reason.

Suppose at a pivotal point of World War II, Winston Churchill had written in the manner of many modern business executives:

> *We're operationalizing this initiative to proceed as effectively, efficiently, and proactively as possible in alignment with our responsibilities to existing population centers and our intention to develop a transformative future for mankind. We'll employ cost-effective, cutting-edge technologies and exercise the highest level of commitment, whatever the obstacles that materialize in various geographic situations.*

Instead he wrote, and said:

> *We shall not flag or fail. We shall go on to the end. We shall fight in France, we shall fight on the seas and the oceans, we shall fight with growing confidence and growing strength in the air, we shall defend our island, whatever the cost may be. We shall fight on the beaches, we shall fight on the landing grounds, we shall fight in the fields and in the streets, we shall fight in the hills; we shall never surrender.*

Which statement engages the senses and therefore the heart, even three-quarters of a century after this particular cause was won? Which carries more conviction? Granted, Churchill was writing a speech, but the statement also works amazingly when read.

TIP

While you probably won't be called on to rouse your countrymen as Churchill was, writing in a concrete way pays off for you too. It brings your writing alive. Aim to get down to earth in what you say and how you say it.

Using short words goes a long way toward this goal. Note how many words of the mock business-writing piece contain three or more syllables. Churchill's piece uses only three. And running both passages through readability checks (see the previous section "Applying readability guidelines") predicts at least a 12th-grade reading level to understand the business-speak with only 2 percent of readers understanding it. By contrast, Churchill's lines require only a 4th-grade reading level and 91 percent of readers understand them.

WARNING

You may often find yourself tempted to write convoluted, indirect, abstract prose — because it's common to your corporate culture, or your technical field or the request for proposal you're responding to. Don't do it. Remind yourself that nobody likes to read that kind of writing, even though he may write that way himself. Take the lead in delivering lean, lively messages and watch the positive response this brings.

Finding action verbs

Good strong verbs invigorate. Passive verbs, which involve a form of the verb *to be*, deaden language and thinking, too. Consider some dull sentences and their better alternatives:

> *All department heads were invited to the celebration by the CEO.*
>
> *The CEO invited all department heads to the celebration.*

> *A decision to extend working hours was reached by the talent management office.*
>
> *The talent management office decided to extend working hours.* Or: *The talent management office is extending work hours.*

> *The idea is an improvement on the original design.*
>
> *The idea improves the original design.*

> *The annual report numbers were contradicted by the auditors.*
>
> *The auditors contradict the annual report numbers.*

Try also to avoid sentences that rely on the phrases *there is* and *there are*, which often bury the meaning of a sentence. Compare the following pairs:

> *There is a company rule to consider in deciding which route to follow.*
>
> *A company rule determines which route to follow.*

> *There are guidelines you should use if you want to improve your writing.*
>
> *Use the guidelines to improve your writing.*

TIP

For most dull passive verbs, the solution is the same: *Find the action.* Be clear about *who* did *what* and then rework the sentence to say that.

You may need to go beyond changing the verb and rethink the entire sentence so it's simple, clear, and direct. In the process, take responsibility. Passive sentences often evade it. A classic example follows:

> *Mistakes were made, people were hurt, and opportunities were lost.*

Who made the mistakes, hurt the people, and lost the opportunities? The writer? An unidentified CEO? Mystery government officials? This kind of structure is sometimes called the *divine passive:* Some unknown or unnamable force made it happen.

To help you remember why you generally need to avoid the passive, here's a favorite mistake. When a group of people were asked to write about their personal writing problems and how they planned to work on them, one person contributed the following:

> *Many passive verbs are used by me.*

REMEMBER

Take the time to identify the passive verbs and indirect constructions in all your writing. Doing so doesn't mean that you must always eliminate them. You may want to use the passive because no clearly definable active subject exists — or it doesn't matter:

> *The award was created to recognize outstanding sales achievement.*

Or you may have a surprise to disclose that leads you to use the passive for emphasis:

> *This year's award was won by the newest member of the department: Joe Mann.*

TIP

Using the passive unconsciously often undermines your writing success. Substitute active verbs. They can be short and punchy, such as *drive, end, gain, fail, win, probe, treat, taint, speed.* Or they can be longer words that offer more precise meaning, such as *underline, trigger, suspend, pioneer, model, fracture, crystallize, compress, accelerate.* Both word groups suggest action and movement, adding zing and urgency to your messages.

Crafting comparisons to help readers

Comparisons help your readers understand your message on deeper levels. You can use similes and metaphors, which are both analogies, to make abstract ideas more tangible and generally promote comprehension. These devices don't need to be elaborate, long, or pretentiously literary. Here are some simple comparisons:

> *Poets use metaphors like painters use brushes — to paint pictures that help people see under the surface.*

> *Winning this award is my Oscar.*

> *Life is like a box of chocolates.*

The new polymer strand is 10 nanometers in width — while the average human hair is 90,000 nanometers wide.

From 15,000 feet up the world looks like a peaceful quilt of harmonious colors where no conflict could exist.

Whatever device you use, effective comparisons do the following:

>> **Create mental images:** You can give readers a different way to access — and *remember* — your ideas and information.

>> **Align things from different arenas:** Using the familiar to explain the unfamiliar can be especially helpful when you introduce new information or change.

MAKING UP FRESH COMPARISONS

Playing with comparisons is a classic schoolroom game, and you can experiment today as a means of finding new ways to express your ideas. Simply think about bringing together two different things so one is seen differently.

Take 15 minutes and assemble a short list of things, activities, or experiences on the left side of a page of blank paper or a screen. For example, you can list your new project, writing your resume, making your boss happy, the new product you're selling, or playing a computer game.

Think about what that item is like — how you can describe it visually or through the other senses. Think about how it makes you feel. Brainstorm about other things that have similar characteristics. Try to avoid clichés and instead come up with something you find interesting.

Write your idea for each item on your list on the right side. Come up with an idea for every item just to give yourself the practice, even if some of your comparisons aren't brilliant. Use your new skill when you're writing an important document, trying to explain something difficult, or making your best persuasive argument.

For example, you might brainstorm for a comparison by finishing statements such as the following:

Winning this contract is as good as . . .

This new service will change your thinking about life insurance, just like X changed Y.

Saving a few dollars by investing in Solution A instead of Solution B is like . . .

>> **Heighten the effect of everyday practical writing:** Just as in well-written fiction, a great comparison in a business document engages the reader's imagination and boosts your message's memorability.

>> **Make intriguing headlines that grab attention:** If you saw a blog post titled, "How Learning to Ride a Bike Is Like Working at Home," you'd be likely to read it just to find out what the two things have in common.

Using Reader-Friendly Graphic Techniques

Good written messages and documents are well thought out, as covered in Chapter 1 in this minibook, and presented clearly and vividly, as shown in the previous sections of this chapter. But there's one more aspect to highlight. Your writing must not only meet audience needs and read well but also look good.

REMEMBER

Whether your material appears in print or online, every message and document you create is a visual experience. More than readability is at stake; readers judge your message's value and credibility by how it looks. Whether you want to write an effective resume, proposal, report — or just an email — design can make or break your writing.

The following sections show you how to use various graphic techniques to maximize your message's appeal. And rest assured, you don't need to purchase special software or other tools to easily implement these good design principles.

Building in white space

To coin a comparison (see the sidebar "Making up fresh comparisons"):

Add white space to your writing for the same reason bakers add yeast to their bread — to leaven the denseness by letting in the light and air.

TIP

Help your writing breathe by providing plenty of empty space. The eye demands rest when scanning or reading. Don't cram your words into a small tight space by decreasing the point size or squeezing the space between characters, words or lines. Densely packed text is inaccessible. If you have too many words for the available space, cut them down. We show you many ways to do that in Chapter 3 in this minibook.

Always look for opportunities to add that valuable white space to your message. Check for white space in everything you deliver. Factors that affect white space include the size of the typeface, line spacing, margin size, and column width, and graphic devices such as subheads, sidebars, and integrated images.

Toying with type

Type has numerous graphic aspects and effects. Following are some of the most powerful, as well as easiest to adjust.

Fonts

Using an easy-to-read simple typeface (or font) is critical. For printed text, *serif fonts* — fonts with feet or squiggles at the end of each letter — are more reader-friendly because they smoothly guide the eye from letter to letter, word to word. However, *sans-serif fonts* (ones without the little feet) are favored by art directors because they look more modern and classy. The sans-serif face Verdana was specifically designed for screen work and often used for it.

TIP

You need to choose your font according to your purpose. For long print documents, serif remains the better choice for the same reason that books still use it — ease of reading. But you can to some extent mix your faces. Using sans-serif headlines and subheads can make a welcome contrast. (For example, Times New Roman and Helvetica work nicely together.) But generally, resist the temptation to combine more than two different typefaces.

WARNING

Avoid fancy or cute typefaces for any purpose. They're not only distracting but may not transfer well to someone else's computer system. They can end up garbled or altogether missing in action. Recruitment officers sometimes find a candidate's name entirely missing from a resume because their systems lack a corresponding typeface and end up omitting these important words.

And never type an entire message in capitals or bold face, which gives the impression that you're shouting. Avoid using italics on more than a word or two because such treatments are hard to read.

Point size

Like font choice, the best point size for text depends on the result that you're trying to achieve. Generally, somewhere between 10 and 12 points works best, but you need to adjust according to your audience and the experience you want to create. Small type may look great, but if you want readers 55 and older to read your annual report, 8-point type will kill it.

Online text suggests a similar 10- to 12-point range for body copy, but calculating the actual onscreen experience for a wide range of monitors and devices is complicated. Online text often looks different on different platforms. Err on the side of a generous point size.

Never resort to reducing the size of your typeface to fit more in. Someone once has to persuade his boss to cut back his "Message from the CEO" because it was longer than the allocated space. He resisted sacrificing more than a few words. Then he was shown what his message would look like in the 6-point type necessary to run the whole thing. He quickly slashed half his copy to create a better presentation.

Margins and columns

For both online and print media, avoid making columns of type so wide that the eye becomes discouraged in reading across. If breaking the copy into two columns isn't suitable, consider making one or both margins wider. Also avoid columns that are only three or four words wide, because they're hard to read and annoying visually.

Be selective in how you justify text. Left-justified text is almost always your best choice for body copy. Right-justified text is difficult to read because each new line starts in a different spot. Fully justified copy (on both left and right) often visibly distorts words and spacing to make your words fit consistently within a block of text (unless it is professionally typeset, like this book). Worse yet, full justification eliminates a good way to add white space through uneven lines.

Keeping colors simple

Using color to accent your document can work well, but keep it simple. One color, in addition to the black used for the text, is probably plenty. See whether an accent color sparks your message by using it consistently on headlines or sub-heads or both.

WARNING

Using a lot of different colors — even on a website — strikes people as messy and amateur these days. Designers prefer simple, clean palettes that combine a few colors at most. So should you. And do not place any type against a color background that makes it hard to read. Backgrounds should be no more than a light tint. *Dropped or reversed-out type* — for instance, white type on a black or dark background — can look terrific but only in small doses, such as a caption or short sidebar. An entire page of reversed-out type, whether in print or onscreen, makes a daunting read.

REMEMBER

If you're producing a substantial document or website in tandem with a graphic designer, never allow graphic effect to trump readability and editorial clarity. To most designers, words are just part of a visual pattern. If a designer tells you the document has too many words, certainly listen; it's probably true and you do want the piece to look good. But just say no if playing second fiddle to the visual undermines your copy. Graphics should strengthen, not weaken, your message's effect and absorbability.

Adding effective graphics

On the whole, if you have good images and they're appropriate, flaunt them. This doesn't really apply to an email or letter, but graphics certainly help long documents and anything read online.

Appropriateness of graphics depends on your purpose. A proposal can benefit from charts and graphs to make financials and other variables clear and more easily grasped. A report may include photographs of a project under way. A blog with a fun image related to the subject is more enticing. Additional possibilities for various media include images of successful projects to support credibility, illustrations of something yet to be built, change documentation, and visualizations of abstract ideas.

Your own resources and time may be limited. But when visual effect matters — to attract readers or when you're competing for a big contract, for example — take time to brainstorm possibilities. Wonderful online resources proliferate, and many are free. With some imagination and research, you can use your computer to produce a good chart or graph.

WARNING

Images must feel appropriate to your readers. If not, you create a negative reaction. Even with websites, research shows that people value the words most and are put off by images unrelated to the subject. And generally stay away from clip art that's packaged with your word-processing software or other design tools. Clip art must be totally appropriate to your medium and message or cleverly adapted to look original or else it instantly cheapens your message in the viewer's eye.

Breaking space up with sidebars, boxes, and lists

Print media in the past decade have increasingly used graphic techniques to draw readers in with as many ways as they can come up with. Today's readers are scanners first. Think of your own behavior when opening up a newspaper or magazine. You most likely scout for what interests you and then read the material, in whole or at least in part, if it appeals to you. When you get bored, you quickly stop reading and start scanning again.

Good headlines and subheads are critical to capture readers' attention and guide them through a document. But you must also pay major attention to writing:

>> Captions accompanying photos and other images

>> Sidebars and boxes offering additional background, sidelights, or information

>> Interesting quotes or tidbits used as pullouts in the margins or inside the text

>> Small tight summaries of the article, or introductions, at the beginning

>> Bulleted or numbered lists of examples or steps

>> Icons (such as the Tip and Remember icons in this book) that denote something of special interest

All these devices serve three important purposes.

>> **Along with images, they break up unrelieved blocks of type that discourage the eye.** In fact, on a printed page, some print editors use the dollar bill test: If you can lay down a bill on a page and it doesn't touch a single graphic device, add one in.

>> **They offer different ways to capture a reader's attention.** A summary, caption, or box may draw you in to read the entire piece, or at least some of it.

>> **Using graphic devices helps to convey ideas and information more clearly and effectively.** People absorb information in different ways. Taking lessons from the online world, today's editors offer readers choices of what they want to read, and where they want to start.

REMEMBER

All these graphic techniques should be part of your writing repertoire. Do you need them for every email you write? Of course not. But strategies elements such as subheads and bullets can still help get your message across. For long documents and materials intended to be persuasive, draw on all the techniques that suit your goals and audience.

Chapter **3**

Improving Your Work

If you expect to create a successful email, letter, or business document in just one shot, think again. Don't ask so much of yourself. Few professional writers can accomplish a finished piece — whether they write novels, plays, articles, websites, or press releases — with their first draft. This especially includes writers known for their simplicity and easy reading.

Editing is how writers write. For them, the writing and editing processes are inseparable because they wouldn't dream of submitting work to anyone that is less than their best. Unfortunately, many people are intimidated by the notion of editing their own work. But equipped with effective methods and techniques, you can edit with confidence.

Mastering hundreds of grammar rules is not necessary to becoming a good editor. Know the clues that reveal where your writing needs work, and you can sharpen what you write so it accomplishes exactly what you want. This chapter gives you the groundwork.

Changing Hats: Going from Writer to Editor

The writer and editor roles reinforce each other.

» In writing, you plan your message or document based on what you want to accomplish and your analysis of the reader (covered in Chapter 1 in this minibook), brainstorm content possibilities, organize logically, and create a full draft. Always think of this piece as the *first draft* because every message, whatever its nature and length, deserves editing and will hugely benefit from it.

>> In editing, you review your first draft and find ways to liven word choice, simplify sentences, and ensure that ideas hang together. You also evaluate the macro side: whether the content and tone deliver the strongest message to your audience and help build relationships. (All this is covered in Chapter 1 in this minibook.) Furthermore, as you make a habit of regularly editing your writing, your first-draft writing improves as well.

>> In proofreading, you review your writing in nitty-gritty detail to find and correct errors — mistakes in spelling, grammar, punctuation, facts, references, citations, calculations, and more.

Don't expect to discard the editing process down the line as you further refine your writing abilities. Professional writers never stop relying on their editing skills, no matter how good they get at their craft.

Improving your editing abilities goes a long way toward improving the effect of everything you write. The following tools and tricks make you a more capable and confident self-editor.

Choosing a way to edit

You have three main ways to edit writing. Try each of the following and see which you prefer — but realize you can always switch your editing method to best suit a current writing task or timeline.

Option 1: Marking up printouts

Before computers, both writers and editors worked with hard copy because it was the only choice. For about a century before computers, people wrote on typewriters, revised the results by hand, and then retyped the entire document. If you were reviewing *printer's proofs* — preliminary versions of material to be printed — you used a shorthand set of symbols to tell the typesetter what to change.

These symbols offered uniformity; every editor and printer knew what they meant. Typing and printing processes have changed radically, but the marks are still used today and remain a helpful way for communicating text changes between people.

TIP

Many professional writers still edit their work on printouts because on-screen editing strains the eyes and makes you more error-prone. You may find that physically editing your copy with universal marks to be more satisfying; you have something to show for your editing efforts when you're finished. Editing on paper can help you switch over to the editor's side of the table. Of course, you must then transfer the changes to your computer.

REMEMBER

Proof marks vary between the US and UK, and some organizations have special marks or special meanings.

Option 2: Editing on-screen

After you draft a document, you can simply read through it and make changes. Younger writers may never have considered any other system. With a few mouse clicks or keystrokes, you can substitute words and reorganize the material by cutting and pasting. The down side to this method of editing is that you're left with no record of the change process. (See the next section for a useful alternative.)

When maintaining a copy of your original text matters, save your new version as a separate document. Amend its name to avoid hassle later, in case a series of revised versions develops.

TIP

Keep your renaming simple yet specific. If the document is titled *Gidget*, title the edited version *Gidget 2*, for example, or date it *Gidget 11.13*. When you edit someone else's document, tack on your initials: *Gidget.nc*, for example. Be sure your titling allows for easy identification of the various versions to avoid time-wasting confusion later.

Option 3: Tracking your changes

Most word-processing software offers a handy feature to record every change you make to the text in a document. In Word 2010, choose Review, then choose Track Changes.

When you choose to track changes, all changes show up on the copy in a color other than black or in small text boxes off to the side (depending on your choice of screen view). Deletions appear as strikethrough text or off to the side.

The system takes some personal trial and error but provides a useful tool for your editing experiments.

When you're tracking changes on an extensively edited document, you can end up with something quite complicated. You can spare yourself the nitty-gritty of every deletion and insertion by selecting to view as Final with All Your Proposed Changes Included. You don't lose your edits; they're just hidden from immediate view.

When you finish editing, save a version that shows the revisions, and then go back to the Review tab and choose Accept or Reject Changes. Accept all changes, or go through your document section by section or even sentence by sentence. You emerge with a clean copy; save this version separately from the original. Proof the new version carefully because new errors creep in when you edit.

TIP

The Track Changes tool can help you improve your writing process and offers a way to share refinement stages with others when needed. (Numerous online tools, such as Google Docs, help you share document development.) But when you ultimately send the message to your audience, be sure your final saved version does not reveal the change process: Turn Track Changes off.

Distancing yourself from what you write

REMEMBER

The first step for a self-editor is to consciously assume that role. Forget how hard some of the material was to draft, or how attached you are to some of the ideas or language. Aim to judge as objectively as you can whether your message succeeds and how to improve it.

PRACTICING THE STRIPPER'S ART: IN WRITING, LESS IS USUALLY MORE

Your goal for every message and business document is "just enough." This applies both to overall content and specific word choices:

- **Content:** Aim to makes your point and achieve your goal without overkill that loses your reader or damages your argument.

- **Words:** A windy presentation dilutes the effect and may slow reading to the point of no return. Aim to state your case, make or respond to a request, present an argument, or accomplish any given purpose in the most concise way.

Build every message with complete words, sentences, and commonly accepted grammar. (Abbreviated messages do have their place, however. See the later sidebar "Texting and instant messaging: When and where to use the style" for details.)

Many documents suggest their own lengths. If you're answering an RFP (request for proposal) that's ten pages long, a one-page response doesn't suffice. You must supply detail and backup. If you're applying for a job, even a well-crafter paragraph can't take the place of a resume. Always take a document's purpose into account to judge its appropriate length and depth.

Your best tool to achieve this distance is the one that cures all ills: time. Chapter 1 in this minibook suggests that for everything you write, allocate roughly one-third the available time to planning, one-third to drafting, and one-third to editing. But ideally, that last third isn't in the same continuous time frame as the first two stages.

TIP

Try to build in a pause between drafting and editing. Pausing overnight (or longer) is highly recommended for major business documents. If your document is long or important, try to edit and re-edit in a series of stages over days or even weeks. Some copy, such as a website home page or a marketing piece, may never be finished. It evolves over time.

For short or less consequential messages, an hour or two between drafting and editing helps. A top-of-your-head email or text message that doesn't seem important can still land you in a lot of trouble if you send it out without vetting. If an hour isn't possible, just a quick trip to the coffee maker to stretch your legs can clear your mind and refresh your eyes.

So put the message away and then revisit it after a planned delay. When you return, you see your words with fresh eyes — an editor's rather than the writer's.

Reviewing the Big and Small Pictures

Your job when self-editing is to review what you wrote on two levels:

>> **The macro level:** The thinking that underlies the message and the content decisions you made.

>> **The micro level:** How well you use language to express your viewpoint and ask for what you want. (This topic is discussed in Chapter 4 in this minibook.)

Assessing content success

Start your edit with a big-picture review, using the fresh eyes and mind you gain by putting the piece aside for a while.

Read through the entire document and ask yourself the following:

>> Is what I want very clear from reading the message?

>> Does the content support that goal?

>> Is anything missing from my argument, my sequence of thoughts, or my explanations? Do I include all necessary backup information?

>> Do I give the reader a reason to care?

>> Do I include any unnecessary ideas or statements that don't contribute to or that detract from my central goal?

>> Does the tone feel right for the person or group with whom I'm communicating?

>> Does the entire message present me in the best possible light?

>> How would I react if I were the recipient rather than the sender?

>> Could my reader misunderstand or misinterpret my words?

TIP

The initial editing challenge is to drill to the core of your message. If you followed the step-by-step process to create the document presented in Chapter 1 in this minibook, check now that you met your own criteria and that every element works to accomplish your goal.

Your objective answers to these nine questions may lead you to partially or substantially revamp your content. That's fine — there's no point working to improve the presentation until you have the right substance.

You may choose to do the big-picture revision right away, or plan for it and proceed to the second stage, which is the micro-level of editing, or crafting the words. It's much easier to make the language more effective when you know exactly what message you want to deliver.

Assessing the effectiveness of your language

You have two ways to get instant, objective feedback on how well you used language.

>> **Use a readability index.** Most word-processing software can give you a good overview of the difficulty of any written piece. As Chapter 2 in this minibook details, Word's Readability Statistics box provides helpful information on word, sentence, and paragraph length; the number of passive constructions; and the degree of ease with which people can read and understand your message. Use these statistics to pinpoint your word-choice problems.

>> **Read it aloud.** Reading what they write aloud is a favored method for many writers. As you speak your writing quietly — even under your breath — you identify problems in flow, clarity, and word choice. Asking someone else to read your words aloud to you can put you even more fully in the listener role.

In addition to telling you whether you achieved a conversational tone, the read-aloud test alerts you to eight specific problems common to poor writing. Solutions to four of these problems are in Chapter 2 in this minibook:

>> **Problem 1:** A sentence is so long it takes you more than one breath to get through it.

Solution: Break up or shorten the sentence.

>> **Problem 2:** You hear a monotonous pattern, with each sentence starting the same way.

Solution: Change some of the sentence structures so you alternate between long and short, simple and complex.

>> **Problem 3**: All or most sentences sound short and choppy, which creates an abrupt tone and dulls the content.

Solution: Combine some sentences to make reading the text smoother.

>> **Problem 4:** You stumble over words.

Solution: Replace those words with simpler ones, preferably words that are one or two syllables long.

The read-aloud method can reveal four additional challenges. Each problem is dealt with in greater detail in following sections. For now, here's a quick overview:

>> **Problem 5:** You hear yourself using an up-and-down inflection to get through a sentence.

Solution: Make the sentence less complicated.

>> **Problem 6:** You hear repeat sounds produced by words ending in *-ize, -ion, -ing, -ous,* or another suffix.

Solution: Restructure the sentence.

>> **Problem 7:** You notice numerous prepositional phrases strung together.

Solution: Change your wording to make fewer prepositions necessary.

>> **Problem 8:** You hear words repeated in the same paragraph.

Solution: Find substitutes.

If you read your copy aloud and practice the fix-it techniques prescribed in Chapter 2 in this minibook and the following sections, you give yourself a gift: the ability to bypass grammar lessons. After you know how to spot a problem, you can use shortcut tools to correct it. Even better, track your own patterns and prevent the problems from happening.

Everyone writes with his or her own patterns. The better handle you gain on your own patterns, the better your writing and the faster you achieve results.

Now for some detail on handling problems 5, 6, 7, and 8.

Avoiding telltale up-down-up inflection

Fancy words, excess phrases, and awkward constructions force sentences into an unnatural pattern when read aloud. The effect is rather like the typical up-down-up-down inflection of the tattletale: **I** know who **DID** it.

Read the following sentence aloud and see what pattern you force on your voice:

All of the writing that is published is a representation of our company, so spelling and grammatical errors can make us look unprofessional and interfere with the public perception of us as competent businesspeople.

Simply scanning the sentences tips you off to its wordiness. This single sentence contains two phrases using *of*, two statements with the passive verb *is*, and three words ending in *-ion*. They produce an awkward, wordy construction. Plus, the sentence contains 34 words — far more than the average 18 recommended — and more than 5 words have three or more syllables (see Chapter 2 of this minibook).

You don't need to be a linguistic rocket scientist to write a better sentence. Just go for simple and clear. Break up the long sentence. Get rid of the unnecessary words and phrases. Substitute shorter friendlier words. One way:

All our company's writing represents us. Spelling and grammar errors make us look unprofessional and incompetent.

After you simplify, you can often find a third, even better way to write the sentence. A third pass may read:

When we make spelling and grammar mistakes, we look unprofessional and incompetent.

Looking for repeat word endings

Big clues to wordy, ineffective sentences come with overused suffixes — words ending in *-ing, -ive, -ion, -ent, -ous,* and *-y.* Almost always, these words are three or more syllables and French or Latinate in origin. Several in a sentence make you sound pompous and stiff. They often force you into convoluted, passive constructions that weaken your writing and discourage readers. (See "Moving from Passive to Active," later in this chapter, for more on activating passive construction.)

TIP

Sprinkle these words throughout your written vocabulary but never let them dominate. Try for one per sentence, two at most. Avoid using a string of these words in a single sentence. Find these stuffy words either visually, by scanning what you write, or orally — read the material out loud and you'll definitely notice when they clutter up your sentences.

In the following sections, you see examples of overly suffixed wording and how to fix it. If you are unenthusiastic about grammar lessons, proceed happily: The goal is to help you develop a *feel* for well-put-together sentences and how to build them. After you notice problems, you can correct them without thinking about rules.

The *-ing* words

Consider this sentence:

> *An inspiring new idea is emerging from marshalling the evolving body of evidence.*

One short sentence with four words ending in *-ing!* Read it aloud and you find yourself falling into that up-down inflection. You can fix it by trimming down to one *-ing* word:

> *An inspiring new idea emerges from the evidence.*

Here's a sentence written for this chapter:

> *Besides, there's something more satisfying about physically editing your copy and using the universal markings.*

The five words ending in *-ing* weren't spotted until the third round of editing! After you see a problem like this, play with the words to eliminate it. Then check that it matches your original intent. The sentence was rewritten this way:

> *Besides, you may find it more satisfying to physically edit your copy with the universal marks.*

When you're both the writer and editor, you're doubly responsible for knowing what you want to say. Fuzzy, verbose writing often results from your own lack of clarity. So when you spot a technical problem, think first about whether a simple word fix will work. But realize that you may need to rethink your content more thoroughly. After you're clear, a better way to write the sentence emerges, like magic.

If you edit someone else's work, knowing the writer's intent is harder. You may not understand what the author is going for, and then it's all too easy to shift her meaning when you try to clarify. You may want to ask the author how to interpret what she wrote. Or make the changes and, as appropriate, check that they are okay with the writer. Don't be surprised if he or she objects. The writer/editor relationship is often a tense and complicated one.

The *-ion* words

The following is cluttered with *-ion* words and incredibly dull:

> *To attract the attention of the local population, with the intention of promoting new construction, we should mention recent inventions that reduce noise pollution.*

Reading aloud makes this sentence's unfriendliness instantly clear. Also note that piling up lots of *-ion* words leads to a very awkward passive sentence structure.

The problem with too many *-ion* words can be more subtle, as in this sentence from an otherwise careful writer:

> *Whether they are organizing large demonstrations, talking with pedestrians in the street, or gathering signatures for a petition, their involvement was motivated by the realization that as individuals within a larger group, they had the potential to influence and bring about change.*

In addition to two words with the *-ion* suffix, the sentence also contains three ending in *-ing.* The result is a rambling, hard to follow, and overly long sentence that feels abstract and distant. This sentence is challenging to fix. One way:

> *They organized large demonstrations, talked with pedestrians, and gathered signatures. Their motivation: knowing that as individuals, they could influence and bring about change.*

Does it say exactly the same thing as the original? Perhaps not, but it's close. And more likely to be read.

Notice that after the *-ion* and *-ing* words were cut down, some of the cluttery phrases become more obvious.

» Of course, pedestrians are *in the street* — so why say it?

» The phrases *for a petition* and *had the potential* are both overkill.

TIP

Always look for phrases that add nothing or offer unnecessary elaboration — and cut them. Your writing will improve noticeably.

The *-ize* words

Similarly to *-ion* and *-ing* words, more than one *-ize* per sentence works against you.

> *He intended to utilize the equipment to maximize the profit and minimize the workforce.*

TIP

In fact, you rarely need these kind of Latinate words at all. In line with the principle of using short, simple words as much as possible, shift *utilize* to *use* and *maximize* to *raise.* And you can more honestly state *minimize* as *cut.*

Modern business language keeps inventing *-ize* words, essentially creating new verbs from nouns. *Incentivize* is a good example. Consider this quote from a government official that appeared in a newspaper article:

> *It would be a true homage to her memory if we are able to channelize these emotions into a constructive course of action.*

Aside from the fact that *channel* is better than *channelize* for the purpose, note how made-up, long words are typically embedded in abstract, verbose thinking.

The *-ent, -ly* and *-ous* words

Words with the *-ent, -ly,* or *-ous* suffixes are usually complicated versions of words available in simpler forms.

A silly example that combines all these forms shows how using long words forces you into that unnatural rhythm, passive structure, and wordy phrases full of unnecessary prepositional phrases.

> *Continuous investment in the pretentiously conceived strategic plan recently proved to be an impediment to the actualization and inadvertently triggered the anomaly.*

WARNING

Unfortunately, much modern business writing is filled with convoluted language, clichés, and hyperbole at the expense of substance. When you try to edit some of it — such as the preceding silly example — you're left with nothing at all. Unfortunately, the fact that no one is impressed with empty writing and no one likes to read it doesn't stop people from producing it.

But research is under way to correlate good writing and communication with the bottom line. Towers Watson, a global management-consulting firm, conducts high-profile surveys on the financial impact of effective communication, and the American Management Association is interested in the ROI–writing connection. Meanwhile, the lesson is clear: Don't write in empty business-speak — it won't reward you.

Pruning prepositions

TIP

Another good way to reduce wordiness is to look for unnecessary prepositional phrases — that is, expressions that depend on words such as *of, to,* and *in.* Here are a few examples along with better alternatives:

> **Original:** *Our mission is to bring awareness of the importance of receiving annual checkups to the people of the community.*
>
> **Revised:** *Our mission is to build the community's awareness of how important annual checkups are.*
>
> **Original:** *But it is important not to forget that you have to still use the rules of traditional writing.*
>
> **Revised:** *But remember, you must still use traditional writing rules.*
>
> **Original:** *He invested 10 years in the development of a system to improve the performance of his organization.*
>
> **Revised:** *He spent 10 years developing a system to improve his organization's performance.*

TIP

Try any and all of the following to cut down wordy phrases:

>> **Use an apostrophe.** Why say the *trick of the magician,* when you can say *the magician's trick?* Why write *the favorite product of our customers,* when you can write *our customers' favorite product?*

>> **Use a hyphen.** Rework *the CEO's fixation on the bottom line* to *the CEO's bottom-line fixation.*

>> **Combine two words and remove an apostrophe:** The phrase *build the community's awareness* can also read well as *build community awareness.*

Cutting all non-contributing words

Extra words that don't support your meaning dilute writing strength. Aim for concise. Use the set of clues described in the previous sections and zero in on individual sentences for ways to tighten. Here's a case in point:

With the use of this new and unique idea, it will increase the profits for the magazine in that particular month.

Extra words hurt the sentence's readability and grammar. Even though the sentence is fairly short already, it manages to jam in two prepositions (*of* and *for*), an altogether useless phrase *(with the use of)*, and an unnecessary word repetition — *new* and *unique*. Of course, the sentence construction is confusing as a result. A better version:

This new idea will increase the magazine's profits in that particular month.

TEXTING AND INSTANT MESSAGING: WHEN AND WHERE TO USE THE STYLE

The terse style of texting and instant messaging follows time-honored traditions.

Probably since the first humans drew on cave walls, people have looked for faster and easier ways to communicate big ideas with written symbols. The Romans chipped their messages into stone tablets and monuments. This was such hard going that they jammed in strings of abbreviations and acronyms that still challenge historians. The ancient Egyptians also depended on word shortcuts to make their point on stone surfaces. They liked abbreviations and often skipped words that were obvious (to them, at least). In the nineteenth century, news was sent by telegraph and people found tapping out every letter of every word too slow. Again, words were abbreviated to their minimal intelligible form or omitted.

There's nothing inherently wrong with finding faster ways to type on tiny keyboards. In fact, many language gurus believe that texting improves writing because it teaches conciseness. But when you assume everyone understands those abbreviations and symbols, you may have a problem.

In general, many older people may not readily read text-style messages (see the information on generation gaps in Chapter 1 of this minibook), and even younger readers may not like it as a common language. Writing in a manner your readers are unlikely to understand simply doesn't make sense.

Further, many readers who are comfortable with texting shortcuts still expect a more formal style in other media, including email. So don't risk your credibility by transferring informal texting strategies to other business writing. Limit texting style to appropriate media and audiences that you're sure will respond in kind.

An objective look at your sentences may reveal words and phrases that obviously repeat the same idea. Here's a sentence written for this chapter, which talks about editing hard copy from a computer printout.

> *Of course, you must then transfer your changes to the original on your computer.*

In context, the original document was clearly on the computer, so the unnecessary phrase was cut:

> *Of course, you must then transfer the changes to your computer.*

Consider this explanation of how Track Changes works:

> *Now when you make a change, the alteration is indicated in a color and any deletion is shown on the right.*

The rewrite:

> *Your changes then show up in color, and deletions appear outside the text on the far right.*

The revision works better because it eliminates unnecessary words and with them, the passive construction of *alteration is indicated* and *deletion is shown*.

Take aim at common phrases that slow down reading. Substitute simple words. The words on the left are almost always non-contributors; choose those on the right.

Wordy	Better
at this time	now
for the purpose of	for, or to
in accordance with	under
in an effort to	to
in order to	to
in regard to	about
in the amount of	for
in the event of	if
in the near future	soon
is indicative of	indicates
is representative of	represents
on a daily basis	daily

Moving from Passive to Active

Most people write too passively. They use too many verbs that are forms of *to be*, which force sentences into convoluted shapes that are hard for readers to untangle. Worse, all those *to be* verbs make writing so dull that many readers don't even want to try. Chapter 2 in this minibook describes passive verbs in context of writing. This section covers the topic from the editing angle.

TIP

Active verbs say everything more directly, clearly, concisely, and colorfully. If you want to transform everything you write quickly, pay attention to verbs and build your sentences around active ones.

Thinking *action*

TIP

Active voice and action verbs are not the same thing grammatically, but this isn't a grammar guide. For practical purposes, don't worry about the distinction. Just remember to cut back on the following word choices:

>> *Is* + an *-ed* ending: As in, *Your attention is requested.*

>> *Are* + an *-ed* ending: As in, *The best toys are created by scientists.*

>> *Were* + an *-ed* ending: As in, *The company executives were worried about poor writers who were failing to build good customer relations.*

>> *Was* + an *-ed* ending: As in, *The ice cream was delivered by Jenny.*

>> *Will be* + *have* + an *-ed* ending: As in, *We will be happy to have finished studying grammar.*

>> *Would be* + an *-ed* ending: As in, *The CEO said a new marketing plan would be launched next year.*

The solution in every case is the same: Figure out *who* does *what,* and rephrase the idea accordingly:

>> *We request your attention.*

>> *Scientists create the best toys.*

>> *Company executives worry that bad writers fail to build good relationships.*

>> *Jenny delivered the ice cream.*

>> *We're happy to finish studying grammar.*

>> *The CEO plans to launch a new marketing plan next year.*

Verbs endings with -en raise the same red flag as those ending in -ed. For example, *I will be taken to Washington by an India Airways plane* is better expressed as *An India Airways plane will fly me to Washington.*

REMEMBER

When you rid a sentence of *to be* verbs, you win a chance to substitute active present tense verbs for boring, passive past tense ones. Many professionals work this tactic out on their own through years of trial and error. Writing in the present tense takes a bit more thought at first but quickly becomes a habit. Use present tense everywhere you can and see your writing leap forward in one giant step.

TIP

Look closely at all your sentences that contain *is, are,* and the other *to be* verbs. See whether an action verb can bring your sentences to life. Often, you can use the present tense of the same verb:

> **Original:** *He is still a pest to the whole office about correct grammar.*

> **Revised:** *He still pesters the whole office about correct grammar.*

At other times, think of a more interesting verb entirely:

> **Original:** *She is intending to develop a surprise party for the boss.*

> **Revised:** *She is hatching a surprise party for the boss.*

Trimming *there is* and *there are*

TIP

Big-time culprits in the passive sweepstakes are the combinations *there is* and *there are.* This problem is easy to fix — just commit never to start a sentence with either. Keep away from *there will be, there have been,* and all the variations. Don't bury them inside your sentences, either.

Check out the following examples and improvements:

> **Original:** *There were 23 references to public relations in the report.*

> **Revised:** *The report cited public relations 23 times.*

> **Original:** *There is a helpful section called "new entries" at the top of the page.*

> **Revised:** *A helpful section called "new entries" appears at the top of the page.*

> **Original:** *It's expected that in the future, there will be easier ways to communicate.*

> **Revised:** *We expect easier ways to communicate in the future.*

In every case, using an active verb does the trick, and almost all reworked sentences are in the present tense.

Cutting the *haves* and *have nots*

Like the *to be* verbs, using the various forms of the verb *to have* signals lazy writing. Find substitute words as often as possible. A few examples and possible rewrites:

> **Original:** *He said he had intentions to utilize the equipment he had been given by the company.*
>
> **Revised:** *He said that he plans to use the equipment the company gave him.*
>
> **Original:** *We have to make use of the talents we have.*
>
> **Revised:** *We must use our own talents.*

Using the passive deliberately

Despite all the reasons for minimizing passive sentences, passive verbs are not bad. You need them on occasions when the actor is obvious, unknown, unimportant, or the punch line. For example:

> *The computer was developed in its modern form over a number of years.*
>
> *After long trial and error, the culprit was finally identified as the Green Haybarn.*

You can also make a case for using the passive voice when you need to frame a message in terms of *you* rather than *we* or *I*. When writing to a customer, for example, you may be more effective to begin as follows:

> *Your satisfaction with the product is what we care about most.*

Rather than this:

> *We care most about your satisfaction with the product.*

The second statement gives the impression that it's all about us. Of course, don't write an *entire* letter like the first opening — just the first sentence.

The passive is also useful when you don't want to sound accusatory. *The bill has not been paid* is more neutral than *You failed to pay the bill.*

Sidestepping Jargon, Clichés, and Extra Modifiers

Relying on words that have little meaning wastes valuable message space and slows down reading. Overused expressions also dilute the effect, and insider language can confuse outside readers. Jargon, clichés, and unhelpful adjectives are hallmarks of unsuccessful business writing.

Reining in jargon

Almost every specialized profession has its *jargon:* terminology and symbols that shortcut communication and, in some cases, make group members feel more professional and inside. If a physicist is writing to other physicists, she doesn't need to spell out the formulas, symbols, and technical language. Her audience shares a common knowledge base.

Similarly, a lawyer can write to colleagues in the peculiar language he and his peers mastered through education and practice. A musician can exchange performance notes with other musicians in a way that means little to non-musicians.

WARNING

The risk arises when people talk or write to anyone other than fellow-specialists and use inside jargon. You forget that the general public does not share your professional language. If, for example, you're a scientist who needs to explain your work to a journalist, report on progress to company executives, order supplies, negotiate employment, or chat at a party, you're best avoiding scientific jargon.

REMEMBER

Outside of specialized fields, we are all generalists. We want to be addressed in clear, simple language that we can immediately understand. Judging by their messages to clients, many attorneys and accountants are among those who forget this basic principle — or perhaps no longer remember how to communicate in plain English.

But business writers face an additional challenge. A specialized, jargon-laden language flourishes full of buzzwords that means little — even to those who use it. For example, a technology company states in a publication:

> *These visible IT capabilities along with IT participation in the project identification process can drive the infusion of IT leverage on revenue improvement in much the same way as IT has leveraged cost cutting and efficiency.*

What does it mean? Who knows? All too often, corporate writers string together a set of buzzwords and clichés that communicate little beyond a reluctance to think.

WARNING

Of course, sometimes a writer or organization deliberately chooses to bury a fact or a truth behind carefully selected words and phrases. Then you might argue that a message built on empty business jargon works well. But don't deliberately distort the truth, write without substance, or mask either situation with bad writing. Doing so just doesn't work, and it may boomerang. This widely circulated Citigroup press release made the bank look ridiculous:

> *Citigroup today announced a series of repositioning actions that will further reduce expenses and improve efficiency across the company while maintaining Citi's unique capabilities to serve clients, especially in the emerging markets. These actions will result in increased business efficiency, streamlined operations, and an optimized consumer footprint across geographies.*

Translation: *We're firing a lot of people to improve our numbers.*

To avoid producing empty business-speak, steer clear of words and phrases such as the following:

best practice	peel the onion
blue-sky thinking	robust
boil the ocean	scalable
boots to the ground	shift a paradigm
core competency	take it to the next level
drinking the Kool-Aid	think outside the box
from the helicopter view	360-degree view
full service	value proposition
optimization	vertical
over the wall	world class

TIP

If you're writing a press release, for a website, or other promotional copy, check it for buzz-wordiness by asking yourself: Could this copy be used by any company, in any industry, to describe any product or service? If I substitute down-to-earth words for the clichés, does the message have meaning? Will my 17-year-old nephew laugh when he reads it?

Cooling the clichés

Jargon can be seen as business-world clichés. English, like all languages, has an enormous trove of general clichés, expressions that are so overused they may lose their effect. A few random examples that can turn up in business communication: *All's well that ends well, barking up the wrong tree, beat around the bush, nice guys finish last, a stitch in time, read between the lines.*

UNCLEAR WRITING IS AGAINST THE LAW!

By long tradition, the worst examples of opaque, confusing, and hard to understand writing come from none other than government. However, plain language movements have gathered steam in a number of countries, including the US and Britain, since the 1970s. Advocates point out that clear writing is essential for people to access services, follow regulations, and understand the law.

In the US, sustained work by several non-profit groups led to passage of the Plain Writing Act of 2010, which requires federal agencies to write all new publications, forms, and publicly distributed documents in a "clear, concise, well-organized" manner that follows the best practices of plain language writing. Extending the law to government regulations is the next effort.

In England, the campaign against small-print, bureaucratic language is similarly vigorous, but a corresponding law has not been passed.

In both countries, efforts to clarify legal writing are underway as well. And an organization called PLAIN — the Plain Language Association International (www.plainlanguage network.org) — serves as a central resource for the plain language movement globally.

A special point of interest: Some studies demonstrate that the guidelines for better writing are basically the same across different languages: short words, short simple sentences, fewer descriptive words, and good graphic techniques (see Chapter 2 in this minibook) work well for Swedish writing, just as for English.

Other interesting US sites include The Plain Writing Association (www.plain-writing-association.org) and the Center for Plain Language (www.centerforplain language.org). These and related websites offer a wealth of useful information and good before-and-after writing examples from both the public and private sectors. Movement leaders hope that promoting clear language in government will have a much-needed effect on corporate writing.

Clichés are so numerous they often seem hard to avoid. Often they're idioms, a popular shorthand was of communicating ideas, found in every language. And they can be used well in context. But be on the lookout for any that don't carry your meaning or that trivialize it. Instead, say what you want more simply, or perhaps develop an original comparison, described in Chapter 2 in this minibook. And never forget that idioms and clichés are rarely understood by non-native English speakers, so try to avoid them when writing to these audiences.

Minimizing modifiers

The best advice on using descriptive words — adjectives and adverbs — came from the great nineteenth-century American novelist Mark Twain:

> *I notice that you use plain, simple language, short words and brief sentences. That is the way to write English — it is the modern way and the best way. Stick to it; don't let fluff and flowers and verbosity creep in.*

> *When you catch an adjective, kill it. No, I don't mean utterly, but kill most of them — then the rest will be valuable. They weaken when they are close together. They give strength when they are wide apart. An adjective habit, or a wordy, diffuse, flowery habit, once fastened upon a person, is as hard to get rid of as any other vice.*

Twain wrote this advice in 1880 to a 12-year-old boy who sent him a school essay, but he's right on target for today's business communicators.

If depending on buzzwords and clichés is Sin #1 of empty business-speak, overuse of adjectives is Sin #2. Consider, for example,

> *The newest, most innovative, cutting-edge solution to the ultimate twenty-first century challenges . . .*

What, another solution?

TIP

Adopt whenever possible the fiction writer's mantra: Show, don't tell. Adjectives generally communicate little. In fiction, and especially scriptwriting, writers must find ways to bring the audience into the experience so they draw their own conclusions about whether a character makes bad decisions, is unethical, feels ugly or pretty, is suffering pain, and so on.

In business writing, *show, don't tell* means giving your audience substance and detail: facts, ideas, statistics, examples — whatever it takes to prove they need your product or idea. Stating that something is innovative proves nothing. Adding an adverb, such as *very innovative,* just multiplies the emptiness.

Take a piece of marketing or website copy, either your own or someone else's, and highlight all the adjectives and adverbs. Then eliminate most or all of the words you identified. Examine what's left. Does it say anything meaningful? If not, can you replace the copy with something real?

Welcome opportunities to replace empty rhetoric with substance! There's no substitute for good content. Use good writing techniques (as presented throughout this book) to make that content clear, straightforward, and lively.

In Chapter 4 in this minibook, you move from sentence building to creating solid paragraphs, solving organization problems, using strong transitions, and fixing the technical problems that typically handicap many business writers.

» **Honing sentences and fine-tuning phrases**

» **Catching and correcting common language mistakes**

» **Proofing what you write**

Chapter **4**

Troubleshooting Your Writing

A s you explore in Chapter 3 in this minibook, good self-editing requires you to look at your writing on two levels — macro and micro. Chapter 3 focuses on how you assess your content and present your material effectively. This chapter drills down to even more specific editing issues: techniques for organizing material and improving sentences and words.

REMEMBER

Each of us has our own writing demons, persistent problems that show up in everything we write. Happily, most of these issues fall into common categories that you can correct with common-sense approaches. Even better, you don't need to master hundreds of grammar rules. This chapter gives you a repertoire of practical fix-it techniques. After you absorb them and begin putting them into practice, they enable you to head off problems *before* they pull you off-message or undermine your success.

Organizing Your Document

Many people, including a number of experienced writers, say that organization is their biggest challenge. If you follow the process outlined in Chapter 1 in this mini-book, which shows you how to plan each message within the framework of your goal and audience, you may be able to sidestep the organization challenge substantially.

But this may not altogether solve your problems, especially when documents are lengthy or complicated, written by more than one person, or simply strike you as confusing or illogical once drafted. You may need to review the organization at that point and reshuffle or recast material. The following techniques help. You can implement them at the writing stage or the editing stage.

Paragraphing for logic

You may remember being told in school to establish a thesis sentence and develop each paragraph from that. If you found this advice dumbfounding, you're not alone.

TIP

Here's a much easier way to look at paragraphs. Just accept the idea that each chunk should contain no more than three to five sentences. If you write your document that way, you easily achieve an inner logic and produce a series of self-contained units, or paragraphs.

If you routinely produce uninterrupted strings of sentences, don't despair: Make the fixes later, during the editing stage. Read over what you've written and look for logical places to make breaks.

Can't decide where to insert breaks? Use the following technique:

1. **Scan your text to find places where you introduce a new idea or fact — or where you change direction.**

    Break the flow into paragraphs at these points.

2. **If your paragraphs are still more than three to five sentences, go through the piece again and make decisions on an experimental basis. You'll check later to see if they work.**

    The three- to five-sentence guideline is a general one that applies to print material. But an occasional one-sentence paragraph is fine and adds variety. When you write for online reading, paragraphs should be shorter.

3. **Look carefully at the first sentence of each newly created paragraph.**

    See whether the new first sentence makes sense in connecting with what follows — or whether it connects better with the preceding paragraph. If the latter, move the sentence up a paragraph and break to a new paragraph where it now ends.

    If a sentence seems not to belong with either paragraph, it may need to stand as its own paragraph — or be rephrased.

4. **Look at your paragraphs again in order and check whether any wording needs adjustment.**

Pay particular attention to the first and last sentences of each paragraph. You want each paragraph to link to the next. Using transitions helps with this. (Read more about these in the later section "Working with transitions.")

If you don't like the sequence of paragraphs when you scan the entire message, fool around with shuffling them. Adjust the language as necessary so that your paragraphs still clearly relate to each other.

TIP

You might find repeated words or entire ideas during this step, so make the necessary cuts and smooth everything out.

REMEMBER

The point of paragraphing is clarity. You want to deliver information in absorbable or usable chunks that lead from one to the next, rather than a single, long, confusing word dump.

Sometimes the reason you have trouble organizing your material is because you don't yet understand it well enough to effectively present it to others. Ask yourself: What *is* my point? What are the components of my argument? Number or list them if you haven't yet done so. (Omit the numbers later if that's better for your purpose.) Also ask yourself whether you are missing critical pieces and need to research for them.

Building with subheads

TIP

Another strategy for organizing, useful on its own or to supplement the paragraphing strategy described in the preceding section, is to add a few simple subheads. Subheads as an excellent graphic technique, as you discover in Chapter 2 in this minibook. They are also useful guideposts for planning what you write and, during the editing process, can be added to help clarify your message.

Suppose you're composing an email telling your staff that new technology will be installed department-wide. The new system is technical, so you anticipate plenty of questions and some resistance. You want your memo to head off many of the possible challenges.

To organize your own thoughts and avoid writer's block, turn your brainstorming of content (see Chapter 1 in this minibook) into a series of subheads. You might write the following:

» System X24A: Rollout starts March 6

» Who is affected?

- >> Advantages of the new system

- >> Changes in how we'll work

- >> Tech training plans

- >> March 6: Department Q & A meeting

Arrange your subheads in a logical order and then fill in the information under each subhead. As you write under each heading, additional topics may emerge that you didn't think of initially — for example, how the new system affects your team's interface with payroll. Find a logical place in your sequence of subheads and add the new one.

In your final message, discard the subheads if you want or leave them in. Subheads usually work well to pull your readers through a message and keep them organized as well. The overall effect on readers, even those who only scan the message, is that they see you have the situation well in hand and have thoroughly thought everything out. This feeling alone inspires greater confidence in both you and the new system, making people more receptive to the change.

REMEMBER

Long, complex documents benefit from the subhead strategy too. For a report or proposal, for example, identify the necessary sections and write a headline, rather than a subhead, for each. Then write a set of subheads for each section.

Drafting headings and subheads is a great way to be sure that you cover all the right bases, identify missing pieces early, and build in good organization from the project's start. You also break up the writing process into doable bits so it's far less formidable.

Use a consistent style for all your headings. The Word program offers built-in styles, so it just takes a click to apply one.

Working with transitions

Transitions, those low-key words and phrases, are like the connective tissue that holds your skeleton together and empowers you to move where you want. Transitions tell readers how all the ideas, facts, and information in a piece of writing connect to each other. They smooth your writing and pull people along in the direction you want to take them.

TIP

Good transitions signal good writing and good thinking. They help you organize your own ideas as a writer. And for the reader, they promote the feeling that your argument is sensible and even unassailable. Transitions are important tools for all writing — and essential for persuasive copy.

Transitions can consist of single words, phrases, or sentences. They can be put to work within a sentence, to link sentences, or to connect paragraphs. Think of them in several categories:

To continue a line of thought — or to shift a line of thought, use the following:

additionally	on the other hand
also	but
and	however
consequently	alternatively
for example	originally
furthermore	nevertheless
mainly	despite
so	in other words
sometimes	conversely

To establish a sequence or time frame, try these:

as soon as	ultimately
at the moment	finally
first . . . second . . . third	later
to begin with	next
to conclude	for now

To reinforce a desired focus or tone, choose one of the following:

disappointingly	it sounds good, but . . .
invariably	counterintuitively
luckily	of particular interest
unfortunately	at the same time

Transitions give you a good way to begin paragraphs or sections, while putting that information in context of the full message. The following are examples of whole sentences that serve as transitions:

Based on this data, we've made the following decisions.

Here's why the problem arose.

We should pay special attention to the sales figures.

We now have four choices.

A number of questions were raised at the meeting. The most significant:

Notice how these introductory statements set up a super-simple way to organize subsequent material, including within long, complicated documents.

As with all writing principles, there can be too much of a good thing. When you give your writing the read-aloud test and it sounds stilted and clumsy, review your transitions — you may need to remove some. Do so and you still have a well-organized, convincing message.

Working in lists: Numbers and bulleting

Lists offer an excellent way to present information in a compact, to-the-point manner. They suit readers' Internet-trained text-skimming habits, and most people like them. They also automatically promote graphic variation, another plus for your document (see Chapter 2 in this minibook).

Numbered lists

Use numbered lists to present sequences of events, procedures, or processes. For example, a numbered list can guide readers on how to do something:

Follow these steps to activate the new software.

1. Turn on your computer.

2. Choose Preferences in your graphics program.

3. Select Formatting, and then . . .

Scout actively for opportunities to organize a sequence by dates or milestones:

1. Jan. 7, Deadline 1: Submit preliminary budget estimates.

2. Feb. 10, Deadline 2: Submit adjusted numbers.

3. March 4, Deadline 3: Finalize department budget.

These techniques may sound simple-minded, but they bestow a clarity that is so unambiguous, few people can misinterpret your meaning.

TIP

You can also use numbered lists in more sophisticated ways. Bloggers use them to present blog posts in a popular and reader-friendly style: a number-centered headline followed by each numbered point, spelled out. For example:

The 7 Tricks for Warp-Speed Writing That Professionals Don't Want You to Know

Many experienced bloggers think up a headline like that first, marshal their ideas around it, and then write the copy. In addition to its reader appeal, this format channels your knowledge in a different way and helps you uncover ideas you didn't know you knew.

Numbering is also a staple for speechwriters:

I'm going to give you five ways to boost your power to close the sale.

The technique works every time because audiences like knowing how much is ahead of them, and they love ticking off the speaker's progress (and their own). It helps people retain information a bit better, too.

You need to know when to stop, though. In a speech, listeners can usually handle no more than five numbered items. In print, as with bullets, limit yourself to seven. (However, something is magnetic about ten.)

Also as with bullets, make items on your lists parallel in structure — begin them with the same part of speech. And they should work visually by being approximately the same length.

Bulleted lists

Between on-screen writing habits and PowerPoint everywhere, writing has become a bullet-heavy experience.

Like numbering, bullet lists convey information tightly and neatly. They're appropriate for summarizing, offering checklists, and providing information-at-a-glance. What's more, readers like them — but only up to a point. Used incorrectly, bullets can kill. Audience interest, that is.

TIP

To successfully use bulleting, take account of these guidelines:

>> **Don't use too many.** Research shows that people can't absorb more than about seven bullets. They tune out after that because each bullet typically makes a separate point and gives little logical connection to hold onto.

If you must present more than seven bullets, break them into more than one list and intersperse some narrative material.

» **Use the same sentence structure for every bullet.** Start each item similarly. Sentence structure must be parallel so as not to confuse readers.

You can begin bullet points with action verbs, such as when you present accomplishments in a resume:

- *Authorized . . .*
- *Generated . . .*
- *Streamlined . . .*
- *Overhauled . . .*
- *Mentored . . .*

» Or you can compose a bullet list that starts with nouns, such as:

When you weekend in Timbuktu, be sure to pack

- *Tropical microfiber clothing*
- *Sunglasses with a good UV coating*
- *Sunhat with extra-long visor*

WARNING

» Don't be lazy and create bulleted lists of unrelated mix-and-match thoughts, like this:

Here are goals to aim for in business writing:

- *You want a conversational but professional tone.*
- *When you quote numbers, check that your readers use those systems.*
- *Don't be emotional or make things up.*
- *Jane is trying to standardize a similar look on charts and graphs. Once she does so, use that standard.*

» You can refine this list by rearranging points two through four to start like the first one:

- *You want to check that all numbers quoted are in line with systems your readers use.*
- *You want to avoid emotion or making things up.*

» But that approach produces an annoying repetition of *you want*. The solution is to find an introductory sentence that covers the points you want to make. For example:

In business writing, try to use a

- *Conversational but professional style*
- *Non-emotional tone*
- *Number systems familiar to your readers*
- *Consistent style for charts and graphs*

>> **Punctuate and format bullets consistently.** In this book, the first phrase or sentence is often bold, followed by a colon (for a phrase) or a period (for a sentence). No one way of formatting is right for every organization and every situation. Figure out your style, or your organization's, and apply it consistently to all your lists.

WARNING

>> **Give bullet points meaning.** Don't depend on bullet points to convince people of something or expect readers to fill in the gaps between them. Bullets are only formatting.

Tell readers what your bullets mean with good narrative writing or a quick introduction that puts the bullets in context. In a bio or resume, for example, using all bullets to describe your assets defies readability. Begin with a well-written overall description of your current job followed by a list of your accomplishments, but put the information in context. For example, a job description can end with *Consistent performance beyond company goals for three years,* followed by your bullet evidence. Use no more than five to seven bullets, stated in parallel sentences.

Don't make formatting decisions, such as using bulleted and numbered lists, lightly. They may be easy to write, but you undermine your success if they don't present your message as clearly as possible. When you use such formatting devices, take a hard look during the editing stage to see if you might present your material better (and be more persuasive) in narrative form.

Catching Common Mistakes

Unlike the common cold, common writing problems can be treated and even prevented. The prescription is simple: Be aware of your own mistakes, which are nearly always consistent.

Improving your grammar is a personal thing, so if you want a solid grounding, scout what's out there in books and on the Internet. Choose a resource compatible with your learning style and dig in. Consider starting out with *English Grammar For Dummies* or *English Grammar Workbook For Dummies*, both by Geraldine Woods.

The grammar-related goals in this minibook are as follows:

>> To raise your consciousness so that you can recognize some of your own problems.

>> To give you practical tips for fixing those problems that require little grammar know-how.

>> To relieve you of some of your worries. What you're doing may be perfectly okay for today's less formal communication.

Infinitely more can — and has — been written about writing it right. See the sidebar "The journalist's grammar guidelines," later in this chapter, for what may be the most succinct rundown ever created.

The following sections tip you off to problems found in even solid writing — all are easily fixed and make the writing more effective. One general guideline to help you relax: When your own writing confronts you with a grammar problem that's hard to resolve or that you can't figure out, write the sentence differently to sidestep the challenge.

Using comma sense

Stop stressing about commas! If visual cues don't work for you, use oral ones. The reading-aloud trick recommended in Chapter 3 of this minibook is a surefire way to find out when you need a comma. Note the difference in the following:

Eat Grandpa!

Eat, Grandpa!

If you read the words aloud to say what you presumably intend — that Grandpa should eat — the first option sounds this way:

Eat (pause and downward inflection) *Grandpa*

A pause signals the comma is needed. And most assuredly, this sentence needs the comma.

Too many commas can also be a problem:

The use of the Internet, is part of a new culture, that more and more of the younger generations are entering into.

Read this sentence and you hear that it works better without pauses where the two commas are placed. They interfere with smooth reading and should be cut.

Badly placed commas in cases like this often signal a wording problem. A better version, once the too-obvious parts are cut:

Using the Internet is part of a new younger-generation culture.

Reading aloud can also cure runaway or run-on sentences that typically depend on misused commas. Here's one:

Grammar is something that everyone can always touch up on, the writers should use simple punctuation, properly place punctuation marks, things like too many commas and semicolons can confuse the reader.

The read-aloud test shows that a sustained pause calls for a new sentence after *touch up on.* The comma between the two middle thoughts doesn't work either because an *and* should connect them. Insert that conjunction and it's clear that you need a period after *marks* because to read meaningfully demands another sustained pause. The result follows:

Grammar is something that everyone can always touch up on. Writers should use simple punctuation and properly place punctuation marks. Things like too many commas and semicolons can confuse the reader.

Another way of fixing this paragraph is to connect the whole second part with a transition and cut some redundancy:

Writers should use simple punctuation and properly place punctuation marks, because too many commas and semicolons can confuse the reader.

Train your ear and with a little practice, you improve your punctuation quickly.

Using *however* correctly

As with commas, reading aloud gives you the clue about how to include *however* in your writing.

Many decent writers undercut themselves with sentences like these:

I'd like to go to the office, however, my car won't start.

Expense reports are due on Jan 15, however, exceptions can be made.

Reading these sentences aloud shows that long pauses are necessary before each *however.* You can break up both statements into two sentences with periods after *office* and *Jan. 15.* The second sentence in each case starts with *However.*

TIP

Alternatively, you can sidestep the "however" problem and also refine your wording by the following:

>> Replacing the *however* with *but*. If this substitution works, go with *but*. It's correct and less stuffy as well.

>> Using *however* only to begin sentences.

>> Moving a *however* that falls in the middle of the sentence to the beginning and see whether the meaning holds. For example:

> *He agreed with Jane, however, she was wrong.*

> *He wants to know, however, so he can plan his vacation.*

Moving *however* to the front makes nonsense of the first sentence. With the second sentence, moving it retains the basic sense.

Matching nouns and pronouns

Using the wrong pronoun is common, even in the work of professionals. *Pronouns* have a simple function — to stand in for nouns so you don't have to keep repeating them. One cause of confusion is when to use *me* instead of *I, he* rather than *him*, and so on. For example:

> *Just between you and I, Jean was correct.*

> *Mark, Harold, and me will go to the conference.*

Both sentences are wrong. One way to figure that out is to switch the wording so the correct pronoun becomes obvious. In the first sentence, if you substitute *us* for *you and I*, it works fine. But if you substitute *we*, the sentence sounds absurd and you're clearly wrong.

In the second sentence, you can choose to say *We will go to the conference,* and the singular for *we* is *I,* so that pronoun is correct. Or you can eliminate Mark and Harold from the scene, in which case you obviously must say *I,* not *me.*

TIP

As a general rule, go with what seems natural; but check yourself out. Try adding or subtracting words, as in the previous examples.

Another cause of confusion is when to use a plural possessive pronoun (like *their*) as opposed to a singular pronoun (*his, its*). In these situations, stay alert to the original noun:

A journalist must always be attuned to their readers' interests.

Everyone should use their discount when ordering online.

Both are wrong because both nouns (*journalist* and *everyone*) are singular, not plural. But the first sentence raises other issues. If I correct the first sentence as follows:

A journalist must always be attuned to his readers' interests.

Will I be accused of sexism? Perhaps, but the jury is still out on how to avoid this. You can do one of the following:

>> Say *his or her readers,* but that repetition gets tiresome.

>> Switch back and forth between the masculine and feminine. This approach works in longer documents.

>> Change the original noun to plural:

Journalists must always be attuned to their readers' interests.

>> Rework the sentence to avoid the problem entirely:

Journalists must always be attuned to reader interest.

You can alter the second sentence to: *Use your discount when ordering online.*

REMEMBER

Some pronoun issues reflect cultural differences. In the US, an organization is considered singular, so you say:

The company is widely criticized for its actions.

But in the UK, the plural is used:

The company is widely criticized for their actions.

Weighing *which* versus *that*

Almost always, choose *that* rather than *which.* The latter word refers to something specific. When you're not sure which to use, try using *that* and see whether the sentence has the same meaning. If it does, keep the *that.* For example:

The report that I wrote at home is on John's desk now.

But if you find that *that* doesn't reflect your meaning, you may mean *which.*

Note that you can write the sentence this way:

The report, which I wrote at home, is on John's desk now.

The second version calls attention to *where* you wrote it. And observe that you need two commas to set off the clause. *Which* always requires two commas unless the phrase appears at the end of the sentence. Another instance:

We provide afternoon breaks, which, we know, help reduce stress.

You're using *which* correctly if you can eliminate the phrase inside the commas (*we know*) without changing the sentence's basic meaning. If you remove the non-essential phrase, the sentence becomes:

We provide afternoon breaks that help reduce stress.

Does this sentence carry the same meaning as the original? Basically yes, but if the "we know" is important, it doesn't. For a sentence to carry your meaning, you must know what you want to communicate.

Pondering *who* versus *that*

Contemporary writing is chock-full of *that's* and very few *who's*. People have become depersonalized into objects. The following sentences are all incorrect:

The new office manager that started on Monday already called in sick.

My friend, that I've known for 20 years, is planning to visit.

The first person that said he was ready changed his mind.

REMEMBER

Always use *who* when referring to people. Inanimate objects and ideas are *that*. You may choose to refer to animals as *who*, but some prefer *that*.

Choosing *who* versus *whom*

Grammar enthusiasts insist that you differentiate between the word used as a subject (*who*) and as an object (*whom*, as in *to whom*). But adhering to the rule can land you in some stuffy places.

To whom should I address the package?

With whom should I speak?

To whom it may concern . . .

The following version of the first two sentences work better for general business writing:

Who should I address this package to?

Who should I speak to?

THE JOURNALIST'S GRAMMAR GUIDELINES

Business writers can learn a lot from journalists, whose full-time work is figuring out how to present ideas and information in the clearest, most succinct, and most interesting way possible. Unfortunately, as the newspaper industry shrinks, it provides an ever-smaller training ground for writers.

This classic list of rules was originally taken from a bulletin board at Denver's *Rocky Mountain News* and has appeared, with different add-ons, in a number of journalism books. *The Rocky Mountain News* stopped publishing in 2009, but many a writer keeps this demonstration of grammar pitfalls on hand.

1. Don't use no double negatives.
2. Make each pronoun agree with their antecedent.
3. Join clauses good, like a conjunction should.
4. About them sentence fragments.
5. When dangling, watch your participles.
6. Verbs has to agree with their subjects.
7. Just between you and I, case is important too.
8. Don't write run-on sentences they are hard to read.
9. Don't use commas, which aren't necessary.
10. Try to not ever split infinitives.
11. It's important to use your apostrophe's correctly.
12. Proofread your writing to see if you any words out.
13. Correct speling is essential(!)
14. Avoid unnecessary redundancy.
15. Be more or less specific.
16. Avoid clichés like the plague.

In the case of the last example, simply don't use such an archaic phrase. Always find a specific person who may be concerned, and use her name. If that's impossible, use a title *(Dear Recruitment Chief)* or a generic address *(Dear Readers)*.

Beginning with *and* or *but*

Like other wording choices addressed in this section, grammatical standards have relaxed, and only the rare individual complains about sentences that begin with *and* or *but*. *The Wall Street Journal* does it, the *New York Times* does it. And so can you.

But don't do it so often that it loses its effect. Starting sentences with these conjunctions adds to your rhythmic variety and gives you a way to add a little verve, especially to online writing. It works best with short sentences.

Because can be used the same way, although I still hear people repeating the schoolroom mantra against starting sentences with that word. And *or* and *yet* can also start a sentence.

Ending with prepositions

An often-quoted piece of wit attributed to Winston Churchill underscores the silliness of strictly obeying some rules:

> *This is the sort of bloody nonsense up with which I will not put.*

Obviously it's more natural to say,

> *This is the sort of bloody nonsense I won't put up with.*

Similarly, sentences such as these that end with prepositions are fine:

> *Leave on the horse you rode in on.*
>
> *See if the answers add up.*
>
> *He's a man I can't get along with.*
>
> *We didn't know where he came from.*
>
> *Don't make fun of grammarians, just because some of their ideas don't go where you want to.*

TIP

Many stock phrases end with prepositions and there's no reason not to use them wherever they fall in a sentence. This especially applies if writing "correctly" requires an unnatural-sounding manipulation of language. The general guideline for business writing is: Use what feels comfortable in conversation.

Reviewing and Proofreading: The Final Check

Before sending your message or document into the world or to its target audience of one, review it at both the big-picture macro level (see Chapter 3 in this mini-book) and the close-in micro level (everything covered in this chapter).

REMEMBER

Editing is essential, but often the process unintentionally shifts meaning and introduces new mistakes. So plan to review any passages you reworked at least one extra time.

Checking the big picture

After you've edited your message or document and are satisfied with the writing, it's time to return to the big picture and assess your overall message in terms of content, effect, and tone. It's not sufficient to send a technically perfect message that isn't geared to accomplishing what you want!

Forgetting all the work and the decisions that went into what you've written and edited, look at your text as a self-contained piece and consider the following:

>> Is my *purpose* — what I want to accomplish — absolutely clear?

>> Does the piece support my sub-agenda? For example, does it promote the relationships I want to build, represent me in the best professional light, and contribute toward my larger goals?

WHEN HAVE I FINISHED EDITING?

Painters have the same question about knowing when they've finished a painting. With writing, stop editing before you begin to change the meaning of your message. And stop before you compress all the life out of it. Overly general, bland writing doesn't work well. Don't cut the examples, anecdotes, or details that engage readers and help them understand.

You're better off saying less but saying it fully. For example, plan a series of emails on a subject rather than jamming the information into one overly long one. Or focus an article on one aspect of a subject and keep the color.

- » Do I get to the point quickly and stay on message? Does every element of the message support the result I want?

- » Does the message move well and smoothly from section to section, paragraph to paragraph?

- » Is the level of detail right? Not too much, not too little, just enough to make my case?

Step even further back and read your document from your recipient's viewpoint:

- » Will the reader know what I want and exactly how to respond?

- » Is the message a good match in terms of tone, communication style, and audience characteristics? Does it focus on what's important to the reader?

- » If I were the recipient, would I care about this message enough to read it — and respond?

- » Did I provide appropriate evidence to support the case I'm making? What unanswered questions could the reader possibly have?

- » If I were the reader, would I give the writer what he or she wants?

- » Can anything in the message possibly be misinterpreted or misunderstood? Could it embarrass anyone?

- » How does it look? Is it accessible and easy to read? Does it have plenty of white space and good graphic devices? Does it need visuals?

- » And finally, will I feel perfectly fine if this document is forwarded to the CEO, tweeted to thousands of strangers, mailed to my grandmother, or printed in a daily newspaper?

Correct any problems using ideas and tips in this book, plus your own common sense. Chapter 1 in this minibook tells you how to understand your goals and your audience and build messages that draw the response you want. Choosing appropriate graphic options is covered in Chapter 2 in this minibook and in the previous sections of this chapter.

Proofreading your work

In professional communication circles, proofreading is seen as separate from writing and editing. But in these economically tight times, copywriters, journalists, and even book authors often wear all three hats. Many publications now outsource their proofing services or eliminate them. If you've noticed a growing number of mistakes in what you read, that's the reason.

TIP

On a daily basis, obviously proofreading is all up to you. But you can still reach out for help. Many writers use a buddy system to back them up on important material, and you can too. A colleague, friend, or partner may be happy to supply editing advice with you in exchange for the same help. As the saying goes, two sets of eyes are better than one.

SUREFIRE PROOFREADING TIPS

Here are some ways to do the best job proofing your own work or someone else's:

1. Use one of the systems explained at the beginning of Chapter 3 in this minibook so your proofreading is systematic and clear.

2. Be sure to keep an original, unedited version.

3. Try to proofread when your eyes and mind are fresh, and take frequent breaks.

4. Proofread more than once — ideally three times — allowing some time between sessions.

5. Carefully check sentences before and after every change you make, because editing often generates new errors.

6. Pay special attention to the places where you find an error, because errors often clump together (perhaps you were tired when you wrote that part).

7. Look for words that are often misspelled. Every grammar book has these lists, and you can easily find one online. (Keep a copy on your desk.)

8. Examine all the little words, including on, *in, at, the, for, to.* They may repeat or go missing without your noticing.

9. Look up all words you aren't sure about. Choose an online dictionary you like, or just Google the word.

10. Triple-check names, titles, numbers, subheads, and headlines.

11. Rest your eyes regularly, especially if you're proofreading on-screen. Looking out a window into the distance helps. So does setting your computer screen to a comfortable brightness.

12. Try enlarging the on-screen type for easier viewing, but not so much that you don't see the entire sentence, paragraph, or section.

13. Read challenging portions of text backward. This approach is often useful with material that is highly technical or contains numbers.

14. Recheck all the places where a mistake would prove most embarrassing: headlines, lead sentences, and quotes.

Creating your very own writing improvement guide

Most writers are highly consistent in the errors they make, so creating a list of your writing shortfalls helps you sharpen — and ultimately speed up — your writing.

Treat yourself to an in-depth session to review either a major document or a batch of smaller messages. Or gather information and insights over time. Better yet, do both.

Start by thoroughly editing your selected work using the various criteria explained in this minibook. Look for patterns of errors and less-than-wonderful writing. You will benefit by addressing these particular problems.

Record the challenges — and the solutions — systematically. An example follows:

My Problems	Solutions
Too many words ending in *ing*	Find substitutes for most and rewrite as necessary
Too many sentences longer than 17 words	Break them up or tighten by cutting
Need to fix sentence rhythm often	Read them aloud and add or cut words so they move better
Too many sentences per paragraph	Break them up
Too many long words	Replace with short ones, mostly
Too much passive voice	Keep an eye on Word's Readability Index; find more interesting verbs that promote an action feel
General wordiness	Cut, tighten, rewrite
Too many qualifiers (*you might, you can, you should*) and extra phrases	Cut the hedge words and write in present tense!

This analysis produces a road map that the writer can use to review everything he or she writes, from an email to a home page to a proposal.

TIP

Get even more specific and add categories, such as words you often misspell or incorrect use of possessives. Scout for solutions in this book and other sources, and equip yourself with tools to lick the problem. Identifying your personal road-blocks goes a long way toward fixing them.

DOESN'T MY COMPUTER CATCH GRAMMAR GOOFS?

Microsoft Word and other word-processing software have grammar-checking features that identify possible mistakes and indicate potential fixes. While these tools can help, accepting the corrections unquestioningly is like trusting a smartphone's word-guessing function.

Pay attention to the corrections and changes your word-processing software wants to make, in both spelling and grammar, and evaluate them thoroughly.

To care about what you write is a different way of thinking. Do you really need to plan, draft, edit, cut, rewrite, add, subtract, edit, and proofread everything you write? You be the judge. But before you decide that most of the process isn't necessary, consider whether or not your reputation and effectiveness are on the line nearly every time you write. They probably are.

Try out the plan/draft/edit process in small ways, such as for everyday messages, and see whether you start getting what you want more often. When you practice the plan/draft/edit process on the small stuff, you're ready to use it for the big stuff: proposals, reports, articles, websites, blogs, and marketing materials.

Chapter 5

Writing Emails That Get Results

L ove it or hate it, you can't leave it — email is the central nervous system of business life all over the world. Companies may declare e-free Fridays or add newer media such as instant messaging or social networks for basic communication, but you probably still find that your work life centers on managing your inbox and outbox.

The volume and omnipresence of email in your life gives you the opportunity to accomplish your immediate and long-range goals, or screw up both. This chapter shows you how to make the most of this powerful medium and sidestep the traps.

REMEMBER

Of course another communication channel may replace email soon, but it hasn't happened yet. In any case, the guidelines in this chapter apply to whatever comes next, maybe with minor adaptations to formatting and style. The essentials of good communication hold steady.

Fast-Forwarding Your Agenda In-House and Out-of-House

If you're wishing for a way to show off your skills, judgment, competence, and resourcefulness and have decision makers pay attention, *shazam* — email is *the* opportunity.

Yes, everyone is overwhelmed with too much email and wants most of it to go away. The reasons are twofold: Most email is unrelated to your interests and needs, and most of it is badly thought out and poorly written. Take a look through your own inbox. You're likely to find that most of it falls into one of those two categories — or both.

Then take a look at your outbox. Ask yourself (and why not be honest) how many messages you carelessly tossed off without planning or editing. You may feel that this is the nature of the medium — here one minute, gone the next, so it's not worth investing time and energy. But email is the tool you depend on to get things done, day in and day out.

Moreover, email has become the delivery system for many forms of communication. In earlier times, you'd write a cover letter to accompany a resume, for example. Today you deliver it electronically. But a cover letter for a job application is still a cover letter — no matter how it's delivered. A short business proposal may also be sent by email, but it, like a cover letter, it needs to be well written. Resist the temptation to write such material in an off-the-top-of-your-head fashion.

REMEMBER

Good emails bring you the results you want. Even more, writing good emails every time — no exceptions — brings you amazing opportunities to reach the people you want to reach with a message *about you*: how intelligent, resourceful, and reliable you are, for example, and how well you communicate. Even those humdrum in-house emails contribute incrementally to your positive image as an efficient professional and give you a long-range advantage way past accomplishing your immediate goal.

Send direct, well-written emails that have a clear purpose and respect people's time, and you get respect back. People notice and respond to well-written messages, though admittedly, most do so unconsciously.

The higher you go in an organization's hierarchy, the more people tend to recognize good writing and value it because they see so little of it these days. Executives are acutely aware of how badly written emails, even on mundane matters, can create the following:

>> Misunderstandings that generate mistakes

>> Needless dissent among employees and departments

>> Inefficiency, because countering unclear messages demands much more communication

>> A staggering waste of collective time and productivity

Smart leaders are even more aware of how poor email messaging can affect an organization's interface with the world at large, resulting in the following:

>> Weakened company image and reputation

>> Disaffected customers

>> Missed opportunities to connect with new customers

>> Long-term damage to relationships with the public, investors, suppliers, lenders, partners, media, regulators, and donors — all of which directly affect the company's bottom line

TIP

Take email seriously and it will give you many happy returns. Decision makers in your workplace who value clear communication will value you all the more. In addition:

>> **Email offers huge opportunities to develop relationships in the course of doing business.** To build and sustain a network of trusted colleagues and contacts in-house and out can only benefit you over the long term.

>> **Email gives you access to the loftiest heights.** Fifteen years ago, the idea that you could directly write to your CEO or the hiring manager of your dream employer was unthinkable. Now you can, and she may read it and even respond — if you make your message good.

>> **Email is your ticket to reaching people all over the world.** Without it, international trade would depend on mail systems and faxes for making initial contact. Surely email is the unsung hero of globalization.

TIP

If you're an independent entrepreneur, a consultant, a freelancer, or an outside contractor, recognize that emails can make or break your enterprise. Written well, emails can help generate what you need: in-person meetings, opportunities to compete for business, new agreements, relationships of trust, and ways to promote what you do.

Getting Off to a Great Start

Your first imperative in drafting an email: Draw your reader to open it — and read it. Sound easy? Not at all, given the sheer volume of messages that motivate most people to press the Delete key. That's another reason why every email you send must be good: You don't want a reputation for sending pointless, hard-to-decipher messages that lead people to ignore the important ones that you craft carefully.

With email, the lead has two parts — the subject line and the opening sentence or paragraph. We explore each in detail in the following sections.

Writing subject lines that get your message read

Take another look at your inbox and scan the subject lines. Note which ones you opened and why. Most of them probably fall into one of these categories:

>> Must-read because of essential information:

   Subject: New location, May 3rd meeting

>> Must-read because of urgency:

   Decision on Plan A needed today

>> Must-read because of who the writer is (in which case, the *From* matters, too):

   From: President White

   Subject: Department reorganization planned

» Want-to-read because you need the information or it may be valuable:

Subject: Free tools to recover deleted files

» Want-to-read because it looks like a good deal:

Subject: Lowest iPhone price ever

» Want-to-read because it's from a trusted source:

From: Kickstarter

Subject: Projects we love: mobile murals

» Want-to-read because it sounds interesting or fun:

From: Bronx Zoo

Subject: Come see our tiger cubs!

REMEMBER

Few messages are required reading. Your challenge in writing email subject lines is to zero in on what's most likely to concern or interest your reader. But you must always be fair. Don't promise something in the package that isn't there after your reader opens it.

To create a good subject line that keeps fingers off that Delete key:

1. **Figure out what's most relevant to your reader in the message — why the person should care.**

2. **Think of the most concise way of saying it.**

3. **Put the key words as far to the left as possible so your recipient understands the meat of your message quickly and easily.**

Subject lines work best when they're as specific as possible. Here are two examples of emails you probably wouldn't open because the subject lines are too vague and general to capture your interest, along with suggestions for improving the message:

Poor: *Important question*

Better: *Where is tomorrow's workshop?*

Poor: *June newsletter*

Better: *New Twitter techniques in June issue*

Ensuring that the most important words appear in your recipient's inbox window and aren't cut off for lack of space — or because the person is reading on a smartphone or other hand-held device — is worth the thought every time. Very few people pay attention to this simple principle, so build this habit to reap a big advantage.

Following are a few examples of truncated subject lines from emails:

The Coach's Corner: 9 ways to . . .

Did you ever wish that y . . .

Express yourself with a perso . . .

Suppose that the full subject line for the last one was *Express yourself with a personalized dish.* Had the line begun *Your personalized dish,* or *Your name on stoneware,* you might have opened the email.

Investing in good, accurate subject lines always rewards you. You may not be able to deliver the whole of your subject in the limited amount of characters your recipient's inbox allows, but try to get the gist across. Ordinarily, you needn't aim to be clever; but if the message is important, spend some time to make the first few words intriguing.

WARNING

If you can't come up with a tight subject line that communicates the core of your message, consider the possibility that your message may not have a core — or any meaning at all — to your reader. Review both the subject line and the entire message to see whether you're clear on why you're writing and what outcome you want.

Be sure to review your subject line after you write the message. You may shift tack in the course of writing. In fact, the writing process can lead you to think through your reason for creating the message and how to best make your case. Drafting the message first and then distilling the subject line is often easier.

TIP

Don't be lazy about changing the subject lines of long message threads. If you don't, people may overlook your new input. Later, both you and the recipient may be frustrated when looking for a specific message. Try for some continuity, however, so it doesn't look like a different topic. If the first email of a series is identified as *Ideas for Farber proposal,* for example, a new subject line might say *Farber proposal update November 3.* Keep the subject lines obviously relevant to everyone concerned.

Most people use email as their personal database to draw on as needed, so always label messages in ways that make them findable.

Using salutations that suit

The greeting you use is also part of the lead. Draw on a limited repertoire developed for letters:

Dear

Hi

Hello

You can use *Greetings* or something else but be sure it doesn't feel pretentious.

Follow with first name or last as appropriate, using the necessary title (Miss, Ms., Mrs., Mr.). For the plural, Mesdames and Messieurs are over the top for English speakers. For groups, you can sometimes come up with an aggregate title, such as *Dear Software X Users, Dear Subscribers,* or *Hi Team.* Don't be homey or quirky. Using *folks,* for example, can grate on people. Avoid generalizations such as *Dear Customer* if you're writing to an individual. These days, people expect to be addressed by name.

TIP

Often, people who know each other well or are transacting business in a series of emails dispense with the title, and simply start the message with the person's name — for example, *John.* That's fine if doing so feels comfortable. In general, don't omit a name and plunge right into your message because you'll miss an important chance to personalize. You can, however, build a name into the opening line, as in, *I haven't heard from you in a while, Jerry, so thought I'd check where things stand.*

Drafting a strong email lead

REMEMBER

The first sentence or two of your message should accomplish the same goal as the lead of a newspaper article: Attract your readers' attention, present the heart of what you want to say, and give them a reason to care. Plus, you need to tell readers what you want.

Because email leads usually include the same information that appears in the subject line, try not to repeat the same wording or the same information. Email copy occupies valuable real estate. Your best chance of enticing people to read the entire message is to make the lead and everything that follows tight.

Your email lead can consist of one sentence, two sentences, or a paragraph, as needed. When the subject line clearly suggests your focus, you can pick up the thread. For example:

> *Subject: Preparing for the August meeting*
>
> *Hi Jenn,*
>
> *Since we need the materials for the Willow conference in less than a week, I'd like to review their status with you ASAP.*

BEST TIME TO SEND EMAIL?

The best time to send an email message is probably 6 a.m., according to research by Dan Zarrella, formerly of the web marketing firm HubSpot. As reported in the *Wall Street Journal,* Zarrella's study of billions of emails showed that the early-bird messages are most likely to be read because people tend to check their inboxes at the beginning of the day, as they do a newspaper. A 6 a.m. message tends to appear high in the inbox, too.

If your email program has a delay delivery feature, you can write your messages at a convenient time and send them out at 6 or so, without having to be there yourself to click the button.

Often you need a context or clarifying sentence before you get to your request:

> *Subject: Timing on design hire*
>
> *Hilary, you mentioned that you'd like to bring in a graphic designer to work on the stockholder report ASAP. However, I won't be able to supply finished copy until April 3rd.*

Note how quickly both of these messages get to the point. Your everyday in-house messages should nearly always do so, whether addressed to peers, subordinates, or immediate supervisors. But never sacrifice courtesy. The right tone is essential to make your message work. That topic is described later in the sidebar "Finding the right tone for email."

In the case of messages to people outside your department or company, you often need to include more framing. Suppose you're responsible for fielding customer complaints and must write to an irate woman who claims your company sold her a defective appliance:

> *Dear Ms. Black,*
>
> *Your letter about your disappointment with the new Magnaline blender has been brought to my attention. I am happy to help resolve the problem.*

REMEMBER

A good subject line and lead rarely just happen: You achieve them by thoughtful planning. That doesn't mean you can't draft the complete email and then go back and strengthen or change the lead. In fact, you may prefer to figure out the main point through the writing process itself. Just be sure you leave time to edit when you proceed that way. See this minibook's Chapters 3 and 4 for more on editing and revising.

Building Messages That Achieve Your Goals

You build a successful email at the intersection of goal and audience. Intuition can take you far, but analyzing both factors in a methodical way improves all your results. Knowing your goal and your audience is especially critical when you're handling a difficult situation, trying to solve a problem, or writing an important message.

Clarifying your own goals

Email often seems like a practical tool for getting things done. You write to arrange a meeting, receive or deliver information, change an appointment, request help, ask or answer a question, and so on. But even simple messages call for some delving into what you really want.

Consider Amy, a new junior member of the department, who hears that an important staff meeting was held and she wasn't invited. She could write the following:

> Tom, I am so distressed to know I was excluded from the staff meeting last Thursday. Was it just an oversight, or should I take it as a sign that you think my contribution has no value?

Bad move! Presenting herself as an easily offended childish whiner undermines what she really wants — to improve her positioning in the department. Instead of using the opportunity to vent, Amy can take a dispassionate look at the situation and build a message that serves her true goal:

> Tom, I respectfully request that I be included in future department meetings. I am eager to learn everything I can about how we operate so I can do my work more efficiently and contribute more. I'd appreciate the opportunity to better understand department thinking and initiatives.

With external communication, knowing your goal is just as important. For example, if you're responsible for answering customer complaints about defective appliances and believe your goal is to make an unhappy customer go away, you can write:

> We regret your dissatisfaction, but yours is the only complaint we have ever received. We suggest you review the operating manual.

If you assume your job is to mollify the customer on a just-enough level, you may say:

> *We're sorry it doesn't work. Use the enclosed label to ship it back to us, and we'll repair it within six months.*

But if your acknowledged goal is to retain this customer as a future buyer of company products while generating good word of mouth and maybe even positive rather than negative tweets, you're best off writing this:

> *We're so sorry to hear the product didn't work as you hoped. We're shipping you a new one today. I'm sure you'll be happy with it, but if not, please call me right away at my personal phone number . . .*

For both Amy's and the customer service scenarios, keeping your true, higher goals in mind often leads you to create different messages. The thinking is big picture and future-oriented: In Amy's case, the higher purpose is to build a relationship of trust and value with a supervisor and gain opportunities. In the unhappy customer case, you want to reverse a negative situation and cultivate a loyal long-term customer.

TIP

Be the best person you can in every message you send. Every email is a building block for your reputation and future. And email is never private: Electronic magic means your message can go anywhere anyone wants to send it — and you can't erase it, ever.

Assessing what matters about your audience

After you're clear on what you want to accomplish with your email, think about your audience — the person or group to whom you're writing. One message, one style does not fit all occasions and individuals. As you discover in Chapter 1 in this minibook, when you ask someone to do something for you in person, you instinctively choose the best arguments to make your case. You adapt your arguments as you go along according to the other person's reactions — her words, body language, expression, tone of voice, inflection, and all the other tiny clues that tell you how the other person is receiving your message in the moment you're delivering it.

An email message, of course, provides no visual or oral feedback. Your words are on their own. So your job is to think through how your reader is most likely to respond and then base what you write on that.

Anticipating a reader's reaction can take a little imagination. You may find you're good at it. Try holding a two-way conversation in your head with the person.

Observe what she says and how she says it. Note any areas of resistance and other clues.

TIP

You also have another surefire way to predict your reader's reaction: Systematically consider the most relevant factors about that person or group. Chapter 1 in this minibook gives you a comprehensive list of factors that may relate to what you want to accomplish.

Do you need to consider so many aspects when you're drafting every email? No, if your goal is really simple, such as a request to meet. But even then, you're better off knowing whether this particular recipient needs a clear reason to spend time with you, how much notice she prefers, if she already has set feelings about the subject you want to discuss, and so on. You can tilt the result in your favor — even for a seemingly minor request — by taking account of such things.

The more major your message is, the more factors you may need to consider. Or perhaps just one facet of the person's situation or personality may be overwhelmingly important. To shape the right message, check out the section on knowing your reader in Chapter 1 for what's relevant to the person and the case at hand. Think about the factors that are most relevant in the context of what you're asking for.

REMEMBER

Audience analysis becomes instinctive with practice. And your better results soon reinforce its value.

Certain characteristics are always important. Considering your reader's age, for example, may seem rude or politically incorrect, but business writers beware — especially with emails. Different generations have genuinely different attitudes toward work, communications, rewards, authority, career development, and much more. If you're a Generation Y'er (born after 1980) or Generation X'er (born 1965 to 1980), you need to understand the Boomer's (born 1946 to 1964) need for respect, hierarchical thinking, correct grammar, courtesy, in-person communication, and more. This topic is described fully in Chapter 1.

I often ask participants in writing workshops to create detailed profiles of their immediate supervisors. Pretend that you're an undercover agent and you're asked to file a report on the person you report to. Take 20 minutes and see what you can put together. First scan the demographic, psychographic, positioning, and personality traits outlined in Chapter 1 and list those you think seem relevant to defining that person (for example, age, position, information preferences, hot buttons, and decision-making style). Then fill in what you know or intuit about the person under each category. You'll probably find that you understand far more about your boss than you think.

Read through the completed profile and you'll see major clues on how to communicate with that important person on a routine basis, as well as how to work with her successfully overall and make yourself more highly valued. You may uncover ways to strengthen your relationship or even turn it around.

Suppose you're inviting your immediate supervisor, Jane, to a staff meeting where you plan to present an idea for a new project. You hope to persuade her that your project is worth the resources to make it happen. First clarify your goal or set of goals. Perhaps, in no particular order, you aim to do the following:

>> Obtain Jane's buy-in and endorsement

>> Get input on project tweaks sooner rather than later

>> Gain the resources you need for the project

>> Demonstrate what a terrific asset you are (a constant)

You know Jane is heavily scheduled and the invite must convince her to reserve the time. What factors about her should you consider? Your analysis may suggest the following:

>> **Demographics:** Jane is young for her position, and the first woman to hold that job. Observation supports the idea that she feels pressured to prove herself. She drives herself hard and works 60-hour weeks.

>> **Psychographics:** She is famously pro-technology, a true believer, and an early adaptor.

>> **Positioning:** She has the authority to approve a pilot program but probably not more. She is most likely being groomed for higher positions and is closely monitored.

>> **Personality/communication style:** She likes statistics. She likes evidence. She's an impatient listener who makes decisions when she feels she has just enough information. Her hottest button is being able to show her own manager that she's boosted her department's numbers. How to do that probably keeps her up at night, along with how to impress her boss for her next promotion. She takes risks if she feels reasonably sheltered from bad consequences.

Presto! With these four points, you have a reader profile to help you write Jane a must-come email — and even more importantly, a guide that enables you to structure a meeting that accomplishes what you want.

Determining the best content for emails

After you know your goal and audience, you have the groundwork in place for good content decisions. You know how to judge what information is likely to lead the person or group to respond the way you want. (See Chapter 1 in this minibook for guidance on how to address groups and construct a reader who epitomizes that group.)

To figure out what you need to say, play a matching game: What information, facts, ideas, statistics, and so on will engage the person and dispose her to say yes?

Think about audience *benefits*. This important marketing concept applies to all persuasive pitches. Benefits speak to the underlying reasons you want something. A dress, for example, possesses features such as color, style, and craftsmanship, but the benefit is that it makes the wearer feel beautiful. When you're planning a message and want it to succeed, think about the audience and goal, and write down your first ideas about matching points and benefits.

FINDING THE RIGHT TONE FOR EMAIL

In everyday emails, your tone contributes hugely to coming across as empathetic, so never overlook it. Chapter 1 in this minibook describes tone as it applies to all writing; here, you find out about tone in electronic communications.

Often you can identify the appropriate tone by briefly thinking about the person you're writing to. Imagine yourself in conversation with him and determine where the atmosphere falls along the spectrum of formal and professionally reserved to casual and friendly.

If you're writing to someone you don't know or to a group, edge toward the more formal but avoid sounding stilted or indifferent. Conveying a degree of warmth and caring is nearly always appropriate because people respond well to that.

Strive for positive energy in all your emails unless for some reason it feels inappropriate. Granted, you have limited ways to express enthusiasm and must balance word choice and content to achieve a positive tone. Punctuation offers the option of exclamation points. Many people use them more freely nowadays because electronic communication offers so few ways to sound excited. But don't scatter them everywhere and make yourself look childish. This recommendation also holds for emoticons, all those cute symbols popularized by texting. Unless you know your reader well, do not use them. Older people especially may regard you as lightweight. Remember, too, that some graphic emoticons don't translate between various technologies and may be auto-replaced with who knows what!

For example, to draw Jane from the preceding section to that meeting, the list may include the following based on your analysis:

>> Evidence that the idea works well somewhere else

>> Information on how cutting-edge technology will be used

>> Potential for the idea to solve a major problem for the department

>> Suggestion that other parts of the company will also be interested and impressed

Many other ideas may be relevant — such as it's great for the environment, and it gives people more free time — but probably not to Jane.

Structuring Your Middle Ground

Think of your email message like a sandwich: The opening and closing hold your content together and the rest is the filling. Viewed in this way, most emails are easy to organize. Complicated messages full of subtle ideas and in-depth instructions or pronouncements are inappropriate to the medium anyway.

Email's typical orientation toward the practical means that how you set up and how you close count heavily — but the middle still matters. Typically the in-between content explains why — why a particular decision should be made, why you deserve an opportunity, or why the reader should respond positively. The middle portion can also explain in greater detail why a request is denied, or provide details and technical backup, or describe a series of steps to accomplish something.

Figure out middle section content by first brainstorming what points will accomplish your goal in terms of your target audience, as outlined in the previous sections. Then do the following:

1. **Write a simple list of the points to make.** One example is the list created to convince Jane to come to a meeting with a positive mindset in the "Determining the best content for emails" section.

2. **Scan your list and frame your lead.**

   Your *lead* is the sentence or paragraph that clearly tells readers why you're writing and what you want in a way most likely to engage their interest. Starting with the bottom line is almost always your best approach for organizing a message. Remember the reporter's mantra: Don't bury the lead.

Skipping the subject line for now, a get-Jane-to-the-meeting message can begin like this:

> Hi Jane,
>
> I'm ready to show you how using new social media can help us increase market share for our entire XL line. After checking the online calendar for your availability, I scheduled the demo for March 5 at 2. Can you meet with me and my team then?

To structure the middle, consider the previously identified points that are most important to Jane:

>> Evidence that the idea works well somewhere else

>> Opportunity to use cutting-edge technology

>> Potential to solve a major problem

>> Potential for wide company interest

You then simply march through these points for the body of the message. For example:

> My research shows that two companies in related industries have reaped 15 to 20 percent increases in market share in just a few months. For us, the new media I've identified can potentially move XL out of the sales doldrums of the past two quarters.
>
> Further, we'll be positioning our department at the cutting edge of strategic social media marketing. If we succeed as I anticipate, I see the entire company taking notice of our creative leadership.

The thinking you did before you started to write now pays handsome dividends. With a little reshuffling of the four points, you have a persuasive memo that is organized and logical. You know your content and how it fits together.

This process may sound easy to do with an invented example, but working with real ideas and facts is even easier.

Your biggest strength in building a successful message in any format is to know your story. Organizing a clear email is rarely a problem after you determine your content. You simply need to know such factors as the following:

>> How the person you want to meet with may benefit by seeing you

>> Why your recipient will find your report or proposal of interest

>> Why the employment manager should read *your* resume

Review the list you assemble, decide which points to include, and put them in a logical order. Your list may include more thoughts than you need for a convincing message, and you can be selective. That's fine. Just enough is better than too much.

This basic premise works with longer, more formal documents as well.

Closing Strong

After you write your lead and the middle, you need to close (and perhaps circle back to fill in or hone your subject line).

TIP

When you use the guidelines in the previous sections to begin messages and develop the middle, your close needs only to reinforce what you want. An email doesn't need to end dramatically. You just want to circle back to the beginning and add any more relevant information to the "ask." For example:

>> If you requested a decision, writing something like the following is sufficient: *I look forward to knowing your decision by October 21st.*

>> If you're delivering a report, your close might be this: *I appreciate your review. Please let me know if you have any questions or if you'd like additional information.*

>> In the case of the memo to Jane, the closing might be simply, *Please let me know if March 5th at 2 p.m. works for you. If not, I'm happy to reschedule.*

Sign off with courtesy and tailor the degree of formality to the occasion and relationship. If you're writing to a conservative person or a businessman in another culture, a formal closing such as *Sincerely* is often best. The same is true for a resume's cover letter, which is essentially a letter in email form and should look like a letter.

But in most situations, less formal end-signals are better, such as the following:

Thanks!

I look forward to your response.

Best regards

Avoid cute signoffs such as *Cheers.* Always end with your name — your first name if you know the person or are comfortable establishing informality. Even if your reader is someone who hears from you all the time, using your name personalizes the message and alerts her that the communication is truly finished.

Your finished message needs one more thing: the subject line. Consider at this point the total thrust of your content. Then decide what words and phrases work best to engage your audience's interest.

The *Jane* subject line, for example, needs to get across that your message is a meeting invitation, suggest what it's about, and emphasize that it is worth her time. Perhaps:

> *Need you there: May 3rd Demo, Social Media Project*

Perfecting Your Writing for Email

Email deserves your best writing, editing, and proofreading skills. Often the message is *who you are* to your audience. You may be communicating with someone you'll never meet, in which case the virtual interaction determines the relationship and the success of the message. At other times, crafting good email messages wins you the opportunity to present your case in person or progress to the next stage of doing business.

REMEMBER

People look for clues about you and draw conclusions from what you write and how you write it. Even if your ideas are good, incorrect grammar and spelling lose you more points than you may suspect, no matter how informal your relationship with the recipient seems.

The following sections run through some top tips for crafting text that perfectly suits email.

Monitoring length and breadth

Keep emails to fewer than 300 words and stick to one idea or question. Three hundred words can go a long way (the memo to draw Jane to the meeting in the previous section was less than 150 words).

Such limits are hard to consistently observe, but you're wise to remember how short people's attention spans are, especially for online reading. That's why you benefit from knowing your central point or request, and opening with it. Don't bury it as a grand conclusion. Nor should you bury any important secondary questions at the end.

WARNING

PRACTICING EMAIL SMARTS

Email is a great facilitator in many ways, but it definitely has limits. Email's easiness can lead you to inappropriate use. Don't use it to do the following:

- **Present complicated issues or subjects:** Of course you can attach a report, a proposal, or another long document to an email, but don't expect an email in itself to produce an investment, donation or other high-stakes buy-in.

- **Wax philosophical or poetic:** Readers look to email for practical communication and are annoyed by windy meanderings — even (or especially) if you're the boss.

- **Spam:** Send email only to people directly concerned with the subject and don't send unnecessary replies. Don't forward cute anecdotes or jokes unless you're sure the particular person welcomes that. And don't forward chain letters: They can upset recipients. Don't forward anything without reading it thoroughly and carefully.

- **Amuse:** Generally avoid sarcasm and irony (and most humor), because it can be misinterpreted against your interests.

Never respond to poorly considered and written emails with poor emails of your own. You don't know who else may see them, and even those who write poorly — perhaps through a feeling of executive privilege — may disrespect you for doing the same. Enjoy feeling superior (without expressing it, of course)! Your excellent emails reward you over the long run as almost nothing else can.

TIP

Aim to make emails as brief and tight as you can. If your message starts to grow too much, reconsider whether email is the appropriate format. You may choose to use the message as a cover note and attach the full document. Or you may want to break the message into components to send separately over a reasonable space of time. But realize that you risk losing your audience if you send a series of messages.

Styling it right

Choose words and phrases that are conversational, friendly, businesslike, and unequivocally clear. Email is not the place for fanciful language and invention. Put your energy into the content and structure of your message.

Try to make your presentation transparent, eliminating all barriers to understanding. Your messages may end up less colorful than they could be, and that's okay. Clear, concise language is especially relevant to messages directed at overseas audiences.

Going short: Words, sentences, paragraphs

The business writing guidelines presented in Chapter 2 in this minibook apply even more intensely to email. You want your message to be readable and understood in the smallest possible amount of time.

Draw on the plain old Anglo-Saxon word stock, mostly one-syllable words. Use two-syllable words when they express ideas better, use three syllables when they're the best choice, but reserve more lengthy and complex words for when they serve a real purpose.

Short sentences work for the same reason. Aim for 10 to 15 words on average. Paragraphs should contain one to three sentences to support comprehension and build in helpful white space.

Using graphic techniques to promote clarity

The graphic techniques discussed here don't require special software or a degree in fine arts. They're simply ways to visually present information and make your writing more organized and accessible.

TIP

Do everything you can to incorporate generous *white space* (areas with no text or graphics) into your writing. Don't crowd your messages and leave them (and the reader) gasping for air. White space allows the eye to rest and focuses emphasis where you want it.

Add subheads

Subheads are great for longer emails. You can make the type bold and add a line of space above it. Subheads for email can be matter of fact:

Why decide now

Step 1 (followed by Step 2 and so on)

Final recommendation

Pros and cons

Background

This technique neatly guides the reader through the information and also enables you as a writer to organize your thinking and delivery with ease.

Drafting all your subheads *before* you write can be a terrific way to achieve good organization. Choose a message that you already wrote and found challenging. Think the subject through to come up with the major points or steps to cover, and then write a simple, suitable subhead for each. Put the subheads in order and add the relevant content under each. (Each section need not be more than a paragraph long.) Now check whether all the necessary information to make your point is there — if not, add it. Your message is sure to become clearer and more cohesive and persuasive.

Providing your own structure in this way may make writing easier, particularly if you feel organizationally challenged. It helps ensure that you don't leave out anything important, too.

Here's an extra trick. If you feel that you have too many subheads after drafting the message, cut some or all of them. You still have a solid, logically organized email. Just be sure to check that the connections between sections are clear without the subheads.

Bring in bulleted and numbered lists

Bullets offer another excellent option for presenting your information. They are

- Readily absorbed
- Fast to read
- Easy to write
- Useful for equipment lists, examples, considerations, and other groupings

WARNING

However, observe a few cautions:

- Don't use more than six or seven bullets in a list. A long stretch of bullets loses all effect; they become mind numbing and hard to absorb.
- Don't use bullets to present ideas that need context or connection.
- Don't mix and match. The items on your list must be *parallel,* so that they begin with the same kind of word — a verb, a noun, or in the case of the first bullet list, an adverb.

Never use bullet lists as a dumping ground for thoughts that you're too lazy to organize or connect. If you doubt this advice, think of all the bad PowerPoint shows you've seen — screens rife with random-seeming bullets.

Numbered lists are also helpful, particularly if you're presenting a sequence or step-by-step process. Instructions work well in numbered form. Give numbered lists some air so that they don't look intimidating — skip a space between each number.

Consider boldface

Making your type bold gives you a good option for calling attention to key topics, ideas, or subsections of your message. You can use bold for lead-ins:

> **Holiday party coming up.** *Please see the task list and choose how you want to contribute . . .*

You may also use bold to highlight something in the body of the text:

> *Please see the task list and choose your way of contributing **by December 10.***

If you overload your message with boldface, you undermine its reason for being. Keep in mind that boldface doesn't always transfer across different email systems and software, so don't depend on it too much for making your point.

Underlining important words or phrases is another option.

Respect overall graphic impact

REMEMBER

Avoid undercutting your content through bad graphic presentation. Plain and simple is the way to go. Use plain text or the simplest HTML — no tricky, cute, or hard-to-read fonts. Don't write entire messages in capitals or italics, and don't use a rainbow of color — that's distracting rather than fun for readers. Avoid that crammed-in feeling. People simply do not read messages that look dense and difficult. Or they read as little of them as possible. Like everything else you write, an email must look inviting and accessible.

Using the signature block

Contact information these days can be complex. Typically you want people to find you by email or telephone. Plus there's your tagline. Your company name. Your website. Your blog. The book you wrote. The published article. Twitter. Facebook. LinkedIn. Professional affiliations and offices.

Decide on a few things you most want to call attention to and refrain from adding the rest. Better yet, create several signature blocks for different audiences. Then you can select the most appropriate one for the people to whom you're writing. Don't include your full signature block every time you respond to a message, especially if you incorporate a logo, which arrives as an attachment. Check your email program's settings so the automatic signature is minimal or absent.

6

Presentations

Contents at a Glance

CHAPTER 1: **Creating Compelling Content**. 449

Getting Your Content Up to Par 450

Adding Variety and Impact. 452

CHAPTER 2: **Honing Your Platform Skills**. 463

Using Your Voice to Command Attention 464

Captivating Audiences with Your Eyes 472

Finding the Right Posture. 475

Making the Right Facial Expressions. 481

Gesturing Creatively 482

CHAPTER 3: **Captivating Your Audience**. 487

Touching on the Laws of Communication Impact 488

Starting with the Law of Primacy. 489

Starting Off on the Right Foot 491

Building Your Introduction. 496

CHAPTER 4: **Keeping Your Audience Captivated**. 503

Standing and Shouting Out: The Law of Emphasis
and Intensity. 504

Involving Your Audience: The Law of Exercise
and Engagement 511

Hitting Their Hot Buttons: The Law of Interest 513

Facing the Consequences: The Law of Effect 515

CHAPTER 5: **Ending on a High Note** 517

Concluding Effectively: The Law of Recency 518

Affecting Your Audience Right to the End 519

Giving a Tactical Conclusion. 521

Engineering Your Conclusion with Building Blocks 524

Chapter **1**

Creating Compelling Content

ontent gives substance to your presentation. When it comes to innovative presentations, content creates a vivid picture for your audience. Throughout this minibook (and in this chapter's title), we use the term *compelling* numerous times. It's a strong, descriptive word meaning to arouse interest in a powerful, irresistible way or urgently requiring attention. Truly compelling information holds your audience in awe of your presentation.

The best type of compelling content affects people intellectually and emotionally from various perspectives. Metaphorically, if a standard presentation gives black-and-white, two-dimensional information, a compelling presentation comes across in rich color 3-D. Great presenters don't just inform, they enlighten; they don't just motivate, they move audiences to action.

The guidelines and information in this chapter help you create irresistible content. We show you how to select and use content that consistently compels your audiences to do what you want them to. We focus on the creative aspects of content, but we include some important tips for organizing and outlining your content, too.

Most people jump into content before, or without, going through the essential process of analyzing and planning and don't get the results they expected or hoped for. Worse yet are people who give slide presentations rather than presentations using slides. Using visuals, rather than text, broadens your choices dramatically. For example, some presenters look through an existing slide deck and simply remove the slides they don't need for their upcoming presentation, when truth be told, most presentations — and especially important presentations — need customized, personalized visuals tailored to the audience.

Getting Your Content Up to Par

Compare your presentation content to a well-written article or script that grabs your attention with the opening or introduction, makes information interesting with descriptive narrative, and solicits an emotional reaction. Content can inform, arouse, stimulate, captivate, persuade, rivet, and illuminate. Compelling content — delivered sincerely, with passion and conviction — can change minds and hearts. Content presented creatively alongside unique images and video gives people a new, enriched perspective on a situation and adds dimension to a topic, thus helping people to commit to and act on your request or recommendation.

Determining your content's purpose

Use your strategy to guide content development. What specifically do you want to accomplish? Think of the effect you want to achieve intellectually and emotionally, such as the following:

>> **Educate:** Enlighten and inform people about a topic they aren't familiar with.

>> **Emphasize:** Highlight, spotlight, or focus on something so your audience easily remembers and appreciates its importance.

>> **Prove:** Give evidence of something and fully convince people of your claims or points.

>> **Reverse:** Change the audience's perceptions or assumptions about something in your topic.

>> **Explain:** Make crystal clear why your claims or perspective on a topic are valid and perhaps the best.

>> **Justify:** Give valid reasons for doing what you propose.

>> **Motivate:** Inspire or urge people to act to improve something.

>> **Entertain:** Stimulate and amuse to make your information interesting and fascinating.

When it comes to your content, determine three to five main points you want to make with your audience. Finally, think how to condense and encapsulate your content and message into just one or two sentences for your audience.

Covering your points in priority order

Some movies and television shows pride themselves on clever, unexpected endings that leave the best for last. Likewise, many presenters think surprising their audience with the most important benefit, message, idea, or negotiating point in their conclusion creates the strongest effect. Instead, we recommend that you cover your topics and information in priority order:

1. **Introduce the most critical and valuable areas of interest to your group first.**

2. **Discuss the details of those topics you know your audience values.**

3. **Present extra, potentially valuable but less important information.**

When you use this priority hierarchy, you cover the most vital areas first when you have the highest attention of your group. If, for some reason, several decision makers or technical experts (who are evaluators and recommenders) have to leave your presentation early, they have heard the most essential and valuable information. If people ask more questions and want more discussion on the priority information, you can choose to not present the least important information or topics and devote more time to what matters most to your group.

You still want to repeat and highlight the priority information throughout your talk and especially during your conclusion.

Navigating content

If you're giving a presentation to a large group at an association meeting, convention, or trade show, your presentation can be sequential and tightly structured. However, if you give a presentation where you expect a lot of questions or requests for more specific information, such as in a sales situation, your content and visuals need a flexible organization so you can quickly and smoothly respond to changing conditions.

What would you do if you find out just a few minutes before beginning an important presentation that instead of having the scheduled 45 minutes, you now have just 15 minutes? In that kind of situation, you must reengineer your presentation. With some careful planning, you can quickly adjust. By preparing the following three levels of information, the more time you have, the deeper you go, whereas if your time is cut short, you cover the first level and choose appropriate information from the other two.

>> **Level 1: Summary:** Communicate your main points and critical highlights. This is the distilled essence of your presentation and can stand alone as a presentation if necessary.

>> **Level 2: Planned:** This level contains the talk you originally planned for your allotted time with content at the appropriate level of detail to fill the allotted time. With less time, choose the most salient points to add to Level 1.

>> **Level 3: Extra:** Prepare more detailed or tangential content and visuals that you use to answer specific questions from the audience.

Most presentation apps let you create *hyperlinks,* which can be graphics or text that you click to jump to other non-sequential visual content in your presentation. Hyperlinks make your presentation impressively interactive because you can swiftly go right to the information or visual you need rather than click through slide after slide until you get to it.

TIP

Don't let extra information go to waste: Consider preparing handouts or publishing the information on your website.

Adding Variety and Impact

You can be a marvelously creative presenter with riveting voice and body language skills, but if your content lacks substance, focus, and relevance, your presentation will miss its mark. In addition to making sure your content fulfills your presentation strategy, you want to present it in creative, interesting, and enjoyable ways. In this section, we describe different types of content and various ways of communicating it.

Think about action movies that keep you on the edge of your seat. Film editors take input from dozens of cameras from different angles and elevations to give variety to a scene. Editors also change entire scenes quickly so as not to let your attention flag for a moment. You seldom see a shot last more than ten seconds! Movie scenes and angles typically change every three to six seconds.

Now think about your presentation. What if your presentation has facts and statistics throughout communicated from a single perspective? Bo-o-o-o-ring. Instead, you want to mix interesting examples, fascinating stories, good video, humorous illustrations, eye-opening comparisons, and metaphors that encapsulate your message in one sentence. Move your presentation along with a rich combination of important information shown from different angles and perspectives to enable people to better understand and appreciate your points.

TIP

You won't want to use all the content types in one presentation. Strive to create the ideal mix that best supports your presentation strategy and goals.

Using facts

Facts are those indisputable things such as names, dates, dimensions, specifications, operating characteristics, and number of employees that are accepted or can be easily verified. When a salesperson says, "Our product has been used in over 170 countries for the last 40 years" and can back that up, that's a plain fact, not a claim or a guesstimate. Lawyers build their cases exclusively on solid evidence from a body of facts and information, never opinions, speculation, or assumptions. Think about what specific set of facts are important to use in your presentation.

REMEMBER

Present the most important facts and make the supporting ones available in a handout or on your website. Using too many facts in your presentation leads to audience confusion and boredom.

Giving examples

Great examples clarify your points, reducing any misconceptions or misunderstandings. They add interest and variety to your information, as well as extra meaning, which amplifies the effect of the conveyed information. Throughout this minibook, we use examples to help you fully understand both meaning and context. Using specific cases and situations illustrate potentially abstract or general concepts.

Use brief, realistic, relevant, and complete examples that interest your audience. Consider prefacing your examples with phrases such as, "For example" or "An example of that would be." Here are just a couple instances when presenters used examples:

» When a politician talks about government waste in spending, she cites several specific, blatant, and shocking examples of money that was foolishly squandered.

» The president of a big metropolitan photography club explains the rules for the new members who want to enter the novice photos category to win a prize. She shows 25 photos from different categories that won recognition in the last three competitions and explains why the judges chose each one. Now, the new photographers have a critical base of reference (ideas and evaluation criteria) to go by.

Citing references

Reference written pieces that support or confirm information you present. Search the web for white papers and government reports that provide detailed information about your topic. Respected publications such as *The Wall Street Journal, Forbes, Fortune, Fast Company, The Economist,* and *Scientific American* provide excellent sources for quotes. Consult specialized trade or industry publications and journals for the latest research and trends. IBM, Strategy & Capgemini, McKinsey & Company, the Boston Consulting Group, Accenture, and many others conduct research and make the results available to the public.

When quoting from these types of publications:

>> Mention the name, issue, and date, the title of the article or report, and the author(s).

>> Use concise excerpts when possible, but if called for, discuss more detailed information such as reading a half-page of the publication.

>> Always relate the key information in the article to the point you stress.

>> Consider using the cover or article page as a visual in your presentation.

Here's a fictional example:

> According to the June 2015 issue of *Aviation Technology News* in an article titled "Are Light Aircraft Ready for Electric Motors," radically lightweight motor designs made of new materials combined with exotic batteries with ten times the energy density of current ones will usher in an era of inexpensive single-engine planes. Let me quote from the article, "Dr. L.W. Chou said his university has established six critical quantum-leap breakthroughs in integrated electric propulsion over the last three years. The entire package is only six months away from commercialization." With the other information I discuss, this article builds yet a stronger case of a growing trend that can open opportunities for us in. . . .

Telling stories

The best speakers in the world agree on the extraordinary power of storytelling in business or even technical presentations because you can include all kinds of content (facts, statistics, examples, explanations) in the format. Stories have a bottom-line moral along with key messages and learnings that reveal purpose. Stories effectively and efficiently convey novel ideas. They illustrate how to solve problems, reach for opportunities, and deal with setbacks, challenges, and outright failures as well as how to pick yourself up to reach new heights of success.

Captivating stories inform, motivate, inspire, and enlighten by triggering an emotional response. Peter Guber, the former chairman and CEO of Sony Pictures, aptly said, "Move listeners' hearts, and their feet and wallets will follow." You can weave a creative tale and use technology, voice, and body language to mesmerize audiences.

When crafting your stories, keep the following tips in mind:

>> A good story involves transformation. The protagonist first faces a conflict and then finds a cure. As the plot progresses, something important changes for the main characters.

>> Your story fits your audience — their needs, wants, and interests — and has a key point or moral they'll appreciate.

>> People relate to and value your story because it envelops them intellectually and emotionally. Your story must address the situation and issues confronting your group.

>> The characters in your story come alive. You explain their pain, fear, concern, hopes, and desires along with their decision making, their struggles, and their ultimate victory or personal and professional change as a result of the conflict or challenge facing them.

TIP

You can find many superb storytellers when you search online for both motivational and also TEDx speakers; let the ways they masterfully use stories in their presentations inspire you. Browse the library at TED talks at www.ted.com/talks/browse. You can also type *speakers bureaus* in to a browser for a list of agencies that represent motivational speakers who specialize in telling great stories. Go to the speakers' websites to view their video demo tapes and see the power of storytelling!

Going by the numbers

Although many presenters know the meaning and relative importance of the numbers they throw at audiences, numbers can be abstract unless you supply a point of reference and bring statistics to life.

Several years ago a US politician sounded the alarm bell that a foreign nation had created the world's fastest supercomputer and that the United States could lose its critical technological edge. He gave the numbers: Speed was 2.5 petaflops (one quadrillion floating point operations per second) or 2.5 followed by 15 zeroes; it had over 7,000 GPUs (graphics processing units); and over 14,000 CPUs (central processing units — the computers). He went on to say it cost almost $90 million and required a little over 4 megawatts to power up. Even though he correctly rounded the numbers, the non-technical audience might have been glassy-eyed until he put it in clearer context and perspective. He said this new computer was 29 million times more powerful than the first Cray supercomputer in 1976!

Make sure the numbers relate to the point you want to make, that they are necessary and add validity to your other information. Be prepared to give the source of your statistics, if asked. Unless exact numbers are critical to make comparisons to baseline numbers, round them. Consider breaking numbers into more recognizable and meaningful units and terms such as per person, average, median, and ranges (minimum to maximum), ratios, or percentages.

TIP

Use the old rule of thumb to simplify numbers: Instead of saying 84.7 percent, say 5 out of 6; instead of 12.5 percent, use 1 out of 8.

Quoting experts

Quotations not only add interest to your talk but also give relevance and support to the points you want to highlight. Use a combination of serious and humorous quotations to add a fresh new look to things your audience values.

Use quotations that directly connect with your points from well-respected, established authorities in their fields from your own country. Keep in mind the old faithful standbys of famous Greek and Roman philosophers, Winston Churchill, Abraham Lincoln, Mahatma Gandhi, Albert Einstein, and humorists such as Will Rogers and Mark Twain. Make use of statements by current business experts, famous authors, celebrities, comedians, and other popular icons in your culture.

Innovative presenters try to find those creative, interesting quotations that add punch and pizzazz to their messages. As with any other type of content, you can use several quotations throughout your talk without overdoing it.

Contrasting and comparing

Contrasts show striking differences between two things. A presenter at a software design conference speaks about advances in 3-D gaming animation where the facial hair, skin, and other physical features of animated characters are almost indistinguishable from photographs of actual people. To illustrate the advances made in this software, he shows a game created 15 years ago compared to today's latest being played on Microsoft Xbox and Sony's PlayStation 4. The difference is shocking in terms of the past technology's lower resolution, lack of realism, lighting, and shading aspects, among other characteristics, capabilities, and performance. This comparison visually communicates the stark differences between old and new. An author and keynote speaker uses contrast to discuss and describe the vast differences between how an open-minded company with an innovative culture operates, grows, and prospers versus a closed company that shuns creativity and innovation and instead embraces the status quo that leads to mediocre operational and financial results.

A comparison, on the other hand, evaluates the qualities of being similar yet different. For example, presenters use comparison when discussing options available to their audiences. Say, for example, a presenter wants to show her internal group of executives that she came up with three program designs to help her organization go through a major change process. She discusses how each specific program, although having the same goals and objectives, has different strategies, resources, and activities with its own mix of pros and cons. She compares the three by describing their attributes and then recommends program number two and explains why she believes this is the optimum choice based upon the stated needs and criteria from the executive board. A carefully crafted comparison aids the audience in their decision making.

Find circumstances in your presentation where stark, eye-opening contrasts and detailed comparisons help to describe, explain, and emphasize your points.

Giving demonstrations

"Seeing is believing," as the saying goes. Demonstrations, when performed properly during a presentation, lend proof to your claims, especially with skeptics or cynics. If you work in sales, marketing, or in a technical capacity, product demonstrations back up and verify your claims about your product being the fastest, most durable, most flexible, easiest to use, lightest, quietest, or whatever feature places your product or service above the competition. Demonstrations add dynamism, drama, and interest to your talk. They create three-dimensional realism that appeals to several senses. Numerous research studies confirm the obvious fact that the more people's senses (sight, sound, touch, smell, taste) are involved in an evaluation process, the easier and faster they can be persuaded. Just look at infomercials and the creativity they use to demonstrate their slicer-dicers, vacuums, or exercise equipment, and you'll understand why they're so successful.

Oftentimes, the more dramatic the demonstration, the more impressive. At the annual Paris Air Show, the world's oldest and largest commercial air show, major manufacturers (such as Boeing, Lockheed Martin, BAE Systems, and Sukhoi Company) demonstrate the capabilities of their military and civilian aircraft to potential customers. You see the best pilots doing what look like impossible maneuvers — straight up takeoffs, hairpin turns, stalls, and steep landings — to prove their machines are the best of the lot.

Demonstrators use a traditional demonstration technique called FAB (feature, advantage, benefit). Suppose that at a trade show for construction and remodeling companies, your company features an industrial-quality cordless drill. You talk about its brushless motors and say, "One key *feature* of our drill is the industry's most advanced brushless motors. The *advantage* is that they are more powerful and durable, and have greater efficiency. The *benefit* to your construction professionals is greater productivity and reliability, which enables them to do more in less time. And that translates into more profits for your company."

When you include a demonstration in your presentation, practice ahead of time so it comes across as realistic and you perform it smoothly and professionally.

TIP

When you can, invite people from the audience to use your product or service as you guide them through the demonstration. Experiencing your claims firsthand removes any doubt an audience member may have.

Defining terms

Definitions ensure understanding of your information. Unless you specifically define terms that may be ambiguous, unknown, or are open to multiple interpretations, your audience may misunderstand your meaning. For example, an aeronautical engineer says, "This potentially quantum leap wing design is *bleeding edge,* not just leading edge." She goes on to say, "Let me define what I mean by bleeding edge . . ."

Obviously, you need to know your audience and their level of knowledge before you start defining terms that may be known to them. If you are unsure, you can subtly build in definitions without insulting the audience's knowledge or experience, as in this example: "Our R&D department is expanding our studies into new forms of *nanotechnology,* which, as you know, is the manipulation of matter on an atomic and molecular level for the fabrication of novel new products with a vast range of applications. Let me give you several jaw-dropping examples of what we're doing." As you develop your content, think of all the terms you may need to define for your audience.

TIP

Rehearse your presentation in front of someone who has a knowledge level similar to your prospective audience and ask him or her to identify terms that may be confusing.

Answering rhetorical questions

Although more of a technique to enhance content instead of a type of content, a *rhetorical question* poses a query without expecting an answer. It creates curiosity, anticipation, or even suspense and gets your audience thinking about the question you just asked.

Say you have skeptics in your audience who don't believe that using your company's new manufacturing and assembly process is a good idea because of disruptions in the changeover due to training time, halted production, and poor return on investment. In this example, after your introduction but before you get into the brief process overview, set the stage with several rhetorical questions that have a touch of devil's advocate in them to get people thinking:

> Your current process has been successful for so long. That's a great testimony to your accomplishments! But nothing stands still for long. Your competitors are biting at your heels to knock you out of the lead position in your industry by implementing significant innovations to make their operations more productive, more efficient, more accurate, and higher quality.

> Can you afford to let them do that at your expense? Of course not!

> Why change right away and go with our comprehensive fabrication and assembly process when others are less costly and take less time to install and start operating?

> Aren't you going to get hassles and disruptions in changing over to our new integrated system with the complexities you perceive it having?

> How can you know for sure you'll get rapid payback and a return on investment that you'll be proud of?

> In the next 45 minutes, let's explore solid answers to those questions, which anyone in your position would naturally have. I say this with a sense of confidence and assuredness: You will be surprised and, I believe, quite pleased with what you hear during our presentation!"

Asking those tough rhetorical questions without expecting answers will pique the audience's curiosity as to how you'll answer them, which means you will have their full attention and can then earn their interest and acceptance.

Explaining yourself

Explanations help your group understand, and perhaps better value, what you discuss. If a description can be said to answer *what,* an explanation answers *why* and *how.* While reviewing your content, look at where explanations are needed to describe the *why* and *how* of your information.

You may use explanations to

>> Explain the cause of and reasons why a problem developed before you discuss your proposed solution, as in, "Let me explain why the problem surfaced and how it affected that organization before I tell you about our carefully engineered solution to eliminate that problem and keep it from occurring again."

>> Explain why a product or service was designed a certain way or why it operates the way it does. For example, "There's a reason we made the structure out of titanium instead of high-strength steel. Let me explain the purpose and benefit of it for you."

>> Interpret anything your audience didn't fully understand by saying something like, "I guess I didn't cover that area as much as I needed to. Let me explain with more clarity and detail how we arrived at those return on investment and net present value estimates."

Making assumptions

Surely you've been cautioned to never assume anything. But in discussing your program, project, or proposed solution, you sometimes have to make and communicate reasonable and likely assumptions when solid facts and data aren't available, especially when you're forecasting situations. You want to tell your audience about your necessary assumptions and why you're making them. It's a way of saying, "Assuming this happens, that will occur."

Explain your assumptions and communicate them only if needed when concrete information isn't available. Make sure to create realistic and probable assumptions. Consider this example of an effective assumption:

The financial return on your investment with our advanced systems is predicated on several likely assumptions or expectations. One: Interest rates will not change or will change very little. According to the Federal Reserve, interest rates will not vary more that one half of a percent over the next year. Two: Your production levels will increase by about an average of 15 percent over the next three years, according to the estimates you gave to me. Three: You'll receive an increase in productivity of about 35 percent if you follow our procedures strictly. Although this improvement isn't a commitment, it is a solid and realistic projection based on the fact that over 90 percent of our 76 customers experienced productivity increases between 30 and 40 percent over the last two years.

Use assumptions when unknowns or unpredictable situations allow you to only guess at future projections or forecasts. Use assumptions sparingly and consider calling them *expectations* or *likelihoods* if the term *assumption* might hurt your credibility.

Showing testimonials

Testimonials help close business deals with new customers and get approval for internal projects, programs, or strategic changes. It's one thing when you say that your training business can get stellar results; it's another when four sincerely satisfied clients brag about what you delivered and describe your team's stellar performance in specific ways. Video testimonials are a powerful way to highlight your product's features and address concerns, doubts, skepticism, or fears people might have. Several brief (one-minute) testimonials from a diverse group of articulate people in jobs and positions that have meaning for your audiences can be a terrific tool to help you convince your group.

Finely crafted testimonials are short stories that present a problem the testifiers faced, their decision-making process (including some hesitations), what critical factors made them buy into your product or program, and the results that made it worthwhile. Although a testimonial should give some important specifics on the virtue of what you advocate, a winning one helps people in the audience relate to the decision-making process others went through and the criteria others used, which can help provide context for your group's upcoming decision.

Include scanned photos of testimonial letters with the key parts highlighted or show comments from satisfied customers on your website in your presentation. Some innovative presenters use a live telephone or Skype call to provide a testimonial from one or more customers or experts who endorse your presentation messages and even let the audience ask questions. If you have such a willing and able person, prepare her carefully by describing your audience and your presentation objectives, strategy, and content along with likely questions (include possible tough ones) from your audience. Skype calls can be risky because of unknowns, but they are powerful if all goes well! And you really want your customer to be frank and truthful, even if some answers disappoint you; otherwise, the call seems like a setup.

Making analogies

French novelist and poet Victor Hugo, who wrote *Les Misérables*, waxed metaphorical with, "Laughter is the sun that drives winter from the human face." Deep, isn't it? Aristotle said "it (a metaphor) is the mark of genius, for to make good metaphors implies an eye for resemblance."

Professional speakers use lots of good metaphors, such as: "Your past should be a springboard, not a hammock," and "A mind is designed to be a storehouse (of ideas), not a wastebasket." One motivational speaker, who cautioned his audience to learn from the past and to never dwell in it, but move on, quoted a poignantly profound metaphor from Richard Kadrey's book, *Kill the Dead*, "Memories are bullets. Some whiz by and only spook you. Others tear you open and leave you in pieces." Memories take on new meaning and perspective.

An *analogy* is a perceived likeness between two things. The only real difference between a metaphor and analogy is the addition of the word *like* to *is.* Shakespeare used his famous metaphor, "All the world's a stage." If he'd used an analogy, it would have been, "All the world's like a stage." Comedian Joey Adams used to say, "A bikini is like a barbed-wire fence. It protects the property without disturbing the view." Innovative presenters look for the right humorous analogy to perfectly illuminate and encapsulate many points into one strong and memorable one.

Chevy's "Like a rock" campaign is an example of an innovative business analogy, not to mention one of the most successful, long-running (1991 to 2004) television commercials of all time. Accompanied by the Bob Seger song, "Like a Rock," scenarios show Chevy trucks taking incredibly brutal punishment and handling it . . . like a rock. The gobs of emotion and Americana jammed into a captivating 30-second commercial produced record sales for Chevrolet.

Steve Jobs said, "When you touch someone's heart, that's limitless." If your metaphor or analogy evokes or awakens feelings in your audience, you can count on a having a lasting effect.

TIP

Look for every opportunity to translate your important information and messages into those clever, colorful, and compelling metaphors and analogies that will be appreciated and long remembered.

Chapter **2**

Honing Your Platform Skills

James Earl Jones, Morgan Freeman, Ben Kingsley, Elizabeth Taylor, Orson Wells, and Meryl Streep are just a few of many other actors who brilliantly used their voices to enchant, scare (Jones was the voice of Darth Vader in the first *Star Wars* movies), tease, express remorse, taunt, show affection or passion, punctuate, surprise, add urgency, and, with consummate skill, project every emotion that human beings can feel and show. Former US president Ronald Reagan used his professional acting skills — body movements and broadcast-quality voice — to look and act the part of the confident world leader, giving speeches that touched the hearts of millions.

Every innovative presentation requires not just excellent technical speaking skills, but personal and imaginative ways to connect with and fascinate, enthrall, motivate, inspire, enlighten, and compel the audience to take action. If you've ever experienced a superb motivational speaker who mesmerized you with captivating stories that evoked belly laughs, tears, and an outpouring of inspiration, you appreciate how masterfully good speakers use their bodies through facial expressions, gestures, movement, and posture, and their voices through rate, tone, pitch, volume, and pauses. They play their nonverbal and vocal skills like fine musical instruments to make their words sparkle, and you remember their messages long after they leave the stage. When they tell an electrifying story, they make it burst alive with the most reliable audio-visual equipment at their command — their words, voice, and body — which gives them exceptional platform presence and command of their topic and audience.

The finest speakers know that subtle changes in volume, voice tone, and pitch, along with articulated body movement, arm gestures, and facial expressions, can convey important emotion cues that powerfully and psychologically reinforce the spoken word, adding greater meaning and substance to their persuasive messages. Finely honed presentation delivery skills rivet your audience's interest and set you far apart from the crowd of ordinary presenters who give just an average or good performance.

This chapter covers the special delivery secrets for your presentation, speech, or videotaping. You learn creative ways to use your voice and body for impressive effect and superior results.

Using Your Voice to Command Attention

Today's busy, multitasking business audiences quickly tune out a monotone, passive speaker who drones on like sleep-inducing white noise. Whether in front of thousands in a stadium or a dozen in the boardroom, a great speaker owns the stage with his or her confidence, self-assurance, and convicted way of presenting information with passion. This secret of performance success revolves around not only being a great public speaker and presenter but also letting your natural, sincere personality shine through while talking. Enthusiasm and speaking dynamics can have many variations and degrees of effect. This doesn't require bouncing off the walls like the late comedian Chris Farley's hysterical *Saturday Night Live* skit playing the over-caffeinated, boisterous motivational speaker Matt Foley who "lives in a van down by the river."

In this section, you discover three rules for using your voice as well as additional speaking tips.

TIP

To professionally hone your delivery skills — one of the seven secrets of performance success — join a speaking club such as Toastmasters and consider taking an acting or presentation skills class and working with a voice coach.

Rule 1: Speak out loud

Volume is the loudness or softness of your voice. It's the amount of energy, intensity, and force you use to emit sounds. Good speaking volume is critical because if you can't be heard, nothing else matters. If people can't hear, they become frustrated, restless, and annoyed. If they have to strain to listen, they tune you out or get up and leave if they can.

SHOWING EMOTIONS

Great presenters and speakers can display intended emotions for effect. The combination of your words and voice and body language in presentations and speeches can convey a gamut of expressive, rich emotions, including the following:

Affection	Contempt	Ferocity	Playfulness
Aggression	Conviction	Frustration	Poise
Agitation	Curiosity	Fury	Regret
Alarm	Defeatism	Gloom	Remorse
Amusement	Delight	Guilt	Revulsion
Anger	Desire	Hurt	Sadness
Annoyance	Disappointment	Interest	Scorn
Anxiety	Dismay	Irritation	Shock
Boredom	Distress	Joy	Surprise
Calm	Empathy	Longing	Triumph
Compassion	Enthusiasm	Optimism	Urgency
Concern	Exasperation	Pain	
Confidence	Excitement	Passion	

Leaders — actual or aspiring — leverage their voice and body language to project an image of competence, confidence, and conviction. A strong, dynamic, and resonant voice shows that you are confident, believe what you're saying, and are enthusiastic about your topic. It may also convey a sense of urgency and commitment. As simple as it sounds, a sufficiently powerful voice gives people the impression that you have the vigor, energy, and even leadership to get the job (you're proposing) done.

Consistently using a low speaking volume, especially if combined with poor eye contact, monotone, and a stiff or defensive posture, is likely to give people the impression that you lack confidence, feel uncomfortable speaking in public, or are nervous or overly meek (or weak).

REMEMBER

Talk loudly enough to be easily heard by everyone, including those farthest away from you at the extreme corners of the room.

Rule 2: Project your voice — without shouting

The first rule is to raise your volume so that your listeners can hear you (especially in the face of background noise in the room or around the area in which you are presenting such as at a trade show). The second rule is to *project* your voice instead of shouting. Speaking loudly by shouting comes across as strained, empty, and unnatural. It may also appear overbearing, harsh, or irritating.

Did you ever wonder how orators in antiquity could be heard by thousands of people without the benefit of amplifying speakers? And how is it that a small dog can bark so loudly and an infant cry with such surprising lung power for so long? These three examples all involve projecting voices using *diaphragmatic breathing* (also called *deep breathing* or *belly breathing*), which is used by yoga practitioners, martial artists, and singers, as well as professional speakers.

Your *diaphragm* is a thin sheet of dome-shaped muscle that separates your lungs from your stomach. In deep breathing, as you slowly and deeply breathe in air through your nose, your abdomen expands (rather than your chest) along with your diaphragm, thus sucking in large volumes of air that fill your lungs. As you exhale slowly, your diaphragm contracts upward pushing air from your lungs.

Visualize the air filling your lungs from your collarbone to the bottom of all your ribs and then that same space emptying from the bottom of your ribs to your clavicle as your exhale. Make your inhalation as long as your exhalation. Do this deep breathing exercise ten times in a row several times a day, ideally while standing or lying flat on your back, or at least sitting up straight with your shoulders pulled back. Work up to a count of ten on both the inhalation and exhalation. After you develop a routine like this, you won't even know you are doing it while speaking, and you'll be amazed at how much better your voice sounds. Good, rich voice projection facilitated by breathing deeply and naturally does not sound like shouting in the least.

TECHNICAL
STUFF

You can compare deep breathing to the woofer of a speaker system that visually moves in and out pushing larger quantities of air than smaller mid-range speakers or a tiny tweeter. Just like the woofer, diaphragmatic breathing enables your lungs to push out greater volumes of air, which produces deeper and richer speaking tones along with a louder volume without straining your throat or sounding harsh. The increased oxygen in your bloodstream relaxes you as well, reducing speaking jitters.

TIP

Deep breathing exercises performed throughout each day not only serve you well when speaking but also provide health and relaxation benefits.

Rule 3: Vary your volume

Although you must speak loudly enough for everyone to hear you, vary your volume to match your intention. Variety of volume as well as speech rate, tone, and pitch are key to making your presentation easy and enjoyable to listen to.

Even if you possess a room-filling, bone-rattling baritone voice, without variation it becomes monotonous and monotone. By changing your volume throughout your presentation, you come across as conversational.

Aim to maintain the volume level that projects your voice to the back of the room and then vary between three and six voice levels — from a whisper to a shout. As a theatrical style technique, many motivational speakers and some highly skilled business presenters selectively speak low enough to whisper. You'd be amazed how — at the right time, in the right way, for the right reasons — that whisper suddenly grabs hold of an audience's attention because they are intensely curious and straining to hear what the whisper might be about. (You read more about this in the next section, "Speaking softly.")

Use volume to emphasize and highlight certain words or terms. When you suddenly increase or decrease your volume, it shocks or alerts your audience to a change that jolts their attention. The rise and fall of your voice indirectly signals differences between major ideas and information and subordinate details that support them.

TIP

Raise your volume when you come to important parts of your presentation such as

>> Benefits of the product, service, program, or project you're proposing

>> Key points, main messages, critical facts, statistics, or other information the audience must understand to appreciate the value of your proposal

>> Recommendations, suggestions, requests, and solutions you offer to the group

>> Quotations, metaphors, examples, comparisons, and contrasts that support your main points

>> Specific aspects of a visual, video, or animated part of the presentation

Speaking softly

Speaking for a time at one volume level and then suddenly lowering your voice and saying important words or numbers softly (and even repeating them) can separate and spotlight them as much as raising your voice. Combine lower volume with a slower speech rate and a pause to command rapt attention.

Determine where in your presentation a whisper would create a dramatic effect that arouses curiosity, suspense, or otherwise builds anticipation to hear more. Your choice of raising or lowering your voice depends on the type of audience, their mood, your presentation goals, and the effect you want to produce.

REMEMBER

Varying your volume, rate, pitch, and tone makes you sound more natural and more interesting.

Adjusting your rate

Rate of speech is how fast you talk in words per minute (wpm) and is also called *speed, pace, tempo,* and *rhythm.* The typical or average speech rate is about 125 wpm. The general recommendation is to speak between 110 to 180 wpm, although not consistently.

TECHNICAL
STUFF

How can you tell if you speak within the 110 to 180 words-per-minute guideline? Read one or two pages of a prepared (scripted) speech or presentation out loud and time yourself for a minute. Count the words you read and divide it by 60 to get your average wpm.

A constant rate of speech almost always accompanies a dull, monotone speaking voice. Using an unvarying speed and pitch works great for a hypnotist ("you are getting very sleepy . . . "), but it's not so effective for a presenter. Like a fine passage of music, which alternates between speeding up and slowing down, your voice should vary in rate throughout your talk. Changing your pace sounds more natural and makes your delivery come across more animated and conversational.

Fast talking at higher speeds can confuse an audience, make it difficult for them to concentrate, or just plain annoy them. Other than your attempts at vocal showmanship, speaking quickly during your presentation suggests nervousness, lack of confidence, irritability, or being rushed — the audience may get the impression you have somewhere else to be! This feeling is magnified when you accompany fast talking with poor eye contact, stiff posture, and lack of gestures. Worse, with certain glib personality types, fast talking can be perceived as slick or smarmy. However, when combined with sincere smiling, meaningful gestures, and effective eye contact, a somewhat faster pace indicates enthusiasm, excitement, and enjoyment.

**TECHNICAL
STUFF**

The term *fast* is relative: Trisha Paytas, a model and actress from Los Angeles, has a black belt in fast talking. She can speak (if you call it that) 710 words in only 54 seconds! It sounds like gibberish until you slow down the recording and find her articulation is nearly flawless!

TIP

Don't pack your presentation with overflowing information if you have a limited amount of time. That forces you to rush through your presentation by talking fast and furiously.

Varying your speaking rate in a presentation is like shifting gears in a car — you use each speed for a purpose as the situations and needs dictate: starting out, going up hill, straightaway cruising, speeding up to pass, or coming to a stop.

The following sections offer tips to help you use the appropriate rate of speech.

When to slow down

A slower pace can help in these situations:

>> **At the beginning of your presentation:** Rather than rushing into your presentation, start slowly. If you have some stage fright, speaking slowly helps, and it makes you come across poised, calm, and composed.

>> **When your audience isn't familiar with your material:** Especially if the information you're presenting is technical, complex, statistical in nature, or has abstract concepts, going slowly helps your audience keep up with you. A slower pace helps with words and complicated terms you're introducing for the first time and those that may be hard to pronounce.

For example, a presenter may want to speak more slowly while discussing an acronym: "Great strides have been made in the last two years with laser technology for medicine, science, construction, and other applications. As you may know, *laser* is an acronym that stands for light [pause] amplification by [pause] stimulated [pause] emission of [pause] radiation." Speaking the acronym slowly lets the meaning and definition sink in.

>> **To add vocal punch when you want to highlight key ideas, main messages, or vital pieces of information:** Slowing down lets significant points sink in for your group. To add weight, use a louder volume and a two-to-three second pause before and after those points. Then, speed up your rate as you add details and filler information to illustrate, give examples, or otherwise describe the essential parts of your presentation.

>> **When declaring your call to action:** When you're requesting donations from the audience, asking to close a sale, or seeing specific support or commitment, you don't want to appear rushed, nervous, or hesitant, which a sudden burst of faster talking may imply.

When to accelerate

Picking up the pace is appropriate at these points:

>> To show extra enthusiasm, excitement, or emotion or as a suspenseful buildup to a secret.

>> When you go over necessary but familiar background material, provide additional details, or do several quick summaries throughout your presentation.

>> To change transitions in your content, as a segue to a quicker pace of talking.

>> During certain parts of an interesting story you tell to make a point. A good storyteller, like a stage performer, uses the ebbs and tides of vocal variety to guide the energy flow of the tale up and down to make stories captivating and forceful.

Even though you vary your speech rate between slower and faster, avoid speaking hiccups (abrupt stops and starts).

Adding a solid punch to a statement

You can use a vocal trick to emphasize something by exaggerating your rate slowdown, while increasing your voice volume and energy. Here's an example of how it works: Say you want to gloss over something. So in an almost trivial, matter-of-fact way (with no tonal energy or variation) you say, "With the total US debt at 20 trillion dollars, we have a major problem." Then follow that statement by saying, "Health insurance costs are also an economic hardship. The average deductible for people is an incredible F-I-F-T-E-E-N T-H-O-U-S-A-N-D D-O-L-L-A-R-S!" See the difference? By using voice tricks, you can de-emphasize the titanic dollar figure — $20 trillion dollars — while pumping up the (relatively) less critical $15,000 amount. It's a psychologically powerful tool.

We're not suggesting that you be devious, we're simply illustrating how, by dramatically slowing your rate down and methodically drawing out each work with a pumped-up volume and passionate expression, you can direct your audience's attention where you want.

Pausing eloquently

The English poet, writer, and novelist Rudyard Kipling aptly said, "By your silence, ye shall speak." And as classical pianist Artur Schnabel profoundly noted, "I don't think I handle the notes much differently from other pianists. But the pauses between the notes — ah, there is where the artistry lies!" Using pauses effectively and dramatically in your presentations reflects your speaking artistry and eloquence.

The main reasons to use pauses are for variety, understanding, and emphasis. A pause is a form of oral punctuation that can help your audience reflect on what you just said. In a way, sudden silence (especially if you've been using a quickened rate of speech) has the same effect as a sudden loud noise. It alerts your audience and makes them attentive to what you say next. When using a pause for emphasis, you want to focus audience attention on your most important pieces of information.

Pauses regulate the rhythm of your speech like that of a natural conversation. They also help you collect your thoughts before moving onto the next piece of information.

Determine when and how long a pause should be to enhance your presentation. Typical pauses last one to two seconds; dramatic, extended pauses last as long as four to six seconds.

Although these commonly termed *pregnant pauses* may seem unnatural for you and uncomfortable for your audience, the longer theatrical-style pauses — done at strategic times in your presentation — can have a very powerful effect. They are often used to give people time to consider the paramount consequences of your statement.

WARNING

Keep in mind that too many long pauses or too many pauses in general can make your presentation choppy.

Consider using a pause either before or after the following types of content:

>> Key points and critical messages

>> Vital facts, statistics, or other shocking information

>> Important quotations

>> A rhetorical or thought-provoking question

>> Key names, dates, events, or titles

>> Essential benefits of your product, service, proposal, plan, or program

>> During the buildup of suspenseful parts of your story

>> Effect and consequences of problems or situations your audience is facing

Proper use of pauses can prevent *sentence run-on*, which is going from sentence to sentence without stopping. Think of a motor mouth without a brake.

If you enumerate points, using a pause in between can help an audience absorb each one. When you use pauses, make sure that you apply them deliberately and cleanly. You don't want to give your audience the impression that you're repeatedly groping for words or hesitating, which can come across as being nervous or unprepared. You want to be articulate, but don't be too deliberate in terms of pausing frequently between words, so that your pace, combined with a slow, even rate of speech, becomes either frustrating or sleep-inducing.

TIP

To add extra punch to your pause, slow down your speech rate and increase your speech volume just before you pause. While you are pausing for several seconds, use good eye contact around the room to reinforce what you said. You can use pause and repetition of your point for a dramatic effect. Raise your volume in steps as you repeat each point for increasing emphasis.

The acclaimed British Shakespearean stage actor Ralph Richardson had this insight, "The most precious things in speech are pauses." Consummate presenters, those who have learned the power of perfectly timed silence, know the value and truth of that. As you watch good movies, television dramas, and plays, for example, see how the seasoned professionals use pauses. You'll be impressed and you can adopt some of those refined techniques.

REMEMBER

Avoid using fillers such as *uh*, *okay*, *uhm*, and *you know* instead of intended pauses. Practice and concentrate on finishing each sentence without a filler, and you'll soon rid yourself of that bad speaking habit.

Captivating Audiences with Your Eyes

Whether in a romantic novel or a spy thriller, much has been written about the mystique of a person's eyes and the effect they can have on people. It's been said that the face is a picture of what lies in the mind and heart with the eyes as the interpreter. You have, of course, heard that the eyes are the mirror of the soul and the expression "They were seeing eye to eye." These sayings reinforce the major role that eye contact plays in human relations, including speeches and business presentations.

The majority of presentation trainers and coaches consider eye contact to be the most important of the nonverbal speaking skills. It is so important that without effective eye contact, you cannot reach your objectives. The numerous benefits of great eye contact include

>> Establishing and maintaining rapport with your audience

>> Setting a positive tone for your presentation

>> Subtly controlling your audience, while holding their attention

>> Reinforcing and emphasizing your key points and ideas

>> Getting immediate feedback on people's reaction to your talk

>> Giving you an enhanced image of credibility, confidence, and charisma

REMEMBER

Eye contact is a personal thing. It shows that you want to connect and that you care.

Understanding the importance of eye contact

Do you trust someone who talks to you but doesn't look you in the eye? Does that make you feel uncomfortable? Well, the same applies to people in your audience. If you don't engage them with eye contact, it not only takes away the personal touch and hurts rapport, but people in your audience will form a negative impression of you — that you are nervous, feel uncomfortable with your topic, are hiding something, or are afraid of the reaction to your talk. But if you make good eye contact, your audience members sense you are enjoying your presentation, like being with them, and are confident in your topic and speaking ability.

REMEMBER

An audience mimics your behavior, so if you display enthusiasm about your topic, they will too.

What's interesting is how you can psychologically keep the interest of people — influence their reactions — by looking directly at them. Next time you give a presentation note this: As you look at people, in almost 100 percent of the cases, they look back at you.

On the one hand, looking directly into someone's eyes pressures them to look back at you. On the other hand, if you look at the walls in the room or stare at the projection screen, people may feel free to look at their smartphone or tablet or otherwise redirect their attention away from you. Even with large audiences, systematically making eye contact with different sections of the room will keep people looking back at you.

Flexibility and adaptability characterize innovative presenters. While maintaining eye contact with as many people as possible, you constantly analyze and gauge how the group is reacting to your talk. The audience's body language, whether positive (sitting on the edge of their seats, nodding in agreement, and smiling) or negative (yawning, looking at watches, fidgeting, frowning), tells you whether they're eagerly listening, anxious to hear more, positively receptive to the information, or bored, restless, frustrated, confused, or irritated. Because you continuously look at people, you can judge whether you need to speed things up, move onto the next area in your presentation, slow down and give more explanations, examples, and details, engage people in discussions, or ask them questions to determine whether they're bothered or are having difficulty understanding something.

Use your eyes for emphasis. When you come to your main points, maintain strong eye contact with your group. To add dramatic effect, you can walk to the center of the meeting room (or stage) to get closer to your audience right before you communicate your critical point, add more voice volume, and pause while you look around the room with direct eye contact. This combination of voice and body movement adds powerful emphasis when needed.

Speaking with your eyes

Tarjei Vesaas, a Norwegian novelist and poet, aptly quipped, "Almost nothing need be said when you have eyes." Obviously, eyes alone, without talking and visuals, won't cut it for your typical business presentation, but your eyes do communicate. Here are some tips for effective eye-speak:

>> When you begin your talk, let your eyes sweep through the audience.

>> Look directly into the eyes of others. Don't look over their heads or anywhere else.

>> Maintain random eye contact around the room — don't make it look contrived by mechanically swinging your head side-to-side and doing eye contact in a predictable, systematic way. As you speak, ask yourself, "Who haven't I looked at yet?"

>> Look at each person for about three to six seconds as if talking to just that individual. If you look for less time, say a second, that's glancing, and if you look longer, people feel uncomfortable — as if they're being singled out.

WARNING

Avoid the following eye-contact no-nos:

>> Staring at your notes, the projection screen, the floor, or anywhere else except your group.

>> Looking only at friendly, supportive people who are nodding, smiling, and otherwise giving you positive feedback; spread your eye contact around the room.

>> Overdoing eye contact with specific people such as the senior managers, prominent and influential people, or the top decision makers. However, when you come to important parts of your presentation, look at the key people to emphasize your point and gauge their reactions.

>> Shifting your eyes. Move your head and even your entire body to look around.

Keeping eye contact with a large audience

You might be asking, "How can we really do effective eye contact with an audience of 500 to 2,000 or even more?" The closer you are to someone — for example, to your immediate front or close left and right sides — the more that person can detect if you are looking directly at him. The farther away you are from someone, the less he can see if you are looking at him eye-to-eye.

When you select one individual in the first row to look at, only a few people think you're looking at them. The trick is to focus on giving individual eye contact to more of the folks in front of you. But don't forget to look at the extremes of the room — right and left, very back, and balcony if there is one.

TIP

Look at the very back of a large room and select one person to gaze at. People in a large radius (perhaps 20 to 40 feet in size) around that person feel that you're looking at them.

Finding the Right Posture

Posture has been deemed a personal display of self-confidence and bearing. It creates a definite impression on listeners. Good posture (along with overall appearance) is important because it's one of the first things the audience notices and judges about you.

The ideal posture to have throughout your presentation is stand erect but relaxed, as if ready for action. Not only does the right posture promote a positive image of yourself, it helps your speech mechanism (throat and lungs) produce strong, resonant sounds.

Giving a bad impression with the wrong posture

Before we suggest some tips on posture and body movement in the next sections, check out some types of posture to avoid.

Timid

A timid posture is characterized by a stooped, slouched, or otherwise listless demeanor that suggests a lack of confidence, energy, or drive. You'll never see dynamic leaders with the posture shown in Figure 2-1.

FIGURE 2-1:
Stand up;
don't be shy.

*Photograph courtesy
of Ray Anthony*

Too casual

When you have both hands in your pockets, hunch over the lectern, sit on the edge of the table with one foot on the ground, or otherwise appear too relaxed, you risk projecting an image of conceit, indifference, or overfamiliarity with the audience. With your hands in your pockets you seem passive, and what's more, you can't gesture. Holding your hands in a steepled position as shown in Figure 2-2 can convey overconfidence or a feeling of superiority.

FIGURE 2-2:
Steepled
hands can be
misinterpreted for
overconfidence or
superiority.

*Photograph courtesy
of Ray Anthony*

Stiff, uncomfortable, or defensive

When you tightly press your legs together or cross them, hang your hands at your side or cup them in front of you, hold your body very rigidly, and have a serious facial expression as shown in Figure 2-3, the audience senses that you're ill at ease, frightened, or possibly inflexible. Likewise, taking a military stance makes you seem as though you're waiting for orders rather than ready to command an audience. When you cross your arms over your chest with a stern look, most people interpret this as being defensive or closed.

FIGURE 2-3: A tense, closed stance can indicate a rigid, closed mind.

Photograph courtesy of Ray Anthony

Clasping your hands together in a plea or prayer position (you may be doing that for real) or the meek fig leaf position as shown in Figure 2-4, imply vulnerability and great discomfort and should be avoided.

Aggressive

Although you don't want to look meek or uncomfortable, standing rigidly with both hands on your hips, your legs far apart, your chin thrust up, and a taut expression on your face makes you appear to be a drill sergeant or an angry parent ready to scold rather than give a presentation. A stance like the one in Figure 2-5 communicates a domineering, overbearing, and opinionated personality.

Standing tall

Good posture shows the audience you're comfortable, relaxed, and professional. You always want to appear confident and in charge without giving even a hint of being authoritative.

FIGURE 2-4:
Avoid this position as it indicates discomfort or vulnerability.

Photograph courtesy of Ray Anthony

FIGURE 2-5:
The scolding parent stance quickly alienates the audience.

Photograph courtesy of Ray Anthony

Overall, your posture when you stand — or sit — should be erect and poised but not stiffly upright or strained. Your shoulders should show that you're relaxed — they should be squared and not hunched. Your body should look alive and stand tall, regardless of your height. Figure 2-6 shows a presenter standing and looking ready and relaxed.

FIGURE 2-6:
Find a comfortable standing position with shoulders pulled back and relaxed (left). You can look assertive *and* relaxed (right).

To position your body, do the following:

1. **Place your feet 6 to 12 inches apart with one slightly in front of the other.**

   Keep your knees loose, not locked.

   Don't cross your legs. That position is unstable, not to mention ungainly.

WARNING

2. **Do a partial shoulder rotation, lifting your shoulders to your ears then pushing them back and down.**

   Your chest will then be open and lifted, which helps with the deep breathing you've been practicing.

3. **Shift your weight to the heels of your feet.**

   Resting on your heels alleviates lower back pain that's common after hours of standing.

4. **Imagine an invisible, taut thread running from the crown of your head to the base of your spine.**

   Leave your arms free to gesture or operate a remote control or laser pointer.

Rocking and rolling

Moving your body during your presentation makes you more animated, more interesting, and can help reinforce some of your key messages. Your movements should be purposeful without distracting body gyrations.

Whether you have a bit of speaking anxiety or are positively excited to be talking to a group, the increased adrenalin can make you move around more, even unconsciously. Comedian Chris Rock walks briskly back and forth on the stage throughout his performance. Walking helps siphon off some of the adrenalin surge anyone speaking in public feels. Perhaps you remember your college professors moving around as they spoke.

WARNING

As a presenter, you want to eliminate the following counterproductive — and distracting — movements:

>> **Swaying** from side to side (often called the *speaker's rumba*) or constantly rocking or stepping forward and backward

>> **Shifting** your weight by repeatedly bending your knees, first one leg, then to the other

>> **Teetering** by raising your body up and down by lifting and lowering your heels or standing on tip-toe

>> **Pacing** around the room in a random way

>> **Swinging** or slapping your arms

>> **Turning** your back to the group for more than a few moments

Moving gracefully and purposefully

Standing in one spot for your entire presentation would be boring and quite difficult to do. Animated movement captivates audiences. Instead of staying stuck behind a lectern, move around the stage or to the front of the room to get close to your audience. If possible, move into and around the group to build rapport and create a more personal tone to your presentation.

TIP

To stress a major point, move to the center of the room, closer to the audience, pause, and then raise your volume while making your key point. The act of moving front and center psychologically implies that you want to share an important piece of information with your group.

A beneficial movement technique is called *move and bolt*. With this technique, you slowly and deliberately walk around the room facing your audience, and then stop as if your feet are bolted to the floor. You remain there without shifting, rocking, or moving for some time before you move again to another area of the room, facing a different part of your audience with your feet again bolted to the floor. This provides animated movement with confidence and purpose and shows your poise in front of your group.

Making the Right Facial Expressions

Facial expressions include movements of your eyes, mouth, eyebrows, forehead, chin, and other parts in any combination that can add meaning to the spoken word. Facial expressions are usually an accurate barometer of how a person is feeling. Smiles, grins, smirks, frowns, grimaces, winks, and raised eyebrows are just a few of the more than one hundred subtle facial expressions that project the attitude and emotional state of a person. By looking at your face, people can tell, for example, if you are

- » Alert
- » Apprehensive
- » Confident
- » Convinced
- » Doubtful
- » Elated
- » Fearful
- » Frustrated
- » Happy
- » Puzzled
- » Relaxed
- » Surprised
- » Tired
- » Worried

As your speaking ability improves, you can tailor your facial expressions to match and reinforce your spoken words.

REMEMBER

Always be aware of how your face communicates. Although it's difficult to control spontaneous facial reactions and hide your feelings, try not to display an unintended negative feeling.

Political and motivational speakers make their faces reflect what they're saying, whether they're telling an amusing anecdote, getting to the sad part of a story, or conveying righteous indignation about some topic. The best facial expression you can use for most business presentations is a smile. As you begin your talk, and periodically throughout it, use a warm, open, and sincere full smile (showing your teeth) to cement a bond with your audience and show that you're relaxed and enjoy being before them.

WARNING

In some cultures, particularly Asian, body postures and facial expressions have different interpretations than in North America. If you present to an international audience at home or abroad, do your homework before your scheduled talk to make sure your presentation is respectful and not inadvertently and unintentionally offensive.

Gesturing Creatively

Gestures are primarily arm and hand movements, sometimes along with body movements such as cocking or nodding your head and moving your eyebrows. The correct gestures enhance the tone and meaning of your words and make your presentation dynamic. Studies show that when you use more gestures than you normally would, your voice becomes livelier, varied, and more animated. Gestures, more than other type of body language, help you convey and reinforce a spoken message. They give immediacy and conviction and add intensity and emotional effect to what you're saying.

TIP

Watch the 2011 Academy Award–winning silent film, *The Artist,* to understand how much you understand from gestures and facial expressions. Or try muting the volume of your television while watching a movie or television show (particularly a drama, mystery, or comedy show). Look at the facial expressions and gestures the performers use and guess what they're communicating. See how gestures speak a powerful language of their own. Combined with words and visuals, the synergy of communication is awesome!

Exploring gesture types

You may be wondering, "What do I do with my hands?" Rest assured, with some imagination, there are practically unlimited gestures you can use in a significant way. Generally, gestures fall into the four categories described in this section.

Size, shape, or dimension

Visualize how using gestures could add to the message in the following two statements:

> "Our new quantum computer is the most powerful of its kind in the world, yet small." (Use gestures to show its height, depth, and width.)

"Graphene is a miracle material, and we're close to manufacturing it in large quantity. It is a honeycomb lattice made of carbon atoms — only one atom thick. This nanotechnology substance is incredibly strong, light, nearly transparent, and an excellent conductor of electricity and heat. A billion layers of it are only this thin." (Use your thumb and forefinger to show the small thickness.)

Direction

Gestures can show that something is up, down, right, left, sideways, slanted, curved, swerving, spiraling, or wavy — for a few examples. Think about how you might use gestures to show something increasing, decreasing, or standing still, such as the following:

"We have a choice. We can choose to grow slowly by playing it extra safe (the presenter extends her entire arm out at a small angle like a bent graph line), or we can innovate, make some mistakes, quickly learn from them, and grow like this." (She now extends her arm out with a much steeper angle upward like a trend line of accelerated growth.)

"Our company's strategy has been disjointed. First we go in this direction (presenter walks to the left). Then we decide to go here (presenter turns and walks in a different direction). If that isn't working, we transition this way (he now walks in the opposite direction). What are we doing experimenting when we should be implementing something that does not look like this (he is now waving his arms in different directions). Here's what we need to do." (The presenter points straight ahead and walks perfectly straight in that direction.)

Motion, movement, or activity

Picture yourself describing and showing people how to play golf, tennis, bowling, or some other sport or training someone how to use a tool or product. You use your entire body with a focus on your arms and hands to illustrate an activity. These gestures make you much more interesting, regardless of your topic. Think about how adding the following movements and motions might better reinforce your points in your presentation:

» Back and forth

» Grabbing

» Holding

» Lifting

» Pulling, pushing

» Round and round

- » Spiraling

- » Stopping

- » Turning, screwing, twisting

- » Zigzagging

Notice how a particular motion can add meaning to these types of examples:

"In a moment, I will show you a video of how our new 3-D printer creates complex designs using our new technology and mechanism. Current printers do this. (The presenter uses an up-and-down and side-to-side motion to demonstrate how a nozzle prints material.) But our system does this. (He now uses both hands in a back and forth way as if he were moving a sheet of metal.) We have a metal plate with over 100 nozzles, each of which can feed a different substance — such as metal, plastic, rubber, or glass — to deposit that material 60 times faster and 300 percent more accurately. Look at the two-minute video to see what I mean."

"Regarding supply-chain management in our company, supply was trying to catch up with runaway demand (presenter uses a gesture of going around and around) and never did quite make it."

Feeling and intensity

These gestures can be captivating when a speaker uses his entire body to help describe, amplify, and focus on an intended, meaningful emotion — enthusiasm, rejection, openness, or frustration — connected to a key point being made. Here are two examples:

"We have got to fight (presenter waves a clenched fist) these suffocating regulations that are destroying our businesses and jobs!"

"Our department must aggressively cut and clash (presenter uses a abrupt chopping motion) this out-of-control waste that's robbing us of profits!"

Making a grand gesture

Make grand gestures by extending your arms far from your body, which enlarges you as a presenter. Use these gestures in front of large audiences to increase your stage presence and charisma. If you want to add dynamics to your body language, expand your gestures outward and animate them as needed. Gestures that keep your arms close to your body are more appropriate for smaller groups where grand gestures would come across as too flamboyant and extravagant for the occasion.

Don't think that your arm and hand gestures have to be animated the entire time you're talking. You can, on occasion, use a specific gesture and hold it in place *(static)* for 3 to 15 seconds, which can be a dramatic, sustained way of communicating a key point.

An organizational change consultant is making a presentation about her idea for a new vision for her client's corporation. She says, "The enticing vision we're discussing is right over the horizon." She raises her arm and points her finger in the direction she's looking toward (as if in the distance). While keeping her arm up, pointing toward the invisible vision, she continues, "Even though that vision is beyond our sight now, we will find it, travel toward it, and reach it. It's a vision that all of you said you would be excited by, and one that is worthy of your hard work. The vision is there (as she slightly pulls her arm back to thrust it forward in the pointed direction) for all of you to see very soon." Think of using static gestures that spotlight and reinforce your spoken words.

WARNING

Avoid the following gestures, which send the wrong message:

>> Keeping your hands in your pockets

>> Holding your arms stiffly at your sides

>> Pointing or wagging your finger at people

>> Folding your arms across your chest

>> Using the same gesture over and over

>> Tightly clutching your notes or folding, rolling, or fiddling with them

TIP

To use gestures to your best advantage, do the following:

>> **Plan** the important gestures you will use.

>> **Practice** gestures to look natural and spontaneous.

>> **Time** your gestures to coincide with a major point.

>> **Reinforce** your messages with appropriate gestures.

>> **Apply** a rich variety of gestures to your talk.

>> **Use** your entire body, not just your arms and hands, to fully gesture.

Eliminating distracting gestures

Even seasoned speaking professionals often have a bit of stage fright or anxiety, especially when giving a new presentation or speech. In new or nerve-wracking circumstances, some mannerisms you don't even know you have come out of hiding. That's why videotaping yourself can be a real (surprising or perhaps shocking) revelation.

Don't let nervous mannerisms hurt your professional image and affect your presentation results. Watch your videotaped presentation and see if you do the following, and then work on being conscious of them in your future presentations:

>> Fidgeting with something in your hands — a marker, a rubber band, a paper clip, a laser pointer, or your slide remote control.

>> Frequently adjusting your jacket or smoothing a part of your clothing or rubbing your clothing as if getting rid of a piece of lint.

>> Taking your glasses on and off or putting a pen in and out of your mouth.

>> Drumming your fingers on the lectern or playing with your microphone or its cord.

>> Tugging at your ear, scratching the side of your face, smoothing your hair, or pulling on your beard.

>> Playing with a necklace or other piece of jewelry or a watch.

Like it or not, chances are you use unconscious gestures even in everyday conversations; if you become more aware of them during daily activities and curb them, you'll be less likely to use them during your presentation. Years ago before laser pointers, you could often see people with retractable pointers continuously extending them and collapsing them without the slightest idea they were doing it. Or some people using a flip chart or white board would hold a big marker in one hand and repeatedly snap the cap on and off.

TIP

Don't despair; you can work on one skill at a time to perfect it, then move onto the next one. The best tool to evaluate and shape your progress is to either audio record or videotape your actual presentations or rehearsals to spot what you do. While looking at your video, pay attention to your volume, rate, and pauses. Check to see what your body — facial expressions, gestures, posture, and body movement — is really saying. Most importantly, analyze how you're relating to your audience, especially with eye contact.

Chapter 3

Captivating Your Audience

Game-changing presentations embody the Five Big Cs:

» Clear

» Concise

» Compelling

» Captivating

» Convincing

Inspiration, motivation, and, perhaps, entertainment take your communications to new heights and success levels. You can imbed those characteristics not only in group presentations but also in everyday conversations and discussions.

The *Laws of Communication Impact* provide the tools to craft stimulating, intellectually persuasive, and emotionally driven communication. You discover how to influence and affect how people think, feel, and even act. When you follow these laws, people eagerly listen to you, better understand what you're saying, and are persuaded to follow your recommendations or requests, adopt your proposed solutions, or buy your products and services.

Touching on the Laws of Communication Impact

The *Laws of Communication Impact* help you engage, fascinate, and intrigue people — even hardcore, buttoned-down business types who may otherwise be inclined to yawn, suffer restless leg syndrome, or work their smartphones during the typical presentation.

This is one of several chapters that provide specific guidelines to boost your creativity and professionalism as you communicate. Use them and see for yourself the amazing results you get.

REMEMBER

The words *information* and *communication* are often used interchangeably. However, they signify quite different things with different results. Of course, you need to provide people with good, solid, useful information. Information is *giving out*. Communication, though, is *getting through*, which should always be your goal.

Innovative presentations create an effect with the audience. Champion presenters creatively use information (including various forms of media) along with their energetic, passionate, and polished delivery style.

If you want to change something in your organization or sell something, you have to get through to people in a potent way to change how they think, feel, and act. In today's frenetic, stressful business world where many are overworked to the point of distraction — a ferret on double espresso has a longer attention span — getting people to give their full, undivided attention and listen to what you're presenting and then agree and act upon your ideas, plans, or proposed solutions is a tall order. The information and examples about the five Laws of Communication Impact give you the ammunition to fight inattention, apathy, and decision-making procrastination.

The Laws of Communication Impact are

1. **The Law of Primacy:** The first thing people see, hear, touch, taste, or experience

2. **The Law of Emphasis and Intensity:** The points, messages, information pieces, and visuals that are critical for your audience

3. **The Law of Exercise and Engagement:** Getting people to interact with you

4. **The Law of Interest:** Communicating that you understand what's important to your audience

5. **The Law of Effect:** Changing or activating people's behavior

6. **The Law of Recency:** The last thing people see, hear, feel, or experience

In this chapter, we explore the dynamics of the first law, the Law of Primacy. We cover the other laws in Chapters 4 and 5 in this minibook.

Whether you're presenting a business topic, giving a motivational speech, or hosting a training workshop, webinar, or virtual meeting, leveraging the Laws of Communication Impact helps you achieve results that far surpass your expectations.

Starting with the Law of Primacy

Think about your first romantic kiss, your first car, your first job, or the first time you achieved something you were so proud of. Now, think about a negative first occurrence, a painful or embarrassing memory. Positive or negative, you remember meaningful firsts of any kind vividly, often for a lifetime. Here, we show you how to leverage the Law of Primacy — of firsts — in an advantageous way: Start your presentation with a B-A-N-G! to wake people up and perk them up.

The *Law of Primacy,* first conceived by Frederick Hansen Lund around 1925, was initially and primarily focused on advertising. This law states that information or impressions first in sequence have a greater effect on people than anything that occurs later. Whether applied to advertising or a sermon, this psychological principle says that people are affected emotionally, intellectually, and behaviorally more by the very first things they see, hear, smell, touch, taste, or otherwise experience than things they encounter later. Imagine seeing a good friend for the first time in a decade, and the very first thing she says to you with a big, welcoming smile is, "You look terrific . . . Wow!" That statement warms your heart and sets the stage and tone for your reunion.

The nature of the Law of Primacy means that you get only one chance to make a first impression. If a speaker delivers a captivating, riveting, and attention-grabbing introduction, it has more influence than anything he says later in his talk — with the exception of a stirring conclusion, which involves the Law of Recency (addressed in Chapter 5 in this minibook). People typically remember the middle part of a presentation the least. A presenter must work harder to maintain, or recapture, a group's naturally fluctuating attention and interest after a strong presentation beginning.

REMEMBER

The adage rings true: You don't get a second chance to make a good first impression.

First impressions — in appearance or behavior — create a strong, often unshakeable opinion of someone. Even before you begin your presentation, you send signals: Your clothes and grooming, your gait, the manner in which you interact with team members or people in the audience, and your overall bearing and body language contribute to the impression others have of you. You make your first

Captivating Your Audience

impression before you even step up to the mic. That's why skilled presenters spend a disproportionate amount of time crafting an interesting, stimulating, and appealing introduction.

The great movie mogul Samuel Goldwyn said that a great movie "starts out with an earthquake and works its way up to a climax." That's great advice for a presentation, too! A strong introduction does several vital things: sets the tone, mood, quality, purpose, intent, and oftentimes the urgency of your presentation. It encourages people to pay serious note to the rest of your talk.

If you can find a way to evoke the audience's curiosity, add suspense or intrigue, ignite their imaginations, add a depth of anticipation — maybe even tantalize them — you will have them firmly in the palm of your hand, with their eyes fixed on you, sitting up straight, and ears perked to eagerly hear what comes next. But if you have a slow or lackluster beginning that comes across as lifeless, rambling, or anxious, the audience will tune out in a heartbeat. Although you can overcome a negative first impression, it takes a great deal of effort to recapture the interest of your audience.

The first two minutes of your presentation or speech say so much about your credibility, image, speaking style, personality, and topic. Done well, the introduction conveys that you are prepared, enthusiastic, poised, and confident, and a consummate professional with competent leadership abilities. Spending extra time preparing, rehearsing, and fine-tuning your introduction pays great dividends. Consider memorizing the first two sentences of your beginning and then continue smoothly in a natural, conversational way.

REMEMBER

How you start determines how you finish!

LAWS OF LEARNING

The Laws of Communication Impact are based upon prior research and models called the *Laws of Learning*, a set of rules that affect the extent to which a person absorbs information, remembers it, acts upon it, or is otherwise mentally, emotionally, or psychologically affected by it. Edward L. Thorndike postulated several Laws of Learning in the early 1900s.

Based on fundamental psychology and the brain's processing of information, these laws were almost universally applicable to the learning process, regardless of age or background of people. Over the years, the laws have been enhanced and modified by others. In this chapter, these general learning laws are adapted and applied to the communication process for presenters and speakers of all kinds.

Starting Off on the Right Foot

Your introduction should be suited to the audience and the situation. Developing and delivering a well-prepared, attention-grabbing introduction has many psychological advantages. Whether you decide to use a straightforward, conservative beginning or a creative kick in the audience's pants depends on your comfort level and the goal for your talk.

Making a dynamic first impression

Regardless of whether you choose a mild or slightly wild start, your introduction should highlight your credibility, professionalism, and expertise and get your group's ears, eyes, and minds focused on your topic. First impressions can be fragile and that's why getting it right from the get-go is critical. Saint Jérôme put it in colorful perspective, "Early impressions are hard to eradicate from the mind. When once wool has been dyed purple, who can restore it to its previous whiteness?"

Following are some metaphors that people have used to describe an effective introduction:

"It's like the first bite into delicious food from a great restaurant, whether it's an appetizer or entree. Wow . . . your taste buds explode with pleasure and expectation of what is yet is to come."

"Experiencing a great speaker from the start is like the takeoff of a plane. Your adrenaline kicks in even if you are sitting down!"

"I have a powerful Ducati motorcycle. When you twist the throttle to accelerate, it's amazing how incredibly smooth, yet thrilling, the launch is. Presentation introductions should be like that."

Use these guidelines to develop your own dynamic and effective introductions:

>> **Make it dynamic.** Nothing is worse for a group than to hear a presentation start off in a dry, boring fashion such that they feel they have to put up with 30 or 45 minutes of dreadfully droning pain. So ask yourself:

- How can I immediately grab the attention and interest of my group?

- What methods can I use to ignite their intellectual and emotional response right from the start?

>> **Keep it concise.** A lumbering, long-winded introduction of your topic is a recipe for failure. As a general rule, limit your introduction to between one and three minutes before going into your topic. Some experts recommend a

flexible, approximate 5 percent rule, which says that in an hour-long presentation, your introduction should be about three to four minutes — or about 5 percent of the allotted time.

>> **Be confident and cordial.** Audiences enjoy a speaker who is relaxed, comfortable, and confident from the beginning. Even if you are somewhat nervous, you can fake it by starting off with a strong voice volume, a slower speech rate, a smile, and good direct eye contact with your audience — look at someone who's smiling or friendly to boost your courage. People respect a speaker who comes across as confidently in charge without being domineering, authoritative, or smug.

>> **Avoid credibility and image killers.** We're sure that you've seen business presenters or public speakers say things like, "I'm not really an expert in this area. I was chosen to fill in for (name), who could not make it. So I will try to get through this presentation using his slides, which I'm not totally familiar with." Or, "I am feeling very nervous right now, so please bear with me because I had to quickly put together this presentation and there may be some minor errors in the slides."

Never start off with an apology or an admission of being inadequate, unworthy, or unqualified (in any way). Don't alert the group, who may otherwise not notice what you perceive as being nervous or unprepared.

>> **Connect with your audience.** Accomplished presenters strive to get their audiences to like, respect, and trust them right away. It may sound like a monumental task to accomplish all three in the first few minutes in front of a group that's never seen you before, but using a friendly speaking style, demonstrating your good intentions, and giving a natural and sincere opening puts the group at ease while arousing their interest.

Using mild-to-wild creativity

Nothing says boring like a predictable, conventional (a nice way of saying slow and dull) introduction to a presentation or speech. Ramping it up just a couple of notches with some creativity can make all the difference. And, in some cases, going from mild to wild with your imagination fires up your audience.

Imaginative, unexpected approaches to starting a presentation are eagerly welcomed by an audience weary of typical talks. The audience appreciates an entertaining, yet professional and relevant, presentation that sets you far apart and above the crowd. Famous comedian and late-night television host Johnny Carson profoundly said, "People will pay more to be entertained than educated." We say, "Do both!"

You may be a bit hesitant to attempt something different and untried because you risk the audience not accepting it. The fact is — and we repeat it again — groups love interesting, enjoyable presentations that display meaningful creativity and captivate and rivet their attention. What are you waiting for? When it comes to being creative in your presentations, and particularly the introductions, your comfort level limits you far more than your imagination. The more you experiment in small ways, the more you feel confident and assured in your ability to successfully apply your imagination. Professional creativity that is neither silly nor lessens your credibility grabs the audience's attention when you begin your talk.

TIP

Start out with milder forms of clever ideas, test them, and then move up the creativity ladder as you become more confident and comfortable with your blossoming communication imagination.

The following sections recount scenarios that ascend the scale from mild to wild. As you read, think about what tactics you could use in your presentations.

Scenario one: Opening with a video

An account manager along with his chemical engineer from a specialty chemical company gives a talk to a group of manufacturing managers from an international company. They begin by just introducing themselves and immediately start showing a 30-second video of several manufacturing operations (that have successfully used their products) with these numbers superimposed over the running video: "Proven Averages: 30 Percent Savings . . . 25 Percent Productivity Increase . . . 50 Percent Return on Investment . . . 4 Month Payback." When the video finishes, the account manager warmly smiles and says, "Those are real numbers that report the benefits that over 70 of our customers have experienced to date. Now we will discuss how your company can and will achieve some remarkable returns from using three of our breakthrough coatings in your manufacturing operations."

This atypical introduction immediately begins with something of obvious value to a potential customer, without a long-winded buildup, a transition, or wasted time. These two presenters raised eyebrows right away and snatched their group's attention from a 30-second, bottom-line oriented video.

Scenario two: Going dramatic

The CEO of a small, innovative software company is one of the key speakers at a business conference. The person who just verbally introduced him walks to the extreme side of the stage, where the speaker has been standing unseen by the audience. He walks the speaker by his arm very slowly and carefully toward the lectern and the audience sees that the speaker is blindfolded. The speaker gropes awkwardly for the location of the microphone to adjust it toward him and the audience wonders what might happen. He begins, "A tsunami of data covers the world, doubling every 18 months. We are drowning in data, but dying of thirst for information that will help run our businesses more effectively. Unknowingly, we wear blindfolds, just like me, that prevent us from seeing the rich sea of information deep within the waves of data flooding our businesses. I'm going to show you how to remove the blindfolds you don't even know you're wearing, giving you the vision to see and use the invaluable, rich information that will make your organizations more productive, more efficient, more innovative — and more successful." As he takes off the blindfold, he smiles and puts up his first slide of a person successfully reading an eye chart for 20/20 vision.

Scenario three: Starting with a story

The director of innovation for one highly effective government agency (yes, it is possible!) was asked to give a presentation to another large, bureaucratic agency that struggles with inefficiencies and waste, which prevent it from meeting aggressive goals set by the administration. After being introduced, she starts in a most unique and unexpected fashion by saying, "Let me tell you a story." She recounts the compelling, captivating tale of three organizations that struggled with essentially the same types of problems that burden this agency. Like a mini-epic, the five-minute story mixes facts and statistics with the personal struggles and emotional highs and lows of the managers who ultimately overcame the obstacles and changed the operations and culture of their organizations.

The presenter tells a story each person in the audience relates to and understands. She mesmerizes the group, but stops short of telling how the story ends to build anticipation and curiosity.

In those brief minutes, she makes a connection with the audience, conveys her understanding of their situation, and instills hope and optimism for a solution. The story gives a valuable, teasing glimpse into how to fix their set of problems. For the next 40 minutes, she describes the plan, process, and solution she advocates. (She does tell them how the story ends — at the end of her presentation.)

Scenario four: Overcoming obstacles

The regional sales vice president for a leading customer relationship management (CRM) application company puts on a public seminar in a hotel and invites sales executives and sales managers from dozens of small to large companies. As attendees walk into the meeting room, they find not the expected rows of chairs and a projection screen but an obstacle course laid out on the floor, as shown in Figure 3-1. Yellow duct tape defines the course interrupted by paper building blocks, signs, plastic figurines, model buildings, and a metal bridge. A large remote-controlled car waits at the start of the obstacle course. Needless to say, this unexpected display intrigues the attendees.

FIGURE 3-1:
An unexpected and entertaining demonstration grabs the audience's interest.

Photograph courtesy of Ray Anthony

When everyone gathers in the room, the vice president says, "Welcome to our seminar! As sales professionals, you know how difficult it can be to navigate the accounts with which you want to do lots of business. You meet gatekeepers, people change jobs, and competitors want to gain an edge over you. Right?" People nod their heads in agreement. He continues, "This morning, we're going to show you how to drive past your competitors, maneuver around all kinds of obstacles, get into that account, and make a difference — quickly. My assistant here will show you how to *really* drive that business."

The VP introduces a young man holding the remote control, and then shouts, "Go!" With that, the fellow drives the car and knocks down the paper blocks that form temporary barriers on the road, navigates over the bridge, steers around the plastic figures of people representing gatekeepers, and passes the finish line in such a quick, masterful way that those in the audience are awestruck with his expert driving. They've never seen anything like it. (The clever VP went to a well-known hobby shop where competitive remote-control racers hang out, and he hired a champ for the demonstration to make it look absolutely easy.)

The group spontaneously erupts in applause and when the din dies down, the VP says, "Our CRM software offers seven specific solutions that will drive your sales organization revenue growth. I'll show you how you can see increases from 15 percent to well over 45 percent within two years. Our median increase for more than 400 customers in this geographic is about 26 percent. Let's start with the first innovative application for you, which is . . ."

Building Your Introduction

A stirring, get 'em excited introduction relies on building-block components in various combinations. Knowing how to develop a structured introduction radically changes your presentations with the potential for over-the-top results.

Depending upon your purpose and the goals of your introduction, think through how to best construct the building blocks. This list shows the components we recommend, numbered not because they are to be completed in that order but to indicate which ones were used to build the introductions in the examples that follow:

1. **Greeting**
2. **Theme**
3. **Introduction(s)**
4. **Housekeeping (goals, agenda, timing, process, handouts)**
5. **Confirm findings**
6. **Executive summary**
7. **Quotation**
8. **Media reference (publication, website, or broadcast media)**
9. **Remarkable or startling facts or statistics**
10. **Questions**
11. **Prop(s)**
12. **Demonstration**
13. **Humor**
14. **Story or anecdote**
15. **Transition**

Connect the blocks in various combinations to create an introduction with purpose (to position your presentation), style, and a tone designed to get your audience to intently listen while establishing your credibility and professionalism.

Sticking with tradition

This straightforward, low-key (but professional) scripted introduction combines components 1, 3, and 4 to build the intro:

1. **(Greeting):** "Good morning. For those of you who don't know me, my name is Jennifer M. and I'm the lead cryogenics engineer on this wonderful project. We certainly appreciate the opportunity to be here today to tell you about our new breakthrough in superconductor technology. And we thank audience members Bill Y. and Yolanda H. for their help in supporting our development of this presentation for you."

3. **(Introductions):** "My engineering and science team are here to assist me in the four major topics that we'll cover. On my left is Jonathan B., who holds a Ph.D. in electrical engineering and has been on our team for the last three years. He'll jump into opportunities around our breakthroughs. Next to him is . . ."

4. **(Housekeeping):** "Our goal today is to give you a condensed but important overview of our new superconductor innovation, which translates into exciting new energy-related products and services for our customers. Looking at your agenda, you can see that we'll focus on four primary areas, with each of my team spending about ten minutes on the topics of . . . . Feel free to ask questions at any time during the presentation or after. Since this is a simplified overview, we have a 25-page handout for those hearty souls who want to dig into the technical details of this key innovation. We'll spend about an hour going through our information using a combination of slides and animations. We also have some interesting videos taken in our laboratory that will give you an overall understanding of our discovery. Jonathan will now get into. . . ."

Spicing it up

The following elements give credibility and punch to your topic and can be used in any combination in your introduction. Assume the presenter has gone through the cordial greeting and other introductory remarks and now transitions into these components of the introduction.

8. **(Media reference):** "The April issue of *Innovative Aircraft Weekly,* the industry's leading publication for small aircraft, highlighted the potential for dramatically escalating sales. In their article, *'The Jetsons Are Almost Here,'* it says, 'We are literally just a few years away from making flying as easy as driving a car, as affordable as owning one, and as safe, practical, and financially feasible as well.'"

7. **(Quotation):** "The well-known Professor of Aeronautical Engineering, Q.J. Razzintop, stated, 'The company that achieves major improvement in avionics, composite aircraft design, simplicity of flight, and low cost of operations will own an industry that explodes exponentially in growth — at least 25 percent per year or more.'"

9. **(Remarkable or startling facts or statistics):** "While our company is only five years old, we have discovered the golden formula for engineering a quantum leap in technology to create an aircraft that will be today's Jetsonmobile. Our engineers found a brilliant way to reduce avionics costs by almost 90 percent and cut fuel consumption by an unimaginable 70 percent with our radically efficient, ultra-reliable, low-cost engine. It normally takes a year to get a flying certification. It would take less than a week with our plane! Last year, about 2,500 small aircraft were sold. Our conservative estimates for our plane's sales exceed 1,000 the first year and 5,000 the second, and the trend curve looks like a vertical takeoff. We have over 156 patents pending that would give us a rare, exclusive, competition-free field lead for at least five years.

"Our management team is the best in the industry, our factory is ready, our employees are all experienced, highly trained experts, and our entire operations and marketing infrastructure is primed for takeoff. The skies are incredibly bright. And so could be your investment in our company. As potential investors, you will learn — in the next 60 minutes — about our superb small aircraft and our company's plans to grow and prosper so you can prosper with us. But most importantly, you will be convinced, I'm sure, that an investment in us will be one of the finest you will ever make. I'm turning the next part over to Denise R., our senior design engineer who has over 30 broad and deep years of experience designing some of the most advanced planes in the world. She will cover our radically bold and supremely tested engineering and designs. Denise . . . ."

Engaging the audience with questions

In this example (of part of an introduction), you pose questions to get a response and ask *rhetorical questions*, those for which you don't expect or want a reply, to stimulate thought or consideration. Startling facts or statistics grab people's interest, so that component is used again in this example. Notice the choice of targeted words used to appeal to the emotional — not just the logical — side of the audience.

10. **(Questions):** "How many of you have made investments in stock, bonds, or other financial instruments within the last five years or so? Please raise your hands. Now, how many of you are satisfied with the returns you got on those investments? I see that only two of you raised your hands, so about 95 percent of you are not happy. Please raise your hand again if you think it's difficult for most of us to survive and maintain a good quality of life in this uncertain and downward economic climate? Okay, now I see everyone's hand up."

9. **(Remarkable or startling facts or statistics):** "Let me tell you about a super survivor. It's called a tardigrade (presenter shows a photo of one). Not too pretty, is it? It's an eight-legged creature about as big as a speck of dust. They

can resist temperatures just above the lowest temperature possible, absolute zero, which is about minus 460 degrees Fahrenheit, to way over the boiling point of water. They can withstand pressures in the deepest part of the ocean that are about 6,000 times that of atmospheric pressure. They can live after being bombarded with radiation hundreds of times greater than what would kill a person or an animal. Tardigrades can live in the searing heat, frigid cold, and the total vacuum of space for weeks, even months at a time. And some have been known to live without food or water for over 50 years! They are the ultimate survivors and seem like the stuff of science fiction, but they are real and some may even exist in the soil in your backyard.

"I tell you about this fascinating creature because a vast majority of economic and financial experts predict that the world economy is entering the most dangerous economic climate experienced since Adam Smith became known as the Father of Modern Economics in the eighteenth century. Unfortunately, we will feel the enormous financial heat, pressure, and likely an empty vacuum in our lives."

10. **(Rhetorical questions):** "So I ask, is it possible to be a survivor in this economy? Is there a way for us to transform our portfolios into a financial tardigrade that can weather the extremes of higher taxes, increasing inflation and prices, and debilitating healthcare costs, among other financial downfalls? Are there any genuinely safe, proven ways to get back on a financial track to not only survive but also actually thrive? The answer is a resounding YES [pause] Absolutely!

"This evening, I will share with you four specific financial strategies combined with our exceptional portfolio of promising and diverse investments that will give you more than hope — they will give you back the optimism and quality of life you so need and deserve. So, let's think like a tardigrade, that little critter who survives and lives through anything! Let's get right into our extensively tested strategies and then the impressive portfolio components."

Adding a little humor

Decades ago, public-speaking courses advised, "Open with a joke." Unfortunately, well-meaning speakers were generally disappointed with the outcomes when they tried it. Unless you're a professional funny person with tested and proven jokes, starting out risking how people might respond can hurt your credibility and tank your ego if the joke falls flat. That's why even giants in the comedy industry test out new jokes in comedy clubs before going onto bigger, high-paying venues. They don't want to bomb either.

Nonetheless, including a somewhat humorous comment, insight, or anecdote that makes people smile while highlighting or reinforcing a point can be useful and can be an entertaining and enjoyable surprise to the audience. Humor, as part of an overall introduction, can add a bit of snap, crackle, and pop to your presentation.

13. **(Humor):** At a conference a presenter, speaking about Grabbing Opportunities, shows a cartoon illustration in his introduction — one he'd tested dozens of times before with excellent results. It shows two cute-looking dinosaurs sitting on a mountaintop surrounded by water. They look at Noah's ark sailing away with the animals gazing over the sides of the ship. One dinosaur dejectedly says to the other, "Oh, crap! Was that TODAY?" Some in the audience laughed out loud, some chuckled lightly, but most smiled as the speaker said, "Now there's an example of a major opportunity missed. See [pause] when was the last time you saw a live dinosaur?" as a few in the audience laughed again. The mild humor (not a joke) both amused and made a memorable point.

Use toned-down, and safer, aspects to amuse as opposed to telling jokes, which many in the audience may have heard before, and which may be met with stark silence and blank looks instead of the intended belly laugh. Always make sure any humor attempts tie into your topic to get people to think about and appreciate your information and messages that follow.

Setting the stage

If you propose a plan or a change of some kind, or are attempting to sell something, try combining the following two components in your introduction. In just about any presentation, it's best to give an executive summary up front to preview the highlights, benefits, and key messages of your presentation so the audience knows what to expect.

5. **(Confirm findings):** "As consultants, you asked us to help develop a change management plan for your organization. You told us that you: one, need to have a more streamlined workflow; two, want to improve employee productivity; three, need employees who respond faster to customer inquiries and requests; four, have to reduce transaction error rates; and five, need an improved system for all your employees to better communicate with each other in a more responsive fashion. Have we accurately and fully summarized your needs as described to us?"

6. **(Executive summary):** "Based upon those needs, our presentation today will highlight our proposed solution, which involves:

- Improving your overall employee productivity by 35 to 40 percent

- Speeding up response to your customers by over 60 percent

- Reducing transaction error rate by an impressive 80 percent or more

- Creating a seven-step process to ensure significantly improved employee communication

"During our presentation, we will also highlight how our proposed changes will minimize disruptions to your operations, communicate to your employees the benefits of these changes, and specify the various payback and returns on investment you can expect within the next six months. Now that I've given you an overview, let's get into specifics starting with . . ."

Starting out bold and interesting

Don't hesitate to get creative, even in boardroom presentations. In this example, the vice president of research and development wants to get approval from the board of directors for more funding to commercialize a significant breakthrough in materials development. In his introduction, he uses a metaphorical theme, a demonstration, and a prop to get his presentation off to a compelling start.

2. **(Theme):** As the vice president begins, "Today's presentation is really about thunder — you either create it or someone steals it from you." With that, he presses his remote control to bring up a video of thunder and lightning accompanied by several deep thunder claps of audio sound echoing around the room. "We have a unique opportunity to create a thunderous new product that could boost our gross revenues by an estimated 30 to 45 percent in the next two years and carve out a huge new market for a radical product we commercialize. With your approval for funding, we can beat our competitors to the market before they steal our thunder."

He then briefly highlights the latest information about their new materials invention that combines nanotechnology and ceramics to produce a lubricant and coating unlike anything on the market. It reduces friction in moving parts by an amazing 95 percent and, as a coating, strengthens metal parts to resist wear in engines and equipment.

11. **(Props):** The VP holds up a two-foot long chain of molecules created with a 3-D printer to represent a blown-up model of the lubricant and coating and says, "This is a model of what our amazing discovery looks like. There is no other molecular structure like it in existence. It's part carbon, as you can see by the red atoms, and part ceramic, as you can see by the blue atoms. I'm going to pass it around for you to look at more closely."

12. **(Demonstration):** The VP of research and development moves to the side of the room where a table and an eight-foot long wooden board is set up like a tabletop. He holds up a hockey puck and says, "This is an ordinary hockey puck with no lubricant on it. Can I get a board member to come up and just push this with a light force on the wooden table?" A woman comes forward and pushes it with moderate force and it travels about two feet. He hands her another puck and says, "This one has our best lubricant and coating on it. Try this one." She does and it goes about four feet. "Now our new 'miracle' product is on this hockey puck. Push it gently." She does and it flies right off the end of the table! You see the stunned and amazed looks on the board members' faces.

The presenter purposely pauses for about eight seconds, looks around the room and says, "Now I am going to discuss what it will take to get this to market quickly, what our expected financial returns look like, and the support and resources for which we need your approval. In the next 30 minutes, I will cover the details you need to make an informed decision to make some thunder and lightning happen." With that, he brings up a four-second video with more lightning accompanied by an audio of room-shaking thunder.

Phrasing transitions

It's often a good idea to use a transition (also called a *segue*) statement as the final part of your introduction to alert your audience that you finished your initial opening and will begin the main body of your presentation with your detailed substance.

15. **(Transition):** Here are examples of transitions:

- "I hope your curiosity is sparked with the introduction of our new product line benefits. Let's get into the specifics of how these exceptional products will transform your operations."

- "You're probably anxious to find out more about the seven ways our proposal can achieve the impressive returns on investment that we teased you with a minute ago. Now you will see as I begin to discuss number one with you . . ."

- "So how will your company actually get those savings and revenue increases in process improvements, which you just glimpsed? Now it's time to move on to the mainline of our presentation starting, with . . ."

» **Adding emphasis and intensity**

» **Getting the audience to interact**

» **Generating interest**

» **Showing cause and effect**

Chapter **4**

Keeping Your Audience Captivated

You've heard the idiom perhaps hundreds of times before, but do you know what it means to "keep the audience on the edge of their seats?" In movie, theater, or sports parlance, it means that people intently follow the action and excitement of a performance, sometimes in a mesmerized way. If it's a story being told or shown (as in a video), it means riveting the audience's attention so that they absolutely must find out what happens next. Entertainment professionals such as producers, actors, comedians, and magicians use suspense, curiosity, surprise, empathy, paradox, humor, and realism to keep people engaged. In innovative presentations when the audience sits on the edge of their seats, you own the room and have the audience's attention and interest locked in tight.

An audience on the edge of their seats focuses on what you say, do, and show. They have laserlike focus on you. They ask many questions to find out more about your topic. Their heads nod in agreement when you cover your key points, and many come up to you after your presentation to talk with you more. You own that group. If you see people glancing around, fidgeting, looking at their phones, conversing with their neighbors, or sitting back with the glazed look of boredom, you've lost possession of the group.

This chapter covers four Laws of Communication Impact: the Law of Emphasis and Intensity, the Law of Exercise and Engagement, the Law of Interest, and the Law of Effect. These laws serve to rev up any audience's attention span and interest. Apply them and you elevate the effectiveness of your presentations to a new level. For each law, we describe innovative presentations that focus on galvanizing and stirring people to committed action, which means getting the results you want.

REMEMBER

These laws can be used in any type of oral or written communication, not just formal business presentations.

Standing and Shouting Out: The Law of Emphasis and Intensity

Suppose you're driving at night, and from far away you see the high-intensity lights of a police car. The brilliantly vivid, flashing, colored lights immediately capture your sight, even with all the traffic around you. They stand out! If you attend a symphony performance and in the middle of the *adagio* — the slow, soft passage of the musical piece — two cymbals clash, that instantaneously adds musical thunder to the ensemble and gives you an auditory jolt. It shouts out! Or you attend a conference in Las Vegas in an air-conditioned casino and then step outside in the July summer to suddenly experience an oven-blast temperature of 118 degrees Fahrenheit that seems to singe your skin. Immediately, you feel the sensation, the overpowering difference that, again, stands out! Each of these audio, visual, or physical sensations exemplifies the Law of Emphasis and Intensity in action. The sudden and strong change you experience with sight, sound, touch, taste, and other sensation affects you in an intense way.

If you want a key statistic, vital fact, or point to vividly stick out in your presentation, use the Law of Emphasis and Intensity. During your presentation, the audience watches and listens to you, so you can appeal to either their visual sense or their auditory sense or both. Physical sensations are a bit harder to conjure during a presentation.

For example, say you fill the page on a flip chart with about 100 round dots using a black felt tip marker. Then in the middle of those dots, you draw one much larger red dot or a big black square. Would eyes be drawn to the red dot or large square immediately among all the other dots? Of course. The non-conforming shape stands out from the uniform crowd of dots. The different color, size, and shape distinguish it among the dots and emphasize it.

The other part of the Law of Emphasis and Intensity involves intensity, be it mental, physical, or emotional. It can be an intense sight, sound, smell, touch, or emotional effect. Think about something you saw, heard, felt, or experienced that surprised, shocked, intrigued, or otherwise got your instantaneous and undivided attention. Intense pleasure or pain, joy or sadness, overwhelming pride or shame — these all share some eruptive feeling, which at times brings a clear, intellectual insight or creates a simple, positive stranglehold on your emotional state.

The more intense the feeling — positive or negative — the more likely you are to remember it. Any sharply vivid or forceful experience causes you to dwell or ruminate upon it long afterward. The intense feeling you get from a rousing standing ovation is unforgettable and drowns you in a sea of churning emotions. The Law of Emphasis and Intensity creates and sustains that sensation.

In any type of presentation, you convey your key points and also disseminate other necessary but less relevant details to explain, describe, or expand on those points or to link key points. During your presentation, you want to draw attention to certain aspects and make sure your audience immediately digests and remembers those aspects more than other supporting pieces of information. You need to use imaginative ways to separate necessary yet supporting information from your most critical message, main point, or key data.

To apply the Law of Emphasis and Intensity to the key points of your presentation, you have to highlight and give special importance and prominence to the point apart and above everything else. As you develop your presentation and identify those key points, think about imaginative ways you can define, stress, and separate the critical points and messages from subordinate information. The next sections give you some ideas to churn your creative juices.

Comparing and contrasting

Despite echoing Composition 101, comparing and contrasting remains an excellent tool to show big differences and highlight and emphasize specific information. When Apple started shipping its radically redesigned and engineered small cylindrical Mac Pro computer server in December 2013, its diminutive size and raw computing power broke major new ground in technology advancements, but its small footprint shocked people. But when photos emerged of the tiny, elegantly designed cylinder computer next to the former huge rectangular box of the previous Mac Pro, the comparative difference stunned and awed audiences — it looked like a lizard next to a dinosaur.

Make a list of adjectives that describe your product, service, or idea in terms of size, color, quantity, speed, age, time, and other aspects, and then make a similar list for your competition or the existing way of doing something. Use comparison and contrast to emphasize the point you want your audience to absorb, remember, and consider when you reach the call to action part of your presentation.

Consider adding an element of controversy, curiosity, intrigue, or purposeful exaggeration to evoke an intense reaction from your audience.

Changing your voice

Your voice is a powerful and persuasive tool. Try repeating the same sentence but place emphasis on different words (indicated with **boldface**) each time. For example:

>> **Our** multi-slice tomographic radiation device can treat up to 15 patients an hour.

>> Our **multi-slice tomographic radiation device** can treat up to 15 patients an hour.

>> Our multi-slice tomographic radiation device can treat up to **15 patients an hour.**

Your voice guides the audience to the points you want to emphasize. Change your vocal inflection as you mention your key message, facts, or statistics. Raising your voice, like a cymbal clash that interrupts an adagio, jolts the audience to attention.

However, after several minutes of a rousing, fevered monologue, a measured statement spoken in a soft tone can have an enormous effect. The key to the Law of Emphasis and Intensity is differentiation. To further separate the ordinary from the important, use a brief, two-to-three second isolating pause both before and immediately after highlighting your significant piece of information.

In addition to inflection and volume, consider repeating that main point for emphasis. Repetition holds the audience's attention on the important point you want to stand out.

Adding pizzazz

Striking, unique, or provocative visuals, photos, and illustrations drive your message home to your audience members. A humorous photo often highlights your point best.

The director of innovation for an international farm, forestry, and construction machinery company gives a presentation to new engineer and technical hires about her company's culture of change and how it has always been ready and willing to embrace new things. She says that ideas — whether incremental or monumental — are the foundation of change and progress, but that it's necessary to unclog the mind of old ways of thinking and doing things that have led to past successes but no longer work in today's environment. With a wry smile, she projects the photo shown in Figure 4-1.

FIGURE 4-1:
Humorous images, when appropriate, reinforce your point.

Photograph courtesy of Ray Anthony

She leaves time for the group to laugh and then follows up with the interesting photo shown in Figure 4-2, which emphasizes her point of keeping an open mind to new opportunities.

FIGURE 4-2:
Use surprising images to stress your point.

Photograph courtesy of Ray Anthony

From a physical standpoint, when a person laughs, especially a hearty guffaw, the facial and abdominal muscles relax and blood and oxygen circulation increase, which lead to better attention.

Highlighting specific aspects

A powerful way to draw attention to an intended part of your text, illustrations, diagrams, photos, or videos is to use other visual attention–getters to precisely emphasize and contrast what you want. Your imaginative ideas can create almost unlimited ways to do that. Here are just a few examples:

>> With text, use a different color, font, size, bold, heavy underline, or italic to make it stand out. Also, consider putting a rectangular box filled in with color around the text. Without overdoing it, have your graphic designer manipulate your text to make it shout. Animating text is a surefire way to make it pop — not to mention a low-cost way to add visual interest to your presentation.

>> Blur out the areas you want to de-emphasize so the part that stays in focus gets the attention.

>> Use a build or dissolve function in your slide show or video to reveal and selectively disclose parts of your visual to construct it sections at a time.

>> If you have a pie chart or a bar chart, make the key sector or bar a bright color, while keeping the rest of the illustration black and white.

>> Spotlight a certain part of a diagram, an illustration, or anything else by enlarging that part over the entire graphic as if a magnifying glass focused on it.

>> Use shapes, colors, and geometric elements to draw the audience's eyes to where you want their concentration. For example, in a process flow chart that displays each step of the process in a box or other geometric shape, change the shape color as you talk about each step in the process. Use color arrows to dissolve onto the visual to point where you want. Consider using color circles, squares, and ellipses to overlay the parts of the visual you want to emphasize.

By using contrasting shapes or colors and showing single parts of the entire image at a time, you guide the viewers' eyes to precisely where you want them to be.

Using special effects

If you're using a presentation software app that lets you overlay (or composite) a QuickTime or other video format file on your slides, consider using stock animations typically called *revealers, motion elements,* or *blinkers.* These animated elements, such as a blinking arrow, lights that go back and forth, and animated circles, immediately bring a viewer's attention to specific text or parts of the photo, diagram, illustration, or chart in a video or static slide. Digital Juice (www.digitaljuice.com) sells many of these.

You can customize powerful ways to direct a viewer's attention to specific pieces of information on your slide or video by using the custom effects of Adobe After Effects or Apple's Motion software. Selectively add audio to one of these animated effects for further emphasis.

WARNING

Don't overdo these creative ways of drawing a viewer's eye to specific parts of your visuals. Special effects should support what you're saying, not replace or overwhelm your message.

Telling a story

People are more likely to remember a story than a list of facts or figures. A short and compelling story brings life to your presentation and can illuminate the critical points you want to showcase. The moral of a well-crafted, captivating tale should convey the message or information you want your audience to remember.

Humor is a captivating way to stress something. An amusing cartoon or illustration with a simple but profound message often turns out to be a sudden sharp insight for your audience. If you tell an amusing anecdote, use the type of humor that makes people not only smile, chuckle, or laugh but also ponder the underlying substance of your key point long after the laughs fade.

Demonstrating your point

Remember show-and-tell day in kindergarten? If you do, you began preparing for demonstrations then. Nothing proves your point as powerfully as showing what you discuss. Years ago when Kevlar bullet-proof vests were coming on the scene, some company owners actually took live-fire shots from a powerful pistol to demonstrate the real protective power of their vests. The manufacturer of a commercial-grade cordless drill pitted its product against a competitor's, connecting each drill to a winch to pull a 4,000-pound tractor. The competitor's drill pulled the tractor about half the distance and stopped as it began to smoke, while the featured product easily pulled the heavy vehicle the entire distance with no damage and a remaining battery charge, obviously highlighting its power, durability, and performance.

Effective demonstrations not only prove the claims you make but also stress the main points you want the audience to know and produce the greatest psychological effect.

Propping up

Physical props support and reinforce both your spoken word and visuals. For example, a sales trainer gives a presentation about how to deal with high-strung, overly sensitive prospects. She takes a large inflated balloon, puts it directly over her head, and compares it to a potential customer's highly inflated but delicate ego. She says if you blatantly disagree with such a person during your sales conversation, her ego will be damaged (as she sticks a pin in the balloon) and you will lose a sale. The abrupt burst with the loud POP! gets people's attention, and long after the training ends, they vividly remember that each time they face a sensitive prospect.

In addition to props, consider using relevant theatrical techniques such as skits, acting, focused lighting, music, and the aforementioned special effects (see "Using special effects" earlier) to add novelty, drama, curiosity, or entertainment around your most important concept.

In addition to props, determine what types of interesting handouts can further showcase what you want. The more concise, creative, and attractive your handouts, gifts, or giveaways, the more likely people are to read or view the main points you want them to absorb and remember.

Tech-ing out

If you lend a tablet to each attendee, you can communicate directly with each person from your computer or tablet. Tell the audience that you're sending something important for them to see for themselves. While you're alerting them, transmit what you want to emphasize, and then discuss it.

If you have a small group of three to six people, you can use a theatrical technique by blanking out your projector or monitor and telling the group you want to show them something close up. You then put the highlighted information or visual on your large tablet screen, move close to each person, and show it from about two to three feet away. This transition from screen to large tablet, combined with your movement and close physical proximity to each person, adds intensity to your information and your relationship to the audience.

Use your stylus and tablet to circle, underline, or put an exclamation point next to what you want to highlight. You can draw something around it or next to it and otherwise think of ways to isolate something on your visual to pull the audience's attention to it. Also consider using your presentation app's laser pointer function on your tablet to highlight key points.

Involving Your Audience: The Law of Exercise and Engagement

As it applies to learning, the Law of Exercise and Engagement states that people who are engaged and active are more interested in continuing an activity, learn more from the activity, and are otherwise affected to a greater degree than those who aren't emotionally involved. For our purposes, we interpret the law to mean that you should have people participate in your presentation.

A presentation, like a conversation, has at least two people — one who speaks and one who listens. However, both situations need balance. If two people have a conversation and one person dominates it, talking solely about his interests without regard for the other person who passively (supposedly) listens, the listener probably isn't interested in what the talker has to say, especially after an extended period tolerating a long-winded monologue. But if the non-stop talker asks the listener a question, makes eye contact, and smiles, the (polite) listener becomes more involved in the discussion. You want to elicit the same reaction from your audience. By showing interest in reciprocally listening, your one-sided monologue becomes a meaningful, active dialogue.

REMEMBER

Speaking about topics that don't interest or aren't pertinent to your audience's needs is a waste of time for everyone.

Involving the audience

An engaged speaker creates an attentive and interested audience. Studies show that people mimic what they see and hear. It's a form of social reciprocity. So, when you show interest in your audience, they in turn show interest in you.

Great speakers use lots of eye contact to connect with their audiences. They encourage questions and comments and ask thought-provoking rhetorical questions. When the room setup permits, move into and among the audience instead of isolating yourself at the front.

Presenters who share stories, examples, quotations, and other specifically tailored content (that addresses the groups needs and wants) capture the audience's attention. (See the earlier section, "Telling a story.") And speakers who call on people in the room to interact with them as much as possible — "Hey, Grace, what are your thoughts on that?" — create a dialogue that makes people feel more attended to as a result. (However, if you don't know the group well, you might make someone uncomfortable being put on the spot like this.)

Some speakers and presenters mingle with individuals before, during, and after their talk. If they know some of the people in the group, they use personal anecdotes about them or friendly humor relating to them. Frequently seeking out a group's opinions, reactions, and ideas helps you turn an otherwise passive audience into an active — and interactive — one and significantly increases the chances of your presentation breeding success.

Encouraging interaction

The exercise part of the Law of Exercise and Engagement, while similar to engagement, indicates a high level of direct involvement. Trainers use learning exercises, case studies, role playing, and questioning to get people to use the information they have acquired in real-world simulation in the classroom — to just do it.

For example, Ray, who sold computers for an international company, would ask potential buyers to bring their real accounting data with them to a demonstration of his company's minicomputers (which were actually sophisticated accounting machines the size of a big desk). With a prospect sitting beside him, Ray would lead the person through the process of inputting the data to do accounts payable, accounts receivable, and general ledger postings. The potential customer would then use the keyboard to type in the data and see for herself just how fast, accurate, easy, and beneficial it would be for her accounting operation. It was not Ray telling or doing it, but the person following the Law of Exercise and Engagement.

The exercise part of this law combines sight, touch, and even sound (in this case the computer's printer gave an impressively quick printout) to present a real situation that convinces the audience of the point you are making. By employing these types of product demonstrations using the Law of Exercise and Engagement, prospects became buying customers.

It's becoming more common, especially in large groups, to use a tablet or an iPad to enable those in the audience to express their opinions, ideas, or questions. In large events, for example, hundreds of people in the audience can tweet comments for you to display on the big screen for all to see in real time.

Whether or not you're a fan of social media, it taps into a desire to share and encourages people to express thoughts and feelings toward an interesting or concerning topic. For many people, liking, commenting, and sharing have become second nature. You can take advantage of the social mentality in your presentation. You can respond as you want to the comments people are making for as long as it's productive or entertaining.

Today's interactive technology allows you to create virtual situations where the audience inputs data or manipulates information or images, along with you, to reach the conclusions you want. Augmented reality apps show the viewer the solutions to the problem or situation at hand.

By providing tablets or laptops that have a presentation or collaboration app pre-loaded (or inviting your attendees to download the app to their own devices before beginning your presentation), your traditional talking-head presentation becomes one involving the Law of Exercise and Engagement. Attendees actively participate and can see for themselves the outcomes you pose and forecast as well as comments and ideas from others in the group. Search for *collaboration* in the App Store and you discover hundreds of apps designed to facilitate interactive brainstorming. Check out BaiBoard (`www.baiboard.com`), a free Mac and iOS app that lets small workgroups collaborate on a shared white board and PDF document annotation, and iBrainstorm (`www.ibrainstormapp.com`), a multi-device collaboration tool that's also free.

We predict that in the near future, most meetings and presentations will effectively take advantage of the Law of Exercise and Engagement, in which involvement is much more two-sided (involving a back-and-forth between audience and presenter) as opposed to presenter-directed, sequentially ordered talks.

Hitting Their Hot Buttons: The Law of Interest

Why do people intently listen to or watch something with rapt attention or enthusiastically engage in an activity? Obviously because they want to. They're interested and enjoy doing it. Simple as that.

When people lose interest, they lose attention, concentration, and focus and become bored or distracted. They start thinking of something else or daydream. At meetings, training workshops, presentations, and speeches, you see people whip out their smartphones or tablets and start to review their emails, send text messages, surf the web, or just work on something else. Although some people try to be discreet, many engage in these activities with total disregard for how you may feel. What was once considered rude before the popular advent and use of addictive digital devices is now accepted as commonplace behavior in many organizational cultures. However, research studies prove that a great majority of those multitaskers who rationalize and justify their selective attention really cannot listen and do something else with equal effectiveness.

If you're giving a presentation and attendees become mentally and emotionally detached, they can miss vital information that affects their decision making and possible desire to commit to what you are asking them to do, such as approve, support, buy, or endorse. They may misinterpret something because of attention gaps in their listening. So, it's important that you strive to keep the interest level high for the people listening or watching.

When it comes to capitalizing upon the Law of Interest, use techniques from the Law of Exercise and Engagement described in the preceding section. Use these extra tips to capture and hold the interest of as many in a smaller group or even larger audience as possible:

>> Do an effective audience analysis to determine the general makeup of the group so that you can personalize and tailor your talk to give them exactly what they need and want. Focus on the priorities your audience wants addressed.

>> Throughout your presentation, tell your audience how they will directly (personally or professionally or both) benefit from your talk. For example, say, "I'm going to show each of you four things that promise to make your job easier, faster, and better. These will reduce your stress, hassles, and tedious workloads."

>> Have as compelling and captivating a presentation introduction as you can. Set the bar high for what follows.

>> Get creative. If appropriate, use fun (but always professional) activities such as information guessing games and interactive exercises to get feedback, ideas, and recommendations based on your presentation. At well-planned segues in your presentation, consider sending useful bits of topic-related trivia, photos, or illustrations from your tablet or laptop to their devices.

>> Ramp up your speech delivery technique. Show energy, enthusiasm, and dynamism to make it easier and more interesting to listen.

>> As much as you can, use stories to communicate fascinating and riveting facts, statistics, testimonials, research results, or analogies that apply to, are meaningful for, or engrossing to your audience. Give vivid examples that entertain, amuse, or emotionally affect people.

>> Use rhetorical, thought-provoking questions at specific junctures in your talk to reignite declining interest. Ask, "Why should you be interested in knowing this?" or "What effect would it have if you began using this new process tomorrow — what three surprising differences would you discover right away?"

>> In a smaller group, use the teacher's trick and call on a specific person (who seems to be inattentive or fixated on her device) to ask a relevant question or get feedback. Be subtle. By casually and randomly going around the room to stimulate discussion, you involve those who may have lost interest and will likely rejuvenate their flagging attention. Bear in mind that a distracted person may reengage or may feel embarrassed or guilty for not contributing to the group discussion.

REMEMBER

Sometimes people drift off because they don't understand what you're saying, so with a small group you can ask, "Does my point make sense to you?"

Facing the Consequences: The Law of Effect

Use the *Law of Effect* to activate or change people's behavior. Politicians, sales and marketing professionals, and others who strive to influence and persuade people to act in certain ways use this law.

Edward Thorndike, the American psychologist known for his work on animal behavior and learning, developed this law. Based upon a stimulus-response reaction, the Law of Effect essentially states that responses that produce an enjoyable or satisfying effect in a particular situation become more likely to occur again in that situation, and responses that produce uneasiness, discomfort, or some other negative effect are less likely to occur again in that type of situation. Common sense, right? If you give an innovative presentation and your audience obviously got a lot out of it, they will be more eager to attend and participate in your future presentations.

You can say that the Law of Effect relates to carrot-or-a-stick rewards and punishments. For example, if a person regularly gets speeding tickets while driving too fast, at some point, after spending lots of time in driving school and court appearances or paying fines and lawyer fees, she's likely to slow down because of the unpleasant and undesirable consequences.

Competent skills trainers, motivational speakers, personal trainers, and business coaches use the Law of Effect to help people learn, develop new skills, build confidence, and be inspired to excel. When it comes to giving a presentation or speech, evoke the Law of Effect in the following ways:

>> From your laptop or tablet, show brief, compelling testimonials or success stories about how your products, services, programs, or innovations generate positive consequences for the users. Likewise, subtly communicate the negative consequences for people who don't take advantage of your recommendations. Before-and-after examples often persuade people to act.

>> If you recommend change of some kind, focus on the (greater) probable positive gain versus the (lesser) possible risk, problems, or inconvenience associated with the proposed change.

>> Compliment and praise people in your audience when they provide constructive comments about your presentation points. This way of psychologically rewarding people's supportive comments encourages more of those in the audience to speak up in ways that approve of and endorse your information.

WARNING

People are fearful of taking unnecessary risks. Be mindful about how you communicate things that may indirectly or subtly invoke fear, anxiety, concern, remorse, or guilt — unless your strategy is designed to solicit negative feelings to further your goals.

» **Following conclusion guidelines**

» **Using conclusive tactics**

» **Building a compelling finale**

Chapter **5**

Ending on a High Note

Today's action movies start like a lit fuse in sticks of dynamite — a sizzling spark heading toward a shock wave with a scene that immediately envelopes you in the unfolding drama, suspense, or action. Many movies have the raw visual firepower and adrenalin-building punch to ignite our attention and transfix us. But the ending of a great movie matters most in creating an explosive experience that effects us emotionally and psychologically. Everything in a good plot builds up to the ending, the close, the climax — and releases it.

If you attend a live performance by a terrific singer or band, you notice that they start off with a lively, heart-pumping, foot-thumping number — their introduction. However, they bring down the house by saving their best, most dynamic song for last — their conclusion — to leave the audience on a high emotional plain. Singers want their fans to cherish their act long afterward, so they sing a blockbuster as their closing song, and some save that blockbuster for the encore, making it the last of the last.

This chapter takes inspiration from movies and concerts to explain how to create and deliver a compelling and rousing conclusion to your presentation or speech.

Concluding Effectively: The Law of Recency

The closing effect — the *Law of Recency* — is the fifth of the Laws of Communication Impact, and carries more weight for your message than the primacy (beginning) effect, because the last thing a person sees, hears, tastes, touches, feels, or experiences is the first thing he or she remembers.

TIP

The acronym LIFO, used by computer scientists, stands for *last in, first out* and applies to list processing and data structures. You can use it to remember how to structure your presentations.

Think about it: You had a great dinner, but you still want that delicious dessert — that last, lingering wonderful taste before you leave the restaurant. Or you're saying goodbye to a potential client, who firmly shakes your hand, gives you a warm, ear-to-ear smile, and says, "This was a terrific meeting. I see us working with your company!" These endings send you out on a high note, long felt and well remembered, don't they? Or, in a converse situation, your boss looks at you sternly and in a cold, steely voice simply says, "Okay," as he walks away after you explained something. That last message also digs in and sticks with you, unfortunately.

For your talk to be a success, you must use the *Law of Recency* to construct a strong conclusion, which has the following features:

» Encapsulates and brings everything together in a simple, concise, and memorable manner

» Highlights your most important points and messages in a convincing and compelling way

AVOID THE FLAPPING SWAN CONCLUSION

Too many presenters let their conclusion trail or suddenly and abruptly die off with weak, disjointed, or indecisive ramblings as if they had not prepared any well-thought-out final remarks. This is what we call the Flapping Swan: A speaker comes to the end of his talk and raises both arms to the side about shoulder height and lets them quickly fall to his hips while saying something like, "Okay . . . that's it, I guess. Ah . . . any questions?" or "That's about all I . . . sort of have to say . . . uhm . . . thanks." Ending this way is definitely neither dynamic nor smooth and certainly not memorable (at least in a positive way).

>> Leaves a group on a high note and motivates them to act upon your recommendation, plan, solution, or idea (the call to action)

>> Cements your rapport and credibility with the audience

>> When necessary, inoculates your group against any subsequent discussions or presentations, such as competitive sales presentations, designed to counter what you advocate

Affecting Your Audience Right to the End

Your conclusion can be soft-spoken or electric, depending on both your personality and your audience, but every type of conclusion should follow the guidelines in this section to be effective.

Conclude, don't include

If you forgot minor, unimportant pieces of information, don't add them to your conclusion as afterthoughts. A conclusion wraps up and tightly summarizes what you said and is not a forum for new information. What's more, if you forget something important and discuss it during your conclusion, your may jeopardize your credibility and leave the audience wondering, "If it was that much of a priority, how could he not have focused on it during the presentation?"

Signal that the end is near

Audiences snap to when they hear the magical words that tell them it's the beginning of the end. When a presenter says something like, "I'm going to wrap up now with my summary and final thoughts," listeners perk up with renewed attention, which you can take advantage of. Use transition statements such as the following:

>> "I'll conclude with the profound quotation of the eminent business giant Catherine Wittner, who said . . . "

>> "The main points I want to leave you with before I end are . . . "

>> "As I finish up, I want to leave you with a stunning four-minute video that perfectly encapsulates and dramatically amplifies the dire importance of my message to you today . . . "

>> "I end today with three recommendations, which are . . . "

End it already

Your conclusion should be direct and concise, yet smooth, not choppy. After you alert your group that you're heading down the homestretch of your talk, conclude with brevity and panache. Some presenters frustrate audiences by giving the impression that things are wrapping up and then continue talking with no sign of ending soon. Some people do this multiple times to the great dismay of the audience.

Be neither meek nor weak

Finish in a confident, strong, and self-assured manner that conveys positivity and optimism. Never apologize or appear submissive as in the following:

>> "I am so sorry it took this long and that we didn't have enough handouts for all of you, but . . . "

>> "I'm embarrassed I forget to prepare details about . . . "

>> "This is a new presentation for me, and also I'm not an experienced speaker . . . "

>> "Thank you for your patience during my talk."

Instead, offer a solution, such as, "If you didn't receive the handouts, please write your email on the list on the table by the exit and I'll send them to you this evening." Or "It was a delight to speak with you today about my new responsibilities."

Leave with a strong message

In certain types of presentations or speeches, a thought-provoking, memorable finale embodies the epitome of the Law of Recency — like the last lyrics of a song or the final words of a play. Consider the following examples of punchy closing statements:

>> "Our company's debt is a disaster teetering on a precipice. We still have time to avoid economic catastrophe, but only if we act right now. Right now!"

>> "Innovation in your corporation is absolutely critical as never before. Apply it, accelerate it, and benefit from it in ways you've never imagined before!"

>> "There are three things to remember about great leadership: Take care of your people [pause], take care of your people [pause], take care of your people. And they will take care of you and your company!"

Giving a Tactical Conclusion

Innovative presentations demand powerful, unique, unpredictable, and thoroughly imaginative conclusions. A genial capstone separates you from the crowd of other presenters. This section provides examples of superb conclusions to spur your creativity and turn a Flapping Swan into a Soaring Eagle.

Repeating a theme (with a twist)

In Chapter 3, which covers the Law of Primacy and explains how to compose a good introduction, one of the examples describes how the CEO of an innovative software company begins his presentation at a business conference by being led blindfolded to the lectern. The theme of his key message drove home the point that extracting useful information from the continuous mega-explosion of data around us is difficult because we can't distinguish between useful and useless — it's as if we're blindfolded.

In his conclusion, the CEO concisely and compellingly summarizes his key points and then says to the group of about 200 people, "Now I have a surprise for you today. Reach under your chair and open the plastic bag." The audience finds a black blindfold with the four main points the CEO emphasized in his summary printed on one side of the cloth.

"Now, I have a couple of more surprises," in which he teases the group. "I'm going to ask you to put on your new blindfold. I have six assistants around the room who will throw soft foam rubber balls to you while blindfolded. Those who catch them will get prizes. Ready? Throw the balls!" he yells out. No one caught one, even by accident. "Take off your blindfolds. Not one of you out of about 200 here today caught one." He said. "Not surprising, is it? I hope you enjoyed this fun exercise that reinforces my point about being blindfolded. I still have one more surprise for you, though. Everyone gets prizes. As you walk outside, pick up a free stylus pen you can use with your smartphone or tablet, a 25 percent discount coupon for our information-gathering software, and a $10 gift card. It was great being with all of you today!" He ended with power and passion. The CEO got a standing ovation and probably lots of business from his talk.

Leaving them smiling

A senior account manager gives an innovative sales presentation using video, animation, and a live demonstration about his company's latest computer-activated plasma- and laser-cutting tools for steel plate to a defense contractor who builds naval combat ships. His crisp summary highlights the extra speed, reliability, and precision of his company's heavy-steel cutting machines that results in reduced waste, increased productivity and quality, and the ability to better meet stringent deadlines and budgets — critical components of getting renewed contracts in the defense industry. Following his summary, he points to a man sitting on the side and says, "I introduced Travis H. in the beginning. While he was quiet throughout my talk, I'd like to bring him up now."

The well-dressed, professional-looking man in his 40s pushes an open cart with a small tablecloth over it, obviously hiding something underneath. Travis opens with, "This is the end of our structured presentation. We hope you understand the excellent information about using our latest equipment to give you the benefits Sam mentioned. Since we have 15 minutes left, we would like to give you a dessert while we briefly chat with you. Don't worry, we'll still finish ahead of schedule." With that, he uncovers the cart and reveals a large cake under a glass cover, which he also removes. "Quality inspection is critical in your industry. Can I get someone up here to do a quality check on this cake?" he asks, as some people laugh while others are curious as to what's going on.

A smiling engineering vice president steps up, looks it over as Travis queries, "Is that cake marked or otherwise defective in any way? Does it look like a tasty, normal cake that our account manager baked just for all of you?" More laughs and smiles from the group as the "inspector" says, "Yeah, it looks okay to me." "Now, check the cart out." Travis requests and continues, "It's a regular cart, with just a flat top holding the cake and nothing under it right?" The VP affirms it.

Travis takes the small tablecloth, covers the front of the cake, and shouts the name of the account manager's company while lifting the cloth straight up to the amazement of everyone. Not only is the cake now bigger with a different color and decoration, but it has 18 perfectly equal slices in it, exactly the number for each person in the group! The account manager steps forward as jaws are still hanging and says, "I told you we offer precision! We'll work the same magic for your company — growth and perfect cuts." To those who asked, he explained that Travis was really a highly skilled magician hired to entertain the group. Needless to say, his innovative presentation was a cakewalk that had a tasty win to it.

Offering impressive incentives

The construction industry is among the most highly competitive of all industries with those who submit the lowest valid bid winning the deal a huge percentage of the time. Lori V., a senior project manager, as shown in Figure 5-1, works for a successful, respected construction firm that made the short list for building an upscale lakeside community of expensive residences, offices, four-star restaurants, and retail stores. She and her team competed against two other firms to win the prized project. Her strategy is simple: Prove they are the absolute best firm to bring the project in on-time, on-target, and on-budget with some important extras. She and her team plan a superb presentation that conveys the expertise, professionalism, teamwork, and valuable creativity their firm brings to the project.

Photograph courtesy of Ray Anthony

The presentation is extraordinary and spellbinding, both different and significantly better than any of the other construction firms. The bid, however, is the highest, although not by an unreasonable margin. Lori has a strategy for that as well. Like any great presenter, she summarizes the highlights and superior benefits of her proposal, which include

>> Her firm's record of successful projects completed

>> Its strong financial health and growth trend

>> Its industry-winning quality awards and safety records

>> The impressive qualifications of the firm's leaders and personnel

For her imaginative finale, her presentation team gives each of the five meeting attendees — the decision makers — a special set of handouts, as shown in Figure 5-2, left. Each includes a model dump truck with a unique binder inside, which you can see in Figures 5-2, right. Lori then uses a standard sales tactic called the *trial close*, "Based on your questions, comments, and body language, I get the impression that you would like to seriously consider us for this large, beautiful project. Have I sensed that accurately?" She sees several smiles and slight head nods, but knows someone will mention the higher price, which two people do. So she counters, "Let's see if we can fix that."

Photographs courtesy of Ray Anthony

She continues, "You'll find two important items in that cool-looking Plexiglas cover handout: a compelling, detailed summary of all aspects that we will excel in for your lakeside development. Secondly, on page 14 you'll find a pleasant surprise! In our previous discussions, you mentioned that you like the idea of further developing the lakefront with numerous amenities and recreations. But you said doing that was in the budget for Phase 2 about three years from now. Well, page 14 details the designs we came up with based on your ideas to do just that." Lori holds up a real-looking bill and says, "My firm is offering you an attractive incentive — a free bonus — of 1 million dollars out of our pockets to further enhance the lakefront and offset part of our higher fee!" She instructs her team to give each of the potential clients the realistic 1 million dollar bill. That spectacular presentation with her unexpected, over-the-top finale clinches the deal.

Although many presentation coaches warn against communicating important incentives at the end of a presentation, Lori's risk-taking pays off, and her team's innovative presentation captivates the audience, giving the 11th-hour unveiling a stronger psychological buying effect with positive results.

Engineering Your Conclusion with Building Blocks

Putting together a well-structured and well-delivered ending amplifies and confirms the excellence of your entire presentation. You can construct a memorable, impressive, send-them-forth-marching conclusion by connecting building block components in various combinations, just like those we suggest for building introductions, as covered in Chapter 3.

REMEMBER

Together, your creative introductions and conclusions are critical in developing and delivering the ultimate innovative presentation. Use the building blocks we suggest, but don't stop there. Use your imagination to come up with something new, unique, maybe even bold and daring. Your conclusion — the last thing they heard — is the first thing they'll remember.

Depending on your presentation's purpose and goals, select and combine these building blocks into an effective conclusion that matches your compelling introduction. Start building your conclusion with these components and then add anything that your imagination cooks up:

1. Theme

2. Quotation

3. Challenge

4. Executive summary

5. Humor

6. News reference (publication, website, or broadcast media)

7. Remarkable or startling facts or statistics

8. Thought-provoking questions

9. Multimedia (video, audio, photo, illustration, animation)

10. Story or anecdote

11. Call to action

The next sections provide several examples of how to connect these building blocks in various combinations to construct a conclusion that adds to the overall excellence of your presentation and elicits the results you want.

Ending with motivation and inspiration

This scenario includes building blocks to pump people up about a challenging situation. A management consultant specializing in innovation and change gives a presentation to managers and professionals on how to best navigate and deal with a big change initiative in their organization. The presenter finishes her summary and now wants to leave the audience with a sense of control, power, and optimism.

She uses two quotations and leverages a metaphor as part of her stirring conclusion, combining three building blocks in this scripted example:

>> **#1, Theme:** "Throughout this project and this presentation, we highlight our theme of victory. It is not contrived or artificial, but a genuine rallying cry to turn this company around 180 degrees — to steer that ship hard to starboard, so we can not only save jobs and security here but also give each of our careers an opportunity to grow and prosper in the most effective ways."

>> **#2, Quotation:** "Attitude, optimism, and a drive to win — in spite of the odds and obstacles facing us — are everything when confronted with a tough challenge, as we have here. Muhammad Ali told one opponent, 'If you even dream of beating me, you'd better wake up and apologize.' We need that kind of confidence and bravado to keep us going when the going seems stopped. We must have an unbeatable attitude and drive to succeed and win!"

>> **#3, Challenge:** "This fine company's CEO and board of directors have committed abundant resources and continuous support to help you turn our ship around and head full speed toward destinations that are full of promise, opportunity, and prosperity for all of us. My challenge to each of you is to look forward to the voyage. Though there will be some choppy and rough seas ahead, hold the helm steady and sure and don't let up or give up for one moment. I challenge you to show your best and be your best during this transformational voyage in which we are setting sail."

>> **#2, Quotation:** "Many of you who have been here for a decade or more have told me that you're worried. That's understandable. Sometimes a situation, though, is at its best when it is shaken and stirred. I will leave you with what I think is a truly profound thought that should sustain us. Anne Morrow Lindbergh, the wife of famed aviator Charles Lindbergh, was herself an aviator and author and one who experienced numerous difficulties and tragedy in her life. She waxed philosophic as she noted, 'Only in growth, reform, and change, paradoxically enough, is true security to be found.' Let's keep that always in mind!"

Advocating a new strategic approach and direction

Organizations must constantly adapt to meet new trends, discoveries, threats, and to take advantage of emerging opportunities. The scenario here is about a vice president of a large research and development group in a Fortune 100 company. He gave an hour-long presentation to a group of over 100 division presidents and senior executives from worldwide locations. He followed the guideline of keeping his summary points between three and five but decided to give adequate detail in the summary to meet his goals of convincing the executives to endorse his new, visionary plan. Here are the building blocks the VP used in his conclusion. But first, his transition statement: "Now it's time for me to wrap up my presentation and summarize."

» **#4, Executive summary:** "Unprecedented, groundbreaking innovations in material science are happening at breakneck speeds and the trends, implications, and consequences will significantly affect our company. I want to leave you with three defining points:

- **Expect radical change.** Nanotechnology, micro-ceramics, and exotic multi-material alloys will dramatically change what we build, process, and use in chemistry, engineering, energy, medicine, travel, environment, space exploration, and literally, every single industry. It will effect the most minute aspects of life and business as we know it.

- **We are positioned for success in that change.** Our company is in an enviable position to leverage the 234 patents we have developed in the last two years to not only take advantage of this change and to master it, but also to lead that change, while both creating and riding the tidal wave for many years to come.

- **We are ready to capitalize on enormous opportunities.** The bold plan that my team created and that I discussed today is meticulously researched, developed, and analyzed in ways to minimize risk, maximize gain, and have an extraordinarily high probability of reaching the estimated goals of revenue increase of $65 billion to $75 billion over five years, annual returns on investment of between 25 to 30 percent, and impressive industry market share gains of at least 8 percentage points.

  For those extremely critical three points, our company is perfectly positioned to be the leader in a monumental way in a monumentally important industry."

» **#6, News reference:** "Coincidentally, in this month's issue of *Advanced Materials Engineering Journal,* in an article titled, 'The Coming Revolution of Exotic Ceramics, Polymers, and Nanotubes,' 20 prestigious university research center directors in America, Europe, and Asia cited how expanded investments in research in precisely the areas in which we have been successfully creating breakthroughs will create sustained massive returns and exploding exponential growth in new, evolving markets."

» **#7, Remarkable or startling facts or statistics:** "During my presentation, I gave you many eye-opening financial figures and statistics to prove and justify what I will ask of this group in a moment. But I saved this rather shocking projection for last: The International Association of Materials Scientists has conservatively projected the worldwide market for commercializing the quantum-leap material innovations we and others are working on to be over $7 trillion in US dollars by 2030. That's trillion, not billion, which is an amazing 10 percent of the world's estimated gross domestic product! That financial value would be larger than the combined worldwide industries of aerospace, computers, electronics, energy, automotive, communications, and construction. The scope of this opportunity is almost unimaginable!"

» **#11, Call to action:** "Because each of you here today is a leader in one of our international business divisions in your country or geographic area, I'm asking you for two important things: One: To strongly support the commercialization of our advanced exotic materials innovations. By support, I specifically mean to convey what we are doing with your new product designers, your operations managers, and your sales and marketing professionals. Another way to support these plans is to start thinking of specific budgets for new products based on our patents. Two: I ask you to take about 15 minutes and fill out a questionnaire. Your answers will be included in my upcoming presentation to our board of directors."

» **#2, Quotation with ending statement:** "I want to thank you for your previous support and dedication, and for your insights on how our company can dominate this new business space. We look forward to your ongoing support, which is so vital to us. It was journalist and author George Will who said, 'The future has a way of arriving unannounced.' Not if we can help it. We intend to loudly trumpet our entry in science and business history!"

Giving the audience a happy ending

Conrad J., president of a national animal rescue organization, gives a fund-raising presentation. His gripping talk shows heart-wrenching photos and disturbing stories of neglected and abused dogs, cats, and other animals. The stories, as expected, melt the hearts of potential donors. The president of the rescue organization wants to end in a special way that shows appreciation for the donors, gives hope and happy endings to many of these wonderful creatures, and leaves his audience ready to donate again. He briefly summarizes his key points and communicates his specific request for making a commitment to generous donations (his call to action) with the following conclusion building blocks:

» **#10, Story or anecdote with music:** Conrad tells stories about the animals, but saves the best one for last. Here is a condensed version of that emotional, heart-tugging tale. Conrad's team selects a moving piece of music to play softly in the background as a subliminal complement to the following anecdote: "Remember the sad story and photos of Pookie, the beautiful Golden Labrador that was literally a day away from death's door? Well, a wonderful family of five from The Woodlands, Texas, adopted him for their

9-year old son, Danny. You see, Danny is autistic. He has numerous communication problems, which limit his social interactions with other children. He demonstrates no interest in playing or showing enjoyment, regardless of the activity.

His heartbroken parents tried everything with no success until [pause] they brought Pookie home from one of our shelters. Sweet Pookie bonded immediately with Danny. It was love at first lick for Danny, too. Pookie is now Danny's most beloved friend, and they do everything together — they're inseparable. Here's a photo of Danny with Pookie (who embraces Danny as he sleeps). This child, once trapped inside himself, is now free as never before! He talks fluently and takes the initiative for social interactions. He laughs, he hugs, he even tells jokes — all because of Pookie. All because you cared to save this beautiful soul of a dog, who saved the life of Danny. This is a genuine miracle that no medicine, no doctor, and no treatment could fix. With your continued donations, we are aggressively expanding this program and many others to bring two-legged and four-legged hearts together!"

Luckily there were boxes of tissues on the tables, because there wasn't a dry eye in the hotel ballroom.

» **#9, Multimedia:** "I can't express enough gratitude for the incredible support you have given and will continue to give to these needy or suffering animals who so deserve a good, healthy, happy, fulfilled life because they give us so much unconditional love, caring, and joy. I know it was uncomfortable and painful seeing the pictures and hearing the stories about Pookie (the dog), Samantha (the cat), Trumble (the horse), and Shadow (the dog). But because of your kindness, I will end showing the photos and short videos of the incredible transformation that results from our caring and our loving. These pictures and 30-second videos are the proof and the thanks they give to you." With that, Conrad concludes with a fast-paced, dynamic, 3-minute multimedia show with 30 photos and 4 videos showing the happy, well-nourished, playful animals running, jumping, and delighting in their renewed vigor and life. This time, the background music is lively and joyful, ending with a close-up photo of Pookie — along with a big, enthusiastic bark from him with the words below, "Thanks to you!"

For this type of happy ending finale, no words alone could have expressed the wonderful work that the rescue shelter provides for these beloved creatures as well as the heartwarming visuals and music does.

Offering an informational conclusion

Many business, technical, or scientific presentations are designed to simply provide information. That information might be about a product or service, a new process, a management technique, a scientific discovery, or anything that the audience may benefit from knowing about. In this example, a consultant gives an extended two-hour presentation to a group of doctors and other medical personnel on new software applications and diagnostic tools to better deal with radical changes in healthcare processes and laws at a medical conference workshop. This ending of this presentation consists of a crisp, concise summary, several thought-provoking questions, a bit of humor, and a different type of call to action. Notice how the presenter uses repetition to emphasize key points right to the finish line.

>> **#4, Executive summary:** "Over the last two hours, we discussed four software applications for your computers, tablets, and smartphones. Keep in mind these four important points:

- One, these applications will make your practice more efficient and profitable.

- Two, we've had the finest firms rigorously test and exhaustively check and certify these apps as error free! (This veiled reference to the problems with the Affordable Care Act website got some laughs.)

- Three, transitioning to these new processes and procedures is much easier and quicker than previous applications — an average of 65 percent quicker.

- Four, these apps are designed to boost the productivity, effectiveness, and quality of all your administrative processing operations. But most importantly, they will give you great peace of mind by better dealing with the myriad of challenging and otherwise frustrating healthcare changes now and in the future."

>> **#5, Humor:** Leaving people with brief humor that makes a definite point can be a nice addition to a conclusion. Here the consultant uses an amusing concise story to set the stage for the next building block of thought-provoking questions. "Oftentimes it pays to get a quick and sure head start on a situation — like this one — that could spiral out of control if you wait too long. It's like the story of the patient who told his doctor that he was thinking of getting a vasectomy. The conscientious physician asked, 'That's a big decision. Have you discussed it with your wife and children?' The patient shot back with a straight face, 'Absolutely! We took a vote and they're in favor 16 to 2.'"

>> **#8, Thought-provoking questions:** These set the stage for the call to action as a result of providing the comprehensive information during the two hours. "So to get that quick start, you may now be asking yourselves these questions:

- What are the next steps to take to begin implementation?

- How will I know that the app is running successfully?

- What's the ideal way to train myself and personnel without disrupting our patients and practice?

- Where do I go to get immediate help in the future?"

» **#11, Call to action:** Instead of asking the group for something in an information-giving presentation, you leave them with some thoughts on how best to use that information in their work or personal lives, as this example shows: "The very next step to take is to pick up a package that consists of several brochures, a typical implementation plan, and a set of instructions and resources to truly make implementation of your apps easy. The packets are on tables on your way out. You will definitely know if your implementation of these apps is successful simply by using them and seeing the results. It's that simple! As far as training, we have a proven plan for that in the handouts along with links to our extensive online courses, where each session lasts only 15 minutes. For help 24 hours a day, we have answers to typical questions on our website, in addition to a live online chat capability with one of our specialists. If you need further assistance, we have the unthinkable: a real live person you can contact via phone or Skype. So, please capitalize upon these great resources to get started. I'm also available after the presentation to answer any questions you have right now. I'll be here as long as there are people who want to talk with me."

» **#2, Quotation:** "As all of you well know, these major healthcare changes can be perplexing, upsetting, and time consuming. As Albert Einstein noted though, 'In the middle of difficulty lies opportunity.' That's exactly what these software apps are — opportunity. Take full advantage of them. I enjoyed being with you over these two hours, and I wish you great success in using these powerful applications to ensure that your practice runs smoothly, efficiently, and profitably!"

7
Negotiation

Contents at a Glance

CHAPTER 1: **Negotiating for Life** 535

When Am I Negotiating? 535

The Six Basic Skills of Negotiating 536

Handling All Sorts of Negotiations 543

CHAPTER 2: **Knowing What You Want** 547

Creating Your Vision 548

Deciding How You Are Going to Achieve Your Vision 555

Preparing Yourself for Negotiation 559

Defining Your Space 563

CHAPTER 3: **Setting Goals** 567

Setting a Good Goal 568

Separating Long-Range Goals from Short-Range Goals 574

Setting the Opening Offer 574

Breaking the Stone Tablet 575

CHAPTER 4: **Asking the Right Questions** 577

Tickle It Out: The Art of Coaxing Out Information 577

Asking Good Questions: A Real Power Tool 580

Dealing with Unacceptable Responses 590

Look for Evidence of Listening 591

CHAPTER 5: **Closing the Deal** 593

Good Deals, Bad Deals, and Win-Win Negotiating 594

Concessions versus Conditions 599

What It Means to Close a Deal 601

Understanding the Letter of the Law 602

Recognizing When to Close 604

Knowing How to Close 605

Barriers to Closing 609

Closing When It's All in the Family 613

When the Deal Is Done 614

Chapter **1**

Negotiating for Life

Negotiating is not a skill to take out once in a while when you have to make a deal. Negotiating is a way to get what you want out of life. You negotiate all day long, whether it's with your co-workers, your spouse, or your kids.

No matter how large or small, how important or minor, how near or far, a negotiation involves six basic skills. After you understand how you can use these skills in a negotiation, you'll use them every time you sit down at the negotiating table.

Even if your dreams or your paycheck seem to hinge on forces beyond your control, you can create a master plan for your life and achieve your dreams — one negotiation at a time.

When Am I Negotiating?

Any time you ask someone to say yes or to do something for you or to get out of the way so you can do it, you're negotiating. You negotiate all the time, whether you realize it or not. You're negotiating when you

>> Ask your boss for a salary increase.

>> Ask the cable guy for a more specific time to show up at your house.

- » Try to hurry up the cable guy when he is late.

- » Decide to marry (part of a lifelong negotiation).

- » Try to enforce a curfew with your kids.

Negotiating occurs in all aspects of life. It happens in your personal life (marriage, divorce, and parenting), in business, in government, and among nations. For example, the United States was in heated negotiations with the Untied Nations council to revise a U.N. resolution on North Korea for conducting a nuclear test. So a negotiation can be on a global scale or on a personal scale, such as "Honey, please put the seat down."

If you're attempting to resolve a dispute, agree on a course of action, or bargain for individual advantage, you're in a negotiation, like it or not. The goal is to reach a resolution that is acceptable to you and that will work for both parties.

The Six Basic Skills of Negotiating

The skills you need to be a successful negotiator in your everyday life are the same skills powerful businesspeople use during major international and industrial negotiations. Sure, you can refine these skills with additional techniques and strategies, and you'll enhance them with your own style and personality. But only these six skills are essential:

- » Thorough preparation

- » The ability to set limits and goals

- » Good listening skills

- » Clarity of communication

- » Knowing how and when to push your pause button

- » Knowing how to close a deal

These six skills are so important that you should should have them on a chart on your wall, just as every chemistry lab has the Periodic Table of the Elements hanging on the wall.

The six basic negotiating skills apply to all areas of life. They can empower you to be happier and more successful in your life by helping you gain more respect, reach better agreements with your business partners and family, and maintain more control in your negotiations.

Preparing

Preparation is the bedrock of negotiation success. You can't be overprepared for a negotiation. Whether you're involved in a business negotiation or a personal negotiation, you must be thoroughly prepared to achieve your goals. Heck, you have to be well prepared just to know what your goals are.

In any negotiation, you must prepare in three areas:

>> Yourself

>> The other person

>> The market

Each one of these aspects deserves your attention. Pay special attention to the first point because you're the most important person in the room. The second item will change as your negotiations change. The third point deserves your lifelong attention.

Prepare yourself

Preparing yourself for a negotiation means knowing yourself and what you want out of life. This step takes some reflection and some planning. With adequate preparation, you boost your confidence and your performance during a negotiation. Know your strengths and weaknesses. For example, are you a good listener, or do you ignore what other people have to say?

What is your life plan? In a perfect world, what will you be doing in three years? This long-range thinking about your own life provides a context for every negotiation you have. After you create a vision of your future, create a plan that includes specific steps to turn your vision into reality. Your negotiations are likely to go astray if you don't prepare your personal, long-range game plan *before* entering the negotiating room. Chapter 2 in this minibook helps you figure out your vision and develop steps to achieve what you want in life.

You also have to prepare yourself for specific negotiating situations. The better you know your own needs, the more easily you can do this. For example, if you're not a morning person, don't let someone schedule a conference call for 7:30 in the morning. For more strategies on making the most of time and places in a negotiation, check out this minibook's Chapter 2.

Prepare for the other person

When you find out who you'll be sitting across from at the negotiating table, research that person. Knowing about the other person can help you build rapport, and you can walk into a room with the comfort and knowledge of having some background on your opponent. One of the most common instances where you should do some research on other person is before a job interview. Perhaps you and your interviewer share a similar past experience. When you show that you know a fact or two about the other person, you usually score points with the interviewer. In a negotiation, showing that you've prepared for the other person also serves as an icebreaker before getting down to the nitty-gritty.

Besides these obvious social benefits, knowledge about the other person lets you know what you're up against. Is this person reasonable? Is this person a bottom-line person, or is quality more important to him or her? Knowing what the other person values helps you emphasize that aspect of your proposal.

It is also important to determine the person's level of authority. If the person is going to have to get approval from folks several rungs up the organizational ladder, you know you'd better provide some written materials or your proposal probably won't be repeated accurately.

Prepare about the marketplace

Research your industry. It's as simple as that. A car dealer knows cars. A chemist knows chemistry. An art dealer knows art. If you're going to negotiate in a world that isn't familiar to you, research it. Know the players, know whom to talk to, and study the terminology. Do whatever it takes to be the smartest guy or gal in the room.

You should definitely have your personal evaluation of everything being negotiated. You should also have a good idea of how the other party values whatever is being negotiated. Don't be afraid to ask questions. You can even ask such questions of the person you're negotiating with. Asking questions shows the other party that you're interested and willing to learn.

Be a constant student of the industry or business in which you work. People who have a spent a lifetime with a company bring added value to the company simply because of their knowledge. The more you know about the business environment in general and your company in particular, the better off you are.

Setting goals and limits

The only way to achieve anything is to set goals. Sometimes your goal setting can be subconscious. This triggers the impulse purchase. You see something you want, you set your goal to acquire it, your hand goes out, you grab it, and it's yours. That is a familiar retail scenario. In the business situation, setting goals is a more serious, labor-intensive process.

When setting goals, you need to have a brainstorming session in which all the possibilities are explored for any given negotiation. Then you pare your list so you have a manageable number of goals to work on. You don't want to overload any single negotiation with all your hopes and dreams for all times. Go into a negotiation with an appropriate list of things to achieve. Chapter 3 in this minibook walks you through this process.

The easiest and fastest way to keep your goals in mind is to write them down. This helps you visualize them and makes them real. Place them somewhere where you will see them on a daily basis. After you've written down your goals, ask yourself why your goals mean so much to you. Goals are led by your inner desires. Let your intuition guide you toward achieving them.

Before starting your next negotiation, ask yourself this simple question: "What do I want out of this negotiation?" Don't be afraid to answer it. Talk it out. Write it down.

After you've nailed down your goals, you need to set limits. Setting your limits simply means to determine the point at which you're willing to walk away from this deal and close the deal elsewhere. For instance, you set limits when you interview for a job by establishing the lowest salary you'll accept.

Setting limits is a scary thing. It takes practice for some people, but if you don't do it, others will take and take and take as long as you keep giving. At some point, you realize that you have given too much — a line has been crossed — all because you did not set your limits.

Listening

The vast majority of people think they are good listeners. Instead of gratifying your ego with self-indulgent reassurance, figure out if you're a good listener. Find out the true state of your listening skills from objective evidence or from those who will be brutally honest with you.

Learning to listen is one of the most important skills to develop when negotiating. Before a negotiation, know the specific areas where you want to gather information. Listen attentively during the meeting. Get the most information you can, and you will have a successful negotiation.

Check your bad listening habits at the door. Always expect to find *something* of value from the other person. The rewards of good listening skills are amazing.

Here are some tips for becoming a good listener:

>> Clear away the clutter in your office.

>> Count to three before responding to a question so that the question (or comment) can sink in.

>> Keep notes.

>> Be sure that you're fully awake and present.

WARNING

If you experience communication problems during a negotiation, it's probably because you or the other party weren't listening.

Part of the listening process involves interaction between the two parties. Don't be afraid to ask questions as you gather your information. When you ask questions, you refine the information you have received from the other party. Questions are a real power tool, and are covered in detail in Chapter 4 in this minibook. If you don't get the information you want to receive, ask a follow-up question. And never, ever interrupt someone who is trying to answer a question you've asked.

Whatever you do, don't accept any substitutes for the information you're seeking. Some folks will try to dodge a question or make a strong general statement instead of answering your specific question. If someone responds to your question without answering it, ask it a little differently, but don't let the other person off the hook.

Being clear

When we say that you should be clear, we mean be clear in what you say and what you do. This sounds easier than it is. You must be sure that your actions, body language, tone of voice, and words all send the same message.

Are you as clear as you can be in your communications? You can rate yourself or ask those you love and trust. A good negotiator is an excellent communicator and understands how others think, feel, and function. But first, you must start by analyzing yourself.

THE SIX NEGOTIATING SKILLS IN ONE FILM

Dog Day Afternoon is probably the best single film on negotiating that you can watch. Millions have seen a young Al Pacino and Charles Durning turn in virtuoso performances as captor and cop in this classic film. Based on the true story of a bank robbery that turned into a hostage situation, the film shows the local police team trying hard to resolve the situation but fumbling a bit. Then the FBI team moves quickly into action and negotiates with skill and training. The events were re-created with incredible accuracy.

Each of the six basic principles of negotiating is clearly demonstrated in this film. Here is a friendly guide through the negotiation without ruining the film.

- **Prepare.** You'll notice right away that the robbers are unprepared for the hostage situation. They came to rob a bank, not to take hostages. In fact, one of the team members bails out immediately in a comic lesson about the importance of building a solid team that is fully prepared. Note how the police immediately and throughout the film try to gather information about the man holding the hostages. They use all the resources of the state to find out who they are negotiating against. Within hours, the cops find out things that shocked the man's mother and his wife.

- **Set goals and limits.** The police set limits before they ever start talking. Their goal is to get the hostages out safely. When a hostage is hurt, they find out how the injury happened. If it was an accident, they continue the negotiation. If it was an execution, they make a frontal assault on the site. Through it all, they never forget their goal, even though they appear willing to do so as far as the captors know.

- **Listen and clarify communications.** This is a constant. Note in the barbershop that someone is always in the background wearing headphones. That officer is monitoring all communications both ways to be sure that they are clear. He does not speak, but he is an integral member of the negotiating team. Also note the body language of the FBI agent when he first meets Pacino's character. The agent, unlike the local policemen, conveys authority and confidence.

- **Push the pause button.** The police have a firm hold on the pause button. One officer's sole job is to observe everyone's emotional state. This officer keeps a check on emotions and removes officers before the strain of the situation overcomes them.

- **Close.** The authorities keep the goal constantly in mind. Notice how many times the police try to close this negotiation.

You can watch this film more than once. Each time, you'll notice something new about the way the skills in this book apply to this type of high-stakes negotiation. It is fun to note something new with each viewing. *Dog Day Afternoon* is so instructive that it is shown at the FBI training school for hostage negotiators in Quantico, Virginia.

To be clear, know your purpose in speaking and cut the mumbo-jumbo. Keep all your commitments. If you say that you're going to get back to someone at 10 a.m., be sure that you get back to him or her at 10 a.m. In the rush of the workday, we often shortchange ourselves and others on clarity. When you say one thing and do another, you may confuse people. Good communicators are consistent communicators.

When you become sensitive to being clear, you can start helping others. You can tactfully bring people back to the point of the conversation and subtly curb the interrupters. When you meet people who are unprepared, you can educate them and bring them up to speed.

As you master the six skills, you model them for others on your team and often to those on the other side of the table. And the negotiation goes all the better for it.

Pushing the pause button

We all have a *pause button* — a little device inside our heads that helps us maintain emotional distance in a negotiation. Some use it more than others. Others don't use it all. The pause button can take many forms — it can be a break during a heated negotiation, or it can be a moment of silence when you don't agree with someone's argument.

When you use your pause button during a negotiation, you prevent yourself from saying things you may later regret. Your pause button also allows you a moment of reflection. When you don't use your pause button, you may jump into a deal too quickly because you didn't spend enough time thinking about your words and actions.

Never let your emotions take control of your actions. Figure out in advance what sets you off. Identify your hot buttons. When you know what upsets you, talk about it with others on your team so you and they are ready if this kind of situation arises. We all have hot buttons, so we may as well deal with them upfront.

If a negotiation looks to be headed south and talks are at a standstill, don't panic. Use your pause button. Think about the steps that got you to this point. Instead of making outlandish demands or angrily storming out of the negotiating room, take a breather and suggest meeting at a later time.

Closing the deal

Sometimes deals don't seem to close even when the parties are more or less in agreement on all the important issues. This situation might happen because someone in the room is being difficult. Maybe the person is being a bully or trying to pull the wool over your eyes. Maybe someone is disrupting the proceedings by yelling or being bossy. Pushing past these problems involves pushing the pause button — hard. Take breaks as often as necessary so everyone has a chance to regroup. You're not the only person in the room who is affected by these people.

Sometime deals get hung up because of the other side's tactics. You probably can list them as well as anyone: a constant change of position, playing good cop/bad cop, having to check with an invisible partner. When you run into one of these behaviors, push the pause button. When you're on a break, analyze your opponent's tactics, and when you return to the negotiating table, ask specific questions of the other side. Listen carefully to get around the obstruction.

Closing is the culmination of the negotiation process, which we focus on in Chapter 5 in this minibook. It's the point where everything comes together, when two parties mutually agree on the terms of the deal. But how soon is too soon to close? The answer: It's never too soon to close. You want to start closing as quickly and efficiently as possible — under reasonable parameters, of course. You don't have to close the whole deal right away. You can close a piece of it by agreeing tentatively and moving on to other issues.

Closing the deal isn't always a smooth process. Sometimes you're dealing with someone who fears making a bad deal or is afraid of his or her boss, who never likes a result no matter how good it is and how hard everyone worked. Again, ask a lot of questions to find out what is going on, and then help this person with his or her problem.

REMEMBER

A good negotiator is often just someone who helps the other side understand all the good points of his or her proposal and gives the other person the tools and arguments to sell the proposal to whoever needs to be sold.

Handling All Sorts of Negotiations

You can apply the six basic skills to every negotiation, no matter what. But some of the negotiations you'll encounter may seem beyond the scope of these skills. Trust me, they aren't. You simply have to remain focused on the six skills.

Negotiating is like tennis. You have to serve the ball whether you're playing a rank amateur or in the finals at Wimbledon. Like the backhand and forehand shots in tennis, your negotiating skills stay with you no matter what court you're on or who your opponent is.

Negotiations can become complex for any number of reasons, and male-female negotiations often have an element of complexity. And as the world seems to grow smaller and move faster, you're likely to face international negotiations and negotiations that take place over the telephone and Internet.

When negotiations get complicated

In simple negotiations, you can apply the six basic skills without too much trouble. But what happens when a negotiation gets complicated? Complex negotiations happen when the negotiation becomes larger in scope, and the amount of work and organization requires more than two people (one on each side of the negotiating table) can handle alone. When the negotiation shifts from a 2-person affair to a 20-person affair, the negotiation is complicated. On a personal level, a negotiation becomes complicated when you invest all your emotion and effort into getting the deal closed. For example, a salary negotiation, although simple in theory, carries a lot of emotional weight behind it.

REMEMBER

No matter the size and factors involved in the negotiation, the six basic skills serve as your core to making the negotiation a success.

International negotiations

International negotiation (or cross-cultural negotiation) is one of many specialized areas in the world of negotiating. The six basic skills are just as critical, if not more critical, in international negotiations as they are when you're negotiating on home turf. International deals require more preparation because you have to tailor your negotiating approach to the customs of the country you're negotiating in.

Preparing for cross-cultural negotiating requires more than just understanding how foreigners close a deal. You have to know the differences in communication, their attitude toward conflict, how they complete tasks, their decision making processes, and how they disclose information. Even the body language in other countries is different from what we're accustomed to in the United States. Eye contact, personal space, and touch vary among countries.

TIP

Research the country's traditions before walking into a negotiating room on foreign soil. Watch foreign language films, read travel guides, and learn key phrases in your counterpart's language during the preparation process. Bridge the communication gap as much as possible. When you start behaving like a native, you'll earn the respect and confidence of your foreign counterpart.

Negotiations between men and women

Communication between the sexes is much different now than it was during our grandparents' time. For one, women are now leaders in large businesses and politics, two worlds once dominated solely by men. As we begin the twenty-first century, the communication gap between men and women has slowly narrowed but fundamental differences still separate the two sexes.

Negotiation on the phone and via the Internet

We're riding on the information superhighway and never looking back.

The landscape of communication has changed dramatically, thanks to the telephone and the Internet. These forms of telecommunication have made communication faster and sometimes simpler. More importantly, they've created a new mode of negotiating. You can now negotiate from the comfort of your own home, in a car while driving to your office, or from a different part of the world.

Negotiating via the telephone and Internet requires the same preparation and etiquette as a face-to-face negotiation. The only difference is that the negotiation happens at the lift of a headset or the push of a button. Although simpler, using the telephone or Internet to negotiate is not as good as negotiating in person. You miss the human interaction, the body language, and the gestures that are so important in gauging others when negotiating in a room.

GIVING PEOPLE TOOLS TO ENHANCE THEIR LIVES

Good negotiating skills translate into good working relationships with employees, clients, vendors, and customers. The ever-challenging task of managing people entails delegating tasks, which means empowering people to get results for which you're ultimately responsible. Managers engage in these negotiations every day. All of us must negotiate in one way or another.

Negotiate fairly and appropriately. You can get what you need and want, and build relationships in the process. You may have to risk upsetting someone for the moment. You may have to risk not being liked by everyone all the time. That comes with achieving results. You always have to choose between comfortable safety and risking discomfort to go for what you want.

Negotiating for Life

Chapter **2**

Knowing What You Want

I f the most important negotiating skill is preparation, the most important thing to prepare is yourself. You must know what you want and don't want in your business and personal life to effectively complete every negotiation you encounter. Negotiating is not a skill you take out once in a while when you have to make a deal. Negotiating is a way to get what you want out of life. Many people blame a lack of negotiating skills for not getting what they want, but that's only part of the answer.

People must also do some long-range thinking about their own lives. When you think about the direction your life is headed, you can see the big picture. Without the big picture, you run the risk of getting involved in a negotiation that doesn't contribute one bit to where you want to be in three or four years. That's a recipe for obtaining a result that makes you unhappy — not because you didn't negotiate well, but because the result doesn't move you along in the direction you want to go.

To use your negotiating skills most effectively, you require a master plan. Think of the *master plan* as a strategy for achieving your hopes and dreams. Everyone should have a master plan; it gives you a choice about where you are on the train of life. You can either sit in the engine driving the train, or you can hang on for dear life off the back of the caboose.

Several steps, large and small, can help you take charge of *all* the negotiations you face in your life. Even if you currently think that you could never take control of certain areas of your life, challenge yourself to entertain the possibility. Consider actors, who do a great deal of waiting. Think of some employees who regard their roles as reactive and not proactive, whose job descriptions entail responding to someone else's needs. The fact that your dreams or your paycheck seem to hinge on forces beyond your control shouldn't stop you from creating a master plan for your life. Create a vision statement and an action plan.

After you have the big picture well in hand, you need to prepare physically and mentally for specific negotiations. This chapter helps with the tasks that are so important for each negotiation that awaits you.

Creating Your Vision

Most corporations and businesses have a mission or vision statement. The US Army's adage is "Be all that you can be." Employers often distribute their statement to employees at every level. They post it on their websites, display it on prominent bulletin boards, and print it in various company publications. Every employee is expected to know this statement. Ask those same employees whether they have a vision statement for their own lives and careers, and far too often the answer is no.

If you want to have the best personal life and a successful career, you need to think about your goals. The good life, no matter how you define it, doesn't just happen. You need to set an agenda for both your short- and long-term goals. Think of your life as a negotiation. The better prepared you are, the smoother the negotiation is likely to go. Even a little planning is more than most people do, so making a small effort now puts you far ahead of the pack.

The first step in creating a master plan for yourself is to identify your vision. A *vision* is an image of a desired future. The word *vision* is from the Latin *videre*, meaning to see. You should state your vision by describing, in present tense, a picture of the future you see for yourself. Your vision should be as rich in detail and as visual as possible. The description must be clear, understandable, and descriptive. Most important, your vision needs to motivate you. You count on your vision to give your life shape and direction.

Here are some vision statements:

>> **Nordstrom:** "To become America's store of choice through the commitment of each employee to provide customers the very best in quality, value, selection, and service."

>> **Microsoft:** "Someday we'll see a computer on every desk and in every home."

>> **A law office:** "To help my clients realize their dreams."

>> **A young businessperson:** "To climb up the corporate ladder in an honest and professional way."

In his book *Think and Grow Rich* (Simon & Brown), Napoleon Hill states that 98 percent of people are in their current jobs because of *indecision* — they never decided what they wanted to do in their lives in the first place. That failure to form a vision of what the future looks like explains why so many people feel that they may have a life purpose, but they have no idea what that life purpose is. Forget about the money; this is just an unfortunate way to spend your life.

REMEMBER

It's important to go through the process of evaluating your vision statement each year. You can assess your vision verbally or in writing, but keeping a written record creates better accountability.

Your vision is a long-term, ongoing, open-ended process. When you read your vision statement, it motivates you to passionately seek to achieve your goals.

Envisioning your future

People who write down their vision of the future are much more likely to live in that dream world someday. The first step to help you think about and achieve your dreams is to write them down. This handy guide is provided to make it easy for you to do that. Sit down by yourself or with your spouse or partner and quietly start to picture your future.

When you picture your future, don't be bound up by your past or what other people tell you or the negatives that have been fed to you over time. You have to think long and deep and wide. You have to think outside the box.

In fact, the puzzle that gave rise to the phrase "think outside the box" is one of our favorites. Here it is. Place nine dots on a sheet of paper (three rows of three dots). Without lifting your pencil, draw four straight, connected lines through all nine dots. Give it a try in Figure 2-1.

Go through each dot once. Keep at it. If you get frustrated, relax and let your imagination flow. Think outside the box. Play with it. The answer is at the end of this section.

Think outside the box as you answer the following questions. They will help you create your ideal picture of the future, so try not to be bound by the constraints of convention. Just as you did in solving the above puzzle, relax and let your imagination flow.

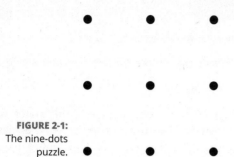

FIGURE 2-1:
The nine-dots
puzzle.

After you have constructed this vision with a good deal of specificity, you are on your way. Every negotiation will be conducted with your own long-range goals in mind. Every decision you make will take this vision into account.

What are you good at?

_____

_____

_____

_____

What positive things have other people said about you? What have they thanked you for?

_____

_____

_____

_____

What would you like to achieve in the next three to five years?

_____

_____

_____

_____

What do you want to avoid?

_____

_____

_____

_____

What do you look forward to doing when you have enough time? (Let your imagination really soar on this one.)

Hobbies:

_____

_____

Volunteer work:

_____

_____

Learning:

_____

_____

Career:

_____

_____

Spirituality:

_____

_____

Where do you see yourself living?

_____

_____

What do you want your legacy to be? What do you want to pass on to others?

Family:

_____

_____

Charities or causes:

_____

_____

Spirituality:

_____

_____

Community:

_____

_____

How do your answers to the preceding questions translate in the marketplace?

_____

_____

_____

_____

What would your ideal day look like if you could structure it your way?

_____

_____

_____

_____

Are you willing to make a commitment?

_____

_____

The preceding list of questions leads you to your vision statement. With luck and enough quiet time, you can develop a clear concept of your future. Then you'll be able to commit to your own future. Creating your vision statement requires you to think outside the box, as they say.

Looking at Figure 2-2, you can easily see why solving this puzzle is called "thinking outside the box." Now when someone tells you to think "outside the box" or "beyond the nine dots," you'll know where the phrase comes from. Take the exercise one step further. How can you cover all nine dots with a single straight line?

Answer: Use a paintbrush!

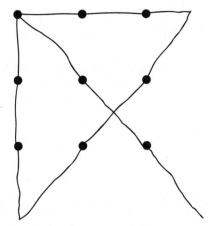

FIGURE 2-2:
The solution to
the nine-dots
puzzle.

TIP

If you really want a vision statement that fits you personally, use the same kind of mindset in creating your vision as you do in solving puzzles and riddles such as this one. Be open to all the alternatives. Don't limit your thinking to the obvious answers. Enjoy exploring all the possibilities as you decide exactly what you want to achieve over the next three years.

Making a commitment

Sure, you have an idea of what a *commitment* is: a binding obligation, a pledge, or a promise. But do you really know how to make and keep a commitment?

People *want* to commit, but they lack the stuff to carry through with that desire. For example, people who say they want to be thin may really *want* to be thin. However, they don't exercise, and they keep eating too much of the wrong things. They don't want to be thin badly enough to commit to the steps they need to follow to *get* thin. The truth is, they *wish* that they wanted to be thin badly enough to *commit* to it. The first step is to commit. You must be so committed to your vision that you will do the hard work necessary to get where you want to go.

Look at what you wrote in the previous exercise (in the section called "Creating Your Vision"). Now write the purpose you see for your life. This is your vision statement. Make sure that what you write inspires you.

_____
_____

_____
_____

UPPING THE STAKES

Here's a harsh definition of commitment: If you don't achieve your objective, someone will cut off your hand. This definition is useful is someone starts blaming others for something when, in fact, the problem would be solved by a little higher commitment from the person doing the complaining.

For instance, Jen insisted that she had done *all* the right things, and the "other guy" was consistently late on a report due to her every Thursday by 5 p.m. The "other guy," in this case, was a co-worker in another department of her company, and she depended on his information. When asked what she did about the late report, she said, "Well, I call him Friday morning and chastise him for not turning in the report." She was someone who prefers to have reasons for *not* getting a job done rather than doing whatever it takes to get it done.

That's when someone stated the definition of commitment and asked her, "What if your hand is cut off at 5:01 on Thursday if you don't have the report from him?" Her demeanor changed. The good solutions flew fast and furious. "I might tell him that the report was due Wednesday. Not only would I tell him it was due Wednesday, but I would probably be a lot nicer to him. I would probably want to know who was in charge of the material for his report in case he died before 5 on Thursday. I would visit his office, ask about his kids, and make sure that the material for my report is in a fireproof filing cabinet."

If the stakes are high enough, you will change your behavior, even if it means taking extra steps — that's commitment. Even with the people who seem most impossible, you can get what you want if you are committed to getting results.

Now evaluate your vision statement:

What are the key words for you?

_____

_____

_____

_____

Do you really own this statement? If not, change it.

_____

_____

_____

_____

How does it strike your senses? If it's not quite bull's-eye, change it.

_____

_____

_____

_____

Keep adjusting your vision statement until you're satisfied. Revisit this chapter in one year. How has your vision changed?

_____

_____

_____

_____

Identifying your values

Your *values* are the principles and standards you live by. They define how you regard others and how you expect to behave toward the people with whom you interact. Figuratively speaking, values define both where you want to go and how you expect to travel.

Values also define your *limits:* the boundaries of behavior you will not cross and that you will not allow others to cross in their dealings with you. The clearer you are with your values, the more you understand what you cherish. Then, making choices about your goals becomes easier. To be a good negotiator, you must be able to look into your own eyes in the mirror *every* morning and know you're living up to your own standards. Values, goals, and limits are tightly connected to each other.

Deciding How You Are Going to Achieve Your Vision

Having a vision and knowing your values are great, but you need to know how you're going to get where you want to go. You have to set a path for yourself so you can eventually live in the picture you've created for yourself.

Note how values come into play in the business world. Small and large companies are specific when translating their missions into action. Think of the *values* (those things treated with importance and respect) affirmed by companies such as McDonald's. The fast-food chain's mascot is a cheerful and colorful clown, and the restaurants have play areas. The food chain is fast, clean, and brightly lit. It caters to youngsters. The company demonstrates its commitment to its corporate vision and values through its action plan.

Internet service companies have also incorporated values into their business models. All major Internet services now provide parental control blockers. These devices help parents keep their children safe from websites that they consider questionable while their kids surf the Internet.

The three-year plan

To negotiate effectively, you need to know why you're engaged in the negotiation in the first place. Three-year plans are an excellent tool for planning your personal and professional life. They're brief enough to follow through on, and they're specific enough to move you toward meeting your vision.

Maybe three years from now you won't achieve everything you planned for, but if you don't give any thought to what you want to accomplish over the next three years, you don't stand a chance of attaining much of anything. Most people who aren't happy with their lives and what they've accomplished during the last five or ten years never bothered to look forward and develop a plan for that time period. Don't let that happen to you. Make a three-year plan and then make sure that your negotiations contribute to achieving that plan.

Think big

Step one in achieving great results is to think big. In every aspect of a specific negotiation and in planning your life, think big. You can always scale back later. When the next year goes by, you don't get to do it over again. So take off the ball and chain; don't let your life be shackled by small thoughts. You can never get more out of life than you choose to.

Think bold

In addition to thinking big, you need to think bold. When your vision seems distant — when the road seems all uphill — you have to be creative. Try tackling the problem in a different way to reach a solution. The *problem* of figuring out how to make your vision become a reality is really an *opportunity*.

LOOK AT THE BIG PICTURE TO FIGURE OUT THE DETAILS

At a negotiation seminar, a questioner with an annoyed look on her face raised her hand while the Keith, the speaker, was in the middle of selling the idea of a three-year plan. "I came here because I wanted to negotiate the purchase of my next car. I've been unhappy with my last two purchases. Will you be addressing *practical* things like that?"

"I just did," was the speaker's immediate response. The woman was nonplussed. "I'm sorry, I guess I missed it," she said, sounding annoyed. Suspecting she hadn't missed a word, Keith asked her what kind of car she was thinking of buying.

"I'm not sure," was her predictable reply. Keith then asked her a series of questions about her life and where it was going. He asked her how soon she was planning to retire, whether she was staying at her present job, how far she drives to work, and what community activities she was involved in.

The answers defined the cars that would fit her needs within four or five models, two or three years of manufacture, and even the fact that she needed a subdued color. She became excited and felt that she had already saved weeks of shopping and agonizing. Keith's point about reflecting on your own life before you enter a specific negotiation was so well made by this exchange that some in the audience thought that the conversation with the woman was preplanned.

She realized that her unhappiness with her previous purchases was because she had been buying cars without thinking about her own life and what she would be doing with the car. That point seems so rudimentary to most people that they don't even realize the lesson: Consider your needs so that every negotiation fits into your life in a positive way. If the negotiation doesn't fit, walk away. It's so simple. Yet people often forget that simple step. They leave themselves out of the picture and then wonder why things don't turn out better for them.

For all the horrible B films that director Edward D. Wood, Jr., produced, his bravado is worth noting. Watch Tim Burton's *Ed Wood,* starring Johnny Depp as the infamous director. Wood is consistently voted the worst director of all time. Burton's film traces Wood's undying optimism to get his films made. Studios refused to finance or distribute his films, but Wood persevered. He thought bold. He rounded up every resource possible and got his films made, despite their minuscule budgets. Ed Wood carried out his vision and transformed his goal into a reality.

Think in sound bites

Refrain from using catch words and phrases during life planning. A life plan should be more tailored and personal, and some phrases act as strong guideposts. Following are a few of my tips for life planning. Think of these phrases after you've established your vision statement and before you've designed an action plan:

>> **The tyranny of *or*:** As people make life plans, they often ask themselves whether they want this *or* that. Try to use the word *and*. The word *or* is limiting. The word *and* is expansive. Frequently, finances require that people choose between desired purchases. When you make a life plan, however, include everything you want in life. You get only one chance to live this life. Live it free of the tyranny of *or*.

>> **The banishment of *just*:** Whatever you do in life, do it well and with pride. Never again say, "I am just a housewife" or "I am just a baker" or "I am just . . ." Banish the word *just* as an adjective to describe you or your life's work. After you have established your vision, never diminish it with *just*.

>> **The law of parsimony:** Although you have times when you want to lend a helping hand to the whole world, you have limited time in *your* life. You can't help everybody. Only help the people who can *use* your help. Those are not necessarily people who *need* your help. Needy people sometimes distract you from your life purpose. Your job is to keep a steely eye on the goals you want to achieve for yourself and your family.

Putting your plan into action

After you are clear about your vision and you take steps to achieve that vision, create your action plan. Your *action plan* includes the specific tasks you need to do, whom you need to help you do them, and when you need to complete each step. Action plans make you more efficient and effective. They enable you to anticipate needs, potential problems, and the time necessary for each step. The process of creating an action plan brings to light any potential obstacles that you may encounter in completing the steps. Then you can be clear about what you need to do to overcome these obstacles.

Here's a recommendation for creating your action plan:

1. **Prioritize each goal.**

Think of your action plan like a meeting agenda. Some goals will carry more weight than others. For instance, maybe buying a house and adopting a pet are part of your three-year plan. Buying a house will probably require more planning and longer discussion than adopting a pet, so finding your new home would take a higher priority.

2. **List the action steps required for you to accomplish each goal.**

After you've prioritized your goals, determine what you need to do to carefully execute each goal. Include as many details as you can think of.

3. **Identify people you need to support you to achieve each action step.**

If it's a family-oriented goal, such as moving homes, you probably want to involve the entire family. In a business-related goal, involve those who will be an asset to the process. When taking steps to achieve a goal, time is of the essence. Don't let someone with a hidden agenda stifle your plan.

4. **Identify potential obstacles to each of the action steps.**

Pause when you identify an obstacle and figure out the best way to overcome it. Solving a problem early in the process saves you the time and hassle of dealing with a potential disaster down the road.

5. **Estimate the completion date for each of the action steps.**

Creating a timeline helps you methodically complete tasks by certain dates. Trying to achieve too much at once can often muddle the goal-setting process.

Preparing Yourself for Negotiation

You are the most important single element in this negotiation. Even if you are the most junior person in the room, your performance at the negotiation is more important to you and your future than any agenda or seating arrangement. Do not shortchange yourself. Keep your confidence up. This just may be the moment that helps you climb the executive ladder. Take a moment to check on yourself, leaving other arrangements for later. This concern for self is an important investment that pays off handsomely. This is your moment to shine (even if you must shine in silence).

A is for alert

To negotiate at your best, you must be well rested and alert. If the negotiation is early in the morning, make sure you eat breakfast. If you feel stressed, do an early-morning workout or meditate. A well-rested and stress-free mind is an alert mind. And when you are alert

» Your concentration and ability to listen improve.

» You're more likely to be quick-witted and able to respond to questions or attacks.

» You won't rush to tie things up so you can get home or get to bed.

Your performance at any negotiation is aided by a good night's sleep. Sometimes getting that sleep is easier said than done. If you find yourself thinking about a negotiation just when you want to go to sleep, try this trick: Pull out a pad and jot down your thoughts. Keep going until you've cleaned out your mind. More often than not, this simple exercise enables you to doze off and secure some much-needed sleep. If you still can't get to sleep after writing down your thoughts, at least you have a crib sheet to help your sleep-deprived mind get through the negotiating session.

Dressing for success

During the 1980s, two books had considerable effect on what people wore to get power and respect. These books, geared toward the professional, have a much wider application if you read between the lines. The first book, *Dress for Success* (P.H. Wyden) by John T. Molloy, chauvinistically addressed only men. The book's popularity led to a sequel, *The Woman's Dress for Success Book* (Warner Books). Both are valuable, if dated, aids for young executives. The theory of both books is to look like the boss.

The startling response to Molloy's books was that, all through the 1980s, droves of young female professionals began wearing dark blue suits, white silk blouses, and big red bows at the neck. Perhaps they were helping themselves up the ladder of success, but the necessity (or perceived necessity) for ambitious young women to transform their appearance to break into the good old boys' club is distressing.

Today, dress styles in the workplace vary widely depending on the type of business. In the entertainment industry, for instance, dress styles are more casual. Visit any animation studio and you will see folks dressed as if they were attending an afternoon barbeque. Clothing styles for the workplace continue to evolve. Some companies still require business attire; others don't. The point is to dress for the occasion. If you're attending an important meeting, you want to look your best to be taken seriously and to be respected.

A writer came into Jill's office to pitch a story idea. He wore a T-shirt, jeans, and flip-flops. Jill's immediate impression was one of laziness. She assumed that his pitch would be as jumbled as his attire — and she was right. The pitch wasn't well thought out. It was carefree and meandering. This is not the impression you want to give the next time you approach the negotiation table.

Don't dress to distract. You are in a negotiation. You want people to listen, and you need their eyes as well as their ears. Here are a few things to keep in mind:

>> Women, you pull the eye away from your face if you wear dangling earrings or expose cleavage.

> » Men, you improve no business environment anywhere with gold chains or a sport shirt open to reveal that remarkable chest.

If a particular type of outfit works for you on vacation or at a party, more power to you. But don't confuse those casual social environments (which may include a bit of negotiating in the course of an evening) with the negotiating environment of the business world.

Of course, every rule has an exception. See the film *Erin Brockovich* for such an example. In the film, Erin, played by Julia Roberts, is hired as a secretary at a small law firm. She dresses in short skirts, revealing blouses, and stiletto heels. Her co-workers don't take her seriously. Little do they know Erin is extremely driven and smart. Her wardrobe becomes second nature as the film progresses. She begins to investigate a suspicious real estate case involving Pacific Gas & Electric Company, which leads her to become the point person in one of the biggest class action law-suits in American history against a multibillion dollar corporation. All this despite her risqué wardrobe.

Mirror your environment as you prepare yourself for your first negotiating session. For example, don't wear a three-piece suit to a place where all the employees, including the executives, wear jeans and polo shirts to work. Respectfully absorb that which is around you. Become a part of the surroundings.

Some negotiators take this tip beyond the way they dress. For instance, some negotiators even adapt to the pace of the speech. In New York, where people tend to talk fast, good negotiators speed up their pace a bit; in the South, where people tend to talk slowly, good negotiators slow it down a few notches. Above all, know that good manners are different from place to place.

Walking through the door

No matter how sleep-deprived, harried, or down-in-the-dumps you may be, always enter the negotiating room with assertiveness. Establish confidence and control from the opening moment. That moment sets a tone for the entire meet-ing. This fact is true even if you are not officially in charge of the meeting. These guidelines can vault the most junior person at a meeting to MVP status almost immediately.

REMEMBER

Never forget the pleasantries. If the last negotiating session ended on a bad note, clear that away first. Otherwise, you run the risk that unrelated matters may ignite the controversy all over again. If you can resolve the situation up front, you can move forward unfettered. Ignoring such a situation just leaves the ill-will hovering over the negotiating table. The bad feelings creep into and influence every conver-sation. The negativity taints all the proceedings until it has been cleared away.

As your hand is on the door of the negotiating room or as you dial the phone number of your counterpart, put on your attitude. Take a beat and lift yourself up to the occasion. Grandmother was right — "Anything worth doing is worth doing well." Toss your head back — literally. Smile, inside and out. Focus on your immediate purposes. Have your right hand free to shake hands with whoever is there. If the meeting requires you to wear one of those awful name badges, be sure to write your name in large letters and place the badge high on your right side so people can easily read it.

Improving your attitude just before the session begins can be one of the most valuable moments you spend in a negotiation.

Here are some tips in case you're in charge of the meeting:

>> **Make sure that all participants are present and ready to listen.** If someone is missing, you face the first dilemma of a meeting leader: to start or not to start the meeting. Follow your gut and the culture in which you're operating. If you are always prompt and have a roomful of folks whose time is valuable (whose isn't?), proceed and educate the laggard later. If the missing person is the boss, well, again, the culture is important. Some bosses would be annoyed that you held up the meeting for them.

>> **State your purpose for having the meeting.** This is like the opening paragraph of a term paper. If there is not a written agenda, outline the important points you will discuss. Knowing what is going to happen helps keep everyone focused.

>> **If there is a written agenda, be sure everyone has one and take a moment to review it.** Put time restraints on each agenda item. Doing so keeps you from lingering on a subject longer than expected and not giving enough time to others.

>> **Make a clear request for agreement on the agenda and the procedure.** Gauge how the other party feels about your agenda. This is an important step on the road to closing a deal and is your chance to start things off with something on which everyone is in agreement.

>> **Acknowledge the participants' attitudes and feelings as they relate to your purpose.** Your objective is to close the deal. To do this, you need to establish empathy from the beginning of the meeting.

>> **Begin according to the agenda.** If you must deviate from your plan at the beginning of the meeting, you'll have a hard time gaining control later.

You've opened the meeting and presented your agenda. You've taken the first step into the negotiation process. Breathe.

Leaving enough time

Deciding how much time to allocate for a negotiation session or for the entire negotiation is always a tricky matter because you aren't in control of the other side. If you want to have the negotiation over by a certain time, say so right up front. If a good reason exists for your desire, state that also. Leaving more time than you actually need for a negotiating session is always better than allocating too little time. If you've overestimated the time, you can always use the extra time for something else.

Defining Your Space

People often spend little time considering the best environment for negotiating, or they rely on rules that make arranging a time and place difficult. For example, when both sides consider it necessary to negotiate in their own office, getting things started is impossible.

If your position is low on the corporate ladder and you feel you have no control over the details of the negotiating environment, giving this issue some consideration is even more important. For example, you may think that the location in which you negotiate for a raise may already be set. Read on. The material covered in this section can help you make even your boss's office a more-receptive negotiating environment.

Negotiating on your home turf

Your own office often provides a powerful advantage because it is your *home turf*. It's your operational base. You have all the information needed at hand. You have a support staff, should you need their expertise or assistance. Your comfort level is going to be at its highest in that environment.

The home turf is so important to the Grundig Pump Company of Fresno, California, that it built a series of guestrooms at its factory and hired staff to look after visitors. You can see the plant, negotiate a deal, and never worry about accommodations, meals, or anything else while you're in town. Grundig set up an ideal negotiating environment. The visitor is freed from the shackles of travel arrangements and home office interruptions. This setup represents the epitome of the oft-stated rule "always negotiate on your home turf."

Beware! Negotiating on your home turf is not always best. Often you're better off in the other person's office. The more time you spend on the other skills covered in this minibook, the less important it is whether you are in your office or someone else's. Sometimes meeting in the other party's office is better for you. If your opponent in a negotiation always claims to be missing some document back at the office, meeting there could avoid that particular evasion. Sometimes bulky, hard-to-transport documents are critical to a negotiation. In that event, the best site for negotiation is wherever those documents happen to be.

Visiting the other person's office always gives you information about that person. A quick glance around the office tells you a lot about the person's interests, usually something about her family situation, whether she is neat or messy, her taste in furnishings, and often, just how busy she really is. You usually can tell something about the person's place in the pecking order of the business. Is her office close to the more powerful people in the organization or far away? How much of the coveted window space does she have? The information you glean from visiting the other person's office allows you to know the person better. And the better you know and understand the other person, the easier it is for you to relate to her. You can never know too much about the person you're facing in a negotiation.

The most important consideration is to be in a place, physically and mentally, where you can listen. Be emphatic on this issue — both for your sake and for the sake of the person with whom you negotiate. If you cannot concentrate on what the other person is saying, negotiating is impossible.

Seating with purpose

Seating arrangements may seem like a silly subject if you've never thought about it before. Sometimes — but not often — the importance of seating can be over-emphasized. Definitely do not leave seating to chance, in spite of the number of people who seem willing to do so. Where you sit during a negotiation can have a big effect on how well you function during a negotiation.

Here are some seating tips:

>> **Sit next to the person with whom you need to consult quickly and privately.** This person is your confidant. You don't want that person sitting across the table and off-center, where you'll need to use hand signals and glances to communicate.

>> **Sit opposite the person with whom you have the most conflict.** For example, if you're the leader of your negotiating team, sit opposite the leader of the other negotiating team. If you want to soften the confrontational effect, you can be off-center by a chair or two. If the shape of the table or room gives

you the opportunity to be on an adjacent, rather than opposite, side to your opponent, choose that position to lessen the confrontational approach.

>> **Consider who should be closest to the door and who should be closest to the phone.** If you expect to use a speakerphone or to have people huddling outside the negotiating room, these positions can be positions of power. The person nearest the phone generally controls its use. The person nearest the door can control physical access to the room.

>> **Windows and the angle of the sun are important considerations, especially if the situation generates heat or glare.** Again, stay within your comfort zone. If the room feels physically uncomfortable, kindly suggest a different room.

Now about the negotiation of prime interest to most readers: asking for a raise. Usually that conversation takes place in your boss's office. Avoid the seat where you normally sit to receive assignments. If your boss has a conversation area, try to move there for the discussion about your raise. Sofas are great equalizers. If your boss is firmly planted behind the desk, however, do two things:

>> Stay standing for a beat or two at the beginning of your presentation, but not after you're invited to sit down. Speaking on your feet is a display of uncompromised self-confidence.

>> When you sit down, move your chair to the side of the desk — or at least out of its regular position. You want to make the statement that this is a different conversation than the normal routine of your boss assigning you a task.

TIP

Try to avoid being lower than your boss when you talk about your compensation. Whenever you can, try be on the same eye level with the person you are negotiating with, even if you normally take direction from that person.

Planning the environment far in advance

If your company is building a new space, get involved in planning the room where most of the negotiating occurs. Fight hard to make it the right size, near the restrooms, and near some areas that can be used for break-out sessions. Everyone has a tendency to cut back on the negotiating space because "we don't use it that much" or "we can make do with less."

All of this is true. However, if you consider the importance to your company of selling, negotiating, or closing a transaction, you cannot overrate the value of this space. This location is where you make money. It is where the deals are made that are at the heart of your business. Don't "do with less" in your negotiating space unless you are willing to "do with less" in your negotiation. Scale down offices if you have to, but don't scale down your negotiation space.

The next time your company designs new office space, look around at great negotiating spaces, such as the one in Figure 2-3. For less formal occasions, this space is furnished with a sofa, a love seat, and two chairs surrounding a large, low coffee table.

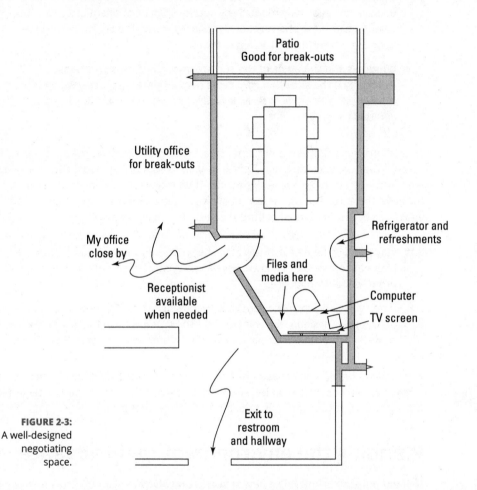

FIGURE 2-3:
A well-designed
negotiating
space.

You don't need a huge budget, but you do need to keep in mind some basic needs. A good negotiating space is more than a huge conference table with a marble top. In fact, the marble top can be too formal for most negotiations. If possible, have break-out rooms nearby, great cross ventilation, and a workstation that can be turned toward the conference area. Everything should be at your fingertips.

» **Evaluating the goals you set**

» **Making an opening offer**

» **Maintaining your goals**

Chapter **3**

Setting Goals

These words are from the song "Happy Talk" in the Rodgers and Hammerstein musical, *South Pacific.* Bloody Mary sings them to Liat and the Lieutenant just after they tell her that they've fallen in love:

You've got to have a dream.
If you don't have a dream,
how you gonna have a dream come true?

Rodgers and Hammerstein taught us a thing or two about goal setting. The entire show is about chasing after your dreams and all the wonderful things that happen when you do. The essence of this great musical is that if you don't work toward your dreams, you regret it for the rest of your life. Sometimes, your dreams — or, in negotiation terms, your *goals* — dawn on you intuitively. Other times, you discover them through more dry, rational processes.

Do you feel fulfilled in your line of business? Are you achieving what you want in life? If not, the problem may be that you're not setting goals, or perhaps your goals are too general. Setting goals — in your life and in your next negotiation — requires spending some time. Goal setting is a natural extension of proper preparation.

You may be scared to set goals (and even more fearful of writing those goals down) because you're afraid of failing. But any athlete can tell you that failure is part of winning. In baseball, if you can make it to first base in just four out of ten times at the plate, you're considered a really good hitter.

You don't have to achieve every goal you set. But if you want to grow consistently, you have to set goals for yourself and for your next negotiation. Setting tangible goals is important if you are to be successful. In specific negotiations, the process is essential.

Setting a Good Goal

Setting goals for yourself, for others, or for your organization is a practical activity that demands preparation and disciplined focus. Setting goals is not wishful thinking. It's not fantasizing. It's not daydreaming. A *goal* is any object or end that you strive to reach. For example, becoming rich and famous may be the result of achieving certain goals, but fame and fortune are not the goals themselves. Deciding to write a bestselling book is not setting a goal; it's daydreaming. Deciding to write a book that is interesting and makes solid contribution is a goal (an ambitious one, but a goal nonetheless). Research shows that individuals who set challenging, specific goals do better than those who don't.

When you set goals, you need to consider what you want to achieve. Setting specific goals gives you an overall perspective that shapes your decision-making process. Use the following lists of questions to help you brainstorm during your goal-setting session.

For business goals, ask yourself the following:

>> What level do I want to reach in my career?

>> What kind of knowledge, training, or skills will I need to reach a certain level in my career?

>> How do I want my partner or other members of the team to perceive me?

>> How much money do I want to earn? At what stage in my career do I want to earn this amount?

>> Do I want to achieve any artistic goals in my career? If so, what?

For personal goals, think about the following:

>> Do I plan on starting a family? If so, when?

>> Do I want to achieve any fitness or well-being goals? For instance, do I want to remain healthy at an old age? What steps do I need to take to achieve this goal?

>> How much time will I reserve for leisure? What hobbies do I want to pursue?

Remember, these goals are about you. You have to pamper yourself every now and then.

Once you have answered some or all of these questions, prioritize your goals in order of importance. Be sure to prioritize until you're certain that the goals reflect your business aspirations or personal aspirations or both.

Here are a few points to keep in mind when thinking about your goals:

>> **Distinguish between a goal and a purpose.** If your purpose in life is to become an Olympic champion, set all of your goals with that ultimate purpose in mind. You must take many steps along the way to becoming a champion of any kind — the training, the dedication, the discipline. Think about your purpose in life; your negotiating goals should contribute to that purpose deal by deal.

>> **Don't confuse goal setting with the process of deciding what to put forward as an opening offer.** (Opening offers are discussed in the "Setting the Opening Offer" section later in this chapter.) You must set your personal goals yourself, before a negotiation begins. Get all the information you can from others about the marketplace and the person with whom you'll be negotiating, but set your own goals. Only you know what your personal dreams are and what will make you happy. Keep a practiced eye on your goals during the course of the negotiation.

TIP

>> **Decide whether a goal is a *good* goal when you set it, not after the fact.** Sometimes people say, "Shucks, we didn't set our goal high enough." If you've ever said that, one or more of the qualities described in the following sections were absent from the goal-setting process. Each of these qualities is important. You don't have to wait until after the negotiation to find out whether your goals are well set. You can judge your goals at the moment you make them by determining whether they contain the qualities presented in the following sections.

Getting active participation from every team member

Whether you're representing someone else in a negotiation or you're part of your company's negotiating team, goal setting is a shared activity. Your first negotiation is with the other team members to be sure that the goals are realistic and understood by everyone on the team. In the entertainment industry, these types of relationships are common.

For example, the agent/writer relationship is one of the tightest relationships in the industry. Agents must know their clients' work and the type of work their writer clients seek. It's important for agents to know this to send their clients to appropriate pitch meetings that will benefit both team members. In essence, agents must know their clients' goals. There is no sense for an agent to send out his or her hot comedy writer to meet with a production company looking for the next great science-fiction project. The writer client doesn't achieve his or her goal of attaining a writing assignment. And the negotiation, or pitch meeting in this case, stalls and goes nowhere. Both agent and writer lose out.

WARNING

When assessing your team, odds are that you have someone on your team whom you would prefer to leave out of a planning session. Perhaps this person's pace is slower than yours, and you're afraid the team's work will slow down. Or the person may be cantankerous and hardly ever agrees with the group. Don't succumb to the temptation to exclude that individual. This person can end up being a stumbling block later when you're close to a decision deadline. Be sure that everyone who is a member of the negotiating team participates to the extent possible in setting the goals. Some people may not be verbal, but make sure that they're on board, even in a passive way. You need everyone to agree on the goals. That way, they are more likely to *own* the goals — and the results.

Steven Spielberg's *Munich* is an excellent example of how important it is for every team member to actively participate in goal setting. The film is set during the 1972 Olympic Games in Munich, where 11 Israeli athletes are taken hostage and murdered by a Palestinian terrorist group known as Black September. In retaliation, the Israeli government recruits five Mossad agents to track down and execute those responsible for the attack. The agents all come from different walks of life, but they share the same goal: vengeance. In the roundtable scene where the group members gather for their first dinner together, the meal starts jovially. But as the scene progresses, the conversation shifts to an intense discussion about the ramifications of their goal. Is vengeance a justifiable option? It's a divisive goal, but despite objections from some of the team members, they ultimately find common ground and proceed with their mission. Without that discussion beforehand, the mission surely would have broken down later.

Even with a personal goal that seems to be your decision alone, you can benefit from consulting with your family or friends. These people are affected by the decision. If you make your friends and family a part of the goal-setting process, they can be invaluable in helping you reach your objective. For example, if you want to write a book, your loved one can join in, if not with content, then with helpful encouragement so you don't let less important tasks get in the way. Telling another person about your goal makes it real and also puts a bit of pressure on you to keep working toward your goal.

Keeping the goals on course

Many people are frustrated at not being heard. If you ask them to participate in the goal-setting process, the list of demands may get excessive. Before long, the list of goals contains demands that are outside the particular negotiation in which you are involved. This result is especially true in workplace negotiations because frustrated employees, when asked to contribute, may feel that this is finally their chance to relieve their frustration. Allowing people with specific agendas to take your goal off course can keep you from getting what you want.

This caveat doesn't contradict the good advice in the saying, "There is no harm in asking." If your goals relate to the specific negotiation, you can choose to add an unrelated matter to the discussion. You can raise an unrelated issue appropriately, but be prepared to abandon it quickly if the reaction is too adverse. Although asking for a few extras probably won't hurt, you should be conscious that you're doing so. Be careful that you don't sabotage the primary goals you're trying to achieve in the negotiation.

Setting the right number of goals

The negotiation itself dictates the number of specific goals you should set. It's amazing how many goals some people can squeeze into even a simple negotiation. Recognize that you can't get everything accomplished in one negotiation. For example, if your priority is to get a raise, don't demand a car allowance, overtime pay, and an assistant all in the same session. By putting too much on the table at one time, you just confuse people. Your boss's eyes will glaze over, and you may not get anything at all.

You want to be realistic about your goal setting. Setting too many goals in a negotiation can make you look ignorant and naive. To combat this situation, walk into the negotiation with a written schematic of your goals. Stay on course with what is written on the page.

Conversely, you don't want to set goals too low. Setting very low goals is as detrimental to a negotiation as setting unrealistically high goals. Setting low goals signals weakness and indifference during a negotiation. The other party will see right through you. You should set goals that are slightly out of your grasp, but not so far that you can't achieve them.

Setting specific rather than general goals

Your goals shouldn't be so abstract that no one — including you — can tell whether you achieved them. To avoid any ambiguity, quantify your goals as much as possible.

If you're selling your home, for example, saying, "I want as much as I can get" is not a good goal. This is probably a true statement, but it doesn't help you achieve anything. A well-stated goal for the price portion of the negotiation must include an exact amount, such as $525,000. If you can't be that specific, you'd better prepare some more.

Along the same line, you can't buy a house listed for $800,000 if your income goal is only $60,000. This kind of contradictory goal will sabotage all the work you put into achieving your goal. You should strive to rid yourself of contradictory goals at every step of the goal-setting process.

Setting challenging yet attainable goals

It is absolutely certain that you never achieve more than your goals. Experiments testing this thesis have shown it to be true. Surprise! At the same time, you must ground your goals in the real world; otherwise you're just daydreaming.

If you're asking $525,000 for your house, and no house in your neighborhood has ever sold for that amount, you'd better have some good reasons for setting your goal that high. Maybe you're in a rising real estate market. Maybe your house is larger or noticeably nicer than any other house in the neighborhood. Maybe a state-of-the-art shopping center is under construction nearby, making your location more desirable than ever before. Any of these factors make a record-breaking price for your home attainable. Without special factors like these, you're wasting your time by starting with such a high goal.

Likewise, you want to be sure that the $525,000 is challenging. If every house on the block sells for $525,000, that price isn't much of a goal — unless your house is noticeably more run-down than the others (in which case, you may want to consider some landscaping or painting first). You may have to do some research to find ways to justify asking a higher price than the others in the neighborhood.

If you find out that major construction is planned for the near future, for example, you can make that part of your sales pitch.

REMEMBER

Too many of us suffer from setting our goals too low. Shoot high or not at all — you can be sure that the other side will never ask you to raise your goals. But remember that you don't have to become rich and famous before breakfast. Goals that are *too* high for the deal lead to frustration and failed negotiations. For the negotiation at hand, consider the marketplace, current values, and your available options.

You can quickly see that setting a challenging yet attainable goal requires that you have a good deal of information — information you always need before you start negotiating. Setting your goals is one way you know whether you're prepared for your next negotiation.

Think of that big thermometer the United Way puts up before every fund-raising drive. The number at the top of the thermometer represents a figure generally a little higher than the previous year, but not too much higher. A better economy, more members participating in the fund-raising drive, or a special event (such as building a new recreation center) justifies an increased amount. As group members raise money, they fill the outline of the thermometer with red paint to show exactly what has been contributed. Whether the organization reaches its goal or not, the thermometer looks very red at the end of the campaign, and those who contributed feel good.

Prioritizing your goals

Be sure to rank your goals in terms of importance. Ideally, you want to achieve 100 percent consensus about the official ranking of your goals. However, different individuals may hold onto their personal agendas. In those cases, let the majority prevail and note explicitly the view of the minority. By making special note of the minority view at the beginning, you record it for the duration. Later, you can allow the repeat discussion, but remind the advocates of the minority view that they were outvoted.

In any negotiation, you rarely achieve all your goals. You must know which goals are the most important. This decision can become contentious. Teams often abandon the critical step of prioritizing in the name of keeping the peace. Unfortunately, such teams only defer the argument to a later time — and probably a worse time, such as the following:

>> When the team needs to hang together

>> When not enough time exists to deal with a side issue

>> When the stakes in the outcome seem higher because they are more immediate

>> When a distraction from negotiating is the most damaging

What a disaster! Bite the bullet and get the team together on this important issue when you settle upon the list of goals.

Separating Long-Range Goals from Short-Range Goals

Set your goals for any particular negotiation with an eye on your long-range life goals, but keep your feet planted firmly on the ground. You want to accomplish the immediate objective of the current negotiation; you also want each negotiation to advance you toward achieving your ultimate life goals. Your goals in any negotiation should help you march along the life path you've set for yourself.

Setting the Opening Offer

The *opening offer* is the first specific statement of what you're looking for in a negotiation. After you've set your goals for the negotiation, you can consider the opening offer. For example, in a job interview, the opening offer is the salary you're seeking. Don't look for any hard-and-fast rules or magic formulas. To determine your opening offer, you should draw heavily on the goals and limits you set and the information you've gathered while preparing for the negotiation.

Your opening offer should be higher than the goals you've set for yourself. But it shouldn't be so outrageously high as to be off-putting to the other side or make you look foolish or inexperienced. Figure 3-1 depicts this relationship graphically.

Whether the amount you state in your opening offer is higher or lower than the amount of your goal depends on whether you're the buyer or the seller (you determine how much higher or lower through good preparation):

>> If you're the seller, your opening offer should never be lower than the goal you set.

>> If you're the buyer, the opening offer should never be higher than the goal you set.

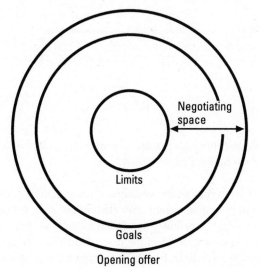

FIGURE 3-1:
The relationship among your goals, limits, and opening offer.

People are quite anxious about the opening offer. They're fearful that they will mess up the entire negotiation by blurting out a demand that is too modest or too ambitious. State your opening offer positively and precisely. You want the ability to measure your achievement. Use your anxiety level as a measure of how well prepared you are. Part of being well prepared is knowing relative values. If you know the value of what you're offering, the opening offer is easy to deduce. You just decide how much negotiating room you want to leave yourself.

TIP

Have your opening offer in mind even if you don't plan to state it openly. This approach speeds your reaction time to whatever offer the other side makes.

Breaking the Stone Tablet

Write down your goals but don't chisel them in stone. Goals can and should change throughout the course of your life. Use your written goals as a road map to your success. Writing them down sets the process in motion and allows you to frequently review your goals.

During a negotiation, you should state your goals as just that. If you state your goal as a take-it-or-leave-it demand, you create a terrible dynamic.

Remember these keys:

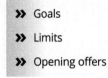

- » Goals
- » Limits
- » Opening offers

If you keep these three concepts separate in your mind, your negotiations begin — and end — on a much happier note.

Even if you never change your goals, you should review them just before you close the deal. Then look at your goals again after closing the deal. If they were too high, or maybe not high enough, consider what information you didn't have before you set your goals that caused you to miss the mark. Don't kick yourself if you decide that your goals should have been higher. Remember the reasons for making the deal you made and learn from the experience.

Chapter 4

Asking the Right Questions

How you ask questions during a negotiation is important because questions open the door to knowledge — knowledge about the other party and knowledge about the negotiation at hand. Questions are the keys to the kingdom. No one ever wasted time asking a smart question.

This chapter covers the art of effective questioning during a negotiation. Asking appropriate questions, knowing when to ask those questions, and knowing when *not* to ask those questions are all techniques you should master. They will lead you to a path of negotiating success. And even if a negotiation is at a standstill, knowing how to ask the right questions creates a discussion between you and the other party. That can lead to positive results if your information is funneled wisely.

Tickle It Out: The Art of Coaxing Out Information

Effective listening requires probing. No one says everything you want to hear in the exact order, depth, and detail that you prefer. You have to ask. No phrase describes the job of questioning better than *tickle it out.* Questions are a way of coaxing out information that you want or need.

In a trial, the question-and-answer format rules the proceedings. Attorneys and the judge can talk to each other in declarative sentences, but all the testimony is presented in the somewhat artificial format of question-and-answer. In court, the purpose of every question should be to obtain specific information. If the question isn't answered directly, it needs to be asked in another way. The rules in the courtroom are specific; as a matter of etiquette, you should apply similar rules in a business meeting. For example, courtesy prohibits you from barraging the other side with rapid-fire questions; court rules prevent the same thing.

Developing the ability to ask good questions is a lifelong effort. If you have the opportunity to observe a trial, notice that the primary difference between the experienced attorney and the less-experienced attorney is the ability of the former to ask the right question at the right time. Almost without fail, the key question is not a bombastic, confrontational inquiry, but a simple, easy-to-understand question designed to extract specific information.

An excellent example of tickling it out occurred in the O. J. Simpson murder trial during the questioning of police officer Mark Fuhrman. Lengthy, soft-spoken questions led up to the simple query, "In the last ten years, have you used the 'n' word?" "No," the officer replied. "Are you sure?" the attorney asked. "Yes, sir," Mark Fuhrman responded. There were no fireworks, no victory dances at that point, but the quiet exchange permanently altered the trial. Because Fuhrman's statement wasn't true, the defense was able to call witness after witness to impeach his testimony. Eventually, the truth about Fuhrman's behavior smashed against that statement so explosively that every other piece of evidence was damaged. Fuhrman and all his co-workers were hurt by those brief words so gently tickled out during questioning.

Remember *Columbo?* The famous detective, performed so consistently by Peter Falk, perfectly demonstrates the key skill of a good negotiator: asking really good questions. You will find Columbo using every type of question and listening to the answer. No single source better demonstrates how to ask questions. You can learn much more from Columbo. Study the man. Let him be your mentor as he entertains you. He also has incredible integrity. He sets his goal and never wavers. His steely determination brings victory in the toughest of circumstances.

Battling the jargon

Don't be shy or embarrassed about asking someone to clarify a statement. Many people use jargon or shorthand when they talk, so you can't always be sure of what they mean.

However, the situation is slightly more difficult when you're both in the same industry. You may feel embarrassed to ask for the meaning under that circumstance, because you think that you *should* know. You can handle this situation by saying, "Just to be sure that we're using our shorthand in the same way, tell me exactly how you define XYZ." When the other person gives you his or her definition, use it. Here are three useful responses when the other party defines a term for you:

>> "That's great! We use that phrase the same way."

>> "Glad I asked; we use that phrase a little differently, but we can go with your definition."

>> "Thanks, I just learned something new."

If you really think the other person is miles off the target and some real damage may be done if you use the word his or her way instead of your way, say: "We should define that term in the written agreement so others won't get confused. You and I know what we are talking about, but we want to be sure that everyone else does, too." Don't get into a battle over definitions.

There's another situation in which you may run into jargon. Some people, particularly doctors, lawyers, and accountants, use jargon to impress others with their knowledge, power, or position.

TIP

As often as not, they use this device on their own clients. Use the preceding techniques to get clear on the conversation. If the problem is chronic, look for another professional to serve your needs.

Clarifying relativity

Requiring others to define relative words is just as important as asking them to explain specific pieces of jargon. *Relative words* are nonspecific, descriptive words that only have meaning in relation to something else.

Here are some examples of relative words that can create a great deal of confusion:

>> Cheap

>> High quality

>> Large

>> Many

>> Soon

>> Substantial

Don't be shy about asking for clarification when someone lays one of these words on you. If the person insists on using generalities, as some people do, press for a range. If you still don't get a specific answer, supply two or three ranges and force the person to choose one.

Let's say your new customer says, "We're thinking of placing a big order with you." That's good news if you and your new customer both use the words "big order" the same way. But you need to ask for specifics. If your customer doesn't answer with a number, you can say, "Do you mean more like ten, or maybe about a hundred, or would it be closer to a thousand?" Whatever the answer is, just say "thank you." Don't belabor the point that you wouldn't call that a "big order." You should make a note of the information, as well.

These situations offer a great opportunity to find out more about the company that you're dealing with. It's a good time to ask questions about the normal size of the orders from this company, why it's changing now, and other pieces of information that will help you service this client much better.

Asking Good Questions: A Real Power Tool

When you listen attentively, you make an incredible discovery. Sometimes, the person is not delivering the information you need. The chief tool of the good listener is a good question. Questions are marvelous tools for stimulating, drawing out, and guiding communication.

Asking a good question is a learned skill requiring years of training. The foundation of good question-asking is knowing what information you want to obtain. Here are seven handy guidelines for asking better questions — questions that are likely to get to the meat of things:

>> **Plan your questions.** Prepare what you're going to ask about, but don't memorize the exact wording; otherwise, you'll sound artificial. A script is too restrictive to flow naturally into the conversation. However, it pays to outline your purpose and a sequence of related questions. If you plan, you can follow the speaker's train of thought and harvest much more information. Pretty soon, the speaker is comfortably divulging information. The question-and-answer format can act as an aid to good communication rather than a block.

>> **Ask with a purpose.** Every question you ask should have one of two basic purposes: to get facts or to get opinions (see Table 4-1 for examples of each). Know which is your goal and go for it, but don't confuse the two concepts.

>> **Tailor your question to your listener.** Relate questions to the listener's frame of reference and background. If the listener is a farmer, use farming examples. If the listener is your teenager, make references to school life, dating, or other areas that will hit home. Be sure to use words and phrases the listener understands. Don't try to dazzle your 5-year-old with your vast vocabulary or slip computer jargon in on your technologically handicapped, unenlightened boss.

>> **Follow general questions with more specific ones.** These specific inquiries, called *follow-up questions,* generally get you past the fluff and into more of the meat-and-potatoes information. This progression is also the way that most people think, so you are leading them down a natural path.

Never doubt how effective the follow-up question can be. It's so powerful that most presidents of the US do not allow reporters to ask them. Pay attention during the next White House news conference. Usually, one reporter asks one question, and then the president calls on the next reporter to avoid a follow-up question from the first reporter. The follow-up question is the one that ferrets out the facts.

>> **Keep questions short and clear — cover only one subject.** Again, this tip helps you shape your questioning technique to the way the mind works. People have to process your question. This is no time to show off. Ask simple questions. Questions are just a way to lead people into telling you what you want to know. If you want to know two different things, ask two different questions. You're the one who wants the information; you're the one who should do the work. Crafting short questions takes more energy, but the effort is worth it. Pretty soon, the other party is talking to you about the subject, and you can drop the questioning all together.

>> **Make transitions between their answers and your questions.** Listen to the answer to your first question. Use something in the answer to frame your next question. Even if this takes you off the path for a while, it leads to rich rewards because of the comfort level it provides to the person you are questioning. This approach also sounds more conversational and therefore less threatening. This is one reason why you should plan your questions, not memorize them.

>> **Don't interrupt; let the other person answer the question!** You're asking the questions to get answers, so it almost goes without saying that you need to stop talking and listen.

The film *The Silence of the Lambs* is an excellent example of each of the preceding elements of the question–and–answer dynamic. In one of the film's pivotal scenes, FBI agent Clarice Starling questions the sinister Dr. Hannibal Lecter in his dungeonlike holding cell. She wants clues about a serial killer on the loose. Lecter offers to provide her with clues if she provides him with stories of her past. Watch how Starling quietly listens to Lecter's questions and how she asks for the clues to help her find the killer. Both parties ask planned, direct, and tailored questions. Watch the question-and-answer scenes in the film for a lesson not only in how to ask questions but also in how to wait patiently for the answer.

TABLE 4-1

The Two Goals of Asking Questions

To Get Facts	To Get Opinions
"When did you begin work on the plan?"	"How good is this plan?"
"How many employees are available?"	"Will the schedule work?"
"What are the dimensions of the house?"	"What do you think of the design?"
"Which car reached the intersection first?"	"Who caused the accident?"

Avoid intimidation

A sharp negotiator who is trying to sell you something may try to use a series of questions to direct you to toward a specific conclusion. Each question is designed to elicit a positive response — a "yes." This sequence of questions leads to a final query posed in the same manner. When you respond in the affirmative to this final question, the negotiation is complete — and you have agreed to your counterpart's terms.

That technique may work for a *one-off negotiation*, a negotiation with someone you never plan to see again (such as when you sell a car through a newspaper ad). It doesn't work so well with people you plan to have a long-term relationship with. You want the other party to understand and be content with the outcome, not to be tricked into signing a piece of paper that he or she may regret later.

WARNING

Some people use questions to intimidate or beat up on others. Someone may ask you, "Why in the world would you want to wear a hat like that?" You may be tempted to take off the hat and use it to pummel that person. The best answer, in such cases, is often no answer. Let a few beats go by and then go on without answering or acknowledging the question. Some conduct is unworthy of your time or energy. Don't try to educate such a person on the niceties of living in a civilized society. It won't work. Keep your eye on your own goal and ignore the diversion.

LEARN FROM NEGOTIATIONS BY ASKING QUESTIONS

To profit from experience, you must be open and willing to learn, even from what some people may consider a failure. What appears to be a failure can lead to new opportunities. That is why so many companies have postmortem meetings, especially after a negotiation that did not go so well. Use open-ended questions as a starting point for the next phase of learning. Here are a few such questions:

- What went well and why?

- What went less well and why?

- What would you do differently now?

- What would you do the same way?

- What went unexpectedly well and why?

- What went unexpectedly badly and why?

- What new assumptions or rules should be made?

- What additional information would have been helpful? How could you have foreseen what happened?

- How can you improve learning in the future?

Ask, don't tell

How you ask questions is important in establishing effective communication. Effective questions open the door to knowledge and understanding. But you must be watchful that asking questions does not evolve into you *telling* the other person instead of *asking.* You have probably heard a question like, "Isn't it true that no one has ever charged that much for a widget?" or better yet, "Can you name one company that met such a deadline?" These are statements masked as questions.

You usually can detect a shift from asking to telling by the tone of voice that the person uses as he or she asks these questions. The art of questioning lies in truly wanting to acquire the information that would be contained in the answer.

Effective questioning leads to the following:

>> **Establishing rapport:** Don't try to impress others with your ideas; instead, establish rapport and trust by eliciting ideas from them and expressing how much you care about hearing their ideas. *Rapport* is the ability to understand

and to connect with others, both mentally and emotionally. It's the ability to work with people to build a climate of trust and respect. Having rapport doesn't mean that you have to agree, but that you understand where the other person is coming from. It starts with accepting the other person's point of view and his or her style of communication.

>> **Better listening, deeper understanding:** Oftentimes while you're talking, other people are not listening but thinking about what they are going to say. When you ask questions, you engage the other person. He or she is much more likely to think about what you're saying. You lead the other person in the direction you want to take the conversation.

>> **Higher motivation, better follow-up:** The right answer will not be imposed by your questions. It will be found and owned by the other person, who will be more motivated to follow it up.

Avoid leading questions

To get the most telling answers and objective information, don't ask leading questions. *Leading questions* contain the germ of the answer you seek. Here is a typical example of a leading question:

> The other person: "I have used that golf club only a couple of times."
>
> You: "How did you like the great weight and balance on that club?"

Because your question contains a glowing editorial of the golf club, the other person will have a difficult time saying anything negative about it, even if that's what he feels. A nonleading question, such as "How do you like it?" is neutral and more likely to elicit the truth. That's what you want to hear. If the other person swallows his true opinion or simply fails to express it to you because of the way you asked the question, you're the loser. The other person hasn't altered his feelings, he just hasn't expressed them. You have lost an opportunity to influence him.

Here are some more examples of leading questions:

>> "Don't you think that such-and-such is true?"

>> "Isn't $10 the usual price of this item?"

>> "Everyone agrees that this widget is best; don't you?"

If phrased in a nonleading way, these questions are more likely to extract accurate information or honest opinions. Here are the same three questions reworded:

>> "What do you think about such-and-such?"

>> "What is the usual price of this item?"

>> "Which widget do you think is best?"

Leading questions don't help you improve your listening skills or get the highest quality information. As a sales tool, however, you may *want* to lead the person to purchase an item on terms favorable to you. When you're closing a deal, the leading question may help lead the other person right to a close. In this section, you're looking at questions to ask to find out what the other party is thinking, *not* to affirm your own views or serve your own financial interests.

In court, leading questions aren't allowed. Witnesses are forced by the laws of evidence to give their own views, not to mimic what the lawyer wants. That's because in court — as in this section — the focus is to find out what factual information the witness has to offer or what honest, independent opinion the witness has formed.

Don't assume anything

We all know that the word *assume* makes an *ass* out of *u* and *me*. When people make flagrant and obvious assumptions, they tend to make a joke about it. What most people don't realize is how many times each day they make routine assumptions about the intention of the other speaker, without double-checking with that person.

Good listening requires that you don't assume anything about the intention of the speaker. This rule is especially true in conversations with family, friends, and work associates. You learn how they use words and often know their verbal shorthand. This familiarity can lead you to presume that you understand a friend's, family member's, or co-worker's point — without carefully considering what this person is saying to you. Be wary of jumping to conclusions about the speaker's intent, especially with the important inner circle of people closest to you.

Lawyers say, "Don't assume facts not in evidence." This legal principle covers a group of questions that are not allowed in a court of law. Following is the most famous example of a question that assumes a fact:

"When did you stop beating your wife?"

This question is actually a trap because the wording implies that you beat your wife in the past. This example demonstrates why such questions impede good communication. The question immediately puts someone on the defensive, and responding accurately is impossible if the underlying assumption is false. If the speaker's purpose is to draw out the truth, these three questions are more objective:

>> "Did you ever beat your wife?"

>> (If yes) "Have you stopped beating your wife?"

>> (If yes) "When did you stop beating your wife?"

In business, leading questions are often viewed as improper. At a minimum, they are challenging, which often leads to hostility. Here is an example:

"Why does your company insist on overcharging on this item?"

Now break down this question so it doesn't assume any facts not in evidence. Again, to get at the information objectively requires three questions. It also eliminates the hostility:

>> "What does your company charge for this item?"

>> "What do other companies charge for this item?"

>> "Why do you think this discrepancy in pricing exists?"

Note that in this example, you and the other person may have different pricing information. Breaking the question down into three parts offers an opportunity to clear up this difference without getting into an argument.

At home, such questions often get viewed as accusations. Because of the emotional ties, such questions can be even more off-putting than they are at work. They can launch an argument pretty quickly. Consider the following question, which assumes a fact that the other party may not agree with:

"Why won't you ever talk about it?"

This particular example shows how such a question seems to assume an unwillingness to communicate. In fact, the other party may want to talk about "it" but doesn't have the skill set, the emotional strength, or the trust to talk about a particular subject. Try breaking this question down so it contains no assumptions. Guess what — it takes three questions again. As you read these questions, play them out in your mind trying to picture the reaction of someone you're close with:

>> "Would you be willing to talk about it sometime?"

>> "What are the circumstances that would make it easy for you?"

>> "How can I help create those circumstances?"

Ask open-ended questions

Unlike simple yes-or-no questions, *open-ended questions* invite the respondent to talk — and enable you to get much more information. Use this type of question when you want to find out a person's opinion or gather some facts during a negotiation. The more you get the other person to talk, the more information you learn. Yes-or-no questions limit choices and force a decision. These types of questions are called *closed questions*.

Here is a simple closed question requiring a yes-or-no answer:

"Do you like this car?"

An open-ended question, on the other hand, encourages the person to start talking:

"What do you like best about this car?"

Try some classic open-ended questions when you need to get information. These questions invite the other party to open up and tell all:

"What happened next?"

"So how did that make you feel?"

"Tell me about that."

TIP

Note in the last example that you can ask a question in the declarative format (as a request rather than as a traditional question). That technique can be useful if you're dealing with a reluctant participant. People who won't answer questions will sometimes respond to a direct order.

REMEMBER

Open-ended questions aren't the only types of questions you can use to get people to talk. Here are some other types of questions to help get responses you need:

>> **Fact-finding question:** This question is aimed at getting information about a particular subject. "Can you tell me the story about how you decided to bring this product to the market?"

>> **Follow-up question:** You ask this type of question to get more information or to elicit an opinion. "So after you do that, what would happen next?"

>> **Feedback question:** This type of question is aimed at finding the difference that makes the difference. "May I say that back to you so I understand the difference between what you are proposing and what I was offering to do?"

Ask again

When a speaker fails to answer your question, you have two choices, depending on the situation.

>> **Stop everything until you get your answer or a clear acknowledgment that your question will not be answered.** Silence can be golden at these opportunities. Most of us are uncomfortable with silence. An individual may feel compelled to answer a difficult question if you remain silent after posing the question. "The next one who speaks loses."

>> **Bide your time and ask the question later.** If the question was worth asking in the first place, it's worth asking again.

Which of these two techniques you use depends on the situation. If the situation is fast paced and the information you requested is fundamental to decision making, use the first technique. You can choose the second technique (to bide your time) whenever you know that you'll have another opportunity to get the information, and you don't need the information right away. Biding your time is always easier and less confrontational, but if you really need a piece of data, don't be afraid to say, "Wait, I need to know . . ."

TIP

A good way to handle someone who doesn't answer your question is to make a little joke out of the situation with a statement such as, "You're leaving me in the dust," or "I need to catch up." No matter how serious the subject matter of the negotiation, a little humor never hurts, especially if you don't spare yourself as a subject of that humor.

If the person makes a little joke back to avoid the question, you may have to shift back to a serious mode. Persevere until you either get an answer to your question or realize that you must go elsewhere. If the other party isn't going to answer your question, make a note of that fact so you remember to use other resources to get the answer you need.

Use your asks wisely

REMEMBER

If you're lucky, the opposing side will answer most of your questions before you ask them. That's why you shouldn't spew out your questions like a machine gun. Have patience. Ask only essential questions. If you don't care about the answer, don't ask. You're granted only so many *asks* in any conversation, so don't use them indiscriminately.

Every child learns the futility of repeating the question, "Are we there yet?" At a negotiating table, you may never "get there" if you have overstepped the asking line. The consequences: The listener becomes oversensitive to your probing, which often translates into resistance to answering your queries. When someone becomes resistant in one area, he or she will be resistant in other areas and, therefore, unreceptive to your general position. That's a high price to pay for asking too many questions.

TIP

To become a good questioner, take some time after a negotiating session to think about the questions you asked. Identify the extraneous questions. Remember that every question should serve a purpose. You're not looking for damage that was done in that particular negotiation; you're evaluating the quality of the questions.

Accept no substitutes

You are listening. You are asking all the right questions at the right time. You are patient. So why aren't you getting the information you need? One of the following possibilities may exist:

» **The person simply doesn't understand your questions.** You might try rephrasing your questions.

» **The person simply doesn't want to answer your questions.** Maybe company policy prevents disclosure of the information. Maybe the person feels uncomfortable discussing a particular subject matter. If you believe this is true, make a note and find out the information elsewhere.

» **The person is not good at answering questions.** The avoidance is not deliberate or devious. Because of bad habits, sloppiness, or laziness, the person neglects to respond to your inquiry. Keep probing.

» **The person doesn't know the answer and is uncomfortable in saying so.** If you suspect this, ask if the other person needs time to research the answer.

» **The person is a pathological liar.** In this case, run. Never negotiate with a liar — you can't win.

Asking the Right Questions

In each of these cases, the result is the same. You're not getting a valuable piece of information. Take the suggested possibilities to get the information you need. Don't give up.

Dealing with Unacceptable Responses

This section discusses techniques people use to avoid providing accurate answers. Do not allow these ploys. When you're alert to these substitutes for honest information, you can demand the real McCoy.

Don't tolerate the dodge

Politicians, as a group, seem specially trained to provide anything but an answer when asked a question. It's almost as though there is some secret college for Congress members where they go to learn about the artful dodge. Just tune into the Sunday morning shows that feature our elected representatives. For example, if someone asks about the state of public education, the representative may launch into a dissertation about family values. It's odd how many interviewers let elected officials get away with avoiding questions Sunday after Sunday.

You don't have to do that. Don't accept the dodge when you ask a question. Recognize this tactic for what it is and repeat the question, this time insisting on a real answer or an exact time when you can expect an answer.

When people say that they have to look into something and get back to you, about the only thing you can do (without making a rather obvious and frontal assault on their honesty) is wait. However, you *can* nail them down to a specific date and time that they will "get back to you." If the question is important enough for the other side to delay (or not answer at all), the issue is important enough for you to press forward. Asking, "When can I expect an answer from you?" is a direct way of obtaining that information. Be sure to make a note of the reply.

Don't accept an assertion for the answer

A person who doesn't want to answer your question may try instead to emphatically state something close to what you're looking for. This technique is common when you're asking for a commitment that the other party doesn't want to make.

Sometimes, an assertion about the past is substituted for an answer about the future. For example, you ask whether a company plans to spend $50,000 on advertising in the next year. You receive an emphatic statement that the company has spent $50,000 each year for the past four years, that sales are rising, and that any company would be a fool to cut back now. Don't settle for such assertions — push for an answer. Say something like "Does that mean that your company has made a final commitment to spend $50,000 for advertising this year?"

REMEMBER

Because assertions are sometimes delivered with a great deal of energy or passion, you may feel awkward insisting on the answer to your question. Not persisting with the inquiry can be fatal to your interests.

Don't allow too many pronouns

Beware the deadly pronoun: *he, she, they,* and the power-gilded *we.* Pronouns can send you into a quagmire of misunderstanding. During a negotiation, force your counterpart to use specific nouns and proper names. This preventive measure avoids a great deal of miscommunication.

With pronouns, you must guess which "they" or which "we" the speaker is talking about. Don't guess. Just throw up your hands and say, with humor, "Too many pronouns." We have never met anyone who begrudged our taking the time to clarify this issue. More often than not, the request is greeted with a chuckle. The potential for confusion is obvious, and everyone appreciates the effort to maintain clarity.

Look for Evidence of Listening

As you listen to the other party in a negotiation, be alert to the occasional indicators that the other person is not really listening to you. If the other person says something like "uh-huh" or "that's interesting," find out immediately whether this response is an expression of genuine interest, a way of postponing discussion, or — equally fatal to communication — a signal that he or she is fighting the dreaded doze monster. Those little demons that tug at the eyelids in the middle of the afternoon cause odd, nonspecific utterances to fall from the lips.

If you suspect the latter, ask a probing question or two to ferret out the truth. Asking, "'Uh-huh' yes you agree, or just 'Uh-huh' you heard me?" is a good way to flush out the noncommittal uh-huh.

When someone says "That's interesting," find out exactly what makes it interesting. Don't be afraid to keep things lively. This approach is much better than having the conversation die right there at the negotiating table.

TIP

If you decide that, indeed, your conversational partner is simply not listening, take a break. Often, a quick stretch or, in a more serious case of the afternoon slumps, a walk around the block will revive you. If a distraction is causing the lagging interest in what you're saying, deal with it. Discuss the preoccupying problem or have the distracted party make that critical call.

Chapter **5**

Closing the Deal

This chapter is about the glory moment when it all comes together — when you close the deal. It's also about closing the deal in a way that makes both sides feel good about the outcome. Both sides should feel as though they've achieved something that is workable and that everyone involved in carrying out the deal will want to make work.

Closing a deal is seldom a single moment with crashing cymbals and loud drum rolls. Typically, closing a deal is a process of reaching agreement on one point after another, adjusting back and forth. Let's face it, the first piece of closing a deal is when two people — who may be far apart in their thinking — sit down and say, "What the heck, we're far apart, but let's at least try to make a deal." The next point of agreement might be that those 10,000 widgets have to be delivered within four months. (Ah, you're right; there are two points of agreement there.) As the discussion progresses the number of widgets may change or the delivery date may change, but slowly a complete agreement is reached.

So the work is more like Michelangelo sculpting a statue of David than David Copperfield pulling a rabbit out of a hat. Yes, sculpting or crafting an agreement, not magic, is the right image. Reaching sound agreements doesn't involve magic but does require hard work, a lot of imagination, and a willingness to let the agreement reach the size and shape that it needs to be instead of trying to force it into some pre-existing notion of what should be.

Most people think of closing the deal as the only satisfactory resolution of a negotiation. However, it's critical to figure out *whether* the deal should close and, if so, how to close it to ensure smooth performance throughout the life of the agreement. This chapter covers the skills and techniques of closing the deal so that it will last.

Closing is a skill that you must develop separately — and keep in mind every step of the way — if you are to become a successful negotiator. We all know people who don't seem to care whether they ever close the deals they are working on. They are delightful at dinner parties. They can be frustrating at the negotiating table. Don't be one of those people. Use your closing skills from the first moment of the negotiation.

Good Deals, Bad Deals, and Win-Win Negotiating

Finding a *win-win solution*, a deal in which both sides are satisfied, is difficult if you don't even know when your own team is winning. You can't believe how many people can't tell the difference between a good deal and a bad deal. More often than not, the person forgot why the deal was made in the first place, or the other party breached the agreement. That situation should never be the case if you use this book:

>> A *good deal* is one that is fair under all circumstances at the time the agreement is made. It provides for various contingencies before problems arise. A good deal is workable in the real world.

What is and isn't fair is subjective. The parties must decide for themselves whether an agreement is fair based on their own criteria. Make sure that everyone is in agreement. Draw the other side out on this basic point before closing the deal. You don't want to sign a deal with someone who is harboring resentments over some aspect of the agreement. Be sure that the other side agrees that the deal is a good one.

>> A *bad deal* is not fair under all the circumstances. It allows foreseeable events to create problems in the relationship after the deal is struck. Some aspect of the agreement looks great on paper but simply doesn't work out in the real world — for reasons that were predictable during the deal-making process.

Each party should assess whether the deal is good or bad. You determine whether a deal is good or bad for you; the other party determines whether that same deal is good or bad for him or her.

Assessing the deal

To be sure that you have a good deal and a win-win situation, take a break just before closing. Ask yourself the following questions:

>> Do you know whom you are dealing with and why he or she wants to make this deal with you?

>> Based on all the information, can the other side perform the agreement to your expectations?

>> Does this agreement further your personal long-range goals? Does the outcome of the negotiation fit into your own vision statement?

>> Does this agreement fall comfortably within the goals and the limits you set for this particular negotiation?

>> Are the people on both sides who have to carry out the agreement fully informed and ready to do whatever it takes to make the deal work?

In the ideal situation, the answer to all these questions is a resounding "Yes!" If you are unsure about any one of them, take some extra time and push your pause button. Review the entire situation. Assess how the agreement could be changed to create a yes answer to each question. Try your best to make the change needed to get a firm yes to each question.

When you have a yes response to each of the preceding questions, close the deal. Don't go for any more changes even if you think that the other person wouldn't mind — you never know! When it's time to close a deal, close it.

Justify your decision to yourself

If you can't alter the deal so that you can answer yes to each question in the preceding section, be thoughtful before closing. If you decide to go forward, write down exactly why you are closing the deal anyway. For example, you may have a project or piece of property that no one wants except the person you are talking to right now. Your choice is to wait a long time because your prospects have declined or accept this deal with its less-favorable terms. Your choice.

Just write down why you are making the choice so you don't become part of that army of people with tales of exploitation. This exercise is particularly helpful to your state of mind if the results don't work out — you have a record as to why you took the deal and you won't be so hard on yourself.

Get more information

If you have a question about the answer to any of the first three questions, get more information either from the other side or from another source. Ask people who may know about the other person. You would be amazed at how much people like to talk when you ask for an opinion and wait. Ask open-ended questions that seek a true opinion, not a leading question that may invite approval without yielding the information that you need. For instance, don't say, "Isn't it great that I am about to close a deal with Joe?" Rather, ask, "Do you think Joe can deliver 10,000 widgets in 60 days?"

Checking out references is one of the most overlooked resources. Many people look at a list of references, assume that the referral will be positive because otherwise the source wouldn't be on the list, and then don't check the references. You can learn a great deal from checking references, even from the most obviously biased sources. Relatives who serve as references are going to say good things, of course. But they can also provide valuable, factual information. For example, a relative may volunteer the names of other people with whom the other side has worked, reveal the other party's experience in the field, or offer information on the other side's financial strength.

If you really listen and draw the reference into a conversation, you will often get an earful when you say, "This has been great. I look forward to working with Mike. Do you have suggestions for things I should look out for to make this relationship work well?"

So check out the other side's references, but do so in a conversational manner and try to draw out facts, not salve for your ego. This often is your last opportunity to avoid a bad deal.

The people you are dealing with are more important than the paperwork you draft. Know your counterpart very well before you enter into a long-term relationship. No lawyer can protect you from a crook. Lawyers can just put you in a position to win your lawsuit. No matter how strong your case is, you don't want to be in a lawsuit. People do bad things all the time, and when they do those bad things to you, bringing a lawsuit won't make you happy to have been in business with that person. Do everything you can to stay out of business with the bad guys.

Don't backtrack

Don't risk the deal by bringing up a new point, no matter how inconsequential the idea may seem. Going back for one more little item that's not all that important may annoy the other side and threaten the entire deal. No one wants to do business with someone who wastes time trying to grab some small, additional advantage instead of closing the deal and moving on when it's time to do so. You may not be after a big point, but that point can sour the relationship if not the deal itself.

A GOOD DEAL AND A BAD DEAL IN *COLLATERAL*

The film *Collateral* is a thriller that contains both a good and a bad deal within the first half-hour of the film. It opens with Tom Cruise exchanging briefcases with a stranger in an airport. Then, intriguingly, it seems to turn into another movie. We meet Max (Jamie Foxx), a cabbie who picks up a customer named Annie (Jada Pinkett Smith). She rattles off the streets he should take to get her to downtown Los Angeles. He says he knows a faster route. They make a deal: The ride will be free if he doesn't get them downtown faster. She agrees. The lengthy scene is like a self-contained negotiation. For Max, the deal is an easy sell. He wins by getting his customer downtown faster.

After dropping Annie off, Max picks up his second customer of the night, Vincent, played by Cruise. Vincent needs a driver to spend all night with him, driving to five destinations. Vincent offers Max six crisp $100 bills as persuasion, and Max agrees to the deal. Max and the audience think this is a good deal. Pause the film and decide for yourself.

The deal turns out to be a bad one. Max didn't ask the key questions. If he had, he may have learned that Vincent is a contract killer. Instead, Max figures this out when a dead body lands on his cab and he discovers Vincent's true motive. Without having clearly reviewed the offer, Max's deal gets increasingly worse at each of the five stops. Max can't turn back at this point, so he must go through with the deal or die. Max's mistake is an important lesson in assessing the deal at hand before closing.

Creating win-win deals

Some negotiations are straightforward, and the interests of each party are clear. For instance, when you're buying a car from someone who wants to sell a car, the negotiation is win-win if you find a price that works for each of you, assuming the wheels don't fall off the day after your check clears. In more complicated negotiations, the motivations are not always so easy to find, at least not the more subtle factors that are driving the negotiation. Sometimes some head scratching and imagination are required to fully understand the interests of the other side.

Win-win is when a deal fills your needs and goals while at the same time filling the needs and goals of the other side. But your counterparts must determine their needs and be sure they are satisfied. You can't play mind reader and divine their needs and then start giving up what you want to make them happy.

Because creative thought is often necessary to arrive at win-win solutions, the best negotiators in a tight spot are people who enjoy games or riddles — people who enjoy figuring things out. This is not to say that the only good negotiators are those with a Sudoku puzzle lying around the house. But it does help if you enjoy the challenge of figuring out what serves both sides.

A sample problem

As a follow-up to the discussion about thinking creatively, this section presents a negotiating problem. This problem is adapted from a story from the Middle East that dates back to the seventh century:

> A wise Arab left 19 camels to his three sons. To the oldest, he left half of his camels. To the middle son, he left a third. To the youngest, he left a sixth. Unfortunately, 19 does not divide by any of the fractions that dear old dad mentioned in his will.

> The three sons quarreled long into the night. (*Quarreling* is unartful negotiating.) One wanted to own the camels communally. One wanted to sell the camels and split the profit. One just wanted to go to sleep. Finally, they consulted with the wise woman of the village. What did she tell them?

Before reading any further, pick up a pencil and try to come up with a solution. Play the role of the wise woman of the village. Go ahead and take a moment to do that now.

If you don't reach a conclusion, here is a hint: This wise woman is smart enough to know that she ought to charge these three lads for solving their problem. Maybe she had attended some ancient law school.

WIN-WIN NEGOTIATING MYTHS

Often, people use the phrase *win-win negotiating* to justify caring too much and too early about a counterpart's feelings and sacrificing their own needs and goals on the altar of conciliation.

No book or informed advocate promotes giving up or subordinating your goals in the name of taking care of the other person. Always assume that two equal adults are in the negotiation — unless of course, you are negotiating with a child. Then you really want to hang on to your objectives. Let the child set the agenda, and you lose before you ever begin.

If you are one of those people who think win-win means skipping over any of the steps in this minibook, now is the time to adjust your thinking. Use all your negotiating skills for every deal you negotiate. Pursue your dreams with passion and with respect for others. There are no shortcuts.

The solution

The wise woman told the three young men to give her one camel as a fee, and the payment would solve the problem. Then she wished the sons well. Each of the sons thought long and hard, and then agreed to give up the camel. This decision left them with 18 camels. The oldest son took his half of the camels (9), the middle son took his third (6), and the youngest took his sixth (3). The wise old woman, to whom they gave the 19th camel, also received their enduring gratitude. Everybody won in terms of camel ownership. But the negotiation was a real win-win because the three brothers lived happily ever after, and the wise old woman had new stature in the village.

This is a great story, but it comes with a caution: The wise woman's solution worked only because the brothers wanted to close the deal in a way that was fair among them, even if the deal meant making a substantial donation to the local shaman. If any one of them was seeking an exact, legal interpretation of the father's will, this solution was nothing more than a mathematical trick. The participants were not fooled; each son truly believed that he received his fair share.

Here, the solution was objectively sound. The answer provided fairness among the brothers, which is what they sought. But an exact division of the 19 camels, according to the father's formula, would have carved up the single camel, which went to the wise woman of the village. This deal worked because all three brothers wanted to accept the expedient solution of giving away one camel.

Note also that the brothers could have fought another night or more over which camels they each received. Or they could have argued about the crazy formula their father used or some other real or imagined affront. But instead, the brothers pushed the pause button and agreed to defer to the wise woman. She used a little sleight of hand, but she solved the problem and received legitimate compensation for her valuable services. Each of the sons got what he wanted: a good feeling about the father's will . . . and some camels. The deceased father had taught his sons one last valuable lesson. Sometimes, even substantial real-life situations are settled with such simple win-win solutions.

Concessions versus Conditions

In a negotiation, you'll make concessions and conditions, so you need to understand the difference between the two. A *concession* is when you give up a point. Don't forget to get something back for it. A *condition* is what you require to grant the concession. For instance, you might say, "I would be willing to knock 20 percent off the price as you asked, if you can guarantee an order of this size each month for the next three months." Most people think that 20 percent is a nice concession. Don't give up that big discount without getting something worthwhile in return. Make sure that the other side earns whatever concession you grant.

WIN-WIN ON THE AIRWAVES

John Kobylt and Ken Chiampou host the number-one talk show, *The John and Ken Show,* in Los Angeles during the important afternoon rush-hour drive time. They were brought to Los Angeles from New Jersey at a mere 10 percent over the minimum union scale. They were glad to take the job because of the opportunity to work in a much larger market. After two years, they thought that they had proven themselves, and they wanted a substantial increase in salary. The station manager agreed that they were well received by the listeners, but pointed out that their ratings had been up and down. The station executive thought that the team had pretty much reached a plateau in ratings. He was happy with that outcome but could do no more than double the hosts' salaries. John and Ken's negotiator was seeking much, much more.

They finally settled on a base salary with bonuses. A modest improvement in the ratings would slightly increase the bonuses. At the high ratings levels that the station didn't think were achievable, the station manager agreed to very high bonuses. When the ratings spiked upward and John and Ken beat all the competition, the station was ecstatic and did not begrudge paying the talented John and Ken much more money than they had originally requested.

Why was the station manager happy to pay more than he would have paid if he had just agreed to the initial demand? The arrangement protected the station from taking a high risk, which would have been burdensome if the team had not performed as predicted. John and Ken were happy because they earned their compensation. This was a true win-win result.

When they started the negotiation, both sides were so far apart on salary points that it seemed they would never get together. Even as the bonus concept was put on the table as an approach, they remained far apart. The negotiation was a struggle. The answer came when the bonus structure changed to small increases at the beginning. An additional 100,000 listeners didn't add much to the salaries. But as the size of the audience grew, 100,000 additional listeners were valuable to the radio hosts.

This solution gave great comfort to the station manager, who didn't mind paying heavily for spectacular results. The agreement gave the clients hope and incentive. Today, everybody is as happy with the results as they were on the day they signed the agreement.

Both sides were sensitive to the needs and desires of the other. A great deal of time was spent educating each other about needs and hopes. What they didn't do was spend time worrying about the people on the opposite side of the table. That is how they got to their win-win result.

In this example, the condition is a guarantee of additional sales. If the other side purchases only the original amount and refuses to give you that concession, it must pay full price. You should always keep this concession/condition balance in mind during a negotiation. You can put a condition on any concession that you're willing to give during a negotiation. In fact, you should receive some specific benefit for each concession.

You can view each request for a concession as a mini-negotiation within the larger negotiation. You give to get. But before you give, always consider what you can ask for in return. View every request to give something to the other side as an opportunity to gain something for your own side. Be stingy with your concessions; they are the coins of the various transactions that take place during a negotiation.

REMEMBER

Don't make any concessions until you have a sense of everything that the other side will demand. You have just so much that you can give up, and of course, there are certain things you want. You don't want to reach the end of the negotiation having given up everything you could give up without receiving everything that you wanted to receive.

TIP

As you negotiate concessions and conditions, try using phrases such as "Assuming we reach agreement on everything else, . . ." or "As long as the overall deal works, . . ." This statement helps your and your counterpart make sure you both get what you want.

What It Means to Close a Deal

A deal closes when the parties agree on enough terms that they can move forward with the performance of the deal. For example, if you agree to pay someone $500 to paint your house a certain shade of green on Saturday using a certain brand of paint, that may well close the deal for the two of you. If you have some trust or history between the two of you, the other details could remain unexpressed. Without history or trust, you would need to specify the quality of the paint and the amount of scraping and sanding that would take place. For yet other people, the deal would not be closed until everything was committed to writing.

This section of the chapter is designed to get you and your opponent to the point where you both feel the deal is closed and are ready to perform under the agreement. It is designed to help you recognize when it is time to stop negotiating the deal and to start living the deal.

Remembering to push the pause button before closing is critical during a negotiation. Take a breather, look over the entire agreement. Make sure it works for you and the other side in the real world. Don't agree to a house-painting contract for Saturday when it has been raining for two weeks and no letup is in sight.

Understanding the Letter of the Law

A short course on contract law is well beyond the scope of this minibook, but you should understand a few key points if you ever negotiate a deal in the business world. These few pages won't make you a lawyer or eliminate the need for a lawyer, but they will make you savvier about the negotiating you do.

Legal definition of a closed deal

Unless you have a specific arrangement to the contrary, no deal is closed until the parties reach an agreement on all the points under negotiation. That is the way US law works. As they say, "It ain't over till the fat lady sings."

Nevertheless, students of negotiation are often upset when only one point remains in contention in a deal, and then the other party begins backing off on some of the points where agreement was reached. But as long as some point is under discussion, the deal remains open and subject to adjustment by either party. Even if an agreement seems to be in place regarding various pieces of the deal, the deal isn't final until both parties reach an agreement on all points. Backing off on previously agreed-to points sometimes happen, even to experienced negotiators.

For example, Kim Basinger agreed to star in *Boxing Helena.* The deal was being extensively negotiated, but the producers had her word that she would perform in the film, so they started raising money by selling the right to distribute the film in various territories around the world. But Basinger changed agents in the middle of the deal. Her new agent *hated* the script. He threw it across the room, calling it garbage. She backed out. The producers sued. Initially, they won. Basinger appealed. Then the producers lost. The court said that the deal still contained open points that were important to Basinger, so either party could back out. In fact, some of the cover letters from the producers' lawyers to Basinger's lawyers said explicitly that the deal wouldn't be final until Basinger agreed to the producers' changes.

To have an enforceable contract, you need agreement on four elements:

>> What you are getting

>> What you are paying for what you are getting

>> How long the contract will last

>> Who the parties are in the contract

Everything else, you can work out along the way. If you're missing any one of those four items, you cannot have an enforceable contract.

Offers and counteroffers

A wide misconception is that you can always accept an offer. When a party makes an offer and you make a counteroffer, the law looks at the transaction in a particular way. The law breaks that simple process into two steps, one of which is implied. Legally, you rejected the initial offer and put a new offer on the table. If you receive a written offer, you can write "accepted" across the document and the deal is done, but be careful when you counteroffer. You are rejecting the offer from the other party. The other party may *let* you accept a previous offer but is not bound to do so. You do not have a legal right to demand that the old offer from the other side stay on the table after you have rejected it and put another offer on the table.

Written versus oral contracts

Samuel Goldwyn once boomed: "An oral agreement isn't worth the paper it is written on." Actually, oral agreements are generally enforceable. The law requires a few contracts to be in writing, such as contracts that sell land, employment contracts for one year or longer, and contracts that convey an interest in a copyright. Generally, contracts do not have to be in writing. The problem is with proving the contents of an oral agreement. If you get into a dispute, be assured that you and the other side will remember the agreement differently.

The dispute often boils down to different renditions of what you said and what the other party said. The situation can be hopeless unless you have something other than your own memory that hints at the terms of the contract. For instance, if you have three checks with "installment 1 of 10," "2 of 10," and "3 of 10" written on the explanation line, those notations are strong evidence of some kind of agreement that called for ten payments in the face amount of the check. The other details may be murky, but that piece of the agreement would be crystal clear, which in turn would give support to the other things that you're claiming to be true.

Legal protection before the contract

So what happens if one or both parties begin to carry out the terms of the deal before a fully enforceable contract is signed? That's okay. On the basis of a technicality, the courts won't abandon someone who acted in good faith. Worst case: The party who performed — that is, the party who painted the house or delivered the goods — will receive the fair market value for the service or product provided. This concept is called *quantum meruit*, which means "what the thing is worth." That's fair.

Recognizing When to Close

The *when* of closing is easy: early and often. Some people don't seem to want or need to close the deal. They are like cows chewing their cud. They just go on and on enjoying the process, burning up time, and never bringing discussions to a close. And then again, like cows, they will put something away and bring it back up later and chew on it some more. Disgusting. Fortunately, you know that closing is a separate skill, and you keep it in mind at every phase of the negotiating process.

Keep the closing in mind as you prepare for your negotiation, as you listen to the other side, and every time you speak. A little piece of your mind should always focus on the closing — on bringing the negotiation to a mutually acceptable solution. You aren't likely to miss an opportunity to close when you view closing as a separate aspect of the negotiation rather than just the lucky result of a negotiation.

The proper moment to make your first effort at closing a deal is when you first sit down.

REMEMBER

Your mantra for closing: early and often. A recent study of salespeople revealed that a very small percentage of sales close after the first effort. Most sales close after at least three efforts to get the order. Try to close any negotiation as early as possible and keep trying until you prevail.

TIP

If you have trouble closing deals, intentionally try to close your next negotiation earlier than you think is possible. You find that no harm is done and that the other side becomes sensitized to the need to conclude matters. Make a game of it. Chart your efforts to close. Your rate of successful closings rises as you become more and more aware of closing as a separate skill to bring out early and often.

Many people find it is easier to close a deal if they set a deadline to do so. Negotiations tend to fall into place at the last minute. Having a deadline is like having a referee at the bargaining table. Remember, every deal has time constraints, so establishing a deadline can help the negotiation come to a smooth end.

WARNING

The phony deadline is a classic negotiating tool used to hurry one side into a quick close. If you suspect a phony deadline, don't sit back and accept it. Instead, test it. Get an explanation.

Knowing How to Close

The purpose of this section is to take the mystique out of closing and to provide some mechanics to make your efforts to close more fluid. It's a beautiful thing to see someone seamlessly switch from a substantive discussion into closing mode and then back.

TIP

With a friend or family member, rehearse the various approaches for closing. The more naturally they roll off your tongue, the easier the attempt will be for you in a real situation. Role play. Describe a typical negotiation situation to a friend and then have your friend challenge you with the objections in this section.

The good closer

Most used car lots have one person who is paid to close deals. You may have encountered a salesperson who, rather than close the deal, introduces you to "the manager." People in the auto industry call this person *the closer.*

People who are constantly resolving conflict and solving problems in their personal lives are thought of as agreeable and cooperative. At the negotiating table, they are considered brilliant. When a negotiator finds a solution to what appears to be a difficult negotiation, the feat brings the problem solver praise all around — including from the folks on the other side of the table.

People who are skilled at wrapping up a negotiation share these characteristics:

>> **Strong closers always seem to find a solution.** The approach may not be the original one, but it gets the desired result. Weak closers tend to get stuck on a position.

>> **Strong closers generally accomplish tasks on time.** Weak closers often procrastinate in many aspects of their lives.

>> **Strong closers rejoice when a deal closes.** Weak closers feel either a sense of loss when the project comes to an end or waves of self-doubt. Either way, closing does not bring unbridled joy to the weak closer in the same way it does for the strong closer.

Good closers are often witty or clever, but they don't have to be. They just need to have the confidence to follow through with the goals and limits they set when they started planning the negotiation. They consider themselves to be effective people. Creating consensus where none exists is a fun activity for the good closer and a struggle for the weak closer. Each one of these qualities is a result of the learned skills set out throughout this minibook. People are all born negotiating successfully: for food, for dry diapers, even for a good burp. Over time, life beats up on some people. Take back your life. Methodically set out to get what you want using the skills in this minibook.

The only three closing strategies you'll ever need

The entire country seems to be in a search of the perfect close — the one that won't fail. Here's the big secret: The three ways to make the sale or to successfully close the negotiation are

>> Ask

>> Ask

>> Ask

The wisdom of the ages works better than some new high-tech secret. No matter how powerful your computer is, what the range of your cellphone is, or how clever your tracking system is, you still have just one way to get the order or close the deal: Ask whether your counterpart will agree to the current terms. If you have trouble asking for commitments, address that issue. Being able to clearly state your need helps in every negotiation and in every other phase of your life.

CLOSING ACCORDING TO SHELLEY "THE MACHINE" LEVENE

See the film adaptation of David Mamet's *Glengarry Glenn Ross*. The film is about four real estate agents working the same sales. The boss stages a contest. The one who sells the most units by the end of the month gets a Cadillac. The second-place salesman gets a pair of steak knives. Third and fourth place get fired. And those who close the deal get good sales leads. The film is a biting look at the failure of the American dream.

Look at Shelley "the Machine" Levene, for example. Played by Jack Lemmon, Shelley was once a hotshot salesman, winning the office sweepstakes month after month. Now he is making no sales at all, and his wife is in the hospital. It's heartbreaking to hear the lies in his sales pitch about how he would feel wrong if the customer weren't able to share in the "marvelous opportunity" he's offering.

In one of Lemmon's best scenes of all time, he makes a house call on a man who does not want to buy real estate. The man knows it, we know it, Shelley knows it. But he keeps trying, not registering the man's growing impatience to have him out of his house. Behind his façade, Shelley has no enthusiasm for what he is doing. The potential customer sees right through Shelley's hard sell. This scene shows the fine line between deception and breakdown. If you don't let your true colors show when closing the deal, the results can be disastrous.

Fortunately for the army of people who give seminars, the nation continues to search for an easy answer to the issue of closing the deal. Maybe you are one of those people who is on such a search. Maybe that's why you bought this book. Meanwhile, earn your success the old-fashioned way: Ask for it. Heck, you should insist on it. Nothing short of persistent, organized inquiry is going to close any negotiation. It just won't happen by itself.

Using linkage to close

Linkage is a great concept to help close a deal when no compromise is in sight on the last point in contention. *Linkage* simply means that you hook a requested concession to something you want so the deal can close.

Here is the kind of situation that cries out for a linkage strategy:

>> The parties on the other side are making a final demand. They can't go any further. They can't give any more than they already have.

>> You don't want to cave in on this point because the deal won't work for you. If you concede, you will not have enough incentive to close the deal.

Here is what you do:

1. **Take a pause.**

   Be sure that the other side is not just bluffing, that he really can't go any further on this point.

2. **Look over the entire transaction. Find an area where you didn't get everything you wanted or find an item that can be changed in your favor to bring balance back to the deal.**

3. **Link the two issues.**

   Tell the other side that you will agree to his request if he will make the adjustment you need in Step 2. The item you link to his request may never have been discussed before. Or, more likely, it was discussed, and you tentatively agreed to drop your desire. But linkage is always acceptable. It makes you the creative problem solver.

REMEMBER

The other side wants the deal to close just as much as you do. When you bring balance to your side without throwing his side out of balance, both parties get something they want. You are a genius. At least, that is what people will say in the moment.

Here are some examples of linkage in response to specific objections:

Objection: "We can't pay this person more than $100,000 next year."

Linkage: "If you could go to $110,000, maybe my client will agree to a two-year contract."

Objection: "There's no way we are going to quit using Joe as our supplier for lead pipe."

Linkage: "Maybe we could sell you half-lots of lead pipe so you can continue to buy from Joe while trying out our company."

Objection: "Your daily fee is too high for just a one-hour speech, even if the conference site is out of town."

Linkage: "Maybe I can also give a seminar in the afternoon, so you feel like you are getting your money's worth."

Linkage is a powerful tool that you can use to help close a deadlocked negotiation. Here are some phrases that are often used to introduce the linkage concept:

"Well, maybe we could look at some of the issues again."

"Well, we may be able to work something out here."

"Tell ya what I'm gonna do."

REMEMBER

Linkage makes you feel like a real top-notch negotiator because it helps you solve a real problem. Neither side can give on the point under discussion, so you find something to trade. The next time you find yourself in a tough spot, use linkage to find your way out.

Barriers to Closing

If you find it difficult to close, the real question is probably not "How do I do this?" but rather "Why do I hesitate instead of going for it?" Merely stating the question helps you to start thinking about the answer.

Overcoming fears

Each person who has a barrier to closing a negotiation or a sale probably has some fears or apprehensions about the process. The most common fears follow:

>> **Fear of failure:** Most people have this fear to some extent. After all, no one likes to fail. In extreme cases, this fear will keep you from asking for what you want in the negotiation. After all, if you don't ever make your request, you can never fail to get it. The deal you're seeking will be a piece of ever-dangling fruit waiting to be plucked.

>> **Fear of rejection:** Everybody wants to be loved. Nobody likes being cast aside. So the fear of rejection can block a person from asking for agreement. No ask, no rejection. It is as simple as that.

>> **Fear of criticism:** Some people live or work in a situation in which they are likely to be criticized when they get back to what should be their support group. One way to prevent those negative words and looks is to never close the deal. Who can criticize a deal while it's still being negotiated?

>> **Fear of making a mistake:** Some people believe that make making a mistake is a sin instead of a normal part of life. The mere possibility of doing something that could be deemed a goof dredges up all sorts of uncertainties and self-doubts. So instead of finalizing the deal, these people shy away from closing the negotiation in a timely fashion.

>> **Fear of commitment:** Now here's a biggie. Closing a deal is a powerful commitment to deliver on a deal. Sometimes closing a deal triggers a short-term commitment such as buying a particular car, but the consequences last for a year or two or five. Sometimes closing a deal results in a commitment that requires participation on both sides for longer than most American marriages last, so it's no surprise that many people get hung up on this idea.

>> **Fear of loss:** Some negotiations last a long time and can be intense. Closing the negotiation means losing that intense relationship.

The real key to success for you may not be an elusive strategy. It may be your own mental blocks to closing a deal. Many people have them. Do your best to deal with your own demons on your own schedule in your own way. But deal with them. Your negotiation skills will improve when you face your fears and refuse to let them get in the way of closing a deal.

This is, of course, much easier said than done. You didn't go out and buy these fears at a department store, so they can't be discarded like an old piece of clothing. But after you identify these fears and start working on saying "good riddance," you're on your way. You may need to talk to a mentor, a therapist, or a trusted family member.

TIP

The disposal of such old baggage is beyond the topic of this book, but you can minimize the effect of such fears, even if you don't purge them completely from your system. One of the following tips may work for you:

>> **Keep in mind the consequences of not going for the close.** When you don't try to close, you end up in the same position as if you had been rejected. You put yourself exactly where you don't want to be.

>> **Think about the criticism you'll receive from those who are looking to you to close this deal.**

>> **Put words to your fear.** You can tell the other side the problem, such as, "Here's the hard part for me. I need to close this deal or call it quits."

>> **Put a deadline on the negotiation up front and talk about it with the other side.** That way, even the person on the other side of the table will be helping you over this hump.

Be sure to keep in mind that the other party may also have some mental blocks to closing. These blocks are the same fears that you may face, and the other side is unlikely to acknowledge how they affect the negotiation. If you sense that the person you're negotiating with has a fear that is blocking a close, don't play shrink — unless you are one. Instead, use one of the techniques just mentioned to help him or her over the fear. You can set a time frame for the negotiation, mention the folks who want the other side to close the deal, or mention the consequences of not closing the deal.

Overcoming objections

The term *objection* is more commonly used in the specialized negotiation of sales. Salespeople around the world want to know how to get over, past, and through objections. They're looking for simple answers to the two most common objections: price and product.

When someone directly states an objection to whatever you're proposing, an opportunity is at hand. You have the opportunity to clear away one more barrier. Every objection you get past puts you closer to your goal of closing the negotiation. An objection — honestly stated — is just another way of inviting you to satisfy some concern or to meet a need that you didn't address earlier in your presentation.

Answering objections is the fun part of a negotiation. You get to use your imagination. You get to reach into your information bank and come up with the answer. Countering objections is the part where you get to show your stuff, and your preparation pays off because you get to explain why.

Using questions to get where you want to go

When you try to close a negotiation and you get an objection, a question is your best friend. Gently probe to find the answers to the following:

>> Is the stated objection really the thing that is bothering the other party?

>> What will the other party do if this deal doesn't close? What is his or her *or else?*

>> Can you meet or beat that alternative?

The frustrating dilemma is that you can't state these questions in a direct manner. You must ask for the information indirectly. You must tease the answer out. For example, look at the first question in the preceding list. You usually can't say, "Come on, tell me what's really bugging you." You have to relax yourself and get the other party to relax so you can get to the source of the concern. Here are some ways to tickle out the information (each question is a variation on the theme):

>> "If we can find agreement on that one item (price, for example) can we close this deal today?" If not, you know something else is bothering the other person.

>> "How about if we . . . ?" Suggest a whole new approach. Use linkage to make the deal work for the other party. (When that works, you know that you've stumbled on what is really bothering the other side.)

>> "In a perfect world, what would this deal look like to you?"

You are inside the negotiation, so you have made some progress. The answers to these questions can turn up all sorts of information you need to know — information you can't ask about directly. Keep digging until you're satisfied that you fully understand the objection. And if you want to improve the questions you ask throughout the negotiation, check out Chapter 4 in this minibook.

Going back to square one

People usually use the phrase "back to square one" to express the loss of a goal or objective. If you run into a blank wall, you may be inclined to shrug your shoulders and say dejectedly, "Well, I guess we're back at square one." Next time that happens, listen to yourself and think of this book. You have just given yourself some great advice. Trouble is, most people don't know great advice when they hear it, even if they hear this wisdom from themselves!

REMEMBER

Square one in negotiating is preparation. When you have a hard time with an objection or can't close the negotiation, you generally need more information about the person you are negotiating with or about your own company or product or about the competition.

The biggest difference between the very successful negotiator and everyone else is in the foundational work he or she does before the negotiation begins. There's no quick fix, magic wand, or sure way to get ahead in life. Unfortunately, no single factor is as directly responsible for success in individual negotiations and success in life as preparation. ("Unfortunately" because a lot of people look at preparation as work.)

Go back and do a little more preparation about yourself and the marketplace. Preparing yourself is covered in depth in Chapter 2 in this minibook so you can understand the unique value you bring to the table. A lot of people don't realize the importance of self-knowledge as it relates to a negotiation. You need to thoroughly understand why your counterpart is in a negotiation with you in the first place.

All these qualities have something to do with preparation. A book titled *Joy of Preparation* would never sell as well as *Joy of Cooking* and *Joy of Sex*, but if you embrace the joy of preparation, it will make an enormous difference in your life. Every minute you spend on preparation is, as they say, money in the bank.

Watch Robert Zemeckis's film *Contact* for a look at overcoming obstacles to close a deal. The film, based on the novel by Pulitzer Prize–winning author and astronomer Carl Sagan, is about a radio astronomer named Dr. Ellie Arroway (Jodie Foster), who discovers an extraterrestrial radio transmission that is clearly from an intelligent alien source. Her research is called the SETI project (Search for Extra-Terrestrial Intelligence). The government doesn't have faith in the project and blocks funding.

Look at the scene where Ellie asks a group of private financiers for continued funding of her research project. The odds are against her, but Ellie walks into the boardroom prepared and determined. She pleads her case to the financiers, and her enthusiasm for her research shines in the meeting. She's persistent without being overbearing. The financiers initially seem reluctant. Ellie is convinced that the deal isn't closed, but as she leaves the boardroom, the financiers stop her and tell her that her funding is secured. The deal closed because Ellie believed in herself.

Closing When It's All in the Family

Parents have an important calling and a rewarding challenge. Mothers and fathers teach values, morals, and appropriate behavior by being positive role models, creating consistent and fair standards of discipline, and enforcing the rules with love and kindness.

These qualities are easy to define, but good parenting takes all the negotiating skills in this book. To reach closing with children means to be explicit about consequences for breaking from expected rules or standards of behavior. First, the standards must be clearly established.

It's a good idea when deciding on rules and standards of behavior to have regular family meetings. As problems and conflicts arise during the week, post them on a meeting agenda sheet on the refrigerator or nearby bulletin board.

The purpose of the meeting is problem solving. Everyone attends and has a voice in suggesting solutions. Many parents are played off against each other, especially when they are separated or divorced. Having everybody in the same room at the same time can prevent that. Decide together on procedures and standards of behavior. These decisions can be posted as family rules.

If everybody is not in the same room at the same time, you may unintentionally create a situation where a family member *assumes* a conclusion that has not been reached. For example, the teenager *really* wants to stay out all night on prom night. The parents are undecided. Dad says, "Sounds like fun. I remember doing that when I was in high school." The teen takes that as a yes and runs with it — straight to Mom, who says "We'll see." The teen goes ahead and makes all the plans, planning a stop to change clothes at someone's house, committing to drive, offering to pitch in with breakfast plans at another's house.

The teen, deep into joyful expectations, assumes that all these plans will definitely close the negotiation with the parental units. When the parents finally research the planned activities and find a lack of adult supervision, Mom says no, and Dad backs her up. Emotional upheaval results. Many teen friends are now inconvenienced, and Mom and Dad are in a weak position — they could be accused of breaching the agreement (which was never really made). Parents need to follow up carefully when closing a deal with teenagers, so no false closure results. Always be clear about what state of decision you are in, even if you say clearly, "I'm not sure yet; don't make any plans."

REMEMBER

Closing is a necessary skill for you to practice consistently with your children. Adults are more equipped to handle uncertainty. Children need to know where they stand — the young live in the here and now. This is as true for the teenager as it is for the 2-year-old. When you have completed all the other skills, and children are clear about your expectations, closing the deal means checking out the child's understanding of the resolution. Encourage the child to say in her own words how she feels after a conflict is resolved, or after something she wants is either given or denied.

When the Deal Is Done

The negotiation is over. The contract is signed. The client is happy. You are being roundly congratulated. Administrative details have yet to be set up, but your job is over — almost.

You have two things left to do for the good of the deal and for your own growth. One is to review the entire negotiation, and the other is to be sure the deal is properly executed. And then the congratulations can begin.

Review the process

As soon as you have a chance to do so, go to a quiet place and think back over the negotiation and consider what you may have done differently. Consider the consequences of the various choices you made. The point is not self-flagellation; it's to conduct a calm review of the entire negotiating history, mentally playing out various options you had along the way. This process is one final review after you have time and distance from the completed negotiation. This is particularly useful after a successful negotiation because you don't have any self-doubt or blame.

Here are some questions to think about during the review:

>> What additional information could you have gathered before the negotiation started? Where would you have obtained that information?

>> Did you know as much as you would have liked to about the other party?

>> Were you as well informed as you needed to be about the marketplace?

>> Were your goals appropriate to the situation? Note that you're not asking if you achieved all your goals. If it happens that you did achieve all your goals, you probably didn't set them high enough.

>> Were your limits appropriate to the situation? Did you learn anything during the negotiation that caused you to change your limits? Did you adjust your limits to keep the deal instead of adjusting your limits based on new information?

>> Did you listen as well as you could have? Were there times where you did not have the patience to hear the other side out?

>> Were you as clear as you could have been throughout the negotiation? Did your lack of clarity ever threaten the deal?

>> How often did you use your pause button? What pause button did you use? What was happening that caused you to use your pause button?

>> Did you start closing right away? How many efforts to close did you make?

These are a lot of questions to answer. They're based on the six basic skills of negotiation (see Chapter 1 in this minibook), so you can also analyze your negotiation using those points.

Set up systems for checking the system

Regardless of whether you are a part of a large organization or are negotiating on your own behalf, don't close the file and consider a negotiation over until you have taken steps to ensure that the agreement will be carried out. You need to make sure that the agreement's execution is ethical, timely, and honest. Precautions you can take include marking a calendar with the dates that various items are due, checking that the people who must carry out the agreement are on board and understand the terms, and making sure that the progress is being reported to the other side.

Most large organizations have a separate department for just that purpose. The department is often called Contract Administration or something similar. Even when departmental staff handles these details, you should call the department after an appropriate amount of time has passed (usually a week or two) and satisfy yourself that the servicing system is in place. If you are a salesperson, you want to be sure that the order is being or has been processed.

You check because if something goes wrong in servicing a contract, the problem reflects badly on you. This is true regardless of how far such matters are from your responsibility. You negotiated the deal. If the terms are not carried out in a professional and timely manner, the other party will remember that the deal he or she made with *you* went sour. Unfair, but true.

Make it your personal responsibility to be sure that the other party is happy. The effort may take a few extra moments and may involve following up with people who should take care of business without prompting. But the benefits of repeat business for you and the preservation of your own good reputation will benefit you many times over. Your personal duty is to live up to the spirit and letter of the agreement. This is a sacred trust. Your word is your bond. Don't ever forget that.

Remember to celebrate!

New beginnings and final endings are celebrated in every culture, even though the events may look very different. The signing ceremony to mark the end of the negotiation and the beginning of the life of the agreement looms large in the United States. Such events feel like a natural time to celebrate. Such celebrations make reopening any discussion on the terms mighty difficult. Americans shake hands even over the smallest agreements and pop champagne corks for the big ones. No matter where you are in the world, people celebrate reaching important agreements. Some go to church, others throw a party, and some light a candle.

It's also important to celebrate when you decide to not close a deal and to walk away from it. Be happy when you do not close a bad deal. Walking away from bad deals is like avoiding a collision in traffic. You breathe a huge sigh of relief and are thankful that you avoided the accident. When you are successful in avoiding a bad deal, celebrate whatever way you know and love best — but celebrate. Celebrate with all the joy and verve that you bring to closing a good deal.

Index

Numerics

3M (Minnesota Mining and Manufacturing Company), 262

80/20 rule (Pareto principle)
  determining where to focus energy at work, 311–312
  identifying top tasks that support goals, 309–310
  overview, 212, 308
  in personal life, 312
  prioritizing daily objectives, 310
  sizing up situation, 309

A

ABC mnemonic, 26

abstractness, concreteness versus (in business writing), 350–351, 370–372

acceptance
  of emotional responses, 42, 59
  leadership and, 36
  mindfulness and, 29

Acceptance and Commitment Therapy (ACT; Acceptance and Commitment Training), 8, 23

acceptance criteria (in scope statements), 134

achieved power, 131

action items, 192–193, 200

action plans, 236, 558–559

action verbs, 163, 367, 372–373, 395–397

active listening, 146, 186–187

active voice, 395–396

ad hoc team meetings, 199–200

Adams, Joey, 462

Adobe After Effects, 509

adversity
  carrot, egg, and coffee bean example, 54
  resilience and, 28–30, 49
  seeking meaning during, 30

Aeschines, 213

agendas (or meetings), 191, 199, 562

alertness (in negotiations), 559–560

Alexander the Great, 209–210

Alger, Horatio, 245

Altair, 255

Amazon, 251

ambition, mindfulness and, 9

America Online, 251

American Express
  mentors, 272
  Travel Related Services (TRS) Division, 210

American Management Association, 392

Ammirati Puris Lintas, 209

amygdala, 19, 29

analogies (in presentations), 461–462

analogous intelligence, 210–211

and, beginning with (in business writing), 418

Anderson, Richard Dean, 206

annual budgets, 144

Anthony, Ray, 512

apostrophes, 392

Apple Computer, 255, 261

Apple Motion, 509

approach mode, 21

Aristotle, 461

Asberg, Marie, 46

ascribed power, 131

Ashridge Executive Education, 36

assumptions
  to clarify WBS components, 162–163
  planning processes of projects, 104
  in presentations, 460–461
  questioning during negotiations, 585–587
  in scope statements
    defined, 134
    documenting, 155

AT&T, 216
audience (for business writing)
  email, 434–436
  identifying, 340, 342–343
audience lists
  categories, 115–116
  complete and up-to-date, 118–120
  formatting, 129–130
  general discussion, 114–115
  overlooked audiences, 117
  purpose of, 116
  sample, 117–118
  templates for, 121–122
Authentic Happiness website, 46
authority
  defined, 129
  lack of direct, in teams, 111
  of project audience, confirming, 129–131
autopilot (mindlessness), 6, 13–14, 44, 80
avoidance mode, 21
awareness. *See also* mindfulness
  ABC mnemonic, 26
  choice of response and, 16
  cooking and eating with, 71
  leadership and, 35
  present-moment focus, 56
  relationships and, 32–33
  of thoughts/feelings and their effects, 7, 11, 16,
    19, 42
  unchanging awareness, 51–52

B

Baby Boomers, 341, 434–435
BaiBoard, 513
Basinger, Kim, 602
Battelle Memorial Institute, 253
BBC, 55
Beauvoir, Simone de, 271
beginner's mind, 66
being in the zone, 288–289
belly breathing (diaphragmatic breathing), 466–467
Ben Franklin stores, 208

benchmarking, 250
benefit-cost analysis, 102–103, 142
Ben-Gurion University, 44
Bernoulli's Principle, 245
big picture viewpoint
  avoidance mode and, 21
  in business writing
    assessing content, 385–386
    giving readers vision, 350
    reviewing document, 419–420
  defining goals, 340
  explaining need for project
    identifying beneficiaries of project, 137–147
    project objectives, 147–151
    scope of work, 146–147
  mindful leadership and, 35, 62
  mindfulness and, 15–16
  in negotiations, 547–548, 557
  open presence and, 62
  three-year plans, 557
Blockbuster, 556
Body Language For Dummies (Kuhnke), 340
boldface (in email), 445
BombBomb, 331
bottom-up attention, 80
boxes (in business writing), 378–379
Boxing Helena (film), 602
brain
  amygdala, 19, 29
  awareness of thoughts and their effect, 16–17
  brainstem, 13
  cerebellum, 13
  energy consumption of, 12
  evolution of, 13–14
  growth in study of mindfulness, 60–61
  higher brain, 13, 19–20
  human negativity bias, 14–15
  increasing productivity, 61–62
  limbic brain, 13, 19
  mental resilience, 29
  neocortex, 13
  neuroplasticity, 15–16, 60

operation and performance of, 12

prefrontal cortex, 19–21

present-focused attention, 52, 55–56, 62–63

primitive brain, 13, 19–20

processing of everyday work tasks, 18–21

recognition and awareness of routine responses, 14

reptilian brain, 13

size of, 12

structures of, 7

brainstem, 13

brainstorming approach (for WBS), 172–173

Breedlove, Sarah, 254

brevity

in email, 442–443

in presentations, 520

of questions, 581

in written project-progress reports, 190

Brockovich, Erin, 561

bubble-chart format (for WBS), 177–178

Buddhism, 23

Buffet, Warren, 345

bulleted lists (in business writing), 409–411, 444

Burger King, 211

Burton, Tim, 557

business requirements documents, 135

Business Week, 260

business writing

editing

clichés, 400–401

document length, 384

general discussion, 381

jargon, 398–399

judging objectively, 384–385

macro level, 385–386

methods for, 382–384

micro level, 385–388

modifiers, 401–402

passive versus active voice, 395–397

prepositional phrases, 387, 392

repeated word endings, 387, 389–391

repeated words, 387, 392–394

role of editors, 381–382

up-down-up inflection, 387–388

when to stop, 419

email

benefits of using, 427–428

best time to send, 432

brevity, 442–443

closing, 440–441

delay delivery feature, 432

general discussion, 425

graphic techniques, 443–445

importance of well-written, 426–427

inappropriate use of, 442

leads, 431–432, 438

length of, 441

middle section content, 438–440

salutations, 430–431

signatures, 445

simplicity, 443

style, 442

subject lines, 428–430, 441

successful, 433–438

grammatical problems

beginning with *and* or *but*, 418

commas, 412–413

ending with prepositions, 418

however, 413–414

journalist's grammar guidelines, 418

noun-pronoun agreement, 414–415

overview, 411–412

which versus *that*, 415–416

who versus *that*, 416

who versus *whom*, 416–418

graphic techniques

boxes, 378–379

colors, 377

general discussion, 375

graphics, 378

lists, 379

sidebars, 378–379

type, 376–377

white space, 375

business writing *(continued)*
  language
    action verbs, 372–373
    comparisons, 373–375
    concrete versus abstract, 370–372
    everyday words and phrasing, 368–369
    reader-friendly words, 369–370
  organizing documents
    general discussion, 403–404
    lists, 408–411
    paragraphs, 404–405
    subheads, 405–406
    transitions, 406–408
  planning
    anticipating readers' questions, 346
    audience, 340, 342–343
    benefits versus features, 349
    concrete versus abstract, 350–351
    connecting instantly, 347–348
    content to fit purpose, 344–345
    goals, 338–340
    imagining readers, 345–347
    plan-draft-edit principle, 337–338
    reader profiling, 342–345
    relationship-building techniques, 355–358
    tone, 351–355
    WIIFM, 348–349
    writing to groups, 345
    writing to strangers, 345
  proofreading, 420–421
  reviewing documents, 419–420
  style
    clarity, 359–361
    conversational, 360, 366–368
    correct, 360
    persuasive, 360
    readability, 361–364
    rhythm, 364–366
    simplicity, 359–361
  writing improvement guide, 422–423
but, beginning with (in business writing), 418

C

calls to action (in presentations), 528, 531
camel inheritance problem, 598–599
capital appropriations plans, 144
Carlson, Chester, 253, 255
carrying out the work stage (of projects)
  confirming authority of audience members, 130
  drivers, 125
  failing to prepare for, 110
  joining projects during, 110
  observers, 126
  overview, 99
  project life cycle stages and, 100
  supporters, 126
CBT (cognitive behavioral therapy), 7
Center for Plain Language, 400
cerebellum, 13
challenges (in presentations), 525
change management
  anchoring self in the present, 51
  embracing change, 51
  expecting change, 30, 51
  flexibility, 99
  identifying those who thrive on change, 55
  resilience, 28–30
  unchanging awareness, 51–52
  using mindfulness, 49–52
  volatility in workplace, 48
  why difficult, 14, 50
Charles (prince), 239
Chevrolet, 462
Chiat, Jay, 255
Christopher, Robert, 262
Chrysler, 216–217
Churchill, Winston, 371
civility, 274
clarity
  in business writing, 359–361
  mental, 33–34

in negotiations, 540–542

of questions, 581

relative words and, 579–580

clichés, 400–401

clients/customers

garnering support for time management, 294–295

as part of project audience, 115

closing deals

assessing deals

backtracking, 596–597

getting more information, 596

justifying decisions to yourself, 595

overview, 595

bad deals, 594

celebrating after, 616

checking execution, 615–616

concessions versus conditions, 599, 601

contract law

definition of closed deals, 602–603

legal protection before contract, 604

offers and counteroffers, 603

written versus oral contracts, 603

within family, 613–614

good deals, 594

linkage strategy, 607–609

negotiating, 541–543

obstacles to

fears, 609–611

objections, 611–613

overview, 593–594

reviewing process, 614–615

strategy for, 606–607

strong closers, 605–606

when to close, 604–605

win-win solutions

creating, 597–599

defined, 594

closing processes (of projects), 100, 107

closing stage (of projects)

drivers, 125

observers, 126

overview, 99

partially completing, 110

project life cycle stages and, 100

supporters, 126

cognitive behavioral therapy (CBT), 7

Colgate-Palmolive, 219–220

collaborators, as part of project audience, 116

Collateral (film), 597

colors

in business writing, 377

in email management, 331

in presentations, 508

Columbia Pictures, 272

Columbia University, 44

Columbo (television series), 578

commas (in business writing), 412–413

commitment

attracting through vision, 247–248

fear of, 610

harsh definition of, 554

to vision, 553

common ground, finding, 221

common sense, 210–211

communication. *See also* business writing; presentations

active listening, 186–187

communications management plans, 201

components of effective, 184–185

defined, 184

email

benefits of using, 427–428

best time to send, 432

brevity, 442–443

closing, 440–441

delay delivery feature, 432

filtering systems, 328–330

general discussion, 327, 425

graphic techniques, 443–445

importance of well-written, 426–427

inappropriate use of, 442

leads, 431–432, 438

length of, 441

communication *(continued)*

    middle section content, 438–440

    multiple addresses, 329

    organizing, 329–330

    responding to, 330–333

    salutations, 430–431

    searching, 330

    signatures, 445

    simplicity, 443

    storing, 329–330

    style, 442

    subject lines, 428–430, 441

    successful, 433–438

  face-to-face, 74, 77–80

  formal versus informal, 188

  as fundamental aspect of the workplace, 52

  general discussion, 183–184

  improved relationships and, 32

  by leaders

    eliciting cooperation of others, 215

    listening, 214

    motivational, 213–214

    virtual leaders, 275–276

    of vision, 213

  maximizing time through effective, 292

  meetings

    ad hoc team meetings, 199–200

    conducting efficient, 192

    following up, 192–193

    general discussion, 190–191, 198–199

    planning, 191–192

    regularly scheduled team meetings, 199

    upper-management progress reviews, 200–201

  non-verbal, 79

  one-way versus two-way, 185–186

  project management and, 101

  self-awareness and, 35

  technology and

    directing attention back to work, 80

    email, 81–82

    forms of, by feedback level, 80

    information overload, 77

    mindfulness and, 78–80

    phoning, 82–83

    smartphone use, 83–84

    social media, 85

    virtual leaders, 275–276

    writing, 85–86, 88

  written project-progress reports

    determining who receives, 193

    drawbacks of, 189

    general discussion, 188

    improving, 189–190

    information to include in, 194

    project dashboards, 197–198

    sample, 195

    writing interesting, 194–196

communications management plans, 201

community involvement, 237

comparisons

  in business writing, 373–375

  in presentations, 457

compassion

  defined, 71

  leadership and, 35–37

  self-compassion, 29, 37

concessions, 599, 601

conclusion (of presentations)

  brevity, 520

  calls to action, 528, 531

  challenges, 525

  conciseness, 520

  confidence, 520

  executive summaries, 527, 530

  facts and statistics, 527–528

  Flapping Swan conclusion, 518

  humor, 530

  incentives, 522–524

  including forgotten points, 519

  leaving audience smiling, 521–522

  media references, 527

  multimedia, 529

  overview, 518–519

  questions, 530–531

quotations, 525, 528, 531
repeating theme, 521
signaling beginning of, 519
stories, 528–529
strong closing statements, 520
themes, 525
concreteness, abstractness versus (in business
    writing), 350–351, 370–372
conditions, 599, 601
confidence
  of leaders, 216
  in presentations
    conclusion, 520
    introduction, 492
consiglieres, 265
consistency, of leaders, 218–219
constraints (in scope statements)
  defined, 134
  limitations
    addressing in statement, 154
    defined, 152
    identifying, 153–154
    types of, 152–153
    vague, 153
  needs
    defined, 152
    identifying, 154
Contact (film), 613
content
  of business writing
    assessing, 385–386
    email, 438–440
    planning to fit purpose, 344–345
  of presentations
    analogies, 461–462
    assumptions, 460–461
    comparisons, 457
    contrasts, 456–457
    definitions, 458
    demonstrations, 457–458
    determining purpose of, 450–451
    examples, 453

explanations, 459–460
facts, 453
hyperlinks, 452
levels of, 451–452
navigating through, 451–452
numbers, 455–456
overview, 449–450
priority of, 451
quotations, 456
references, 454
rhetorical questions, 458–459
stories, 454–455
testimonials, 461
of scope statements, 133–134
contingency plans, 181
contractions (in business writing), 367
contractors, as part of project audience, 116
contracts
  defined, 135
  definition of closed deals, 602–603
  legal protection before, 604
  offers and counteroffers, 603
  written versus oral, 603
contrasts (in presentations), 456–457
Corning Glass Works, 262
Corrigan, Mairead, 240
counteroffers, 603
cover letters, 339
Covey, Stephen, 317
creativity
  free association and, 62
  mindfulness and, 39–41
  in presentations, 492–495, 514
  specificity and, 150–151
  stages of creative process, 40
  using mindfulness to improve, 41
Csikszentmihalyi, Mihaly, 40
culture and diversity issues
  appropriateness of tone in business writing,
    352–353
  benefits of diversity, 268
  eliciting cooperation, 268

culture and diversity issues *(continued)*
  eliciting cooperation through trade, 270–271
  emerging as leader from cultural groups
    mentoring, 272
    overview, 271–272
    practicing diversity from ground up, 272
    striving to want more diversity, 272
    toleration, 272–273
  encouraging diversity, 229
  international negotiations, 545
  listening, 268–270
  negotiations between men and women, 544
  overview, 267–269
  posture and facial expressions, 482
  putting needs of group first, 268–269
  technology and virtual leadership, 275–276
  working internationally
    capital and decision making, 274–275
    committing best and brightest, 274
    de minimus rule, 274
    general discussion, 273

D

Davidson, Richard, 29
de minimus rule, 274
deadlines (in negotiations), 605
decision making
  acting ethically, 69
  avoiding putting off, 293
  delegating to team
    choosing up sides, 227
    general discussion, 225
    mental play clock, 231–232
    recruiting and training, 228–229
    rethinking problems, 230–231
    SWOT analyses, 226–227
  effect of regular breaks and eating properly, 44
  five-step approach to, 45
  giving team increasing latitude, 233–234
  mindfulness and, 43–45
  prefrontal cortex and, 19
  setting reasonable goals, 223–225

settling team disputes, 232–233
using mindfulness to improve, 45
value-based time decisions
  chores and responsibilities, 303
  general discussion, 302–303
  leisure activities, 303–306
decoded messages, 185
decomposition, 116, 158–159. *See also* work breakdown structure
deep breathing (diaphragmatic breathing), 466–467
definitions (in presentations), 458
delay delivery feature (in email), 432
delegation
  choosing up sides, 227
  email management, 332
  general discussion, 225
  mental play clock, 231–232
  prioritization and, 316–317
  recruiting and training, 228–229
  rethinking problems, 230–231
  SWOT analyses, 226–227
deliverable/activity hierarchy, 166–167
deliverables. *See* objectives/deliverables
Delivering Happiness: A Path to Profits, Passion, and Purpose (Hsieh), 38
demographics
  considering for business emails, 435–436
  considering for business writing, 341–342
demonstrations (in presentations), 457–458
  introduction, 501–502
Demosthenes, 213
dependability, of leaders, 218–219
Depp, Johnny, 557
Derow, Peter, 223
Detroit Lions, 249–250, 259
Diana (princess), 239
diaphragmatic breathing (deep breathing; belly breathing), 466–467
Digital Juice, 509
discount rate, 103
Disney, Walt, 254
Disneyland, 254

distribution lists, project audience versus, 114

diversity. *See* culture and diversity issues

divine passive, 373

dodging questions, 590

Dog Day Afternoon (film), 541

dopamine, 75

dress

  diversity and dress code, 270–271, 273

  for negotiation, 560–561

Dress for Success (Molloy), 560

drive to succeed, 215–216

drivers

  agreement on objectives, 149

  categorizing audience as, 123

  defined, 122

  determining expectations and needs of, 141–142

  identifying project initiators, 139

  when to involve, 124–125

dropped (reversed-out) type (in business writing), 377

Drucker, Peter, 79

Durning, Charles, 541

E

Eaton, Bob, 217

Ecclesiastes, 212

Ed Wood (film), 557

Edison, Thomas, 53

editing business writing

  clichés, 400–401

  document length, 384

  general discussion, 381

  jargon, 398–399

  judging objectively, 384–385

  macro level, 385–386

  methods for

    marking up printouts, 382–383

    on-screen, 383

    tracking changes, 383–384

  micro level, 385–388

  modifiers, 401–402

  passive versus active voice

    action, 395–396

    deliberate use of passive, 397

    have and *have not*, 397

    there is and *there are*, 396–397

  prepositional phrases, 387, 392

  repeated word endings

    -ent words, 391

    -ing words, 389–390

    -ion words, 390–391

    -ize words, 391

    -ly words, 391

    -ous words, 391

    overview, 387, 389

  repeated words, 387, 392–394

  role of editors, 381–382

  up-down-up inflection, 387–388

  when to stop, 419

80/20 rule (Pareto principle)

  determining where to focus energy at work, 311–312

  identifying top tasks that support goals, 309–310

  overview, 212, 308

  in personal life, 312

  prioritizing daily objectives, 310

  sizing up situation, 309

Einstein, Albert, 41

elaboration, as part of creative process, 40

Elway, John, 207

email

  benefits of using, 427–428

  best time to send, 432

  brevity, 442–443

  closing, 440–441

  delay delivery feature, 432

  feedback level, 80

  filtering systems, 328–330

  general discussion, 327, 425

  graphic techniques

    boldface, 445

    lists, 444–445

    simplicity, 445

email *(continued)*
    subheads, 443–444
    white space, 443
  importance of well-written, 426–427
  inappropriate use of, 442
  leads, 431–432, 438
  length of, 441
  middle section content, 438–440
  multiple addresses, 329
  multitasking, 89
  organizing, 329–330
  responding to
    automatically, 333
    color coding, 331
    by deferring, 332
    by deleting, 331–332
    general discussion, 330
    immediately, 332
    via telephone, 331
    via video email, 331
    via voice text, 331
  salutations, 430–431
  searching, 330
  sent and received per day, 426
  signatures, 445
  simplicity, 443
  storing, 329–330
  style, 442
  subject lines, 428–430, 441
  successful
    anticipating reader's reaction, 434–435
    audience analysis, 434–436
    clarifying goals, 433–434
    determining best content, 437–438
    reader profiling, 435–436
    tone, 437
  using mindfully, 81–82
emotional intelligence
  employee promotion and, 52
  leadership and, 35–36
encoded messages, 185

end users
  identifying, 140–141
  identifying true, 118
  as part of project audience, 115, 117
engagement, of employees, 38–39
English Grammar For Dummies (Woods), 411
English Grammar Workbook For Dummies (Woods), 411
-ent words (in business writing), 391
Erin Brockovich (film), 561
ethics
  behaving in ethical manner, 69–70
  benefits of acting ethically, 69
evaluation, as part of creative process, 40–41
examples (in presentations), 453
executing processes (of projects)
  defined, 100
  performing project work, 106
  preparing to begin, 105–106
executive summaries (in presentations)
  conclusion, 527, 530
  introduction, 500–501
experience, as source of vision, 244
explanations (in presentations), 459–460
external audience, as part of project audience, 115–116
eye contact
  for emphasis, 473–474
  importance of, 472–473
  large audiences, 475
  what to avoid, 474
eye-speak, 474

F

FAB (feature, advantage, benefit) demonstration technique, 458
Facebook, 49
face-to-face communication
  digital downtime, 77–78
  disadvantage of technology, 74
  feedback level, 80

involving project audiences, 127

mindful communication, 78–80

facial expressions (in presentations), 481–482

facts and statistics (in presentations)

conclusion, 527–528

defined, 453

introduction, 498–499

Falk, Peter, 578

falling awake, 31

Fantasy Baseball, 255

Farley, Chris, 464

Farr, Mel, 249–250, 259

feasibility studies, 138

feature, advantage, benefit (FAB) demonstration technique, 458

Federal Communications Commission (FCC), 216

FedEx, 255

Ferguson, Sarah, 239

Fields, Debbi, 261

fight-or-flight response, 11, 15, 20, 53

fillers, verbal (in presentations), 472

filtering systems (for email), 328–330

first drafts (in business writing), 382

First Things First (Covey, Merrill, and Merrill), 317

Flapping Swan conclusion, 518

Flesch, Rudolph, 363

Flesch Readability Index, 361–363

flex time, 321–322

Flutie, Doug, 207

focus. *See also* mindfulness

benefits of, 34

career ambitions and goals, 9

for employees, 33–34

lack of, 34

listening and, 32

multitasking, 20, 34

on next footstep, 24–26

on positives, 30

power of, 10–11

prefrontal cortex and, 19

on present, 51

productivity and, 41–42

quiz scores, 35

on self, 24–25

sharpening with time off, 289

on short term, 37–38

on single task, 90

technology and, 74

types of, 62

using mindfulness to improve, 34, 61–62

Focus: The Hidden Driver of Excellence (Goleman), 61, 80

Fog Index, 363

follow-up questions (in negotiations), 581

Forbes, Malcolm, 216

Forbes Magazine, 216

Ford, William Clay, 249

formal communications, 188

Foster, Jodie, 613

Foxx, Jamie, 597

Fredrickson, Barbara, 29

Freedom program, 91

Frog Design, 255

Fuhrman, Mark, 578

Fuller, Buckminster, 211

functional managers, as part of project audience, 120

G

Gates, Bill, 261

Geneen, Harold, 258

General Electric (GE), 51, 245

Generation X'ers, 341, 434–435

Generation Y'ers, 341, 434–435

Gerstner, Louis V., Jr., 210

gestures (in presentations)

for dimension, 482–483

for direction, 483

distracting, 485–486

for feeling, 484

grand, 484–485

for motion, 483–484

Glengarry Glenn Ross (film), 607

goals
  of business writing, 338–340
  of email, 433–434
  focus and, 9
  in leadership
    setting reasonable goals, 223–225
    short-term goals, 241
    synthesizing goals, 212
  in negotiations
    active participation of team, 570–571
    challenging yet attainable goals, 572–573
    changeableness of goals, 575–576
    goals of questioning, 582
    keeping on course, 571
    long-range versus short-range goals, 574
    number of goals, 571–572
    opening offer, 569, 574–575
    overview, 567–568
    prioritizing goals, 573–574
    purpose versus goals, 569
    questions to ask, 568–569
    setting goals, 539, 541
    specific versus general goals, 572
  in personal life
    balancing household tasks with at-home hobbies, 314–315
    family traditions, 313
    investing in personal relationships, 313–314
  in time management
    identifying top tasks that support goals, 309–310
    long-term career goals, 310
    measurable goals, 323
    qualitative goals, 323
    setting goals to give self direction, 287
Goldwyn, Samuel, 490, 603
Goleman, Daniel, 61–62, 80
good judgment, of leaders, 218–219
Google, 7
Gorbachev, Mikhail, 212
Gordian knot, 209–210
Grameen Bank, 270

grammatical problems (in business writing)
  beginning with *and* or *but*, 418
  commas, 412–413
  ending with prepositions, 418
  however, 413–414
  journalist's grammar guidelines, 418
  noun-pronoun agreement, 414–415
  overview, 411–412
  which versus *that*, 415–416
  who versus *that*, 416
  who versus *whom*, 416–418
grants of opportunity, 239
graphic techniques (for business writing)
  boxes, 378–379
  colors, 377
  email
    boldface, 445
    lists, 444–445
    simplicity, 445
    subheads, 443–444
    white space, 443
  general discussion, 375
  graphics, 378
  lists, 379
  sidebars, 378–379
  type
    columns, 377
    fonts, 376
    margins, 377
    point size, 376–377
  white space, 375
graphical view (organization-chart format) (for WBS), 176
graphics (in business writing), 378
group learning, 220
groups, as part of project audience, 115
Grove, Andrew, 249, 259
Grundig Pump Company, 563
Guber, Peter, 455
A Guide to the Project Management Body of Knowledge (PMI), 97
Gunning, Robert, 363

H

Haig, Alexander, 234
Haloid Company, 253
Hammerstein, Oscar, II, 567
happiness
  of employees, 38–39
  using mindfulness to improve, 39
"Happy Talk" (song), 567
Harvard Business School, 210
Harvard University, 9, 56, 83
have and *have not* (in business writing), 397
Hawn, Goldie, 10
Hayes, Steven, 8
Hebb, Donald, 26
Hein, Piet, 230
hierarchy diagram (organization-chart format) (for WBS), 176
higher brain, 13, 19–20
Hill, Napoleon, 549
Hirsch, Leon, 218
housekeeping (in presentations), 497
Hsieh, Tony, 38
HubSpot, 432
Hugo, Victor, 461
human negativity bias, 14–15, 82
humor (in presentations)
  conclusion, 530
  introduction, 499–500
hyphens (in business writing), 392

I

IBM, 210, 261
iBrainstorm, 513
imagination, as source of vision, 245
incentives (in presentations), 522–524
incubation, 40–41
indented-outline format (for WBS), 176–177
inferences, checking, 187
inflation, 103
informal communications, 188

information
  assessing deals by getting more, 596
  communications management plans, 201
  importance of
    to good planning, 258
    to project management, 101
  project manager's role and, 108
  questioning when not forthcoming, 589–590
  for scope statements, searching for, 145–146
  sharing
    for group learning, 220
    with project audiences, 106, 127
  sources of for scope statements, 145–146
  using to build team spirit, 235–237
information overload, 76–77
-ing words (in business writing), 389–390
initiating processes (of projects)
  benefit-cost analysis, 102–103
  defined, 100
  questions to ask, 101–102
insight
  communication and, 32, 79
  as part of creative process, 40
inspiration, 212–213
instant messaging
  feedback level, 80
  writing style, 393
Intel, 249–250, 259
intellectual honesty, of leaders, 217–218
intelligence (in leadership)
  coming up with novel ideas, 212–213
  finding distinctions, 211–212
  finding similarities, 210–211
  flexibility in response to situations, 207–208
  getting at truth of contradictory information, 209
  putting concepts together in new ways, 212
  ranking importance of information, 209–210
  seizing opportunities, 208–209
  vision, 206–207
intentions regarding mindfulness, 63–64

interest
  defined, 131
  power-interest grids, 132
  of project audience, assessing, 131–132
internal audience, 115
internal rate of return, 103
International Campaign to Ban Landmines, 237, 239
International Monetary Fund, 270
Internet stock bubble, 251
interruptions, 292–294, 309
intimidation, 582
introduction (of presentations)
  components of, 496–502
  concise, 491–492
  confident, 492
  confirming findings, 500
  connecting with audience, 492
  cordial, 492
  creative, 492–495
  demonstrations, 501–502
  dramatic, 494
  dynamic, 491
  entertaining, 494–495
  executive summaries, 500–501
  facts and statistics, 498–499
  greetings, 497
  housekeeping, 497
  humor, 499–500
  media references, 497
  props, 501
  questions, 498–499
  quotations, 497
  stories, 494
  themes, 501
  transitions, 501–502
  type to avoid, 492
  unexpected, 494–495
  videos, 493
-ion words (in business writing), 390–391
iOpener Institute, 46
ITT, 258
-ize words (in business writing), 391

J

Jackson, Andrew, 217
jargon
  in business writing, 398–399
  clarifying during negotiations, 578–579
Jay and the Americans, 245
Jaycees (United States Junior Chamber), 236
Jesse, Jackson, Sr., 268
Jobs, Steve, 255, 462
John Wanamaker department store, 245
Jones, James Earl, 463
Journal of Computer-Mediated Communication, 79
judges, 44
judgment
  acknowledgement of emotional response without, 17, 59, 65
  writing non-judgmentally, 86
Juran, Joseph M., 308
juries, 238
just, banishment of (in negotiations), 558
justification (in scope statements)
  ability to address needs, 142–143
  beneficiaries, 139–140
  defined, 133
  drivers' expectations and needs, 141–142
  emphasizing project's importance, 143–145
  end users, 140–141
  project champion, 140
  project initiator, 137–139
  related projects, 143
  relationship to organization's priorities, 144
  searching for information, 145–146

K

Kabat-Zinn, Jon, 7, 64, 90
Kadrey, Richard, 462
key performance indicators (KPIs), 144
Kill the Dead (Kadrey), 462
King, Martin Luther, Jr., 246, 268
Kipling, Rudyard, 470
knowledge, as source of vision, 244–245
known unknowns, 180–181

Kodak, 45
Kohl, Helmut, 212–213
Kornfield, Jack, 90
Kotter, John P., 210
KPIs (key performance indicators), 144
Kroc, Ray, 254

L

Lampe, Marc, 70
Land, Edwin, 255
land mines, 237, 239
Langer, Ellen, 56
Laws of Communication Impact
  Law of Effect, 515–516
  Law of Emphasis and Intensity
    comparisons, 505–506
    contrasts, 505–506
    demonstrations, 509–510
    highlighting specific aspects, 508
    humor, 506–508
    overview, 504–505
    props, 510
    special effects, 509
    stories, 509
    technology, 510–511
    voice skills, 506
  Law of Exercise and Engagement
    audience involvement, 511–512
    encouraging interaction, 512–513
    overview, 511
  Law of Interest, 513–515
  Law of Primacy
    components of introductions, 496–502
    creativity, 492–495
    dynamic introductions, 491–492
    overview, 489–490
  Law of Recency
    brevity, 520
    components of conclusions, 524–531
    conciseness, 520
    confidence, 520

Flapping Swan conclusion, 518
    incentives, 522–524
    including forgotten points, 519
    leaving audience smiling, 521–522
    overview, 518–519
    repeating theme, 521
    signaling beginning of conclusion, 519
    strong closing statements, 520
  overview, 487–488
Laws of Learning, 490
leadership
  culture and diversity issues
    benefits of diversity, 268
    eliciting cooperation, 268
    eliciting cooperation through trade, 270–271
    emerging as leader from cultural groups, 271–273
    listening, 268–270
    overview, 267–269
    putting needs of group first, 268–269
    technology and virtual leadership, 275–276
    working internationally, 273–275
  decision making
    delegating to team, 225–232
    giving team increasing latitude, 233–234
    setting reasonable goals, 223–225
    settling team disputes, 232–233
  leading as a follower
    asking on behalf of group, 237
    avoiding confrontation with management, 238
    community involvement, 237
    general discussion, 235
    improving simple things, 235
    logos, 238
    using information to build team spirit, 235–237
  leading when not expected to succeed
    auditing accounts, 241
    events beyond your control, 241
    rallying troops, 240–241
    short-term goals, 241
  leading when position is honorary, 238–240

leadership *(continued)*
  mindful
    employees, 35–37
    mindfulness exercise for leaders, 36–37
    self-awareness and, 35
  problem solving versus assigning blame, 214
  quiz regarding, 206
  readjusting expectations, 224
  traits common to great leaders
    communication, 213–215
    confidence, 216
    dependability and consistency, 218–219
    drive to succeed, 215–216
    finding common ground, 221
    general discussion, 205
    good judgment, 218–219
    intellectual honesty, 217–218
    intelligence, 206–213
    learning environment, 220
    sense of urgency, 216–217
    trust, 219–220
  vision
    basis in reality, 258–260
    checklist for launching enterprises, 263
    components of, 255–258
    as doable dream, 253–255
    dynamism of, 265–266
    failure of, 251
    harnessing opportunities, 260–265
    human element of, 246–248
    ideas versus, 255
    linking present to future, 251–252
    simplicity, 255
    sources of, 243–245
    standards of excellence, 248
    staying ahead of the game, 248–250
Leadership IQ: A Personal Development Process Based on a Scientific Study of a New Generation of Leaders (Murphy), 213
leading questions (in negotiations), 584–585
leads (in email), 431–432, 438
learning environment, promoting, 220
Leigh, Janet, 604

leisure activities
  balancing household tasks with at-home hobbies, 314–315
  digital downtime, 78
  effect of regular breaks, 44
  sharpening focus with time off, 289
  value-based time decisions and
    experiences gained, 306
    factoring in monetary and time costs, 304–305
    general discussion, 303
    rewards, 304
Lemmon, Jack, 607
Les Misérables (Hugo), 461
letting go
  free association and, 62
  overview, 67
"Like a Rock" (song), 462
limbic brain, 13, 19
limits and limitations
  ability to set, 539, 541
  addressing in statement, 154
  defined, 152
  defining, 555
  identifying, 153–154
  opening offer and, 575
  types of, 152–153
  vague, 153
linkage strategy, 607–609
listening
  active, 146, 186–187
  evidence of, 591–592
  by leaders, 214
  in negotiations, 539–541
  questioning during negotiations, 584
  by virtual leaders, 276
  to voices different from own, 268–270
  to words and emotions behind them, 32
lists (in business writing). *See also* audience lists
  breaking up space with, 379
  bulleted, 409–411, 444
  in email, 444–445
  numbered, 408–409, 444–445

logos, 238
long-range plans, 144
Lund, Frederick Hansen, 489
Lutz, Bob, 217
-ly words (in business writing), 391

M

Madame C.J. Walker Company, 254
mailing lists, 328
Mamet, David, 607
Man of La Mancha (musical), 253
Manhattan Project, 253
Mark, Reuben, 219
market requirements documents, 135
Markkula, Mike, 255
master plan (for negotiations)
  achieving vision
    action plans, 558–559
    general discussion, 555–556
    three-year plans, 556–558
    values, 556
  defined, 547
  environment
    general discussion, 563
    home turf, 563–564
    planning far in advance, 565–566
    seating arrangements, 564–565
  overview, 547–548
  preparing self
    alertness, 559–560
    allocating time, 563
    dress, 560–561
    entering room, 561–562
    when in charge of meeting, 562
  vision statements
    commitment, 553
    evaluating, 554–555
    examples of, 548–549
    indecision and, 549
    overview, 548–549
    questions to consider, 550–552
    thinking outside the box, 549–550, 552–553

values, 555
  vision, defined, 548
Mattel, 272
MBCT (Mindfulness-Based Cognitive Therapy), 7–8, 23
MBSR (Mindfulness-Based Stress Reduction), 7–8, 23
McCabe, Ed, 211
McDonald, Dick and Mac, 253–254
McDonald's, 211, 253–254, 556
McGowan, William, 216
MCI, 216
McKenna, Regis, 255
McKinsey & Company, 210
McKnight, William, 262
meaning
  seeking during adversity, 30
  sense of, connected to work, 64–65
meditation, 10
meeting minutes, 138, 145, 153, 192–193, 199
meetings
  ad hoc team meetings, 199–200
  conducting efficient, 192
  following up, 192–193
  general discussion, 190–191, 198–199
  involving project audiences, 127
  planning, 191–192
  regularly scheduled team meetings, 199
  upper-management progress reviews, 200–201
Mehrabian, Albert, 351
mental clarity, 33–34
mentoring, 272
Mercer Management Consulting, 212
Merrill, A. Roger, 317
Merrill, Rebecca R., 317
microprocessors, 249
Microsoft, 548
Microsoft Disk Operating System (MS-DOS), 261
Microsoft Word
  Focus mode, 88
  grammar checking feature, 423
  Readability Index, 361–363
  Track Changes tool, 383–384

Millennials, 341
A Mindful Nation (Ryan), 7
mindfulness
  ABC mnemonic, 26
  acting ethically, 69–70
  attitudes
    acceptance, 67
    alternative, 11
    beginner's mind, 66
    letting go, 67
    non-judgmental, 65
    non-striving, 66
    patient, 65–66
    trust, 66
  benefits of
    activities enhanced by, 8
    brain structures, 7
    creativity, 39–41
    decision making, 43–45
    employee happiness and engagement, 38–39
    general discussion, 6–9, 27, 37–38
    leadership, 35–37
    mental clarity and focus, 33–34
    mental resilience, 28–30
    productivity, 41–43
    relationships, 31–33
    staff turnover, 45–46
  brain
    awareness of thoughts and their effects, 16–17
    evolution of, 13–14
    human negativity bias, 14–15
    increasing present-focused attention, 62–63
    increasing productivity, 61–62
    neuroplasticity, 15–16
    processing of everyday work tasks, 18–21
    recognition and awareness of routine responses, 14
  challenges to
    concerns about what others think, 23
    habits and mindsets, 24
    right time and place, 23–24
  defining, 6–7

  exercises
    beginner, 25
    body scan, 87–88
    for increasing present-focused attention, 63
    for managing difficulties, 59–60
    mindful minute, 50
    mindfulness of breath, 31
    for those in leadership position, 36–37
    thought bubble, 57
    three-step body check, 53
  focusing on next footstep, 24–26
  general discussion, 5
  intentions regarding, 63–64
  introducing at work, 22–23
  living mindfully, 70–71
  mindset adjustment
    approaching rather than avoiding difficulties, 58–60
    focusing on present moment, 55–56
    treating thoughts as mental processes, 56–58
  monitoring effects of, 68
  myths regarding, 9–10
  origins of, 7–8
  power of focusing attention, 10–11
  practicing at home, 22, 70–71
  practicing daily, 67–68
  research into, 60–61
  technology
    communicating mindfully through, 78–88
    defined, 73
    focusing on single task, 89–90
    programs to enhance focus, 90–91
    pros and cons of, 74
    rebalancing use of, 76, 78
  uncertainty in workplace and
    change, 49–52
    new ways of working, 51–52
    resilience, 53–55
    VUCA acronym, 48–49
Mindfulness at Work conferences, 7
Mindfulness at Work For Dummies (Alidina and Adams), 7

Mindfulness journal, 35

Mindfulness-Based Cognitive Therapy (MBCT),
7–8, 23

Mindfulness-Based Stress Reduction (MBSR),
7–8, 23

mindlessness (autopilot), 6, 13–14, 44, 80

mindset
approaching rather than avoiding difficulties,
58–60

breaking down habits and mindsets to do things
differently, 24

concerns about what others think, 23

finishing work on time, 49

focusing on present moment, 55–56

nudging to build resilience, 30

right time and place for practicing mindfulness,
23–24

treating thoughts as mental processes,
56–58

wishing others well, 33

Minnesota Mining and Manufacturing Company
(3M), 262

mission statements. *See* vision statements

modifiers, minimizing (in business writing),
401–402

Molloy, John T., 560

monitoring and controlling processes (of projects),
100, 106–107

monkey mind, 56

monks, 67

Moore, Gordon, 249–250, 259

Moore's Law, 249

Mount Everest, 24

Mrs. Field's Cookies, 261

MS-DOS (Microsoft Disk Operating System), 261

multimedia (in presentations)
conclusion, 529

introduction, 493

multitasking
avoiding, 34

myth of, 20

technology and, 74, 89

Munich (film), 570

Murphy, Emmett C., 213

N

The Naked Spur (film), 604

NASA, 238

natural leaders, 205

neatness, 283

needs (in project management)
confirming project can address, 142–143

defined, 152

of drivers, determining, 141–142

identifying, 154

negative option response, 328

negativity
acknowledgement and awareness of negative
feelings, 28, 42, 55, 58

amygdala and, 29

dealing with, 58

human negativity bias, 14–15, 82

managing inner critic, 86

negotiating
closing deals
assessing deals, 595–597

bad deals, 594

celebrating after, 616

checking execution, 615–616

concessions versus conditions, 599, 601

contract law, 602–604

within family, 613–614

good deals, 594

linkage strategy, 607–609

obstacles to, 609–613

overview, 593–594

reviewing process, 614–615

strategy for, 606–607

strong closers, 605–606

when to close, 604–605

win-win solutions, 594, 597–599

goals
active participation of team, 570–571

challenging yet attainable, 572–573

changeableness of, 575–576

keeping on course, 571

long-range versus short-range, 574

negotiating *(continued)*
  number of, 571–572
  opening offer, 569, 574–575
  overview, 567–568
  prioritizing, 573–574
  purpose versus, 569
  questions to ask, 568–569
  specific versus general, 572
managing people and, 545
master plan
  achieving vision, 555–559
  defined, 547
  environment, 563–566
  overview, 547–548
  preparing self, 559–563
  vision statements, 548–555
questioning
  art of, 577–580
  asking versus telling, 583–584
  assumptions, 585–587
  brevity and clarity, 581
  evidence of listening, 591–592
  follow-up questions, 581
  general discussion, 577
  goals of, 582
  interruptions, 581
  intimidation, 582
  leading questions, 584–585
  learning from, 583
  limiting to essential questions, 589
  open-ended questions, 587–588
  planning questions, 580
  purpose in, 580
  repeating questions, 588
  tailoring questions to listener, 581
  transitions, 581
  unacceptable responses, 590–591
  when needed information isn't forthcoming, 589–590
reasons for, 535–536
skills for
  clarity, 540, 542
  closing deals, 542–543

  goal- and limit-setting, 539
  listening, 539–540
  overview, 536
  pause button, 542
  preparing, 537–538
types of
  complicated, 544
  general discussion, 543
  international, 544
  between men and women, 544
  via phone or Internet, 545
neocortex, 13
net present value (NPV), 103
New Economics Foundation, 39
newsletters, 328
Newsweek, 223
Newsweek International, 238
Nightingale, Earl, 295
Nike, 332
noise, 185
non-striving attitude, 66
Nordstrom, 548
noun-pronoun agreement (in business writing), 414–415
Noyce, Robert, 249, 259
NPV (net present value), 103
numbered lists (in business writing), 408–409, 444–445
numbers (in presentations), 455–456

O

objectives/deliverables
 in scope statements
   defined, 134, 158
   general discussion, 147
   identifying all, 149–150
   making clear and specific, 148–149
   resistance to, 150–151
   serendipity versus, 150
   SMART acronym, 149
 in WBS
   deliverable/activity hierarchy, 166–167
   focusing on results when naming, 163

observers
  categorizing audience as, 123
  defined, 123
  when to involve, 125–127
Ommwriter, 88
one-off negotiations, 582
one-way communication, 185
online resources
  Authentic Happiness website, 46
  cheat sheet (companion to book), 2
  collaboration apps, 513
  Digital Juice, 509
  Freedom program, 91
  plain language websites, 400
  readability tests, 362
  RescueTime, 91
  SelfControl for Mac, 90
  TED talks, 455
  updates or changes to book, 2
  Wisdom 2.0 Conference, 90
"Only in America" (song), 245
open competitions, 231
open-ended questions, 587–588
opening offers, 569, 574–575
opportunities
  creating idea-promoting atmosphere, 262
  intelligence in leadership, 208–209
  moving from ideas to plans, 263–265
  overview, 260–261
  searching out, 261–262
  spotting, 261
or, tyranny of, 558
Oracle of Delphi, 209
oral contracts, 603
organization-chart format (hierarchy diagram; graphical view) (for WBS), 176
organizing and preparing stage (of projects). See also work breakdown structure
  drivers, 125
  observers, 126
  overview, 98–99
  project life cycle stages and, 100
  supporters, 126

Ouchi, William, 257
-ous words (in business writing), 391

P

Pacino, Al, 541
Palo Alto Research Center (PARC), 255
paragraphing (in business writing), 404–405
paraphrasing (in project management), 187
Pareto, Vilfredo, 308
Pareto principle. See 80/20 rule
Paris Air Show, 457
parsimony, law of, 558
passion
  leadership and, 36
  work orientation, 65
passive voice and sentences (in business writing)
  action, 372–373, 395–396
  deliberate use of passive, 397
  have and have not, 397
  there is and there are, 396–397
Paterson, Tim, 261
patience, 65–66
pause button (in negotiations), 542, 602
pausing, 470–471
Paytas, Trisha, 468–470
Peace People, 240
perfectionism, 325
personal organization
  general discussion, 279
  keys to
    evaluating key work areas, 283
    general discussion, 282–283
    neatness habits, 283
    "refusing to excuse," 284
  planning
    activating subconscious mind, 280–281
    gathering needed materials, 281–282
    handling items once, 281–282
    overview, 279–280
    peace of mind and, 280
    return on time spent, 281

persuasiveness (in business writing), 360

PFC (prefrontal cortex), 19–21

Plain Language Association International (PLAIN), 400

Plain Writing Act of 2010, 400

Plain Writing Association, 400

plan-draft-edit principle, 337–338, 423. *See also* editing business writing; planning

planning

  in business writing

    anticipating readers' questions, 346

    audience, 340, 342–343

    benefits versus features, 349

    concrete versus abstract, 350–351

    connecting instantly, 347–348

    content to fit purpose, 344–345

    goals, 338–340

    imagining readers, 345–347

    plan-draft-edit principle, 337–338

    reader profiling, 342–345

    relationship-building techniques, 355–358

    tone, 351–355

    WIIFM, 348–349

    writing to groups, 345

    writing to strangers, 345

  in leadership

    ability to create plans, 257–258

    importance of information to good planning, 258

    importance of team participation to good planning, 258

    moving from ideas to plans, 263–265

    systematic planning, 217

  personal organization and

    activating subconscious mind, 280–281

    gathering needed materials, 281–282

    handling items once, 281–282

    overview, 279–280

    peace of mind, 280

    return on time spent, 281

  in project management

    communications management plans, 201

    contingency plans, 181

    long-range plans, 144

    meetings, 191–192

    scheduling strategic planning time, 321

planning processes (of projects). *See also* meetings; scope statements; work breakdown structure; written project-progress reports

  assumptions, 104

  defined, 100

  overview, 104–105

platform skills (in presentations)

  eyes

    eye contact, 472–475

    eye-speak, 474

  facial expressions, 481–482

  general discussion, 463–464

  gestures

    for dimension, 482–483

    for direction, 483

    distracting, 485–486

    for feeling, 484

    grand, 484–485

    for motion, 483–484

  posture

    aggressive, 477–478

    casual, 476

    general discussion, 475

    good, 477–479

    movement, 479–480

    tense, 477

    timid, 475–476

    uncomfortable, 477–478

  voice

    displaying emotion, 465

    general discussion, 463

    pausing, 470–471

    projecting, 466–467

    rate of speech, 468–470

    speaking softly, 468

    variation, 467–468

    vocal emphasis, 470

    volume, 464–466

Polaroid, 255

Post-it notes, 262

post-traumatic stress disorder, 29

posture (in presentations)

  aggressive, 477–478

  casual, 476

  general discussion, 475

  good, 477–479

  movement, 479–480

  tense, 477

  timid, 475–476

  uncomfortable, 477–478

power

  defined, 131

  power-interest grids, 132

  of project audience, assessing, 131–132

prefrontal cortex (PFC), 19–21

pregnant pauses (in presentations), 471

prepositional phrases (in business writing), 387, 392

prepositions, ending with (in business writing), 418

presentations

  content

    determining purpose of, 450–451

    hyperlinks, 452

    levels of, 451–452

    navigating through, 451–452

    overview, 449–450

    priority of, 451

  content types

    analogies, 461–462

    assumptions, 460–461

    comparisons, 457

    contrasts, 456–457

    definitions, 458

    demonstrations, 457–458

    examples, 453

    explanations, 459–460

    facts, 453

    numbers, 455–456

    quotations, 456

    references, 454

    rhetorical questions, 458–459

    stories, 454–455

    testimonials, 461

  Laws of Communication Impact

    Law of Effect, 515–516

    Law of Emphasis and Intensity, 504–511

    Law of Exercise and Engagement, 511–513

    Law of Interest, 513–515

    Law of Primacy, 489–502

    Law of Recency, 518–531

    overview, 487–488

  platform skills

    eyes, 472–475

    facial expressions, 481–482

    general discussion, 463–464

    gestures, 482–486

    posture, 475–480

    voice, 463–471

primary sources, 145

primitive brain, 13, 19–20

printer's proofs, 382

prioritization

  80/20 rule

    determining where to focus energy at work, 311–312

    identifying top tasks that support goals, 309–310

    overview, 308

    in personal life, 312–315

    prioritizing daily objectives, 310

    sizing up your situation, 309

  assessing progress, 322–324

  daily, 315–318

  general discussion, 307–308

  making adjustments, 324–325

  of negotiation goals, 573

  time-blocking system

    dividing day, 319–320

    factors affecting, 318

    flex time, 321–322

    personal activities, 320

    results from, 319

    self-evaluation and planning time, 321

    work activities, 320–321

privacy policies, 328

processes, projects versus, 98

procrastination, 292–293

product requirements documents, 135

product scope description (in scope statements), 134, 146–147

productivity, mindfulness and, 41–43

products, as component of projects, 96–97

professional societies, as part of project audience, 116

programs, projects versus, 98

project audience
  assessing power and interest of, 131–132
  audience lists
    categories, 115–116
    complete and up-to-date, 118–120
    formatting, 129–130
    general discussion, 114–115
    overlooked audiences, 117
    purpose of, 116
    sample, 117–118
    templates for, 121–122
  confirming authority of, 129–131
  defined, 114
  drivers
    categorizing audience as, 123
    defined, 122
    when to involve, 124–125
  general discussion, 113
  guidelines for involving, 128
  methods for involving, 127
  observers
    categorizing audience as, 123
    defined, 123
    when to involve, 125–127
  supporters
    categorizing audience as, 123
    defined, 122
    when to involve, 125–126
project champions, 124, 140
project charters, 135
project dashboards, 197–198
project exclusions (in scope statements), 134

project initiators, 137–138

project management
  communication
    active listening, 186–187
    communications management plans, 201
    components of effective, 184–185
    general discussion, 183–184
    meetings, 190–193, 198–201
    one-way versus two-way, 185–186
    written project-progress reports, 188–190, 193–198
  defining
    closing processes, 107
    executing processes, 105–106
    initiating processes, 101–102, 104
    monitoring and controlling processes, 106–107
    overview, 100–101
    planning processes, 104–105
  keeping track of projects, 168
  project audience
    assessing power and interest of, 131–132
    audience lists, 114–122, 129–130
    confirming authority of, 129–131
    defined, 114
    drivers, 122–125
    general discussion, 113
    guidelines for involving, 128
    methods for involving, 127
    observers, 123, 125–127
    supporters, 122–123, 125–126
  project champions, 124
  project managers
    effective, 111–112
    excuses for not following project-management approach, 108–109
    general discussion, 107
    potential challenges, 110–111
    "shortcuts" to avoid, 109–110
    tasks of, 107–108
  project title, 136–137
  projects
    components that define, 96–97
    diversity of, 97

general discussion, 95
stages of, 98–100
scope statements
  acceptance criteria, 134
  assumptions, 134, 155
  as binding agreement, 134
  constraints, 134, 151–154
  contents of, 133–134
  documents related to, 135
  formatting, 155–156
  justification, 133, 137–146
  objectives/deliverables, 134, 147–151
  product scope description, 134
  project exclusions, 134
  scope of work, 146–147
work breakdown structure
  assumptions to clarify planned work, 162–163
  categorizing work, 173–174
  decomposing in detail, 158
  defined, 159
  deliverable/activity hierarchy, 166–167
  determining needed detail, 161–162
  developing, 160–161, 171–173
  focusing on results when naming deliverables, 163
  formatting, 176–178
  general discussion, 157–158
  identifying risks, 180–181
  improving quality of, 178
  labeling entries, 174–175
  levels of, 159
  schemes for, 170–171
  size of project and, 164
  special situations, 167–170
  surveys using, 164–165
  templates for, 179–180
  titling activities with action verbs, 163
  WBS dictionary, 182
Project Management Institute, 97
project managers
  effective, 111–112
  excuses for not following project-management approach, 108–109

general discussion, 107
as part of project audience, 115
potential challenges, 110–111
"shortcuts" to avoid, 109–110
tasks of, 107–108
project processes. *See also* meetings; scope statements; work breakdown structure; written project-progress reports
  closing processes, 100, 107
  executing processes
    defined, 100
    performing project work, 106
    preparing to begin, 105–106
  initiating processes
    benefit-cost analysis, 102–103
    defined, 100
    questions to ask, 101–102
  monitoring and controlling processes, 100, 106–107
  planning processes
    assumptions, 104
    defined, 100
    overview, 104–105
project profiles, 135
project requests, 135
project stages
  carrying out the work stage
    confirming authority of audience members, 130
    drivers, 125
    failing to prepare for, 110
    joining projects during, 110
    observers, 126
    overview, 99
    project life cycle stages and, 100
    supporters, 126
  closing stage
    drivers, 125
    observers, 126
    overview, 99
    partially completing, 110
    project life cycle stages and, 100
    supporters, 126

project stages *(continued)*
  organizing and preparing stage
    drivers, 125
    observers, 126
    overview, 98–99
    project life cycle stages and, 100
    supporters, 126
    work breakdown structure, 157–182
  starting the project stage
    drivers, 125
    observers, 126
    overview, 98
    project life cycle stages and, 100
    supporters, 126
project title, 136–137
projecting voice (in presentations), 466–467
projects. *See also* project management
  components that define, 96–97
  diversity of, 97–98
  general discussion, 95
  processes and programs versus, 98
  stages of, 98–100
pronouns (in negotiations), 591
proof marks (in business writing), 382–383
proofreading business writing, 382, 420–421
props (in presentations), 501
psychographics
  considering for business emails, 435–436
  considering for business writing, 342
public, as part of project audience, 116
pull communications, 185
punctuality, 192
Puris, Martin, 209
push communications, 185

Q

QDOS, 261
quality
  assuring, 106
  defined, 97
questions
  anticipating readers' questions, 346

  in negotiations
    art of, 577–580
    asking versus telling, 583–584
    assumptions, 585–587
    brevity and clarity, 581
    follow-up questions, 581
    general discussion, 577
    goals of, 582
    interruptions, 581
    intimidation, 582
    leading questions, 584–585
    learning from, 583
    limiting to essential questions, 589
    open-ended questions, 587–588
    to overcome objections, 611–612
    planning questions, 580
    purpose in, 580
    repeating questions, 588
    tailoring questions to listener, 581
    transitions, 581
    when needed information isn't forthcoming, 589–590
  in presentations
    conclusion, 530–531
    introduction, 498–499
    rhetorical questions, 458–459, 498–499, 515
QuickTime, 509
Quixote, Don (fictional character), 253
quiz scores, mindfulness and, 35
quotations (in presentations)
  conclusion, 525, 528, 531
  introduction, 497–499
  overview, 456

R

Rabi, Isidor I., 253, 255
Radicati Group, Inc., 426
Radio Corporation of America (RCA), 245
Rally's, 211
rate of speech, 468–470
Raychem, 207–208
Raytel, 207–208

RCA (Radio Corporation of America), 245
readability (of business writing)
  assessing readability level, 362–364
  editing process, 386
  everyday words and phrasing, 368–369
  matching reading level to audience, 361–362
  overview, 361
  readability research, 363
  reader-friendly words, 369–370
reader profiling, 342–345, 435–436
Reagan, Ronald, 234, 463
recasting problems, 231
references (in presentations)
  conclusion, 527
  introduction, 497
  overview, 454
references, checking (in negotiations), 596
"refusing to excuse," 284
regularly scheduled team meetings, 199
regulators, as part of project audience, 116
relationships
  caring for others, 33
  employees', 31–33
  garnering support for time management
    from co-workers and customers, 294–295
    from family and friends, 294
  investing in personal, 313–314
  listening to words and emotions behind them, 32
  practicing mindfulness at home, 70–71
  regulating emotions, 32
  techniques for building through business writing
    general discussion, 355–356
    personalization, 356
    you frame, 356–358
  technology and, 74
  using mindfulness to improve, 33
relative words (in negotiations), 579–580
religion, mindfulness and, 9
repeated word endings (in business writing)
  -ent words, 391
  -ing words, 389–390
  -ion words, 390–391

-ize words, 391
-ly words, 391
-ous words, 391
overview, 387, 389
repeated words (in business writing), 387, 392–394
reptilian brain, 13
requesters, as part of project audience, 115
RescueTime, 91
resilience
  acceptance and, 29
  amygdala and, 29
  building through mindfulness, 53–55
  carrot, egg, and coffee bean example, 54
  creativity and, 29
  defined, 28
  of employees, 28–30
  growth and, 29
  managing VUCA, 49
  rumination and, 54
  self-compassion and, 29
  using mindfulness to build, 30
resources, as component of projects, 96–97
retreats, 9
reverse engineering, 231
reverse marketing, 231
rhetorical questions (in presentations)
  introduction, 498–499
  overview, 458–459, 515
rhythm
  in business writing
    long and complicated, 365–366
    overview, 364–365
    short and choppy, 365
  personal, 288–289
Richardson, Ralph, 472
risk
  as component of projects, 97
  known unknowns, 180–181
  risk-management status in progress reports, 194
  unknown unknowns, 180–181
RJR Nabisco, 210
Roberts, Julia, 561

Rock, Chris, 480

Rocky Mountain News, 417

Rodgers, Richard, 567

Rogers, Will, 221

rumination, 54

Ryan, Tim, 7, 10

S

Saatchi, Charles and Maurice, 248

Saatchi & Saatchi, 248

safety (in workplace), 229

Sagan, Carl, 613

Saldich, Bob, 207–208

salutations (in email), 430–431

Sandberg, Sheryl, 49

sans-serif fonts (in business writing), 376

Sarnoff, David, 245

SAT (Scholastic Aptitude Test), 210

Saturday Night Live (television series), 464

scale problem, 263

schedules, as component of projects, 96–97

schemes (for WBS), 170–171

Schnabel, Artur, 470

Scholastic Aptitude Test (SAT), 210

scope statements

  acceptance criteria, 134

  assumptions

    defined, 134

    documenting, 155

  as binding agreement, 134

  constraints

    defined, 134

    limitations, 152–154

    needs, 152, 154

  contents of, 133–134

  documents related to, 135

  formatting, 155–156

  general discussion, 151–152

  justification

    ability to address needs, 142–143

    beneficiaries, 139–140

    defined, 133

    drivers' expectations and needs, 141–142

    emphasizing project's importance, 143–145

    end users, 140–141

    project champion, 140

    project initiator, 137–139

    related projects, 143

    searching for information, 145–146

  objectives/deliverables

    defined, 134

    general discussion, 147

    identifying all, 149–150

    making clear and specific, 148–149

    resistance to, 150–151

  product scope description, 134

  project exclusions, 134

  scope of work, 146–147

Scotch tape, 262

seating arrangements (for negotiations), 564–565

secondary sources, 145

seeking behavior, 75

Segal, Zindel, 7

Seger, Bob, 462

self-awareness, 35

self-compassion, 29

SelfControl for Mac, 90

sense of urgency (in leadership)

  informal proposals, 216–217

  systematic planning, 217

  team of advisors, 217

sentence run-on (in presentations), 471

serendipity, 150

serif fonts (in business writing), 376

Shakespeare, William, 462

sidebars (in business writing), 378–379

signatures (in email), 445

The Silence of the Lambs (film), 581–582

simpatico factor, 343

simplicity

  in business writing, 359–361

  in email, 443, 445

Simpson, O. J., 578

Skype, 461

SMART acronym, 149

smartphones, using mindfully, 83–84

Smith, Fred, 255

Smith, Jada Pinkett, 597

social media

  feedback level, 80

  information overload, 77

  using mindfully, 85

Solidarity movement, 234

Sony Pictures, 455

South Pacific (musical), 567

South Shore Bank, 270

spam, 328, 442

speakers bureaus, 455

specifications documents, 135

Spielberg, Steven, 570

stakeholders, project audience versus, 114

Star Wars (film series), 463

starting the project stage (of projects)

  drivers, 125

  observers, 126

  overview, 98

  project life cycle stages and, 100

  supporters, 126

statements of work, 135

statistics. *See* facts and statistics

Stewart, James, 604

stories (in presentations)

  conclusion, 528–529

  introduction, 494

  overview, 454–455

subheads (in business writing)

  breaking up space with, 378–379

  building with, 405–406

  email, 443–444

subject lines (in email), 428–430, 441

subjectivity, 270

suppliers, as part of project audience, 116

support and maintenance personnel, as part of project audience, 117

support groups, as part of project audience, 117

supporters

  agreement on objectives, 149

  categorizing audience as, 123

  defined, 122

  identifying project initiators, 139

  when to involve, 125–126

surveys, 164–165

SWOT analyses, 226–227

synthesizing goals, 212

T

Tan, Chade-Meng, 82

teams and teamwork

  ad hoc team meetings, 199–200

  assigning roles, 105

  benefits of acting ethically, 69

  challenge of new people on new teams, 110–111

  defining performance of essential functions, 105–106

  delegating to team

    choosing up sides, 227

    general discussion, 225

    mental play clock, 231–232

    recruiting and training, 228–229

    rethinking problems, 230–231

    SWOT analyses, 226–227

  face-to-face communication, 79

  giving and explaining tasks, 105

  giving team increasing latitude, 233–234

  introducing members to each other and project, 105

  lack of direct authority, 111

  members as part of project audience, 115

  participation of members in setting negotiation goals, 570–571

  project audience versus team members, 114

  regularly scheduled team meetings, 199

  requirement of for good planning, 258

  settling team disputes, 232–233

  using information to build team spirit, 235–237

  vision, and ability to create teams, 255–257

Teasdale, John, 7

technical requirements documents, 135

technology

  addictive nature of, 75, 81

  change in workplace due to, 49

  communicating mindfully through

    email, 81–82

    overview, 78–80

    phoning, 82–83

    smartphone use, 83–84

    social media, 85

    writing, 85–86, 88

  defined, 73

  digital downtime, 76–78, 509

  distraction caused by, 61

  email

    benefits of using, 427–428

    best time to send, 432

    brevity, 442–443

    closing, 440–441

    delay delivery feature, 432

    feedback level, 80

    filtering systems, 328–330

    general discussion, 327, 425

    graphic techniques, 443–445

    importance of well-written, 426–427

    inappropriate use of, 442

    leads, 431–432, 438

    length of, 441

    middle section content, 438–440

    multiple addresses, 329

    multitasking, 89

    organizing, 329–330

    responding to, 330–333

    salutations, 430–431

    searching, 330

    sent and received per day, 426

    signatures, 445

    simplicity, 443

    storing, 329–330

    style, 442

    subject lines, 428–430, 441

    successful, 433–438

    using mindfully, 81–82

  focusing on single task, 89–90

  handling and storing documents, 282

  information overload, 76–77

  practicing mindfulness at home, 71

  programs to enhance focus, 90–91

  pros and cons of, 74

  rebalancing use of, 76, 78

  social media

    feedback level, 80

    information overload, 77

    using mindfully, 85

  unmindful use of, 52

  virtual leadership and, 275–276

TED talks, 455

Teilhard de Chardin, Pierre, 246

telephone

  feedback level, 80

  multitasking, 89

  negotiations via, 545

  using mindfully, 82–83

templates

  for audience lists, 121–122

  for work breakdown structure

    drawing previous experience, 179

    improving, 179–180

testimonials (in presentations), 461

text messaging

  feedback level, 80

  multitasking, 89

  writing style, 393

that (in business writing)

  which versus, 415–416

  who versus, 416

themes (in presentations)

  conclusion, 521, 525

  introduction, 501

Theory Z: How American Business Can Meet the Japanese Challenge (Ouchi), 257

there is and *there are* (in business writing), 372, 396–397

Think and Grow Rich (Hill), 549

Thorndike, Edward L., 490, 515

thought spirals, 16–17

threat/risk avoidance, 15

3M (Minnesota Mining and Manufacturing Company), 262

three-year plans
  looking at big picture, 557
  overview, 556
  thinking big, 556
  thinking bold, 556–557
  thinking in sound bites, 558

time management
  email
    filtering systems, 328–330
    general discussion, 327
    multiple addresses, 329
    organizing, 329–330
    responding to, 330–333
    searching, 330
    storing, 329–330
  garnering support for
    from co-workers and customers, 294–295
    from family and friends, 294
    general discussion, 293–294
  knowing self
    assessing strengths and weaknesses, 286
    assigning monetary worth to time, 287–288
    identifying rhythms, 288–289
    setting goals, 287
  motivation for, 295–296
  obstacles to
    communication, 292
    decision making, 293
    general discussion, 291
    interruptions, 292
    procrastination, 292–293
  personal organization
    general discussion, 279
    keys to, 282–284
    planning, 279–282

prioritization
  80/20 rule, 308–315
  assessing progress, 322–324
  daily, 315–318
  general discussion, 307–308
  making adjustments, 324–325
  time-blocking system, 318–322

routine and freedom, 291

system for
  general discussion, 289–290
  organizing surroundings, 290–291
  scheduling and time-blocking, 290

valuing time
  boosting hourly value through work efforts, 301–302
  calculating hourly income, 299–300
  gaining perspective, 298–299
  general discussion, 297
  making value-based time decisions, 302–306

Time Warner, 272

time-blocking system. *See also* time management
  dividing day, 319–320
  factors affecting, 318
  flex time, 321–322
  general discussion, 290
  personal activities, 320
  results from, 319
  self-evaluation and planning time, 321
  work activities, 320–321

time-equals-money concept
  assigning monetary worth to time, 287–288
  boosting hourly value through work efforts, 301–302
  calculating hourly income, 299–300
  gaining perspective, 298–299
  general discussion, 297
  helping children understand, 305
  making value-based time decisions
    chores and responsibilities, 303
    general discussion, 302–303
    leisure activities, 303–306

Titanic (ship), 245

Toffler, Alvin, 76

toleration, 272–273

Tolle, Eckhart, 90

Tom Cruise, 597

tone (of business writing)
  appropriateness of, 352–353
  authenticity, 353
  awareness of personal mood, 354–355
  conversational, 366–368
  email, 437
  overview, 351–352
  respectfulness, 353–354

top-down approach (for WBS), 171–172

top-down attention, 80

Towers Watson, 392

tracking systems, 106

transitions
  in business writing, 406–408
  in negotiations, between answers and questions, 581
  in presentations, 501–502, 519

trial close, 523

Truman, Harry, 217

trust
  creating atmosphere of, 219–220
  developing, 66
  sacredness of, 219

turnover, reducing through mindfulness, 45–46

Twain, Mark, 400

two-way communication, 185–186

type (in business writing)
  columns, 377
  fonts, 376
  margins, 377
  point size, 376–377

U

UCLA Mindful Awareness Research Center, 60

UCSD Center for Mindfulness, 60

UMASS Medical School for Mindfulness, 60

United States Junior Chamber (Jaycees), 236

United Way, 573

University of Liverpool, 55

University of Pennsylvania, 46

University of San Diego, 70

unknown unknowns, 180–181

up-down-up inflection (in business writing), 387–388

upper management, as part of project audience, 115

upper-management progress reviews, 200–201

US Army, 29, 548

U.S. Surgical, 218

V

values, 555

vendors, as part of project audience, 116

Vesaas, Tarjei, 474

video chat, 80

Vietnam Veterans of America, 237

Virgil, 208

vision
  achieving in negotiation
    action plans, 558–559
    general discussion, 555–556
    three-year plans, 556–558
    values, 556
  basis in reality
    overview, 258–259
    responding to diminishing resources, 260
    thinking beyond available resources, 259–260
  checklist for launching enterprises, 263
  communication of, 213
  components of
    ability to create plans, 257–258
    ability to create teams, 255–257
  defined, 548
  as doable dream, 253–255
  dynamism of, 265–266
  failure of, 251
  harnessing opportunities
    creating idea-promoting atmosphere, 262
    moving from ideas to plans, 263–265

overview, 260–261

searching out opportunities, 261–262

spotting opportunities, 261

human element of

attracting commitment and energizing, 247–248

overview, 246

reminder of reasons for joining group, 246–247

ideas versus, 255

leadership and, 206–207

linking present to future, 251–252

simplicity, 255

sources of

experience, 244

imagination, 245

knowledge, 244–245

overview, 243–244

standards of excellence, 248

staying ahead of the game

being a visionary, 249–250

benchmarking, 250

general discussion, 248–249

vision statements

commitment, 553

evaluating, 554–555

examples of, 548–549

indecision and, 549

overview, 548–549

questions to consider, 550–552

thinking outside the box, 549–550, 552–553

values, 555

vision statements (mission statements)

commitment, 553

evaluating, 554–555

examples of, 548–549

indecision and, 549

overview, 548–549

questions to consider, 550–552

thinking outside the box, 549–550, 552–553

values, 555

vision, defined, 548

visualizing, 186–187

voice skills (in presentations)

displaying emotion, 465

general discussion, 463

pausing, 470–471

projecting, 466–467

rate of speech, 468–470

speaking softly, 468

variation, 467–468

vocal emphasis, 470

volume, 464–466

Volvo, 244, 269

VUCA (volatility, uncertainty, complexity, ambiguity)

defined, 48

managing at work, 48–49

W

Walesa, Lech, 234

Walker, Charles J., 254

Wall Street Journal, 432

Walmart, 208–209

Walton, Sam, 208–209

Washington, George, 247

Watson supercomputer, 12

WBS. *See* work breakdown structure

WBS dictionary, 182

Welch, Jack, 51

What's In It For Me (WIIFM), 128, 348–349

which versus *that* (in business writing), 415–416

white space

in business writing, 375

in email, 443

who (in business writing)

that versus, 416

whom versus, 416–418

WIIFM (What's In It For Me), 128, 348–349

Williams, Betty, 240

Williams, Jody, 237, 239

Williams, Mark, 7

win-win negotiating, 598

win-win solutions, 594. *See also* closing deals

wisdom, 71

Wisdom 2.0 Conference, 90

The Woman's Dress for Success Book (Molloy), 560

Wood, Edward D., Jr., 557

work breakdown structure (WBS)

  assumptions to clarify planned work, 162–163

  categorizing work, 173–174

  decomposing in detail, 158

  defined, 159

  deliverable/activity hierarchy, 166–167

  determining needed detail, 161–162

  developing

    brainstorming approach, 172–173

    overview, 160–161

    top-down approach, 171–172

  focusing on results when naming deliverables, 163

  formatting

    bubble-chart format, 177–178

    indented-outline format, 176–177

    organization-chart format, 176

  general discussion, 157–158

  identifying risks, 180–181

  improving quality of, 178

  labeling entries, 174–175

  levels of, 159

  schemes for, 170–171

  size of project and, 164

  special situations

    conditionally repeating work, 167–168

    contracts for services, 169–170

    long-term projects, 169

    work with no obvious break points, 168–169

  surveys using, 164–165

  templates for

    drawing previous experience, 179

    improving, 179–180

  titling activities with action verbs, 163

  WBS dictionary, 182

work orders, 135

work orientations, 65

work packages, 159–160

World Bank, 270

Wozniak, Steve, 255

Wright, Wilbur and Orville, 245

writing. *See also* business writing

  involving project audiences, 127

  mindfully, 85–86, 88

writing improvement guide, 422–423

written contracts, 603

written project-progress reports

  brevity, 190

  determining who receives, 193

  drawbacks of, 189

  general discussion, 188

  improving, 189–190

  information to include in, 194

  project dashboards, 197–198

  sample, 195

  writing interesting, 194–196

Wrzesniewski, Amy, 65

X

Xerox, 253, 255–256

Y

Yale University School of Management, 65

you frame, 356–358

Z

Zappos, 38

Zarrella, Dan, 432

Zemeckis, Robert, 613

About the Authors

Shamash Alidina, MEng MA PGCE, is CEO of Learn Mindfulness International, offering training and teacher training in mindfulness for the general public, as well as life and executive coaches, yoga teachers, doctors, nurses, and other health professionals. Shamash has trained extensively in mindfulness at Bangor University's Centre for Mindfulness in the UK, and with Dr. Jon Kabat-Zinn and Dr. Saki Santorelli in New York. He holds a Masters Degree in Engineering (Imperial College) and a Masters Degree in Education (Open University), with a focus on Brain and Behavior.

Shamash has appeared on television, on radio, and in magazines and newspapers, including on the BBC and in the *Daily Express*. He is an international speaker, addressing audiences at places such as Cambridge University's conference on Mindfulness in the Workplace, the Mind and Its Potential conference in Sydney, and the Healthy Living Show in Auckland. Shamash is the author of the international bestsellers *Mindfulness For Dummies* and *Relaxation For Dummies* (Wiley).

See all Shamash's courses and workshops at www.learnmindfulness.co.uk or email him directly at shamash@learnmindfulness.co.uk. Catch Shamash on the social networks at: www.twitter.com/shamashalidina, www.facebook.com/learnmindfulness, and www.linkedin.com/in/learnmindfulness.

Juliet Adams has spent most of her career working with organizations on leadership and strategic learning programs, organizational development, and change projects. She has worked on national projects for the police and several standards setting bodies. She now runs her own successful consultancy, A Head for Work, specializing new approaches to leadership, where she develops programs and e-learning content for leading organizations.

In recent years, Juliet has become increasingly involved in bringing mindfulness to the world of work. She is the founder of Mindfulnet.org, a leading web-based independent mindfulness information resource. She arranged the first Mindfulness at Work conference at Robinson College Cambridge in 2012. She is author of "The Business Case for Mindfulness in the Workplace". She teaches mindfulness to groups of staff in the workplace and coaches one-to-one with senior staff.

Stan Portny, president of Stanley E. Portny and Associates, LLC, is an internationally recognized expert in project management and project leadership. During the past 35 years, he's provided training and consultation to more than 200 public and private organizations in consumer products, insurance, pharmaceuticals, finance, information technology, telecommunications, defense, and healthcare. He has developed and conducted training programs for more than 100,000 management and staff personnel in engineering, sales and marketing, research and development, information systems, manufacturing, operations, and support areas.

Stan provides on-site training in all aspects of project management, project team building, and project leadership. In addition, Stan can serve as the keynote speaker at your organization's or professional association's meetings. To understand how Stan can work with you to enhance your organization's project-management skills and practices, please contact him at Stanley E. Portny and Associates, LLC, 20 Helene Drive, Randolph, NJ 07869; phone 973-366-8500; e-mail Stan@ StanPortny.com; website www.StanPortny.com.

Marshall Loeb is the former managing editor of *Fortune* and *Money* magazines, as well as the former editor of the *Columbia Journalism Review*. His program "Your Dollars" was broadcast daily on the CBS Radio Network and his "Your Money" column was published in newspapers across the country. Marshall has won every major award for excellence in business journalism and is currently an online columnist for CBSmarketwatch.com and Quicken.com.

Stephen Kindel has served as a senior editor at *Financial World* magazine and *Forbes*, as well as associate editor at *Newsweek International*. Stephen has held several executive-level positions for various companies in marketing and strategy. He has consulted for a number of companies migrating their businesses to the web.

Dirk Zeller has been teaching, coaching, and training success, sales, and time management strategies to executives, managers, and salespeople since 1998, when he founded Sales Champions and Real Estate Champions. He is one of the most sought-after speakers in time management, peak performance, and sales. He has spoken on five different continents to hundreds of thousands of people.

Dirk is one of the world's most published authors on success, time management, productivity, sales, and life balance. He is the author of ten top-selling books, including *Telephone Sales For Dummies* and *Success as a Real Estate Agent For Dummies* (Wiley). He has more than 500 published articles to his credit, and over 250,000 people read his weekly newsletter. You can reach Dirk at Sales Champions, 5 NW Hawthorne Ave., Ste. 100, Bend, OR 97701. Phone: 541-383-0505. Email: info@saleschampions.com and info@dirkzeller.com. His website is www.sales champions.com.

Natalie Canavor is a nationally known expert on business writing whose mission is to help people communicate better so they can get what they want — whether that means a job, a promotion, or a successful business. Natalie creates practical writing workshops for businesspeople, writers, and professionals in every walk of life. Her unconventional approach meshes the best strategies from many writing venues: feature articles and columns, video scripts, websites, presentations, print and online marketing materials, and copywriting. She finds that given a planning structure and set of down-to-earth techniques, most people can dramatically improve their writing.

Natalie is the author of *Business Writing in the Digital Age* (Sage Publications), a textbook for advanced and graduate-level students of business and public relations. And with Claire Meirowitz, she co-authored *The Truth About the New Rules of Business Writing* (Financial Times Press), a quick guide to better writing. Natalie is happy to consult with organizations that see the value of raising the bar on writing, and travels to present custom workshops for businesses, associations, and other groups. Find her at Natalie@businesswritingnow.com.

Ray Anthony is a national leading authority in advanced presentation engineering, training, consulting, and executive coaching, and a dynamic keynote speaker. He founded and is president of the Anthony Innovation Group in The Woodlands, Texas. Ray's clients include numerous Fortune 500 companies, the CIA, NASA, and the military. An expert in business creativity and innovation, he has a passion for helping people use creativity in ways that will boost their careers, bring extra prosperity to their organizations, and enrich their lives.

Ray has written over 60 articles on numerous topics in leading publications and authored seven books on sales and presentation techniques and organizational change and innovation. His books include *Killer Presentations with Your iPad* (McGraw Hill Professional), co-authored with Bob LeVitus, and *Talking to the Top* (Prentice Hall). Ray has been showcased in various magazines and newspapers as well as a guest on numerous radio and television programs.

Barbara Boyd writes mostly about technology and occasionally about food, gardens, and travel. She's the co-author, with Joe Hutsko, of the first, second, and third editions of *iPhone All-in-One For Dummies* and the third and fourth editions of *Macs All-in-One For Dummies*. She's also the author of *AARP iPad: Tech to Connect* and *iCloud and iTunes Match in a Day For Dummies* (all published by Wiley). She co-authored (with Christina Martinez) *The Complete Idiot's Guide to Pinterest Marketing* (ALPHA). Barbara was a contributor to *Killer Presentations with Your iPad*, written by Ray Anthony and Bob LeVitus.

Barbara worked at Apple from 1985 to 1990 as the first network administrator for the executive staff. She then took a position as an administrator in the Technical Product Support group. She learned about meeting facilitation and giving presentations during that time and produced quarterly offsite meetings. She went on to work as a conference and event manager and later as an associate publisher at IDG (International Data Group). Before leaving the San Francisco Bay area, she worked as the marketing director for a small graphic design firm. In 1998, she left the corporate world to study Italian, write, and teach.

Michael C. Donaldson, in his successful entertainment law practice, represents writers, directors, and producers. He was co-chairman of the Entertainment Section of the Beverly Hills Bar Association and is listed in *Who's Who of American Law*. His book *Clearance and Copyright* (Silman-James Press) is used in 50 film schools across the country.

Michael travels extensively to universities, annual meetings, and corporate head-quarters throughout the United States, Asia, and Europe to lead workshops on the topic of negotiating. Michael's expansive knowledge of negotiating coupled with his energetic and engaging style delivers powerful results to each seminar attendee. You can contact him at Michael C. Donaldson, 2118 Wilshire Blvd, Ste. 500, Santa Monica, CA 90403-5784.

Publisher's Acknowledgments

Acquisitions Editor: Amy Fandrei

Project and Copy Editor: Susan Pink

Technical Editor: Michelle Krazniak

Editorial Assistant: Serena Novosel

Production Editor: Selvakumaran Rajendiran

Cover Image: © Tischenko Irina/Shutterstock